Arts
& Ideas

reproduced on the cover
Jan Vermeer. *Concert,* detail. c. 1660.
Oil on canvas, entire work 28 × 24¾″ (71 × 63 cm).
Isabella Stewart Gardner Museum, Boston.

cover design
Marlene Rothkin Vine

Arts & Ideas

6th edition

William Fleming

Syracuse University

Holt, Rinehart and Winston

New York Chicago San Francisco Atlanta Dallas
Montreal Toronto London Sydney

Editor   Rita Gilbert
Picture Editor   Joan Curtis
Developmental Editor   Karen Dubno
Project Assistant   Barbara Curialle
Production Manager   Nancy Myers
Designer   Marlene Rothkin Vine
Associate Designer   Karen Salsgiver
Map Illustrator   Robert Porter

Publisher: Judith L. Rothman

Library of Congress Cataloging in Publication Data

Fleming, William
    Arts & Ideas
    Includes index.
    1. Arts—History.   I. Title.
NX440.F56   1980   700'.9   79-20123
ISBN 0-03-046531-1

Copyright © 1980, 1974, 1963, 1955 by Holt, Rinehart and Winston
All rights reserved.
Composition and camera work by York Graphic Services, Inc., Pennsylvania
Color separations by Lehigh/Electronic Color, Illinois
Printing and binding by R. R. Donnelley & Sons Company, Ohio
    2 3 4   039   9 8 7 6 5

Preface

Arts & Ideas is a history of the humanities—art, architecture, music, literature, and philosophy—from the ancient world to the present day. It highlights the major styles of arts and letters as they crystallized in centers of civilization at moments of high cultural achievement, such as 5th-century B.C. Athens and Renaissance Florence.

The underlying concept of *Arts & Ideas* is the belief that deeper human understanding can be acquired by studying the creative revelations of artists, poets, philosophers, and composers, from our own time and from the past. More broadly, the arts, when considered in their natural humanistic and cultural context, can reveal the panorama of ever-changing human images and attitudes, as people and artists over the centuries express their conceptions of themselves, their social surroundings, and their place in the universal scheme of things. All join in the ceaseless quest to create significance for life. The ultimate objective is the understanding of self and society through familiarity with evolving visual, verbal, and tonal imagery.

Throughout the book, as the separate works of art build into a synthesis of style periods, various human images emerge. What were the citizens of Athens striving for in the classical period? How did the Greco-Roman view of the world differ from that of the early Christians? What changing constellations of concepts and events led to the medieval experience? In what images and reflections did the Renaissance world reveal itself? How are the contrasting aristocratic and middle-class ideals reconciled in the arts of the 18th century? What changes of self and society came about in the industrial age? And what courses are open to modern men and women as they explore the expanded horizons of human history, as they confront the problems of the present and probe the challenges of the future?

Readers familiar with previous editions of *Arts & Ideas* will find a number of innovations. Of the 555 illustrations in the book 116 are in full color. Moreover, the color reproductions, rather than being isolated on separate pages, are now printed adjacent to their textual discussions. Also new to this edition are 10 full-color maps, inserted so that readers can follow the changing geography of the world along with the changing arts and philosophies of its populace.

Each of the major stylistic phases covered in *Arts & Ideas* can be considered as a kind of period-piece drama of human civilization. Thus, the maps will mark the theaters where the action takes place. Five new part introductions will serve as overtures, noting the main currents at the opening of each period. The revised and updated chronologies at the beginning of each chapter function as programs, listing at a glance the background of important events that will occur and the cast of characters who will make their appearance. Introductory sections in the chapters follow in the manner of curtain raisers, which attempt to capture something of the social spirit of the time. The succeeding sections, like the several acts of a play, then present the architectural, sculptural, pictorial, literary, and musical expressions of the period. The final portion, or epilogue, of each chapter will be in the nature of a style synthesis, designed to bring the arts of each time into significant relationships within the scope of the history of ideas.

As the pragmatic philosopher John Dewey has so trenchantly expressed it, there is no immaculate conception of ideas. First comes to mind the inspired work of the great artists whose creative contributions throughout the ages have illuminated not only their own periods but ours as well, brightening the lives of all those who have eyes to see, ears to hear, and minds to understand. Then, in the research and writing of this study, one becomes aware of the immense indebtedness incurred to so many archaeologists and scholars whose diligent digging over the centuries has uncovered, brick by brick, piece by piece, the parts of the cultural jigsaw puzzle that make it possible to reconstruct and interpret the images of past periods.

My heartfelt gratitude must also be expressed to all those colleagues, associates, and friends who, over the years, have contributed so much to the nourishment and growth of this brainchild. I am thinking especially of my distinguished and learned friend Abraham Veinus and of my other colleagues in the Department of Fine Arts here at Syracuse University: Sidney Thomas, David Tatham, Meredith Lillich, Frank Macomber, George Nugent, Ellen Oppler, and Peg Weiss. Elsewhere my warm thanks go to Dan Wheeler for his sterling work on previous editions, to Patricia Newman for many cogent suggestions, and to Clyde Young for his help in preparing the manuscript. A number of teachers from across the United States have been particularly generous with their advice on this, the silver anniversary edition of *Arts & Ideas*. These include: Duncan M. Courvoisier of American River College; Linda M. Fisher of Florida Junior College at Jacksonville; Mary E. Giles of California State University, Sacramento; Helga H. Harriman and William M. McMurty of Oklahoma State University; Nancy McCollum of El Paso Community College; Deborah E. Patterson of Edison Community College; James R. Sunwall and Richard Wear of the University of Florida; and Rosemary Whitaker of Colorado State University.

Special thanks are due to the staff at Holt, Rinehart and Winston: particularly to my editor, Rita Gilbert, for her astute supervision of this project from start to finish; to Karen Dubno for her adroit editorial work; to Joan Curtis for her keen eye in ferreting out and organizing the illustrations; to Marlene Rothkin Vine for the elegant design of the book; to both Marlene Rothkin Vine and Karen Salsgiver for the appealing layout; to Barbara Curialle for her perspicacious management of details throughout the editorial process; and to Nancy Myers, for having masterminded the physical production of this volume.

Syracuse, New York   W. F.
August 1979

Contents

1
Genesis of the Arts

The Presence of the Past

"The thing that hath been, it is that which shall be; and that which is done is that which shall be done: and there is nothing new under the sun." So wrote the wise author of the Old Testament book Ecclesiastes (1:9). He seems to be thinking of the way history holds up the mirror to humanity, reflecting the present and future as well as the past, reflecting human achievement as well as potential. The search for roots and beginnings is really the quest for continuations. For how can human beings know where they are going unless they know where they have been? How can they understand the present until they know the past? The past, in fact, is never really discarded, only expanded, encompassed, and eventually transcended. As the French philosopher Henri Bergson described it, time is "the continuous progress of the past, which gnaws into the future, and which swells as it advances."

The Italian painter Giorgio de Chirico expresses this idea poetically in *Le Muse Inquietante* (Fig. 1). The title of this painting can variously be translated as *The Disquieting Muses, The Disturbing Muses,* or even *The Menacing Muses.* Usually a painting with specific subject matter, whether an impressionistic seascape or a portrait of mother and child, tries to capture and crystallize a single moment in time, to distill the essence from a constantly changing situation. In this dreamscape, however, Chirico expands the concept of time to embrace the distant past as well as a dimly seen future.

In Chirico's painting one sees three ancient Greco-Roman statues symbolizing the Muses, those mythical maidens who preside over the arts. With

1. Giorgio de Chirico. *The Disquieting Muses.* 1917. Oil on canvas, 37¾ × 25⅞″ (96 × 66 cm). Private collection.

1

CHRONOLOGY
Prehistory, Egypt, and the Ancient Near East

(all dates approximate)

PREHISTORY B.C.	
33,000–10,000	Paleolithic period (Old Stone Age)
15,000–10,000	Cave paintings and carvings in southwestern France and northern Spain
10,000– 4,000	Neolithic period (New Stone Age) Geometric art

EGYPT B.C.	
4000	Egypt united into one country
3100–2686	Early Dynastic period
2686–2181	Old Kingdom (3rd–6th Dynasties)
2650	Imhotep, architect and physician, built step pyramid of Saqqara for King Zoser (3rd Dynasty)
2590–2568	Pyramid of Khufu (Cheops)
2540–2514	Pyramid of Khafre (Chefren), Great Sphinx

2133–1991	Middle Kingdom (11th–12th Dynasties) Golden age of arts and crafts
1567–1085	New Kingdom, or Empire (18th–20th Dynasties)
1503–1482	Reign of Queen Hatshepsut. Temple of Amon, Karnak
1379–1362	Reign of Akhenaton (Amenhotep IV). Bust of Queen Nefertiti
1361–1352	Reign of Tutankhamon
1290–1225	Colossi of Rameses II
672	Assyrian conquest
525	Persian conquest
332	Conquest by Alexander the Great
332– 30	Macedonian and Greek dynasties
51– 30	Reigns of Ptolemy XIII and Cleopatra
30	Egypt became Roman province

NEAR EAST B.C.	
4000–3000	Sumerian art began

3000	Foundation of Troy I. Metal working developed
3000–1750	Babylonians
1792–1750	King Hammurabi's law code
1400–1200	Hittite Empire
1350–1000	Assyrian art began
1250–1200	Moses flourished
1025– 922	United Kingdom of Israel
1025–1000	Saul reigned
1000– 968	David reigned
968– 937	Solomon reigned
922– 783	Two Kingdoms Israel to 793 Judah to 597
884– 612	Assyrian Empire
612– 539	Neobabylonian period
605– 562	Nebuchadnezzar II, king of Babylon
575	Ishtar Gate, Babylon, constructed
539– 333	Persian Empire of Cyrus, Darius, and Xerxes
333	Conquest of Near East by Alexander the Great

wry humor the artist supplies one with a balloon in place of a head. Another wears a hatrack, an object found in ladies' closets at the turn of the century. Beside these figures are various stage props associated with performances of a type of 18th-century theater known as *commedia dell'arte*. Architecturally one discovers the medieval battlements of a castle and a Renaissance arcade together with a modern factory building and a strange futuristic tower. The setting is the main square of Ferrara, the Italian city where the artist was then living, and the castle is that of the Este family, the former rulers of the region. Chirico renders the scene with an eerie emptiness and heightens the effect with the mysterious deep perspective and the elongated shadows cast by the setting sun. He called such visions "metaphysical pictures," implying that their meaning lies beyond mere physical representation. By assembling objects ranging from ancient to modern, from the past, the present, and a projected future, he creates an image of what philosophers refer to as "the eternal now."

An even wider expanse of time is the theme of *Time Is a River without Banks* (Fig. 2), painted by Marc Chagall, Chirico's Russian colleague. In this fantasy, geological millions of years are suggested by the course of the river, evolutionary development by the half-bird, half-fish creature, the briefer human span by the clock, and a more personal, subjective perception of the flow of musical time by the floating violin being played by a disembodied hand.

The old saying that the past repeats itself is verified when two works from the past and present are compared. The Swiss sculptor Alberto Giacometti, working in the 1940s, created a sensation when such tall, thin forms as his *Man Pointing* (Fig. 3) first appeared. The extreme elongation of his fragile figures and the rugged, rough-hewn quality of their surfaces seem to set up strange vibrations in the surrounding space. But how modern is this idea? Long ago, the ancient Etruscans of central Italy arrived at a similar rendering of the human body to symbolize the spirit of the dead (Fig. 4). Although the Etruscan figure is smaller in proportion, its bronze material and general treatment are similar to the Giacometti. Such objects derive from tombs dating from the 1st and 2nd centuries B.C.

The 20th century, more than any other period, is heir to all the ages. The continuous discoveries of archaeologists, anthropologists, and historians constantly bring to light precise knowledge of the remote past and thereby increase our inherited cultural wealth. For instance, before the late 18th century, Greek art was known principally through the adaptations and copies made by the ancient Romans. The Western world first glimpsed the great Greek originals of the 5th century B.C. in the early 19th century, when Lord Elgin transported many of the Parthenon sculptures from Athens to London. Similarly, the Old Stone Age wall paintings of the cave people of Altamira in northern Spain were accidently discovered as

below: 2. Marc Chagall. *Time Is a River without Banks.* 1930–39. Oil on canvas, $39\frac{3}{8} \times 32''$ (100 × 81 cm). Museum of Modern Art, New York (anonymous gift).

right: 3. Alberto Giacometti. *Man Pointing.* 1947. Bronze; height 5'10½" (1.79 m), base 1' × 1'1¼" (.30 × .34 m). Museum of Modern Art, New York (gift of Mrs. John D. Rockefeller 3rd).

below right: 4. Votive figurine. Etruscan, 2nd–1st century B.C. Bronze, height 7½" (19 cm). Museo di Villa Giulia, Rome.

recently as 1879. As a result, the frontiers of art and civilization were pushed back by some 30,000 years.

The foundations of Western civilization are to be found in the life and arts of ancient Egypt and Mesopotamia, yet our interest in and knowledge of the ancient Near East are quite recent. Egyptian art first influenced modern taste in the 18th century in the form of rococo fancies. Popular and scientific interest gained momentum with Napoleon's expeditions, grew steadily throughout the 19th century, and eventually produced the discovery in 1922 of Tutankhamon's tomb. Its rich yield of art works had remained hidden for well over 3000 years. The Mesopotamian civilizations occupied scholars and collectors throughout the 19th century, but the high points of discovery came only with the early 20th-century excavations of Babylon and the unearthing of the Sumerian royal tombs at Ur in 1922.

The past is thus constantly alive and ever present. In order to achieve a fuller understanding of the arts, therefore, we must view them within this expanded contemporary time framework. So to the question of what is old and what is new, the answer must inevitably be that everything is both old *and* new—all art is a kind of cumulative momentum of a past that permeates the present, a continuous mixture of ideas and motifs, media and techniques, shapes and forms.

Constants and Variables

Artists, like scientists, are concerned with both constants and variables. Over thousands of years human nature has remained relatively constant. Like the ancients, we marvel at the fertility of life, the miracle of birth, the process of growth and maturity, the experience of joy and sorrow, the mystery of death. Like the people of antiquity, we are attracted by sights and sounds that delight the eye and ear; we wonder at the change of seasons, the awesomeness of the seven seas, and the vast expanse of starry skies. Like the ancient Greeks, we still try to come to terms with our own inner nature, to adjust to society and become part of the social scene, and to speculate on our place in the universal scheme of things. And like the peoples of the past, we still try to express these continually recurring themes in our poetry, music, art, and architecture.

5. Barnett Newman. *Genesis—The Break.* 1946. Oil on canvas, 24 × 27″ (61 × 69 cm). The Lone Star Foundation, Inc., New York.

6. Michelangelo.
Creation of the Sun and Moon,
detail of Sistine Chapel ceiling. 1511.
Fresco. Vatican, Rome.

If human nature is a constant, human invention is a bedazzling variable. In the past few decades we have seen the arrival of jet transportation, the development of atomic energy, the computerization of information, and the beginning of satellite communications and space exploration. It is doubtful, however, that the thrill of supersonic air speed is any greater than when the ancients first rode on horseback, when the Industrial Revolution produced the iron horse, when gunpowder was first invented, or when new continents were first explored in the age of discovery. Electronics and photojournalism have brought the whole world before our eyes. We can now watch astronauts walking on the surface of the moon and computer-controlled shovels scooping up soil samples on Mars. Yet people have always communicated—another constant—and the development of speech, language, writing, and the printed word are equal causes for wonderment. The ever-shrinking horizons have reduced our world to a planetary community. The process has also contracted our sense of time so that knowledge about the arts of the past has molded the present into an extended historical now.

One concern of the artist that has remained constant throughout the course of the arts is the nature of creativity. The poet Carl Sandburg expressed this concern of all artists by wondering when the "borderland of dream and logic, fantasy and reason, where the roots and tentacles of mind and personality float and drift" suddenly crystallizes into "a scheme, a form, a design, an invention, a machine, an image, a song, a symphony, a drama, a poem." In *Genesis—The Break* (Fig. 5) Barnett Newman, one of the masters of modern American painting, turns for his subject to the creative act itself. The stark blacks and whites in this reconstruction of the primal creative force suggest God separating light from darkness, the essential from the trivial, bringing order out of chaos, form from the void. In this titanic struggle, one can imagine a celestial body taking shape out of nothingness.

During the Renaissance Michelangelo Buonarroti struggled with the same theme in Rome while painting the scenes from Genesis on the Sistine Chapel ceiling. In the *Creation of the Sun and Moon* (Fig. 6) he personifies the universal creative force suspended between the finite world and infinity. The figure of the Creator, seen both from the front and in mirror image, seems to describe a cosmic orbit as the celestial bodies are spun off amid the starry firmament.

Both artists remind us that human beings are also creators and that creativity means bringing forth new forces and forms that cause change. From the void of the mind and the chaos of experience, the artist conceives various hints of order, even if that order is contrived chaos as some contemporary works might at first appear to be. By selecting objects at random—whether from classical ruins, the junkyard, or the supermarket—artists are using their age-old prerogative to find poetry where no one has ever seen or experienced it before.

An apt instance is in the work of the American sculptor Duane Hanson. With marvelous directness, a sharp eye for minute detail, and an enormous love of the life he sees around him, Hanson portrays the people we all observe in everyday life. *Supermarket Shopper* (Fig. 7) is a humorous embodiment of conspicuous consumption. As the artist comments: "She began my satirical period. She is a symbol of the overconsuming housewife pushing a cart filled with every kind of imaginable item that she can buy in a supermarket. . . ."

Landscape, of course, is another constant of art. It can be traced from ancient times, through the 17th-century Dutch painters, to the 19th-century romantics and impressionists. In the 1970s Alfred Leslie,

one of the new American realists, continues this tradition. His point of departure is the work of the romanticist of the Hudson River school Thomas Cole, who painted *The Oxbow* (Fig. 8) in 1836. Leslie sought out the various places where Cole had set up his easel a century and a half before and proceeded to paint a series of modern versions of the same scenes. In the instance reproduced in Figure 9, it is the so-called Oxbow, a bend in the Connecticut River as seen from Mt. Holyoke in Massachusetts.

The difference between the romantic and realistic points of view is striking. Cole creates a contrast of moods, with the approaching storm on the left and the rest of the landscape still bathed in sunshine. He is following the *picturesque* tradition of painting the wild, elemental, awesome moods of nature. Here he projects into his painting a feeling of solitude and the longing to find peace and comfort amid the beautiful and sublime aspects of nature. Leslie, on the other hand, paints what he actually sees. The atmosphere and weather are stable, suggesting no particular emotional overtones. He also includes such anti-picturesque details as the interstate superhighway that slashes through the scene in the background.

Leslie, like many of his fellow realists, takes advantage of the latest developments of color photography to aid both the eye and the memory when he refines his composition back in the studio. Working from photographs, however, is far from new in the history of art. The 19th-century French landscapist Gustave Courbet found the camera an important aid in his studio. Later Paul Cézanne, who developed his great still-life paintings painstakingly over a period of months and even years, used photographs of his carefully studied compositions as an invaluable record of his original intentions long after the apples, onions, and flowers had decayed and faded away.

All art begs the age-old question, What is real? Each generation of artists has come to grips with reality in one form or another. The impressionists saw reality in fleeting atmospheric effects. In the mid-19th century Courbet and Manet, who called themselves realists, found it in casual, everyday subjects and in forest scenes. Leonardo da Vinci's reality is reflected in his meticulously accurate drawings of human anatomy; Michelangelo's is in the powerful musculature of his heroic figures. The ancient Romans found reality in their forthright, uncompromising, unflattering portraits, the ancient Greeks in the mathematical proportions of their sculptured gods and goddesses, and the Cro-Magnon cave people in

7. Duane Hanson, *Supermarket Shopper*. 1970.
Polyester resin polychromed in oil, with clothing,
steel cart, groceries; life-size.
Courtesy O. K. Harris Works of Art, New York.

above: 8. Thomas Cole. *The Oxbow.* 1836. Oil on canvas, $4'3\frac{1}{2}'' \times 6'4''$ (1.31 × 1.93 m).
Metropolitan Museum of Art, New York (gift of Mrs. Russell Sage, 1908).

below: 9. Alfred Leslie. *View of the Oxbow on the Connecticut River as Seen from Mt. Holyoke.*
1971–72. Oil on canvas, $5'11'' \times 8'9\frac{1}{4}''$ (1.82 × 2.7 m).
Collection Peter Ludwig, Aachen, West Germany.

their carefully rendered naturalistic representations of the animals that roamed the primeval forests. Since defining reality is a necessary struggle for artists of all periods, we have, in effect, come full circle, back to the beginning, and surely "what has been is that which shall be."

Today's modernity is but tomorrow's history. Ever since Adam and Eve left the Garden of Eden, crisis and change have been built into the human experience. As the old saying goes, the more things change, the more they remain the same. What is important for the contemporary artist and audience, however, is the easier access to the vast body of the world's literature, art, and music. With so many media, so many levels of taste, and so many frames of reference available, both the artist and audience now have an almost unlimited number of choices.

In this larger geographical and historical now, the arts today are what contemporary audiences choose to look at, listen to, and read, whether ancient or modern. A survey of recital and symphony programs and of the recordings people buy will quickly reveal that Bach, Mozart, and Beethoven are still the most popular classical composers. In this sense they are as relevant as such avant-garde figures as John Cage with his theatrical improvised happenings and Karlheinz Stockhausen with his electronically synthesized fantasies (see Chap. 22). Only a short time ago observers were warning of the imminent death of such time-honored institutions as symphony orchestras and opera companies, which were labeled museums where only the works of the past were preserved. Yet both symphony and opera are alive and well today with full public support, constantly expanding seasons, and ever-increasing audiences. Likewise, when we view great picture collections in the museums of the world, the El Grecos and Rembrandts still communicate to us with the force of living art quite as much as the Barnett Newmans and Giorgio de Chiricos.

The presence of the past is also apparent in the host of ancient media that are now being rediscovered and adapted to contemporary expression—mosaics, various fresco techniques, encaustics, painting in tempera and in stained glass—all hundreds, even thousands, of years old. These media hold their own amid many new modes and methods, but contrary to the popular notion they are certainly not the message. The fundamental experience of what it is to be human—to be alive, to see, to hear, to love, to laugh, to feel, to think—is what counts. In a work of art the consideration is not the medium, the subject matter, or any of the observable details, but the contribution the work can make to our lives, the sharpening of our perceptions, the suggestions to our sensations, feelings, and imagination.

Past, present, and future are thus finely woven into the fabric of contemporary life as well as of history. They are simply different dimensions of the human experience, and in order to understand the artistic manifestations of these different dimensions the viewer, reader, and listener must know how to supply the various frames of reference. So the arts that move us, speak to us, delight us, whether of the past or present, whether Oriental, European, or American, are a basic part of our immediate experience. All move and live and have their being within the extended historical perspective of contemporary knowledge and awareness in this astonishing time machine called the 20th century.

Onward into the Past

Stone Age Beginnings

Many and varied are the faces of art, and together they reveal the basic urges and aspirations of human beings. The search for sights and sounds that delight the senses is only one of these many faces. Cave artists may have drawn animals to sharpen their eyes before the chase. African tribal members donned the masks of their ancestors to invoke their strength in the struggle for life. Aborginal tribes fashioned idols and fetishes to protect them from evil spirits. Medicine men sang magic incantations to restore health. In times of drought the American Indian performed rain dances. Egyptian rulers built and embellished tombs to provide for their needs beyond the grave.

Through monuments, statues, paintings, dance rhythms, and the sounds of music, people reveal the divinity of their gods, the might of their rulers, the force of nature. For art begins in myth and magic, in images and image making, in tombs and temples, in war whoops and anguished outcries, in mating calls and work songs. The artistic search may lead to dark caverns and sunny shores, to sanctuaries and castles, to the abodes of the living and the dead. Whether carving out a shelter on a rocky ledge, laying out sites for religious rites, or burying the dead, human beings—through art—concern themselves with the natural and supernatural, the real and unreal, the seen and unseen, the past and future, the transitory and eternal.

The first human expressions in the arts are clouded over by the mists of prehistory. Whether people sought safety in the confines of the caves or built huts of mammoth bones and animal skins, early societies have from the first been involved with architecture. Making shelters for the body, refuges for the spirit, and sanctuaries for the gods were the earliest concerns. Ever since men and women saw their reflections in still pools, the desire to represent

left: 10.
Paleolithic cave painting.
c. 15,000–10,000 B.C.
Approximately life-size.
Lascaux (Dordogne), France.

below: 11.
Venus of Willendorf.
c. 30,000–10,000 B.C.
Limestone, height 4⅜″ (11 cm).
Natural History Museum, Vienna.

nature and human nature suggested itself to early peoples. The bone whistles, flutes, and drumsticks found in caves and graves tell of the power of sound to evoke moods and echo the footsteps of man, woman, and beast in mysterious rites. Strange crisscross lines, V-shaped markings, and dots and circles on bone, ivory, and cave surfaces reveal that the Cro-Magnon people created some sort of visual language that recorded a vast variety of observed detail, possibly notes of seasonal changes, records of births, and the like.

Through the magic of images, early peoples dealt with hunting and being hunted, with life and death, with existence and extinction (Fig. 10). Cave artists represented what they actually saw with such accuracy and immediacy that later literate societies have never excelled the sheer strength of the pictorial record left from prehistory. The herds of beasts and spirited specimens painted and carved on cave walls and ceilings tell of the precarious place of the cave people in a world dominated by brutish forces. The artists made these startlingly lifelike animals by outlining and shading them with charcoal, then adding colors in reddish brown and yellow ochre clays. Though horses and antelopes appear in herds, the art of grouping figures or organizing images into complete compositions seems to have been of little or no importance.

These animal images may have been created simply for the pleasure of making a living likeness. More probably they were symbols standing for the processes of nature. Their placement in remote underground grottoes suggests sanctuaries where religious rituals and ceremonies were performed. Evidence that lances were hurled at the paintings also points to primitive hunting rites. For the cave people,

art served life, art and reality were one, and the image was the animal. By imitating their prey exactly, hunters could gain power over it. The idea was to create a double and then assault it. They could then bring their true quarry to bay.

All across Ice Age Europe female images have been found. The featureless face of the figure known as the Venus of Willendorf (Fig. 11) exudes pride and

contentment. She bends over her large breasts and clasps them with tiny arms. In this and other such sculptures, the voluptuous contours, fleshy hips, huge bosoms, and exaggerated sex characteristics suggest mother goddesses of some fertility cult. Thus many thousands of years before the beginnings of recorded history, the Ice Age people produced art that embraced naturalism and realism, abstraction and expressionistic distortion.

Naturalistic animal and human images did not serve the purposes of later, more complex societies. For them, signs and symbols served better than reality to depict the unseen forces of wind and weather, the spirits of good and evil, the souls of the dead. The mask reproduced in Figure 12 was designed to be worn by an African tribesman as he danced by firelight to the accompaniment of drums. The small, round, protruding mouth, the enlarged eyes, and the long triangular nose are not intended to represent a living person but to conjure up the presence of an invisible spirit. By impersonating the unseen presence, by enacting ritual steps and gestures, tribal peoples could come in contact with the vital rhythms and controlling influences of their world. To the tribe, the masked dancer was an ancestral hero, a god to be pleased, or a demon to be pacified. Through such fetishes and idols, divine beings and mythical heroes resided among the living and enabled the tribe to assume their powers and skills, win victories at arms, or ensure a good harvest.

African tribal art was one of the "discoveries" of 20th-century anthropologists and artists. It helped initiate the movement toward both abstraction and the distortion of reality for expressive purposes. Picasso's *Woman's Head* (Fig. 13), one of a series of studies for his *Demoiselles d'Avignon* (see Fig. 455), is an apt example.

As seen in a bronze horse from the very early period of Greek art called "geometric" (Fig. 14), the artist was not so much concerned with reproducing the living likeness as with grasping the essence, the concept of the horse. Such objects are found in temple precincts, where they were brought as *votive offerings* by worshipers who petitioned or thanked the deities for divine favors—for victory in a race, fertility of a farm, restoration to good health.

Similarly, the female form as revealed in Figure 15 is simplified and abstracted into a compact, flattened shape. The intent of these "island idols" is not known. Since they cannot stand upright they are not statuettes. Found in tombs, where they were placed beside the body, these carved figures may be goddesses, fertility forms, guides to the underworld, or spirits of the dead. The artist has stamped a preconceived geometrical outline on the material, which is the fine-grained white crystalline marble found in the Cyclades Islands near Crete. The smooth surface treatment is broken by the sharp angular arrangement of the arms, the long straight noses, and the conventional flat-topped heads devoid of other facial features.

The *conventions* of a period are the inherited, invented, and prescribed formulas that the people who formed its culture generally understood. The traditional arrangement of areas and rooms in a temple or dwelling, the larger-than-life representations and rigid postures of gods and rulers, the appearance of a masked deity or hero to pronounce the prologue and epilogue of a Greek drama, the required fourteen lines of a sonnet, the repeated rhythmic patterns of dances, the way characters speak in rhymed meters in poetic drama and sing their lines in opera—all are conveniences that became conventions through their acceptance by a representative

below: 14. Horse. Greek "geometric" style,
c. 750 B.C. Bronze, height 6¼" (16 cm).
State Museums, West Berlin.

right: 15. Idol, from Amorgos, Cyclades Islands.
c. 3000 B.C. Marble, height 30" (76 cm).
Ashmolean Museum, Oxford.

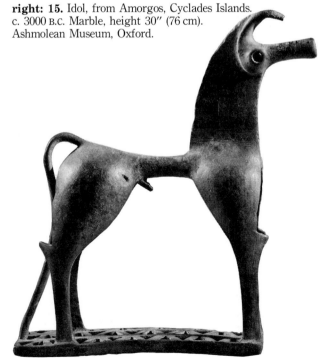

number of people whose commonly held values and attitudes formed a culture.

The work of a period or particular artist is often criticized because it seems conventional or full of clichés. But all art is based on the observations of some rules. When everything is too much as expected, it tends to be repetitious and boring; however, if all is completely unanticipated, it becomes bewildering. Competent artisans of any time can master the basic media, the necessary techniques, the accepted conventions of their era. Only the true artist knows how to depart from the rules meaningfully and how to break them brilliantly. Conventions are a body of habits, but a significant work is a stroke of genius. Conventions are perspiration; art is inspiration. Conventions are predictable; greatness is unpredictable. Conventions are the heritage of tradition; innovations are the mark of change.

The shift in prehistory from a nomadic to a communal life, from a food-hunting to a food-gathering

Genesis of the Arts 11

society, from an animal-chasing to a cattle-breeding economy is reflected in the arts by the shift from naturalistic or direct imitation of nature to a more geometric art based on formal principles and traditional conventions. Concrete images yielded to abstract forms, naturalism to stylization, imitation to idealization, the actual to the metaphorical. In short, the rendering of reality was replaced by accepted conventions. These are the polar extremes in relation to which the art of all following periods tended to express itself—the faithful portrayal of the natural appearance and "speaking" likeness on the one hand, and the conceptual, geometric, stylized conventions of the established formulas on the other.

Ancient Egyptian Art

A wise mixture of accepted formulas and accurate observation of life is found in the art of ancient Egypt. Through impressive temples and spacious palaces, magnificent statues and murals, representations of priestly ceremonies and royal processions, the artist could give flesh and blood to the concepts of divinity, kingship, and priestly authority. Originality and innovation were discouraged, which caused artists, for the most part, to concentrate on technique and skill of execution. Yet the paintings on the walls of Egyptian tombs show a keen eye for informal activities and naturalistic detail.

Egyptian society was like a pyramid with the Pharaoh as its peak. As a descendant of the sun he ruled with absolute authority and was responsible only to his gods and ancestors. The Pyramid of Khufu (Cheops in Greek) is the largest and grandest of funerary monuments, meant to last forever (Fig. 16). The statistics are staggering. Combining the basic geometrical forms of the square and triangle, it was built of 2.3 million blocks of stone, each weighing about 2.5 tons (2.3 metric tons). The stupendous structure covers more than 13 acres (5.2 hectares), encloses a volume of 85 million cubic feet (2.4 million cubic meters), and is completely solid except for two small burial chambers. To line it up with the four corners of the world, it was surveyed so accurately that each of its 755-foot (299-meter) sides faces one of the cardinal points of the compass. So skillfully is the stone cut that joinings are scarcely visible. For centuries the pyramids have been convenient quarries, so that now the original smooth facing of varicolored sandstone and granite remains in only a few places. For sheer simplicity and endless durability, these masterly solids are likely to outlast anything humankind has produced.

The companions of this mighty monument are the pyramids of Khufu's dynastic successors and lesser members of the royal line. The guardian of this city of the dead is the inscrutable Sphinx (Fig. 16), which combines the resting body of a lion with a human head. It is placed beside the tomb of King Khafre (Chefren in Greek), whose pyramid is second in size only to that of his father. Facing the rising sun, the Sphinx's body symbolizes immortality (the Pharaohs were often buried in lion skins), while the face is thought to be a portrait of the deified King Khafre himself.

The priestly caste made its architectural mark in Egypt's temples. From its origins in the practice of occult magic, this group gradually gained in scientific knowledge and social influence. Cloaked in veils of secrecy, the priests were skilled in geometry and mathematics, knew the heavens and the movements of stars, and could predict the time when the Nile would overflow and bring renewed life to fields and gardens. At first, the priests had their temples carved out of the living rock, but gradually they caused them to assume stylized architectural forms. Approaching by broad avenues, worshipers entered through massive *pylons,* or gateways, into a forecourt beyond which lay mysterious *hypostyle* halls (Fig. 17) and inner sanctums where the roofs rested on forests of columns with strange hieroglyphic inscriptions.

A colossal statue of Rameses II (Fig. 17) typifies the aloof, rigid, unchangeable images of the Pharaohs. Serenely above it all, this sculptured form provides no suggestion of movement to disturb its ma-

18. Tuthmosis. *Queen Nefertiti.* c. 1370 B.C. Painted limestone with inlaid glass eye, height 20″ (51 cm). State Museums, West Berlin.

jestic calm. Strict convention dictated the stance, with its severe frontality, stylized ceremonial beard, and hands placed upon the knees. As the direct descendant of Horus, god of the skies, Rameses appears as the absolute ruler and judge of his people.

The sole exception to these rigid and stylized representations of Pharaohs occurs during the reign of Amenhotep IV, who rejected the many gods and rituals of his ancestors, adopted monotheism, and changed his name to Akhenaton ("Beneficial of the Aton," the universal and sole god of the sun). The unfinished bust of his beauteous queen, Nefertiti, was found at Tell el Amarna in the workshop of the sculptor Tuthmosis (Fig. 18). Despite the royal headdress, regal dignity, conventional elongated neck, and bright paint, the living likeness of a real personality with genuine human warmth shows through. On close examination, the queen can be seen as a woman well past the bloom of youth but not yet prey to the ravages of age. Breaking with formal conventions, as well as with precedent, Akhenaton allowed himself to be portrayed informally as he offered his queen a flower and fondled his baby daughter, with Nefertiti holding two infant princesses on her lap. Despite the restoration of polytheism, this informality carried over briefly into the reign of his successor, King Tutankhamon, famed because his is the only Pharaonic tomb found in modern times almost intact and unplundered. On the back of Tutankhamon's throne

(Fig. 19), the King is shown in a relaxed attitude talking with his wife while the sun god bestows his divine blessing with many raylike hands.

The dominant fact of Egyptian life was death. And the art forms assume the shapes of mummy cases, stone sarcophagi, death masks, sculptured portraits, pyramids, tombs—all associated with death. The purpose was not to gladden the eye of the living, but to provide for the needs of the dead in the afterlife. Death for prominent Egyptians did not mean extinction but rather a continuation of life beyond the grave. To achieve immortality the body had to be preserved and the tomb elaborately furnished. The inner walls, floors, and ceilings were covered with hieroglyphic inscriptions that identified the deceased and recounted his or her titles and honors, and with portrayals of the deceased surrounded by family and friends and occupied with his or her favorite pursuits. The tomb's occupant was shown supervising work in the fields, making offerings to the gods, sailing a boat, hunting or fishing, watching the dance, listening to music, or playing games. In wall paintings and reliefs, fruit and game were provided for the table and handmaidens and manservants to take care of all needs. Everything was designed to make the deceased feel completely at home.

As seen in tomb paintings (Figs. 20, 21), the Egyptian artist was concerned only with the picture plane, not with creating illusions of depth, modeling the figures in three dimensions, or showing them against a background. According to the usual conventions, the heads are always drawn in profile, but the eyes (several thousand years before Picasso) are repre-

top: 19. Back of Tutankhamon's Throne, from Thebes. c. 1365 B.C. Wood covered with gold leaf and colored inlays of faience, glass, and stone; back width 21″ (53 cm). Egyptian Museum, Cairo.

above: 20. *Offering Bearers,* from Tomb of Sebekhotep, Thebes. c. 1500–1300 B.C. Tempera on mud plaster, width c. 30″ (76 cm). Metropolitan Museum of Art, New York (Rogers Fund, 1930).

right: 21. *Musicians with Double Aulos, Lute, and Harp,* from Tomb of Nakht, Thebes. 18th dynasty (c. 1420 B.C.). Height 15⅝″ (40 cm).

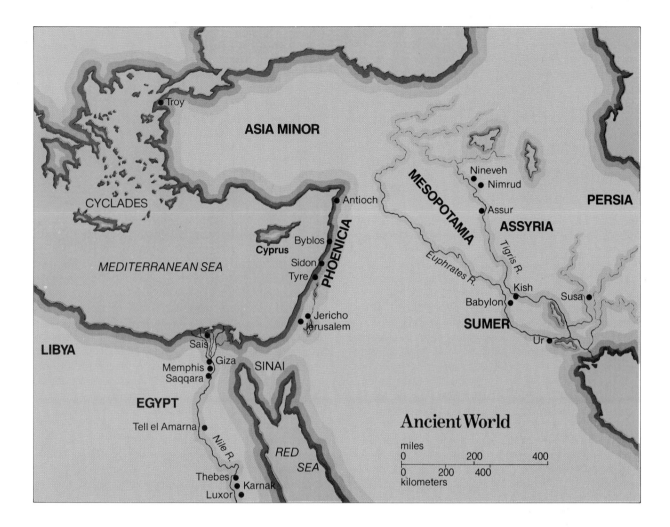

The following labels appear on the map:

Troy

ASIA MINOR

CYCLADES

Antioch

Nineveh • Nimrud

MESOPOTAMIA

PERSIA

Assur

ASSYRIA

Byblos
Cyprus

Sidon

PHOENICIA

Tyre

MEDITERRANEAN SEA

Euphrates R.

Tigris R.

Kish

Babylon

Susa

SUMER

Jericho
Jerusalem

Ur

LIBYA

Sais

Memphis • Giza
Saqqara

SINAI

EGYPT

Tell el Amarna

Nile R.

RED
SEA

AncientWorld

miles
0   200   400

0   200   400
kilometers

Thebes
Karnak
Luxor

Ancient World

sented front face. The torsos are frontal, but the arms and legs offer a side view. And though the figures are shown from the right side, they have two left feet so that both big toes are toward the front. If a pool or river is included in a landscape, the view of it is from above, but fish, ducks, plants, and trees in and around it are shown sideways. Important personages always appear larger than their families, followers, or servants. Once these conventions are taken for granted, the scenes appear remarkably lifelike. Naturalistic detail is rendered so accurately that botanists and zoologists can recognize each separate species of plant and animal life. The Egyptian artist also knew how to portray the fur and feathers of animals and birds by breaking up the color surfaces with minute brushstrokes of various hues. Egyptian tomb art is thus a recreation of life as it was experienced in the flesh, and these still-vital, colorful murals provide an amazingly complete and comprehensive picture of how people behaved in an ancient civilization.

Dynamics of History

Mainstreams of Influence

Art history, like philosophy and science, is concerned with causes and effects. Thus, in reviewing the major styles of Western culture, one should keep in mind the mainstreams of influence. The dynamics of contact and conquest affect both the condition of life and the expression in art. But conquest is a double-edged sword. On one side the conquerors stamp their image on the conquered; on the other the overlords absorb many of the forms and expressions characteristic of the subjugated peoples.

Egypt and Mesopotamia developed as landlocked powers and closed societies that, with little dependence on outside forces, were nurtured from inner reserves. But the Greeks were seafaring folk and, like the Romans after them, had to look beyond their shores for the maritime trade, commercial ventures, and colonization essential to their survival. The

Greeks came in contact with Egyptian and Mesopotamian scientific and artistic traditions and then absorbed, refined, and transformed them into their own unparalleled achievements. Rome, as the cultural melting pot of antiquity, successfully merged the ideas, building methods, ornamental motifs, plastic and pictorial traditions, literary and musical expressions of the Greek, Near Eastern, Egyptian, North African, and Etruscan cultures, together with significant contributions of their own.

Arts and Society

Since artists must represent their world as they themselves see it, their work becomes a reflection of their time from a particular point of view. Their temples, statues, pictures, poems, or pieces of music are indications of how sensitive members of that society imagine, dream, think, feel, and communicate. In this light a building is not a mere pile of sticks and stones, steel and glass, no matter how interesting the shapes these materials may assume. Rather, it is a created environment, a form of action for some social activity. Masses and voids, solids and hollows, create rhythms in space. It could be said that the architect is the ballet master who writes the figure of a dance that all who enter the structure must perform. From architectural engineering it is possible to tell how much a people know about their environment, how advanced scientific knowledge was, whether they were hunters or farmers, kings or commoners. The Ishtar Gate of ancient Babylon (Fig. 22), for instance, shows that the Assyrians knew the principle of the arch and vault long before the Romans came on the scene. Dating from the time of King Nebuchadnezzar II, the gate was part of a proud wall that the King had built to enclose his temples. Made of glazed brick, the gate's monumental decorations depict a stately procession of lions and dragons, stylized horses and graceful gazelles.

No art, however, is independent of its companion arts. Architecture finds its natural ally in sculpture as embellishment that relieves that strict functionalism of a structure. Sculpture can provide focal points of interest and give meaning to a building. In ancient times reliefs and freestanding statues were a visual reflection of the activity the architectural setting was designed to house. In a more exalted sense a statue becomes the image of the heroic or godlike ideal toward which a people is striving.

Paintings, frescoes, and mosaics supply the pictorial dimension. In them one discovers the profile of an age as well as the hopes and fears of the people who created them. Poetry and music crystallize the rhythms of human activity in songs and dances that reflect work and play, joy and sorrow, as well as the deepest longings and highest aspirations of the human heart.

Whether architect, sculptor, painter, poet, or musician, the artist begins the creative process with the vanishing point of the void—empty space and undefined time—then *composes* in the literal sense of selecting materials, placing them together, building them up. The procedure is from the singular toward the plural, from unrelatedness to relatedness, as the artist reaches out toward the order and unity of a particular style.

Unity and Diversity

The search for unity within historical style periods, or at least for a logical grouping of diversities, is crucial for both defining style and criticizing art. Cultural expressions, in the manner of the classical unities of Greek drama, usually occur within definite limits of time, place, and action. The search for the underlying ideas that motivate human activities can often reduce to simplicity what appears on the surface as a confusing multiplicity of directions. And because the arts are usually experienced simultaneously, not separately, it is often wiser to seek understanding from many directions rather than from one. If a common pattern of ideas can be found, then aspects that previously proved baffling may suddenly fall into place and acquire meaning.

Such ideas may be originated by artists themselves, either individually or as a group, or by single or collective patrons who have the insight, means, and energy to pursue complicated projects to completion. Such a patron might be a ruler with the vision of Pericles, who presided over the cultural climax of ancient Athens; an enterprising medieval abbot or bishop who envisaged a great monastery or cathedral complex; a family of merchant princes, such as the Medici, who brought Renaissance Florence to its creative peak; or a religious order like the Jesuits, who spread the Counter-Reformation baroque style in the wake of their missionary activities. The 20th century has witnessed the Commonwealth of India commissioning the Swiss-born architect Le Corbusier to design and construct Chandigarh, an entirely new capital city for the East Punjab, complete with every public and private facility. In New York, the heirs of a modern industrialist have sponsored an architectural complex in Rockefeller Center that compares in grandeur with the imperial forums of ancient Rome. And many public agencies and private contributors have joined forces to erect in New York the Lincoln Center "acropolis" that embraces a group of opera houses, concert halls, repertory theaters, libraries, museums, and educational and cultural centers.

22. Ishtar Gate (restored), from Babylon. c. 575 B.C. Enameled sun-dried brick, height 48′9″ (15 m). Near Eastern Museum, State Museums, East Berlin.

Whenever a center has attained a degree of civilization, has developed a prosperous economy, has produced a number of promising individuals, has fostered an adequate educational system, has in its midst groups of artists and artisans, a significant cultural expression may occur. When this happens, it is usually because some individuals with powerful convictions have reacted so strongly to the challenge of their time that they are catapulted into dominating positions.

Various explanations have been advanced for this phenomenon, such as the theory that outstanding persons stamp their image upon an age, and that genius is the primary causal influence on history. Social realists, however, contend that environmental forces shape the characters and actions of the indi-

viduals involved. The truth probably lies somewhere between these extremes of nature and nurture. The interplay between powerful personalities and the stimulus of their times brings about the explosion commonly described as genius.

Techniques of production are the private problems of particular artists. Composition, however, is common to them all. An architect puts building materials together, a poet words, a musician tones. But contrary to the views of some purists, they do not do so merely in order to express themselves but in order to communicate thoughts, fantasies, social comments, satirical observations, self-revelations, images of order, and the like. Their works—temples, statues, murals, odes, sonatas, symphonies—are addressed not to themselves but to their fellow human beings.

The choice of medium, the way of handling materials, the language used to express thoughts, personal idioms and idiosyncrasies, mode of vision, manner of representing the world, all add up to a vocabulary of symbols and images that define an artist's individual *style*. In a broader sense, however, a style must include similar expressions in many media, whether in visual, verbal, or tonal forms. Artists working within a given time and place share a common sociocultural heritage; therefore, it follows that each has a common point of departure. In the arts, as in politics, there are conservatives who try to preserve traditional values, liberals who are concerned with current trends, and progressives who point to coming developments. The individual artist may accept or reject, endorse or protest, conform or reform, construct or destroy, dream of the past or prophesy the future, but the taking-off point must be the artist's own time. The accents with which artists and their contemporaries speak, the vocabularies they choose, the passion with which they champion ideas, all add up to the larger synthesis of a style.

Time, Place, and Idea A positive approach in the search for unity, then, can be established on the coincidence of *time, place,* and *idea.* Artists, while working in separate fields, are a basic part of a society, living within a certain geographical and temporal center, and collaborating in varying degrees with each other and with the larger social group. The closer the coincidence of these factors, the closer the relationship will be. Composite works of art—forums, monasteries, cathedrals, operas—are always collaborative in nature and must be made to express the several interests they are designed to serve. Liturgical needs, for instance, have to be taken into account in the design of a cathedral, and the sculptural and pictorial schemes must fit into an iconographic, or symbolic, program and the overall *architectonic,* or structural, plan. Hence in one *time* and in one *place,* the arts of architecture, sculpture, painting, music, literature, and liturgy share a common constellation of *ideas* in relation to the contemporary social order and its spiritual aspirations.

True history is no mere record of dates, treaties, battles, kings, and generals. Aristotle long ago recognized this vital fact when he placed poetic truth higher than historical truth. The political experience of a nation is but one phase of its whole life. If one desires to know the spirit and inner life of a people, one must look at its art, literature, dances, and music, where the spirit of the whole people is reflected. While kings, dynasties, and dictators rise and fall, and political revolutions and battles seem abruptly to settle the affairs of nations, the arts, as the expression of the living unity of a people, reveal the continuity of life. Romain Rolland has rightly observed: "Art, like life, is inexhaustible; and nothing makes us feel the truth of this better than music's ever-welling spring, which has flowed through the centuries until it has become an ocean."

Through the study of the arts in relation to the life and time out of which they spring, a richer, broader, deeper humanistic understanding can be achieved. The past, as reflected in the arts, exists as a continuous process, and any arbitrary separation from the present and future disappears in the presence of a living work. True critical judgment of art, or indeed of any other human activity, can never be a catalogue of minutiae, a record of isolated moments. Understanding can come only when one event is related to another, and when their sum total is absorbed into the growing stream of universal life from which each particular moment derives its significance. In their natural relationship, the arts become the study of people reflected in the ever-changing images of men and women as they journey across historical time, search for reality, and strive to achieve the ideals that create meaning for life.

All creative activity begins in the mind's eye and ear of the artist, but a work of art that does not communicate meaning is stillborn. Art, then, is a two-way process involving both creator and recreator. The activity of the recreator, to be sure, may be less than that of the artist, but it is a dynamic activity nevertheless. The experience of responding to a work of art conjures up corresponding sets of perceptions, images, and impressions of one's own. To play this part in the creative act, the recreator must learn the visual, verbal, and auditory vocabularies that make communication possible and that distinguish the finer nuances of sight and sound. Imagination and knowledge must be summoned to supply the frame of reference and the aura that once surrounded the work of art in its original context. Hence it is necessary to know the period and style, the social and religious circumstances, the patronage system and personal situation within which the artist worked. These pages, then, have been written to guide the viewer, reader, and listener on the quest for enjoyment, knowledge, and understanding of the humanistic experience.

I
THE
CLASSICAL
PERIOD

The Greco-Roman classical period spanned about 1000 years. It extended from the glorious age of Pericles, when Greek culture reached its zenith, witnessed the expansion of Greek settlements under Alexander the Great, saw the rise of Roman power and the grandeur of the Roman Empire, and concluded with the decline and fall of Rome.

Instead of accepting mythological and religious explanations of the nature of their world, the early Greek philosophers boldly struck out to examine the physical world for themselves. Pythagoras discovered a unity in nature based on numbers; this led to a picture of the universe based on the music of the spheres, in which the heavenly bodies respond to mathematically predictable measurements. Socrates' relentless pursuit of truth, goodness, and beauty made him the hero of his pupil Plato, the supreme idealist, for whom the world of ideas was preeminent. Aristotle's approach was more down-to-earth. He systematized the entire scope of knowledge in his works on logic, ethics, politics, poetics, biology, physics, and metaphysics. For 2000 years he remained the highest philosophical and scientific authority in the Western world.

While Greek thought was mainly theoretical, the later Romans were adept at applying general principles to practical problems. They developed the science of engineering, architecture, and public-works projects to a fine degree. Their practicality was reflected in their administrative genius.

Classical Greek civilization did not rise without challenges. At first the eastern Mediterranean was dominated by the Persian empire, and the flourishing Greek cities in Asia Minor fell under Persian control. When Darius I invaded the Greek mainland, however, his Persians were turned back in the Battle of Marathon. Later the Persians regrouped under Xerxes, defeated the Greeks, and plundered Athens. Undaunted, the Greeks lured the Persian fleet into the strait of Salamis just west of Athens, defeating them in 480 B.C. This ended the Persian threat to the mainland and marks the transition from the archaic, or old, period to the classical phase.

Instead of rebuilding and reconstructing their old shrines, the Greeks cleared the rubble and embarked on an ambitious new building program. They also formed the Delian League, a defensive alliance to protect them from future Persian attacks. When its treasury was moved from the island of Delos to Athens by Pericles, the league became the basis for an Athenian empire. The ambitions of the Athenians, however, awakened the jealousies of neighboring city-states, notably Sparta. The resulting Peloponnesian War ended with the defeat of Athens. Thereafter the decentralization of power among small city-states paved the way for the conquest of the Greek peninsula by Philip of Macedon. His son Alexander expanded the Greek empire by conquering Egypt, Persia, and western Asia right up to the Ganges River.

Alexander's death in 323 B.C. marks the beginning of the Hellenistic period. The great conqueror left an empire too huge to be ruled by one head. The main parts fell to his principal generals— Ptolemy taking Egypt, Seleucis Persia, and Attalus the northern part of Asia Minor. The mainland Greek population dispersed to occupy the conquered territory. Eventually, Greek power was so thinly spread that it challenged the ambitious Romans, who by the end of the Second Punic War (201 B.C.) had largely conquered the Greeks.

By their brilliance in organization and warfare the Romans emerged as the strongest power in Italy. After founding a republic, they gradually expanded their command to include the entire Mediterranean world and most of Europe. The genius of Julius Caesar brought all of Gaul and parts of Britain and Germany into the Roman orbit and the government of Rome under his personal control. After his assassination, his grandnephew Octavian assumed command of the army and, in a triumvirate with Mark Anthony and Lepidus, overthrew the Republic. Later Octavian defeated Anthony and Cleopatra in the Battle of Actium and became the sole ruler of the Roman Empire with the title Caesar Augustus.

Under the guidance of the great emperors, beginning with Trajan and Hadrian and continuing with Antoninus Pius and Marcus Aurelius, Rome reached the pinnacle of her power. The whole known Western world was thus brought into a unified system of law and order with peace and prosperity prevailing. The Roman achievements in public administration, city planning, and architecture are legendary.

After this enlightened period Roman stability was undermined by the gathering of land and wealth into the hands of a few, threats of rebellion by distant conquered peoples, the breaking up of religious unity and rise of Christianity, invasions by barbarian tribes, and a decline of population. Emperor Constantine saw the coming dissolution and established a more easily defended capital in the eastern city of Byzantium, renaming it Constantinople. This division of the empire into eastern and western halves, each with its own emperor, further weakened Roman stability. Rome was repeatedly sacked by successive waves of Gauls, Huns, and Vandals. When the situation became unbearable, the West Roman Emperor Honorius moved his capital northward to Ravenna. In 476 A.D. the Ostrogoths, a Germanic people from the Danube valley, captured the city and caused the collapse of the West Roman Empire.

Greco-Roman as well as Judeo-Christian societies were based on the principle of patriarchy, in which the father image dominated family, social, political, and religious life. Circumstances conspired, however, to bring women of exceptional abilities to the fore. There were the reigns of queens Hatshepsut and Cleopatra in Egypt and Artemesia in the Hellenistic kingdom of Caria. Sappho, considered to be the greatest Greek lyric poet, was hailed by Plato as "the tenth Muse." Women of the patrician class became prominent in Roman times but played their roles behind the scenes rather than in the public eye. With such exceptions, there is no record that women were active in public life or in the production of art before the medieval period.

2
The Hellenic Style

Athens, 5th Century B.C.

The land of Hellas, a small city-state dedicated to Athena, goddess of wisdom, saw the birth of a new spirit—a spirit destined to quicken the human heart and mind then, now, and for ages to come. Here in Athens for a brief span of time were concentrated the creative energies of many geniuses. There were leaders capable of securing Athens' victory in the struggle to dominate the Mediterranean world (see map, p. 52); statesmen with the perception to make Athens the first democracy in an era of tyrants; philosophers committed to search for an understanding of the physical, social, and spiritual nature of the environment they lived in; and artists who conceived daring expressions in stone, word, and tone.

In 480 B.C. the Athenians had turned the tide against the powerful Persians, but only after their city had been reduced to rubble. Without hereditary rulers, government rested on the shoulders of the citizen class, and the rule of the *demos,* the "people," became the order of the day. Here the statesman Pericles and the philosopher Socrates heard the wisdom of Anaxagoras, who taught that the universe was governed by a supreme mind that brought form out of the chaos of nature. He also taught that people, by thinking for themselves, could likewise bring order into human affairs.

After the destruction of their city, the Athenians boldly faced the future. They launched a new building program that surpassed anything the world had ever seen and that would serve as an eternal model.

Like many other ancient cities, Athens had developed around an *acra,* or "hill," originally found suitable as a military vantage point. A long-ago victory on this fortified hilltop, known as the *acropolis* (Fig. 23),

23. Acropolis, Athens, from southwest.

CHRONOLOGY
The Hellenic Period

GENERAL EVENTS B.C.

c.1600–c.1100		Mycenaean period
	c.1184	Fall of Troy to Achaeans
	c.1100	Dorians and Ionians invaded Greek peninsula, conquered Achaeans. End of Mycenaean period, beginning of Hellenic civilization
c.800–	c.650	Geometric period; Homer; Eastern contacts
	776	First Olympic games; beginning of Greek calendar
	c.700	Hesiod wrote *Theogony* (basis of Greek mythology)
c.650–	c.500	Archaic period
	534	Playwriting competitions began at Athens
	c.494	Persians under Darius invaded Greece
	c.490	Athenians defeated Persians at Marathon
	480	Persians under Xerxes defeated Spartans at Thermopylae. Athens sacked and burned. Athenians defeated Persian fleet at Salamis
	477	Delian League set up under Athenian leadership
468–	450	Cimon (c.505–450), general, leader of conservative aristocratic party, dominated Athenian politics
	454	Delian League Treasury moved to Athens
449–	429	Pericles (c.490–429), leader of popular party, ruled Athens
437–	404	Peloponnesian War between Athens and Sparta
	413	Athenians defeated at Syracuse, Sicily
	404	Athens fell to Sparta. End of Athenian empire
	387	Plato founded Academy
359–	336	Philip of Macedon gained control of Greek peninsula
	336	Alexander the Great succeeded Philip as king of Greece
	335	Aristotle founded Lyceum
335–	323	Alexander the Great conquered Near East, Asia Minor, Persia, India
	146	Corinth destroyed by Romans
	86	Athens sacked by Romans under Sulla

ARCHITECTURE AND SCULPTURE B.C.

	c.650	Ionic temple of Artemis built at Ephesus
	c.600	Kouros from Sounion carved
	c.550	Korai of Samos carved
	c.530	Archaic Doric temples built at Athens, Delphi, Corinth, Olympia
	c.489	Doric Treasury of Athenians built at Delphi by Callicrates (?)
	c.470	*Charioteer of Delphi* cast
c.470–c.450		*Zeus (Poseidon?)* cast
467–	449	New temple to Athena on Acropolis (predecessor to Parthenon) being built by Callicrates. Work halted on accession of Pericles
c.465–	457	Temple of Zeus built at Olympia
	450	Phidias appointed overseer of works on Athenian acropolis
448–	440	Temple of Hephaestus (Theseum) built by Callicrates (?)
447–	432	Parthenon built by Ictinus.
		Parthenon sculptures carved under Phidias
437–	432	Propylaea built by Mnesicles
427–	424	Temple of Athena Nike built by Callicrates
421–	409	Erechtheum built by Mnesicles
	334	Choragic monument of Lysicrates built

ARCHITECTURE AND SCULPTURE A.D.

	c.117	Temple of Olympian Zeus completed

PHILOSOPHERS B.C.

c.582–c.507		Pythagoras
500–	428	Anaxagoras
485–	411	Protagoras
469–	399	Socrates
427–	347	Plato
384–	322	Aristotle

HISTORIANS B.C.

c.495–	425	Herodotus
c.460–	395	Thucydides
c.434–c.355		Xenophon

HISTORIANS A.D.

	c.100	Plutarch (c.46–c.115) wrote *Parallel Lives*
c.140–	150	Pausanius visited Athens. Later wrote description of Greece

SCULPTORS B.C.

c.490–c.432	Phidias
c.460–c.450	Myron active
c.460–c.440	Polyclitus active
c.390–c.330	Praxiteles
c.350–c.300	Lysippus active

PAINTERS B.C.

c.480–c.430		Polygnotus (noted for perspective drawing)
	c.440	Apollodorus, the "shadow painter," flourished (modeled figures in light and shade)

WRITERS AND MUSICIANS B.C.

	c.600	Sappho flourished
525–	456	Aeschylus
496–	406	Sophocles
480–	406	Euripides
c.444–	380	Aristophanes

24. Agora, Athens, with reconstruction of Stoa (left) of Attalus II of Pergamon. c. 150 B.C.

had been attributed to the help of the gods. This caused the people to regard the acra as a sacred place, one to be crowned with an appropriate monument. Civic buildings, palaces, and temples were erected, and the people in the city below looked up with pride toward the acropolis that recorded their history, represented their aspirations, and had become the center of their religious, cultural, and civic ceremonies.

From the beginning, the Athenian acropolis was never static, and its successive buildings reflected the city's changing fortunes. Once it had been the site of a palace for the legendary king Erechtheus. Later it shifted from a military citadel and royal residence to a religious shrine, especially sacred to Athena as the city's protectress. This change is described by the poet Homer when he notes in the *Odyssey:* "Therewith gray-eyed Athene departed over the unharvested seas, left pleasant Scheria, and came to Marathon and wide-wayed Athens, and entered the house of Erechtheus."

Spreading out from the base of the acropolis was the *agora* (Fig. 24), a meeting and a market place, with rows of columns, public buildings, market stalls, gardens, and shade trees. This 10-acre (4-hectare) square was the center of the city's bustling business, social, and political life. Here could be found country folk selling their wares, citizens discussing the news, foreign visitors exchanging stories, and magistrates conducting routine city affairs.

On a typical day, the philosopher Socrates could be heard arguing with the sophists, whom he called "retailers of knowledge," for as his pupil Plato was to point out, the merchandising in the agora was "partly concerned with food for the use of the body, and partly with food of the soul which is bartered and received in exchange for money." The sophists were concerned primarily with the art of persuasive speech, but some professed to teach wisdom as well. As manipulators of public opinion, they often became intellectual opportunists who would use any argument so long as it turned their trick. In his disputations, Socrates showed that sophistry was more a matter of quibbling on the surface over words than of penetrating deeply into the world of ideas. By pricking some of the sophists' pretensions with the sting of his wit, Socrates gained his immortal reputation as the "gadfly" of Athens.

On the southern slope of the acropolis was the theater of Dionysus (Fig. 25), the sanctuary dedicated to the god of wine and frenzy and patron of the drama. Here, more than 2000 years before Shakespeare, the Athenians gathered to marvel at the plays that mirrored their world in dramatic form. Annually, through their applause they chose the winner of the coveted poetry prize that had been won no less than thirteen times by Aeschylus, the founder of heroic tragedy. Sophocles, his successor and principal poet of the Periclean period, quickened the pace of Greek drama by adding more actors and action. Euripides, last of the great tragic poets, explored the full range of emotions, endowing his plays with such passion and pathos that they plumbed the depths of the human spirit. After the great Periclean age was past, the comedies of Aristophanes proved that the Athenians still were able to see the humor of life.

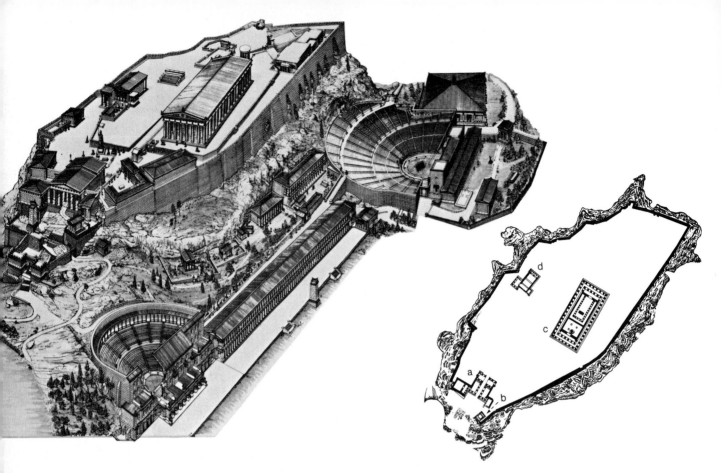

Above the theater, on the rocky plateau of the acropolis, was a leveled site, about 1000 feet (304 meters) long and 445 feet (135.2 meters) wide, where the temples were constructed (Fig. 26). Under Cimon and his successor Pericles, this was a place of ceaseless activity by builders, sculptors, painters, and other craftsmen. The necessary materials were available in abundance: Paros and other Aegean islands yielded good stone; from nearby Mt. Pentelicus came the fine-grained, cream-colored marble ideal for building and carving; Mt. Hymettus in Athens itself had a blue-white rock, excellent for embellishments; while the dark gray limestone of Eleusis could be used for contrasting effects. Later Plutarch was to declare in his biography of Pericles that as the buildings rose stately in size and fair in form, the craftsmen were "striving to outvie the material and the design with the beauty of their workmanship, yet the most wonderful thing of all was the rapidity of their execution. Undertakings, any one of which singly might have required, . . . for their completion, several successions and ages of men, were every one of them accomplished in the height and prime of one man's political service."

Pericles had the daring and wisdom to foresee that the unity of a people could rest on philosophical ideas and artistic leadership as well as on military might and material prosperity. A seafaring people,

left: 25. Acropolis, Athens. Reconstruction drawing as of end of 2nd century A.D.
Upper right, Theater of Dionysus, 4th century B.C.; lower left, Odeion of Herodes Atticus, 2nd century A.D.
Reconstruction by Al. N. Oikonomides.

right: 26. Plan of Athenian acropolis, with Propylaea (a), Temple of Athena Nike (b), Parthenon (c), and Erechtheum (d).

the Athenians had always looked beyond the horizon for ideas as well as goods to enrich their way of life. In the Delian League, once the Persian threats were ended, the Athenians joined with the broader community of Greek-speaking peoples of the mainland, the Aegean islands, and the coast of Asia Minor to defend themselves and to achieve cultural unity.

When the Delian treasury was brought to Athens and its ample funds became available for her building program, the city was assured leadership in the arts as well as in other practical and idealistic enterprises. Thus, Athens became a city whose acknowledged wealth was in its dramatists Aeschylus, Sophocles, and Euripides; its architects Ictinus, Callicrates, and Mnesicles; its sculptors Myron, Polyclitus, and Phidias; and such painters and craftsmen as Polygnotus, Apollodorus, and Callimachus.

The acropolis was, then, both the material and spiritual treasury of the Athenians, the place which held both their worldly gold reserves and their religious and artistic monuments. Work continued with undiminished enthusiasm until by the end of the 5th century B.C. the acropolis had become a sublime setting, worthy of the goddess of wisdom and beauty. It was also the pedestal that proudly bore the shining temples dedicated to her.

Architecture

The Acropolis
and the Propylaea

On festive occasions, the Athenians would leave their modest homes to walk along the Panathenaic Way (Fig. 27), the main avenue of their city, toward the acropolis. Towering above them was the supreme shrine—the acropolis where they worshiped their gods, commemorated their heroes, and recreated themselves. Accessible only by a single zigzag path up the western slope, the ascent was never easy. In Aristophanes' *Lysistrata,* a chorus of old men bearing olive branches to kindle the sacred fires chant as they mount the hill: "But look, to finish this toilsome climb only this last steep bit is left to mount. Truly, it's no easy job without beasts of burden and how these logs do bruise my shoulder!"

As the procession neared the top, the exquisite little Temple of Athena Nike appeared on a parapet to the right (see Fig. 37), and ahead was the mighty Propylaea, the imposing gateway to the acropolis (Fig. 28). This project, undertaken shortly after the completion of the Parthenon, was entrusted by Pericles to Mnesicles, who had been chief assistant to Ictinus, the principal architect of the Parthenon. Ictinus himself probably had a hand in planning the Propylaea, whose further relationship to the Parthenon can be found in the proportions of its forms, in the presence of certain features of the Ionic order in a dominantly Doric structure, and in the main axis that the Propylaea shares with the larger monument.

The Propylaea was built entirely of Pentelic marble except for some dark contrasting Eleusinian stone in the frieze. It was thus a spacious gateway with wings extending on either side to an overall width of about 156 feet (47.5 meters). An enclosure on the left was a picture gallery, and an open room on the right contained statues. In the center was the porch consisting of six Doric columns with the middle two spaced more widely apart as if to invite entrance. Between the columns facing the city and the corresponding ones on the opposite side facing the acropolis plateau was an open vestibule with columns of the more slender Ionic order, which permitted greater height and space for exhibitions and the waiting crowds (Fig. 29).

above: 27. Athenian Agora with Panathenaic Way. Reconstruction. Royal Ontario Museum, Toronto.

below: 28. Mnesicles. Propylaea (view from east), Acropolis, Athens. 437-432 B.C.

bottom: 29. Propylaea, cross section (after H. D'Espouy).

30. Ictinus and Callicrates. Parthenon, Athens. 447–432 B.C. Pentelic marble, height of columns 34′ (10.36 m).

Through the gateway of the Propylaea the procession entered the sacred area. Amid the revered monuments to the gods and heroes and looming above them was the colossal statue of Athena Promachus, said to have been fashioned by Phidias from the bronze shields of defeated Persian enemies. The tip of her spear is said to have gleamed brightly enough to guide homecoming sailors over the seas toward Athens. On the right was the majestic Parthenon, on the left the graceful Erechtheum.

The Parthenon

Doric Order At first glance, the Parthenon seems to be a typical Doric temple (Fig. 30). Such a shrine was originally conceived as an idealized dwelling to house the image of a deity. Under a low-pitched gabled roof, the interior was a windowless rectangular room called the *cella,* which sheltered the cult statue of the deity to whom the temple was dedicated. The *portal,* or doorway, to the cella was on one of the short ends, which extended outward in a *portico,* or porch, faced with columns to form the *façade,* or front. Sometimes columns were erected around the building in a series known as a *colonnade.* The construction was simple: a platform of three steps, the top one known as the *stylobate,* from which rose the upright *posts* that supported the *lintels,* or horizontal beams. When these columns and lintels were made of marble, the weight and size of the superstructure could be increased and the *intercolumniation,* or span between the supporting posts, widened. The history of Greek temple architecture was largely the refining of this *post-and-lintel* system of construction, which permitted the architects a steadily increasing freedom as time went on.

The *capital,* or crown, of the Doric column is in three parts: the necking, the echinus, and the abacus (Fig. 31). The purpose of any capital is to smooth the passage between the vertical shaft of the column and the horizontal portion of the building above. The *necking* is the first break in the upward lines of the shafts, though the fluting continues up to the outward flare of the round, cushionlike *echinus.* This, in turn, leads to the *abacus,* a block of stone that squares the circle, so to speak, and makes the pro-

31. Comparison of Doric (a) and Ionic (b) orders.

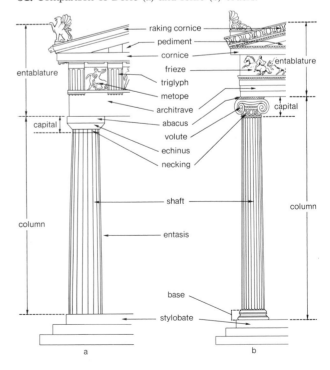

gression between the round lower and rectangular upper members.

Above the columns and below the roof is the *entablature.* Directly above the abacus is the *architrave,* a series of plain rectangular blocks. These stretch from the center of one column to that of its neighbor to constitute the lintels of the construction. They also support the upper parts of the entablature—frieze, cornices, and pediment. At this point, sculpture is called into play for decorative purposes, beginning with a carved band known as a *frieze.*

In the Doric order, the frieze is made up of alternating triglyphs and metopes. The rectangular *triglyphs* are so named because of their three grooves (*glyphs*), two in the center and a half groove on either side. They are the weight-bearing members, and, by rule, one is placed above each column and another in the space between. The sameness of the triglyphs contrasts with the differently carved relief panels of the *metopes.* This alternation creates an interesting visual rhythm, which illustrates the classical principle of harmonizing the opposites of unity and variety.

The frieze is protected by the overhanging *cornice* (and enhanced by its shadow), and the *raking cornice* rises gablelike from the side angles to the apex in the center. The triangular space enclosed by the cornices is called the *pediment,* which is recessed or set back to create a shelf on which freestanding sculpture can be placed to climax the decorative scheme.

On closer inspection, the Parthenon is not so much a typical Doric temple as it is the culmination of the long evolution of the Doric order with adaptations conforming to the needs of its time and place. Since the Parthenon was to serve both as a shrine to Athena and as the treasury of the Delian League, the plan called for a double cella (Fig. 26). The larger room on the east was to house Phidias' magnificent gold-and-ivory cult statue of Athena, and that on the west was to be the treasury. It was this western cella that technically was the *parthenon,* or chamber of the virgin goddess. Later the name was given to the whole building. The outer four walls of the cella were embellished by a continuous frieze, a decorative device borrowed from the Ionic order.

A *peristyle,* or colonnade, of freestanding columns completely surrounded the temple. The columns were placed far enough from the cella walls to permit an *ambulatory,* or passageway. On each side, along its 228 feet (69.5 meters) of length, were seventeen columns, and along the 104-foot (31.7-meter) width in front and back were eight columns—hence the Parthenon is called *octastyle.* (The number of columns used on the porch of a Greek temple was determined by the size of the building rather than by any rigid rule. The usual number was six, although some temples had as few as two, others as many as ten or twelve.) On both the east and west ends of the Parthenon, between the outer colonnade and the entrance portals to the cella, were six additional columns that formed the inner porches.

The outer surfaces of the columns have twenty grooves, or *flutes,* which form concave vertical channels from the bottom to the top of the shaft. Fluting serves several purposes, the first being to correct an optical illusion. When seen in bright sunlight, a series of ungrooved round columns appear flattened. In addition to maintaining the round appearance, the fluting makes a constant play of light and shadow and creates a number of graceful curves to please the eye. The increased number of vertical lines quickens the visual rhythm, and the eye is led upward toward the sculpture of the entablature.

Except for such details as the wooden roof beneath the marble tiles and the wooden doors with their frames, the entire Parthenon was built of Pentelic marble. When freshly quarried, this fine-grained stone was cream colored, but as it has weathered through the centuries its minute veins of iron have oxidized, so that today the color varies from light beige to darker golden tones, depending on the light.

In the original design, bright colors played an important part. The triglyphs were tinted dark blue and parts of the molding were red, as is known from ancient sources. The sculptured parts of the metopes were left cream colored, but the backgrounds were painted. In the frieze along the cella walls, the reins of horses were bronze additions, and the draperies of figures here and on the pediments were painted. Such facial features as eyes, lips, and hair were done in natural tints.

For the sheer technical skill of its construction, the Parthenon is astonishing. No mortar was used anywhere; the stones were cut so exactly that when fitted together they form a single smooth surface. The columns, which appear to be monoliths of marble, actually are constructed of sections called *drums,* so tightly fitted by square plugs in the center that the joinings are scarcely visible.

The harmonious proportions of the Parthenon have long been attributed to some subtle system of mathematical ratios. But despite close study and analysis no geometrical formula has so far been found that fits all the evidence. However, there is a recurrence in several instances of the proportion of nine to four (9:4). This proportion has been noticed in the length of the building (228 feet [69.5 meters]) relative to its width (104 feet [31.7 meters]) when measured on the stylobate, or top step; in the width of the cornice contrasted to the height of the raking cornice at the center; in the distance between the axial center of one column and the next (about 14 feet [4.2 meters]) as compared to the diameter of the column at its base; and in the bottom diameter of the columns relative to the width of the triglyphs.

Deviations from Regularity   At the same time, many irregularities defy mathematical logic. Any visitor to the Parthenon can observe that the columns stand somewhat closer together at the corners. Also apparent is the gentle arching of the stylobate from corner to corner—the center point on the short ends being about $2\frac{3}{4}$ inches (7 centimeters) higher than the corners and the long sides rising about 4 inches (10 centimeters) higher. Above the columns the architrave supporting the entablature echoes this curve. Noticeable too is the slight outward swelling of the column shafts as they rise (about $\frac{11}{16}$ of an inch [1.7 centimeters]) and a tapering off toward the top, making a curved effect known as *entasis*. Entasis creates the impression of elasticity, as if the "muscles" of the columns bulged a bit in bearing the load imposed by the building's superstructure.

Though somewhat less than true, it has often been stated that not a single straight line is to be found in the Parthenon. If exaggerated and compressed, the lines of the façade would resemble the drawing reproduced in Figure 32, which suggests that the architect Ictinus intended the Parthenon to be more graceful and visually gratifying by virtue of the dominance of curved lines over straight.

Deviations from regularity exist elsewhere in the Parthenon. The thickness of the corner columns, for instance, is about 2 inches (5 centimeters) greater than that of neighboring columns. This increased sturdiness and stability provides optical compensation for their being seen against light-filled, open space, rather than against the solid mass of the cella wall, and for their serving as final members of both lateral and longitudinal colonnades. In the spacing between columns, exact measurement reveals variations as great as $1\frac{1}{2}$ inches (3.8 centimeters). In addition, the columns lean inward to such an extent that they are some 3 inches (7.6 centimeters) off plumb. The deliberateness of this departure from exactitude is confirmed by the cella walls, which on the outside also tilt inward, while inside they are strictly perpendicular to the ground. It has been estimated that if continued upward, the lines of the Parthenon's columns would converge to meet at a point approximately 1 mile (1.6 kilometers) above.

In Doric temples, triglyphs rest, like the ends of cross beams, on the architrave in positions halfway between and just over the tops of columns, leaving the spaces between them to be filled with metopes, which on the Parthenon are marble plaques bearing scenes carved in relief. In contradiction of this rule and its functional origin, the triglyphs amd metopes of the Parthenon gradually squeeze one another slightly out of position toward the extremities of the colonnades so that the corners can be closed by two triglyphs joined at right angles.

Such discrepancies are due to a variety of historical, social, and aesthetic factors, rather than to inept workmanship or to a structural system whose logic has been lost. Like many great works of architecture, the Parthenon reflects the rivalry of political factions, the rising ambitions of rulers, and in general, the changing fortunes of the people who produced it. And here—as it so often occurs—what seems an imperishable masterpiece, in which every detail accords with the intentions of an original preconceived plan, actually emerges as the product of a master builder, Ictinus, in whom genius combined faculties for theoretical calculation and creative invention with an equal capacity for imaginative adaptation and creative improvisation.

The evidence is that Ictinus labored to avoid the rigidity and repetitiousness of the strict Doric order and to make the Parthenon organically coherent rather than merely mechanically consistent. The building can be thought of as a monumental sculpture, compact and firmly structured but resilient and elastic in the relationships among its component parts. This invests the whole with an organic vital quality like that of life itself. Considered in this way, the Parthenon becomes more visual than logical, more the work of inspired stonemasons than of mathematicians. In short, the Parthenon is a work of art, not a cold abstraction.

In its time, the Parthenon stood out as a proud monument to Athena and her people and the attain-

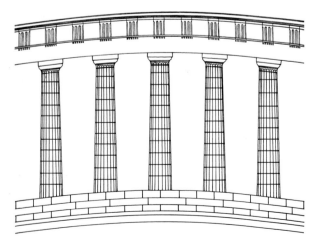

32. Schematic rendering of the Parthenon exaggerating the curvature and irregularities in the scale.

33. Mnesicles (?). Erechtheum (view from southeast), with Propylaea at left, Athens. c. 421–409 B.C. Pentelic marble; length 37′ (11.28 m), width 66′ (20.12 m).

ment of Pericles' ideal of "beauty in simplicity." Begun in 447 B.C. as the first edifice in that great statesman's building program, it was dedicated during the Panathenaic festival ten short years later at a time when the star of Athens was still in ascendancy. It and its companion buildings on the acropolis would be standing today with only the usual deteriorations of time were it not for a disaster in the year 1687. At that time, a Turkish garrison was using the Parthenon as an ammunition dump, and during a siege by the Venetians a random bomb ignited the stored gunpowder, blowing out the central section. From that time on, the Parthenon has been a noble ruin. Today, after numerous partial restorations, its outline is still clear. In its incomparable proportions and reserved poise it remains one of the imperishable achievements of the human mind.

The Erechtheum

Ionic Order   After Phidias' gold-and-ivory statue was so handsomely housed in the Parthenon, the city fathers wished to provide a place for the older wooden statue of Athena that was thought to have fallen miraculously from the sky. They also wished to venerate the other heroes and deities that formerly shared the acropolis with her. Hence a new building of the Ionic order (Fig. 33) was erected. The city records described it as "the temple in the acropolis for the ancient statue."

The site chosen was where Erechtheus, legendary founder of the city, had once dwelled. As recounted by Homer, Erechtheus was born from Earth, the grain giver, and was befriended and fostered by Athena, who "gave him a resting place in Athens in her own rich sanctuary; and there the sons of the Athenians worship him with bulls and rams as the years turn in their courses. . . ."

The Erechtheum, as the building was thus called, was also the spot where Athena and the sea god Poseidon were supposed to have held their contest for the patronage of the land of Attica and the honors of Athens. This story is depicted in the sculptures on the west pediment of the Parthenon. As the two deities asserted their claims, Poseidon brought down his trident on a rock, from which sprang a horse, his gift to humanity. A spring of salt water gushed forth to mark the event. When Athena's turn came, she brought forth the olive tree, and the gods awarded her the victory. Later, Erechtheus, whom she protected, tamed the horse and cultivated the olive that gave the Athenians oil for their cooking, a spread for their bread, ointment for their bodies, and fuel for their lamps.

Since the sacred olive tree, the salt spring, the mark of Poseidon's trident on the rock, and the tomb of Erechtheus were all in the same sacred precinct, the architect Mnesicles had to design the temple around them. Combining these separate functions makes the plan of the Erechtheum (Fig. 26) as complex as that of the Parthenon is simple. The rectangular interior, some $31\frac{1}{2}$ feet (9.5 meters) wide and $61\frac{1}{4}$ feet (18.7 meters) long, had four rooms for the various shrines on two different levels. One was $10\frac{3}{4}$ feet (3.3 meters) higher than the other. Projecting outward from three of the sides were porticoes, each of different size and design. The east porch has a row of six Ionic columns almost 22 feet (6.7 meters) high.

ornaments. The fine columns of the north porch (Fig. 34) rest on molded bases carved with a delicate design. The necking has a band decorated with a leaf pattern. Above this is a smaller band with the egg-and-dart motif, followed by the volutes and then a thin abacus carved with eggs and darts. The columns support an architrave divided horizontally into three bands, each receding slightly inward. The architrave thus consists of a continuous carved frieze rather than the alternating Doric triglyphs and metopes. Above rises a shallow pediment without sculpture.

An admired and much-imitated doorway leads into the cella of the Erechtheum. The lintel above is framed with a series of receding planes and combines the decorative motifs that appear elsewhere in the building. As seen in the band that runs around the cella (Fig. 36), these include (from lower to upper) honeysuckle, bead-and-reel, egg-and-dart, another bead-and-reel, and leaf-and-tongue motifs.

The north porch (Fig. 34) has a like number but with four in front and two on the sides; while the smaller porch on the south (Fig. 35) is famous for its six *caryatids,* the sculptured maidens who replace the customary columns.

Ionic columns (Fig. 31), unlike those of the Doric order, are more slender and have their greatest diameter at the bottom. Their shafts rest on a molded base instead of directly on the stylobate, and they have 24 instead of 20 flutings. Most striking, however, is the Ionic capital with its *volutes,* or scroll-like

South Porch   Facing the Parthenon, the south porch of the Erechtheum, with its caryatids (Fig. 35), is smaller than the others, measuring only some 10 by 15 feet (3 by 4.6 meters). Above three steps rises a 6-foot (1.8-meter) parapet on which the six maidens, about one and a half times larger than life, are standing. In order to preserve the proportions of the building and not appear to overburden the figures, the frieze and pediment were omitted. Grouped as if in a procession, the figures seem engaged in a stately forward motion, with three on one side lifting their

right legs and those on the other their left. The folds of their draperies suggest the fluting of columns; and while the maidens seem solid enough to carry their loads, there is no stiffness in the stances.

Just as the cella frieze of the Parthenon reenacts the Panathenaic festival, so these maidens may relate to the ritual of the Erechtheum. A sculptural fragment from an older temple on the acropolis shows a priestess leading a procession in which four maidens balance a long chest on their heads. Since the temple bears the name of their warrior king, the caryatids seem to suggest a ceremony for the heroic dead.

On their acropolis, the Athenians brought to the highest point of development two distinct Greek building traditions—the Doric with the Parthenon, and the Ionic with the Erechtheum and the Temple of Athena Nike (Fig. 37). By combining the two architectural orders in the Propylaea and displaying them separately in the Parthenon and the Erechtheum, the Athenians made symbolic reference to their city as the place where the Dorian people of the western Greek mainland and the Ionian people of the coast of Asia Minor across the Aegean Sea had for centuries lived together in peace and harmony.

In the following century, another order was added: the Corinthian. The columns of the Corinthian order are taller and more treelike than the Ionic. They are distinguished by their ornate capitals with double rows of acanthus leaves and fernlike fronds rising from each corner and terminating in miniature volutes. Too ornate for the generally restrained Hellenic taste, the Corinthian order had to wait for Hellenistic and Roman times to reach its full development, as seen in the ruins of the Temple of Olympian Zeus (Fig. 38).

right: 37. Callicrates.
Temple of Athena Nike, Athens.
c. 427–423 B.C.
Pentelic marble;
length 17′9″ (5.41 m),
width 26′10″ (8.18 m).

above: 36. Decorative band from the Erechtheum showing (bottom to top) honeysuckle, bead-and-reel, egg-and-dart, bead-and-reel, and leaf-and-tongue motifs. Glyptothek, Munich.

left: 38. Temple of Olympian Zeus, Athens. 174 B.C.–A.D. 130. Pentelic marble, height of columns 56′6″ (17.22 m).

The Hellenic Style **31**

as it went along. Never satisfied with routine efforts, the sculptors strove constantly to approach the ideal of excellence in craftsmanship.

Metopes of the Doric Frieze   The metopes of the Doric frieze play an important part in the architectural design of the Parthenon. They provide a welcome variety of figures to relieve the structural unity. Their predominantly diagonal lines contrast well with the alternating verticals of the triglyphs and the long horizontals of the architrave and cornice just below and above. In order to take full advantage of the bright sunlight, the sculptors chiseled these metopes in *high relief,* a technique by which the figures are deeply carved so as to project boldly outward from the background plane.

The subject of the figures in the south frieze is the battle of the Lapiths and centaurs after a centaur has kidnapped a Lapith bride at a wedding feast. In one of the most skillfully executed (Fig. 39), the rich spreading folds of the mantle form a fine unifying framework for the human figure. In turn, both make a striking contrast with the awkward angularity of the grotesque centaur.

Cella Frieze   The inner frieze (Figs. 40–42) that ran along the outer walls of the cella was a continuous band about 3¾ feet (1 meter) high, over 500 feet (152 meters) in length, and included some six hundred figures. Since this frieze was placed behind the colonnade and directly below roof level, where it had to be viewed from up close and at a steep upward angle, some sculptural adjustments were called for. The technique, of necessity, was *low relief,* in which the figures are shallowly carved. Because shadows in this indirect light are cast upward, the frieze had to be tilted slightly and cut so that the lower parts of the figures project only 1¼ inches (3 centimeters) from the background plane, with the relief gradually becoming bolder toward the top where the figures extend outward about 2¼ inches (5.7 centimeters). The handling of space, however, is so deft that as many as six horsemen are shown riding abreast without confusing the separate spatial planes.

Other adjustments can be observed. The horses, when seen at eye level, are too small in comparison with their riders. When viewed from below and in indirect light, however, they would not seem out of proportion. The use of color and metal attachments for such details as reins and bridles also helped to accent parts and projected the clarity of the design.

Sculpture

The Parthenon Marbles

The Parthenon sculptures have a special significance, because they rank high among the surviving originals of the 5th century B.C. The Parthenon statuary that has survived falls into three groups: the high-relief metopes of the Doric frieze, the freestanding pediment figures, and the low-relief cella frieze. Phidias' celebrated gold-and-ivory cult statue of Athena has long since disappeared, and inferior later copies convey little of the splendor attributed to it by the ancients.

As architectural sculpture, the friezes and pediments should not be judged apart from the building they embellish. By providing diagonal lines and irregular masses as well as figures in motion, they offset the more immobile vertical and horizontal balances of the structural parts. The original location of these sculptures must also be kept in mind by the modern viewer. They were meant to be seen outdoors in the intense Greek sunlight and from the ground some 35 feet (10.6 meters) below. While some of the frieze work is still in place, most of it is now in museums, where it is seen in dim artificial light and at eye level.

The craftsmanship of the Parthenon marbles reveals the unevenness in quality common to all group projects. Some sculptures are obviously from the hand of a master; others seem the routine products of artisans. The metopes were completed first. These were in turn surpassed by the finer quality of the pedimental figures and finally by the cella frieze. This progressive growth in sculptural skills shows that the work on the Parthenon gathered momentum

above: **40.** Frieze of west cella,
Parthenon. c. 440 B.C. Marble.

left: **41.** *Horsemen,* detail of
Parthenon west cella frieze.
c. 440 B.C. Marble, height 43″ (109 cm).

below: **42.** *Poseidon and Apollo,*
detail of Parthenon east cella frieze.
c. 440 B.C. Marble, height 43″ (109 cm).
Acropolis Museum, Athens.

All the heads, whether the figures are afoot or on
horseback, have been kept on the same level in order
to preserve unity of design as well as to provide a
parallel with the architectural line. (This principle,
known as *isocephaly,* will also be encountered later in
Byzantine art [Figs. 119, 127, 128]).

The cella frieze, unlike the traditional mythological subjects elsewhere in the Parthenon sculptures,
depicts the Athenians themselves participating in the
festival of their goddess. One of the oldest and most
important festivals, the Panathenaea was held in mid-
August. The scene depicted is the Greater Panathenaea, which took place every four years. Larger
than the annual local procession as it included
delegations from other Greek cities, the Greater
Panathenaea was the prelude to poetical and oratorical contests, dramatic presentations, and games.

On the western side (Figs. 40, 41), which is still in
place, last-minute preparations for the parade are in
progress as the riders ready their horses. The action,
appropriately enough, starts just at the point where

43. *Birth of Athena.*
Reconstruction of Parthenon east pediment.
Acropolis Museum, Athens.

above: 44. *Dionysus,* from Parthenon east pediment.
c. 438–432 B.C. Marble, over life-size.
British Museum, London
(reproduced by courtesy of the Trustees).

the live procession, after passing through the Propylaea, would have paused to regroup. The parade then splits in two, one file moving along the north and the other along the south side. After the bareback riders come the charioteers; and as the procession approaches the eastern corners, the marshals slacken the tempo to a more dignified pace. Here are musicians playing lyres and flutes, youths bearing wine jugs for libations, and maidens walking with stately step. The two files then meet on the east side, where magistrates wait to begin the ceremonies.

Even the immortal gods, as seen in the panel depicting Poseidon and Apollo (Fig. 42), are present to bestow their Olympian approval on the proceedings. The high point of the ritual comes in the center of the east side with the presentation of the *peplos,* the saffron and purple mantle woven by chosen maidens to drape the ancient image of Athena.

Pedimental Sculptures The pedimental sculptures, in contrast to the friezes, are freestanding figures, carved in the round. The themes of both pediments have to do with Athena. That on the west, facing the city, depicts her triumph over Poseidon (see p. 29). That on the east pediment (Fig. 43) recounts the story of her miraculous birth, the event that was celebrated each summer at the Panathenaea. While only a few fragments of the western pediment remain, enough survives of its eastern counterpart to convey an idea of its original state.

From various sources it is known that the eastern scene is Mt. Olympus, and that Zeus, father of the gods, was seated in the center. On one side stood the fire god Hephaestus, splitting open the head of Zeus to let Athena spring forth in full battle array. The sudden appearance of the goddess of wisdom, like a brilliant idea from the mind of its creator, disturbs

the Olympian calm. As the news spreads from the center to the sides, each figure is in some way affected by the presence of divine wisdom in their midst. Iris, the messenger of the gods (Fig. 45), rushes toward the left with a rapid motion as revealed by her windswept drapery. Seated on a chest, Demeter and Persephone are turning toward her, and the rich folds of their costumes reflect their attitudes and interest. The reclining Dionysus, with his panther skin and mantle spread over a rock (Fig. 44), is awakening and looking toward the sun god Helios, the horses of whose chariot are just rising from the foaming sea at break of day.

Three goddesses (Fig. 46) on the opposite side have postures that bring out their relationship to the composition. The one nearest the center of the pediment, aware of what has happened, is about to rise. The middle figure is starting to turn toward her. The

opposite below: 45. *Demeter, Persephone, and Iris,*
from Parthenon east pediment.
c. 438–432 B.C. Marble, over life-size.
British Museum, London
(reproduced by courtesy of the Trustees).

below: 46. *Three Goddesses,*
from Parthenon east pediment.
c. 438–432 B.C. Marble, over life-size.
British Museum, London
(reproduced by courtesy of the Trustees).

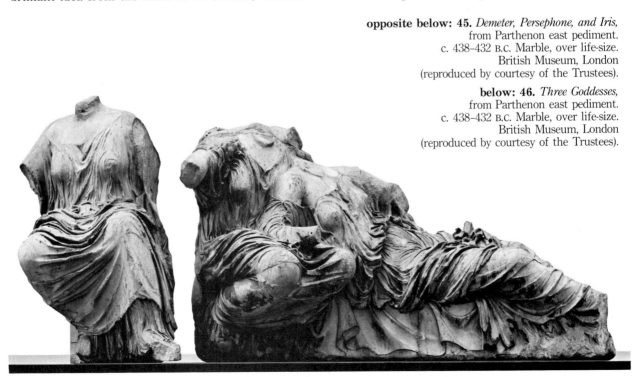

47. *Moon Goddess' Horse,* from Parthenon east pediment. c. 438–432 B.C. Marble, life-size. British Museum, London (reproduced by courtesy of the Trustees).

reclining figure at the right, still in repose, is unaware of the event, as is her counterpart Dionysus on the far left. Like the feminine group on the left, these figures form a unified episode in the composition, and their relation to the whole is made clear in the lush lines of their flowing robes. This undulating linear pattern and the way it transparently reveals the anatomy of the splendid bodies beneath mark a high point in the art of sculpture.

At the far right of this group the chariot of the moon goddess Selene was seen descending. Now only the expressive downward-bending horse's head (Fig. 47) remains to show by his spent energies that it is the end of the day.

Perhaps the most admirable aspect of the entire pediment composition is the ease and grace with which each piece fulfills its assigned space. Fitting suitable figures into a low isosceles triangle and at the same time maintaining an uncrowded yet unified appearance was a problem that long occupied Greek designers. One oversize figure usually dominated the center, with seated or crouching figures on either side and reclining ones in the acute side angles.

The pediment space of the Parthenon stretches about 90 feet (27.4 meters) and rises over 11 feet (3.4 meters) in the center. The chariots of the rising and setting sun and moon define the time span as that of a single day. Furthermore, the background of Mt. Olympus and the single event identify time, place, and action in keeping with the classical unities (a principle that will be treated more fully in the section on drama).

The ascending and descending chariots give a contrasting upward and downward movement on the extreme ends, while the reclining and seated figures lead the eye to the apex, where the climax takes place. The action that follows disperses the middle figures outward once more toward the sides. The varied postures, rich plastic modeling, and flowing lines connect all the figures with such a unified mo-

tion that, even though the center ones are now missing, the meaning is quite clear.

Overall Sculptural Program   Taken as a whole, the Parthenon marbles present a picture of the Greek past and present and of their aspirations for the future. The attempt of the Greek people to interpret their dark ancient myths in contemporary terms is found here in their sculptures as well as in their philosophy, poetry, and drama.

The metopes on the east frieze portray the primeval battle of the gods and giants for control of the world, and the triumph of the Olympians hailed the coming of order out of chaos. The metopes on the south frieze show the oldest inhabitants of the Greek peninsula, the Lapiths, subduing the half-human centaurs with the aid of the Athenian hero Theseus. This victory signaled the ascendancy of human ideals over the animal side of human nature. In the north group, the Homeric epic of the defeat of the Trojans is told, while in the west metopes the Greeks are seen overcoming the Amazons, those ferocious women warriors who symbolized the Asiatic enemies and, in this case, allude to the Athenian defeat of the Persians at Marathon. In the east pediment, the birth of the city's patroness Athena is seen; while the west pediment tells the story of the rivalry of Athena as goddess of the intellect and Poseidon as patron of maritime trade, suggesting the conflict of two ways of life—the pursuit of wisdom and of material wealth.

The Panathenaic procession of the cella walls brings history up to date by depicting a contemporary subject. Here the proud Athenians could look upward and see their own images carved on a sacred temple, an echo of the living procession that marched along the sides of the temple on feast days. The climax came after they had gathered at the east porch and the portals of the temple were opened to the rays of the rising sun, revealing the image of the goddess herself. Shining forth in all her gold-and-ivory glory, Athena was the personification of the eternal truth, goodness, and beauty for which her faithful followers were striving. With her help, Greek civilization had overcome the ignorance of the barbarians. The bonds between the goddess and the citizens of her city were thus periodically renewed, and the Parthenon as a whole glorified not only Athena but the Athenians as well.

The Course of Hellenic Sculpture

The tremendous distance encompassed by the art of sculpture from the archaic, or preclassical, phase prior to the 5th century B.C. to the end of the Hellenic style period in the mid-4th century can be seen clearly when examples are compared.

Male Figures The *Kouros* (Fig. 48) represents the archaic sculptural type of youthful athlete, victor in the games, moving toward the temple to dedicate himself. The advancing left foot provides the only suggestion of movement in the otherwise rigid posture. The anatomy of the torso is severely formal and close to the block of stone from which it was carved. The wide shoulders and long arms attached to the sides provide a rectangular framework. The long vertical line from the neck to the navel divides the chest; while the diamond-shaped abdomen is defined by four almost-straight lines, a heritage of the formalized geometrical conventions of the archaic period. About a century later, a similar figure (see Fig. 63) reveals how the rigid posture has softened, the muscles relaxed, and the spirit enlivened.

The *Doryphorus,* or *Spear Bearer,* by Polyclitus (Fig. 49), in contrast, moves with greater poise and freedom. Originally in bronze, it is now known only through routine marble copies. The sculptor won fame in ancient times for his attempts to formulate a *canon,* or body of rules, for the proportions of the human figure. The exact way Polyclitus' theory worked is not known, but the Roman architect Vitruvius mentions that beauty consists "in the proportions, not of the elements, but of the parts, that is to say, of finger to finger, and of all the fingers to the palm and wrist, and of these to the forearm, and of the forearm to the upper arm, and of all . . . to each other, as . . . set forth in the Canon of Polyclitus."

Whether the *module,* or unit of measure, was the head, the forearm, or the hand apparently varied from statue to statue. Yet once the module was adopted, the whole and all its parts were expressible in multiples or fractions of it. As Vitruvius illustrated the canon, the head would be one-eighth of the total

left: 48. *Kouros,* from Sounion.
c. 615–590 B.C. Marble, height 11′ (3.35 m).
National Museum, Athens.

center: 49. Polyclitus. *Doryphorus (Spear Bearer).*
Roman copy of original of c. 450–440 B.C.
Marble, height 6′6″ (1.98 m). National Museum, Naples.

right: 50. Praxiteles. *Hermes and the Infant Dionysus.*
c. 340 B.C. Marble, height 7′1″ (2.16 m). Museum, Olympia.

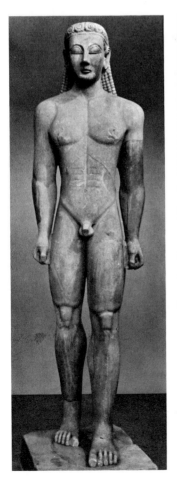

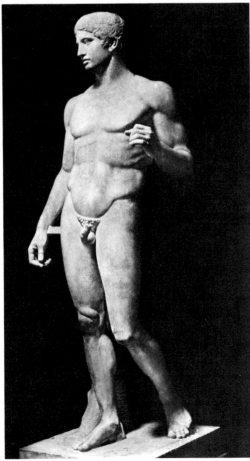

above left: 51. *Charioteer,* from Sanctuary of Apollo, Delphi. c. 470 B.C. Bronze, height 6'11" (2.11 m). Museum, Delphi.

above right: 52. *Zeus (Poseidon?).* c. 460–450 B.C. Bronze, height 6'10" (2.08 m). National Museum, Athens.

left: 53. Myron. *Discobolus (Discus Thrower).* Roman copy after bronze original of c. 460 B.C. Marble, life-size. National Museum, Rome.

height. The face would be one-tenth, subdivided, in turn, into three parts: forehead, nose, and mouth and chin. The forearm would be one-quarter the height, and the width of the chest equal to this length of forearm. Like the optical refinements of the Parthenon, however, Polyclitus' canon was not a mechanical formula. It allowed for some flexibility; the dimensions could be adjusted for a figure in movement or for one designed to be seen from a certain angle.

Praxiteles' *Hermes and the Infant Dionysus* (Fig. 50), coming at the close of the Hellenic period, is the ultimate in poise and polish. Unlike the rather restrained *Doryphorus,* Hermes rests his weight easily on one foot. The relaxed stance throws the body into the familiar S-curve, a Praxitelean pose widely copied in later Hellenistic and Roman statuary. From the stiffness of the stolid archaic *Kouros* and the strength of the stocky *Doryphorus,* the sculptor Praxiteles has arrived at complete mastery of his material. Through the soft modeling and suave surface treatment, Praxiteles suggests the blood, bone, and muscles beneath the skin and gives his cold marble material the vibrancy and warmth of living flesh.

The *Charioteer of Delphi* (Fig. 51) and the *Zeus* found at Artemision (Fig. 52)—two of the rare Hellenic bronze originals—and the Roman marble copy of Myron's lost bronze *Discobolus* (Fig. 53), or *Discus Thrower,* reveal a transition in style from quiet monumentality to energetic action within a twenty-year time span in the mid-5th century. The splendid *Charioteer* once was part of a larger group that included several horses. Although in action, the figure has something of the monumentality and equilibrium of a fluted column due to the vertical folds of its lower garment. The commanding figure of *Zeus,* poised to throw a thunderbolt, reveals in its powerful musculature the massive reserves of strength of a truly godlike physique. In Myron's *Discobolus,* the taut yet elastic muscles of the athlete are poised momentarily

between a backward movement and forward thrust. The vigorous motion is admirably contained by the curved arms that enclose the composition and confine the activity to a single plane.

Female Figures   The archaic *Kore* from Samos (Fig. 54) is one of a file of maidens, originally in a temple courtyard, carrying small animals as votive offerings. Her severely cylindrical figure is quite abstract in that everything extraneous has been eliminated and only the essential formal and linear elements retained. The rhythmically repeated lines of the skirt contrast with the curves of the upper drapery to create a pleasing linear design.

left: **54.** *Kore,* from Samos. c. 550 B.C. Marble, height 5'3" (1.6 m). State Museums, East Berlin.

center: **55.** Phidias. *Athena Lemnia.* Roman copy after original of c. 450 B.C. Marble, height 6'6" (1.98 m). Body, Albertinum, Dresden; head, Civic Museum, Bologna.

right: **56.** Praxiteles. *Aphrodite of Cnidos.* Roman copy after original of c. 320 B.C. Marble, height 6'8" (2.03 m). Vatican Museums, Rome.

57. School of Scopas (?). *Dionysian Procession.* 4th century B.C. Marble. National Museum, Athens.

The *Athena Lemnia* (Fig. 55) is a superior marble copy of Phidias' original bronze statue that stood on the Athenian acropolis. Phidias here created a mood that is more lyrical than epical, and in ancient sources the statue was referred to regularly as "the beautiful." The serene profile, softened by the subtle modeling, surely approaches the ideal of chaste classical beauty.

Praxiteles' *Aphrodite of Cnidos* was proclaimed by Greco-Roman critics as the finest statue in existence. It is known only through such an inferior copy as Figure 56. The "smile playing gently over her parted lips" and the "soft melting gaze of the eyes with their bright and joyous expression" that the Roman writer Lucian so admired in the original can now only be imagined. Praxiteles, however, departed from the draped goddesses of the previous century by boldly portraying the goddess of love in the nude. By so doing, he created a *prototype,* or original model, that influenced all subsequent treatment of the undraped female figure.

Drama

Greek drama was a distillation of life in poetic form, represented (or imitated, to use the ancient term) on the stage. In these vivid presentations, members of the audience through their representatives in the chorus became vicarious participants in events happening to a group of people at another time and in another place.

Like all great works of art, Greek drama can be approached on many different levels. At one level, it can be a thrilling story of violent action and bloody revenge. At another, it is a struggle between human ambition and divine retribution, or a conflict of free will and predestined fate. At still another, it becomes a moving experience that ennobles through lofty language and inspired poetry.

Plots were always taken from mythology, heroic legends, or stories of royal houses. Since these age-old themes were forms of popular history known in advance, the dramatist could concentrate more on purely poetic functions than on plot development, providing dramatic commentaries on old tales and reinterpreting them in the light of recent events. The playwright could thus inspire by conjuring up the heroic past, as did Aeschylus in *The Persians;* express individual sentiments in the light of universal experience, as did Sophocles in *Antigone;* invite reexamination of ancient superstitions, as did Euripides in *The Bacchants;* or place current problems in broader historical perspective by reminding the audience that present difficulties had parallels in times past.

Origins

The origins of the Greek dramatic form were rooted in the religious rites associated with the worship of Dionysus (the Bacchus of Roman mythology). He was the god of wine and revelry, whose cult festivals coincided with spring planting and fall harvesting seasons (Fig. 57). From primitive magical practices, the rituals gradually grew in refinement until they became a vehicle for powerful creative expression. When theaters came to be built, they were located in a precinct sacred to Dionysus. His altar occupied the center of the circular *orchestra,* where the chorus sang and danced. The audience which gathered paid their tribute to him by their presence.

In the beginning, Greek drama had only a chorus, whose function, according to the philosopher Nietzsche, was to conjure up the divine vision in which it "beholds its lord and master Dionysus . . . [and] sees how he, the god, suffers and glorifies himself." The vision beheld by the chorus eventually came to be acted out, and the alternation between group *choruses* and individually declaimed *episodes* became the basis of the dramatic form. Put another way, the choral songs were at first a group narration of great deeds. Later, the words attributed to the hero were sung and mimed by the leader of the chorus. Then a second and a third actor were added, and the dialogue of the enacted episodes achieved equal emphasis with the alternating choruses.

Hellenistic and Roman drama were later to upset this classic balance by emphasizing the action and roles of individual performers, but in Hellenic times the voice of the chorus and that of the principal actors were equal in importance. As the group chanted its *strophes* and *antistrophes* ("turns" and "counterturns"), it effected transition from scenes, reminded of the past and foretold the future, reflected public opinion, voiced the dramatist's own commentary, and, above all, by acting as its proxy, made the audience feel a part of the play.

The Theater of Dionysus at Athens (Fig. 25), like the better-preserved one at Epidaurus (Fig. 58), had an *auditorium* hollowed out of a hillside to accommodate approximately 18,000 spectators. The semicircular tiers of seats half surrounded the orchestra and faced the *skene,* a scene building or raised platform, on which the actors played their roles. The skene had a permanent architectural façade with three doors for the actors. The chorus entered and exited at the corners below. The stylized façade of the skene, suggesting a temple or palace, was suitable for most dramatic situations, since the action almost always took place in the open. The chorus, for example, usually represented worshipers at a shrine, townspeople or petitioners before a palace, a mob, or a group of prisoners. The actors moving in and out of the portals above took the parts of priests, heroes, or members of royal families. When the situation demanded another setting, the chorus or an actor would "paint" the scene with a few words so that other sets were unnecessary.

Structure and Scope

A typical Greek play opens with a *prologue,* spoken by one of the actors. The prologue sets the scene, outlines the plot, and provides a taking-off point for the action that is to follow. The substance of the drama then unfolds in a sequence of alternating choruses and episodes (usually five episodes enclosed

58. Polyclitus the Younger. Theater, Epidaurus. c. 350 B.C. Diameter 373′ (113.69 m), orchestra 66′ (20.12 m) across.

by six choruses) and concludes with the *exodus* of the chorus and an *epilogue.* Actors wore masks (Fig. 59) of general types that could be recognized instantly by the audience. The size and outdoor location of the theaters made facial expressions ineffective, and the swift pace of Greek drama required the player of a king or peasant to establish immediately a type and character. Masks also proved useful when an actor took more than one part, bringing him immediate acceptance in either role.

Restraint and simplicity were the rule in Greek staging. As with the later Elizabethan theater, scenery was conspicuous by its absence. The only visual illusion seems to have been the *mechane,* a crane that lowered to the stage those actors portraying gods. This *deus ex machina,* or "god from the machine," in later times became a convenient way of solving dramatic problems that were too complex to be worked out by normal means.

Direct action never occurred on stage. Any violent deed took place elsewhere and was reported by a messenger or another character. The plays proceeded by narration, commentary, speculation, dialogue, and discussion. All these devices—plot known in advance, permanent stage setting, use of masks, offstage action—served two principal purposes: to accent the poetry of the play and to give the freest possible scope to the spectator's imagination.

Greek drama unfolds as a sequence of choral song, group dances, mimed action, and dialogue coordinated into a dramatic whole. Poetry, however, always remains the central dramatic agent. It should also be noted that the Athenians experienced their plays and poetry only in oral presentations. While manuscript copies of literary and philosophical works were available to scholars, books in the modern sense did not exist. Much of the beauty and power of the plays was derived from the heightened experience of poetic recitation as well as from the Greek tongue itself. Not an accentual language, Greek allows a wide variety of metrical patterns capable of expressing every nuance of action and mood. In experiencing a Greek drama in translation, therefore, modern readers must let their imagination supply the melody, color, and flowing rhythms of the original language as well as the missing factors associated with a live theatrical production.

The scope of Greek drama was tremendous. It extended from majestic tragedy of heroic proportions, through the pathos of *melodrama* (in its proper meaning of "drama with melody"), all the way to the riotous *comedies* of Aristophanes. Conflict, however, is always the basis for dramatic action, and the playwrights set up tensions between such forces as murder and revenge, crime and retribution, cowardice and courage, protest and resignation, pride and hu-

59. Pronomos Painter. *Actors Holding Their Masks.* Detail of red-figured painting showing the cast of a satyr play on exterior of volute krater. Ruvo, Italy. c. 410 B.C. Terra-cotta, height 29½″ (75 cm). National Museum, Naples. (from *Classical Greek Art, Arts of Mankind* series. Paris: Editions Gallimard).

mility. When, for instance, a hero is confronted with his destiny, the obstacles he encounters are at once insurmountable and necessary to surmount. In the conflict that follows, the play runs an entire range of emotions and explores the heights to which human life can soar and the depths to which it can sink. In Sophocles' *Oedipus Rex,* for instance, the hero starts at the peak of his kingly powers and ends in the abyss of human degradation. Each character in a true drama, moreover, is drawn three-dimensionally so as to reveal a typically human mixture of attractive and repulsive, good and bad, traits.

The *protagonist,* or central character, of a Greek play can fulfill the requirements of tragedy only when portraying some noble figure—one "highly renowned or prosperous," as Aristotle puts it—who is eventually brought to grief through a personal flaw in psychological makeup and by some inevitable stroke of fate. The reasons for this must be made apparent to the audience gradually through the process of "causal necessity." A common person's woes might bring about a pathetic situation but not a tragic one in the classical sense. When a virtuous hero is rewarded or the evil designs of a villain receive their just deserts, obviously there is no tragic situation. When a blameless person is brought from a fortunate to an unfortunate condition or when an evil person rises from misery to good fortune, there is likewise no tragedy because the moral sense of the audience is outraged.

Aeschylus, Sophocles, and Euripides

Under Aeschylus, its founder, Greek tragedy sought to comprehend the mystery of the divine will, so inscrutable to mortals—as in his *Agamemnon.* By establishing a working relationship between mortals and their gods, he tried to reconcile the conflict between the human and the divine and find a basis for personal as well as social justice. The implications of the early Aeschylean tragedy were thus strongly ethical, showing clearly that the drama was still identified in his mind with theological thought. The forms of Sophocles' plays were distinguished by their flawless construction, while their lofty content was based on the course of human destiny as seen in the light of the moral law of the universe.

Euripides, said the philosopher Aristotle, sought to show people as they are, while Sophocles had depicted them as they ought to be. In some ways, the works of Euripides may not be so typical of the Hellenic style as those of Aeschylus or Sophocles, but his influence on the subsequent development of the drama, both in Hellenistic and later times, was incalculably greater.

The Bacchants, the last of Euripides' ninety-odd plays, was written at a time when the darkness of disillusionment was descending on Athenian intellectuals toward the end of the disastrous Peloponnesian War. In it he gives voice to some of the doubts and uncertainties of his time. Like most masterpieces, it is in some respects atypical, while in others it seems to stem from the deepest traditional roots of the theater's origin. Despite some inner inconsistencies and a certain elusiveness of meaning, *The Bacchants* has all the formal perfection and poetic grandeur of the loftiest tragedies. The strange, wild beauty of the choruses, the magic of its poetry, and the complex interplay between the human and divine wills endow it with all the necessary ingredients of the theater at its best.

Aristotle's Commentary   After the great days of Aeschylus, Sophocles, and Euripides were over, Aristotle, with knowledge of their complete works in-

stead of the relatively few examples known today, wrote a perceptive analysis of tragedy and more broadly of art in general in his treatise *Poetics.* According to him, true drama, indeed all other works of art, must have form in the sense of a beginning, a middle, and an end.

Unity of time, place, and action is also desirable. Sophocles' *Oedipus Rex,* for example, takes place in a single day (albeit a busy one); all the scenes are set in front of the palace at Thebes; and the action is direct and continuous without subplots. Other Greek plays encompass a longer span of time and have several settings. As Aristotle pointed out, these unities were useful but by no means hard and fast rules.

In the episodes, convention held that three actors on stage at one time was the maximum. If the play required six parts, the roles were usually apportioned among three actors. As the action proceeds, the conflict between *protagonist* and *antagonist* emerges, and the play should rise to its climax in the middle episode. Through the proper tragic necessity, the hero's downfall comes because he carried the seeds of his own destruction within his breast. After this turning point, the well-planned anticlimax resolves the action once more into a state of equilibrium.

Tragedy, according to Aristotle, had to be composed of six necessary elements, which he ranked as follows: Plot, "the arrangement of the incidents"; Character, "that which reveals moral purpose"; Thought, "where something is proved to be or not to be"; Diction, "the metrical arrangements of the words"; Song: which "holds the chief place among the embellishments"; and Spectacle. Finally, Aristotle summed up his definition of tragedy as "an imitation of an action that is serious, complete, and of a certain magnitude; in language embellished with each kind of ornament, the several kinds being found in separate sections of the play; in the form of action, not of narrative; with incidents arousing pity and fear, wherewith to accomplish its *katharsis* ["purgation"] of the emotions."

Music

The word *music* today carries the connotation of a fully mature and independent art. It must be remembered, however, that symphonies, chamber music, and solo instrumental compositions, where the focus is almost entirely on abstract sound, are relatively modern forms. The word *music* is still used to cover the union of sound with many other elements, as in the case of popular songs, dance music, military marches, and church music. It also describes the combination with lyric and narrative poetry, as in songs and ballads; with bodily movements, as in the dance and ballet; and with drama, as in opera.

60. Douris. *Instruction in Music and Grammar in an Attic School.*
Red-figured painting on exterior of kylix.
c. 470 B.C. State Museums, West Berlin.

In ancient Greece, *music* in its broadest sense meant any of the arts and sciences that came under the patronage of the Muses, those imaginary maidens who were the daughters of the heavenly Zeus and the more earthly Mnemosyne. Since Zeus was the creator and Mnemosyne, as her name implies, the symbol of memory, the Muses and their arts were thought to be the results of the union of the creative urge and memory, half divine, half human. This was simply a way of saying that music was recorded inspiration.

As Greek civilization progressed, the Muses, under the patronage of Apollo, god of prophecy and enlightenment, gradually increased to nine. The arts and sciences over which they presided came to include all the intellectual and inspirational disciplines that sprang from the fertile minds of this highly creative people—lyric poetry, tragic and comic drama, choral dancing, and song. Astronomy and history were also included. The visual arts and crafts, on the other hand, were protected by Athena and Hephaestus—intelligence tempered by fire. Plato and others placed music in opposition to gymnastic or physical pursuits, and its meaning in this sense was as broad as our use of the general terms *liberal arts* or *culture.*

The Greeks also used *music* more narrowly in the sense of the tonal art. But music was always intimate-ly bound up with poetry, drama, and the dance and was usually found in their company. At one place in the *Republic,* Socrates asks: "And when you speak of music, do you include literature or not?" And the answer is yes. Thus, while it is known that the Greeks did have independent instrumental music apart from its combination with words, evidence suggests that the vast body of their music was connected with literary forms.

This does not imply, of course, that music lacked a distinct identity or that it was swallowed up by poetry, but rather that it had an important and honored part in poetry. Plato, for instance, remarks: "And I think that you must have observed again and again what a poor appearance the tales of the poets make when stripped of the colours which music puts upon them, and recited in simple prose. . . . They are like faces which were never really beautiful, but only blooming; and now the bloom of youth has passed away from them[.]"

Music and Literature

Greek music must therefore be considered primarily in its union with literature, as illustrated in the vase painting *Instruction in Music and Grammar in an Attic School* by Douris (Fig. 60). The clearest statement of this again is found in the *Republic,* where it is pointed out that "melody is composed of three things, the words, the harmony [by which is meant the sequence of melodic intervals], and the rhythm." In discussing the relative importance of each, Plato states that "harmony and rhythm must follow the words." The two arts thus are united in the single one of *prosody*—that is, the melodic and rhythmic setting of a poetic text.

The Greek melodies and rhythms are known to have been associated with specific moods, or *modes*—scales constructed by adjusting the pitch of tones within the octave as with the more modern major and minor modes, from which they are descended. The modern major scale, or mode, can be found on the piano by playing the white keys from middle C to the next C above (eight tones, or an *octave*). Similarly, the minor scale, or mode, goes from A (two white keys below middle C) to the A above. The ancient Greek Dorian mode extends from D (one white key above middle C) to the D above.

The great variety of Greek modes allowed poets and dramatists to elicit a gamut of emotional responses from their audiences. Although ethical and emotional orientations have changed over the centuries, the basic modal and metrical system of the Greeks has, in effect, continued through all subsequent periods of Western music and poetry.

Music, in both its broad and narrow senses, was closely woven into the fabric of the emotional, intellectual, and social life of the ancient Greeks. The art was also considered by them to have a fundamental connection with the well-being of individuals personally as well as with their social and physical environment. There is no more eloquent tribute to the power of art in public affairs than that made by Socrates, who said, "When modes of music change, the fundamental laws of the State always change with them."

Education for young people in Greece consisted of a balanced curriculum of music for the soul and gymnastics for the body. The broad principle of building a sound mind in a sound body is still one of the ideals of education. Even the welfare of the soul after death had musical overtones, since immortality to many Greeks meant being somehow in tune with the cosmic forces, and being at last able to hear the "music of the spheres."

All these notions had to do with the physical world being some way in harmony with the world of the spirit—the metaphysical world—and the soul being an attunement of the body. According to the Greek myth of Orpheus, who is depicted in a fine red-figured vase of the early 5th century B.C. (Fig. 61), music even had the miraculous power to overcome death. This thought found an enduring place in Western literature, and no writer has expressed it

61. *Orpheus among the Thracians.* Attic red-figured vase. c. 440 B.C. State Museums, West Berlin.

more sensitively than Shakespeare in *The Merchant of Venice* (Act V, scene 1):

> . . . look, how the floor of heaven
> Is thick inlaid with patines of bright gold:
> There's not the smallest orb which thou behold'st
> But in his motion like an angel sings,
> Still quiring to the young-eyed cherubins;
> Such harmony is in immortal souls;
> But, whilst this muddy vesture of decay
> Doth grossly close it in, we cannot hear it.

Music Theory

The most important Greek contribution to music is without doubt a theoretical one—that of coordinating the mathematical ratios of melodic intervals with their scale system. The discovery, attributed to Pythagoras, showed that such intervals as the octave, fifth, and fourth had a mathematical relationship. This can easily be heard when a tuned string is stopped off exactly in the middle. The musical interval between the tone of an unstopped string and the one that is divided into two equal parts will then be the octave, and the mathematical ratio will be 1:2. Then if a segment of the string divided into two parts is compared with one of a string divided into three parts, the resulting interval will be the fifth, and the ratio 2:3. If one compares the tone of the triply divided string with one divided into four parts, the interval will be the fourth, and the ratio 3:4. Hence, mathematically 1:2 equals the octave; 2:3, the fifth; 3:4, the fourth; 8:9, the whole tone; and so on.

Music to Pythagoras and his followers thus was synonymous with order and proportion and rested on a demonstrably rational basis. This tremendous discovery seemed to be a key that might unlock the secrets of the universe, which, they reasoned, might likewise be reduced to numbers and be constructed according to the principles of a musical scale. This idea found its way into all aspects of Greek intellectual life, and even Plato built up a conception of the cosmic harmony of the world on these musical principles in his *Timaeus*. It is possible that the architects also incorporated these laws into the proportions and designs of their buildings. The Roman architect Vitruvius, for instance, was thoroughly familiar with Greek musical theory.

Music and Drama

Knowledge of Greek music must be gleaned from a variety of sources, such as occasional literary references, poetry and drama, visual representations of musical instruments and music making in sculpture and painting, theoretical treatises, and some very fragmentary surviving examples of the music itself. When all the separate sources are combined, a faint notion of what Greek music actually was like can be had. From them, it is apparent that music's highest development undoubtedly was in its union with the drama. Athenian dramatists were by tradition responsible for the music, the training of the chorus, and the staging of their plays as well as for the writing of the script. In addition, they often played some of the roles. The great dramatists had to be composers as well as poets, actors, playwrights, and producers.

In reconstructing the Greek drama, one must imagine a Greek audience to whom the drama was a lively aural and visual experience of choral singing and dancing, of vocal and instrumental music, as well as of dialogue and dramatic sequence. Today, with all the choruses and dances missing, such a play as *The Suppliants* of Aeschylus is like the text of an opera without the musical score. This play is so clearly a lyric drama that the music itself must have been a full partner in conveying the poet's meaning. Euripides' *The Bacchants,* on the other hand, has far greater dramatic substance, but even here the emotional intensity of the individual scenes often rises to such a pitch that music had to take over where the words left off—just as when a person is so overcome with feeling that words fail and inarticulate sounds and gestures are all that can be mustered.

The Chorus   The weight of the musical expression fell primarily on the chorus, which was the original basis of the dramatic form and from which all the other elements of the drama evolved. We have at last realized, said Nietzsche in his analysis of Greek drama, "that the scene, together with the action, was fundamentally and originally conceived only as a *vision,* that the only reality is just the chorus, which of itself generates the vision and speaks thereof with the entire symbolism of dancing, tone, and word." The chorus performed both in stationary positions and in motion. As the chorus circulated about the orchestra, where the choral songs, dances, and group recitatives took place around the altar of Dionysus, its song was accompanied with appropriate gestures. The forms of the choruses were metrically and musically very elaborate and were written with such variety and invention that repetitions either within a single play or in other plays by the same poet were very rare.

Interestingly enough, the sole surviving relic of Greek music from the 5th century B.C. is a fragment of a choral *stasimon,* or "stationary chorus," from Euripides' *Orestes* (Fig. 62). All ancient Greek manuscripts come down through the ages from the hands of medieval scribes who omitted the musical notation of the earlier copies because it was no longer comprehensible to them. In this instance, the musical notation was included, but all that is left is a single sheet of poorly preserved papyrus.

From ancient accounts it is known that the music of Euripides differed considerably from that of his predecessor Aeschylus and his contemporary Sophocles. Euripides was educated in the "new" music by Timotheus, while Sophocles received his instruction from the more conservative rival Lampros. The new music was criticized because it was so complex that the words were unintelligible. The text was thus on its way to becoming of as little consequence as the text of an opera chorus of today, whereas traditionally it had dominated the music. Evidence to support this development is found in the literary content of Euripidean choruses, which sometimes have little or no direct connection with the action.

Fragmentary though this scrap of evidence is, these few notes from Euripides' *Orestes* are enough to tell their own story. That the intervals called for are in half and quarter tones means that Euripidean choruses were musically complex enough to demand highly skilled singers. The mode is Mixolydian, which is described by Aristotle in his *Politics* as being "mournful and restrained." The words that accompany the fragment perfectly express this sentiment, and, when properly performed, the fragment still conveys this mood. Other than this single relic of choral recitative, the music of the 5th century must

62. Fragment of a choral stasimon from Euripides' *Orestes*. c. 200 B.C. Papyrus, $3\frac{1}{2} \times 3\frac{3}{8}''$ (9 × 8.5 cm). Austrian National Library, Vienna.

remain mute to our ears, and we can only echo the words of John Keats in his "Ode on a Grecian Urn": "Heard melodies are sweet, but those unheard are sweeter."

Ideas

Each of the arts—architecture, sculpture, painting, poetry, drama, and music—is, of course, a distinct medium of expression. Each has its materials, whether of stone, bronze, pigments, words, or tones. Each has its skilled craftsmen who have disciplined themselves through years of study so they can mold their materials into meaningful forms. But every artist, whether architect, sculptor, painter, poet, dramatist, or musician, is also a child of a specific time and place, who in youthful years is influenced by the social, political, philosophical, and religious ideas of the period and who, in turn, on reaching maturity contributes creative leadership in a particular field.

No art exists apart from its fellows, and it is no accident that the Greeks thought of the arts as a family of sister Muses. Architecture, to complete itself, must rely on sculpture and painting for embellishments. Sculpture and painting, for their parts, must search for congenial architectural surroundings. Drama embraces poetry, song, and the dance in the setting of a theater.

This interdependence of the arts was all quite clear in ancient times, as Plutarch's quote of Simonides indicates: "Painting is silent poetry; poetry is painting that speaks." When the philosophers Plato and Aristotle examined the arts, they looked for common elements applicable to all. And they were just as keen in their search for unity here as they were for unity among all the other aspects of human experience.

Certain recurring themes appear in each of the arts of the Hellenic period as artists sought to bring their ideals to expression. Out of these themes emerges a trio of ideas—humanism, idealism, and rationalism—that recur continually in Athenian thought and action. These three ideas, then, provide the framework that surrounds the arts and encloses them in such a way that they come together into a significant unity.

Humanism

"Man," said Protagoras, "is the measure of all things." And, as Sophocles observed, "Many are the wonders of the world, and none so wonderful as man." This, in essence, is humanism. With the human being as yardstick, the Greeks conceived their gods and goddesses as perfect beings, immortal and free from physical infirmities but, like themselves, subject to very human passions and ambitions. The gods, likewise, were personifications of human ideals: Zeus stood for masculine creative power, Hera for maternal womanliness, Athena for wisdom, Apollo for youthful brilliance, Aphrodite for feminine desirability, and so on down the list. Because of their resemblance to the gods, the Greeks gained greatly in self-esteem. When gods were more human, as the saying goes, men and women were more divine.

The principal concern of the Greeks was with human beings—their social relationships, their place in the natural environment, and their stake in the universal scheme of things. In such a small city-state as Athens, civic duties fell upon each individual. Every responsible person had to be concerned with politics, which Aristotle considered to be the highest social ethics. Participation in public affairs was based on the need to subordinate personal aspirations to the good of the whole state. A person endowed with great qualities of mind and body was honor-bound to exercise these gifts in the service of others.

Aeschylus, Socrates, and Sophocles were men of action who served Athens on the battlefield as well as in public forums and theaters. One responsibility of a citizen was to foster the arts. Under Athenian democracy the state itself, meaning the people as a whole, became the principal patrons of the arts.

Politically and socially, the life of the Athenians was balanced between aristocratic conservatism and liberal individualism, a balance maintained by the democratic institutions of their society. Their arts reflected a tension between this aristocratic tradition, which resisted change and emphasized austerity, restraint, and stylization in the arts, and the new dynamic liberalism, which put greater emphasis on emotion, the desire to cultivate ornateness, and a taste for naturalism. The genius of Phidias was his ability to achieve a golden mean between these opposites; the incomparable Parthenon was the result.

Humanism also expressed itself in kinship with nature. By personifying all things, animate and inanimate, the Greeks tried to come to terms with unpredictable natural phenomena and to explain the inexplicable. Their forests were populated with elusive nymphs and satyrs, their seas with energetic tritons, and their skies with capricious zephyrs. All were imaginative explanations and personifications of forces beyond their control.

These personifications, as well as the conception of the gods as idealized human beings, created a happy condition for the arts. By increasing their understanding of nature in all its aspects, the Hellenes also enhanced their own humanity. Even when the scientific philosophers sought to reduce the universe to basic matter—earth, air, fire, water—the body and soul were still identified with the basic stuff of the natural world. To create an imaginary world that is also a poetic image of the real world will always be one of the pursuits of the artist. And the Greeks thought of art as a *mimesis*—that is, an imitation or representation of nature. Since this also included human nature, it implied a recreation of life in the various mediums of art.

Particularly congenial to this humanistic mode of thought was the art of sculpture. With the human body as the point of departure, such divinities as Athena and Apollo appeared as idealized images of perfect feminine and masculine beauty. Equally imaginative were such deviations from the human norm as the goat-footed Pan, the half-human, half-horse centaurs, and the many fanciful creatures and monsters that symbolized the forces of nature.

The Greeks were more thoroughly at home in the physical world than the later Christian peoples, who believed in a separation of flesh and spirit. The Greeks greatly admired the beauty and agility of the human body at the peak of its development. In addi-

tion to studies in literature and music, Greek youth was trained from childhood for competition in the Athenian and Olympic games. Since it was through the perfection of their bodies that human beings most resembled the gods, the culture of the body was a spiritual as well as physical activity.

The nude male body in action at gymnasiums was a fact of daily experience, and sculptors had ample opportunity to observe its proportions and musculature. The result is embodied in such well-known examples as the statues of athletes attributed to Polyclitus, such as the *Doryphorus* (Fig. 49) and the *Discobolus* by Myron (Fig. 53). The *Kritios Boy* (Fig. 63), found on the acropolis, is one of the rare marble originals of this period. The slight turn of the head and the easy stance with the weight placed on one foot give the figure a supple grace and animation. As an instrument of expression, the male nude reached a high point in the 5th century B.C. The female form, however, had to wait for similar inspired treatment until the next century.

Any humanistic point of view assumes that life here and now is good and is meant to be enjoyed. This attitude is the opposite of medieval self-denial, which viewed the joys of this life as snares of the devil, believing that true good could be attained only in the unseen world beyond the grave. While the Greeks had no single belief about life after death, the usual one is found in the underworld scene of Homer's *Odyssey* when the spirit of the hero's mother explains that "when first the breath departs from the white bones, flutters the spirit away, and like to a dream it goes drifting." And the ghost of Achilles tells Odysseus that he would rather be the slave of the poorest living mortal than reign as king over the underworld. Greek *steles*, or gravestones, usually depicted the deceased in some characteristic worldly attitude—a warrior in battle, a hunter with his favorite horse or dog, or a lady choosing her jewelry for the day's adornment (Fig. 64).

The spiritual kingdom of the Greeks was definitely of this world. They produced no major religious prophets, had no divinely imposed creeds, no sacred scriptures as final authority on religious matters, no organized priesthood. Such mottoes inscribed on the sacred stones of Delphi as "Know thyself" and "Nothing in excess" were suggestions that bore no resemblance to the thunderous "Thou Shalt Nots" of the earlier Ten Commandments.

Knowledge of their gods came to the Greeks from Homer's epics and Hesiod's book of myths. The character and action of these gods, however, were subject to a wide variety of interpretations, as is clear from the commentaries of the 5th-century drama. This nonconformity indicated a broad tolerance that allowed free speculation on the nature of the universe.

lines on a map but with a cultural unity of independent peoples sharing common ideals. The continuous flow of time also seemed unreal, and their unconcern with a precise historical past is evident in the imperfection of their calendar and in the fact that their historians Herodotus and Thucydides were really chroniclers of almost-contemporary events.

Greek geometry was designed to measure static rather than moving bodies, and their visual arts emphasized the abiding qualities of poise and calm. Greek architecture humanized the experience of space by organizing it so that it was neither too complex nor too grand to be fully comprehended. The Parthenon's success rests on its power to humanize the experience of space. Through its geometry, such visual facts as repeated patterns, spatial progressions, and distance intervals are made easy to see and to understand. The simplicity and clarity of

left: 63. *Kritios Boy.* c. 490–480 B.C.
Marble, height 34″ (86 cm).
Acropolis Museum, Athens.

right: 64. Grave stele of Hegeso. c. 410–400 B.C.
Marble, height 4′11″ (1.5 m).
National Museum, Athens.

Indeed, the Greeks had to work hard to penetrate the divine mind and to interpret its meaning in human affairs. Ultimately, their ethical principles were embodied in four virtues—courage, meaning physical and moral bravery; temperance, in the sense of nothing too much or, as Pericles put it, "our love of what is beautiful does not lead us to extravagance"; justice, which meant rendering to each person what was due; and wisdom, the pursuit of truth.

Humanism and the Arts   Just as the Greek religion sought to capture the godlike image in human form, so also did the arts try to bring the experience of space and time within human grasp. Indefinite space and infinite time meant little to the Greeks. The modern concept of a nation as a territorial or spatial unit, for instance, did not exist for them. Expansion of their city-state was not concerned with

Greek construction were always evident to the eye, and by defining the indefinite and imposing a sense of order on the chaos of space, the architects of Greece made their spaces clearly intelligible.

Just as architecture humanized the perception of space, so the arts of the dance, music, poetry, and drama humanized the experience of time. These arts fell within the broad meaning of *music,* and their humanistic connection was emphasized in the education of youth. For as Plato said, "rhythm and harmony find their way into the inward places of the soul, on which they mightily fasten, imparting grace, and making the soul of him who is rightly educated graceful."

The triple unities of time, place, and action observed by the dramatists brought the flow of time within definite limits and are in striking contrast to the shifting scenes and continuous narrative styles of later periods. The essential humanism of Greek drama is found in its creation of distinctive human types; in its making of the chorus a collective human commentary on individual actions of gods and heroes; in its treatment of human actions in such a way that they rise above individual imitations to the level of universal principles; and, above all, in the creation of tragedy, in which the great individual is shown rising to the highest estate and then plunging to the lowest depths, thereby spanning the limits of human experience.

In sum, all the arts of Greece became the generating force by which Athenians consciously or unconsciously identified with their fellow citizens and with the entire rhythm of life about them. Through the arts, human experience is raised to its highest level; refined by their fires, the individual is able to see the world in the light of universal values.

Idealism

When artists face the practical problem of representation, there are two main courses. They can choose to represent objects either as they appear to the physical eye or as they appear to the mind's eye. In one case, they would emphasize nature, in the other, imagination; the world of appearances as opposed to the world of essences; the real as opposed to the ideal. The avowed realist is more concerned with *concretion*—that is, with rendering the actual, tangible object with all its particular and peculiar characteristics. The idealist, on the other hand, accents *abstraction,* eliminating all extraneous accessories and concentrating on the essential qualities of things. A realist, in other words, tends to represent things as they are; an idealist, as they might or should be. Idealism as a creative viewpoint gives precedence to the idea or mental image, tries to transcend physical

limitations, aspires toward a fulfillment that goes beyond actual observation, and seeks a concept closer to perfection.

Both courses were followed in the Hellenic style. One of Myron's most celebrated works was a bronze cow said to be so natural that it aroused amorous reactions in bulls, and calves tried to suckle her. Such a work would certainly have been in line, in the literal sense at least, with the Greek definition of art as the imitation of nature. In contrast, the painter Parrhasius agreed with Socrates that since it was impossible to find perfection in a single human model, it was necessary to "combine the most beautiful details of several, and thus contrive to make the whole figure look beautiful."

Plato's Ideal Forms   The case for idealism is argued in Plato's dialogues. He assumes a world of eternal verities and transcendental truths but recognizes that perfect truth, beauty, and goodness can exist only in the mental world of forms and ideas. Phenomena observed in the visible world are but reflections of these invisible forms. By way of illustration, parallelism is a concept, and two exactly parallel lines will, in theory, never meet. It is impossible, however, to find anything approaching true parallelism in nature, and no matter how carefully a draftsman draws them, two lines will always be unparallel to a slight degree and, hence, will meet somewhere this side of infinity. But this does not destroy the concept of parallelism, which still exists in the mental image or idea of it.

Plato's *Republic,* to cite another example, is an intellectual exercise in projecting an ideal state. No one knew better than Plato that such a society did not exist in fact and probably never would. But this did not lessen the value of the activity. The important thing was to set up goals that would approach his utopian ideal more closely than did any existing situation. "Would a painter be any the worse," he asks, "because, after having delineated with consummate art an ideal of a perfectly beautiful man, he was unable to show that any such man could ever have existed? . . . And is our theory a worse theory because we are unable to prove the possibility of a city being ordered in the manner described?"

Plato's idealistic theory, however, leads him into a rather strange position regarding the activities of artists. When, for instance, they fashion a building, a statue, or a painting, they are imitating, or representing, specific things that, in turn, are imitations of the ideal forms, and hence their products are thrice removed from the truth. The clear implication is, of course, that art should try to get away from the accidental and accent the essential, to avoid the transitory and seek the permanent.

Aristotle, on the other hand, distinguished between various approaches in art. In his *Poetics,* he observes that "we must represent men either as better than in real life, or as worse, or as they are. It is the same in painting. Polygnotus depicted men as nobler than they are, Pauson as less noble, Dionysius drew them true to life. . . . So again in language, whether prose or verse unaccompanied by music. Homer, for example, makes men better than they are; Cleophon as they are; Hegemon the Thasian, the inventor of parodies, . . . worse than they are." Aristotle applied the same standard to drama, pointing out that "Comedy aims at representing men as worse, Tragedy as better than in actual life." In the visual arts, the distinction, then, is between making an idealized image, a realistic image, or a caricature. Aristotle clearly implies that idealism as expressed in Homer's heroic poetry, Polygnotus' noble paintings, and Sophocles' moving tragedies constitutes the highest form of art.

Idealism and the Arts   At its high point in the latter half of the 5th century B.C., the Hellenic style was dominated by the idealistic theory. The Greek temple was designed as an idealized dwelling place for a perfect being. By its logical interrelationship of lines, planes, and masses, it achieves something of permanence and stability in the face of the transitory and random state of nature.

In portraying an athlete, a statesman, or a deity, the Hellenic sculptor concentrated on typical or general qualities rather than on the unique or particular. This was in line with the Greek idea of personality, which it was felt was better expressed in the dominating traits than in individual oddities.

In sculpture, as well as in all the other arts, the object was to rise above transitory sensations to capture the permanent, the essential, the complete. Thus the sculptor avoided representing the human being in infancy or old age, since immaturity and postmaturity implied incompleteness or imperfection and hence were incompatible with the concept of ideal types. The range of representations extends from athletes in their late teens through images of Hermes, Apollo, and Athena, who are conceived in their early maturity, to Zeus, father of the gods, who appears as the fully developed patriarch in all the power of mature manhood. It must also be remembered that few of the Hellenic sculptor's subjects were intended to represent human beings as such. The majority were fashioned to represent gods, who, if cast in human form, must have bodies of transcendent beauty.

In some way, even the intangible tones of music participated also in the ideal world by way of the mathematical relationships on which they are based.

A melody, then, might have something more permanent than its fleeting nature would indicate.

One of the main functions of the drama was to create ideal types, and, while the typical was always opposed to the particular, somehow the one arose from the other. The interpretation of this interplay was assigned to the chorus, and the drama as a whole shared with the other arts the power of revealing how the permanent could be derived from the impermanent; how the formula could be extracted from the process of forming; how a permanent quality could be distilled from universal flux; how the type could be found in the many specific cases; and how the *archetype,* or highest type, could arise from the types.

In the extreme sense, the real and ideal worlds represent blind chaos and perfect order. Since the one was intolerable and the other unattainable, it was necessary to find a middle ground somewhere. Glimpses of truth, beauty, and goodness could be caught occasionally, and these intimations should help people to steer a course from the actual to the ideal. By exercising the faculties of reason, judgment, and moral sense, human beings can subdue the chaotic conditions of their existence and bring closer into view the seemingly far-off perfection.

The Socratic theory of education, expressed in the balance between gymnastic for the body and music for the soul, was designed as a curriculum leading toward this end. The Greek temple, the nobly proportioned sculptural figures, the hero of epic and tragedy, and the orderly relationships of the melodic intervals in music are all embodiments of this ideal. Politician, priest, philosopher, poet, artist, and teacher all shared a common responsibility in trying to bring the ideal closer to realization. As Socrates said, "Let our artists rather be those who are gifted to discern the true nature of the beautiful and graceful; then will our youth dwell in a land of health, amid fair sights and sounds, and receive the good in everything; and beauty, the effluence of fair works, shall flow into the eye and ear, like a health-giving breeze from a purer region, and insensibly draw the soul from earliest years into likeness and sympathy with the beauty of reason."

Rationalism

Rational and irrational forces exist within every society as well as within every person. The question remains whether the state or individual tries to solve problems by reason or emotion. "Things are numbers," Pythagoras is supposed to have said, and by this statement to have affirmed that something solid and permanent underlies the shifting appearances of things. A few generations later, Anaxagoras went a step farther by stating that "mind has power over all

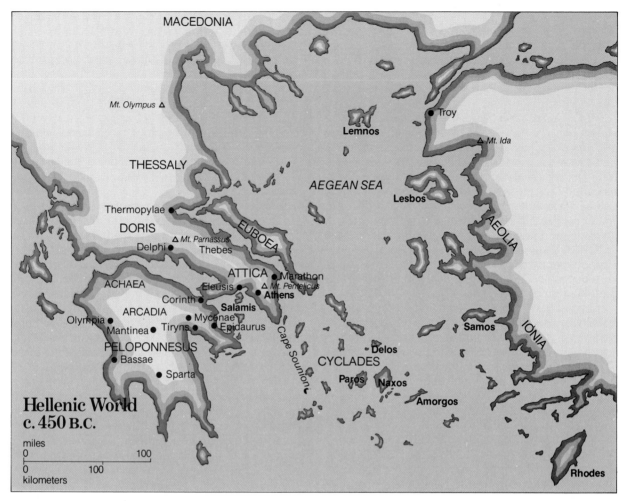

Hellenic World
c. 450 B.C.

MACEDONIA

Mt. Olympus △

THESSALY

Thermopylae

DORIS

△ Mt. Parnassus
Delphi   Thebes

ACHAEA
Corinth
ARCADIA
Olympia   Mycenae
Mantinea Tiryns Epidaurus
PELOPONNESUS
Bassae

Sparta

ATTICA Marathon
Eleusis △ Mt. Pentelicus
Salamis Athens

AEGEAN SEA

Lemnos

Troy
△ Mt. Ida

Lesbos

AEOLIA

Samos

IONIA

Cape Sounion

Delos
CYCLADES
Paros Naxos
Amorgos

Rhodes

miles
0   100
0   100
kilometers

things that have life." His disciple Socrates continued the argument and kindled in his followers a burning love of truth, not because truth was useful for worldly success but because truth is an ideal to be pursued for its own sake. The good life in the heyday of Greek civilization embraced not only the ethical principles of courage, temperance, and justice, but also wisdom, a virtue achieved by the free exercise of one's rational faculties.

In the Hebraic and Christian traditions, mortal error lay in breaking the moral law, but to the Greeks, original sin was a lack of knowledge. The tragedy of Oedipus in Sophocles' drama *Oedipus the King* is his ignorance that does not permit him to know he is murdering his father, marrying his mother, and begetting children who are also his own siblings. His downfall therefore comes through his ignorance, and his fate is the price he has to pay.

In *The Bacchants,* too, the general theme is the conflict between the known and the unknown. Agave is led to murder her own son because she voluntarily surrenders her reason to an irrational cult. Her son

Pentheus' downfall comes because his reason was not strong enough to comprehend the emotional and irrational forces that motivated the members of his family and his subjects. Since Pentheus could not understand these forces, he could not bring them under control and thus lacked the wisdom and tolerance necessary in a successful ruler. The entire Greek philosophical tradition concurred in the assumption that, without knowledge and the free exercise of the faculty of reason, there is no ultimate happiness for humanity.

By thinking for themselves in the spirit of free intellectual inquiry, the Greeks to a great extent succeeded in formulating reasonable rules for the conduct of life and its creative forces. This faith in reason also imparted to the arts an inner logic of their own, since when a craftsman's hands are guided by an alert mind, the work can penetrate the surface play of the senses and plunge to deeper levels of universal experience. For all later periods, this balance between the opposites of reason and emotion, form and content, reality and appearance becomes the basis for any classical style. For such subsequent classical movements as the Renaissance and 19th-century neoclassicism, the guiding principle is symmetry, proportion, and unity based on the interrelationship of parts with one another and with the whole.

Plato's Suspicions of the Arts The qualities of balance, clarity, and simplicity that the Greeks set up as standards of excellence in all the arts depended upon the selective faculty of a well-ordered mind. As Plato put it, "beauty of style and harmony and grace and good rhythm depend on simplicity—I mean the true simplicity of a rightly and nobly ordered mind and character." Plato's attitude toward the arts that did not meet these specifications was highly critical. And since inspiration is as necessary a condition of creativity as standards, Plato was afraid that some works of art tended to be more the product of divine madness than of reason.

Aristotle, without compromising his rational position, was able to distinguish between historical and poetic truth, fact and fancy, but Plato severely criticized poetic license. He was disturbed, for instance, by such architectural refinements as the carefully calculated distortions for purposes of creating the appearance of perfection. Since only the world of mathematics seemed fixed and logical, the world of appearances was deceptive, as proved by such illusions as a straight stick appearing bent when thrust into water. The artist, to Plato, sometimes seemed to minister to the deficiencies rather than the strengths of human nature. "Thus," he writes, "every sort of confusion is revealed within us; and this is that weakness of the human mind on which the art of conjuring and of deceiving by light and shadow and other ingenious devices imposes, having an effect like magic."

The philosopher also pointed out that "in works either of sculpture or painting, which are of any magnitude, there is a certain degree of deception; for if artists were to give the true proportions of their fair works, the upper part, which is farther off, would appear to be out of proportion in comparison with the lower, which is nearer; and so they give up the truth in their images and make only proportions which appear to be beautiful, disregarding the real ones."

Furthermore, that which is true of the deviations of visual lines applies also to the variations in the rhythms of recited poetry and performed music. If mathematical regularity prevails, the result is dull and mechanical. In music, pitch must also waver slightly in order to approximate the human voice and sound natural and interesting. This Plato also considered irrational. He felt that the only hope was for "the arts of measuring and numbering and weighing

[to] come to the rescue of human understanding." For Plato, then, the excellence or inferiority of the several arts depends upon the manner in which they make use of mathematical principles.

Rationalism and the Arts In spite of the suspicions of the philosophers, the Hellenic artists were no less concerned than Plato with the pursuit of an ideal order, which they felt could be grasped by the mind through the medium of the senses. Greek architecture, in retrospect, turns out to be a high point in the rational solution to building problems. The post-and-lintel system of construction, as far as it goes, is eminently reasonable and completely comprehensible. All structural members fulfill their logical purpose. Nothing is hidden or mysterious. The orderly principle of repetition on which Greek temple designs are based is as logical in its way as one of Euclid's geometry propositions or Plato's dialogues. It accomplishes for the eye what Plato tries to achieve for the mind.

The tight unity of the Greek temple met the Greek requirement that a work of art be complete in itself. Its carefully controlled but flexible relationships of verticals and horizontals, solids and voids, structural principles and decorative embellishments give it a relentless internal consistency. And the harmonic proportions of the Parthenon reflect the Greek image of a harmoniously proportioned universe quite as much as a logical system.

Sculpture likewise avoided the pitfalls of rigid mathematics and succeeded in working out principles adapted to its specific needs. When Polyclitus said "the beautiful comes about, little by little, through many numbers," he was stating a rational theory of art in which the parts and whole of a work could be expressed in mathematical proportions. But he also allowed for flexible application of the rule, depending on the pose or line of vision. By such a reconciliation of the opposites of order and freedom, he reveals the kinship of sculptors with their philosophical and political colleagues who were trying to do the same for other aspects of Athenian life.

Rational and irrational elements were present in both the form and content of Greek drama, just as they were in the architecture of the time. In the Parthenon, the structurally regular triglyphs were interspersed with panels showing centaurs and other mythological creatures. The theme of these sculptures was the struggle between the Greeks as champions of enlightenment and the forces of darkness and barbarism. In the drama, the rational Apollonian dialogue existed alongside the inspired Dionysian chorus. However, even in the latter, the intricate metrical schemes and the complex arrangements of the parts partake of rationalism and convey the dramatic content in a highly ordered composition. In the dialogue of a Greek tragedy, the action of the episodes must by rule lead inevitably and inexorably toward the predestined end, just as the lines and groupings of the figures must do in a composition like that on the east pediment of the Parthenon.

In the union of mythological and rational elements, tragedy could mediate between intuition and rule, the irrational and rational, the Dionysian and Apollonian principles. Above all, it achieves a coherence that meets Aristotle's critical standard of "a single action, one that is a complete whole in itself with a beginning, middle, and end, so as to enable the work to produce its proper pleasure with all the organic unity of a living creature."

Just as the harmony of the Parthenon depended on the module taken from the Doric columns, so Polyclitus derived his proportions for the human body from the mathematical relationship of its parts. In similar fashion, melodic lines in music were based on the subdivisions of the perfect intervals derived from the mathematical ratios of the fourth, fifth, and octave. So also the choral sections of the Greek drama were constructed of intricate metrical units that added up to the larger parts on which the unity of the drama depended. In none of these cases, however, was a cold distillation the desired effect. In the architecture of the Hellenic style, in the statues of Polyclitus, in the dramas of Aeschylus, Sophocles, and Euripides, and in the dialogues of Plato, the rational approach was used principally as a dynamic process to suggest ways for solving a variety of human and aesthetic problems.

It was also the Greeks who first realized that music, like the drama and other arts, was a mean between the divine madness of an inspired musician, such as Orpheus, and the solid mathematical basis on which the art rested acoustically. The element of inspiration had to be tempered by an orderly theoretical system that could demonstrate mathematically the arrangement of its melodic intervals and metrical proportions.

Finally, it should always be remembered that the chief deity of the city was Athena, goddess of knowledge and wisdom. Even such a cult religion as that of Dionysus, through the Orphic and Pythagorean reforms, tended constantly toward increased rationalism and abstract thought. While Athena, Dionysus, and Apollo were all born out of a myth, their destinies found a common culmination in the supreme rationalism of Socrates and Plato, who eventually concluded that philosophy was the highest music.

"We are all Greeks." So said Shelley in the preface to his play *Hellas.* "Our laws, our literature, our religion, our arts, have their roots in Greece." Merely the mention of such key words as *mythology, philosophy, democracy* points immediately to their Greek source. So also do the familiar forms of architecture, sculpture, painting, poetry, drama, and music have their taproots in the age-old soil of Hellas, the land where the Hellenic style was nurtured and brought to fruition.

As the Athenians looked into the mirror of their arts, they could see reflected the long road they had traveled from the dark past of prehistory, with all its primitive practices and mythological superstitions. In the light of their radiant present, they confidently shared the direction of their world with their gods who, to be sure, were immortal but not all-powerful. Since even deities had limitations, human help was urgently needed. The constant search for justice and wisdom was bringing the divine and human worlds closer together into a single universal harmony, and in the process, the gods were humanized and men and women reached out toward divinity.

The Socratic notion of truth, for example, was not brought down from a mountain or imposed from above by either priest or god. It was evolved with practice and effort by the application of rational principles in a *dialectical,* or give-and-take, process. Since the arts of the Athenians were addressed to reasonable beings, they were more persuasive if they possessed balance, order, and proportion than if they tried to impress by the ponderous mass of a pyramid or the colossal height of a projected tower of Babel.

Athenian idealism found expression in the eternal trinity of truth, beauty, and goodness, each in its way a facet of the ideal oneness attainable by the human mind. The approach to these ideals was not through mystical rites but through the process of dialectics, aesthetics, and ethics. Through these avenues, it was possible to discern on the distant horizon an intelligent, beautiful, and moral living space, broad enough to ensure the expansion of Athenian institutions and arts into a sphere of excellence seldom equaled and never excelled before or since.

Such, then, was the remarkable configuration of historical, social, and artistic events that led to this unique flowering of culture. Although circumstances conspired to bring about a decline of political power, Athens was destined to remain the teacher of Greece, Rome, and all later peoples of Western civilization. And the words of Euripides still ring down the corridors of time:

Happy of old were the sons of Erechtheus,
Sprung from the blessed gods, and dwelling
In Athens' holy and untroubled land.
Their food is glorious wisdom, they work
With springing step in the crystal air.
Here, so they say, golden Harmony first
Saw the light, the child of the Muses nine.

3

The Hellenistic Style

Pergamon, 2nd Century B.C.

Like the earlier city of Athens, Pergamon (or Pergamum) in Asia Minor developed around its acra, the fortified hilltop that became the residence of its rulers and a sanctuary. The Pergamene acropolis was a geographical site with even greater natural advantages than that of Athens. Thus it played a significant role in the growth of the city. Strategically located on a plain near the Aegean Sea, Pergamon developed a prosperous export trade. The fertile plain, formed by the flowing together of three rivers, was easily defensible from the hill. The city itself, surrounded as it was by the wide sea, high mountains, and precipitous ravines, was unassailable except from its southern approach. Here, in a situation of unusual beauty, grew the city that was to play such an important role in the Hellenistic period.

After Athens fell to Sparta in 404 B.C., Greece veered away from the small democratic city-state as the basic political unit toward more autocratic forms of government. Philip of Macedon first succeeded in bringing the mainland of Greece into a single kingdom. Then his son Alexander the Great embarked on a course of conquest leading to a short-lived empire. With great centers of the empire separated as widely as Syracuse on the island of Sicily, Alexandria on the banks of the Nile, and the cities of Asia Minor on the east coast of the Aegean (see map, p. 59), Greek thought became varied and international in scope.

The Hellenistic period proper covers the two centuries between the death of Alexander in 323 B.C. and the Roman conquest of Greece in 146 B.C., but in effect it continued through a transitional Greco-Roman era down to 27 B.C., the beginning of the Augustan Age in Rome. Throughout these two centuries, cultural leadership remained in the hands of the Greeks, but as they came in contact with such a variety of native influences, their culture became progressively more cosmopolitan. Hence, the distinction is drawn between the earlier and purer Hellenic and the later, more diffused Hellenistic styles.

In Asia Minor, significant art centers developed at Halicarnassus, Ephesus, Rhodes, and especially at Pergamon. The unique position of the latter was largely due to the energy and political wisdom of the Attalid kings, whose early recognition of the rising power of Rome led to an advantageous alliance with that city of the future. Pergamon was thus both an important center of civilization in its own right and one of the principal bridges over which the Greek tradition passed into the Roman Empire.

The planning of Greek cities apparently goes back no further than the middle of the 5th century B.C. The fame of "wide-wayed Athens" rested on its Panathenaic Way, a street about 12 feet (2.7 meters) broad. Just wide enough for five or six persons to walk abreast, it made easier the processions to the acropolis, theaters, and marketplace. Otherwise, the streets of Athens were narrow alleys barely broad enough to permit the passage of a driver with a donkey cart. Unpaved in any way, they must have been as dry and dusty in summer as they were damp and muddy in winter and spring. The Athenian residential section was only a mass of mud-brick houses in which rich and poor lived side by side in relative squalor. Only in the agora and on the acropolis did spaciousness develop. But even here buildings were planned with full attention to their individual logic and little or none to their relationship as a group. Each building thus existed as an independent unit, not as part of a coherent whole.

CHRONOLOGY
The Hellenistic Period

Greek city plans, while a vast improvement on their haphazard predecessors, were based on the application of an inflexible crisscrossing grid pattern that paid little or no attention to the irregularities of the natural site. When a hill was within the city limits, the streets sometimes became so steep that they could be climbed only by difficult stairways. While the residential sections of the ancient city of Pergamon have only now begun to be excavated, it is known that they followed such a regular system. Under Eumenes II, the city reached its largest extent, and the thick wall he built around it enclosed over 200 acres (81 hectares) of ground—more than four times the territory included by his predecessor. Ducts brought in ample water from nearby mountain springs to supply a population of 120,000. The system was the greatest of its kind prior to the Roman aqueducts.

The main entrance to Pergamon was from the south through an impressive arched gateway topped by a pediment with a triglyph frieze. Traffic was diverted through several vaulted portals that led into a square, where a fountain refreshed travelers. From here, the road led past the humbler dwelling places toward the lower marketplace, which bustled with the activities of peddlers and hucksters of all sorts. This market was a large open square surrounded on three sides by a two-story colonnade behind which were rows of rooms that served for shops. Moving onward, the road went past buildings that housed the workshops and mills for pottery, tiles, and textiles. Homes of the wealthier citizens were located on higher positions off the main streets overlooking the rest of the city. At the foot of the acropolis another square opened up, which could boast of a large fountain and a fine view.

On a dramatic site almost 1000 feet (305 meters) above the surrounding countryside rose the Pergamene acropolis (Fig. 65), a stronghold that ranked among the most imposing in the Greek world. Up the slopes of the hill, on terraces supported by massive retaining walls and fortifications, were the buildings

65. Acropolis, Pergamon.
Reconstruction by H. Schlief.

and artifacts that gave the city its reputation as a second Athens. By ingenious use of natural contours, the Pergamenes had developed settings for a number of buildings, which not only were outstanding as individual edifices but which, by means of connecting roadways, ramps, and open courtyards, were grouped into a harmonious whole. Here on a succession of rising levels were gymnasiums, athletic fields, temples, assembly places, public squares, wooded groves, and an amphitheater. Above them all, flanked by watch towers, barracks, arsenals, storage houses, and gardens, stood the residence of the kings of Pergamon.

Architecture

Triple Gymnasium

On the three lowest of the artificially created terraces of the Pergamene acropolis were a series of open grounds, enclosed by colonnades and buildings, which comprised a triple gymnasium—one for each general age group. The spacious outdoor areas included a playground for boys, an athletic field, and a race course. Provision was also made for dressing rooms, baths, and indoor sports. And, as the education center of the city, the gymnasium also included classrooms and lecture halls. It is significant that such gymnasiums provided mental as well as physical exercise. Their pleasant locations in groves and gardens, in fact, were responsible for the names of such famous schools of philosophy as Plato's Academy and Aristotle's Lyceum, just as the *stoa,* or shady colonnade facing a public building, became the name of the Stoic school of thought.

At the Pergamon gymnasium, statues have been found of such mythological figures as Asclepius, son of Apollo and physician of the gods, and Hygeia, daughter of Asclepius and guardian of the health of growing youths, as well as sculptured representations of athletes at their games. A small adjacent temple was dedicated to one of the patron deities of sports, possibly Hermes, the fleet-footed messenger of the gods, or Heracles, mythological model of strength; and nearby were statues of Nike, goddess of victory, altars for votive offerings, and busts of prominent athletes who won the Olympic and other Greek games.

Upper Agora and Altar of Zeus

Above the gymnasium was the upper agora (Fig. 65, lower left), an open square that served both as an assembly place and as a market for such quality merchandise as the renowned Pergamene pottery and textiles. Above the agora spread the broad marble-paved terrace on which stood the Altar of Zeus, with its famous frieze depicting in marble slabs the battle of the gods as personifications of light and order against the giants as representatives of darkness and chaos. Dating from about 180 B.C., this artistic triumph of the reign of Eumenes II was declared by many contemporary authorities to be one of the seven wonders of the ancient world. Since both its structure and sculptures are of major importance, this edifice will be discussed in the following section.

Athena Precinct and Theater

Above the Altar of Zeus was the precinct dedicated to Athena Polias, or Athena protectress of cities and guardian of laws and city life. Her shrine (Fig. 65, center) was a graceful Doric temple, smaller than the Parthenon, with six-columned porches on either end and ten columns on each side. This level was framed by an L-shaped, two-storied colonnade that formed an open courtyard in which stood the bronze monument that celebrated the victory of Attalus I, father of Eumenes, over the Gauls (Figs. 66, 67). This colonnade served also as the façade of the great library of Pergamon, which appropriately was placed here in the precinct of Athena, goddess of reason, contemplation, and wisdom. The most precious part of the library was housed in four rooms on the second-story level stretching about 145 feet (44 meters) in length and 47 feet (14.2 meters) in width. On their stone shelves, some of which still exist, rested the ancient scrolls, estimated to have numbered about 200,000 at the time of the Attalids. The Pergamon library ranked with that of Alexandria as one of the two greatest libraries of antiquity. Later, after the major portion of the Alexandrine collection of half a million volumes had been burned in an uprising against Caesar, Mark Anthony made a gift to Cleopatra of the entire library of Pergamon.

Below the Athena precinct was the theater (Fig. 65, center left), constructed under Eumenes II about 170 B.C. The auditorium with its 78 semicircular tiers of stone seats could hold 10,000 spectators and was carved out of the hillside. Below was the circular section of the orchestra, where the chorus performed around a small altar dedicated to Dionysus, and the rectangular scene building for the actors.

Royal Residence

Just as the Attalid kings dominated the life of their city and constituted the apex of the social pyramid of their kingdom, so the royal residence crowned the highest point in their capital city. Later, after the realm came under the domination of Rome, part of the palace was destroyed to make way for the large Corinthian temple honoring Emperor Trajan that is shown in the top foreground of Figure 65.

From their hilltop residence the kings of Pergamon could survey much of their rich domain. From the mountains to the north came the silver and copper that furnished the metal for their coins—so necessary in promoting trade and paying soldiers. From the same region came also supplies of pitch, tar, and timber—greatly in demand for the building of ships—as well as marble for buildings and sculptures. A panorama thus unfolded around them, starting with the heights of Mt. Ida and the surrounding range (down whose slopes flowed the streams that watered the fertile valleys and broad plains), all the way to the bright waters of the Aegean Sea, beyond which lay the shores of the Greek motherland.

Like the legendary Croesus, the Attalids of Pergamon were famed for their fabulous wealth, and "rich as an Attalid" was a phrase used by Horace and other Roman writers. But by later standards, the Attalids lived in relative modesty. The residence generally referred to as the "royal palace" was actually a loose grouping of small buildings, set amid wooded groves and gardens, that shifted from time to time with the changing fortunes of the kings. Included in the group were living rooms opening out into columned courtyards, chambers devoted to the dynastic cult, a barracks for the royal guard, a treasury, and storerooms for goods, grain, and arms.

The love of display, however, was less in evidence in royal residences than in the great public buildings the Attalids erected and in the ostentatious gifts they made to such cities as Athens and Rome. More important to the Attalid kings than the size and luxury of their dwelling was the close link with the temples of the gods that its location afforded. Both symbolically and practically, their residence was located here in order to dominate the city that spread out below them. From there all eyes would be attracted to the magnificent group of edifices. Thus the populace would look upward psychologically as well as actually to the kings and gods who ruled them.

The planning of Pergamon thus cleverly promoted the idea of the monarchy towering above it. There, topographically as well as politically, stood the king, aloof from his people and associated by them with the gods. Even while living, he was accorded such divine prerogatives as a cult statue, with perfumed grain burning on an altar before it, and an annual celebration in his honor. This semidivine status, connected with the king's right to rule, served the practical social purposes of commanding obedience to his laws, facilitating the collection of taxes (often under the guise of offerings to the deities), and uniting the peoples and factions who lived under him. Assisting in this deification were the scholars and artists the king attracted to his court, whose works were regarded with awe by native and foreigner alike.

The pomp and display that marked Hellenistic life was a distinct departure from the simplicity and nobility of the more austere 5th century B.C. Grandeur became grandioseness, and many monuments were erected not to revere the gods but to honor kings who, even in their own lifetimes, assumed semidivine status. The accent was no longer on abstract ideals but on the glorification of individuals.

With the changing times, however, definite advances in the art of building were taking place. Domestic architecture was emphasized, and Pergamene architects went beyond the simple post-and-lintel method of the Hellenic period by employing the arch and vault in city gates and in underground water and sewer systems. Architecturally as well as culturally, Pergamon forged the link between the Greek and Roman periods.

Hellenistic World
c. 323-146 B.C.

Sculpture

While sculptural works of all kinds are known to have existed in profusion throughout the city of Pergamon, the examples that claim the attention of posterity were located on two of the terraces of the acropolis. In the Athena precinct just below the royal residence, bounded by the temple on one side and the L-shaped colonnades of the library on two others, was a spacious courtyard in which Attalus I erected the sculptural monuments commemorating his victories. The groups he commissioned were in place during the last quarter of the 3rd century B.C. On the terrace below, in the first quarter of the 2nd century B.C., his son and successor Eumenes II built the Altar of Zeus (Fig. 68) with its famous frieze.

Historically, the two periods have been distinguished as the First and Second schools of Pergamon. Since they were separated by less than half a century, however, some sculptors possibly worked on both projects, and if not, they must have had a hand

in training their successors. All the bronze originals of the First School have disappeared and can be studied only in the marble copies made by later Hellenistic or Roman artists. Most of the sculptures from the Second School survive, because of the fortunate results of the late 19th-century German excavations, and may be seen today in the Pergamon Museum in East Berlin.

First School of Pergamon

The principal works of the First School were two large monuments in bronze, each of which was composed of many figures. One commemorated the victories of Attalus over the neighboring Seleucid kingdom. Only a few details of this group survive. The other honored his earlier and greater victory over the nomadic tribes of Gauls, which swept down from Europe across the Hellespont into the region north of Pergamon. From this province, called Galatia after them, the Gauls were a constant threat to the Greek

cities lying to the south. While his predecessor had bought them off by paying tribute, Attalus I refused to do so. He met their subsequent invasion with an army, and the outcome of the battle, fought about 30 miles (48 kilometers) to the east of Pergamon, was decisive enough to repel the Gauls for a generation. Its consequences were felt far and wide, and all the cities and kingdoms of the Greek world breathed a little easier.

The fierce Gauls had inspired such general terror that their defeat was associated in the popular mind with something of a supernatural character. The name of Attalus was everywhere acclaimed as *Soter* ("Savior," the victor), and after incorporating the lands he had gained, he asssumed the title of king. Thereafter, as King Attalus the Savior, he continued to capitalize on his fortunes by embarking on a program of beautifying his city with the services of the best available Greek artists. Sharing the same patroness, Athena, Pergamon began to acquire the status of a second Athens, and its ruler that of a political and cultural champion of Hellenism.

Parts of the monument that Attalus erected to the memory of his victory over the Gauls can be seen in numerous museums. The *Dying Gaul* (Fig. 66) and the *Gaul and His Wife* (Fig. 67) are the most famous of the individual units to survive from antiquity. The collective whole was a large group that rested on a circular platform some 10 feet (3 meters) in diameter. In the center rose a cylindrical base, about 7 feet (2 meters) high, on which were placed the victorious Pergamenes, while their opponents were found below on three descending steps.

The *Dying Gaul* (Fig. 66) is a fine example of Hellenistic emotional expression. He is the trumpeter who sounded the call for relief. Mortally wounded, the warrior has agonizingly dragged himself out of the thick of the battle to struggle alone against death. His eyes are fixed on the ground where his

above: 66. *Dying Gaul.*
Roman copy after bronze original of c. 225 B.C.
Marble; height 3′ (.91 m), length 6′3″ (1.91 m).
Capitoline Museum, Rome.

below: 67. *Gaul and His Wife.*
Roman copy after bronze original of c. 225 B.C.
Marble, height 6′11″ (2.11 m). National Museum, Rome.

right: **68.** Menocrates of Rhodes.
Altar of Zeus (restored),
from Pergamon.
Begun c. 180 B.C. Marble.
State Museums, East Berlin.

below: **69.** Plan of Altar of Zeus.

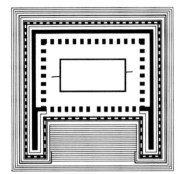

sword, the trumpet, and other pieces of his equipment are lying. He supports himself weakly with one arm, proud and defiant to the end, while his life's blood flows out of the gaping wound in his side. The anguished expression in the face has an intensity not encountered before in Greek art. The strong but rough musculature of his powerful body, so different from that of the supple Greek athletes, marks him as a barbarian. Further contrast is found in his hair, which is greased so heavily that it is almost as thick as a horse's mane, and in the collar of twisted gold worn around his neck.

All these carefully recorded details show the interest of the period in individuals as such, in the features that distinguish one person or group from another. Above all, they show the artist's desire to awaken the sympathies of the observer. By the process of empathy, the sculptor involves the observer in the situation. The contemporary audience would have felt both attraction and repulsion toward such a subject and hence would have experienced a strong emotional reaction. The litter of the battlefield beside the Gaul, as well as other realistic details, is not used so much for its own sake as to convey a sense of immediacy in the experience of the beholder. At the same time, the viewer was invited to look beyond the physical wounds and behold the spiritual anguish of the proud but defeated warrior, so reluctant to accept his fate.

The expressive impact of the *Gaul and His Wife* (Fig. 67) is no less powerful. The custom of the Gauls was to take their women and children with them on their campaigns. Realizing his defeat, and too proud

to be taken a slave, this Gaul has just killed his wife and looks apprehensively over his shoulder at the approaching enemy as he plunges his sword into his own neck. The mood of despair is heightened by the sweeping lines of the woman's drapery, which droops downward in deep folds, casting dark shadows. In both these surviving representations, strong feeling is aroused in the observer by the noble figures who stare death so courageously in the face.

Second School: Altar of Zeus

To the Second School of Pergamon are assigned all the works that fall within the reign of Eumenes II, the patron under whom Pergamon achieved the highest point of its power and glory. Like his father before him, Eumenes II had his victories over the Gauls, and in the Altar of Zeus (Fig. 68) he continued the tradition of erecting votive works. It was at once the greatest single monument of the city and one of the few top-ranking architectural and sculptural works of the Hellenistic period. It, too, was intended to glorify the position of the king and to impress the entire Greek world with Eumenes' contribution to Hellenism in the struggle against the barbarians.

Because of the diligent efforts of the German excavators, it is possible to appraise the Altar of Zeus almost in its original state. Beginning in 1878, piece by piece each fragment was painstakingly unearthed, and after a half-century of study, the entire monument was reconstructed in the Pergamon Museum in Berlin. Famed throughout the ancient world, the altar was described in the early years of the Christian era by St. John as "Satan's seat" (Rev. 2:13). The reference seems to have been prompted by the resemblance of the structure to an immense throne and by the pagan gods and demons depicted in the frieze. While the principal interest is focused on the sculpture, the building itself also commands attention.

Structure The actual altar on which animal sacrifices and other offerings were burned was a large stone podium standing in the inner courtyard. The altar was surrounded by a U-shaped enclosure known as a *temenos* (Fig. 69). The building rested on a *podium,* or platform, with five steps, above which was the great frieze more than 7 feet (2 meters) in height and 450 feet (137 meters) in length. It ran continuously around the entire podium, bending inward on either side of the stairway, and diminishing in size as the steps rose. Below, the frieze was framed by a molding and, above, by a *dentil range* (see Figs. 70, 71), a series of small projecting rectangular blocks. These bricklike blocks served also to support an Ionic colonnade that surrounded the structure and paralleled the frieze. Above the colonnade appeared a friezeless entablature with a second dentil range supporting the roof. Crowning the whole was a series of freestanding statues of deities and mythological animals placed at various points along the outer edges of the roof.

The concept of space that underlies the Altar of Zeus differs from that of the 5th century. In the earlier period, the altar was placed outside the temple, and rituals took place against the exterior colonnades. In the Hellenistic period, the concept of space included an interest in depth. Thus, in the Altar of Zeus, the spectator looked into a courtyard that enclosed the altar, and not toward a background plane. The wider space between the columns also invited the eye toward the interior, whereas the closer spaced columns of the 5th century promoted the continuity of the plane. Since the Hellenistic concept incorporates the same structural members as the earlier Greek style, the Altar of Zeus is more a variation on 5th-century forms than a radical departure from them. The columns, entablatures, and interior walls, consistent with the Greek tradition, clearly define the spatial limits. There is as yet no hint of the unbounded or infinite.

The general effect produced by the Altar of Zeus as a whole is of a traditional Greek temple turned upside down. The simple dignity of the older Doric temple—the Parthenon, for example—depended upon its structural integrity. The columns served the logical purpose of supporting the upper members, and the sculptured sections were high above where they embellished but did not dominate the design. At Pergamon, the traditional order was inverted. Considered more important than the columns, the decorative frieze was put below, only a little above eye level, in order to be seen more easily. For the sake of tradition, the colonnade was included, but placed above the frieze where it had no structural purpose. Structurality as a guiding principle had yielded to decoration for its own sake, and the art of architec-

ture, in effect, had given way to the art of sculpture. In the case of the Parthenon, the decorative frieze was included to give some variety to what might otherwise have been monotonous unity. In that of the Altar of Zeus, on the other hand, the variety of the frieze was so overwhelming that the regularity of a colonnade was needed to preserve the unity. The quiet Greek architectural drama, in other words, had become an architectonic melodrama.

Frieze The subject of the frieze is the familiar battle of the gods and giants. In the typical depiction of this scene, it was customary to include the twelve Olympians and an equal number of opponents, but here the unprecedented length of available space demanded more participants. Almost certainly scholars of the library were called upon to compile a catalogue of divinities, together with their attendants and attributes, in order to have enough figures to go around. This increase in the usual number of mythological figures, however, apparently taxed the knowledge of the average Greek, because carved names were provided beside the unfamiliar figures.

Further scholarly influence is found in the allegorical treatment of the ancient battle theme. Literal belief in the gods was largely a thing of the past, and the local scholars interpreted them as personifications of the forces of nature. Thus the gods represented orderly and benign phenomena, and the giants represented such calamities as earthquakes, hurricanes, and floods.

The narrative begins on the inner part of the podium, facing the stairs. Moving parallel with the stairs, it proceeds along the south and around the corner to the east. Along the way are introduced the principal characters in the drama—Zeus and his fellow gods, whose mortal combat is with Chronus, father of Zeus, and his supporters, the wicked titans and giants. There are also Helios, the sun god, Hemera, the winged goddess of day, her brother Aether, the spirit of air, and the moon goddess. Such others as Hecate, goddess of the underworld, Artemis, the heavenly huntress, and Heracles, father of Telephus, the legendary founder of Pergamon, are included as well. The struggle is between the forces of darkness—the giants—and the spirits of light.

In the four panels reproduced in Figure 70, Zeus is seen, appropriately, in combat with no less than three titans at once. His powerful figure, wrapped in a swirling mantle, is rearing back to smite the giants with his spear and thunderbolts. While most of Zeus' arm is missing, his hand is seen in the upper left corner of the panel. The titan in the lower left has already been overcome by a thunderbolt, which is shown as a pointed spear with a handle of acanthus leaves. The second giant is on the other side, his body

70. *Zeus Hurling Thunderbolts,*
detail of Altar of Zeus frieze.
c. 180 B.C. Marble, height 7'6" (2.29 m).

tense with terror before the blow falls. In the slab to the right, Porphyrion, king of the titans, is shown from the back. From his animal ears to his serpent legs, he is a fearsome sight as he shields himself with a lion skin from both Zeus' eagle above and the thunderbolts that the mighty god is about to hurl.

Next comes the fine group depicting the part played by Athena, protectress of the city (Fig. 71). Her figure is shown in the second slab. Bearing a shield on her left arm she grasps a winged giant by the hair with her right and forces him to earth where her sacred serpent can inflict the mortal wound. A moment of pathos is provided by the giant's mother, the earth goddess Gaea, who is seen as a torso rising from the ground. Though she is on the side of the gods, the earth mother implores Athena with her eyes to spare the life of her rebellious son. Gaea's attributes are seen in the horn of plenty she carries in her left hand, a cornucopia filled with the rich fruits of the earth—apples, pomegranates, and grapes with vine leaves and a pine cone. Over her hovers the goddess Nike, symbolizing the victory of Athena.

From this climax in the sky, the action on the shadowy north side of the frieze gradually descends into the realm of the water spirits. They drive the fleeing giants around the other corner of the stairway into the sea where they drown. Here are the representations of the rivers of Greece. Around the face of the west side and up the stairs are other creatures of the sea. The tumultuous action opens on the right side with the divinities of the land and ends here on the left with those of the sea. They are separated by the wide stairs as well as by their placement at the beginning and the end of the dramatic conflict between the forces of good and of evil.

The frieze as a whole is a technical feat of the first magnitude and was executed by a school of sculptors, many of whose names are inscribed below as signatures for their work. In addition to the figures, such details as swords and belt buckles, saddles and sandals, and the cloth for costumes are carved and polished to simulate the textures of metal, leather, and textiles, respectively. The bold high-relief carving, deep undercutting that allows the

71. *Athena Slaying Giant,*
detail of Altar of Zeus frieze.
Marble, height 7'6" (2.29 m).

figures to stand out almost in the round, and rich modeling effects that make full use of light and shadow reveal complete mastery of material.

To sustain such a swirl of struggling forms and violent movement over such a vast space is a minor miracle. The traditional Doric frieze could depend for unity on the momentary action in the metopes regularly interrupted by the static triglyphs. Here at Pergamon the unity relies on the continuity of the motion itself. The slashing diagonal lines and sharp contrasts of movement are grouped into separate episodes by the device of coiling snakes. Winding in and out, they are at once the visual punctuation marks that separate the scenes and the connecting links of the composition. They lead the eye from one group to another and promote a sense of constant writhing motion.

Stylistic Differences

Comparing the great frieze with the *Dying Gaul* and *Gaul and His Wife,* one can note a style trend from the First to the Second school. Both allude to the constant wars between the Pergamenes and Gauls. But, in contrast to the almost morbid preoccupation with pain in the earlier monument, the gods on the Altar of Zeus slay the giants with something approaching gaiety and abandon. Thus instead of having sympathy for the victims, the viewer wonders at the ingenious ways the gods dispatch their enemies.

Both monuments accent pathos, but whereas in the earlier examples the compassion of the observer is awakened simply and directly, the great frieze deals with its subject, the battle of the gods and giants, as a thinly disguised allegory of the war between the Pergamenes and Gauls. The Pergamenes in the guise of the gods have become superhuman figures, while the giants, whose features closely resemble earlier Gallic types, are now monsters.

Instead of the frank realism of the previous generation, then, the tale is told in the language of melodrama accompanied by visual bombast. It is put on the stage, so to speak, and done with theatrical gestures and histrionic postures. The emotional range is, correspondingly, enormous, beginning with the stark horror of monsters with enormous wings, animal heads, snaky locks, long tails, and serpentine legs, which recall the grotesque prehistoric creatures who inhabited the primordial world. After being terrorized by the sight of such bestial forms, the contemporary audience must have melted into sympathy for the earth mother pleading mercy for her monstrous offspring, and then gone from tears to laughter at the inept antics of some of the clumsy giants. And after hissing the villains, the viewers must have applauded the gods coming to the rescue.

This theatrical exaggeration of reality extends to the representation of bodily types. The functional physique of the *Dying Gaul* has become the Herculean power of the professional strong man who finds himself more at home in the arena than he does on the battlefield.

The perception of deeper space entered into the sculptural composition of the Altar of Zeus as well as into its architectural composition. Just as with the architectural composition the eye is being drawn into an enclosed interior, so with the sculpture, the eye does not move only from side to side, as in a plane, but is constantly led back and forth into spatial depth. Because it was painted blue, the marble background no longer offered a solid boundary but dissolved into atmosphere. To escape the plane, some of the figures of the great frieze project outward in such high relief as to be almost in the round; others even step outward from the frieze and support themselves by kneeling on the edge of the steps. The heavy shadows cast by the high-relief carving further intensify this effect. Thus the two-dimensional plane of the Hellenic style was expanded here to suggest some recession in depth.

A general comparison of Hellenistic art with the Athenian art of the 5th century B.C. leaves one with the impression of discord rather than harmony; an overwhelming magnitude rather than dimensions constrained within limited bounds; a wild emotionalism in the place of a rational presentation; virtuosity triumphing over dignified refinement; melodrama superseding drama; variety ascending over unity. The Athenian culture, in short, placed its trust in human beings; the Hellenistic, in super beings. No longer the masters of their fate, Hellenistic people were engulfed in the storms and stresses of grim circumstances beyond their control.

Paintings, Mosaics, and the Minor Arts

Owing to the enduring qualities of stone, more ancient sculpture has survived than art works in any other form. Buildings were torn down for their materials and replaced by others. Statues in bronze, precious metals, and ivory were too valuable in their essential material to survive as such. Libraries either were burned or had their volumes disintegrate in the course of time, so that their books survive only in imperfect copies made by medieval scribes or as fragmentary quotations in other volumes. The musical notation contained in ancient manuscripts could not be understood by these copyists, who eventually omitted it. Mosaics and pottery have fared better, but they, too, were either broken up or carried off by conquerors and collectors.

72. *Hercules Finding His Infant Son Telephus.* A.D. c. 70. Fresco from Herculaneum, probably a copy after a Pergamene original of 2nd century B.C. National Museum, Naples.

Pergamene Painting and Roman Adaptations

Of all the major visual arts in antiquity painting has suffered most from the ravages of time. The number of surviving examples is sufficient to give only a hint of what this art must have been at its best. The impression is thus easily gained that sculpture was the most important of all the arts. Literary sources, however, verify the effectiveness of painting and the high esteem in which it was held by the ancients. The fame of individual painters and the critical praise for their works make it clear that painting was on a par with architecture and sculpture.

Pausanias, a writer of Roman times, described the works of the legendary 5th-century B.C. Athenian painters Polygnotus and Apollodorus. The former worked out the principles of perspective drawing, and the latter was renowned for his use of light and shade and the finer gradations of color. Pausanias also mentioned many paintings at Pergamon. The excavated fragments at Pergamon reveal that the interior walls of temples and public buildings frequently were painted with pictorial panels and had streaks of color that imitated the texture of marble. Other scattered fragments of paintings show that the Pergamenes loved bright colors, such as yellows, pinks, and greens that contrasted with deep reds, blues, and browns.

The palace paintings used motifs of actual animals, such as lions and charging bulls, and imaginary ones, such as tritons and griffins. Interiors of rooms were often decorated with painted friezes similar to sculptural ones; and walls, especially of small rooms, were painted with panels and columns which cast realistic shadows in order to create the illusion of spaciousness. The writers of antiquity mention that the subjects of paintings were often drawn from mythology (Fig. 72) or literary sources, such as the *Odyssey*. It is also known that Hellenistic painting

frequently dealt in *genre scenes,* that is, casual, informal subjects from daily life.

Although the original paintings no longer exist, and only fragments of mosaics and vase painting survive, well-preserved copies of Pergamene work have been found in the Greek cities of southern Italy, notably Herculaneum. This city supposedly was founded by Hercules, whose son Telephus founded Pergamon. A "family" relationship thus existed between the two centers. Herculaneum, in fact, became a later middle-class version of the earlier richer and aristocratic Pergamon.

Both Herculaneum and nearby Pompeii were suddenly buried in a rain of cinders and a hail of volcanic stone that accompanied the eruption of Mt. Vesuvius in A.D. 79. When rediscovered in the 18th century, the two cities yielded many paintings and mosaics preserved almost intact. The prevailing taste was Hellenistic, and the well-to-do patrons, preferring traditional subjects, usually commissioned copies of famous paintings rather than original works of art.

Hercules Finding His Infant Son Telephus (Fig. 72) is an adaptation of a Pergamene original. The winged figure in the upper right is pointing out to Hercules his son Telephus, who is seen in the lower left among wild animals and suckling a doe. The place is the legendary fertile land of Arcadia, personified by the stately seated figure. Beside her are the fruits of the land, and at her back a playful faun is holding a shepherd's crook and blowing the panpipes. The coloring for the most part is sepia and reddish brown, relieved by lighter blue, green, and whitish tints. The figures appear against the background plane of the sky that projects them forward in the manner of relief sculpture. The drapery and modeling of the flower-crowned Arcadia recall the carving of a marble relief, while the powerful musculature of Hercules' body is cast in the manner of a bronze statue in the round.

Since ancient sculpture usually was painted in vivid colors, and reliefs sometimes had landscapes painted in the backgrounds, the arts of painting and sculpture obviously were closely identified in the Hellenistic mind, and they should perhaps be thought of more as complementary arts than as independent media. Paintings were more adaptable to interiors, while weather-resistant stone made marble reliefs better for out-of-doors. From the existing evidence, however, it is clear that the visual intention and expressive effect of both arts were closely associated and that neither could claim aesthetic supremacy over the other.

Mosaics and Lesser Arts

Mosaics, the art of which goes back to remote antiquity, were highly favored at Pergamon for the flooring of interiors and for wall paneling. As with later Roman work, geometrical patterns were preferred for floors, while representations of mythological subjects, landscapes, and genre scenes were used for murals. Such compositions are formed of small cubes or pieces of stone, marble, or ceramic known as *tesserae* that are set in cement.

One mosaic (Fig. 73) by the artist Hephaiston covered the entire floor of a room. It has a blank center surrounded first by a colorful geometrical design of black, gray, red, yellow, and white marble tesserae. Beyond this is a wavelike pattern of black and white. Then enclosing the whole is a border about a yard (0.9 meter) wide with a foliated, or leaflike, design of such rich variety that in its 44-foot (13.3-meter) expanse there is no repetition. Against a dark background are intertwined colored flowers, exotic lilies, vine leaves and various fruits, all with delicate shadings. In some places grasshoppers are feeding on acanthus leaves; in others small winged *putti,* or Cupidlike boys symbolizing love, are playing among the vines.

Copies of many Pergamene designs have been found at Herculaneum, Pompeii, Naples, and Rome. The floor mosaic depicting the Persian warrior Darius fleeing from the forces of Alexander the Great after his defeat in the battle of Issus (Fig. 74) is a Pompeian mosaic version of the 2nd century B.C. after a well-known earlier Hellenistic painting. According to the Roman writer Pliny the Elder, the most famous mosaicist of antiquity was Sosus, who worked at Pergamon. Among his most widely copied designs was one of doves drinking from a silver dish. A favorite design of his for the floors of dining rooms

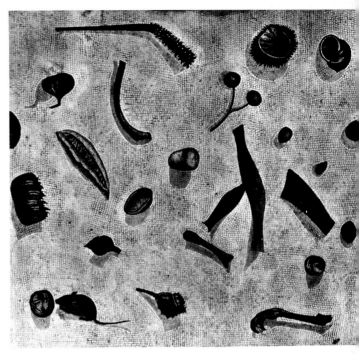

75. Sosus. *Unswept Dining Room Floor,* detail of later Roman copy of Pergamene original mosaic of 2nd century B.C. Vatican Museums, Rome.

showed vegetables, fruit, fish, a chicken leg, and a mouse gnawing on a nut (Fig. 75).

Pergamon was also noted for its textiles, dyed with special chemical and mineral substances, its metalwork of silver and bronze, and its carved gems, as well as for the ceramics it produced in both practical ware and terra-cotta figurines.

Music

Pergamon was identified with the musical tradition of the nearby northern Asia Minor region known as Phrygia, which had its own characteristic idioms, modes, rhythms, scales, and instruments. As early as the 5th century B.C., the Greeks in Athens were divided in their views as to the relative merits and propriety of the native Dorian musical tradition of the Greek mainland and of the increasing influence from foreign centers. In particular, the wild and exciting music of Phrygia was now gaining in popular favor.

Phrygian Music

Melodies in the Phrygian mode apparently induced strong emotional reactions, and the introduction of a musical instrument called the Phrygian pipe had a similar effect in inflaming the senses. This pipe was a

above: **76.** *Contest of Apollo and Marsyas.*
Relief from Mantineia, Greece. c. 350 B.C.
Marble, height 38¼″ (97 cm).
National Museum, Athens.

right: **77.** *Marsyas.* Roman copy
after Pergamene original.
Marble, life-size. Glypotothek, Munich.

below: **78.** *Knife Sharpener.*
Roman copy after Pergamene original.
Marble, life-size. Uffizi, Florence.

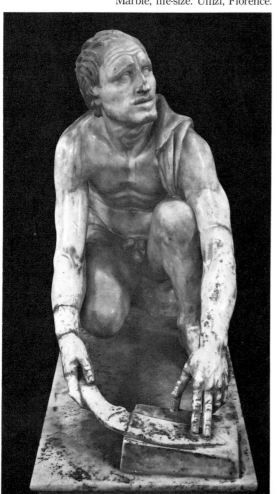

double-reed instrument with a peculiarly penetrating sound, somewhat like the modern oboe. Properly, the single version of the pipe is known as the *aulos* and the double version (shown in Fig. 76, right) as the *auloi.* In English translations of ancient Greek words, both are often incorrectly rendered as "flute." Dorian music, on the other hand, was associated with such stringed instruments as the lyre and the cithara (Fig. 76, left), the latter being mistranslated as the harp.

Both the lyre and the cithara in the Dorian music and the aulos in the Phrygian were used principally to accompany the songs, melodies, and choruses of the two modes and only to a much lesser extent were played as solo instruments by skilled performers. Lyre playing was especially associated in the Dorian tradition with the Apollo cult. The Greeks attributed to this body of music the quality of *ethos,* or ethical character. The aulos, as the instrument of Dionysus, was associated with *pathos,* or strong emotional feeling, and had a sensuous quality conducive to enthusiasm. To the Athenians, this meant a division in their aspirations and ideals—one instrument and mode of singing were associated with clarity, restraint, and moderation; the other with emotional excitement and aroused passions.

Musical Contests

The resultant division of opinion was expressed in the many sculptural representations of the musical contest between the Olympian Apollo and the Phrygian satyr Marsyas. According to an ancient myth, Athena was the inventor of the aulos. One day as she was playing, however, Athena caught sight of her reflection in a pool of water. So displeased was she with the facial grimaces the aulos caused her to make that she threw it away in disgust. Marsyas, happening along, found it and was so enchanted by its sounds that he challenged Apollo, the immortal patron of the Muses, to a contest. The god chose to play on the dignified lyre, won the contest easily, and proved once again that mortals are no match for the gods. As a punishment Apollo had his challenger skinned alive.

A 4th-century relief from Mantineia of the school of Praxiteles represents the contest in progress (Fig. 76). On one side, calmly awaiting his turn, is the seated Apollo with his lyre; on the other, Marsyas is ecstatically blowing on the aulos. Between them is the judge, or music critic, standing patiently but with knife in hand. The Pergamene versions left out the contest and showed the victorious Apollo on one side, the unfortunate Marsyas in the center strung up by the wrists to a tree (Fig. 77) and, on the other side, the crouching figure of a Scythian slave, whetting a knife with keen anticipation (Fig. 78). The choice of the punishment as the part of the myth to be represented—and the evident enjoyment with which this Hellenistic artist tackled the gruesome subject—was designed to tear the emotions to shreds.

Music in Hellenistic Life

While historical facts about the actual musical life of Pergamon are few, it is known that here, as in other Hellenistic centers, the practice of music was given a high place in the arts. Both boys and girls received musical instruction in their educational institutions, and sang hymns as they marched in processions or participated in religious observances. The curriculum included musical notation and the chanting of poetry to the accompaniment of the cithara. The chief educator of the city, the *gymnasiarch*, was also expected, among his other duties, to arrange for the appearances of visiting poets and musicians.

The Hellenistic era was one of increasing professionalism in activities that had previously been performed by free citizens as part of their public duties and honors. Participation in athletic contests and performances of certain dances, which earlier had

been done only by those of noble birth, were taken over by specialists who often commanded high fees for their services. Professional associations of performing artists, known as the Dionysiac *technites,* had a membership made up of stage managers, actors, mimes, dancers, and musicians who participated in theatrical productions. These groups functioned as *guilds,* or unions, and the master craftsmen accepted talented apprentices who understudied them. The Attalids and other Hellenistic monarchs encouraged and protected these technites with an eye toward improving and maintaining the quality of their theatrical and musical performances.

Tralles, a city of the Pergamene kingdom, provides some general information and one of the best musical examples of antiquity. Less than 100 miles (160 kilometers) from Pergamon, Tralles was a subject-city of the Attalids, who maintained there a residence usually occupied by the high priest of the city as their representative. This Phrygian town was saved from the threat of defeat and enslavement at the hands of the Gauls by the victory of Eumenes II in 168 B.C. Like many other cities of the region, Tralles was so grateful for its deliverance that it instituted annual gymnastic and musical festivals in honor of the Pergamene kings. One of these was the Panathenaea, which honored Athena as the protectress of Pergamon; another was the Eumenaia, which honored the monarch himself. From inscriptions it appears that the Eumenaia was a musical contest.

At Tralles, in the latter part of the 19th century, a tombstone was unearthed that bore an inscription of some four lines of poetry accompanied by clear musical notation. It was an epitaph inscribed on a slab of stone by a man named Seikolos for the grave of his wife Euterpe. On transcription it turned out to be the words and music of a short but presumably intact tune in the Phrygian mode from the 2nd century B.C. After hearing about the wild and orgiastic character of Phrygian music, the listener will find this short song a model of sobriety. The mood, in fact, is more melancholy than intoxicating and, since it was carved on a tombstone, the elegiac character would seem to be altogether appropriate.

This somber little song (above), well over 2000 years old, was of a popular type known as a *skolion,* or drinking song. It was sung after dinner by the guests as the cup was passed around for toasts and sacrificial drinks to the gods. The word *skolion* is derived from the Greek meaning "zigzag." It referred to the manner in which the lyre and cup were passed back and forth, crisscrossing the table as each of the reclining guests sang in turn.

The simplicity of this example marks it as the type of tune expected in the repertory of every acceptable guest rather than as one of the more elaborate ballads intended to be sung by professional entertainers. In spirit and mood it is not unlike "Auld Lang Syne," and the occasions on which it was sung would parallel those when we sing the venerable Scottish tune. The substance of the words is the universal one of eat, drink, and be merry for tomorrow we die, which expresses a convivial philosophy of the Epicurean type. Technically, it is in the Phrygian mode with the upper and lower extremes falling on the E above middle C and the E an octave above. This spans a full octave. The tone most often stressed is A. It thus becomes the mean between the higher and lower reaches of the melody and consequently functions as its tonal center.

Ideas

Many striking differences have been noted between the Hellenistic and earlier Hellenic styles. Although both styles are Greek, the Hellenic was a more concentrated development in the small city-states of the Greek mainland, whereas the Hellenistic is a combination of native Greek and such regional influences as those of the Near East, North Africa, Sicily, and Italy. The spread of Hellenistic art over several centuries and the entire Mediterranean world makes any quest for stylistic unity difficult. It is remarkable, in fact, that there is any unity at all.

In addition, the contrast between Hellenic and Hellenistic styles is never extreme but rather like a tilting of the cultural scale in one direction or another. The generalized social humanism of Athens becomes the particularized personal *individualism* of Pergamon and other centers. The noble Hellenic idealism breaks down into a *realism* that looks at the world more in terms of immediate experience than under the aspect of eternity. The uncompromising rationalism of Socrates, Plato, and Aristotle yields to an *empiricism* of scientists, scholars, and artists interested more in the development of methods and techniques and in the application of scientifically acquired knowledge to practical affairs than in the spirit of free inquiry. The tendencies that underlie the various art enterprises at Pergamon in particular and the Hellenistic period in general, then, are to be found in a pattern of interrelated ideas, of which individualism, realism, and empiricism are parts.

Individualism

The individualistic bias of Hellenistic life, thought, and art was an aspect of humanism, but it contrasted strongly with the broader social accent of the Hellenic period. In politics, the rough-and-tumble public discussions of free citizens and decisions arrived at by voice vote were superseded by the rule of a small group headed by a king who enjoyed semidivine status. Another evidence of individualism was the cult of personal hero worship that started with Alexander the Great and continued with the kings who succeeded him in the various parts of his far-flung empire. It was reflected in the popular biographies of great men and in the building of lavish temples and monuments glorifying not the ancient gods but monarchs and military heroes. The famous Mausoleum (Fig. 79) for King Mausolus of Halicarnassus (Fig. 80) is a good example. It was also reflected in the sculptor's accent on individual characteristics, diverse personality traits, and racial differences.

In the earlier Hellenic centers, poets, playwrights, and musicians were mainly skilled amateurs; even in sports the emphasis was on active participation. In the Hellenistic period, however, a rising spirit of professionalism is noted in the fame of individual writers, actors, musical performers, and athletes. As a result people became passive spectators rather than active participants.

Epicureanism and Stoicism   The search for truth in Athens was a social activity of argumentation participated in by all comers. It took place in public squares or in the shady groves of an academy or lyceum where Plato and Aristotle discoursed with colleagues and students. Truth, it was felt, could not be arrived at individually but only through give and take, question and answer, examination and cross-examination, dialogue or dialectical processes. In Hellenistic times, these strenuous mental gymnastics were replaced by the more personal contemplation and self-reflection practiced in the Epicurean and Stoic philosophies.

The thought of Epicurus found ready acceptance in the rich cities of Asia Minor. Epicurus had taught that the highest good was "freedom from trouble in the mind and from pain in the body" and that the pursuit of pleasure was the goal of life. The stern idealism of Socrates thus gave way to a comfortable *hedonism,* the belief that pleasure is the chief good in life. But since some pleasures exceed others, the mind and critical faculties are needed to distinguish among those that give more lasting satisfaction. Epicurus also held that happiness for the individual lay in the direction of the simple life, self-sufficiency, and withdrawal from public affairs. This, in effect, denied

left: 79. Pythios. Mausoleum at Halicarnassus. 359–351 B.C. Length 106′ (32.31 m), width 86′ (26.21 m). Reconstruction drawing.

below: 80. *Mausolus,* from Mausoleum at Halicarnassus. c. 353 B.C. Marble, height 9′10″ (3 m). British Museum, London (reproduced by courtesy of the Trustees).

the social responsibilities of citizenship and encouraged escapism and extreme individualism.

The Stoic philosophers too sought self-sufficiency. They felt that through endurance human beings could rise above both pleasure and pain. Only by cultivating virtue and accepting duty, they taught, can true freedom and mastery of life be attained. Stoicism won growing acceptance in the Hellenistic world. In Roman times it was a major world view.

Individualism and the Arts   Since the state was so wealthy, Hellenistic people took greater enjoyment in personal and home life. Poverty had been thought honorable in ancient Athens, where rich and poor lived as neighbors in modest homes. Hellenistic prosperity, however, allowed a more luxurious standard of living for a larger percentage of the population. Hellenistic architects, then, took special interest in domestic dwellings. Painters and mosaicists were called upon to decorate the houses of the well-to-do. Sculptors created figurines with informal, sometimes humorous, subjects, because they were more adaptable to the home than monumental formal works. Together with potters and other craftsmen, all contributed to the life of luxury and ease of a frankly pleasure-loving people.

Hellenistic artists were more interested in exceptions than rules, in the abnormal than the normal, in diversity than unity. In portraiture, they noted more the physical peculiarities that set an individual apart than those that united an individual with others. Even the gods were personalized rather than generalized, and the choice of subjects from daily life showed the artists' increased preoccupation with informal, casual, everyday events. They were also more concerned with environmental influences on the human condition than with the ability to rise above one's limitations. Hellenistic artists, by recognizing the complexity of life, gave their attention to shades of feeling and to representing the infinite variety of the world of appearances.

Hellenistic thought entered on a new and more emotional orientation. Instead of looking for the universal aspects of experience that could be shared by all, Hellenistic philosophers held that each person

81. Agesander, Athenodorus, and Polydorus of Rhodes. *Laocoön Group.* Late 2nd century B.C. Marble, height 8′ (2.44 m). Vatican Museums, Rome.

has feelings, ideas, and opinions that are entirely different from those of others. Thus each must decide what is good and evil, true and false. Instead of seeking a golden mean between such opposites as harmony and discord as did their Hellenic predecessors, Hellenistic philosophers became psychologists, analyzing the self and laying bare the causes of inner conflict. The joy, serenity, and contentment of the Hellenic gods and athletes were social emotions that could be shared by all. The sorrow, anguish, and suffering of Hellenistic wounded warriors and defeated giants were private, personal feelings that separated a person from the group and invited inward reflection. It was an old variation on the theme—laugh and the world laughs with you, weep and you weep alone.

Reflecting this new orientation, artists turned from the ideal of self-mastery to that of self-expression, from the concealment of inner impulse to outbursts of feeling—in short from ethos to pathos. It was said of Pericles that he was never seen laughing and that even the news of his son's death did not alter his dignified calm. A strong contrast to this Olympian attitude is provided by the late Hellenistic *Laocoön Group* (Fig. 81), where the balance of reason and emotion is replaced by a reveling in feeling for

its own sake. What is lacking in self-restraint and regard for the limitations of the sculptural medium, however, is amply made up for by the vigor of treatment and virtuosity of execution.

The preoccupation of Pergamene artists with such painful and agonizing subjects as the defeated Gauls, the punishment of Marsyas, and the battle of gods and giants reveals the deliberate intention to involve the spectator in a kind of emotional orgy. Misfortune becomes something that can be enjoyed by the fortunate who participate in the situation with a kind of morbid satisfaction. The French writer and moralist La Rochefoucauld said: "We all have the strength to endure the misfortunes of others." Aldous Huxley similarly observed that when the belly is full men can afford to grieve, and "sorrow after supper is almost a luxury."

In the spirit of Stoic philosophy, life and suffering were to be endured with a grim satisfaction akin to morbid enjoyment. The artists of the frieze of the Altar of Zeus, for instance, were incredibly inventive in the ways they found for the gods to inflict pain and death. The composition approaches encyclopedic inclusiveness in the various modes of combat by the gods and the capacity for suffering by the giants. Nothing like it appears again until the Romanesque Last Judgments (see Fig. 154) and Dante's *Inferno*.

Realism

The increasing complexity and quicker pulse of Hellenistic life weakened the belief in the underlying unity of knowledge and abiding values that produced the poise of Hellenic figures and the unemotional calm of their facial expressions. The world of concrete experience was more real to the Hellenistic mind than one of remote abstract ideals. Taking a more relativistic view of things, people now looked to variety rather than unity and took into account individual experiences and differences.

Hellenistic artists sought to present nature as they saw it, to depict minute details and ever finer shades of meaning. The decline of idealism was not so much the result of decadence as it was a matter of placing human activities in a new frame of reference, reexamining the goals and redefining the basic values of humanity. Confronted with the variety and multiplicity of this world, Hellenistic artists made no attempt to reduce its many manifestations to the artificial simplicity of types and archetypes.

Hellenic artists portrayed their subjects standing aloof and rising above their environmental limitations, but in Hellenistic art men and women find themselves beset on all sides by natural and social forces and are inevitably conditioned by them. The writhing forms on the great frieze reveal some of the conflicts and contradictions of Hellenistic thought. The gods in this work became projections of human psychological problems. The earlier Hellenic gods appeared to have the world well under control, and the calm, poised Zeus in Figure 47 exhibits no sign of stress or strain as he hurls his thunderbolt. The deities of the Altar of Zeus, however, are fighting furiously, and things verge on getting out of hand.

Realism and Architecture   In the Athenian architecture of the 5th century B.C., each building, however well in harmony with its site, was an independent unit, and the architects were little concerned with any precise relationship to nearby buildings. Indeed, to have admitted that one structure was dependent upon another in a group would have diminished its status as a self-contained whole and thus rendered it incomplete by Hellenic standards. On the Athenian acropolis, each temple had its own axis and its independent formal existence—in keeping with the conception that each separate work of art must be a logical whole made up of the sum of its own parts. Only such concessions to nature as were necessary for structural integrity were made. To the artist alone belonged the power of creating symmetrical form and balanced proportion, and the perfection of each building had to stand as a monument to the human mind and, as such, to rise above its material environment rather than be bound by it.

Hellenistic architecture moved away from the isolated building as a self-contained unit and toward a realistic recognition that nothing is complete in itself but must always exist as part of an interrelated pattern. City planning is in this sense a form of realism, and Hellenistic buildings were considered as part of the community as a whole. In the case of the Pergamene acropolis, the relationship of each building was carefully calculated not only in regard to its surroundings but also to its place in the group.

Realism and Sculpture   In sculpture, the members of each group were likewise subject to their environment, and the individual is portrayed as an essential part of the surroundings. By painting in backgrounds and by using higher relief, Hellenistic sculpture becomes more dependent on changing light and shade for its expressive effect, allows for movement in more than one plane, and suggests greater depth in space. In earlier sculpture, a figure always bore the stamp of a type, and personality was subordinate to the individual's place in society. A warrior, for example, had a well-developed physique, but his face and body bore no resemblance to a specific person. He could be identified by a spear or shield and was more a member of a class than a person in his own right.

82. *Old Market Woman.* 2nd century B.C. Marble, height 4′1½″ (1.26 m). Metropolitan Museum of Art, New York (Rogers Fund, 1909).

The Hellenistic desire to render human beings as unique personalities and not as types required a masterly technique capable of reproducing such particular characteristics as the twist of a mouth, wrinkles of the skin, physical blemishes, and individualized facial expressions. Faces, furthermore, had to appear animated and lifelike, so that the subject of a realistic portrait could be distinguished from all others. Faithfulness to nature also meant the accurate rendering of anatomical detail. Like a scientist, the sculptor carefully observed the musculature of the human body so as to render every nuance of the flesh. The *Old Market Woman* (Fig. 82), for example, reveals the body of a person worn down by toil. The bent back, sagging breasts, knotty limbs are the results of the physical conditions under which she has had to live. A portrayal such as this would have been unthinkable to an earlier artist.

In the handling of materials, the older Hellenic sculptors never forgot that stone was stone. But their realistic zeal often led later Hellenistic craftsmen to force stone to simulate the softness and warmth of living flesh. The story of the legendary sculptor Pygmalion who chiseled his marble maiden so realistically that she came to life could have happened only in the Hellenistic period, and the sensuous figure of the

Aphrodite of Cyrene (Fig. 83) surely bears this out. The easy grace and charm with which Praxiteles had rendered his gods and goddesses (Figs. 50, 56) reach a climax in such elegant and polished figures as this Aphrodite and the famous *Apollo Belvedere* (Fig. 84).

Hellenistic emphasis on realism appealed greatly to the forthright Roman conquerors of Greece. Its appeal was largely responsible for the survival of the Pergamene art now known to us.

Empiricism

The rationalism of Hellenic thought as developed by Socrates, Plato, and Aristotle had emphasized the spirit of free intellectual inquiry in a quest for universal truth. Epicureanism and Stoicism, by contrast, were practical philosophies for living. The abstract logic of the earlier period yielded to an empiricism that was concerned more with science than wisdom. It focused on bringing together the results of isolated experimentation and on applying scientific knowledge to the solution of practical problems. More broadly, it stressed fact gathering, cataloguing source materials, research, collecting art works, and developing criteria for judging the arts.

Epicurus, by eliminating the notion of divine intervention in human affairs, and by his physical explanations of natural phenomena, laid the philosophical basis for a scientific materialism. The scientific achievements of the period are truly impressive. Hellenistic mathematics extended as far as conic sections and trigonometry, and such astronomers and physicists as Archimedes and Hero of Alexandria knew the world was round as well as its approximate circumference and diameter. Hellenistic scientists had a solar calendar of $365\frac{1}{4}$ days, invented a type of steam engine, and worked out the principles of steam power and force pumps. Indeed, the modern mechanical and industrial revolutions might well have taken place in Hellenistic times had not slave labor been so cheap and abundant. The progressiveness of the period is also seen in its commercial developments that led to new sources of wealth.

The scientific attitude of Hellenistic thought found brilliant expression in the musical field by the development of the theoretical basis of that art. While philosophers and mathematicians of the earlier period had made many discoveries and had had brilliant insights into the nature of music, it remained for the Hellenistic mind to systematize them and construct a full and coherent science of music. Under Aristoxenos of Tarentum, a disciple of Aristotle, and under the great geometrician Euclid, the theory of music reached a formulation so complete and comprehensive that it became the foundation for Western music. While it is impossible to go into the intricacies of the Greek musical system here, one should keep in mind that it was in this theoretical field more than in any other that a lasting musical contribution was made.

Rise of Antiquarianism   After establishing his great library, Eumenes II gathered about him many of the outstanding Greek scholars of his day. They were dedicated to the task of preserving the literary masterpieces of former days, making critical editions of the works of ancient poets and dramatists, selecting material for anthologies, cataloguing collections, copying manuscripts, writing grammatical treatises, and compiling dictionaries. In their scholarly endeavors, they held the works of the ancients above those of their own time. As a consequence their literary production began to be addressed more to other scholars than to the general populace.

Such a restricted audience of cultivated readers could not be supplied by Pergamon alone but had to be sought for throughout the vast Greek world. By mutual consent, the pure and majestic Attic Greek of Pericles, Euripides, and Plato became their "common dialect" and the artificial medium of communication between the cultured classes. With this emphasis on a tongue that was no longer spoken, the living language in which writers could address their fellow citizens began to be regarded as a local dialect.

This was a period of *antiquarianism,* or concern with things old and rare, of scholarly rather than creative writing, of book learning instead of inspiration. Only systematic, exhaustive research, for instance, could have produced the program of the great frieze encircling the Altar of Zeus, which is a veritable catalogue of Greek mythology, complete with footnotes and annotations. The Attalids not only collected art but actually engaged in archaeological excavations, another antiquarian activity, and for the first time the living sculptor and painter were confronted with a museum filled with noted works from the glorious past. As a result, copying the masterpieces of Myron, Phidias, and others became an industry that thrived throughout antiquity until the coming of organized Christianity. The age raised the social position of the artist. As in literature and music, it established the history of art and formulated aesthetic standards, so that now art was worthy of attention in intellectual and social circles.

The Road to Rome

A reputation for learning had direct bearing on the political purposes of the Pergamene government. The more famous their capital became for its intellectual and cultural enterprises, the higher its prestige in the Greek world would be. The career of Eumenes II's brother, who eventually succeeded him as Attalus II, is a case in point. As a skillful general, he was invaluable to the Pergamene regime, yet at the conclusion of a successful war he took five years off to study philosophy at the academy in Athens. Furthermore, the proudest boast of the Attalids after their military victories was that they were the saviors of Hellenism from the barbarians. This claim, of course, had to be fortified by the development of their capital as a center of arts and letters.

To advertise the cultural achievements of his realm, Eumenes II chose his librarian, the famed grammarian Crates of Mallus, as his ambassador to Rome. By defending humanistic learning, and by stimulating Roman desire for more knowledge about Greek philosophy, literature, and art, Crates made a lasting impression on the future world capital.

With literary talents being diverted into the editing of manuscripts, scholars delving into the history of the past, art collectors digging for buried treasure, and musicians writing theoretical treatises, Pergamon was well on its way toward becoming an archive and a museum. In time, this antiquarianism was bound to reduce artistic developments to a system of academic formulas and rules—all of which is symptomatic of a hardening of the artistic arteries and the eventual decline of the creative powers. When, therefore, in 133 B.C. Attalus III willed his kingdom to Rome, he was actually presenting that city with a living museum. The vast art holdings of the Attalids soon were on their way to Italy, where the interest and admiration they commanded, when shown in public exhibitions, were destined to have a powerful effect on the taste of the Romans. With them went the Hellenistic craftsmen who would embellish the new world capital with a wealth of public buildings, carvings, murals, and mosaics (Fig. 85).

85. *Imperial Procession,* detail of Ara Pacis Augustae (Augustus' Altar of Peace), Rome. c. 13 B.C. Marble, height 5′3″ (1.6 m).

4
The Roman Style

Rome, 2nd Century A.D.

The Antonine Age was "the period in the history of the world during which the condition of the human race was most happy and prosperous. . . ." So wrote the English historian Gibbon in *The Decline and Fall of the Roman Empire*. Under Trajan, Hadrian, and Marcus Aurelius, Gibbon continues, "the Empire of Rome comprehended the fairest part of the earth and the most civilized portion of mankind." This favorable state of affairs he attributed to the Romans' genius for law and order, their cultivation of tolerance and justice, and their capacity for wise government.

The Arch of Trajan at Benevento (Fig. 86) recalls some of this vanished grandeur by proclaiming the virtues and accomplishments of the first great emperor of Gibbon's chosen period. The arch was commissioned by the Roman Senate to celebrate the completion of the Via Traiana, a 200-mile (320-kilometer) highway over the mountains that linked Rome with the large port of Brindisi. It honored an outstanding achievement in engineering as well as the chief engineer of the Empire. Such a gateway, marking the start of the long road to the East, challenged the Roman imagination (see map, p. 91).

The Romans' sense that their individual destinies, as well as those of their city and state, were closely bound up with the surrounding territories found logical expression in just such a monument. Among ancient city-states Rome was unique in its solution to the problem of how to maintain its municipal integrity and at the same time manage a far-flung empire. In evolving the institutions by which this political unity could be made compatible with such wide diversity, Rome achieved its greatest distinction.

Monumental arches usually marked the conclusion of a successful military campaign, by which distant barbarian tribes were subdued or some new civilized people were brought into the Roman orbit. In the instance of the Arch of Titus in Rome, the returning conqueror, along with his army, a train of captives, and the trophies of war, passed through the arch to the cheers of the multitudes.

Trajan's Arch was modeled architecturally after that of Titus, including such details as the attached *Composite* columns, a Roman combination of the Ionic and Corinthian orders. It differs in spirit from the Arch of Titus, however, in that the sculptures celebrate the arts of peace rather than of war. The reliefs that so liberally cover its surface were arranged in characteristic Roman fashion so as to inform and instruct as well as to delight the eye.

On the side facing the town of Benevento and more-distant Rome (Fig. 86), the panels deal with Trajan's domestic policy. He is seen making land grants in the newly conquered Danube region to veterans of his wars; standing in the midst of prosperous merchants grateful for the new harbor he built for them at Ostia, the port of Rome; and receiving the praise of the Senate and the people in the Roman Forum. Across the lintel moves a triumphal procession, and on either side of the keystone hover figures with crown and banners who represent victories. Above, Jupiter and Juno and Minerva (known in Roman mythology as the Capitoline Triad) are seen extending their welcome to the Emperor. As a gesture of approval, Jupiter is turning over his thunderbolt to Trajan. This dignity is a recognition of the latter's great power as well as a sign that worship of the emperor was supplanting worship of the Olympian deities. The group is placed next to the inscription, which adds to Trajan's usual string of titles that of *Optimo*, "the best," which is said to have pleased him especially since he shared it only with Jupiter.

Toward the seaport side of the arch are the scenes pertaining to Trajan's foreign policy. Germany is seen taking the oath of allegiance; various Oriental rulers are sending tributes through their envoys; and the Emperor is establishing state-sponsored benefits for the relief of poor children. Above, a figure symbolizing Mesopotamia is paying him homage, and the divinities of the Danube territory are welcoming him.

The basic principles of design are evident in the reliefs. Although each panel depicts a separate episode, unity is achieved in the repetition of Trajan himself. Variety is obtained by shifting the human and geographical environment. Changes of place are indicated partly by the activities and partly by the background, which signify a setting in Rome by some familiar buildings, a country place by trees, and a remote locality by exotic river gods. The subject matter is obviously propaganda for imperial rule—even to the extent of often showing the Emperor as a figure of superhuman size—but the restrained manner of presentation keeps this aspect from becoming too conspicuous. The actual sculpture is technically well handled, though there is a tendency to accent linear detail at the expense of unity and repose.

While monumental arches did not have a practical purpose, their form exemplifies the building principle that underlies the Roman achievements in architecture. With the arch the Romans constructed their vaults and domes that carried architecture forward well into modern times. The fact that Trajan's Arch was built in a provincial town south of Rome on the road to and from the great centers of the East—Athens, Pergamon, Alexandria, Ephesus, and Antioch—is a reminder of the route by which the heritage of the classical Mediterranean world became a part of Western cultural tradition. By military conquest, by annexation, by inheritance, and by voluntary action—one by one the proud old city-states and

86. Arch of Trajan, Benevento. A.D. 114.

kingdoms became a part of greater Rome. Likewise all the ideas, institutions, and art forms of this vast region were sifted through the ingenious Roman mind. Integrating these with notable contributions of her own, Rome gradually achieved a prominence in culture, expressed in her literature, architecture, and sculpture, along with her political eminence.

Architecture

Forum of Trajan

Following his accession as emperor in A.D. 98, Trajan began a grandiose project in Rome: the construction of a new forum (Figs. 87, 88). Just as the Empire had

below: 87. Apollodorus of Damascus. Forum of Trajan, Rome. A.D. c. 113–117. Length 920′ (280.42 m), width 620′ (188.98 m). Reconstruction by Bender. Museum of Roman Civilization, Rome.

right: 88. Apollodorus of Damascus. Plan of Forum of Trajan.

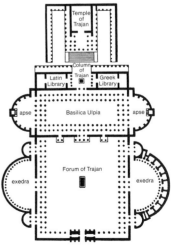

CHRONOLOGY
Roman Period—Republic and Empire

GENERAL EVENTS B.C.

	753	Legendary date of Rome's founding
c.616–	c.509	Etruscan period. Tarquin kings reigned
	c.500	Roman Republic founded; Tarquins dethroned
	c.450	Romans colonized Italy
	390	Gauls sacked Rome
280–	275	Greek power in Italy weakened
264–	241	First Punic War; Rome annexed Sicily, Corsica, Sardinia
218–	201	Second Punic War; Hannibal invaded Italy; Carthage ceded Spain to Rome
150–	146	Third Punic War; Carthage destroyed; African province created
	133	Pergamon bequeathed to Rome
100–	44	Julius Caesar. Conquered Gaul (58–51); crossed Rubicon, occupied Rome, became dictator (49); founded Julian family dynasty of future emperors; Forum of Julius Caesar begun (c.48); campaigned in Egypt, Asia Minor, Africa, Spain (48–45); Julian calendar (45); assassinated (44)
c.50–	c.10	Vitruvius active; wrote treatise *De Architectura*
	43	Second Triumvirate formed—Anthony, Octavian (Augustus), Lepidus
	31	Naval battle at Actium; Anthony and Cleopatra defeated
27–A.D.14		Augustus (Octavian) reigned. Start of Empire, built Forum and Mausoleum of Augustus, Ara Pacis, Baths of Agrippa, Theater of Marcellus, Basilica Julia
	4	Birth of Jesus; crucified A.D. c.29

GENERAL EVENTS A.D.

54–	68	Nero reigned. Built Baths of Nero, Domus Aureus
	70	Titus took Jerusalem; temple destroyed
	79	Vesuvius erupted; destroyed Pompeii, Herculaneum
79–	81	Titus reigned. Colosseum finished; Temple of Vespasian, Arch of Titus built
96–	180	Antonine Age, or "Era of Five Good Emperors" (Nerva, Trajan, Hadrian, Antoninus Pius, Marcus Aurelius). Roman Empire at height of power
98–	117	Trajan reigned. Dacian campaigns (101–106); harbor at Ostia built (103); Via Traiana from Benevento to Brindisi, and Baths of Trajan built (110); Forum of Trajan and Column erected, Arch of Trajan at Benevento begun (113); conquered Armenia, Parthia; Empire extended to Persian Gulf and Caspian Sea (113–117)
c.100–c.120		Apollodorus of Damascus, architect, active. Completed bridge over Danube (105)
117–	138	Hadrian reigned. Temple of Olympian Zeus at Athens completed (117); Roman Pantheon built (120–124); Villa of Hadrian at Tivoli built (c.120–127); Hadrian's tomb begun (135)
138–	161	Antoninus Pius reigned. "House of Diana" at Ostia
161–	180	Marcus Aurelius reigned. Stoic philosopher, wrote *Meditations* (c.174)
211–	217	Baths of Caracalla

80 B.C.-A.D.14 "GOLDEN AGE" OF ROMAN LITERATURE

106–	43	Cicero, statesman, orator, essayist
c.96–	55	Lucretius, poet, philosopher, *On Nature of Things*
87–	57	Catullus, lyric poet
70–	19	Vergil, *Aeneid, Eclogues*
65–	8	Horace, *Odes*
59–A.D.17		Livy, *History of Rome*
43–A.D.17		Ovid, *Art of Love, Metamorphoses*

A.D.14–117 "SILVER AGE" OF ROMAN LITERATURE

3 B.C.–A.D.65		Seneca, philosopher, dramatist
c.20–	66	Petronius, *Satyricon*
23–	79	Pliny the Elder, naturalist, encyclopedist
c.50–	c.90	Epictetus, Stoic philosopher
35–	95	Quintilian, *Institutes of Oratory*
40–	c.102	Martial, epigrammatist
c.46–	120	Plutarch, *Parallel Lives*
55–	c.117	Tacitus, historian, *Annals, Germania*
c.60–	c.135	Juvenal, *Satires*
62–	113	Pliny the Younger, writer, administrator; delivered *Panegyric* to Trajan before Roman Senate (100)
75–	c.150	Suetonius, *Lives of the Caesars*
	c.160	Apuleius flourished, philosopher, *Golden Ass*

grown in his time to its greatest extent, so the population of Rome had risen to over a million, creating a need for larger and more imposing public buildings. The old Roman forum of the Republic had long been inadequate, and several extensions had been undertaken in the early years of the Empire. But Trajan's project was so ambitious that it equaled all previous forums combined, bringing the total area covered by such structures to over 25 acres (10 hectares).

Needless to say, the magnificence of the new forum was in every way comparable to its size. Trajan entrusted the project to Apollodorus, a Greek architect–engineer from Damascus, famous for the construction of a stone bridge over the widest part of the Danube river before Trajan's second Dacian campaign. But Apollodorus' Greek origin did not necessarily indicate a Hellenistic bias on the Emperor's part. All other known architects in Rome at this time (including those who collaborated on the project) were Romans, and Apollodorus was thoroughly familiar with Roman building tradition.

Typically Roman in conception, a forum combined a system of open courtyards and buildings all grouped in a specific relationship (Fig. 88). The reconstruction drawing of the Athenian acropolis (see Fig. 25) shows the Parthenon and Erechtheum had little more in common than the site on which they stood. But no part of a forum existed in isolation, and in the case of Trajan's Forum everything was conceived from the beginning on a large scale and with an eye to symmetry. The whole was divided by a central axis running from the center of the arched gateway, through the middle of the square, through the entrance to the basilica (whose axis is at right angles to the whole forum), to the base of the monumental column called Trajan's Column, and finally up the steps of the temple to the altar at the back.

Entrance to the forum was made through a majestic triple archway into the large paved rectangular courtyard, enclosed on three sides by a wall and colonnade and on the fourth by the Basilica Ulpia, whose entrances stood opposite those of the archway.

89. *Marcus Aurelius.* A.D. 161–181. Gilt bronze, height 9′10″ (3 m). Piazza del Campidoglio, Rome.

Standing in the exact center of the open square was an impressive bronze statue of Trajan on horseback. Though no longer in existence, it is known to have resembled the surviving bronze equestrian portrait of Marcus Aurelius (Fig. 89), who sits astride his splendid mount with a sense of balance and a thoughtful appearance worthy of the patient Stoic philosopher and author of the widely read *Meditations.*

Flanking the square on the east and west sides were semicircular recesses known as *exedrae* outlined by tall Doric columns. Similar in shape were the series of market stalls rising upward into the two hills. The best preserved are those on the side toward the Quirinal Hill. They are six stories in height and constructed of brick (Fig. 90). On the forum floor

90. Apollodorus of Damascus. Forum of Trajan, Rome. Northeast exedra and market hall. A.D. c. 113–117.

91. Apollodorus of Damascus. Column of Trajan
and ruins of Basilica Ulpia, Rome.
Column of Trajan, A.D. 106–113. Marble;
height of base 18′ (5.49 m), height of column 97′ (29.57 m).

tectural form, the Roman basilica is one link in the long chain of Mediterranean structures that began with domestic dwellings, Egyptian hypostyle halls, and Greek temples, and that continued with Christian basilicas.

The large rectangular interior of the Basilica Ulpia, named for Trajan's family, was marked by a double colonnade in the Corinthian order than ran completely around the building. It supported a balcony and a second tier of columns that, in turn, supported the beams of the timbered roof (Fig. 92). This large central hall served as a general meeting place as well as a business center. The semicircular interior recesses called *apses* housed the courts of law. They were possibly roofed over with hemispherical vaults and set apart from the central hall by screens or curtains.

Beyond the basilica were two libraries, one for Greek and the other for Latin scrolls. They were separated by a courtyard that enclosed the base of Trajan's Column (see pp. 86–89).

Temple of Trajan   After Trajan's death his adopted son and successor, Hadrian, built at the end of the main axis of the forum the Corinthian temple that climaxed the grand design. Architecturally, it was a version of the Maison Carrée at Nîmes in southern France (Fig. 93). Like other Roman temples, this one honoring Trajan and the Maison Carrée rested on *podiums,* or masonry platforms, and had porches in the front. These porches were much more prominently featured than those in Greek temples. The well-preserved example at Nîmes likewise shows only the columns of the porch standing free, while the rest are attached to the cella. This indicates that columns were needed less for structural strength than for embellishment.

The practice of deifying rulers and erecting temples to them was widespread in Hellenistic times and began in Rome as early as the reign of Augustus. The type of statue that stood in such a temple can be seen in the portrait of Augustus that was found near Prima Porta (Fig. 94), a suburb of Rome. He stands in the imposing attitude of an *imperator,* or "commander-in-chief," addressing his troops. Carved on the *cuirass,* or metal breastplate of his armor, are scenes in low relief recounting the outstanding achievements of his reign and pictures of the gods and goddesses who conferred their favors upon him.

At Augustus' side is a cupid astride a dolphin. Both allude to the goddess of love, Venus, who was

92. Apollodorus of Damascus.
Basilica Ulpia, Forum of Trajan, Rome. A.D. 113.
Reconstruction drawing of interior.

were more than 150 booths—for vegetables, fruits, and flowers. Above were large vaulted halls where wine and oil were stored. Spices and imported delicacies were sold on the third and fourth floors. The fifth was used to distribute food and money out of the imperial treasury. And on top were tanks supplied by fresh water from an aqueduct where live fish could be bought.

Basilica Ulpia   Adjacent to the open square was the Basilica Ulpia (Fig. 91), of which only the rows of broken columns remain. The term *basilica* was applied rather generally to large public buildings and is approximately equivalent to the modern word *hall* used for meeting places. Since court sessions were also held in a basilica, the term *hall of justice* is likewise related to one of its functions. As an archi-

93. *Maison Carée,* Nîmes, France. 16 B.C.
Marble; base 117 × 59′ (35.66 × 17.98 m),
height of podium 11′ (3.35 m),
height of columns 30′6″ (9.3 m).

born in the sea (see Fig. 83, where her Greek counterpart Aphrodite also has a dolphin at her side). Here the symbols serve to remind the Romans of the divine origin of their emperors. Vergil, the principal poet of his period, traced Augustus' ancestry all the way back to Aeneas, the legendary founder of Rome, whose father was the mortal Anchises but whose mother was none other than the immortal Venus.

Much of Roman religion was a family affair, honoring the living *pater familias,* or "father of the family," as well as the nearer and more remote ancestors. A room in every residence was set aside for this purpose, and the custom was responsible for a

whole genre of sculpture—portrait busts such as the one entitled *Porcia and Cato* (Fig. 95). In contrast to the generalized and somewhat idealized image of Augustus as the statesman and imperator, this unpretentious portrait of ordinary citizens is remarkably realistic. Both kinds of sculpture, however, served essentially the same purpose—as paternal images to be admired with reverence and even awe. The emperors were felt to deserve the universal reverence of the whole Roman family, since they were considered *pater patriae,* or "fathers of their country." Erecting a temple to a distinguished Roman emperor was done in much the same spirit as building the Washington Monument or the Lincoln Memorial in Washington, D.C. In ancient Rome certain days were set aside for the offering of food and drink in simple family ceremonies. On the day for

above: 94. *Augustus of Prima Porta.* c. 20 B.C.
Marble, height 6′8″ (2.03 m). Vatican Museums, Rome.

right: 95. *Porcia and Cato* (?), portraits of a Roman couple.
c. 1st century B.C. Marble, height 27″ (69 cm).
Vatican Museums, Rome.

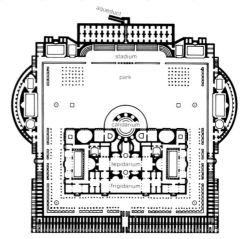

left: **96.** Tepidarium (heated central hall), Baths of Caracalla. A.D. 211–217. Reconstruction drawing by Spiers.

below: **97.** Plan of Baths of Caracalla, Rome. Length 750' (228.6 m), width 380' (115.82 m).

honoring the emperor, the rites at his temple were more formal, occasionally including animal sacrifice, a procession, festivities, and amusements. Religion to the Romans was the tradition and continuity of the family and, in the larger sense, the history and destiny of Rome itself.

With the exception of the temple, the Forum of Trajan was completed during his lifetime and was dedicated by him for the use of the people of Rome in A.D. 113. Its many parts—the triumphal entrance archway, the courtyard and its equestrian statue, the market buildings, the Basilica Ulpia, two libraries, a monumental column, and the temple—add up to an architectural composition on a grand scale, designed to accommodate activities on many levels. Beginning with a shopping center and place to transact business, the forum continued with a general meeting place and the halls of justice, moved on to places for quiet contemplation, study in the libraries and the reading of history in visual form on the column, and, finally, came to rest in the precinct for honoring the Emperor and worshiping the Roman gods.

Imperial Baths

While the forums took care of the more serious pursuits of his people, Trajan never forgot that circuses often were as important as bread in promoting the happiness of his subjects. One of every emperor's duties, in fact, was to provide for public amusement out of his private purse. Only the very wealthy could afford entertainment in their own homes, so the people as a whole had to look for their recreation outside. To this end many baths, theaters, and stadi-

ums had been built all over the city. The variety of architectural forms and human activities they encompassed has never been surpassed. To this day the highest praise that can be given an elaborate public festival is to call it a "Roman holiday."

Imperial baths provided the people with far more than hot, cold, and tepid swimming pools. They offered such other facilities as dressing rooms, gymnasiums, restaurants, bars, and shady walks. Guests also could attend plays, witness athletic contests, listen to public lectures, read in one of the libraries, or stroll about the galleries where statues and paintings were exhibited. The baths were, in short, the people's palaces where citizens could enjoy together what only the rich could afford separately. Favored also as places to show the booty and souvenirs from foreign conquests, they are the sites where much ancient statuary has been found, such as the *Laocoön Group* (see Fig. 81). These baths also had important hygienic advantages. With the habit of daily bathing established, the people of Rome were cleaner than those of any other city before or since.

Trajan added to the already existing public baths a large establishment also built by Apollodorus. Although the ruins of his *thermae* ("baths") are not so well preserved as the later Baths of Caracalla and Diocletian, enough is known to establish a clear picture of what they were like. The large central hall was the earliest known use of concrete *cross vaulting,* the principle of which can be studied in Figure 103 and in the similar central hall of the Baths of Caracalla (Figs. 96, 97). It measured 183 feet (55.7 meters) in length with an open space between the walls of 79 feet (24 meters). From the illustration, it

98. Colosseum, Rome.
A.D. 72–80.
Long axis 620′ (188.98 m),
short axis 513′ (156.36 m),
height 160′ (48.77 m).

can be seen that the barrel vault that runs lengthwise is three times intersected at right angles by shorter vaults extending across the width of the hall. Besides spanning larger interior spaces without the obstruction of supporting piers and columns, this type of construction offered the advantage of ample lighting through a *clerestory,* a row of windows in the upper part of a wall, which used thin strips of translucent yellow marble in place of glass. Modern architects, when erecting such huge edifices as the Union Station in Washington, D.C., and Grand Central Terminal in New York City, found no better models among large secular structures than these Roman baths.

99. Pont du Gard, Nîmes, France. Early 1st century A.D.
Length 902′ (274.93 m), height 161′ (49.07 m).

Colosseum and Aqueducts

The Colosseum (Fig. 98), which dates from the late 1st century, was the scene of rather garish forms of mass entertainment, including gory gladiatorial contests between men and wild beasts. The oval form of the Colosseum covers about 6 acres (2.4 hectares) and could seat about 50,000 spectators at one time. Around its circumference run some eighty archways, which served so efficiently as entrances and exits that the entire bowl could be emptied in a matter of minutes. The Roman talent for organization is evident here not only in such practical respects but also extends to the structure and decorative design. Three architectural orders are combined in the successive stories of the same building. The attached columns on the lower range are the "home-grown" variation of the Doric, known as the Tuscan. Those on the second tier are Ionic. Those on the third, Corinthian. On the fourth, which rises to a height of 157 feet (47.7 meters), are found shallow, flat Corinthian piers known as *pilasters* between which runs a row of sockets for the poles over which a canvas awning was stretched to protect the spectators from sun and rain.

The building material of the Colosseum was a concrete made from broken pieces of brick, small rocks, volcanic dust, lime, and water. It could be poured into molds of any desired shape, including channels for use in aqueducts (Fig. 99). The exterior was originally covered with marble facing; the structure would be in good condition today had it not been used later as a quarry for building materials right up to the 18th century. Still, the Colosseum is one of the most impressive ruins to survive from Roman times.

above: 100. Pantheon, Rome.
A.D. c. 120.
Height of portico 59′ (17.98 m).

left: 101. Giovanni Paolo Pannini.
Interior of the Pantheon, Rome. c. 1750.
Oil on canvas, 4′2½″ × 3′3″
(1.28 × .99 m).
National Gallery of Art, Washington, D.C.
(Samuel H. Kress Collection).

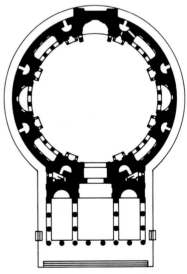

102. Plan of Pantheon.

Its popularity as a model can be seen in the numerous football stadiums on college campuses.

In order to assure enough water for his baths, Trajan found it necessary to improve the old system of aqueducts and to add a new one, 35 miles (56 kilometers) long, that is still in use today. A more beautiful example of a Roman aqueduct is the Pont du Gard at Nîmes (Fig. 99), which survived from the 1st century A.D. A system of underground and open concrete channels was constructed to bring water from its mountain source to the town 25 miles (40 kilometers) away. Functioning on the principle of gravity, the ducts were sloped in the desired direction. In this instance the water was carried almost 300 yards (274.2 meters) across the valley at a height of more than 160 feet (48.8 meters). The graceful lower range of arches support a bridge that is still in use, while the upper series of large and small arches support the water channel.

The Pantheon

The Roman sense of social organization extended into the field of religion with the Pantheon (Fig. 100). While the name might imply a temple to all the gods, in effect the Pantheon became a mirror of the world order, with statues placed in niches to personify the sun, the moon, and the so-called planetary deities— Mercury, Venus, Mars, Jupiter, and Saturn. The Emperor Hadrian himself had a hand in the design of this distinguished edifice, and he occasionally presided over meetings of the Roman senate held in its splendid and masterly interior (Fig. 101).

The Pantheon's geometry is based on the union of a cylinder and a hemisphere over a circular ground plan (Fig. 102), with the interior diameter and the height of the dome both being a little more than 140 feet (42.7 meters). The clarity of form achieved by the equality of dimensions, as well as by the simplicity of design, is evident to the casual eye.

The satisfying sense of spatial proportion and the harmonious impression of the interior result from the merger of applied scientific skill and aesthetic feeling. In the Pantheon as well as in the great halls of imperial baths, the Romans advanced architecture to the point where it achieved significant interiors. Unlike other classical temples, the Pantheon presents an aspect inviting entrance.

The inner surface of the dome is characterized by *coffers*, indented panels which serve the dual purpose of diminishing the weight of the dome and furnishing the basis for its decoration. In the center of each coffer was a gilded bronze star, a motif that related the dome symbolically to the sky. Much of the once-elegant interior, with its walls faced with many-colored marbles of glowing ochre with red, green,

and black contrasts, is still visible. Gone, however, are the gilded bronze tiles that once spread across the coffered inner dome like an expansive starry sky mirroring the heavens.

The sole source of light is the single 29-foot (8.8-meter) round opening in the middle of the dome. This *oculus,* or "eye," as it was called, can be interpreted as an allusion to the all-seeing eye of heaven. Soaring almost 150 feet (45.7 meters) above the colorful mosaic flooring, it creates a great shaft of illumination that bathes the interior in light of high intensity.

As seen today, the Pantheon exterior is stripped of its former rich and colorful marble covering. The bronze plates of the portico ceiling, the gilded bronze tiles that covered the entire exterior of both the drum and the dome, and the monumental statues of the gods within have all disappeared. Despite mutilations, however, the Pantheon is the best-preserved single building from the ancient world and the oldest structure of large proportions with its original roof intact. It still holds its own as one of the world's most impressive domed buildings, despite such outstanding competition as Hagia Sophia in Constantinople (Fig. 126), the Cathedral of Florence (Fig. 207), St. Peter's in Rome (Fig. 237), and St. Paul's in London (Fig. 357). Its descendants are numberless—the Villa Rotonda (Fig. 262), Thomas Jefferson's home at Monticello, the rotunda he designed for the University of Virginia (Fig. 394), the Pantheon in Paris, certain features of the Capitol rotunda in Washington, D.C., and the Low Memorial Library at Columbia University in New York, to name but a few of the buildings inspired by the Pantheon.

The Roman
Architectural Contribution

The Roman contribution to architecture was fourfold: (1) building for use, (2) development of the arch and vault as a structural principle, (3) emphasis on verticality, and (4) design of significant interiors. In the first case, Roman architecture was marked by a shift in emphasis from religious buildings to the civil-engineering projects that had such an important bearing on the solution of the practical problems of the day. This did not mean that the Romans neglected their shrines and temples or that they lacked religious feeling. As in the 19th and 20th centuries, however, the main architectural expression was to be found in secular rather than religious structures. In this category come the basilicas, aqueducts, roads, bridges, even the sewer systems, which so admirably served the practical purposes of the Romans.

Second—and perhaps most important of all—was the Roman exploitation of the possibilities inherent in the arch as a building principle to achieve the

103. The *arch* is a curved structural member used to span a space between two vertical elements, such as posts (piers) or walls (A). Wedge-shaped blocks, called *voussoirs* (a), give the arch its form and stability by virtue of their compressed relationship to each other and to the *keystone* (b) at the apex of the semicircle. The curve of the arch rises from the *springing* on either side of the opening (c). The *compression* of its stones is better able than the *tensile* strength of a *lintel* on posts (B) to resist the downward thrust of the load above. It does this by directing the weight in a lateral direction and by transmitting the load to the ground through the arch and the vertical elements supporting it. Placed one after the other, a series of arches make a *tunnel vault* (C). Two tunnel vaults intersecting each other at right angles (D) create a *cross vault,* also known as a *groin vault* (so called for the groin line [E] along which the vaults join). The square or rectangular space they define is called a *bay* (d). Intersecting each other around a central axis, a series of arches would form a *dome* (F).

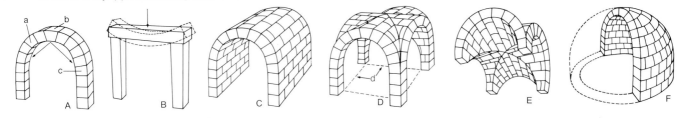

previously mentioned objectives. The construction of a true arch by means of the wedge-shaped blocks known as *voussoirs,* as well as some of the implications of the system, can be seen more easily in Figure 103 than explained in words. When such arches are placed side by side in a series, the resulting arcade can be used for such structures as aqueducts and bridges, as seen in the Pont du Gard (Fig. 99). When placed in a series, from front to back, the result is a *barrel vault* (also called a *tunnel vault*), which can be seen in the Arch of Trajan at Benevento (Fig. 86) and which was useful for roofing interiors. When two barrel vaults intersect each other at right angles, as seen in Figure 96, the result is a *cross vault* (or *groin vault*). When a series of arches span a given space by intersecting each other around a central axis, the result is a dome, as exemplified in the Pantheon (Fig. 101). In greatly oversimplified form, these constitute the technical principles behind the Roman architectural achievement.

Third, by their technical advances the Romans were able to increase the height of their buildings in proportion to the growing size of their large structures. The six-story market buildings of Trajan's Forum were an impressive demonstration of the practical advantages of such verticality, which allowed the combination of many small shops into a single structure in a crowded city location. The multifamily apartment houses in Ostia and Rome were also cases in point. The trend was to be seen, too, in the great height of the halls in the Baths of Trajan and Caracalla and of the Pantheon. The pleasing proportions that such height gave these buildings was made possible by cross vaulting and the dome.

Last, the enclosing of large units of interior space was made necessary by the expansion of the city's population. The direction of architectural thought in

meeting this need can easily be seen by contrasting a Greek agora with the Forum of Trajan, a Hellenistic theater with the Colosseum, or the Parthenon with the Pantheon. Special attention to space composition and the problems of lighting are evident in the planning of such interiors as those of the Basilica Ulpia, the Pantheon, and the halls of the great baths. In all instances, the Romans treated space as a tangible reality to be molded into significant designs.

Sculpture: Trajan's Column

To commemorate Trajan's victories in the two campaigns against the Dacian people of the lower Danube region, a monumental column was erected in the Emperor's forum by the Senate and people of Rome. It was placed in the small opening off the Basilica Ulpia between the two libraries (Fig. 91). Its base was originally surrounded by a colonnade that supported an upper gallery from which better views of the sculptures could be obtained. The diameter of the column varies from 12 feet (3.7 meters) at the base of its shaft to 10 feet (3 meters) at the top. As a whole it rose to a full height of 128 feet (39 meters), including the 18-foot (5.5-meter) base, the 97-foot (29.5-meter) shaft, and a 13-foot (4-meter) colossal statue of Trajan that originally stood at the top. The latter disappeared long ago and has since been replaced by a standing figure of St. Peter. Inside the column is a circular staircase that winds upward to the top and is lighted by small windowlike slits cut into the frieze. According to tradition, Trajan chose the monument as the site of his burial, and his ashes were placed in a chamber under the column.

The column itself is of the Doric order and is constructed in several sections of white marble. Its surface is entirely covered by a spiral band, carved in low relief, which winds from bottom to top in 23 revolutions. Reading from left to right, the story of the two Dacian campaigns unfolds in a continuous strip about 50 inches (127 centimeters) wide and 218 yards (199 meters) long. More than 2500 human figures make their appearance in this visual narrative, in addition to horses, boats, vehicles, and equipment of all kinds.

The hero of the story is, of course, the soldierly Trajan, who is shown fulfilling his imperial mission as the defender of Rome against the advances of the barbarians. The Empire was always willing to include any people who accepted the values of Mediterranean civilization, but it could tolerate no challenge. When an important barbarian kingdom was founded in Dacia, Trajan regarded it as a threat and set out to bring it under Roman control. While it took two campaigns to do the job, the lasting result of this Romanizing process is seen in the name of one of the nations of the region—Romania.

Trajan's brilliance as a commander was well known, and on this column and other similar monuments his reputation certainly did not suffer for lack of public advertisement. In the frieze, he seems to be everywhere at once and is portrayed as a bold and steady figure in complete command of the situation, whatever its nature. Sharing top billing with their general is the Roman army. Their opposite numbers are Trajan's antagonist, the Dacian king Decebalus, and his barbarian hordes.

The beginning of the campaign is placed on the banks of the Danube in a Roman camp guarded by sentries and supplied by boats (Fig. 104). As the Romans set forth across a pontoon bridge, a river god personifying the Danube rises from a grotto and lends his support by holding up the bridge. From this point the action moves with singular directness toward the inevitable climax: the triumph of Roman arms. The following scenes show Trajan holding a council of war; clad in a toga pouring a sacrificial drink to the gods; and standing on a platform as he addresses his troops (Fig. 105). The army is shown pitching a camp on enemy soil; burning a Dacian village; and in the midst of battle. At the psychological moment Jupiter appears in the sky, throwing bolts of lightning at the enemy to disperse them in all directions. The aftermath is then shown with the soldiers crowding around the Emperor and holding up the decapitated heads of the enemy; surgeons are seen caring for the wounded; and winged Victory makes her appearance.

Continuous Narrative

The scenes are designed to promote the continuous flow of action as smoothly as possible. For reasons of

above: 104. *Trajan's Campaign against the Dacians,* detail of Trajan's Column. A.D. 106–113. Marble, height of frieze band 4′2″ (1.27 m).

below: 105. *Trajan Addressing Assembly of Troops,* detail of Trajan's Column.

clarity the scenes have to be differentiated. The artist does this through some ninety separate appearances of Trajan, which always signal a new activity. Other devices employed are an occasional tree, to set off one scene from another, and new backgrounds, indicated in some places by a mountain, in others by a group of buildings, and so on.

The comparison of this type of spiral relief has aptly been made with the form of the unfolding papyrus and parchment scrolls that the educated Romans were accustomed to read. Trajan is known to have written an account of his Dacian campaigns, much as Julius Caesar had done in the case of his Gallic wars, but the document is lost. Since commentaries on this bit of history are so fragmentary, the column has become one of the principal sources of information about it. The impression viewers receive is so vivid that they feel almost as if they had experienced the campaign with Trajan.

The reliefs have a definite likeness to literature in their manner of telling a story by the process of visual narration. The methods the Romans used in such cases have been distinguished as "the simultaneous" and "the continuous." The simultaneous method is the same as that used by the Greeks in the east pediment and frieze of the Parthenon, for example, where all the action takes place at a given moment that is frozen into sculptural form. It thus observes the classical unities of time, place, and action. The continuous, or cyclic, method was developed by the Romans for just such a series of scenes as Trajan's wars. Unity of action is obtained by the telling of a life story, or it can be broadened to include a couple of military campaigns, as in this instance. The unities of time and place are sacrificed as far as the whole composition is concerned but are preserved in the separate scenes. While the origin of this continuous style is still a matter of scholarly dispute, no one has challenged the effective use the Romans made of it. Its spirit is close to their keen interest in historical and current events, and its value for the purposes of state propaganda is obvious.

Style

Despite the direct narrative content of the spiral frieze, the style is not realistic. For effects, the artist depended upon a set of symbols as carefully worked out as the words used by writers of epics. The use of a series of undulating lines, for example, indicates the sea. A jagged outline on the horizon stands for a mountain. A giant rising up out of the water represents a river. A wall can mean either a city or a camp. A female figure whose draperies are folded in the shape of a crescent moon informs the observer that it is night.

In such symbolism, liberties with perspective inevitably occur, and it is quite usual to find a man taller than a wall and an important figure, such as the Emperor, much greater in size than those around him. This technique does not rule out such clearly recognizable things as the banners of certain Roman legions as well as the details of their shields and armor. The Trajan frieze points unmistakably in the direction of the pictorial symbolism used later by Early Christian and medieval artists, who doubtless were influenced by it.

Much of the work will seem crude if placed beside the sculptures of Hellenistic artists who were still active in Rome. But this relief is clearly and intentionally an example of Roman popular art, and as such it was addressed to that large segment of the populace not accustomed to getting its information and enjoyment from books. Its location between two libraries also indicates a recognition that history could come from pictorial sources as well as from Greek and Latin scrolls.

The elegant and placid forms of Greek gods were not apt to arouse the emotions of those Romans who sought amusement in the gladiatorial contests held in the Colosseum. While the educated minority could admire dignity and restraint in their sculpture, the vast majority had to be aroused by just such an energetic action-filled story as this, involving people like themselves. Thus viewed, Trajan's frieze is fresh, original, and astonishingly alive.

The artist who designed the frieze was clearly a master of relief sculpture, able to depict with ease, in extremely low relief, whole armies, pitched battles, and the surrounding landscapes and sky. The care in execution is consistent, and even though the reliefs at the top were almost certainly out of view, the quality remains the same.

Standing in its prominent location from Trajan's time to the present, this column and the similar one of Marcus Aurelius have had incalculable influence on later art. The continuous mode of visual narration was taken over directly into the catacomb paintings of the Early Christians. It was continued in illuminated manuscripts, religious sculptures, and the stained glass of the medieval period. And it can still be found going strong in the comic strips of daily newspapers. Even the motion picture owes a certain debt to the technique worked out here in the 2nd century A.D. In this book, examples of the direct influence of this narrative mode include the Roman Christian tomb of Junius Bassus (Fig. 109); the mosaics relating the story of Christ in the church of Sant' Apollinare Nuovo in Ravenna (Figs. 116–119); the Bayeux Tapestry, which tells the story of the Norman conquest of England (Figs. 159, 160, 162); Giotto's frescoes on the life of St. Francis of Assisi (Figs.

106. *Gladiatorial Contest,* showing orchestra with hydraulic organ, trumpet, and horn players. Mosaic from Zliten, North Africa. A.D. c. 70.

194–197); and the studious duplication of Trajan's Column made under Napoleon for the Place Vendôme (Fig. 393).

Music

The practice of poetry and music enjoyed higher favor among educated Roman amateurs than did dabbling in the visual arts. Suggesting a plan for a building or some of its decorative details was all right for a member of the patrician, or upper, class but from there on it was the architect's and carpenter's business. Women of the patrician class achieved prominence in Roman times and may also have participated in such activities. With sculpture and painting wealthy people could make an impression as collectors, but the actual chiseling and painting were for artisans and slaves. When it came to writing verse or singing to the accompaniment of the lyre, however, amateurs were plentiful in the highest ranks of society.

The emperors themselves were included in the ranks of skillful amateurs. While Trajan's recreations seem to have been as strenuous as some of his military activities, those of his immediate successors included literary and musical pursuits. Hadrian wrote poetry in both Greek and Latin, but it remained for the last of the Antonines, Marcus Aurelius, to make an enduring reputation as a writer and philosopher. Hadrian, Antoninus Pius, and Caracalla were proficient on the cithara and hydraulic organ. Their musical ability, however, was not destined to put that of their predecessor Nero into the shade.

Instruments and Performing Groups

While much is known about Roman literature, no actual examples of Roman music survive. All knowledge of it must be gathered from occasional literary references, from sculptures, mosaics, and wall paintings that show music-making situations, and from some of the musical instruments themselves. From these sources, it is clear that the Romans heard much music and that no occasion, public or private, was complete without it.

A mosaic showing a small Roman instrumental ensemble performing in an amphitheater during a gladiatorial contest has been found in excavations in North Africa (Fig. 106). One musician is shown playing the long, straight brass instrument known as the *tuba,* or "trumpet." Two others are playing the circular *cornu,* or "horn." Still another is seated at the *hydraulus,* or "water organ." Equipped with a rudimentary keyboard and stops, this highly ingenious instrument produced sounds by forcing air compressed by two water tanks through a set of bronze pipes. Some of these instruments were 10 feet (3 meters) high. They were used mainly in open-air arenas where their tone must have resembled that of the calliopes, once so popular in circus parades.

In keeping with the Roman idea of grandeur, the size of their musical instruments was greatly increased. The writer Marcellinus described a performance in which hundreds of players took part, some of whom were said to have performed on "lyres as big as chariots." Owing to their usefulness in warfare, an ever-increasing volume of sound was demanded of wind instruments. Battle signals were relayed by means of trumpet calls, and the more the legions, the bigger and brassier became the sound. This is verified by the philosopher and teacher Quintilian, who asks a typical rhetorical question, then proceeds to answer it with a characteristic flourish: "And what else is the function of the horns and trumpets attached to our legion? The louder the concert of their notes, the greater is the glorious supremacy of our arms over all the nations of the earth."

The large audiences accustomed to gather in amphitheaters also played a part in stepping up the volume of individual instruments and in developing sizable vocal and instrumental groups. Writing in the 1st century A.D., the dramatist Seneca notes that the size of the vocal and instrumental groups was such that sometimes the singers and players in the arena outnumbered the audience. Soloists would be lost in such vast surroundings. There are also descriptions of large groups of singers accompanied by various wind instruments and the hydraulic organ.

Music in Speech and Drama

Quintilian also points out some of the practical applications of music to the art of oratory. He particularly emphasizes the development of the voice because "it is by raising, lowering, or inflexion of the voice that the orator stirs the emotions of his hearers." He then cites the example of one of the great speakers of the past who had a musician standing behind him while making his speeches, "whose duty it was to give him the tones in which his voice was to be pitched. Such was the attention which he paid to this point even in the midst of his most turbulent speeches, when he was terrifying the patrician party."

Music was also a part of every theatrical performance. While the Roman drama omitted the chorus that the Greeks had stressed, its dialogue was interspersed with songs accompanied by the *tibia,* an ancient wind instrument originally fashioned from the leg bone of an animal. Such musical portions, however, were not composed by the dramatists, as they had been in the Athenian tradition, but were delegated to specialists in this field. The importance of choruses and bands for military morale was not overlooked, and a functional type of military music existed in addition to the trumpet calls to battle. Popular groups played music at games and contests, and strolling street musicians were part of the everyday scene.

The fact that not a single note of any of this music exists today testifies that Roman music was primarily a performing art. While the practicing

musicians may very well have composed their own songs and pieces or made variations on traditional tunes, none seem to have been concerned with writing them down—and if they had done so, the later Church fathers would very likely have had these pagan melodies committed to the flames. So, like the folk music that existed only in oral tradition until the coming of modern notation and recording devices, the art of Roman music died with the people who practiced it.

Ideas

As a part of the mainstream of classical culture, Roman civilization shared many of the basic ideas that produced the Hellenic and Hellenistic styles. Significantly, the Romans widened the scope of the arts to include not only works that were aimed at the expert but also those that carried broad mass appeal. The two ideas that differentiate the Roman from earlier classical styles and that dominate the Roman expression in the arts are the genius for organization and the frank spirit of utilitarianism, evident in a conception of the arts as a means to popular enjoyment and the solution of practical problems.

Organization

The Roman ability to organize is shown in the building up of a systematic world order, which embraced a unified religion, a unified body of laws, and a unified civilization. Military conquest was, to be sure, one of the means employed. However, the allowance of a maximum of self-government to subject peoples and the latitude given to local customs, even to tribal and cult religions, are proof of the Romans' realistic approach to governing and their toleration. Their desire for external unity did not imply internal uniformity, and their frank recognition of this fact was at the root of their success as administrators.

Applications to Architecture   With this ability to organize religious, legal, social, and governmental institutions, the Romans' greatest contribution in the arts clearly would lie in the direction of architecture. This organizational spirit, moreover, is revealed most decisively in their undertaking of large public-works projects, such as the building of roads, ports, aqueducts, and the like. It is also seen in their manner of grouping buildings on a common axis, as in the Forum of Trajan, which was so directly in contrast to the Hellenic idea of isolated perfection. It appears, similarly, in the organization of business activities in common centers, and the various forms of recreation in the baths. The technical application and development of all the possibilities of construc-

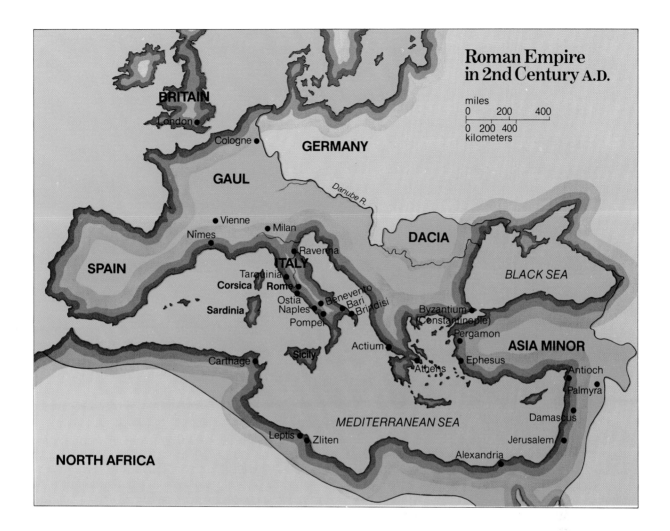

Roman Empire in 2nd Century A.D.

tion by means of the arch and vault is another example. The combination of the Ionic and Corinthian capitals to form the Composite order, the only distinctive Roman contribution to the classical orders, is yet a further example. So is their combination of three orders on the exterior of the same building, as in the Colosseum, where the Tuscan-Doric order is used on the first story, Ionic on the second, and Corinthian on the third and fourth. Equally impressive in this regard are the development of the multifamily apartment house, the attention given to the efficient assembling and dispersing of large numbers of people in such buildings as the Colosseum, and the invention of a supermarket, such as the six-storied example in Trajan's Forum. A final example is in the erection of a supertemple for the principal gods, as in the Pantheon.

Expansion of Interior Space　The same organizational spirit is reflected in the expansion of interior space, as in the Basilica Ulpia, the Pantheon, and the

great halls of the baths, in order to accommodate ever-larger numbers of people. The Greek idea had been to define space in planes. Thus, the exteriors of their temples were designed as backdrops for processions and religious ceremonies. Those who worshiped Athena at the Parthenon were concerned primarily with its external colonnade, not the interior. Space in this sense was defined but not organized. In the Pantheon, however, interior space was enveloped and made real (Fig. 101). To the Greeks, space always remained a formless void to be controlled and humanized, but the Romans recognized the possibilities of molding three-dimensional space, enclosing it and giving it significant form.

The Romans sought to enhance this spatial feeling in many ways. They showed a sensitivity to scale and a tendency to design buildings in related structural units. They exploited color by the use of *polychrome,* or many-colored, marbles, which enlivened interiors and which added to the perception of depth. They used illusionistic wall paintings to suggest the

107. *View of a Garden.* c. 20 B.C. Wall painting from Villa of Livia at Prima Porta. National Museum, Rome.

third dimension (Fig. 107). They also gave increased attention to lighting problems. All this the Romans accomplished without sacrificing the classical clarity of form.

The same feeling, furthermore, is carried over into sculpture, where the tangibility of the spatial environment is reflected in the backgrounds of reliefs by means of buildings and landscapes that suggest depth. The 5th-century B.C. Grecian style, by contrast, consciously omitted any such frame of reference. In addition to this, the organization of time into a continuum, as in the spiral series on the Column of Trajan, shows a new concept of sequential order translated into the pictorial medium.

Broadening Appeal of the Arts   Still another facet of this Roman organizational ability is found in the allowance for a wide range of taste in the arts. There were styles that appealed to the educated few and those that held the attention of the middle and lower classes. In one case it was directed to the eye and ear of the expert; in the other it was frankly popular in its appeal. The conservative tastes of the first group embraced the tried-and-true values of Greek art; hence they either collected antique statues and paintings, or they commissioned new works to be executed in the older style. Exquisite Greek craftsmanship held little interest for the majority, who needed a large bronze equestrian statue or a monumental triumphal arch to capture their atten-

tion. In Trajan's Forum, due allowance was made for this variety of taste, with the Greek and Latin libraries placed on either side of a court and a column in between, where the story of Trajan's campaigns was related in a carefully worked out popular language of symbols designed to awaken the curiosity of the multitude.

The disdain of the conservative group for popular art was well stated by Athenaeus, a Greek scholar and teacher who resided in Rome A.D. c. 200. He defended the virtues of the older cultural tradition and frequently made unflattering comparisons between the higher standards of the past and those that prevailed in his day. "In early times," he wrote, "popularity with the masses was a sign of bad art; hence, when a certain aulos-player once received loud applause, Asopodorus of Phlius, who was himself still waiting in the wings, said 'What's this? Something awful must have happened!' The player evidently could not have won approval with the crowds otherwise. . . . And yet the musicians of our day set as the goal of their art success with their audiences."

Just as in the case of architecture, sculpture, and painting, the Romans were heirs to the Greek musical tradition. The ancient theories survived in philosophical speculation, and Greek music teachers were employed by preference in the homes of the wealthy. The only musical compositions to survive from this period, for instance, are three hymns by Mesomedes, a Greek musician attached to Hadrian's court. Those who cultivated this more austere style felt that music was meant to educate and elevate the mind, but the popular taste lay in quite another direction.

The music making that Athenaeus and his conservative group scorned was obviously the very kind that the majority of Romans enjoyed at their public festivals, military parades, games, sporting contests, races, and to some extent the theater. The modern parallel would be the split that exists between audiences interested in chamber music, symphony concerts, and the opera, and those attracted by bands at football games, Broadway musicals, popular jazz, and hard rock. What the Romans accomplished here was to broaden the base of the appeal of the arts and gear them to different types of audience. They thus succeeded in providing for the entertainment of a large city population, just as their buildings and civil-engineering projects took care of the physical needs of the populace.

Utilitarianism

In referring to the administrations of the last two Antonine emperors, Gibbon declared that "their united reigns are possibly the only period of history in which the happiness of a great people was the sole object of government." The basis of this claim is to be found in the way the Romans managed to steer a middle course between the Scylla of Greek theoretical abstractions about the nature of an ideal state and the Charybdis of religious speculation on the joys of the world to come, which was to characterize the subsequent Christian phases of the Empire. Speculation on the eternal verities could uplift the mind, but the understanding of human behavior was rewarded by more immediate advantages.

In the late Antonine Age, Rome had reached a balance based on an acceptance of the Stoic doctrine of "live and let live" and the Epicurean idea of pleasure as an index to the highest good. The transfer of these doctrines of individualism to the forms and policies of a government meant a high degree of tolerance and a recognition that the standard of excellence in either a law or a work of art was the greatest good for the greatest number.

The construction of elegantly proportioned temples was therefore not so important as the building of bridges (Fig. 108). Maintaining a luxurious private palace was secondary to providing people's palaces, such as the public baths and theaters. A private collection of sculpture was subordinate to public exhibitions in city squares and galleries, where the statues could be seen and enjoyed by many. A play, poem, or piece of music that awakened only the sensibilities of the cultured minority did not rank so

108. Bridge (Pons Aelius), Rome. A.D. 134. Hadrian's Tomb (Castel Sant' Angelo), A.D. 135–139.

high on this scale as those that were applauded by the multitude. In short, the practical arts were favored over the decorative arts, material goods superseded more remote spiritual blessings, and utility was valued over abstract beauty (though the two are by no means mutually exclusive).

Since the Romans were little concerned with ideal forms, it was not an accident that their greatest successes occurred in the arts of government rather than in the fine arts. As Vergil said in the *Aeneid:* "Let others melt and mold the breathing bronze to forms more fair . . . or trace with pointed wand the cycled heaven, and hail the constellations as they rise; But thou, Oh Roman, learn with sovereign sway to rule the nations." As was said earlier, the art which proved most congenial to Roman aspirations was that of architecture, especially in its utilitarian aspects as found in the field of civil engineering. Building a 200-mile (320-kilometer) highway over the mountains, moving part of a hill over 100 feet (30.4 meters) high to make way for a forum, providing a sewer system for a city of over a million inhabitants, bridging the Danube at its widest point, perfecting such a new building material as concrete—all these were taken in stride.

When it came to sculpture, the Romans saw that subject matter served the purposes of the state by praising the virtues and deeds of the emperors. Such epic poems as Vergil's *Aeneid* performed a similar service in the literary medium; and, as Quintilian

109. Sarcophagus of Junius Bassus. A.D. c. 359.
Marble, 3'10½" × 8' (1.17 × 2.44 m). Vatican Grottoes, Rome.

said, the loud sounds of the brass instruments proclaimed the glory of Roman arms.

Other applications of this utilitarianism are found in the brilliant exploitation of such technical devices as the arch and vault. Their success in solving practical problems is proved by the number of roads, aqueducts, and bridges that are still serving their purpose today (Fig. 108). In sculpture the application of the continuous-narrative method was more psychologically practical. This way of telling a tale promoted a sense of continuity in time and anticipated later Christian and secular pictorial forms.

Effective as utilitarianism was, it was purchased at the price of conflict between structure and decoration, external and internal values, and functional and nonfunctional aspects of art. The Romans built and decorated well, but the two activities somehow failed to achieve a harmonious coexistence. This is well illustrated by the somewhat hollow claim of Augustus, who in an earlier period had boasted that he found Rome a city of brick and left it a city of marble. Actually, Rome was still a city of brick, stone, and concrete under an Augustan marble veneer. None of these materials needs a disguise, or even an apology, as proved by the rhythmical grace of the functional arches of the Pont du Gard (Fig. 99). Hence Augustus had no need to imply that Roman structures were solid marble like the Parthenon. As a whole, then, Roman architecture was at its best when it stuck to its frank utilitarianism, undertook vast engineering projects, and successfully solved the practical problems of construction.

Older cultural centers, such as Athens and Pergamon, were so far off the beaten track that their more restrained classical purity did not exert any appreciable influence on the forms of Western art until the archaeological discoveries of the 18th and 19th centuries. All intervening phases of classicism were, in effect, revivals of the Roman style. With the establishment of the Roman building methods, Western architecture was firmly set on its course, and it steered in substantially the same direction until the technological discoveries of the 19th and 20th centuries. Consequently, it must be emphasized once more that Rome was the gateway through which all the styles, forms, and ideas of Mediterranean civilization passed in review. After being transformed by the process of selectivity—and by flashes of genuine originality—into a uniquely Roman expression, they proceeded onward through the arch into medieval culture by way of the new Roman imperial capitals of Byzantium in the East and Ravenna in the West.

Rome in imperial times was also the western center of Christendom from the first century onward. Because Christianity was at first an underground religion, the art had to be hidden in underground passages known as catacombs. Later, when Constantine legalized Christianity, large churches known as basilicas were built. Surviving from this time are many elaborately carved marble tombs, or *sarcophagi,* depicting biblical subjects (Fig. 109).

When Rome declined as the center of world empire, it still remained the capital of Christendom. As the object of pilgrimages, its architectural, sculptural, and literary monuments were bound to exert a massive influence on those who were drawn at one time or another toward the city. Because of this enduring preeminence no important Western city exists without a bit of Rome in it. It is therefore with full justification that Rome has been and still continues to be called the Eternal City.

II
THE MEDIEVAL PERIOD

The medieval period, or Middle Ages, was so named by later Renaissance historians to account for the nearly 1000-year span between the fall of Rome in A.D. 476 and the revival of classical learning in the 15th century. In western Europe the time is roughly divided by art historians into four main classifications: early Christian (300–600), Carolingian (750–950), Romanesque (1000–1150), and Gothic (1150–1300).

In the medieval world the East Roman Empire remained a powerful force until its capital, Byzantium (Constantinople), fell to the Ottoman Turks in 1453. In western Europe the power vacuum produced by the fall of Rome was followed by migrations of restless barbarian peoples into new territories and the establishment of many tribal kingdoms. Meanwhile, a new Roman power, the Church, was converting these peoples to Christianity, restoring order, and imposing a new code of law.

While the Greco-Romans had been more concerned with prosperity and pleasure in this world, the early Christians concentrated on bliss and beauty in the next. They believed that earthly life was a period of trial and error beset by the snares of the devil to trap the faithful. Overcoming temptation and sin meant heavenly rewards; yielding led to hellish tortures amid fire and brimstone. Medieval thought turned away from the rational, scientific, and materialistic world view of the ancients and created a system based on faith, spiritual values, and miracles.

Early Christian theology rested on a synthesis of Greek philosophy and the Hebrew Scriptures as interpreted by such Church fathers as St. Ambrose, the bishop of Milan, who became a great moral force; St. Jerome, who translated the Bible from the original languages into the common Latin tongue of the people; St. Augustine, who wrote the influential books *City of God* and his *Confessions;* and Gregory the Great, who organized the papacy into the central administration of the Church and made it into a powerful political as well as religious institution. Together their works established what is known as the patristic tradition. This meant that the authority of the Bible and the teachings embodied in the works of the Church fathers were the final authority.

Innovation and originality were discouraged. Philosophy took the form of learned commentaries and some variations on ancient sources. In architecture traditional forms had to be preserved, but local adaptations often produced striking results. Art forms were almost exclusively under the patronage of the Church. No artist was allowed a free hand, but work varied from one generation and place to another. In music Gregorian melodies were the official body of church music. Yet new voices could be woven in and around the traditional tunes, a practice that allowed wide latitude for musicians.

Medieval philosophy culminated in the thought of the scholastics. These teachers included Abelard, Albertus Magnus, and Thomas Aquinas. Their principal concern was in applying Aristotelian logic to prove such propositions as the existence of God, the immortality of the soul, and the nature of good and evil. Those who could not understand the complexities of logical proof could accept the articles through revelation and faith.

The structure of medieval society assumed the forms of monasticism, feudalism, the building of cities, and the rise of national monarchies. Of great importance was the monastic movement, whereby those who valued spiritual pursuits banded together in isolated communities to lead Christian lives away from the paths of temptation. Some monks were skilled farmers. Others kept the torch of knowledge alight by copying ancient books, collecting libraries, establishing schools, and building monastic complexes that included the great abbey churches.

Feudalism reflected a strict stratification of society and an economy based on the ownership and productivity of the land. Everyone's place was fixed by birth, from great nobles down to small landlords, peasants, and serfs. The only upward mobility was in the Church, where such a figure as Abbot Suger could rise from obscure beginnings to become the confidant of French kings and rule as regent during one of the Crusades.

The Gothic period witnessed the rise of cities in northern Europe. Here the merchants and artisans became distinct social groups, organizing themselves into guilds, similar to trade unions, that regulated prices, set forth a code for business practices, and assured the quality of production. In Paris, Rheims, and other cities great Gothic cathedrals rose. These soaring towers of stone and stained glass reflected the communal efforts of the towns and people that built them. Women were employed in craft workshops; on the aristocratic level the code of chivalry simultaneously accorded them a high status, and Mary as Queen of Heaven became the ideal of womanhood. The beginnings of nationhood were to be seen in the growth of monarchies in France, England, and Spain. In 1215 the Magna Charta was signed by King John of England. This meant that the laws of the land applied even to English kings, who now had to share power with the nobles. Later this led to the establishment of a representative form of government known as a parliament.

The Romanesque period had seen the movement of people along pilgrimage routes toward Rome, Jerusalem, and Santiago de Compostela. Along the way they stopped to honor various saints at their shrines and to revere their relics. The conquest of Palestine by the Moslems made pilgrimages to the Holy Land hazardous if not impossible. Earlier, Mohammed had conquered Mecca in A.D. 630 and started a movement that took the Mediterranean world by storm. The Islamic empire eventually extended from Spain, through north Africa, and as far east as India. Science and mathematics were pursued with zeal by Moslem scholars, who developed the style of writing numbers called Arabic numerals. The conquest of Palestine led to 150 years of strife during the Crusades when, with papal sanction, successive waves of western Europeans invaded the Holy Land. The results were inconclusive, but the Crusades checked Moslem expansion, opened up new east-west trade routes, and brought Europeans into contact with Islamic civilization with mutual benefits.

5
The Early Roman Christian and Byzantine Styles

Ravenna, Late 5th and Early 6th Centuries

Many an old Roman coin bears the inscription *Ravenna Felix*—"Happy Ravenna." By a felicitous stroke of fate, this previously unimportant little town on Italy's Adriatic coast became the stage on which the great political, religious, and artistic dramas of a century and a half of world history were enacted.

Ravenna was, in turn, the seat of the last Roman emperors of the West, the capital of a barbarian Ostrogothic kingdom, and the western center of the East Roman Empire. A more forbidding site could hardly be imagined. To the east lay the Adriatic Sea, to the north and south wide deltas of the river Po, and the only land approach was through marshes and swamps. Yet when the barbarian hordes had Rome in a state of almost constant siege, it was this very isolation that led Emperor Honorius to abandon Rome in A.D. 402 and seek in Ravenna a fortress where his hard-pressed legions could be supplied by the East Roman Empire through the nearby port of Classe (see map, p. 115).

Even with all its natural advantages, Ravenna could hold out against the barbarians only until the year 476. Odoacer then succeeded in entering the all-but-impregnable city and put an end to the West Roman Empire. The Ostrogothic kingdom of Theodoric, Odoacer's successor, was even more short-lived, and Ravenna fell once more in 540, when Justinian's armies of the East Roman Empire conquered the Italian peninsula and for a brief time reunited the old Empire. Meanwhile a third force, the more enduring power of the Roman papacy, was becoming increasingly influential.

Diverse historical traditions as well as wide geographical distances separated Rome in the west, Byzantium in the east, and the nomadic Ostrogoths in the north. Early in the 4th century, after he had made Christianity an official state religion, Emperor Constantine had moved his court to Byzantium, christening the city the "new Rome." Later, this second capital was called Constantinople in his honor, and soon the East and West Roman empires were going their separate courses. With the encroachments of northern barbarians, a three-way struggle for power began among Justinian, Theodoric, and the pope.

More than the sea stretched between Ravenna and Constantinople, higher mountains than the Alps stood between it and the restless northern barbarians, and greater obstacles than the Apennines separated it from Rome. Theological barriers, in fact, proved more impassable than seas or mountains, because this was the age that was laying the foundations of basic religious beliefs. In some respects the controversies in Ravenna foreshadowed the later separations of Christianity into Eastern Orthodox and Roman Catholic, and Catholic and the much later Protestant denominations.

At this time, the main doctrinal battle centered on the nature of the Trinity, and especially on Christ's role as the second person in the Trinity. The Ostrogoths, having been converted by Arius of Alexandria (c. 256–336), believed that since He was created by God the Father, Jesus was subordinate and not of one substance with God. Despite this denial of the Trinity, the Arians revered Christ as the noblest of created beings, but human rather than divine. In Byzantium, it was held that Christ as the Word Incarnate

ROME

284-	305	Diocletian, emperor
306-	337	Constantine, emperor
	313	Edict of Milan legalized Christianity
	c.313	Lateran Basilica begun on site of present San Giovanni in Laterano
c.324–c.333		Old St. Peter's Basilica begun on Vatican Hill
c.330–c.350		Tomb of Santa Costanza, daughter of Constantine. Later rededicated as church
c.332–c.340		Santa Maria Maggiore Basilica begun
c.340-	397	St. Ambrose; bishop of Milan
340-	420	St. Jerome; translated Latin Vulgate Bible
354-	430	St. Augustine; bishop of Hippo (North Africa); author of *Confessions* (397), *City of God* (426)
	385	San Paolo fuori le Mura ("St. Paul's outside the Walls") Basilica built. Destroyed by fire 1823 and rebuilt
	402	Rome abandoned by Emperor Honorius as capital of West Roman Empire
	410	Visigoths sacked Rome
	455	Vandals sacked Rome
	476	Odoacer sacked Rome; fall of West Roman Empire

590-	604	Gregory the Great, pope; Roman Catholic liturgy codified; Gregorian chant established

RAVENNA

395-	423	Honorius, West Roman emperor
	402	Ravenna, under Emperor Honorius, became capital of West Roman Empire
c.402-	450	"Neonian" Baptistry for Roman Christians
c.425–c.440		Mausoleum of Galla Placidia
c.475-	524	Boethius; Theodoric's minister; translator of Greek treatises; author of *The Consolation of Philosophy*
476-	540	Ravenna capital of Ostrogothic kingdom
	476	Odoacer conquered Ravenna; fall of West Roman Empire
476-	493	Odoacer, king
c.480-	575	Cassiodorus; Theodoric's minister; after 540 founded monastery at Vivarium, Italy
493-	526	Theodoric, king
	493	Church of Sant' Apollinare Nuovo begun
	c.526	Mausoleum of Theodoric built
	c.527	Church of San Vitale begun
c.530-	539	Church of Sant' Apollinare in Classe
	540	Belisarius entered Ravenna as conqueror; end of

		Theodoric's Ostrogothic kingdom
	546	Maximian appointed archbishop of Ravenna; ruled as Byzantine exarch
	547	San Vitale completed

BYZANTIUM (CONSTANTINOPLE)

c.324–c.330		Constantine made Byzantium capital of East Roman Empire
	325	First Council of Nicaea
329-	379	St. Basil; bishop of Caesaria; liturgist of Eastern Orthodox Church
c.345-	407	St. John Chrysostom; patriarch of Constantinople; liturgist of Eastern Orthodox Church
518-	527	Justin, East Roman emperor
527-	565	Justinian the Great, East Roman emperor
	c.527	Church of Sts. Sergius and Bacchus begun
	c.527	Church of San Vitale begun at Ravenna
532-	537	Church of Hagia Sophia built by architects Anthemius of Tralles and Isidorus of Miletus
	533	Justinian's *Digest of Laws*
534-	540	Belisarius, Justinian's general, conquered Italy; entered Ravenna; end of Ostrogothic kingdom

was of one single substance with the Father and hence of divine nature only. The Roman papacy found a middle ground between the two extremes and took the position that, since the Word was made flesh, Christ possessed both divine and human natures and was a full member of the Trinity. Today, such theological controversies seem remote, but in the early centuries of Christianity they were of sufficient intensity to shake empires, depose kings, and cause decades of war.

Paralleling the political and religious controversies, a conflict of art styles took place within Ravenna as successive rulers built and embellished the city. In the 6th century, Ostrogothic Arian heretics, Byzantine patriarchs, and members of the Roman hierarchy, together with the schools of artists each patronized, had different cultural heritages, aesthetic goals, and ways of looking at the world.

During the days when the Roman Empire was united, cultural influences came from all parts of the

Mediterranean world, and with due allowance for regional diversity, Roman art achieved a recognizable unity. But with the disintegration of Roman power, the adoption of Christianity as an official religion, and the separation of the Empire into eastern and western centers, a reorientation in the arts took place. Though there were many overlapping elements, owing to a common heritage, two distinct styles began to emerge. Hence, when reference is to all the art of this period, the designation will be Early Christian. The term Early Roman Christian will be used to distinguish the Western style from the declining old pagan Roman arts, on the one hand, and from the subsequent Romanesque and Gothic styles of the later medieval period on the other. Byzantine will designate the parallel Eastern style.

Architecture and Mosaics

Ravenna's replacement of Rome as a capital city demanded a building program that would transform a minor town into a metropolis. No ruler could afford to be outdone by predecessors. Therefore, the West Roman emperors and Empress Galla Placidia, whose tomb is seen in Figure 110, erected significant secular and religious structures. Then the barbarian king Theodoric, after he came to power, sought to be more Roman than the Romans. As he wrote to an official in Rome, he wished his age to "match the preceding ones in the beauty of its buildings." And the great Justinian, after the Byzantine conquest, made architectural contributions corresponding to his imperial dignity.

110. Mausoleum of Galla Placidia, Ravenna. c. 425.

Rectangular Basilicas: Sant' Apollinare Nuovo

Theodoric included in his building program a church to serve his own Arian sect. Originally dedicated by him to "Our Lord Jesus Christ," this church (Fig. 111) today bears the name of Sant' Apollinare Nuovo, honoring Apollinarus, patron saint of Ravenna and, by tradition, the disciple and friend of St. Peter. The floor plan is a severely simple one (Fig. 112). There is a division of space into a vestibule entrance, known as the *narthex;* a central area for the congregation to

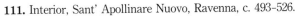

111. Interior, Sant' Apollinare Nuovo, Ravenna, c. 493–526.

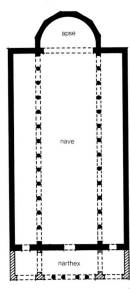

above: 112. Plan of Sant' Apollinare Nuovo.

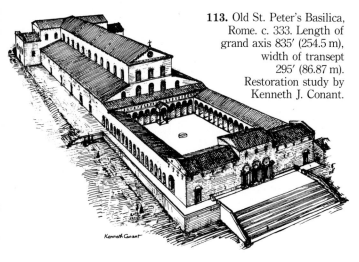

113. Old St. Peter's Basilica, Rome. c. 333. Length of grand axis 835′ (254.5 m), width of transept 295′ (86.87 m). Restoration study by Kenneth J. Conant.

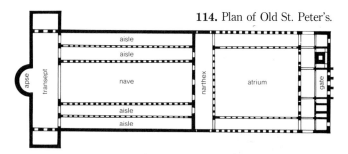

114. Plan of Old St. Peter's.

aisle
aisle
nave
aisle
aisle
apse
transept
narthex
atrium
gate

assemble, known as the *nave,* separated from the side aisles by two rows of columns; and a semicircular *apse,* which framed the altar and provided seats for the clergy.

Older pagan temples, with their small, dark interiors, were not suitable models for Christian churches that had to house large congregations. Ancient Greek ceremonies had taken place outdoors around an altar with the temple as a backdrop. The principal architectural and decorative elements of

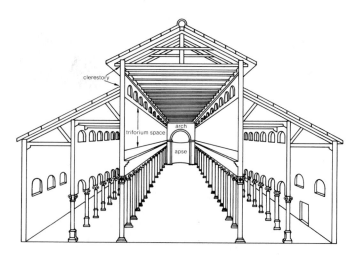

clerestory
triforium space
arch
apse

115. Section view of a typical Early Roman Christian basilica.

the classic temples—colonnades, frieze, pediments—faced outward. The Christian basilica turned the Greek temple outside in, leaving the exterior quite plain, and concentrated attention on the interior colonnades and the painted or mosaic embellishments of the walls and semidomed apse.

The most complete of these Early Christian basilicas was Old St. Peter's (Figs. 113, 114), so called because it was destroyed in the 16th century to make way for the present basilica of Bramante, Michelangelo, and Maderno (see Fig. 237). Planned from the year 324, when it was dedicated by Constantine, built over the presumed tomb of the Apostle, and as the largest church of the period, Old St. Peter's, until its demolition, ranked as the key monument of Western Christendom.

To provide for all Christian activities, Old St. Peter's brought together elements of Roman domestic, civic, and temple architecture into a new harmonious composition. Approached by a flight of steps, entrance to the open *atrium* was made through an arched gateway. This courtyard, derived from old Roman country villas, was surrounded by roofed *arcades,* or series of arches, supported by columns. It provided space for congregations to gather, facilities for the instruction of converts, and offices for church officials. In its center was a fountain for the ceremonial washing of hands. The side of the atrium toward the church became the *narthex* that serves as a frontispiece to the church proper. Through the portals of the narthex, entrance was made to the nave and side aisles (Fig. 115). This spacious nave was 80 feet (24.4 meters) wide and resembled the rectangular law courts of Roman public basilicas (see Fig. 92). It was flanked on either side by two aisles 30 feet (9.1 meters) wide and a procession of columns that led the eye along its 295-foot (89.9-meter) length to the *triumphal arch* (so called because of its derivation from similar Roman imperial structures, such as that in Fig. 86). Beyond this was the wide *transept,* the "arms" set at right angles to the nave and an area that functions as a second nave, followed by the semicircular apse.

The ground plan (Fig. 114), then, was roughly T-shaped or cruciform, resembling a long Latin cross with short arms. From beginning to end, the design of Old St. Peter's swept along a horizontal axis of 835 feet (254.5 meters) and opened out at its widest point in the 295-foot (89.9 meter) transept.

Vertically, a basilica (Fig. 115) rises above the nave colonnades through an intermediate area called the *triforium* that extends to the level of the roofing over the side aisles. Above this is the *clerestory* with its rows of windows that light the interior and with its masonry that supports the wooden beams of the shed roof. In keeping with the sheltered and inward orientation of these early basilicas, no windows gave view on the outside world. Those at the clerestory were too high and too deeply set to allow even a glimpse of the sky. It was inner radiance of the spirit rather than natural light that was sought.

Roman and Byzantine Mosaics　Sant' Apollinare Nuovo, unlike Old St. Peter's, which had to accommodate a standing congregation of 40,000 or more, was designed as the private chapel of Theodoric's palace. Only the nave now remains intact, all other parts being restorations or later additions. As such, its modest architecture would attract only passing attention. However, the magnificent mosaics that decorate its nave wall are of major importance in art history. Although they present a harmonious design, the mosaics actually were made in two different periods and styles.

The mosaics of the earlier period were commissioned by Theodoric and are Early Roman Christian craftsmanship. "Send us from your city," Theodoric had written through his secretary Cassiodorus to an official in Rome, "some of your most skilled marble-workers, who may join together those pieces which have been exquisitely divided, and connecting together their different veins of color, may admirably represent the natural appearance." After Justinian's

conquest, the church was rededicated and all references to Arian beliefs and Theodoric's reign were removed. Half a century later, part of the frieze above the nave arcade was replaced by mosaics in the Byzantine style.

Completely covering both walls of the nave, the mosaic work is divided into three bands (Fig. 111). Above the nave arcade and below the clerestory windows, a wide and continuous mosaic strip runs the entire length of the nave in the manner of a frieze. It depicts two long files of saints (the Byzantine part) moving in a majestic procession from representations of Ravenna on one side and Classe on the other (the Early Roman Christian part). The second band fills the space on either side of the clerestory windows with a series of standing toga-clad figures.

At the top level, panels depicting incidents in the life of Christ alternate with simulated canopylike niches over the figures standing below. The middle and upper bands are of Roman craftsmanship. The scenes in the upper band constitute the most complete representation of the life of Christ in Early Christian art. On one side, the story of the parables and miracles is told, among them the *Good Shepherd Separating the Sheep from the Goats* (Fig. 116), an allusion to the Last Judgment. In this and other scenes Christ appears youthful, unbearded, with blue eyes and brown hair. On the opposite side, scenes of the Passion and Resurrection are presented. In the

116. *Good Shepherd Separating the Sheep from the Goats.* c. 520. Mosaic. Sant' Apollinare Nuovo, Ravenna.

Last Supper (Fig. 117) showing Christ and the disciples reclining in the manner of a Roman banquet, He is seen as a more mature and bearded figure. In all instances He has the cruciform halo with a jewel on each arm of the cross to distinguish Him from the attending saints and angels. His dignified demeanor and purple cloak also tend to show Him in the light of royal majesty.

Standing like statues on their pedestals, the figures in the middle band are modeled three-dimensionally in light and shade and cast diagonal shadows. They apparently were once identified by inscriptions over their heads. The removal of their

names suggests they may have been prophets and saints revered by the Arian Christians.

The great mosaic frieze above the nave arcade starts on the left and right of the entrance with representations of the port of Classe and Ravenna, respectively. In the crescent-shaped harbor with three Roman galleys riding at anchor, Classe is seen between two lighthouses. Above the city walls some of the ancient buildings are discernible, and from the gate issues the procession of virgin martyrs.

On the opposite side is Ravenna with Theodoric's Palace in the foreground (Fig. 118). Under the word *Palatium* is the central arch where once was a portrait of Theodoric on horseback. Under the other arches, outlines and traces of heads and hands indicate that members of his court were also portrayed, and Theodoric was again depicted in the city gate at the right. But when the Ostrogothic kingdom came to its abrupt end, these personages were replaced by simulated Byzantine textile curtains. Above the palace are several of Theodoric's buildings with the Church of Sant' Apollinare Nuovo itself on the left.

As with the cella frieze of the Parthenon, this procession reflects the ritual that regularly took place in the church. According to the early custom, the congregation gathered in the side aisles, with women on one side and men on the other. At the offertory they went forward through the nave to the altar carrying with them their gifts of bread and wine for the consecration. In a stylized way, the procession frieze reenacts this part of the service on a heavenly level. On the left (Fig. 119), 22 virgins are

118. *Theodoric's Palace.* c. 520. Mosaic. Sant' Apollinare Nuovo, Ravenna.

119. *Procession of Virgin Martyrs.* c. 560. Mosaic. Sant' Apollinare Nuovo, Ravenna.

led forward by the Three Wise Men to the throne of the Virgin Mary, who holds the Christ Child on her lap. Arrayed in white tunics with richly jeweled mantles, the virgins carry their crowns of martyrdom in their hands as offerings.

In a similar manner, 25 male martyrs on the right are escorted by St. Martin of Tours into the presence of Christ, who is seated on a lyre-backed throne. The eye is led along by the upward folds and curves of their costumes as they step along a flowered path lined with date palms that symbolize both Paradise and their martyrdom. All is serene and no trace of their earthly suffering is seen. Their heads, though tilted differently to vary the design somewhat, are all on the same level in keeping with the Greco-Byzantine convention of isocephaly. (See Chap. 2, p. 33, for discussion of a Hellenic example).

In the procession only St. Agnes is accompanied by her attribute, the lamb. Otherwise the faces reveal so little individuality they could not be identified without the inscriptions present in the composition.

A completely different artistic feeling is revealed when these Byzantine figures are compared with the earlier Roman work in the bands above. The unshaded lines of the Byzantine design form a frankly two-dimensional pattern, while the garments of the Roman personages fall in natural folds that model the forms they cover in three-dimensional fashion. All the figures in the upper two bands wear simple unadorned Roman togas, while the saints below are clad in luxurious, ornate Byzantine textiles decorated with rare gems. The Roman figures appear against such natural three-dimensional backgrounds as the

green Sea of Galilee, hills, or a blue sky. The Byzantine virgins and martyrs, however, are set against a shimmering gold backdrop with uniformly spaced stylized palms. The candor, directness, and simplicity with which the Roman scenes are depicted likewise contrast strikingly with the impersonal, aloof, and symbolic Byzantine treatment of the nave frieze. Differences of theological as well as stylistic viewpoints are involved, since the Arian-Roman panels accent the Redeemer's worldly life and human suffering, and the Byzantine frieze accents His divinity and remoteness from worldly matters.

The art of mosaic, in general, depends for its effectiveness on directing the flow of light from many tiny reflectors. After the placement of the panels, the design, and the colors have been determined, the mosaicist must take into account both the natural source of light from windows and artificial sources from lamps or candles. Accordingly, the mosaicist fits each *tessera,* or small cube made of glass, marble, shell, or ceramic, onto an adhesive surface, tilting some this way, others that, so that a shimmering luminous effect is obtained.

Central-Type Churches: San Vitale

Little more than a year's time elapsed between the death of Theodoric and the accession of Justinian as emperor in Constantinople. In the politics of that day, the building of a church that would surpass anything undertaken by Theodoric would serve both as an assertion of Justinian's authority in Italy and as evidence of the weakening power of Theodoric's Ostrogothic successors. Almost immediately, therefore, Justinian decided to build the church of San Vitale at Ravenna (Fig. 120).

At first Justinian's position in the capital of the West Roman Empire was anything but certain, and the project languished. Eventually, the use of force was needed to assert his Italian claims, and his armies entered the city in the year 540. Thereafter, construction of San Vitale proceeded swiftly, and seven years later the church was ready for its dedication by Archbishop Maximian. Its plain red-brick exterior is proof that as little attention was paid to the outside of San Vitale as to that of any other church of the period. But with its rich multicolored marble walls, carved alabaster columns, pierced marble screens, and, above all, its sanctuary mosaics, the Church of San Vitale is a veritable jewel box.

Architecturally, San Vitale is a highly developed example of the central-type church (Fig. 121), differing radically from Sant' Apollinare Nuovo. Yet it has all the usual features of the basilica, including a narthex entrance, circular nave, surrounding side aisles, and a triumphal arch leading into a sanctuary with an apse and two side chambers. The striking difference, however, between an oblong basilica and a centralized church is the direction of its axis. In the former, the axis runs horizontally through the center of the building, dividing the church lengthwise into equal halves, the eye being led toward the apse. In the central-type building the axis is vertical, leading the eye upward from the central floor space to the dome. Were it not for the addition of the oblong narthex on the west and the apse on the east, San Vitale would be a simple octagon.

The two side chambers of the apse are usually associated with Eastern Orthodox churches. Their presence here points to the fact that San Vitale was designed as a theater for the Byzantine liturgy. The northern chamber was designated the *prothesis,* to indicate its use as the place where the communion bread and wine were prepared for the altar. In Eastern Orthodox usage, the sacrificial aspect of the mass assumed a dramatic character, and the sacramental bread was "wounded, killed, and buried" on the table of the prothesis before it appeared on the altar, where it symbolized the resurrection of the body. The southern chamber is called the *diakonikon* and served as the vestry and as a place to store the sacred objects used in the orthodox service.

Structural Counterparts   In order to understand San Vitale and central-type churches, one must look at similar buildings at Ravenna and elsewhere. While the ancestors of the rectangular basilica were Roman domestic and public buildings, the centralized church derives from ancient circular tombs such as Hadrian's colossal monument on the banks of the Tiber (see Fig. 108). The ancient preference for the circular mausoleum can be explained partly by its symbolism. Immortality was frequently represented by the image of a serpent biting its tail—that is, a living creature whose end was joined to its beginning. Another ancestor is the round classical temple, such as the Pantheon (see Figs. 100–102).

The idea of a church built in the same form as a tomb is by no means as somber as it might seem. In the Christian sense, a church symbolized the Easter tomb, reminding all of the resurrection of Christ. In His memory, churches were dedicated to martyrs and saints who were believed to be partaking of the heavenly life with Him, just as the faithful hoped that they themselves would one day be doing. The ancient Orphic cult had stressed the idea of the body being

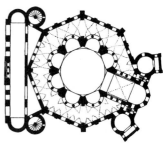

left: 120. Exterior of apse, San Vitale, Ravenna. c. 527–547. Diameter 112′ (34.14 m).

above: 121. Plan of San Vitale.

122. *Baptism of Christ and Procession of Twelve Apostles.* c. 520.
Dome mosaic.
Arian Baptistry, Ravenna.

the tomb of the spirit. Hence, death and resurrection were aspects of one and the same idea, and the martyr's death was a mystical union with Christ. Indeed, the altar itself was a tomb or repository for the sacred relics of the saint to whom the church was dedicated. Early altars in the catacombs actually were sarcophagi that served also as communion tables. Thus, in the rites of the church, the earthly past of Christ, His apostles, saints, and martyrs was commemorated, and, at the same time, the glorious heavenly future was anticipated.

The eight-sided Christian baptistry was taken over directly from the octagonal bathhouses found in ancient Roman villas. There the pool was usually octagonal and the structure around it assumed that shape. Early Christian baptisms involved total immersion, and the transition from bathhouse to baptistry was easy and natural. Since baptism is a personal and family affair, not calling for the presence of a congregation, baptistries usually are small.

The Arian Baptistry was built in Theodoric's time in the same style as the earlier "Neonian" Baptistry for the Roman Christians. Both are domed structures with the chief interest centered on the fine interior mosaics. Both have similar representations of the baptism of Christ on the interior surfaces of their *cupolas,* or domes. That of the Arian Baptistry (Fig. 122) shows the ceremony being performed by

St. John the Baptist, while the river Jordan is personified as an old man in the manner of the ancient pagan river gods (see Fig. 104).

Around the central scene are the twelve apostles, who move processionally toward the throne of Christ. Just as the virgins and martyrs reenacted the offertory procession above the nave arcade of Sant' Apollinare Nuovo, so the apostles here mirror the baptismal rites on a more heavenly level. They group themselves around the center above where Christ is being baptized, just as the clergy, family, and sponsors gathered about the font below for the baptism of some Ravenna Christian. Here is yet another example of the *iconography,* or subject matter, of the decorative scheme reflecting the liturgical activity that took place within the walls of the building.

Balancing domes over square or octagonal supporting structures was a preoccupation of 6th-century architects. The Romans had found one solution in the case of the Pantheon—resting the dome on supporting cylindrical walls—but in Ravenna later builders found two other solutions. The exquisite little mausoleum of Galla Placidia (Fig. 110), which dates from about A.D. 425, was built in the form of an equal-winged Greek cross. Its dome rests on *pendentives*—that is, on four concave spherical triangles of masonry rising from the square corners and bending inward to form the circular base of the dome

123–124. Circular domes can be raised over rectangular buildings by *pendentives* or *squinches.* Pendentives are vaults in the form of spherical triangles that connect arches springing from corner piers and unite at the apex of the arches to form a circular base upon which the dome rests. Squinches are stone lintels placed diagonally across corners to form a continuous base for the dome. Often the squinch is supported from below by masonry built up in wedge or arch formation.

left: 123. Pendentives
(shaded area)
supporting a dome.

right: 124. Squinches
(shaded area)
supporting a dome.

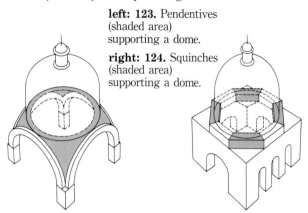

(Fig. 123). The role of the pendentives is to encircle the square understructure and make the transition to the domed superstructure. The Ravenna baptistries exemplify the same pendentive solution, but in their cases the domes rest on octagonal understructures.

Another solution stemming from the same early period is based upon a system of *squinches,* or pieces of construction placed diagonally across the angles of the square or octagonal walls of the understructure so as to form a proper base for a dome (Fig. 124). This was the method employed for the doming of San Vitale. The eight piers of the arcaded central room below rise and culminate in an octagonal drum on which, by means of squinches, the dome rests.

Above the nave arcade and beneath the dome, the builders of San Vitale included a vaulted triforium gallery running around the church and opening into the nave (Fig. 125). This gallery, which was called the *matroneum,* was for the use of women, who were more strictly segregated in the Byzantine rites.

The Eastern parallels of San Vitale are found in Justinian's churches at Constantinople—Sts. Sergius and Bacchus, among others. The great Hagia Sophia ("Sancta Sophia," or "Holy Wisdom"), however, is the foremost monument of the Byzantine style. As a combination of great art and daring engineering, Hagia Sophia has never been surpassed. Externally it is practically square with bulging *buttresses,* or masonry supports, and swelling half-domes mounting, by means of pendentives, to a full dome on top. Internally, from the narthex entrance on the west, the space opens into a large nave, and the eye is led horizontally to the apse in the east (Fig. 126). While the most ambitious Gothic cathedral nave never spanned a width of more than 55 feet (16.8 meters), the architects of Hagia Sophia achieved an open space 100 feet (30.5 meters) wide and 200 feet (60.9 meters) long.

From this discussion it should be obvious that the dome of the central-type structure unifies the separate structural members, and that the eye perceives this unity at a glance. In the interior of San Vitale (Fig. 125) the dome and its supports are clearly visible and the structure is therefore self-explanatory. Psychologically, this equilibrium is important for it produces a restful effect, which is in direct contrast with the restless interiors of later Gothic cathedrals (see Fig. 175). There the dynamic surge depends partly on the fact that the exterior buttressing is not apparent. Indeed, the dome of San Vitale is an interior fact only, because on the outside its octagonal base has been continued upward and roofed over.

125. Interior, San Vitale, Ravenna. 527–547 (clerestory decorations, 18th century).

Decorative Design   In the apse of San Vitale, facing the altar from opposite sides, are two panels in mosaic that portray the leading figures of the early Byzantine rule in Ravenna. On one, Emperor Justinian appears in the midst of his courtiers (Fig. 127). On the other, facing him as an equal, is Empress Theodora in all her sovereign splendor (Fig. 128). It is significant that the finest existing portrait of the great Emperor should be in mosaic rather than in the form of a sculptured bust, a bronze figure on horseback, or a colossal statue. It is just this medium that could best capture the unique spirit of his life and times. Concerned with the codification of Roman law, presiding at religious councils, and reconciling different political points of view, Justinian based his rule on the skillful use of legal and theological formulas as well as on naked military might. He is, then, represented as a symbol of unity between the spiritual force of the Church on one hand and the temporal power of the state on the other.

Preceding Justinian in the procession are the clergymen, among whom only Archbishop Maximian is identified by name. His crucifix is held up as an assertion of his power as the spiritual and temporal lord of Ravenna. On the Emperor's other side are his courtiers and honor guard holding their jeweled swords aloft. The shield with its Chrismon insignia points to the status of the soldiers as defenders of the faith. The Chrismon was a widely used monogram of the time, made up of the Greek letters *Chi* (X) and *Rho* (P), which together form the abbreviation of Christ. Somewhat more allegorically, the letters become a combination of the Cross and the shepherd's crook, which symbolize the Savior's death and pastoral mission.

In the center of the procession stands Justinian, clothed in all his magnificence and crowned with the imperial diadem. The observer knows immediately that this is no ordinary royal personage but rather one who could sign his name as the Emperor Caesar Flavius, Justinianus, Alamanicus, Francicus, Germanicus, Anticus, Alanicus, Vandalicus, Africanus, Pious, Happy, Renowned, Conqueror and Triumpher, ever Augustus. Great as Justinian's military exploits were, however, it is his works of peace that have endured. In addition to a vast building program, the Byzantine Emperor is remembered for his monumental code, the *Digest of Laws,* which prevailed for centuries throughout the Western world.

On her side, the Empress Theodora (Fig. 128), richly jeweled and clad in the imperial purple, is seen as she is about to make her entry into the church from the narthex. Possibly because of her humble origin as the daughter of the feeder of the bears at the circus of Constantinople and her stage career as an actress, Theodora appears more royal than the King. Her offering recalls a remark by Procopius, the chronicler of Justinian's reign. He said that she fed the geese of the devil while on the stage and the sheep of Christ when she sat on the throne. On the hem of her robe the offertory motif is carried out by the embroidered figures of the Three Wise Men, the first bearers of gifts to Christ. Since the Wise Men of old as well as Justinian and Theodora came from the East, this motif served as a reminder to the people of Ravenna that the source of wisdom and power lay in that direction.

These two mosaic portraits are especially precious because they are among the few surviving visual representations of the vanished glories of Byzantine courtly ceremonies. The regal pair appear as if participating in the offertory procession at the

126. Interior, Hagia Sophia, Istanbul (Constantinople). 532–537. Height of dome 183′ (55.78 m).

The Early Roman Christian and Byzantine Styles   **107**

127. *Emperor Justinian and Courtiers.* c. 547. Mosaic. San Vitale, Ravenna.

dedication of the church, which took place in the year 547—though neither was actually present on that occasion. Such ceremonial entries were a part of the elaborate Byzantine liturgy, and both the Emperor and Empress are shown as the bearers of gifts. On his side, Justinian is carrying the gold *paten,* which was used to hold the communion bread at the altar, while Theodora is presenting the chalice that contains the wine. Since their generosity was responsible for the building, decoration, and endowment of San Vitale, the allusion is to gifts of gold as well.

In keeping with the rigid conventions of Byzantine art, all the heads appear in one plane. Those of Justinian and Theodora are distinguished by their halos, which in this case not only refer to their awesome power but also are a carry-over of the semidivine status assumed by the earlier Roman emperors. Even though they are moving in a procession, they are portrayed frontally in the manner of imperial personages accustomed to receiving the homage of their subjects. In spite of the stylized medium, the eye can follow the solemn procession as it moves in

dignified measure, carried forward by the linear pattern in the folds of garments. The elegant costumes add to the richness of the scene, emphasizing by their designs the luxury of their Oriental origins.

In addition to the mosaics, the decorative design of San Vitale includes carved alabaster columns, *polychrome,* or multicolored marble wall panels, pierced marble choir screens, and many other details. The capitals of the columns are carved with intricate patterns, such as that in Figure 129.

The influence of San Vitale on subsequent western European architecture dates from the time of Charlemagne's conquest. So impressed was Charlemagne with this church that he not only carried off at least half of its original marble and mosaic decorations but also adopted its plan for his imperial chapel at Aachen. When the harmonious proportions of the building as a whole are combined with the rich optical effects of the mosaics, polychrome marble, and ornamental sculptures, San Vitale, as the counterpart of Hagia Sophia, is the high point of Byzantine art in the West.

128. *Empress Theodora and Retinue.* c. 547. Mosaic. San Vitale, Ravenna.

left: 129. Byzantine capital, San Vitale, Ravenna. c. 547.

Sculpture

From its status as a major art in Greco-Roman times, sculpture declined to a relatively modest place in the ranks of Early Christian arts. Instead of constituting a free and independent medium, it became primarily the servant of the architectural and liturgical forms of the Church. Even its classical three-dimensionality was in eclipse, and sculpture tended to become increasingly pictorial and symbolic as it assumed a teaching role in Early Christian usage.

When sculpture moved indoors, it underwent a radical change in relation to light and shade. A statue in the round, for instance, was either placed against a wall or stood in a niche, which prevented its being seen from all sides. The closeness in time and place to the pagan religions also served to channel Christian visual expression in other directions.

The Early Roman Christian and Byzantine Styles **109**

130. *Good Shepherd.* c. 350. Marble, height 39″ (99 cm). Vatican Museums, Rome.

With the influence of such pronouncements as the First Commandment that forbade the making of "graven images," it is remarkable that the art survived as well as it did.

A rare surviving example of three-dimensional Early Roman Christian sculpture is the *Good Shepherd* (Fig. 130). Figures of peasants carrying calves or sheep to market are frequently found in ancient Greek and Roman genre sculpture. In the Christian interpretation, however, the shepherd is Christ, the sheep the congregation of the faithful, and, when a jug of milk is included, the whole image refers to the Eucharist.

Characteristic Forms and Representations

Sculpture, in general, proved adaptable to the new demands and purposes. In the new frame of reference, architectural sculpture—capitals of columns, decorative relief panels, carved wooden doors, and, to some extent, statues in niches—continued with appropriate modifications. The principal emphasis, however, shifted toward objects associated with the new form of worship, such as altars, pulpits, pierced marble screens, and carved ivory reliefs. Smaller items, such as precious metal boxes for relics, lamps, incense pots, communion chalices, jeweled book covers, and patens, all with delicately worked designs, began to ally the former grand classical art more closely with that of the jeweler.

One of the strongest influences on Early Christian design was the new orientation of thought toward symbolism. As long as the religions of Greece and Rome were oriented toward the human form, sculptors could represent the gods as idealized human beings. But in Christian terms, how could they represent in concrete form such abstractions as the Trinity, the Holy Spirit, the salvation of the soul, or the idea of redemption through participation in the Eucharistic sacrifice? The solution could come only through use of parables and symbols. Thus the Christian idea of immortality could be rendered through biblical scenes of deliverance—Noah from the flood, Moses from the land of Egypt, Job from his sufferings, Daniel from the lion's den, the men from the fiery furnace, and Lazarus from his tomb.

In Early Christian relief panels, plant and animal motifs were included less for naturalistic reasons than to convey symbolic meaning. The dove represented the Holy Spirit, the peacock stood for Paradise, and so on. The Cross is seldom found in Early Christian art, since it recalled a punishment used for the lowest type of criminal. Instead, the Chrismon symbol already seen on the shield of Justinian's soldiers (see Fig. 127) was used. A fish, or the Greek word for it, *ichthys,* is often found as a reference to Jesus making His disciples fishers of men. The letters of the word also constituted an abbreviation for Jesus Christ Son of God, Savior. Such symbols and lettered inscriptions caused sculpture to assume the aspect of engraved designs on stone surfaces, which carried special meaning and mystical significance to the initiated worshipers.

Carved Stone Tombs   One of the chief forms of Early Roman Christian sculpture is the carved stone sarcophagus. The custom of burial above ground was carried over from late Roman times, and a special Christian incentive came from the desire for interment within the sacred precincts of the church. The relics of saints reposed in the altar. Tombs of bishops and other dignitaries were housed in the church. Those of the laity were usually placed out in the atrium. Survivals of this latter custom continue well into modern times with burials taking place in churchyards.

A fine Early Christian example is provided by the sarcophagus of Archbishop Theodore (Fig. 131). The front panel shows the combination of the Chrismon symbol with that of the first and last letters of the Greek alphabet, *Alpha* and *Omega,* another reference to Christ, taken from His statement that He was both the beginning and the end. Their inclusion here on a tomb indicates the end of earthly life and the beginning of the heavenly one. Flanking the symbols are two peacocks symbolizing Paradise and, on either side, a graceful vine pattern in which the small birds feeding on grapes refer symbolically to communion. The inscription reads in translation, "Here rests in peace Archbishop Theodore." On the lid are repetitions of the monogram below, here surrounded by the conventional laurel wreath symbolizing immortality. The end of the sarcophagus that shows in Figure 131 is carved to symbolize the Trinity. From the urn at the bottom springs the tree of life indicating the Father. Above it appear the cross for the Son and the descending dove as the Holy Spirit. The cross is repeated above on the end panel of the lid.

Maximian's Cathedra   By far the most impressive single example of sculpture of this period is the chair which is thought to be that of Archbishop Maximian (Fig. 132), Justinian's viceroy who is portrayed beside him in the mosaic panel in San Vitale (Fig. 127). Such an episcopal throne is called a *cathedra,* and the church in which it is housed is termed a *cathedral.* When a bishop addresses his congregation from it, he is said to be speaking *ex cathedra.* A cathedra may also be called a *sedes* (the Latin word for "seat"), from which word is derived the noun *see,* which once meant the seat of a bishop but now means the territory in the charge of a bishop. Originally *sedes* meant a chair denoting high position. Roman senators used such chairs on public occasions, and modern politicians still campaign for a "seat" in the senate or legislature. Both Jewish rabbis and Greek philosophers taught from a seated position; hence the reference in modern colleges to a "chair" of philosophy or history.

Maximian's cathedra consists of a composition of ivory panels, carefully joined together and delicately carved. Originally, there were 39 different pictorial panels, some of which told the Old Testament story of Joseph and his brethren, and the others, the story of Jesus. The chair is thought to have been presented to Maximian by Justinian, and the different techniques employed in the various panels indicate collaboration of craftsmen from Anatolia, Syria, and Alexandria. On the front panel, below Maximian's monogram, is a representation of St. John the Baptist flanked on either side by the Evangelists (Fig. 132). The Baptist holds a medallion on which a lamb is

above: 131. Sarcophagus of Archbishop Theodore. 6th century. Marble, 3'3½" × 6'9" (1 × 2.06 m). Sant' Apollinare in Classe.

below: 132. Cathedra of Maximian, front view. c. 546–56. Ivory panels on wood frame, 4'11" × 1'11⅝" (1.5 × 0.6 m). Archepiscopal Museum, Ravenna.

carved in relief, while the Evangelists hold their traditional books.

The elegant Byzantine carving of the front panel—with its complex grapevine motif intertwined with birds and animals denoting the tree of eternal life, the peacocks symbolizing heaven, the symmetrically arranged saints, and the luxuriant linear pattern of their classical drapery—lends itself best to just such a static, formal, stylized design. In the Joseph story illustrated in the side panels, however, the overriding concern is with an active narrative as related in a series of episodes. Content and vivid detail then rise above purely formal considerations.

While sculpture is not the outstanding Byzantine art, such intricate tracery and arabesque patterns become highly important. Since ivory does not make monumentality either possible or desirable, such details as these, handled with precision, are richer and more satisfying than the work as a whole.

At this formative phase, the Western and Eastern styles are not so separate and distinct as they tend to become in the later medieval period. The situation is also complicated by the fact that Roman artists could be summoned to work in Constantinople just as easily as Byzantine artists could be called to Rome or Ravenna. In general, however, one can conclude that the trend in the West was toward the long, rectangular basilica, while the East developed the central-type structure. In mosaics and sculpture, the Early Roman Christian style stays closer to the heritage of classical naturalism, with figures modeled three-dimensionally and appearing against landscape backgrounds. It also shows a preference for simpler designs employing recognizable motifs. The Byzantine style, on the other hand, moves more in the direction of flat two-dimensional surfaces, gold backgrounds, nonrepresentational designs, abstract geometrical forms, and luxurious arabesque patterns.

Music

From the writings of Theodoric's learned ministers Boethius and Cassiodorus, some knowledge about the status of musical thought in 6th-century Ravenna can be gained. Like the writings of the Church fathers and other literary figures of the day, however, these reveal much about the theory of the art and little about its practice.

Theoretical Discussions

Boethius was a tireless translator of Greek philosophical and scientific treatises into Latin, among which were no less than thirty books by Aristotle alone. When he fell from favor and was imprisoned,

Boethius wrote *The Consolation of Philosophy,* which became one of the most influential medieval books. Called by Gibbon "a golden volume not unworthy of the leisure of Plato or Tully [Cicero]," the *Consolation* later found its way into English via translations by Alfred the Great and Chaucer. Boethius' was a universal mind, capable of discoursing on anything from the mechanics of water clocks to astronomy.

Boethius' treatise on music became the common source of most medieval essays on the subject. In transmitting the best of ancient Greek musical theory, it became the foundation stone of Western musical thinking. Like the ancients before him, Boethius believed that "all music is reasoning and speculation," and hence more closely allied with mathematics than with the auditory art that music is today.

Boethius divided music into three classes, the first of which was the "music of the universe," by which he meant the unheard astronomical "music" of planetary motion. The second was "human music," which referred to the attunement of the mind and body, or the rational and irrational elements of the human constitution, in the manner of a Greek harmony of opposites. The third was instrumental music and song, of which he had the philosopher's usual low opinion, considering only the theoretical aspects of the art as pursuits worthy of a gentleman and scholar. The only true "musician" in his opinion was one "who possesses the faculty of judging, according to speculation or reason, appropriate and suitable to music, of modes and rhythms and of the classes of melodies and their mixtures . . . and of the songs of the poets."

Cassiodorus wrote in a similarly learned vein after he had retired from public life to the haven of his monastery at Vivarium. But while he was still involved in the affairs of Theodoric's kingdom, he was constantly called upon to solve every conceivable administrative problem. Among these was a request from Clovis, king of the Franks, for a *citharoedus*—that is, a singer who accompanied himself on the stringed instrument of the classical lyre type known as the cithara (see Figs. 76, 135). In search for such a musician, Cassiodorus turned to his fellow senator Boethius, who was in Rome at the time. His letter first launches into a flowery discourse on the nature of music, which he describes as the "Queen of the senses." It continues with endless discussions of its curative powers, how David cast out the evil spirit from Saul, the nature of the modes, the structure of the Greek scale system, and the history of the art. Then he comes to the lyre, which he calls "the loom of the Muses," and after going off on a few more tangents, he finally gets to the point. "We have indulged ourselves in a pleasant digression," he says, making the understatement of the millennium, "because it is always agreeable to talk of learning with the learned; but be sure to get us that *Citharoedus,* who will go forth like another Orpheus to charm the beast-like hearts of the Barbarians. You will thus obey us and render yourself famous."

Church Music

Knowledge about the church music of Ravenna at this time is based on conjecture and must be gathered from a variety of sources. From the writings of the Church fathers it is evident that great importance was attached to music in connection with divine worship. The problem was how to separate a proper body of church music from the crude idioms of popular music on one hand, and from the highly developed but pagan art music of Rome on the other. From St. Paul and the Roman writer Pliny the Younger, in the 1st and 2nd centuries respectively, it is known that the earliest Christian music sounded very much like the ancient Jewish singing of psalms. A fragment of an Early Christian hymn from the latter part of the 3rd century has been found at Oxyrhynchos in North Africa. From the Greek text and ancient musical notation, it is possible to establish its stylistic connection with the late Hellenistic musical tradition.

Hebrew, Greek, and Latin sources thus provided the basis for Early Christian music, just as they had done in the cases of theology and the visual arts. Out of these diverse elements and with original ideas of their own, the Christians of the Eastern and Western churches over the centuries gradually worked out a synthesis that resulted in a musical art of great power and beauty. The 6th century witnessed the culmination of many early experimental phases. At its close, the Western form of the art found official formulation in the body of music known as Gregorian Chant. In its various changes and restorations, as well as in its theoretical aspects, this system has remained the official basis of Roman Church music up to the Second Vatican Council that ended in 1965. Closely related forms are still in use throughout the Christian world, where free adaptations of its melodies have enriched the hymn books of nearly every denomination.

Arian Liturgy   Knowledge about the Arian liturgy, such as that which was practiced at Sant' Apollinare Nuovo during Theodoric's reign, is very obscure, because all sources were destroyed when the orthodox Christians gained the upper hand and stamped out the Arian heresy. From a few negative comments, however, it is known that hymn and psalm singing by the congregation as a whole was among the practices.

Aeterne rerum Conditor (after Dreves)
(hymn of St. Ambrose)

Arius, the founder of the Arian sect, was accused of insinuating his religious ideas into the minds of his followers by means of hymns that were sung to melodies derived from drinking songs and theatrical tunes. Such hymns were frowned upon in orthodox circles because they were too closely allied with popular music. Furthermore, the Arian way of singing them was described as loud and raucous, indicating that they must have grated on the ears of the more civilized Roman Christians.

Ambrosian Liturgy   The popularity of these musical practices, however, was such that the Arians were making too many converts. So in the spirit of fighting fire with fire, St. Ambrose, bishop of Milan, where the Arians were strong, compromised by introducing hymn and psalm singing into the Milanese church service.

A firsthand account of this practice is contained in a passage from St. Augustine's *Confessions.* In the 4th century, when Bishop Ambrose was engaged in one of his doctrinal disputes with the Byzantine Empress Justina, he and his followers at one point had to barricade themselves in a church for protection. "The pious people kept guard in the church, prepared to die with their bishop," wrote St. Augustine. "At the same time," he continues, "was it here first instituted after the manner of the eastern churches, that hymns and psalms should be sung, lest the people should wax faint through the tediousness of sorrow: which custom being retained from that day to this, is still imitated by divers, yea, almost by all thy congregations throughout other parts of the world."

The practice spread widely and was incorporated into the Roman liturgy during the following century. Since Ravenna was the neighboring see to that of Milan, the musical practices there must have been quite similar.

Some half-dozen hymns can be attributed to the authorship of St. Ambrose. Whether he also composed the melodies is not so certain, but they at least date from his time. From the example of *Aeterne rerum Conditor* (above), it can be seen that the extreme simplicity and metrical regularity of these vigorous Ambrosian hymns made them especially

Alleluia (Ambrosian chant of Byzantine origin) (after Wellesz)

suitable for congregational singing. The mosaics of Sant' Apollinare Nuovo show files of male and female saints on opposite sides of the nave arcade (Fig. 111). Below them, the men of the congregation were grouped on one side, while the women and children gathered on the other, thus forming two choirs.

The psalms were sung in two ways: antiphonally and responsorially. When the two choruses sing alternate verses, then join together in a refrain on the word *alleluia* after each verse, the practice is referred to as *antiphonal psalmody*. When the priest or leader chants one verse as a solo, and the choirs perform the next verse as a choral response, it is called *responsorial psalmody*. Both were widespread practices in the Western church, including Ravenna.

Byzantine Liturgy Since Sant' Apollinare Nuovo and San Vitale were designed for different purposes, it follows that their music must also have differed. As a part of the Byzantine liturgy, the music heard at San Vitale would have been like that of the cathedral in Constantinople. As in the West, congregational singing was included there at first, but, with the abandonment of the offertory procession, congregational singing was gradually replaced by that of a professional choir. Music for congregational singing must always be kept relatively simple, but with a truly professional group all the rich potentialities of the art can be explored and developed.

Since San Vitale, like Hagia Sophia, was under the direct patronage of the emperor, and since both formed a part of Justinian's grand design, provision for a group capable of performing the music of the Byzantine liturgy could hardly have been overlooked. The principal difference between the music of the Eastern and Western churches is that between a contemplative and an active attitude. The contemplative aspect of the Eastern liturgy is illustrated by a remark of St. John Chrysostom, who said that "one may also sing without voice, the mind resounding inwardly, for we sing not to men, but to God, who can hear our hearts and enter into the silences of the mind." This attitude contrasts strongly with that of St. Ambrose, who said in connection with the participation of the congregation in song: "If you praise the Lord and do not sing, you do not utter a hymn. . . . A hymn, therefore, has these three things: song and praise and the Lord."

In a static form of worship, greater rhythmic freedom is possible, while the chant that accompanies a procession must have more metrical regularity. The singing of a professional choir, furthermore, implies an elaborate and highly developed art, while the practice of congregational singing means the avoidance of technical difficulties. The difference, then, is the difference between the sturdy Ambrosian *syllabic* hymn (see p. 113)—that is, with a syllable allotted to each note—and the *melismatic* alleluia of Byzantine origin (above left)—that is, with each single syllable prolonged over many notes in the manner of a *cadenza*.

Byzantine music had a distinctive style of its own, comparable in this respect to that of the visual arts. The elaborate melismas of the latter example would have been heard in San Vitale and in other Byzantine churches at the end of the 6th century. It was precisely such excessively florid alleluias that were ruled out by the Gregorian reform which was to occur in the early 7th century.

Ideas

Since all the surviving monuments of Early Christian art are religiously oriented, it follows that the various sources of patronage, the geographical locations, and the liturgical purposes are the factors that determine the forms of architecture, the iconography of mosaics, the designs of sculpture, and the performance practices of music.

The Early Roman Christian and Byzantine styles were both Christian, and all the arts of the time lived, moved, and had their being within the all-embracing arms of Mother Church. But her Western and Eastern arms pointed in different stylistic directions. The disintegrating Roman power in the West led to decentralization of authority and allowed a wide range in local and regional styles, while the Byzantine emperors kept tight autocratic control of all phases of secular and religious life. Early Roman Christian art was more an expression of the people. It involved all social levels, its quality varied from crude to excellent, and it was more simple and direct in its approach. Byzantine art, however, was under the personal patronage of a prosperous emperor who ruled both as a Caesar and a religious patriarch. Only the finest artists were employed; and the arts, like the vertical axis of a centralized church, directed

Europe at Death of Theodoric, 526

miles
0   200   400

0   200   400
kilometers

FRISIANS

SAXONS

SLAVIC PEOPLES

THURINGIANS

KINGDOM OF FRANKS

Tours

LOMBARDS

WEST ROMAN EMPIRE

Ostrogoths

BURGUNDIANS   KINGDOM OF OSTROGOTHS

Milan

Ravenna
Classe

BASQUES

SUEVES

KINGDOM OF WEST GOTHS

Trade Route

Rome

BLACK SEA

Constantinople
(Byzantium)

ANATOLIA

Nicaea

Caesarea

EAST ROMAN EMPIRE

Vivarium

Tralles

Miletus

SYRIA

KINGDOM OF VANDALS

MEDITERRANEAN SEA

Alexandria

attention to the highest level and tended to become more removed from the people and more purely symbolic. As the arts of both West and East pass by in review, two ideas seem to be the clues to their understanding: authoritarianism and mysticism.

Authoritarianism

Ravenna in the 6th century was the scene of a three-way struggle among a barbarian king who was a champion of Roman culture, a Byzantine emperor who claimed the prerogatives of the past golden age, and a Roman pope who had little military might but a powerful influence based on the succession of spiritual authority derived from Christ's apostles. As the conflict shaped up, it was among an enlightened worldly liberalism, a traditionalism based on a divinely ordered social system, and a new spiritual institution with a genius for compromise.

In the course of the century, the Ostrogothic kingdom was vanquished by the Byzantine Empire.

However, after a brief period of domination, Byzantine power in the West crumbled, and the political and military weakness that followed became the soil that nurtured the growth of the new Rome. By the end of the century, Gregory the Great had succeeded in establishing the papacy as the authority that eventually was to dominate the medieval period in the West, while the Eastern Empire continued in its traditional Byzantine forms of organization.

The principle of authority was by no means foreign to Christianity, which grew to maturity in the later days of the Roman Empire. With Christianity an official state religion under the protection of the emperors, Christian organization increasingly reflected the authoritarian character of the imperial government. Roman Christian philosophers, such as Boethius and Cassiodorus, cited the authority of Plato and Aristotle on all matters. Theologians accepted the authority of the divinely inspired Scriptures and the commentaries on them by the early Church fathers.

The thought of the period was expressed in constant quotations and requotations, interpretations and reinterpretations of ancient Hebrew, Greek, Latin, and early Christian authors. No one was willing or able to assume complete and independent authority for a position; on all issues one had to cite ancient precedents. The intellectual climate produced by these Church fathers paved the way for the mighty struggle for political and spiritual authority. The only remaining question was what form the authority was to assume, and who would exercise it.

Authoritarianism and the Arts Justinian, who claimed the authority and semidivine status of the old Roman emperors, lived in an atmosphere so unchanging and conservative that the words *originality* and *innovation* were used at his court only as terms of reproach. Despite the high price, Byzantine civilization purchased only a blanket uniformity. The principal creative energies of the period were channeled into aesthetic expression, largely because there was no other direction in which to move.

Only in the arts was any variety and freedom to be found. Here again the art of both Church and state was under the sole patronage of the emperor. It was then all the more remarkable that such a flowering as that which produced Hagia Sophia in Constantinople and San Vitale in Ravenna could have taken place. In both of these instances, the methods of construction were experimental, and the solution developed in response to the architectural and decorative problems was uninhibited and daring.

The Byzantine concept of authority was embodied in the architectural and decorative plans of both Hagia Sophia and San Vitale. The central-plan church, with its sharp hierarchical, or ranked, divisions that set aside places for men and women, clergy and laity, aristocrat and commoner, was admirably suited to convey the principle of imperial authority. The vertical axis culminated in a dome that overwhelmed Byzantine subjects by reminding them, when they were in the presence of the Supreme Authority, of their humble place in the scheme of things. The august imperial portraits in the sanctuary showed them that, outside the clergy, only the emperor and empress and those who occupied the top rungs of the social ladder might approach the altar of God. They might not even presume to bring forward gifts to the altar in the offertory procession. Since all material things came within the province of Caesar, the exalted duty of making the offering was his alone.

Byzantine worshipers, furthermore, were not even allowed to raise their voices in God's praise, as it was also the emperor's prerogative to provide a chorus of qualified professional musicians whose

privilege this was. The attitude of reverence was not only to God alone but also to His representatives on earth. The imperial portraits left no doubt about that. The majesty of God was felt through the infinite power of government. By means of the solemn rituals of sacred and courtly ceremonies, both spiritual and secular authority were imposed on the Byzantines from above. Their place in this world was inexorably determined; and their human dignity was in proportion to the blandness of their acceptance of a unified ideal of one Christian empire with one Church, one emperor, and one body of laws.

On the other hand, as typical forms of the basilica, Sant' Apollinare Nuovo (Figs. 111, 112) and its companion Sant' Apollinare in Classe (Figs. 133, 134) indicated a contrasting conception of both God and human beings. As the twin rows of columns on either side of the nave marched forward, they carried the eyes and footsteps of the faithful with them. The approach to the sacred precincts was encouraged rather than forbidden, and even the gift of the poor widow's pittance (Mark 12:41-42; Luke 21:2) was acknowledged in one of the mosaic panels above.

Just as the congregation had gone forth from the doors of their homes to the house of the Lord, in the mosaics the processions of saints likewise moved out of the gates of the twin cities of Classe and Ravenna. The rites they attended were not so incomprehensible and fearsome that they had to be enacted behind curtains and choir screens, as they had been in the Byzantine liturgy. In the West they took place in the open, and ordinary men and women enjoyed the privilege of ministering to the Lord. The spatial divisions of the oblong basilica, to be sure, still allowed for differences of status, such as that of men and women, choir and clergy. The allowance for all to participate in the sacred service, however, modified the authoritative concept, so that there was some religious freedom.

Mysticism

The art of the 6th century in Ravenna, like that of such other important centers as Constantinople and Rome, makes the transition from the classical Greco-Roman to the medieval world. While some of the ancient grandeur remained, the accent on symbolism laid the foundation for the coming medieval styles. The physical was replaced by the psychical, the rational road to knowledge by intuitive revelation.

World of Symbols Many of the older art forms were carried over and reinterpreted in a new light. The Roman bathhouse became the Christian baptistry where the soul was cleansed of original sin, and the public basilica was redesigned for church mys-

right: **133.** Exterior of apse, Sant' Apollinare in Classe. c. 530.

below left: **134.** Interior of apse, Sant' Apollinare in Classe. c. 530.

below right: **135.** *Christ as Orpheus.* 4th century A.D. Marble, height 40¼″ (102 cm). Byzantine Museum, Athens.

teries. Mosaics, which formerly were used for Hellenistic and Roman floors and pavements, became the mural medium for mystical visions. The shepherd of classical genre sculpture became symbolically the Good Shepherd. Classical bird and animal motifs became symbols for the soul and the spiritual realm. Music became a reflection of the divine unity of God and mortals, and the classical lyre, because of its stretched strings on a wooden frame, was reinterpreted by St. Augustine as a symbol of the crucified flesh of Christ. Orpheus, by means of its sounds, had descended into the underworld and overcome death. Christ is therefore frequently represented as playing on the lyre (Fig. 135), and at Sant' Apollinare Nuovo he is seated on a lyre-backed throne.

The concept of space turned from the limited classical three-dimensional representation of the natural world to an infinite Christian two-dimensional symbolic world. Invisible things rose in importance above those that could be seen with the eyes. While

the classical mind had regarded the world objectively from without, the Early Christian mind contemplated the soul subjectively from within. Socrates once asked an artist whether he could represent the soul. The reply was: "How can it be imitated, since it has neither shape nor colour . . . and is not visible at all?" St. Augustine also observed that "beauty cannot be beheld in any bodily matter."

Such mystical visions could be perceived only through symbolism. While natural science had been the foundation stone of ancient philosophy, symbolic theology became the foundation of Christian philosophy. Whereas Greek drama (which was a form of religious experience) had reached its climax step by step with remorseless logic, the Christian drama (as expressed in the liturgy) kindled the fires of faith and arrived at its mystical climax by intuitive means. The denial of the flesh and the conviction that only the soul can be beautiful doomed classical bodiliness and exalted bodilessness. Instead of capturing and clothing the godlike image with flesh and blood, the new concern was with releasing the spirit from the bondage of the flesh.

Liturgy as Embodiment of Mysticism   The liturgy was the great creation and the all-inclusive medium shaped during this period to convey the otherworldly vision. The thought, action, and sequence of the rites of Constantinople, Ravenna, Rome, and other centers determined to a large extent the architectural plans of churches, the symbolism of the mosaics, and the forms of the sculpture and music. At this time, the fruits of generations of contemplative and active lives gradually ripened into mature structures. The content of centuries of theoretical speculation united with the practical efforts of countless generations of writers, builders, decorators, and musicians to produce the Byzantine liturgy in the East and the synthesis of Gregory the Great in the West. Removed from its primary religious association and seen in a more detached aesthetic light, the liturgy as a work of art embodies a profound and dramatic insight into the deepest longings and highest aspirations of the human spirit.

During the 6th century the controversy still raged as to whether Christ's nature was essentially human or divine. The more the Eastern view emphasized Christ's divinity, the more remote He became. One of the prayers of St. John Chrysostom begins: "O Lord, our God, Whose power is inconceivable and glory incomprehensible, Whose mercy is immeasurable and tenderness to man unspeakable. . . ."

Such a conception makes highly presumptuous any attempt to comprehend the divine essence by reason or by direct representation. Hence the mosaics of San Vitale weave such abstract symbols as that of the Chrismon into a rich arabesque of ornate designs. Strict symmetry and other means were employed to raise the representation out of the plane of reality and thus to widen the immeasurable gulf between divinity and humanity. The dim lighting, the golden glow of the mosaics, the mysterious symbols whose meaning it was the privilege of Christians to contemplate—all helped conjure up this incomprehensible and invisible divinity. The most sacred rites took place behind carved alabaster screens. The words addressed from Maximian's carved ivory chair took on a superhuman impressiveness. All these conveyed the mystical idea and awakened the vision of eternity in the minds of the beholders.

The Early Roman Christian and Byzantine styles were responses to the need for new verbal, visual, and auditory modes of expression. In both cases, there was a shift from the forms designed to represent this world to those capable of conjuring up otherworldly visions. Through the poetry of language, the dancelike patterns of step and gesture, and the exalted melodies of the chant, the gripping drama of humanity embodied in the liturgy was enacted in awe-inspiring theaters that were furnished with an impressive array of stage settings, decor, costumes, and props created by the inspired hands of the finest craftsmen and artists of the time. The liturgy is, moreover, a continuous pageant. It lasts not only for a few hours, but unfolds with constant variation during the continuous sequence of solemn and joyful feasts through the weeks, months, and seasons of the calendar year, the decades, centuries, and millennia.

6
The Monastic Romanesque Style

The Monastery at Cluny, Late 11th and Early 12th Centuries

The most typical expression of the Romanesque period was the monastery. The life of ancient Athens and Pergamon had culminated in the clusters of their acropolis buildings, that of Rome had been realized in its forums and civil-engineering projects, while Constantinople and Ravenna had evolved the basilica and palace as the Church and state sides of a divinely ordered social system. In the Gothic period that succeeded the Romanesque it was to be the cathedral.

As Christianity had spread northward after the fall of the West Roman Empire, southern classical forms had met and merged with those of the northern barbarian peoples. This union of the older settled Roman civilization, with its ideals of reason, restraint, and repose, and the newly awakened spirit of the north, with its restless energy and brooding imagination, resulted in the Romanesque. This new style reached its maturity between the years 1000 and 1150.

Lacking the security of strong central governments and without the advantages of flourishing cities and towns, the monastic movement sought peace of mind in the abbey as a haven from the storm-tossed seas of the chaotic social surroundings. In these centers off the beaten path were built miniature worlds that contained a cross section of Romanesque life. Besides serving as a religious shrine where pilgrims could gather to revere sacred relics, the monastery was the manufacturing and agricultural center of its region as well as a seat of learning, a source for civilization where the only libraries, schools, and hospitals of the time were to be found.

The largest and grandest of all Romanesque monasteries was the abbey at Cluny. In Figure 136 Kenneth J. Conant has reconstructed its appearance

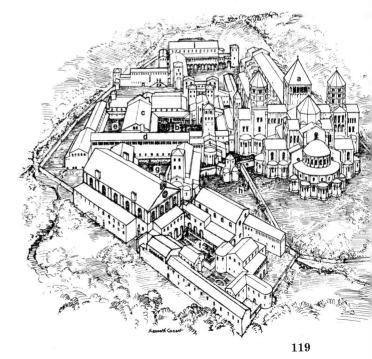

136. Abbey of Cluny, from southeast. c. 1157.
Reconstruction by Kenneth J. Conant.
Third Abbey Church, with lantern tower over crossing of nave and major transept (a); Cloister of Pontius, main cloister (b); refectory (c); monks' dormitory (d); novices' cloister (e); visitors' cloister (f);
Cloister of Notre Dame (g); monks' cemetery (h); hospice (i); craftsmen's quarters and stables (j).

CHRONOLOGY
Monastic Romanesque Period

GENERAL EVENTS

480–	543	St. Benedict founded European monasticism; c.529 built abbey at Monte Cassino, Italy
768–	814	Charlemagne ruled at Aix-la-Chapelle (Aachen); Carolingian Period initiated
c.792–	800	Centula monastery built by Charlemagne
c.796–	804	Palatine Chapel at Aix-la-Chapelle built
	800	Charlemagne crowned Holy Roman emperor in Rome by pope
	c.800	St. Gall (Switzerland) monastery begun
	910	Abbey of Cluny in Burgundy, France, founded
927–	942	Odo, abbot of Cluny, reputed author of musical treatises
	962	Otto the Great (936–973) crowned Holy Roman emperor
994–	1049	Odilo, abbot of Cluny
c.995–c.1050		Guido of Arezzo, author of musical treatises, inventor of staff notation
1000–	1150	Romanesque period at height
1049–	1109	Hugh of Semur, abbot of Cluny
	1050	Holy Roman

		Empire at height; ascendancy of papal power
	1063	Pisa Cathedral begun
	1066	William, duke of Normandy, conquered England; reigned as king of England, 1066–87
1071–	1112	Pilgrimage church at Santiago de Compostela, Spain, built
	1072	St. Peter Damian died
1073–	1085	Gregory VII (Hildebrande), pope
	1077	Emperor Henry IV bowed to Pope Gregory VII at Canossa; Abbot Hugh of Cluny mediated
	c.1080	Church of Sant' Ambrogio begun at Milan
c.1080–	1160	Church of St. Sernin built at Toulouse, France
1088–	1099	Urban II; Cluniac pope
1088–	1130	Great Third Church at Cluny built (1088 Cluny III begun under Hugh of Semur by architect Hezelo; 1095 apse dedicated by Pope Urban II; 1120 church finished; 1125 nave vaults partially

		collapsed; 1131 church dedicated by Pope Innocent X)
	1095	Urban II preached the First Crusade
1096–	1120	Abbey Church of La Madeleine at Vézelay built (1096 church begun; 1104 original Romanesque choir and transept dedicated; 1110 nave finished; 1120 narthex begun and nave revaulted after fire; c.1130 tympanum over the central portal of narthex; 1132 dedicated)
	1098	Cistercian order founded; opposed Cluniac order; St. Bernard of Clairvaux was its principal spokesman
	1109	Pontius became abbot of Cluny
	1122	Peter the Venerable became abbot of Cluny
c.1130–	1135	Gislebertus carved sculptures at St. Lazare, Autun
1168–	1188	Matteo carved Pórtico de la Gloria at Cathedral of Santiago de Compostela, Spain

at the pinnacle of its power and fame. Within these walls, men of contemplation were to be found beside men of action; those who were world-weary dwelled side by side with those who knew little of life beyond the cloister; saints brushed shoulders with criminals who sought refuge from the prosecution of secular authorities.

Those who were drawn to the vocation of monk were firm believers in the seeming paradox in Christ's words: "For whosoever will save his life shall lose it: but whosoever will lose his life for my sake, the same shall save it" (Luke 9:24). By taking the triple vows of poverty, chastity, and obedience, the monk automatically renounced such worldly pursuits as individual material rewards, the pleasures of the senses, the personal satisfactions of family life, and even the exercise of his own free will. According to the Rule of St. Benedict, the founder of European

137. Cloister, Abbey of St. Trophîme, Arles. c. 1100.

monasticism, a monk "should have absolutely not anything; neither a book, nor tablets, nor a pen—nothing at all . . . it is not allowed to the monks to have their own bodies or wills in their power."

In order to provide such a life, a monastery had to be planned so that the monks would have all that was necessary for both their bodily existence and their spiritual nourishment. The objective was to be as independent of Caesar as possible so as to render their all unto God. The Benedictine Rule did not prescribe the exact form that a monastic building should take, and, nominally, each abbey was free to solve its problems according to its needs, the contours of its site, and the extent of its resources. But tradition often operated as rigidly as rules, and with local variations most monasteries followed a common pattern. If one allows for the exceptional size and complexity due to its status as mother house of a great order, the plan of Cluny can be accepted as reasonably typical.

Since the life of a Cluniac monk was one of almost continuous religious duties alternating with periods for contemplation, the soul of the monastery was in its abbey church, and its heart was in its cloister (Fig. 137). The church served primarily as the scene of the constant devotional activities of the monks day and night throughout the year. Only secondarily was it a shrine for the streams of pilgrims who arrived from near and far to revere relics of saints.

Cluny was rich in relics, and on the feastdays of the saints, pilgrims flocked there as they did to other famous shrines, such as that of the Apostle James at Santiago de Compostela in Spain (see map, p. 134). European pilgrimage routes were traveled mainly by foot. There were hospices at 20-mile (32-kilometer)

intervals where after a day's journey, travelers could eat and sleep. Pilgrims from England had to cross the Channel. Those from Germany traveled south by way of the St. Bernard Alpine passes. Pilgrims to the Holy Land went by ship from Genoa, Venice, or Silicly with stops at Cyprus, Constantinople, or Rhodes.

Next in importance to facilities for the church services was the provision for the contemplative life that centered on the cloister. The cloister is found, typically, in the center of the abbey and south of the nave of the church. The other monastic buildings cluster around it. The usual cloister was an open quadrangular garden plot enclosed by a covered arcade on all four sides. The somewhat irregular shape of the cloister at Cluny in the 12th century resulted from the ambitious building program required by the rapid growth of the monastery. Since this renowned marble-columned cloister no longer exists, the one of St. Trophîme at Arles will serve as an example (Fig. 137).

Such a complete abbey as Cluny had to provide for many other functions. The daily life of the monks demanded a refectory where they could eat their meals in common, plus kitchens, bakeries, and storage space. There was also a chapter hall where they could transact their communal business, and a dormitory adjacent to the church, for services were held during the night as well as by day. Three small cloisters were included—one for the education of novices (young future members of the order), another for visiting monks and religiously inclined laymen who sought refuge from the world, and a third, near a cemetery, for the aged and infirm brothers. The *hospice,* or guesthouse, provided accommodations for visitors who flocked in during the pilgrimage season. There were also quarters for blacksmiths, carpenters, cobblers, and the like, as well as stables for dairy cattle and other domestic animals.

The plan of Cluny was thus a coherent system of adjoining quadrangles that embraced courts and cloisters whose variation in size and importance accommodated the differing activities they were designed to serve. Altogether, it was a highly complex and at the same time logical plan for a complete community. It took into account the ideals, aspirations, practices, and everyday activities of a group that gathered to work physically and spiritually toward a common end.

Architecture

Hugh of Semur, greatest of the Cluniac abbots, succeeded Odilo in the year 1049. Under Hugh, Cluny was destined to attain a period of such splendor that it could be described by an enthusiastic chronicler as "shining on the earth like a second sun." Taking as his model the accepted feudal organization of society, in which smaller and more dependent landowners swore allegiance to the larger and more powerful landlords in return for protection, Hugh began to bring many of the traditionally independent Benedictine monasteries into the Cluniac orbit. With the express approval of the popes, Hugh gradually concentrated the power of the whole order in his hands and transformed Cluny into a vast monastic empire that extended from Scotland in the north, Portugal in the west, Jerusalem in the east, and Rome in the south. In the Church hierarchy he was outranked only by the pope. In the secular world he was the peer of kings.

Hugh figured prominently in most of the historical events of his day. He even acted as intermediary between an emperor and a pope on the famous occasion at Canossa, when Henry IV came on bended knee to beseech Gregory VII for forgiveness. Hugh's greatest moment, however, came when Pope Urban II, who had received training as a monk at Cluny under Hugh's personal guidance, was present to dedicate the high altar of his great new abbey church. Honor after honor was bestowed upon the monastery by this Cluniac pope, who was also the preacher of the First Crusade.

Third Abbey Church
at Cluny

With such a rapidly expanding monastic order Hugh had to undertake a massive building program. The ever-increasing number of Cluniac monks and the growing importance of Cluny as a pilgrimage center made the older second church inadequate. So to rival the legendary temple of Solomon and to eclipse all other churches in Western Christendom, Hugh, with his architect Hezelo, began the immense new Third Abbey Church.

In contrast to the simpler Early Christian basilicas (compare Figs. 111, 112), Romanesque abbey churches show remarkable extensions before and beyond the nave (Fig. 138). The three-aisled narthex entrance has grown to the size of a large church in itself. It was, in fact, called variously the "church of the pilgrims" and the "minor nave." Besides accommodating these devout visitors, the narthex was the assembly place for the clergy who marched in the grand processions on high holidays, such as feastdays of saints.

The spacious five-aisled nave itself allowed pilgrims and townspeople to gather for religious services, while the space beyond was expanded for the large monastic community. Instead of a single transept there are now two. Extending outward from both the major and minor transepts are chapels dedicated to various saints, each the size of a small church. The apse is enlarged to accommodate the huge high altar, and an *ambulatory,* or passage for pilgrims and processions, is provided to reach the *apsidal chapels* that radiate outward from the apse, as the term implies. An exterior view of these apsidals can be seen in Figure 139.

Unlike later Gothic cathedrals, the exterior of the abbey church was unadorned by sculpture. All such embellishments were concentrated on the interior. Even the western façade remained bare, since it was designed for an introspective, cloistered community and had no need to extend sculptured invitations to the world outside, as did later city churches.

On entering the nave (Fig. 140), the mighty proportions of the huge basilica loomed up. From the entrance portal to the end of the apse, it extended a distance of 415 feet (126.5 meters). The entire horizontal axis from front to back, including the narthex, reached an overall length of 615 feet (187 meters). The nave itself had eleven *bays,* or arched units between the supporting columns, that stretched forward a distance of 260 feet (79 meters). Each bay was separated by a group of columns clustered around supporting piers. As the architectural counterpart of the monks, they marched in solemn procession toward the climax of the building at the high altar. In width, the nave spread outward 118 feet (35.9 meters) and was divided into five aisles. This division responded in part to the need to provide extra space for altars, since it was now the custom for each monk to say mass every day.

The outside aisles, extending all the way around the church and choir, gave pilgrims access to these

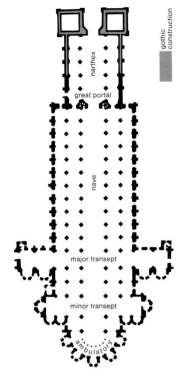

138. Plan of Third Abbey Church of Cluny. c. 1120.

gothic construction

narthex

great portal

nave

major transept

minor transept

ambulatory

139. Exterior of apse, St. Sernin, Toulouse. c. 1080. Height of lantern tower 215′ (65.53 m).

140. Hezelo. Nave, Third Abbey Church of Cluny. 1088–1130. Reconstruction by Kenneth J. Conant.

numerous altars and, more especially, to the smaller chapels in the choir without disturbing the monastic liturgy. The aisles also provided more room for the grand processionals that distinguished the Cluniac liturgy and that demanded ever more impressive and spacious settings.

It can be seen in Figure 140 that a stone screen was placed across the nave to close off the space set aside for the monks' choir. The great height of the church was such that the screen did not break the impression of a unified whole. The eye was drawn aloft to the tall columns around the high altar and above them, in turn, to the towering figure of Christ, which, gazing downward as if in a vision, was painted in the fresco technique on the interior of the half-dome of the apse.

Whereas the Early Roman Christian basilicas basically were horizontally directed, the Romanesque examples, because of the northern influence, raised the levels of the nave upward vertically. Gradually, this resulted in more and more accent being placed on the parts of the building above the nave arcade. At Cluny, a double row of windows was found, the lower of which was filled in with masonry, while the upper remained open and served as the clerestory for illumination. Though it had numerous windows, the church drew criticism from later Gothic builders as being too dark. Its thick walls and massive propor-

141. Tympanum, Abbey Church of La Madeleine, Vézelay. c. 1120–32.

tions allowed little direct sunlight to penetrate into the church itself. This was not of great importance, because so much of the monastic liturgy took place at night when the interior was illuminated by candlelight. Churches designed for city people who worshiped by day naturally had to pay more attention to lighting problems.

The nave at Cluny was spanned by ribbed barrel vaulting, 32 feet (9.8 meters) in width, supported by slightly pointed arches. Rising a full 98 feet (29.8 meters) above the pavement, the vaults were the highest achieved up to this time. But the emotional exuberance of attaining such height outran the engineering knowledge needed to maintain it, and a part of the Cluny vaulting soon collapsed. Out of this accident came experimentation with external buttressing so that when the vaults were rebuilt, a range of supports with open round arches was placed outside on the aisle roofs. Cluny thus achieved the distinction of being the first church to have external buttresses supporting its nave vaults. With its pointed arches and high vaulting in addition to external buttresses, Cluny combined for the first time three of the features that future builders would employ to make the unified system characteristic of the great Gothic cathedrals: high ribbed vaulting, pointed arches, and flying buttresses.

The decorative plan of the church was carried out on a scale comparable in quality to the grandeur of its spatial dimensions. More than 1200 sculptured capitals surmounted the columns of the structure, while carved moldings outlined the graceful pointed arches of the nave arcade. Most of the sculpture was painted in rich colors that gave an added glow to the splendor of the interior, and the whole church was paved with mosaic floors inlaid with images of saints and angels or with abstract designs.

All this magnificence did not go unchallenged. St. Bernard, the vigorous opponent of the Cluniac order, disapproved violently of such extravagances. By doing so in writing he inadvertently left a first-hand account of the glory of Hugh's church soon after it was finished. In a letter to one of the Cluniac abbots, he deplored (with Cluny in mind) "the vast height of your churches, their immoderate length, their superfluous breadth, the costly polishings, the curious carvings and paintings which attract the worshiper's gaze and hinder his attentions." His feeling was that "at the very sight of these costly yet marvelous vanities men are more kindled to offer gifts than to pray. . . . Hence the church is adorned with gemmed crowns of light—nay, with lustres like cart-wheels, girt all round with lamps, but no less brilliant with precious stones that stud them. Moreover we see candelabra standing like trees of massive bronze, fashioned with marvelous subtlety of art, and glistening no less brightly with gems than with the lights they carry. What, think you, is the purpose of all this? The compunction of penitents, or the admiration of beholders?"

Cluny Abbey stood proudly until the year 1798, when a wave of anticlericalism swept France in the wake of the Revolution, causing the abbey to be sacked and burned. All the buildings except a single transept wing were blown up by gunpowder, and the rubble was sold as common building stone. Some sculptural fragments survive, and the spirit of the great monastery lives on in the influence it exerted on such related structures as St. Trophîme at Arles (Fig. 137), St. Sernin in Toulouse (Fig. 139), and La Madeleine at Vézelay (Figs. 141–143).

Sculpture

Some of the finest sculpture that dates from the period of Cluny's grandeur is in the abbey church of La Madeleine at Vézelay. The nave and narthex are contemporary with Hugh's church at Cluny, and the intelligent restoration in the 19th century by the French medieval archaeologist Viollet-le-Duc accounts for their present good condition. While its proportions are considerably smaller than those of the great basilica at Cluny, La Madeleine today is the largest Romanesque abbey church in France. Rich in historical associations, it derived its principal fame in medieval times as the repository of the relics of St. Mary Magdalene.

The principal interest at Vézelay, however, is the seemingly inexhaustible wealth of sculptured capitals and, above all, the relief compositions over its three portals leading from the narthex into the nave and side aisles. For the first time since antiquity, monumental sculpture appears. In Romanesque churches it was used in the *tympanums* (the space enclosed by the lintel and arch) over the portals, the largest and most intricate sculpture being used in the tympanum over the central doorway.

Tympanum at Vézelay

The splendid tympanum over the central portal at Vézelay (Fig. 141) is from the first quarter of the 12th century. In its iconography and design, it is by far the most complex Romanesque tympanum, yet the logical division of space keeps the composition from seeming cluttered or confused. Here, as elsewhere, Romanesque designers and sculptors looked for their subjects and models in the drawings and miniature paintings that illustrated the texts of the Scriptures in monastic libraries. Such illuminated manuscripts provided convenient models that the monks could show to the sculptors who were to carry out the projects. At Vézelay, the robe of Christ, as well as those of the apostles, reveals a pattern of clear, sharp, swirling lines that stems from pen drawings in manuscripts of the time.

The interpretation of the tympanum scene may be found in the vision of St. John as recorded in Revelation (22:1–2): "And he shewed me a pure river of water of life, clear as crystal, proceeding out of the throne of God and of the Lamb. In the midst of the street of it, and on either side of the river, was there the tree of life, which bare twelve manner of fruits, and yielded her fruit every month: and the leaves of the tree were for the healing of nations."

The figure of Christ dominates the composition, seated, as St. John says, on "a great white throne," but not so much to judge mortals as to redeem them. While the figure is supremely majestic, Christ is not crowned. The streams issuing from his fingers descend upon the barefooted apostles, who bring spiritual understanding through the books they hold in their hands and physical healing through the divine mercy which they transmit to humanity. On one side of Christ's head, the water referred to in the quotation flows forth, while on the other are the branches of the tree.

The 12 fruits, one for each month, are found among the 29 medallions in the middle band of *archivolts,* the series of arches that frame the tympanum. A figure treading grapes, for example, represents September; October is symbolized by a man gathering acorns for his pigs. The months themselves, besides being connected with these labors, are also symbolized by the signs of the zodiac that, in turn, remind humans of the limited time they have in which to attain salvation. A few of the other medallions picture strange exotic beasts taken from the *bestiaries,* those curious books of the time that recounted the lore about animals actual and fabulous. A survival from antiquity can be noted in the medallion (lower right) that depicts a centaur.

The inner band of the archivolt is divided into eight irregular compartments that contain figures representing the nations which the leaves of the tree of life are intended to heal. The one on the top left, next to the head of Christ, contains two dog-headed men, called by the Spanish prelate and scholar Isidore of Seville in his *Etymologies* the "Cynocephaloi," a tribe supposed to have inhabited India. The corresponding compartment on the right side shows the crippled and bent figure of a man and that of a blind woman taking a few halting steps as she is led forward. In the other compartments, the lame supported on crutches are found along with lepers, who point toward their sores.

Along the lintel below, a parade of the nations converges toward the center. While the compartments above picture those in physical distress, here are the pagans and heathens who need spiritual aid. Among these strange peoples who populate the remote regions of the earth are a man and woman (in the far right corner) with enormous ears and feathered bodies. Next to them is a group of dwarfs or pygmies, so small they have to mount a horse by means of a ladder. On the far left, half-naked savages are hunting with bows and arrows, while toward the left center some heathens are shown leading a bull to sacrifice.

In the center stands St. John the Baptist holding a medallion with the image of the lamb on it. This is doubtless intended to convey the explanation that the "river of water of life" is baptism, the way to salvation that all must take if they want to enter into eternal life. It is an appropriate symbol to adorn the portal leading into the nave. For the interior of the church with its glowing colors and jeweled decorations was often likened to the heavenly city, the New Jerusalem so eloquently described by St. John: "And the gates of it shall not be shut at all by day: for there shall be no night there. And they shall bring the glory and honour of the nations into it" (Rev. 21:25-26).

The open books of the apostles seated next to St. Peter on the left recall the following verse that states that all who enter it are the ones "which are written in the Lamb's book of life" (Rev. 21:27). Furthermore, in a monastic church especially, the monks would have been conscious of the final reference to these gates: "Blessed are they that do his commandments, that they may have the right to the tree of life, and may enter in through the gates into the city" (Rev. 22:14). The awakened interest in foreign countries and peoples was doubtless due to the influence of the early Crusades, which were then being preached.

Capitals at Vézelay

At Vézelay, the imaginative scope displayed in the abundance of sculptured capitals is breathtaking. Biblical scenes, incidents from the lives of the saints, allegorical commentaries, and the play of pure fantasy are found throughout the narthex and the nave. One of the capitals in the nave shows the angel of death striking down the eldest son of Pharaoh (Fig. 142). Another shows a bearded figure pouring grain into a handmill that a barefooted man is turning (Fig. 143). The real meaning of this scene would be lost to obscurity were it not for a chance remark in the writings of Suger, the abbot of St. Denis near Paris, who visited Cluny and Vézelay before beginning to rebuild his abbey church. He noted that the corn is the old law, which is poured into the mystic mill by

142–143. Nave capital sculptures, Church of La Madeleine, Vézelay. c. 1130.

142. *Angel of Death Killing Eldest Son of Pharaoh.*   **143.** *Mystic Mill: Moses and St. Paul Grinding Corn.*

by an ancient Hebrew prophet, probably Moses, and is being ground into the meal of the new law by St. Paul.

Unlike the statuary of antiquity that was made of marble or bronze, French Romanesque capitals are usually of soft sandstone and limestone. Their purpose was mainly to decorate interiors that did not have to resist the elements. The soft material, furthermore, was better adapted to the pictorial forms of Romanesque sculpture. Its plasticity responded more quickly to the imaginative demands made on it than a harder stone could have done.

Works in Metal

While the examples discussed are stone carvings, the general category of Romanesque sculpture in this period should be broadened to include works in metal. Only a few examples of this kind have survived, because they were made of such precious materials as gold, silver, and copper, adorned with enamel work and studded with precious gems.

Cluny, according to an early inventory, had a golden statue of the Virgin seated on a silver throne and wearing a jeweled crown. Churches also needed chalices, plates, and pitchers for the sacred services. On important feast days, books with ivory or metal covers encrusted with jewels (Fig. 144) were used on the high altar, where also rested reliquaries fashioned to contain the relics of saints. Candelabras, incense burners, and metal choir screens added their beauty to the sacred precincts.

Romanesque sculpture always remained an integral part of the architectural design and is inseparable from the whole. The walls, ceiling, portals, columns, and capitals were not merely mute structural necessities. They were places where carved images communicated messages and meanings—where stones spoke to monk and pilgrim alike in the eloquent language of form, line, and color.

Painting and Other Monastic Crafts

Miniatures of modest proportions on the parchment pages of books and monumental murals in the apses of abbey churches were the two extremes of the art of painting in the Romanesque period. The one craft known definitely to have been consistently practiced by the monks themselves was the copying, illustrating, and binding of books, activities that took place in a large communal room called the *scriptorium.* This tradition, which dates from the time of Cassiodorus, was followed by all Benedictine houses, and those in the Cluniac order fostered it with both diligence and enthusiasm.

Manuscript Illumination and Murals

While the Cluniac copyists were known for the beauty of their lettering and the accuracy of their texts, a monk skilled in his craft would certainly not have been content merely to copy letters all his life. A blank place in the manuscript provided him with both the space and the challenge to fill it in. At first, these spaces were filled with nothing more than fanciful little pen drawings or an elaborate initial letter at the beginning of a paragraph. Gradually, the drawings grew into miniature paintings, and the initial letters became highly complex designs.

The luxurious development of this art of illuminating manuscripts seems to have been one compensation for the austerity of Benedictine life. As the practice became more widely accepted, specialists in the various phases began to be designated. A painter of small illuminated scenes was called a *miniator,* while one who did initial letters was known as a *rubricator.*

Cluniac manuscripts were done with the utmost delicacy. Miniatures were painted in many colors, and halos of saints or crowns of kings were made with thin gold leaf. The letter Q in an evangeliary from St. Omer is an intricate example of the illuminator's art (Fig. 145).

Such flourishes of the pen by expert copyists on their parchment pages and the gradual refinement of the painstaking miniature art of illumination had effects far beyond the medium for which either was intended originally. They became the models for the large murals that decorated the walls and apses of churches and for the sculpture that embellished the spaces above portals and columns. Later, they were the prototypes of designs for stained glass windows in Gothic cathedrals.

Contrasting with the diminutive illuminations in manuscripts were the huge frescoes painted on the surfaces of barrel-vaulted ceilings, arches, and semi-domed apses of churches of the Romanesque period.

above: 145. Initial page with letter Q, from Evangeliary of Abbey at St. Omer. c. 1000. Manuscript illumination. Pierpont Morgan Library, New York.

left: 146. *Christ in Glory.* c. 1103. Fresco (apse mural), height 13′ (3.96 m). Cluniac Chapel, Berzé-la-Ville, France.

Except for a few fragments, all the large paintings at Cluny itself have disappeared. Notable examples, however, are found elsewhere. In a chapel at nearby Berzé-la-Ville, a residence built for Hugh's last years, there is an apse mural modeled after that in the Third Abbey Church (Fig. 146). Christ is clothed in a robe of white over which is draped a red mantle. While blessing the sixteen surrounding apostles and saints with His right hand, He gives St. Peter a scroll containing the law with His left. The heavenly setting is suggested by the dark blue background of the *mandorla,* an almond-shaped contour, which is studded with golden stars, and by the hand of God the Father, which hovers above Christ holding a crown.

Handcrafts

Besides the arts of building, stone carving, and painting, many crafts were practiced in the workshops of Cluny and the other monasteries. These included embroidering altar cloths and vestments, weaving, ceramics, goldsmithing and other metal crafts, leather tooling, and the casting of bells. The constant experimentation and research carried on in these centers resulted in a continuous improvement in the methods employed, including better ways of manufacturing glass, and in the invention of chemical formulas for stained glass.

Just how extensively the monks themselves took part in the actual production of such handcrafts at Cluny or elsewhere is not definitely known. There is no evidence, for instance, that a monk ever worked as a sculptor in stone. The capitals and relief sculpture were executed for the most part by freelance carvers who went from place to place in groups wherever building activity was in progress. Likewise, similar work in other media was probably performed by itinerant craftsmen or by lay workers from the region. However, the iconographic schemes—that is, the images and symbols depicted—were always worked out under the direct supervision of the monks, some of whom may have possessed the necessary skills so that they could train the craftsmen working under them. The variety and subtle character of the work, therefore, often is as much the monks' as if they had taken the chisel or other tools into their own hands. Wherever a name has survived in connection with sculpture, painting, or other work, it is usually that of a monk who is said to have "made" it. But "made" could mean anything from donating the material or suggesting the subject to supervising the work in progress or even to doing the carving or painting itself.

The monastic attitude toward decorating a church is well summed up by Theophilus, a writer on the various crafts of this time. He addressed his fellow monks and noted their artistic contribution to the worship of God, saying:

> . . . you have confidently approached the house of God, have decorated with utmost beauty ceilings or walls with various work, and showing forth with different colours a likeness of the paradise of God, glowing with various flowers, and verdant with herbs and leaves, and cherishing the lives of the saints with crowns of various merit, you have, after a fashion, shown the beholders everything in creation praising God, its creator, and have caused them to proclaim him admirable in all his works. Nor is the eye of man even able to decide upon which work it may first fix its glance; if it beholds the ceilings, they glow like draperies; if it regards the walls, there is the appearance of paradise; if it marks the abundance of light from the windows, it admires the inestimable beauty of the glass and the variety of the costly work. . . .

Music

Odo of Cluny, abbot from 927 to 942, brought the monastery its earliest musical distinction through actively fostering choral music. Documents tell of more than a hundred psalms being sung there daily in his time; and on his tours of inspection to other monasteries, he devoted much of his energies to the instruction of choirs. His great success made it necessary for his teaching methods to be written down, and from this circumstance something about the early status of music at Cluny can be ascertained.

Development of Notation

Odo's great accomplishments include the arranging of the tones of the scale into an orderly progression from A to G. By thus assigning to them a system of letters, he was responsible for the earliest effective system of Western musical notation. Odo's method, as expounded in his treatise, also included the mathematical measurement of *intervals,* the difference in pitch between tones, on the *monochord.* This instrument, consisting of a single string stretched over a long wooden box and frets for varying the length of the string, made it possible to demonstrate the relationship between string lengths and intervals.

Before Odo's time, the chants used in the sacred service had laboriously to be learned by rote; and if any degree of authenticity was to be achieved, they had to be taught by a graduate of the Schola Cantorum that Gregory the Great had established in Rome. The treatise declares that by teaching the singers to perform by reading notes, they soon "were singing at first sight and extempore and without a fault anything written in music, something which until now ordinary singers had never been able to do, many continuing to . . . study for fifty years without profit."

Refinements on Odo's method were made in the 11th century by another monk, Guido of Arezzo. His treatise, which was in the library of Cluny, made it clear that he embraced the Cluniac musical reforms. He also freely acknowledged his debt to the work of his great predecessor, the Abbot Odo, "from whose example," he said, "I have departed only in the forms of the notes." This slight departure by Guido was actually the invention of the basis for modern musical notation on a staff of lines where tones of the same pitch always appear on the same line or space.

Odo's work also led to Guido's system of *solmization,* which assigned certain syllables, derived from a hymn to St. John, to each degree of the scale:

147–150. Ambulatory capital,
Great Third Abbey Church of Cluny, 1088–95.
Ochier Museum, Cluny.

147.
*First Tone
of Plainsong.*

C	D	F	DE	D
Ut	que	-ant	la	-xis
D	D	C	D E	E
re	- so	-na	-re fe	-bris
EFG	E	D	EC	D
Mi	- ra	ge	-sto	-rum
F	G	A G	FED	D
fa	- mu	-li tu	- o-	rum,
GAG	FE	F	G	D
Sol	- ve	pol	-lu	-ti
A	G A	F	GA	A
la	- bi	-i re	-a	-tum,
GF	ED	C	E	D
San	- cte	**Io**	-an	-nes.

Later the syllable *si,* compounded from the first two letters of the Latin form of "St. John" (*Sancte Ioannes*), was added as the seventh scale degree. In France, these syllables are still used just as in Guido's time. In Italy and elsewhere, the first note *ut* is replaced by the more singable *do.*

The most remarkable fact about Odo's and Guido's treatises is that both champion music as an art designed to be performed in the praise of the Creator and to enhance the beauty and meaning of prayer. Previously, Boethius, along with most early writers on music, had considered music a branch of mathematics that could reveal the secrets of the universe. Guido, however, made a point of stating that the writings of Boethius were "useful to philosophers, but not to singers," and both Odo and he intentionally omitted heavenly speculations. Cluny, therefore, emerged as a center of practical music making rather than as a place where scholars pondered on music as a theoretical science.

148.
Second Tone.

Music Pictured in Sculpture

The story of music at Cluny was also told visually with compelling beauty in two sculptured capitals that survive from the apse of Hugh's great church. In the sanctuary, the architectural climax of the whole edifice, was a series of columns grouped in a semicircle around the high altar, and the capitals of these pillars constituted the high point of late 11th-century sculptural skill. One capital presented on its four faces the theological virtues; another, the cardinal virtues. On a third were pictured the cycles and labors of the monk's year in terms of the four sea-

149.
Third Tone.

150.
Fourth Tone.

sons. His hopes for the hereafter were portrayed by the four rivers and trees of Paradise. Finally, his praise for the Creator was expressed with figures to symbolize the eight tones of sacred psalmody.

On the first of the eight faces of these twin capitals (Fig. 147) is inscribed: "This tone is the first in the order of musical intonations." The figure is that of a solemn-faced youth playing on a lute. Here the symbolism of the stringed instrument stems from the belief in the power of music to banish evil, as David had cast out Saul's evil spirit when he played to him.

The second tone (Fig. 148) is represented by the figure of a young woman dancing and beating a small drum. The inscription reads, "There follows the tone which by number and law is second." Such percussion instruments are known to have been used to accompany medieval processions on joyful feast days in the manner described in Psalm 68: "The singers went before, the players on instruments followed after; among them were damsels playing with timbrels."

The next inscription (Fig. 149) says: "The third strikes, and represents the resurrection of Christ." The instrument here is of the lyre type with a sounding board added, which is one of the 11th-century forms of the psaltery, the legendary instrument with which David accompanied himself as he sang the psalms. This instrument with its gut strings stretched over the wooden frame roughly resembles a cross and was used as a symbolic reference to Christ stretched on the Cross.

The fourth figure (Fig. 150) is that of a young man playing a set of chime bells. The accompanying inscription reads: "The fourth follows representing a lament in song." The Latin word *planctus* denotes a funeral dirge. The practice of ringing bells at burials is pictured in the contemporary representation of the burial procession of Edward the Confessor from the Bayeux Tapestry (see Fig. 160), where the figures accompanying the bier carry small bells.

Early Forms of Polyphony

While Gregorian plainsong was a purely melodic style and continued to be practiced as such, during the Romanesque period the choral responses began to show variations in the direction of singing in several parts at different levels of pitch. The 9th, 10th, and 11th centuries thus saw the tentative beginnings of the *polyphonic,* or "many-voiced," style that was to flourish in the Gothic period and in the Renaissance.

Unfortunately, the polyphonic practice of the pre-Gothic period is known only through theoretical treatises. From the rules they give for the addition of voices to the traditional chant, however, some idea of

Parallel Organum (10th century) (from *Scholia Enchiriadis*)

the early forms of polyphony can be determined. As might be expected, the influence of mathematics and the Pythagorean number theory were found in the musical usages of the time (see Chap. 2, p. 45). The perfect intervals of the octave, fifth, and fourth were preferred over all others, since their mathematical ratios indicated a closer correspondence with the divine order of the universe.

In a treatise dating from the beginning of the 10th century, the type of choral response known as *parallel organum* (above) is discussed. The original Gregorian melody was maintained intact. However, at pitch levels of the fourth, fifth, and octave above and below, the principal voice was paralleled by these so-called organal voices. Parallel organum, in effect, built a mighty fortress of choral sound around the traditional Gregorian line of plainsong. By thus enclosing it within the stark and gaunt but strong perfect intervals, parallel organum achieved a massive and solid style quite in the spirit of the other Romanesque arts.

The music of this time was yet another expression of the praise of God. When related to the great buildings, the richly carved sculpture, the illuminated manuscripts and painted murals, it fits into the picture as a whole. Consequently, when the choir section of a monastic church was being planned, every effort was made to provide a resonant, acoustically vibrant setting for the perpetual chant. Hugh's great church was especially famous for its acoustics. The curved ceiling vaults and the great variety of angles in the wall surfaces of the broad transepts and cavernous nave gave the chant there a characteristic tone color that can be reproduced only in a similar setting. The effect of a monastic choir of several hundred voices performing joyous songs with all its heart and soul must have been overwhelming.

Cluny's sculptured capitals depicting the tones of plainsong represent an obvious synthesis of the arts of sculpture, music, and literature into an appropriate architectural setting. Their expressive intensity, moreover, bespeaks both the motion and emotion typical of the Romanesque style in general. As such, they are representative products of a people capable of the long and difficult pilgrimages and the fantastic effort associated with the organization of the First Crusade. These sculptures reveal something of that unconquerable energy, and especially of a vigorous attitude toward the act of worship, that must have been channeled into a performance style which was emphatic in feeling. They are, in fact, the embodiment of the spirit expressed by St. Augustine, who called upon the faithful to "Sing with your voices, and with your hearts, and with all your moral convictions, sing the new songs, not only with your tongue but with your life."

Ideas

The key to the understanding of the Romanesque as a living and active art is a knowledge of the opposing forces that created it. As the Roman Christian influence spread northward, it encountered the restless surging energies of the former barbarian tribes. In effect, a Church that respected and admired tradition and encouraged an unchanging order was absorbing peoples with an urge for experimentation and action. The resulting innovations gave ancient forms new twists and turns.

When builders combined the horizontal Early Roman Christian basilica, for example, with northern towers and spires, they took the first step toward Romanesque architecture. Further development of the style was the direct result of this union of southern horizontality and northern verticality, reflecting as it did the broad spirit of the late Roman humanism and the soaring northern aspirations.

The musical counterpart is found in the joining together of southern monophony and northern polyphony, which occurred when the Mediterranean tradition of singing one melody in unison met the northern custom of singing in several parts. The result was the experimentation with primitive forms of counterpoint and harmony that characterized the music of the Romanesque period.

This meeting of southern unity with northern variety, and its slow maturation over the centuries, was thus responsible for the first truly European art style: the Romanesque. The ideas that underlie the monastic aspect of the style are an outgrowth of those motivating the earlier period in Ravenna. The mysticism of the previous period moved into an otherworldly phase; and Early Christian authoritarianism resulted in the rigid stratification of society into strict hierarchies. The two basic ideas, then, crystallize as asceticism and hierarchism.

Asceticism

The monastic way of life demanded the seclusion of the countryside as an escape from the distractions of the world. Since the monk conceived earthly life to be but a stepping-stone to life beyond, living required only the barest essentials. The very absence of physical luxury led to the development of a rich inner life, and the barren soil of rural isolation almost miraculously produced an important art movement. Poverty, chastity, and humility became virtues as the result of moral rather than aesthetic impulses, but the very severity of monastic life stimulated imaginative experience, and individual self-denial reinforced communal energies.

The attitude of turning away from the world found its architectural expression in the plain exteriors and rich interiors of monastic churches. Thus, the net effect of asceticism was to increase the fervor of the spirit and to express this with great intensity. Two favorite Cluniac saints were the Paul and Anthony who had gone farthest into the forbidding African desert; it was they who had the most fantastic visions and the most dreadful temptations.

The spread of social centers into widely scattered monastic communities likewise lent a peculiar intensity and a wide variety to the expressive forms of the Romanesque. The arts, consequently, were not intended to mirror the natural world or to decorate the dwelling place of an earthly ruler but, rather, to conjure up otherworldly visions of divine majesty. Hence, all the arts found a common ground in their desire to depict aspects of the world beyond.

Symbolism and Otherworldliness   The monks developed an art of elaborate symbolism addressed to an educated cloistered community familiar with sophisticated allegories. The growth of such a symbolic language—whether in architecture, sculpture, painting, or music—could only have been promoted by an abbot like Hugh, whose learning was so universal that he succeeded in adding "philosophy to ornament and a meaning to beauty." By contrast, the later Gothic arts were directed toward the humble of the world and the unlettered people beyond the cloister. While the sculpture and stained glass of the Gothic cathedral were destined to become the Bible in stone and glass for the poor, in a monastic church the comparable forms were always aloof and aristocratic and at times intentionally subtle and enigmatic. This does not mean that Romanesque art was overly intellectualized and remote from the experience of those to whom it was addressed. On the contrary, it was very directly related to the intensity of the inner life and the visionary otherworldly focus of the religious communities that developed it.

Greco-Roman sculpture was successful in its way precisely because the classical mind had conceived the gods in human form. As such they could be rendered so well in marble. When godhood was conceived as an abstract principle, a realistic representation of it became essentially impossible. Rational proportions were of no help to the Romanesque mind, since it was considered impossible to understand God intellectually. God had to be felt through faith rather than comprehended by the mind. Only through the intuitive eye of faith could His essence be grasped. Hence He had to be portrayed symbolically, not represented literally, since a symbol could stand for something intangible. Physical substance was secondary, and soul stuff primary; but the latter could be depicted only in the imagination.

A life so abstractly oriented and motivated by such deep religious convictions could never have found its models in the natural world. The fantastic proportions of Romanesque architecture, the eccentric treatment and distortions of the human body in its sculpture, the unnecessarily elaborated initials in the manuscript illuminations, and the ornate melismas added to the syllables of the chant all signified a rejection of the natural order of things and its replacement by the supernatural. The book of the Bible most admired was Revelation, containing as it did the apocalyptical visions of St. John. It is not surprising, then, that the pictorial element in sculpture and painting in both large and small forms reflected Romanesque emotions with such intensity that the human figures seem to be consumed by the inner fires of their faith. Reason seeks to persuade by calm or serene attitudes, but such animated figures as those of the prophets at Souillac (Fig. 151) and Moissac seem to be performing spiritual dances in which their slender forms stretch to unnatural lengths with gestures more convulsive than graceful.

The Romanesque monk thus dwelt in a dream world where the trees that grew in Paradise, the angels who populated the heavens, and the demons of hell were more real than anything or anybody he beheld in everyday life. Even though he had never seen such creatures, he never doubted their existence. Indeed, the monsters whose fearsome characteristics were described in the bestiaries, and which were represented in the manuscripts and sculptures, had a moral and symbolic function far more real to him than any animals of mere physical existence. All these imaginary creatures existed together in a jungle of the imagination where the abnormal was the normal and the fabulous became the commonplace (Figs. 152, 153).

Hierarchism

A strict hierarchical structure of society prevailed throughout the Romanesque period. It was as rigid in its way inside the monastery as was the feudalism outside the cloistered walls. The thought of the time was based on the assumption of a divinely established order of the universe, and the authority to interpret it was vested in the Church. The majestic figure of Christ in Glory carved over the entrance portals of the Cluniac abbey churches, and echoed in

above: 151. *Isaiah,* west portal, Church of Notre Dame, Souillac. c. 1110.

right: 152. *Demon of Luxury,* nave capital sculpture, Church of La Madeleine, Vézelay. c. 1130.

far right: 153. Detail of Figure 152.

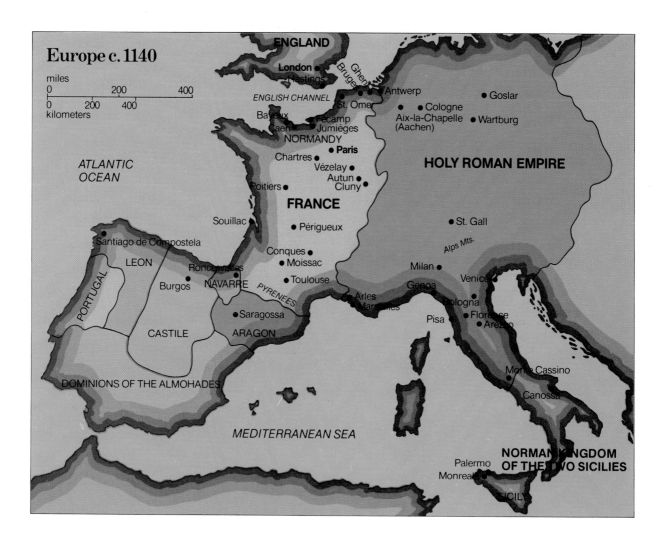

Europe c. 1140

the mural compositions painted on the interiors of their half-domed apses, proclaimed this concept.

Christ was no longer the Good Shepherd of Early Christian times but a mighty king, crowned and enthroned in the midst of His heavenly courtiers, sitting in judgment on the entire world (Fig. 154). The keys to His heavenly kingdom, as seen in the Vézelay tympanum (Fig. 141) and the apse painting at Berzé-la-Ville (Fig. 146), rest firmly in the grasp of St. Peter, the first of the popes according to the Roman tradition. As if to lend additional emphasis to this doctrine, St. Peter at Berzé-la-Ville is seen receiving a scroll containing the divine laws from the hands of Christ. The papacy of medieval days always found its most powerful support in the Cluniac order, and through such aid succeeded in establishing a social order based on this mandate from on high.

The authority of the Church was nowhere better expressed than in these monumental sculptural and mural compositions that from their place of promi-

nence warned those who beheld them of their position on the road either to salvation or to damnation. The milestones marking the path were placed there by the Church, whose clergy alone could interpret them and assure the penitent that he or she was on the way to the streets of gold instead of the caldrons of fire. The frequency with which the apocalyptic vision of St. John was represented, with apostles and elders surrounding the throne of Christ, was evidence of the reverential respect for the protective-father image in the form of the bearded patriarch.

In such a divine order, nothing could be left to chance. All life had to be brought into an organizational plan that would conform to this cosmic scheme of things. The stream of authority, descending from Christ through St. Peter to his papal successors, flowed out from Rome in three main directions. The Holy Roman emperor received his crown from the hands of the pope; in turn, all the kings of the Western world owed him homage, as did all on downward,

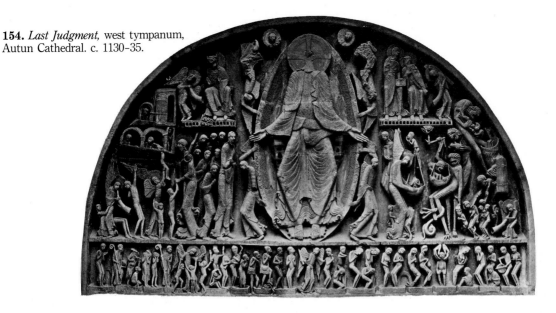

154. *Last Judgment,* west tympanum,
Autun Cathedral. c. 1130–35.

from the great lords to the humblest serf, for all had a preordained place in this great cosmic plan. Next, the archbishops and bishops received their miters in Rome, and in their bishoprics they were feudal lords in their own right. Under them, the so-called secular clergy, from the parish priest to the deacon, owed their allegiance to the superiors from whom they received their orders. Finally, the monastic communities under their abbots also owed their allegiance to the pope; and through their loyal support of the papacy, the Cluniac order grew so strong that its abbot was, other than the pope, the most powerful cleric in Christendom.

Cluniac Feudalism   Beginning as a small independent monastery, Cluny was from the first exempted from tribute to any power save that of the pope alone. But instead of remaining an independent unit like other Benedictine abbeys, Cluny adopted the feudal principle by expanding and absorbing other monasteries until it dominated monasticism.

As the head of a monarchical system, the Cluniac order was the most powerful unifying force of the time, not only in religious and political affairs but in architectural, artistic, and musical thought as well. Through this adherence to the feudal system, it became a great landowning institution, and in an economy where land was the sole source of wealth, the monasteries became the principal commissioners of works of art. In a world where faith triumphed over reason and where the sole road to salvation was through the Church, the Cluniac order acted as the mainstay of the Roman tradition and spread its authority, doctrines, and liturgy all over Christendom.

The ranks of the monks were drawn mainly from the aristocratic class, whose members were among the few free to choose their own way of life. All the higher Church offices were held principally by men from noble families, often by younger sons not eligible under the law of primogeniture, which favored the eldest son, to inherit the feudal estates. The vow of poverty applied only to individual ownership; collectively, a monastic community resembled a feudal manor. It was only in later times that the mendicant, or begging, orders of monks attempted to interpret the vow of poverty literally. Hence, Romanesque art was an aristocratic art, and it remained so throughout the period with patronage concentrated in the hands of its abbots and bishops.

The Romanesque abbey church was organized according to a rigid hierarchical plan that mirrored the strict order of precedence in the processionals of the liturgy for which it was the setting. By its insistence on visible proportions, it signified the invisible plan of a divinely ordered world. The monastic buildings that surrounded it were similarly significant in their regularity. They were designed to enclose those who expressed their willingness to conform to such a regulated life, and thus to constitute a reflection of the divinely established plan for salvation.

The very spaciousness of the abbey church was far in excess of anything that was needed to accommodate the few hundreds who normally worshiped there. It was, however, the monument that mirrored the unshakable religious convictions of the Romanesque mind; and, as the house of the Lord and Ruler of the universe, it became a palace surpassing the dreams of glory of any king on the face of the earth. In the insecurity of the feudalistic world, Romanesque people built fortresses for their faith and for their God, which were designed to withstand the attacks of heretics and heathens as well as the more

155. Sant' Ambrogio, Milan, from west. c. 1181.
Length, including atrium, 390′ (118.87 m);
width 92′ (28.04 m).

elemental forces of wind, weather, and fire. Furthermore, the abbey church was the place where the heavenly Monarch held court, and where His subjects could pay Him their homage in the divine services that went on day and night, year in and year out.

This hierarchical principle, moreover, applied not only to the social and ecclesiastical levels but also to the basic thought processes. Authority for all things rested firmly on the Scriptures and the interpretations of them by the early Church fathers. Rightness and fitness were determined by how ancient the tradition was, and scholarship consisted not so much in exploring new intellectual paths as in interpreting traditional sources. To the educated, this process took the form of learned commentaries; to the uneducated, it was expressed in the cult of relics. Thousands took to the dusty pilgrimage roads and traveled across France and Spain to touch the legendary tomb of the Apostle James at Compostela. In the arts, this veneration of the past made mandatory the continuance of such traditional forms as the Early Roman Christian basilica and the music of the Gregorian chant.

Survival of Creative Vitality   This traditionalism, curiously enough, never led to stagnation or uniformity. In making learned commentaries on the Scriptures, the writers unconsciously, and sometimes quite consciously, interpreted them in the light of contemporary views. And as the untaught populace traveled about Europe on pilgrimages and later went to the Near East on the Crusades, it absorbed new

ideas that eventually were to transform the provincialism of feudal times into a more dynamic social structure.

All the arts, however, exhibited an extraordinary inventiveness and such a rich variety as to make the Romanesque one of the most spontaneous and original periods in history. Diversity rather than unity was the rule of Romanesque architecture. Regional building traditions and the availability of craftsmen and materials contributed to the varied pattern. At St. Mark's in Venice (Fig. 259) there is a combination of the multidomed Byzantine style with Greek-cross ground plans. In Spain, the Moorish influence is felt; in northern Italy, Sant' Ambrogio at Milan (Fig. 155) has the rich red brickwork and square belfry towers typical of Lombardy; while in central Italy, the Romanesque is characterized by zebra-striped exteriors composed of alternating strips of dark green and cream-colored marbles, as at the Baptistry of Florence (Fig. 207) and the Cathedral of Pisa.

Romanesque structures never became types as did Greek temples, Byzantine churches, and the later Gothic cathedrals. Each building and each region sought its own solutions. Through constant experimentation, Romanesque architects found the key to new structural principles, such as their vaulting techniques. By gradually achieving complete command of their medium, they progressed in their building techniques from the earlier heavy fortress-like structures to the later edifices of considerable elegance.

Meanwhile, the decorators groped toward the revival of monumental sculpture and mural painting. The need for larger and better choirs likewise led to the invention of notational systems, and the emotional exuberance in worship made many modifications of the traditional chant, which eventually culminated in the art of counterpoint. In all, the creative vitality exhibited in each art medium is a constant source of astonishment.

Within the formal framework provided by the abbey church, architectural detail, sculpture and other decorative arts, music, and liturgy combined as integral parts of the overall architectonic design. The nave and transepts were designed as a resonant hall for the chant, just as the tympanum over the entrance portal and the semidomed interior of the apse were designed as the settings for sculptural and painted mural embellishments. The sculptural representations of plainsong on the ambulatory capitals in the Third Abbey Church at Cluny show a union of music and sculpture, while their inscriptions add a literary dimension. All the arts converge into the unified structure of the liturgy, since all were created in the monastic concept for service in the glorification of God.

7
The Feudal Romanesque Style

The Norman Conquest and the Bayeux Tapestry

While a monastery was a haven of peace, a feudal manor was an armed fortress. While the cloistered brothers were laying up treasures in heaven, the feudal lords were harvesting theirs on earth. And while the monk was a man of prayer, the landed baron was a man of war.

Surviving examples of secular art from the Romanesque period are so rare that each is practically unique. The treasures of a monastery or cathedral were under the watchful eye of the clergy, and religious restraints against raiding Church property usually were strong enough to prevent wanton destruction. The same cannot be said for secular property. Feudal castles constantly were subject to siege, and those that survived frequently were remodeled in later centuries with the changing fortunes of their successive owners. Among the best preserved of these Romanesque residences are the Imperial Palace near Goslar, Germany (Fig. 156); the Wartburg

Castle, where Tannhäuser's famous songfest took place; and parts of the Palace of the Normans in Sicily, notably the Dining Hall of Roger II, with its emblematic animals and traditional symbols of feudal heraldry (Fig. 157).

Towns did grow up in the protective shadows of a castle, a monastery, or a cathedral, but only a few urban dwellings remain, such as those at Cluny (Fig. 158). Their arched doorways facing the street sometimes were decorated by sculptured hunting scenes or representations of an artisan's trade—a cobbler bending over his workbench, for example, or a merchant showing cloth to a client. Of interior decorations—mural paintings, wall hangings, furniture, and the like—almost nothing is left. And, since poetry and music were intended to be heard rather than read by these feudal people, little of either was written down.

History, however, is filled with accidents. For example, the single large-scale example of secular pictorial art, the famous Bayeux Tapestry, survives because it was designed for a church instead of a castle. The only French epic poem before the Cru-

156. Imperial Palace at Goslar, Lower Saxony, Germany. Begun 1043, rebuilt 1132. Chapel of St. Ulrich (far left), 11th century.

CHRONOLOGY
Feudal Romanesque Period

sades, the *Song of Roland,* owes its present existence to some monastic scribe who happened to write it down either for a minstrel with a poor memory or because he wanted to preserve it after it had ceased to be sung. The one authentic melody to which such poetry was chanted is extant because it was included as a jest in a 13th-century musical play. And the so-called Tower of London, a *keep* or fortress, that William the Conqueror constructed, is still intact because of its later use as a royal residence and prison and because it housed an important chapel.

The most complete example of pictorial art is the so-called Bayeux Tapestry, one of the most eloquent documents of the time. Here, in visual form, the story of the winning of England by William the Conqueror is told from the Norman point of view. It presents a vivid picture of the life and attitudes of the feudal period. The term *tapestry* is not quite accurate though it is somewhat justified in this case because the cloth did function as a wall hanging. Since the design is applied in woolen yarn to a coarse linen surface rather than woven into the cloth itself, the work is more correctly described as an embroidery.

Such cloth decorations were used to cover the bare stone walls of castles, but in this case the extraordinary dimensions—20 inches (51 centimeters)

157. Mosaic of centaurs, leopards, and peacocks, from Dining Hall of Roger II. Palace of Norman Kings, Palermo. c. 1132.

wide and 231 feet (70.4 meters) long—and its possession over the centuries by the Bayeux cathedral indicate that this tapestry or embroidery was intended to cover the plain strip of masonry over the nave arcade of that building. It was probably the product of one of the renowned English embroidery workshops and apparently was completed about twenty years after the great battle it describes.

The central figure is, of course, William the Conqueror, who indelibly stamped his powerful personality on the north European scene throughout the latter half of the 11th century. The span of time is from the closing months of the reign of Edward the Confessor to that fateful day in 1066 when the Conqueror made good his claim to the throne by putting the English forces to rout at the Battle of Hastings.

The Bayeux Tapestry, in its surviving state, is divided into 79 panels, or scenes. The first part (panels 1–34) is concerned with William's reception of Harold, an English duke, whose mission to Normandy allegedly was to tell William that he would succeed Edward the Confessor as king of England. In one of these scenes, William and Harold are seen at Bayeux (Fig. 159), *where Harold took an oath to Duke William.* (The italics here and later are literal translations of the Latin inscriptions that run along the top of the Tapestry above the scenes they describe.) Placing his hands on the reliquaries that repose on the two altars, Harold apparently swears to uphold William's claim, although the exact nature of the oath is left vague. This is, however, the episode that later became the justification for the English campaign—because Harold, false to his supposed sworn word, had had himself crowned king.

In these early panels, in the upper and lower borders, a running commentary on the action contin-

ues a tradition begun in manuscript illuminations. Here the commentary is in the form of animal figures that were familiar to the people of the time from bestiaries and sculpture, and often the allusion is to certain fables of Aesop. The choice of the fox and crow, the wolf and stork, and the ewe, goat, and cow in the presence of the lion all have to do with treachery and violence and serve to point out the supposed treacherous character of Harold.

William is seated serenely on his ducal throne, foreshadowing his future dignity as king. The scene, furthermore, truly is located in the Bayeux cathedral, the exterior of which is shown in the curious repre-

158. Romanesque house, Cluny. c. 1159.

159. *Harold Swearing Oath,* detail of Bayeux Tapestry.
c. 1073-88. Wool embroidery on linen;
height 1'8" (.51 m), entire length 231' (70.41 m).
Town Hall, Bayeux.

sentation to the left of the seated William. Bayeux's bishop was none other than Odo, William's half-brother, who in all probability commissioned the tapestry. Odo possibly intended that the tapestry be exhibited each year on the anniversary of William's conquest, and thus forever to commemorate the glory of that occasion—and, of course, the bravery of the bishop and builder of the church.

The main course of the action in the Bayeux Tapestry moves like the words on a printed page—that is, from left to right. At times, however, it was necessary to represent a pertinent episode apart from the principal action. In these instances the pictorial narrator simply reversed the usual order and moved the scene from right to left, thus, in effect, achieving a kind of visual parenthesis and avoiding any confusion with the flow of the main story.

Such a reversal is used in the scene depicting the death and burial of the Confessor (Fig. 160). On the right near the top is *King Edward in his bed* as he *addresses his faithful retainers.* On one side of him is a priest; Harold is on the other; while the queen and her lady-in-waiting are mourning at the foot of the bed. Below, under the words *here he has died,* the body is being prepared for the last rites. Moving toward the left, the funeral procession approaches *the church of St. Peter the Apostle,* the Romanesque predecessor of Westminster Abbey in London, which Edward had built and dedicated only ten years before, while the hand of God descends in blessing. The procession includes monks reading prayers and two assistants ringing the funeral bells.

When William received word that Harold had been crowned, he immediately determined on invasion, and the second part of the Tapestry (panels 35-53) is concerned with the preparations for his revenge up to the eve of the battle. After all was in readiness, he set sail. The ships seen in the Tapestry are similar to those in which William's restless Viking ancestors invaded the French coast two centuries before (Fig. 161). It was in just such ships that Leif Eriksen and his fellow mariners apparently reached the eastern coast of North America earlier in the same century.

After the landing, the grand finale begins with the assembling of forces for the great battle (panels

54-79). The Norman side has both archers on foot and knights on horseback, while the English infantry fight in close formation with immense battleaxes, small spears, and clubs with stone heads. The Normans move in from left to right and the English from the opposite direction. The climax of the battle is reached in a wild scene at a ravine, where men and horses are tumbling about while the *English and French fall together in battle.* Shortly after, Harold is killed, and the fighting concludes with the *English turned in flight.* The lower border in these scenes spares none of the horrors of warfare. Dismembered limbs are strewn about, scavengers strip coats of mail from the bodies of the fallen, and naked corpses are left on the field.

The design of the Bayeux Tapestry is dominantly linear and, like the illuminated manuscripts of the time, is rendered in two dimensions with no suggestion of spatial depth. The coarseness of the linen and the thickness of the wool, however, create interesting textural contrasts. The eight shades of woolen yarn—three blues, light and dark green, red, buff yellow, and gray—make for a vivid feeling of color, which is not used for natural representation but to

160. *Death and Burial of Edward the Confessor,*
detail of Bayeux Tapestry.

enliven the design. Some men have blue hair, others green, and horses often have two blue and two red legs. Faces are merely outlined, though some attempt at portraiture is made in the various likenesses of William (Fig. 162).

Details, such as costumes, armor, mode of combat, and the deployment of troops in battle, by contrast, are done with great accuracy. For this reason, the Tapestry is a never-ending source of amazement and one of the most important historical documents on the manner of life in the 11th century—so much so that its historical value is often allowed to overshadow its quality as a work of art. Admittedly crude and at times naïve, the Bayeux Tapestry does not elaborate details. It concentrates on telling its story, and the sweeping effect of the whole takes precedence over any of its parts.

The Bayeux Tapestry is a work of infinite variety. In the handling of the narration, after a slow beginning with frequent digressions, the designer went on in the middle panels to the rather feverish preparations that culminated in the breathless climax of the battle. In both tempo and organization, the Tapestry can stand comparison with the best works in narra-

161. Oseberg Burial Ship. c. 825. Oak; length overall 70′1⅝″ (21.38 m), beam 16′7″ (5.05 m). University Museum of Antiquities, Oslo.

162. *William's Feast,* detail of Bayeux Tapestry. c. 1073–88. Wool embroidery on linen; height 1′8″ (.51 m), entire length 231′ (70.41 m). Town Hall, Bayeux.

tive form, visual or verbal. The details, whether in the main panels or in the upper or lower borders, are handled so imaginatively that they not only embellish the design but add visual accents, comment on the action, and further the flow of the plot. Scenes are separated one from another by buildings that figure in the story and by such devices as the stylized trees that are mere conventions. So skillfully are these arranged that the continuity of the whole is never halted, and the observer is hardly aware of their presence. All in all, a successful work of art designed for such a long and narrow space is a feat of visual virtuosity, and it leaves no doubt that it is the product of a master designer.

Song of Roland

A *chanson de geste* is a "song of deeds," an action story in poetic form sung by a minstrel to the accompaniment of a viol or lyre. It is an epic poem in Old French, the medieval language of the French people, rather than in the scholarly Latin. The *Chanson de Roland,* or *Song of Roland,* is narrated in an abrupt, direct manner, and transitions between episodes are sudden and unexpected. A warlike atmosphere surrounds the characters, including the fighting Archbishop Turpin as well as the Archangels Gabriel and Michael who, like the Valkyries in the German epic *Song of the Nibelungs,* swoop down on the battlefield to bear the souls of fallen warriors to heaven.

Though set in an earlier time (the actual event took place in 778), the *Song of Roland* is, both in form

and spirit, the product of the warlike feudalistic 11th century, and various recorders of historical events of that time mention it in connection with the Battle of Hastings. Guy of Amiens, one of William and Matilda's courtiers, who died ten years after the battle, was the author of a Latin poem about a *jongleur,* or singing actor, by the name of Taillefer. This "minstrel whom a very brave heart ennobled," Guy relates, led William's forces into the battle throwing his sword in the air, catching it again, and singing a Song of Roland. The English historian William of Malmesbury, writing about fifty years after the battle, tells that William began to sing the *Song of Roland* "in order that the warlike example of that hero might stimulate the soldiers."

The *Song of Roland* is thus an action-filled story, set in the time of Charlemagne and the Carolingian period. It relates incidents from the campaign in northern Spain where that Emperor had been battling the pagan Saracens for seven long years. Roland, Charlemagne's favorite nephew, and the twelve peers, the flower of French knighthood, had been left in charge of the rear guard, while Charles and the main body of the army were crossing the Pyrenees back into France. Betrayed by a false kinsman, Ganelon—a situation strongly paralleling the episode of William and Harold in the Bayeux Tapestry— Roland is attacked near Roncesvalles by overwhelming pagan forces. The outnumbered rear guard is cut to pieces, and Roland, before dying a hero's death, sounds his ivory horn summoning his uncle and his army from afar.

The third part of the poem has to do with the vengeance of Charlemagne, just as the corresponding section of the Bayeux Tapestry relates that of William. All is action and heroism, with swords flashing, helmets gleaming, drums beating, horns blowing, banners snapping, and steeds prancing. The story of the battle proceeds in what amounts to a blow-by-blow account, echoing frequently with such statements as "fierce is the battle and wondrous grim the fight."*

First one hears of the preparations in the camp of Charles. The poet, using a cumulative technique, describes the ten battalions one by one. Knight is added to knight, battle group to battle group, weapon to weapon, in order to build up the full monumentality of the occasion in the listeners' minds and imaginations. All the forces of Western Christendom are eventually drawn up on Charlemagne's side—the French, Normans, Bavarians, Germans, Bretons, and so on. The virtues of the men invariably are those of bravery, valor, and hardiness. They have no fear of death; never do they flee the battlefield; and their horses are swift and good.

Then quite suddenly and without any transition the reader is in the midst of the pagan hordes. Twenty Saracen battalions are described, and in order to show how the Christians were outnumbered, still another ten are added. The fearsomeness of the enemy however, is not due to their numbers alone but to their ferocious character as well. The only admirable quality allowed them is that of being good fighters; otherwise they are hideous to behold, fierce and cruel, and love evil. Yet in spite of this the poet can say of both Christian and pagan forces, "Goodly the armies."

The physical appearance of the people from these strange lands is fantastically exaggerated. The Myconians, for instance, are men with "huge and hairy polls,/ Upon whose backs all down the spine in rows,/ As on wild boars, enormous bristles grow." Of the warriors of the desert of Occian, it is said, "Harder than iron their hide on head and flanks,/ So that they scorn or [either] harness or steel cap." Later, during the battle, these same men of Occian "whinny and bray and squall," while the men of Arguille "like dogs are yelping all."

The religious life of the enemy is just as much misunderstood as their appearance. The pagans are represented as polytheists who worship as strange an assortment of gods as was ever assembled—Apollyon, Termagant, and Mahound. When things are not going well from their point of view, they upbraid these gods. The statue of Apollyon is trampled underfoot; Termagant is robbed of his carbuncle, a precious stone; and Mahound is cast "into a ditch . . . For pigs and dogs to mangle and befoul." Later, when Marsilion, the king of Spain dies, the listener hears that he "yields his soul to the infernal powers." Such descriptions could not have been written after the Crusades had brought Western warriors into contact with Moslem culture. Like the foreigners depicted on the Vézelay tympanum (Fig. 141), then, the imagery of the *Song of Roland* is filled with naïve wonder.

With the lines of battle thus drawn, the setting is described in a single line: "Large is the plain and widely spread the wold." Then as the conflict begins, battalion falls on battalion, hewing and hacking. Christian knights hurtle against pagan knights the whole day until the battle is reduced to a personal encounter between Charlemagne and his opposite, Baligant the Emir:

> At the Emir he drives his good French blade,
> He carves the helm with jewel-stones ablaze,
> He splits the skull, he dashes out the brains,
> Down to the beard he cleaves him through the face,
> And past all healing, he flings him down, clean slain.

After this the pagans flee and the day is won.

The lines of the original Old French proceed according to a crude rhyming scheme of assonance in which the final syllables of each line correspond roughly in sound. The last words of each line of one of the stanzas will suffice to illustrate this principle of assonance: *magne, Espaigne, altaigne, remaigne, fraindre, muntaigne, m'enaimet, reclaimet, ataignet.*

Much of the direct character and rugged strength of the poem is due to rigid avoidance of literary embellishment. This is observable in such minute details as the forward motion within such single lines as: *So sent Rollanz de tun tens ni ad plus.* Nothing is allowed to block the progress of these sturdy military monosyllables. So consistent is this quality of starkness throughout the poem that it even extends to the portrayal of the characters themselves. Each is the embodiment of a single ideal and human type: Ganelon is all treachery and hatred; Roland is bravery to the point of rashness; Oliver, Roland's close companion, is reason and caution; and Charlemagne, outstanding in his solitary grandeur, represents the majesty of both Church and state. Through each one of these devices separately and through all of them together, the poem as a whole rises to the heights of epic art. Its language, style, and form thus well fit the brave deeds of the heroic men with whom its narrative is concerned.

---

*All quotations from *The Song of Roland,* translated by Dorothy L. Sayers, published by Penguin Books, © Executors of Dorothy L. Sayers, 1937, 1957.

The Art of Minstrelsy

"A verse without music is a mill without water," said Folquet of Marseilles, the *troubadour* (a lyric poet or poet-musician, often of knightly rank) whom Dante immortalized in his *Divine Comedy.* Poetry in medieval times was a popular art form in which verses were chanted by a jongleur to the accompaniment of a viol or lyre. No festive occasion was complete without this minstrel who sang *chansons de geste* and lays, told tales and fables, played on a variety of musical instruments, performed dances, and astonished and delighted the audience with juggling and sleight-of-hand tricks.

Records of these jongleurs go back many centuries. It is known that jongleurs gathered at Fécamp in Normandy in the year 1000. It is also known that they met together regularly during the slack season of Lent, when the Church forbade their public performances, to learn one another's tricks and techniques, and increase their repertories with new tales and songs. A lively account of their place in medieval society is contained in a description of a wedding feast in Provence, which says: "Then the *joglars* stood up, each one anxious to make himself heard; then you could hear instruments resounding in many a key. . . . One played the Lay of the Honeysuckle, another that of Tintagel, another that of the Faithful Lovers, another the lay that Ivan made. . . . Everyone performed at his best and the noise of the instrumentalists and the voices of the narrators made a considerable uproar in the hall."

The jongleurs of the 11th century were not of noble birth as were most of the later troubadours and their northern French and German counterparts, the *trouvères* and *minnesingers,* but they were welcomed in every castle and abbey. Records reveal that some women were included in the ranks of jongleurs and troubadours. Under the patronage of the feudal nobility, lyrical poetry and music were to bloom in the 12th and 13th centuries into the full-fledged art of the troubadours, trouvères, and minnesingers. Courtly tournaments, brave knights winning fair ladies, and aristocratic poets making music with minstrels enlivened the nobles' entertainments in the Gothic period (Fig. 163). The practice of holding songfests also began at this time.

Since 11th-century secular music forms were just emerging, the models undoubtedly were derived from certain formulas used in the performance of church music. The simple repetitive melodies of the *chansons de geste,* together with the assonanced stanzas and insistent rhythms of the poetry, had much in common with the litany—though, of course, the subject matter differed radically. It is greatly to be regretted that the musical setting of the *Song of Roland* has not been preserved. While jongleurs could refresh their memories of longer epics from the manuscripts they carried in the leather pouches that they wore, these manuscripts included no musical parts. Hence it is assumed that the melodies were so simple there was little need to write them down.

The music of the *chansons de geste,* according to medieval sources, consisted of a short melody with one note to a syllable, repeated over and over for each verse in the manner of a litany or folk song. At the end of each stanza was a melodic appendage, which served as a refrain much like the *alleluias* between the verses of psalms and hymns. In the manuscript of the *Chanson de Roland* the puzzling letters AOI appear after each of the 321 stanzas, while in the songs of troubadours and minnesingers

163. *Heinrich Frauenlob Directing a Minstrel Performance,* from the Manesse Manuscript of German minnesingers. 14th century. University Library, Heidelberg.

Chanson de geste melody
(11th century)

Adam de la Halle
(after Gennrich)

Au · di · gier, dit Raim · ber · ge, bou · se vous di.

Aucassin et Nicolette,
Stanza, or *laisse* (13th century)

Adam de la Halle
(after Gennrich)

Qui vau · roit bons vers o · ir_____ del de ·
de deus biax en · fans pe · tis. Ni · co ·

port du duel cai · tif
le · te Au cas · sins. . .

164. Tower of London, aerial view. 1078–90.

the letters are EUOUAE or some variant. EUOUAE is an abbreviation of *sa-e-c-**u**-lor-**u**-m* **a**-*m*-**e**-*n,* the last two words of the Latin version of the lesser Doxology (the full text of which is "Glory be unto the Father, the Son, and the Holy Spirit, as it was in the beginning, is now, and ever shall be, world without end. Amen."), and thus is a link between the troubadour's refrain and some Gregorian melody.

The single authentic example of a *chanson de geste* melody that survives is in a little pastoral play from the 13th century by Adam de la Halle, where it is quoted humorously by one of the characters (above). The short melody is repeated for each line of the stanza, following which there would have been a short cadenza, or refrain, for either the voice or an instrument. The operation of this refrain principle is found in a song from *Aucassin et Nicolette,* a French *chantefable* (above). Written about a century later, it is similar in style to that of the *chanson de geste.* The melody of the first eight measures is repeated for each line of the stanza, each time to different words. The refrain in the final three bars is then either sung or played between each of the verses and again at the end. The extreme simplicity of these melodies indicates that the music alone would not have held an audience. The dominant interest was epic poetry, and the minstrel's performance of it with appropriate action, gestures, and vocal inflection.

Norman Architecture

The architecture of the Normans was sufficiently important to give one aspect of the Romanesque style the name of Norman. The building done in 11th-century Normandy not only had a lasting effect on that region of France but also reached a logical conclusion in the fortresses, castles, abbeys, and cathedrals that the Normans later built in England. Since the Romanesque style in England dates from the Norman Conquest, it is still referred to there as the Norman style.

Norman architecture, like many other facets of Norman culture, resulted from the union of the rugged pagan spirit of the Vikings and the Gallic Christian remnants of the disintegrated Carolingian empire. As a representative product of these people, their architecture reflects blunt strength and forthright character. Both the Carolingian and Viking societies were nomadic. Charlemagne and his successors as well as the dukes of Normandy down to William's time frequently shifted their residences, and the insecurity of the times discouraged building in general. But as the feudal system reached its mature stage and a more settled order became possible, the Norman conquerors turned to the assimilation and development of the vast new lands they had acquired instead of seeking further conquests. William's policy thus shifted from offensive to defensive. Earlier he had discouraged the construction of castles and sanctioned only monasteries; now he proposed to impress his new subjects with solid and unconquerable fortresses as well as feats of arms.

The Tower of London

The Tower of London (Fig. 164), or more specifically the White Tower (Fig. 165), was begun by the Conqueror about 1078 and finished by his successor in order to defend and dominate the town. Its form was that of a Norman keep, and as such it was something new to England. The Tower is simply a massive, square, compact stone building, divided into four

above: **165.** White Tower, London. c. 1081–90. Height 92′ (28.04 m).

right: **166.** Plan of the White Tower.

stories which rise 92 feet (28 meters) with a turret at each corner. A glance at the plan (Fig. 166) will show some of its many irregularities. Its four sides, for instance, are unequal in length, and its corners are therefore not exactly right angles. Three of its turrets are square, while one is round. The one on the west rises 107 feet (32.6 meters), while that on the south is 118 feet (36 meters) high. The walls vary from 11 to 15 feet (3.4 to 4.6 meters) in thickness. In addition, the interior is divided from top to bottom in two unequal parts by a wall running through from north to south.

The bareness of its original exterior (it has been changed over the centuries) was well suited to the White Tower's function as a fortress, but the austerity, or severity, of the interior was a commentary on the bleakness and general lack of physical comforts of medieval life. The Tower was divided into four stories by means of wooden floors, and its darkness was relieved only by narrow, slitted, glassless windows. They were more important as launching sites for arrows than as sources of light and air.

After Norman times, other buildings were added until the whole became a system of outward spreading fortification with the old Norman keep as its heart. From William's time on, the Tower has been in continuous use as fortress, palace, or prison.

The main floor of the White Tower has three divisions: a large council chamber, which also doubled as a banqueting hall, a smaller presence chamber, and the well-preserved St. John's Chapel (Fig. 167). Like a miniature church, this chapel has a

barrel-vaulted nave of four bays. On either side are aisles that command interest because of their early use of cross vaulting. The columns of the nave arcade are thick and stubby, and the cushionlike capitals have only the most simple scalloped carving by way of decoration. Above is a triforium gallery, which was used by the queen and her ladies, with slitlike windows that serve as a clerestory.

Abbey Churches at Caen

At Caen in Normandy, two buildings were under the personal protection of William and Queen Matilda and designated as their respective burial places: St. Étienne, or Abbaye-aux-Hommes (Fig. 168), and Ste. Trinité, or Abbaye-aux-Dames. Since both were abbey churches, they properly belong in a discussion of the monastic Romanesque style, but here they serve to complete the picture of the Norman style.

Begun just prior to the conquest, St. Étienne has a well-proportioned west façade. Four prominent buttresses divide the section below the towers into three parts that correspond to the central nave and two side aisles of the interior. Vertically, the façade rises in three stories, with the portals matching the level of the nave arcade inside, while the two rows of windows above are at the triforium and clerestory levels, respectively. The windows are mere openings and in themselves are quite undistinguished. But the functional honesty in this correspondence of exterior design and interior plan was a Norman innovation that came into general use in the Gothic period.

167. St. John's Chapel, White Tower, London. 1078–97.

The twin towers belong to the original design, but their spires are later additions. As with the usual Norman church, the towers are square and in three stories. Thus they repeat on a higher level the triple division of the façade below. The first story is of solid masonry. The second has alternate blind (that is, blank) and open arches. The greater open space of the third story contributes to its function as a belfry and relieves the general heaviness. Otherwise the bareness and heaviness of the façade in general is a fitting prelude to the gloomy grandeur of the interior (Fig. 169). The church as a whole is as thoroughly rugged and masculine in character as its founder and typifies the spirit of the Norman people and their forceful leader.

When the bare façade of St. Étienne is compared to the exterior of the Tower of London, it becomes apparent that the lack of decoration was a conscious part of the design of both. One façade impresses by its bold outlines, sturdiness, and straightforward honesty, the other by its strength and bluntness.

Though the Norman accent on structure rather than embellishment was to be replaced soon after the Crusades by Saracen innovations, it did lead to advances in the art of building. In their churches, although the clerestory windows were small, the Normans achieved more adequate lighting than in previous Romanesque structures. More unified inte-

riors were attained by connecting the three levels of the nave arcade, triforium, and clerestory by single vertical shafts between the bays that run from floor to ceiling. Both these features, as well as the harmonious spatial divisions of such a façade as that of St. Étienne, were incorporated into the Gothic style.

Still, when the work of the Normans is placed alongside that of their Burgundian contemporaries, it seems crude by comparison. The Normans were as blunt and brash as the Cluniacs were ingenious and subtle. The difference, in short, is that between men of action and men of contemplation.

Ideas: Feudalism

The Bayeux Tapestry, the *Song of Roland,* the abbey churches at Caen, and the White Tower in London are representative of the Romanesque style, and all are related in time, place, and intent. Each was a high point in the development of Norman culture, falling between the dates of the Battle of Hastings in 1066 and the First Crusade in 1095. The *Song* was sung at the battle; the Tapestry was designed soon after the battle whose tale it tells (and both reveal the same form and spirit); and the abbey churches and the Tower were built when William's success and prosperity after the conquest were at their height. This relationship coincided with the climax of feudalism, and it is in the terms of this all-embracing concept that the individual works have their unity.

All the separate concepts of the Norman world were contained in the overpowering central idea of

below: 168. Façade, St. Étienne (Abbaye-aux-Hommes), Caen. c. 1064–1135. Nave 157′ 6″ × 32′ 10″ (48.01 × 10.01 m), height of towers 295′ (89.92 m).

169. Interior, St. Étienne.

feudalism. Like the concentric rings of the inner and outer fortifications of the Tower of London (Fig. 164), individuals in a feudal society were but tiny circles in an expanding cosmic scheme of things that determined their relations to their superiors, their peers, and their inferiors. Correspondingly, the ethic that bound the whole together was *fealty,* a kind of blind loyalty, with right and wrong being fixed by physical force rather than by reason and principle. The feudal system provided a proper place for every person in a strict hierarchy, with barons holding their power from their overlords, ecclesiastical or secular; dukes holding their realms from their king; and the king, emperor, and pope holding the earth as a *fief,* or feudal estate, from God.

Feudal Virtues

The feudal virtues were faith, courage, and blind loyalty to peer and superior. Any departure from this code was treachery and had to be dealt with by isolation and defeat. Treachery and defection from the code had to be decided on the field of battle, with God awarding victory to the righteous cause. Enemies, however, were granted the distinctions of honor and bravery, provided their lineage was in order, otherwise it would have been socially impossible to do battle with them. In the *Song of Roland,* no one below the rank of baron figures with any degree of prominence; similarly, the abbeys of William and Matilda were intended primarily for persons of rank, and by the foundation of these churches the royal pair pledged their feudal oath to God.

In their subject matter, the *Song of Roland* and the Bayeux Tapestry have many points in common. As the *Song* opens:

> Carlon the King, our Emperor Charlemayn,
> Full seven years long has been abroad in Spain,
> He's won the highlands as far as to the main;
> No castle more can stand before his face,
> City nor wall is left for him to break,
> Save Saragossa in its high mountain place;
> Marsilion holds it, the king who hates God's name,
> Mahound he serves, and to Apollyon prays:
> He'll not escape the ruin that awaits.

If the simple substitution of William for Charles, England for Saragossa in Spain, the barrier of the sea for that of the mountain, and Harold for Marsilion is made, the situation becomes the contemporary one that the Tapestry so vividly portrays. Later at the battle of Roncesvalles the dominant trio is Roland, Oliver, and the fighting Archbishop Turpin, in whom it is not difficult to recognize their parallels at Hastings: William and his half brothers, Robert of Mortain and the irrepressible Bishop Odo.

In both *Song* and Tapestry, the cause for war allegedly was religious. In one, it was Christianity versus paganism; in the other, the breaking of a sacred oath when Harold became king—and both causes were sanctioned by the pope. In the poem as well as the tapestry, religious symbols figure prominently. Durendal, Roland's sword, is his most sacred possession, having within it a tooth of St. Peter, blood of St. Basil, hair of St. Denis, and a fragment of the Virgin's robe—all souvenirs of his pilgrimage to the Holy Land. At this time, relics had overwhelming importance. In the Tapestry, Harold's seizure of the kingly power was treacherous mainly because the oath had been sworn on the reliquaries in Bayeux Cathedral. Harold's perjury and breaking of a vow sworn under such sacred conditions was sufficient cause for invasion.

Both Tapestry and poem are set in a man's world of clear-cut loyalties and moral and physical certainties. Chivalry in each is based on the ways of fighting men. The code of Roland and Oliver, and of William and Odo, was clearly, "My soul to God, my life to the king, and honor for myself." It remained for the Gothic period to add, "My heart to the ladies." Roland's dying thoughts, for instance, are occupied with his family and lineage; his king, Charlemagne; his country, the fair land of France; and his sword, Durendal (Fig. 170). Surprisingly, he makes no mention of the woman he has promised to marry, the Lady Aude.

170. *Death of Roland,* from *Le Miroir Historial.* Beauvais, 15th century. Manuscript illumination. Musée Condé, Chantilly.

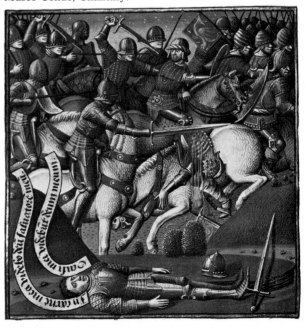

Earlier, the exasperated Oliver had reproached Roland for his rashness in not summoning aid sooner, and at that time he swore:

Now by my beard . . . if e'er mine eyes
Again behold my sister Aude the bright,
Between her arms never you think to lie.

No true or courtly love is this, only the feudal baron bestowing his female relatives like his goods and property on those whose faith and courage he has cause to admire. Later, after Charles returns to France, the poor Lady Aude inquires about the fate of her fiancé. The King tells her of his death and as a consolation prize offers her the hand of his son Louis, whereupon the lady falls dead at his feet. Whether she dies of grief for Roland or from the indelicacy of Charlemagne's suggestion is left open to conjecture. Since scarcely more than a dozen of the 4000-odd lines of the poem are devoted to her, the historian Henry Adams was justified in observing: "Never after the first crusade did any great poem rise to such heroism as to sustain itself without a heroine."

Curiously enough, on the Saracen side Marsilion's queen takes an important part in the affairs of state after her husband is incapacitated. Nowhere on the Christian side is a woman given anything like a similar status. And in the Bayeux Tapestry, the only place where a woman is mentioned by name is the enigmatic inscription *Where a cleric and Aelfgyva,* apparently introduced to give a motive for the minor episode describing an invasion of Brittany. While a few female figures are found in the borders and in attendance at the death of the Confessor (see Fig. 160), none have any prominence. Both works are thus as bold and direct as the poetry and art of the coming Gothic period was delicate and subtle. Roland and his counterparts in the Tapestry fought for king and country, while the knightly heroes of the later period entered the lists for a loving glance from a pair of blue eyes, a fleeting smile, or the fragrant roses tossed from a lady's chamber.

Ruggedness of Feudal Art

Formal considerations of the *Song of Roland* and the Bayeux Tapestry are in keeping with their rugged character. The emphasis everywhere is on the concrete rather than the abstract, content rather than form, and separate narrative episode over structure.

Symmetry in the *Song* and Tapestry is seldom considered. The lines of the poem, for example, are rough-hewn but heroic pentameters, which group themselves into irregular stanzas (known as *laisses*) averaging fourteen lines in length. Similarly, the space given to individual scenes in the Bayeux Tapestry, like the irregular size of the compartments in the archivolt of the Vézelay tympanum (Fig. 141) and the unequal height of the arches in a Romanesque cathedral wall, takes no account of proportion and balance in a unified design.

Details in the *Chanson,* the Tapestry, St. Étienne, and the Tower of London thus remain crude and unpolished. The Romanesque in general and the Norman period in particular are characterized by forming, building, experimenting, and reaching out toward new modes of expression.

In architecture, the process of building was more important than what was built. The emphasis in the Tapestry on representations of castles, fortifications, and specific buildings, like the Bayeux cathedral and the abbey churches at Caen, suggests the image of a builder's world and a century of architectural activity and progress. The forthright, direct narration of deeds in the *Song* and Tapestry finds its architectural counterpart in the functional honesty of the style of the Tower and William's church at Caen. Just as the action-filled story of the *Chanson* and Tapestry takes precedence over literary form and decorative flourish, so the structural honesty of the building process, as exemplified in the Tower and St. Étienne, becomes the leading characteristic. The process of lengthening balladlike poetry into the epic *chanson de geste* capable of sustaining attention through the long Norman winter evenings, or of extending a few pictorial panels into a heroic tapestry depicting a major historical episode in its entirety, was essentially the same as the process of piling up tall towers that could pierce the gloomy northern skies.

The image of the Norman world as it thus builds up through the various arts is not essentially a complex one. There was little of the mystical about these clearheaded Viking adventurers. They caught on quickly to any progressive development of the time, whether it was the discarding of their rather inflexible mother tongue in favor of the more expressive French or the adopting of many of the Cluniac moral and architectural reforms.

Whatever the Normans did, they did always with characteristic determination and energy. Thus the rugged man of action in William unites with the military monosyllables of the *Chanson,* the frank, almost comic-strip directness of the Bayeux Tapestry, and the rough-hewn stones of the Tower and abbeys to make a single monolithic structure. Each was concerned with forms of action, and whether in picture, word, or stone, the epic spirit is present. Deed on deed, syllable on syllable, stitch on stitch, image on image, stone on stone—each builds up into the great personality, heroic epic, impressive Tapestry or gaunt tower. In the process a Norman feudal structure of monumental proportions is revealed.

8 The Gothic Style

Île-de-France, Late 12th and 13th Centuries

In contrast to the shores of the Mediterranean, where such splendid centers of culture as Athens, Alexandria, Antioch, Constantinople, and Rome flourished for centuries, northern Europe had been little more than a rural region with a few Roman provincial outposts and, later, a scattering of castles, monasteries, and villages. Before the 13th century not one medieval center north of the Alps could properly have been described as a city.

Toward the end of the 12th century, however, Philip Augustus as king of France was promoting the destiny of Paris as his capital, enclosing it with walls and paving some of its streets with stone. The work was continued under his successors, and by the end of the 13th century Paris was the capital of a kingdom of growing importance. With its splendid Cathedral of Notre Dame, its university famed for the teaching of Abelard, Albertus Magnus, Thomas Aquinas, and Bonaventura, and with its flourishing mercantile trade capable of supporting about 150,000 inhabitants, Paris could well claim the status of a capital city. When it is remembered, however, that Constantinople was the hub of the rich East Roman Empire and had been a city of over 1 million since Justinian's time, the status of this first northern urban center is seen in proper perspective.

The growth of Paris, while more rapid than other northern centers, was far from an isolated instance. For a full century, the town as a social unit had been gaining importance over the manorial estate, and the literature of the time mentions Ghent with its turreted houses, Lille and its cloth, Tours and its grain,

and how all were carrying on commerce with distant lands. With the exception of such occasional references, however, the life of medieval French towns would have remained a closed book had it not been for the visual record preserved in the castles of their feudal lords, in the monasteries, and, above all, in the cathedrals.

The prototype of the Gothic cathedral has been recognized in the abbey church of St. Denis just outside Paris. This monastery was under the direct patronage of the French kings and was their traditional burial place. Around the middle of the 12th century its abbot was Suger, a man whose talents were as remarkable as his origin was obscure. The trusted confidant of two kings, he ruled France as

France c. 1150–1300

regent while Louis VII was away on a Crusade. When he undertook the rebuilding of his abbey church, his great personal prestige, as well as its importance as the royal monastery, enabled him to call together the most expert craftsmen from all parts of the kingdom. Suger's church thus became a synthesis of all the ideas that had been tried and found successful by the Romanesque builders.

Posterity has had reason to rejoice that the abbot's enthusiasm for his project caused him to write extensively about it, for his book is an invaluable source of information about the architectural thought of the time. In 1130, when St. Denis was in the planning stage, as was mentioned, Abbot Suger had made a prolonged visit to Cluny to learn from firsthand observation about its recently completed church. His commentary on the iconography of the windows and sculpture of St. Denis suggests that he took a personal hand in this part of the project, but of the architect who carried out the building no mention is made. St. Denis is notable not so much for its innovations as for its successful combining of such late Romanesque devices as the pointed arch and ribbed groin vault, and flying buttresses.

Many late Cluniac Romanesque churches had used these features separately, but not before Suger's church had they been grouped into a logically consistent structural system. The abbot's position at the French court, as well as the proximity of his church to Paris, assured the widest possible circulation of his ideas. Hence, St. Denis became the model for many of the Gothic cathedrals that were built in the region shortly afterward.

The Île-de-France (see map, p. 150), the royal domain with Paris as its center, was the setting in which the Gothic style originated and where, over a period extending approximately from 1150 to 1300, it reached the climax of its development. The name of this region referred to the royal lands under the direct control of the French king. The rest of what is now France was still under the dominion of various feudal lords. By heredity, marriage, conquest, and purchase, the Île-de-France gradually had grown over the years into the nucleus of the future French nation. Like a wheel with Paris as its hub, it radiated outward about 100 miles (161 kilometers), with spokes extending toward the cathedral towns of Amiens, Beauvais, Rheims, Bourges, Rouen, and Chartres.

The loftiest expression of the medieval period is seen in these miracles of soaring stone—the crystallized expressions of community effort, religious exaltation, and emotional and intellectual forces of the people who created them. Gothic architecture, moreover, is a struggling, striving, dynamic urge that reaches upward to embrace infinity. Though the

171. Eugène Viollet-le-Duc. Drawing of a Gothic cathedral with full set of seven spires.

building process often spanned several centuries, there are no finished Gothic cathedrals. Completion can take place only in the imagination of the observer. The 19th-century French medieval archaeologist Viollet-le-Duc once projected such a complete cathedral with seven spires—one pair on the west façade, another on the north and on the south transept, and a climactic spire over the crossing of the nave and transept (Fig. 171).

Unlike an abbey church, a cathedral is located in a populated area where it comes under the administration of a bishop, whose official seat it is. A cathedral cannot rise from a plain like a monastic church; it needs the setting of a town where it can soar above the roofs and gables of the buildings that cluster around it. The barren exterior of an abbey forbids, while the intricate carving on the outside of a cathe-

CHRONOLOGY
Gothic Period in France

GENERAL EVENTS		
1096– 1291	Crusades: European Christians fought Moslems and Saracens; extended Christianity; opened up trade routes	
	1137	Louis VII began reign as king of France; married Eleanor of Aquitaine
	1140	Abbey Church of St. Denis, original model of Gothic cathedrals, begun by Abbot Suger
	1142	Abelard, master of School of Notre Dame in Paris, died at Cluny
c.1150–c.1170		University of Paris founded
1163– 1235		Cathedral of Notre Dame in Paris built
	c.1163	Oxford University founded; Cambridge University soon thereafter
1180– 1223		Philip Augustus reigned as king of France; enclosed Paris with walls; promoted Paris as his capital city

1194– 1260	Chartres Cathedral built after fire destroyed earlier Romanesque cathedral with exception of narthex, west portals, two towers, three stained glass windows; 1260 cathedral dedicated by Louis IX	
	1210	Rheims Cathedral rebuilt
	1215	Magna Charta signed in England
	1220	Amiens and Rouen cathedrals begun
	1223	Louis VIII crowned king of France
	1225	Beauvais Cathedral begun; choir finished in 1272
	1226	Louis IX became king of France under regency of his mother, Blanche of Castile
	1236	Regency of Blanche of Castile ended
	1240	Ste. Chapelle, royal chapel of French kings, begun in Paris
	1250	Albertus Magnus taught at University of Paris

	1274	Scholastic philosophy at height. St. Bonaventura and St. Thomas Aquinas died
PHILOSOPHY		
1079– 1142		Abelard
c.1193– 1280		Albertus Magnus
1221– 1274		Bonaventura
c.1225– 1274		Thomas Aquinas
MUSIC		
c.1122– 1192		Adam of St. Victor, joint author of hymns with St. Bernard of Clairvaux
	c.1150	Leonin active at Cathedral of Notre Dame in Paris
	c.1183	Perotin active at Cathedral of Notre Dame in Paris
c.1237–c.1288		Adam de la Halle, author and composer of *Le Jeu de Robin et Marion,* a pastoral play with music
	c.1240	"Summer is icumen in," oldest surviving piece of secular polyphony, written

dral awakens curiosity and invites entrance. As the center of a cloistered life, a monastic church is richest in its dim interior, while the most elaborate decoration of a cathedral points toward the dwelling of the people.

The tall towers of a Gothic cathedral need space from which to spring and room to cast their shadows. Their spires beckon the distant traveler to the shrine beneath and direct the weary steps of the toiling peasant homeward after a day in the fields. The bells they enclose peal out to regulate the life of a whole town and its surrounding countryside. They tell of weddings and funerals and of the time for work and rest and prayer.

A cathedral is, of course, primarily a religious center, but in a time when spiritual and worldly affairs were closely interwoven, the religious and secular functions of a cathedral were intermingled.

Its nave was not only the place for religious services but, on occasion, a town hall where the entire populace could gather for a meeting. The rich decorations that clothe the body of the cathedral told not only the story of Christianity but also the history of the town and of the activities of its people. The cathedral was thus a municipal museum on whose walls the living record of the town was carved.

Inside, the iconography of a cathedral dedicated to Notre Dame ("Our Lady") was concerned mainly with religious subjects. Since the Virgin Mary was also the patroness of the liberal arts, her cathedral often constituted a visual encyclopedia whose subjects ranged over the entire field of human knowledge. The pulpit was not only the place from which sermons were preached but also a podium for lectures and instruction. The sanctuary served as a theater in which the constantly changing sequence of

172. Chartres Cathedral, from southeast. c. 1194–1260.

the religious drama was enacted. The choir was not only the setting for liturgical song but, in addition, a concert hall or opera house, where intricate polyphonic choral works, or *motets,* could be performed and the melodies of the religious dramas chanted.

Outside, the deep-set portals provided stage sets for the mystery plays appropriate to the season, and the porches became platforms from which minstrels and jugglers could entertain their audiences. The stone statues and stained glass were useful not only as illustrations for sermons but also as picture galleries to stimulate the imagination.

Chartres (Fig. 172), unlike Paris, was never a center of commerce but a small bishopric in the midst of a rural district well off the beaten path. Its greatest distinction came from its shrine of the Virgin Mary where annually thousands congregated from far and wide to celebrate the feasts of the Virgin, the grand celebrations that were unique to the Cathedral of Chartres.

Here, as elsewhere, the cathedral was not only the spiritual center of the lives of the townsfolk but the geographical center of the medieval town as well. Towering over all, its great shadow fell upon the clustering church buildings that included the bishop's palace, the cathedral school, a cloister, a hospice, or lodging for travelers, and an almshouse for help to the poor. Its west façade formed one side of the marketplace, and from the cathedral square radiated the narrow streets on which were located the houses and shops of the townspeople. As members of guilds, or associations of craftsmen, the people of the town contributed their labor and products to the cathedral when it was being built and through their guilds donated windows and statuary. They also undertook to fill such continuing needs as candles for the altars and bread for the communion service.

The cathedral itself, toward which all eyes and steps were drawn, represented a group effort of the stonecutters, masons, carpenters, and metalworkers, all of whom gave of their time, skill, and treasure to build it. It thus was the greatest single product a town and its craftsmen could produce.

As a great civic monument the cathedral was the pride of the community, and the ambitions and aspirations of citizens determined its character and contours. In those days, the importance of a town could be measured by the size and height of its cathedral as well as by the significance of the religious relics its cathedral housed. Consequently, civic rivalry was involved when the vaulting of Chartres rose 122 feet (37.2 meters) above the ground. Next came the cathedral at Amiens, which achieved a height of 140 feet (42.6 meters). Finally Beauvais became the loftiest of all with the crowns of its high vaults soaring over 157 feet (47.9 meters).

The extraordinary religious enthusiasm that prompted the undertaking and construction of these immense projects is well brought out by several medieval writers. Allowing for the enthusiasm of a religious zealot, as well as for the probably symbolic participation of the nobles in manual labor, Abbot Haimon's words reflect the spirit of these times.

Who has ever heard tell, in times past, that powerful princes of the world, that men brought up in honor and wealth, that nobles, men and women, have bent their proud and haughty necks to the harness of carts, and that, like beasts of burden, they have dragged to the abode of Christ these waggons, loaded with wines, grains, oil, stone, wood, and all that is necessary for the wants of life, or for the construction of the church? . . . When they have reached the church, they arrange the waggons about it like a spiritual camp, and during the whole night they celebrate the watch by hymns and canticles. On each waggon they light tapers and lamps; they place there the infirm and sick, and bring them the precious relics of the Saints for their relief.

Architecture
of Chartres Cathedral

West Façade

When the harmonious proportions of the west façade of the Cathedral of Notre Dame at Chartres (Fig. 173) are first observed, everything appears as right as an eternal truth. Yet what seems so certain, so solid, so monumental is actually the end result of fire salvage, a long process of growth, and a goodly amount of improvisation. Four centuries, in fact, separate the earliest parts from the latest, and the interval between saw rapid construction in time of prosperity, lag in time of poverty, work inspired with religious ardor, and cruel destruction by fire.

The stylistic difference between the two unsymmetrical spires is one of the most striking features of

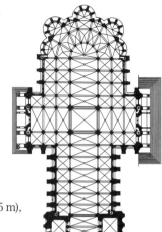

below left: 173.
West façade,
Chartres Cathedral.
Portals and lancet windows
c. 1145;
south tower (right) c. 1180,
height 344' (104.85 m);
north spire (left) 1507–13,
height 377' (114.91 m).
Length of cathedral 427' (130.15 m),
width of façade 157' (47.85 m).

right: 174. Plan of Chartres Cathedral.

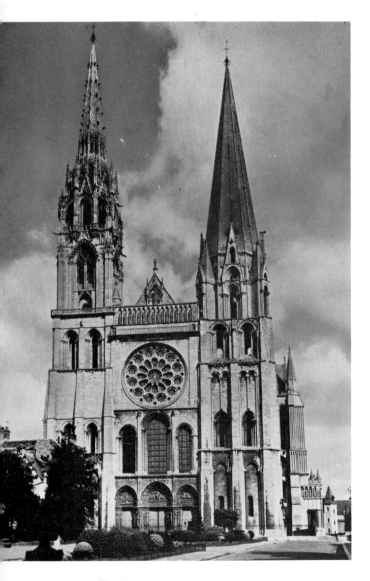

the Chartres façade. The supporting towers, as a part of the previous church, are approximately contemporary. The upper part and the spire of the one on the right, however, date from the time the later parts of the Romanesque abbey church at Cluny were being finished. Their counterparts on the left are contemporary with the laying of the foundations for St. Peter's basilica in Rome in the early 16th century.

Close inspection will reveal such minor flaws as the discrepancy between the proportions of the portals and the scale of the façade as a whole, the rose window being set slightly off center; and the awkward joining of the gallery and arcade of kings above it with the tower on the right. In spite of these differences, the façade bears out the initial impression of unity surprisingly well. Its space is so logically divided as to become an external promise of the interior plan (Fig. 174). Horizontally, the three entrance portals lead into the nave while the flanking towers face the aisles. Vertically, the portals correspond to the nave arcade within, the lancets to the triforium gallery, and the rose window to the clerestory level. By this means, the spatial composition maintains a close relationship between the inner and outer aspects of the structure.

Rising above the twin towers are the tall, tapering spires that seem both a logical and necessary continuation of the vertical lines of the supporting buttresses below and a fitting expression of the Gothic spirit of aspiration generally. The façade of Chartres, however, is rare in having a pair of spires. In Paris, Rouen, Amiens, and elsewhere, spires were projected but never completed; and at Strasbourg, one tower has a spire while the other does not.

The two towers at Chartres make an interesting contrast between the attitudes of the early and late architects. In the older one on the south (right), the builder felt that the joining of tower and spire should be made as smoothly as possible and did so by adding a story between the three levels of the tower below and the single shaft of the spire above. Here the eight dormerlike windows project from the roof, each being surmounted by alternating higher and lower miniature spire forms of its own. These overlap the base of the larger spire, break the line, and add to the rhythm of the vertical movement. The transition from the square supporting tower to the octagonal form of the spire, and the continuation of the straight lines rising from ground level to the receding sloping lines of the spire, which culminate 344 feet (104.8 meters) above, is accomplished with finesse. The later Gothic architect, whose task was to replace the old wooden spire that had burned, was more concerned with intricacy of design and with sending the slimmer and more elegant spire 33 feet (10 meters) higher than its neighbor. While both excel in terms of their own stylistic contexts, it is the old south tower, still sound after seven centuries and almost as many fires, that commands the most admiration.

Nave

When one enters Chartres Cathedral through the central portal, the broad nave (Fig. 175) spreads out to a width of 53 feet (16 meters), making it one of the most spacious of all Gothic naves. On either side are amply proportioned aisles with their stained glass windows that allow a rich flood of light to enter.

Interior Construction   The plan (Fig. 174) reveals that, in comparison with the abbey church at Cluny (Fig. 138), the Gothic architect has practically dispensed with walls. Instead of running parallel to the nave, the *piers,* vertically rising masonry supports, are now at right angles to it, and the area between is bridged over with vaults. This allows open space for glass to light the interior at both ground and clerestory levels. The walls, instead of serving to bear the weight of the superstructure, now exist mainly to enclose the interior and as a framework for the glass.

Through the language of form and color, in representations of religious subjects, the wall space communicates with the worshipers. On a sunny day the beams of filtered light transform the floor and walls into a constantly changing mosaic of color. Together with the clerestory windows, the shafts of mysterious light serve also to accent the structural system of arches, piers, and vaults in such a way as to contribute to the illusion of infinite size and height. And since the eye is naturally drawn to light, the interior gives the impression of being composed entirely of windows (Fig. 176).

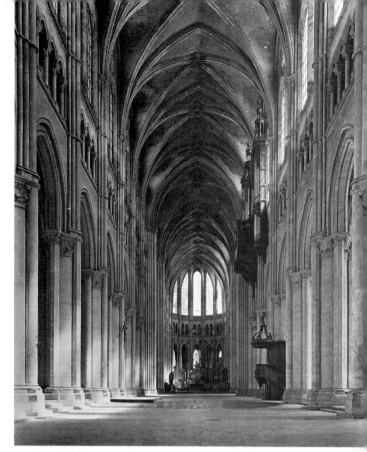

175. Nave and choir, Chartres Cathedral. c. 1194–1260. Length of nave 130′ (39.62 m), width 53′ (16.15 m), height 122′ (37.19 m).

From the center of the nave, attention is drawn next to the arcade of six bays marching majestically toward the crossing of the transept and to the choir beyond. The immense piers consist of a strong central column with four attached colonnettes of more slender proportions clustered around it. As Figure 175 shows, piers with cylindrical cores and attached octagonal colonnettes alternate with piers with octagonal cores and attached cylindrical colonnettes. An interesting rhythm of procession and recession is set up, and a further variation is provided by the play of light on the alternating round and angular surfaces of the piers.

The space above the graceful pointed arches of the nave arcade is filled by a series of smaller open arches that span the space between the bays (see Fig. 176). Behind them runs the triforium gallery, a passage using the space above the internal roofing over the aisles and under the slanting external roof that extends outward from the base of the clerestory. Above the triforium runs the clerestory level, which now fully accomplishes its purpose. The triple pattern of two tall, pointed *lancet windows* below and a circular one above allows a maximum of space for the glass and a minimum for the masonry.

right: 176.
North clerestory wall of nave,
Chartres Cathedral.
c. 1194–1260.

below: 177. Transverse section
of nave (left) and diagram
of vaulting (right),
Chartres Cathedral.
Drawing by Goubert.

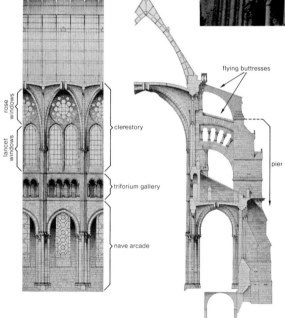

rose windows

lancet windows

flying buttresses

clerestory

pier

triforium gallery

nave arcade

of the vaults toward the ground as efficiently as possible. The heavier transverse ribbing is carried past the clerestory and triforium levels by the large central shaft, while the smaller cross ribs are borne by the groups of slender colonnettes that extend downward and cluster around the massive central piers of the nave arcade below.

Chartres is about midway in the cumulative trial-and-error process by which the Gothic system was eventually perfected. The central piers of the nave arcade are still somewhat bulky, as though the architect did not feel entirely free to be daring. Greater slenderness was achieved at Rheims and Amiens. The tendency toward slimness and height continued until its limit was achieved at Beauvais.

Exterior Supports   Externally, there is an opposite number to each of these interior members (Fig. 178). The purpose of the flying buttress is to carry the thrust of the vaulting at specific points outward over the aisles to the piers that are set at right angles to the length of the nave. The function of flying buttress, *pinnacle,* or small spire, and pier is now clarified. From the observer's point of view, just as in the interior of the cathedral the eye is drawn irresistibly upward by the rising vertical lines, so on the outside it follows the rising vertical piers to the pinnacles, along the procession of the flying buttresses toward the roof of the transept, and on to infinity.

Covering the span of the nave is the triumph of the Gothic builders, the broad quadripartite, or four-part, vaulting (Figs. 175, 177), which at Chartres rises 122 feet (37 meters) above the ground level. It is this principle of vaulting that underlies all Gothic thinking and, in turn, explains all the supporting facts of shafts, colonnettes, clustered columns, piers, and pointed arches. Each of these comes into play to direct the descending weight of the intersecting ribs

The purpose of the pointed arch also becomes clear now. The Romanesque architects of Burgundy had used it at Cluny mainly as a decorative motif to promote a feeling of height and elegance (see Fig. 140). Gothic architects, however, pointed their arches to raise the crowns of the intersecting ribs of the vaulting to a uniform height so as to achieve greater structural stability. The tendency of the round arch is to spread sideways under the gravitational force of the weight it bears. A pointed arch, being steeper, directs the thrust of its load downward and onto the upright supporting members (Fig. 179). By the ever-increasing skill with which they used the device of the pointed arch, Gothic builders were able to achieve a constantly increasing height. This, in turn, led to loftier vaults and more ethereal effects.

When all these various devices—pointed arch, rib vault, flying buttress, triforium gallery, walls maintained by spacious arcades, window spaces maximized at all levels—came together in a working relationship, Gothic architects were able to bring the dead masses of masonry into an equilibrium of weights and balances. Gothic architecture is thus a complex system of opposing thrusts and counter-thrusts (Fig. 178) in which all parts exist in a logical relation to the whole. The weight and position of each stone had to be considered in terms of what was above and below it, so that its force could be properly transmitted along the various levels until it eventually was grounded. If any part should give way, the entire structure would be endangered. It is all the more remarkable when one remembers that Gothic builders used mortar and concrete in the joinings only as reinforcement and as a kind of structural insurance.

This logic of interior and exterior supports could not always take into account the irregularity of a cathedral's site. Over the years the ground might settle at certain points, or some of the piers and

178. South nave exterior, Chartres Cathedral. c. 1194–1260.

buttresses might be undermined by floods, thus putting the whole structure in danger. It also was impossible to make the vaults at high levels heavy enough to withstand wind and weather. At Chartres and elsewhere, the thin-webbed masonry had to be protected by the addition of wooden roofs. At Chartres these roofs actually burned several times without, however, destroying the stone vaults underneath. The builder of Chartres achieved such stability that the structure has never had to be reinforced. It stands today substantially as it did seven centuries ago. Rheims Cathedral has fared equally well by

179. The *pointed arch* and *ribbed groin vault* are fundamental to Gothic architecture, making it a light and flexible building system that permits generous openings in walls for large, high windows. The result is well-illuminated interior spaces. Whereas the less stable, lower round arches spread the load laterally (a), pointed arches, being more vertical, thrust their load more directly toward the ground (b). Too, pointed arches can rise to any height, but the height of semicircular arches is governed by the space they span. In (c) and (d) the space, or *bay*, that has been vaulted is rectangular in shape, rather than square. In (c) the round arches create a dome-shaped vault whose forms and openings are irregular and restricted. In (d) the pointed arches rise to a uniform height and form a four-part Gothic vault with ample openings.

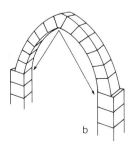
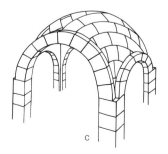
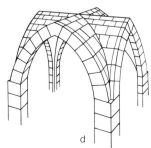

a   b   c   d

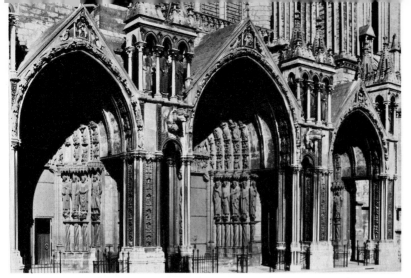

surviving the centuries, two fires, and an artillery bombardment in World War I. Gothic cathedrals, in fact, have so far borne out the hopes of people who desired to raise buildings that "have nothing to fear from fire till the day of judgment."

Transept, Choir, and Apse

At Chartres, the wings of the transept terminate in triple portals (Fig. 180) that in size and magnificence surpass those of the western façade, parts of which had survived from the previous church. The north and south portals in the 13th-century style, however, are framed by row upon row of richly sculptured receding archivolts that bring a maximum of light and shadow into play. The shape of such sections was partly determined by the tastes of individual donors. The north transept with its portals, porch, and stained glass was the gift of the royal family of France, primarily Blanche of Castile and her son Louis IX (Fig. 181), while its southern counterpart was donated by their archrival, the Duke of Brittany. When the cathedral was dedicated in the year 1260, Louis IX was present with such an assembly of bishops, canons, princes, and peasants as had rarely been seen before.

Beyond the transepts extend the spacious choir and sanctuary, surrounded by a double-aisled ambulatory that gives easy access to the apse and its necklace of radiating chapels. The increasingly elaborate Gothic liturgy demanded the participation of more and more clerics, and the cavernous recesses of the huge structure were needed to accommodate an ever-growing number of choristers. The apsidal chapels are also a distinctive feature of a developed Gothic plan, so that pilgrims could have access to the various altars where the revered relics of saints were kept in reliquaries.

The Cathedral of Notre Dame at Chartres, as well as earlier churches that stood on the same site, was

closely associated with the cult of the Virgin Mary. Its most famous relic was the legendary veil of the Virgin which, by tradition, had been presented to Charlemagne by the Byzantine Empress Irene. Another chapel enshrined the skull of St. Anne, the Virgin's mother, which was brought back by Crusaders and given to the church in 1205. This relic explains the many representations of St. Anne in statuary and stained glass and the pilgrimages in her honor, which were second only to those of the Virgin.

The most important chapel in Gothic cathedrals was the *Notre Dame,* or Lady Chapel, devoted to Mary. It was usually placed on the main axis of the nave beyond the center of the apse, with chapels of other saints grouped on either side. All these considerations caused the parts beyond the transepts to expand to unprecedented proportions.

Interior Lighting

Gothic interiors need little more decorative detail than the vertical lines of the structural members, the variety of representations in stained glass, and above all, the flow of light. At Chartres, the lighting is so organized as to achieve a gradual crescendo. It proceeds from the dark violet and blue lancets and rose window in the west through the brighter tones of the aisle and clerestory windows of the nave, past the flaming reds of the transept rose windows to the high intensity of the five red and orange lancets, the tall pointed windows in the apse. These apsidal windows soar above the altar and capture the rays of the morning sun.

Romanesque abbey churches were lighted mainly from within by lamps and candles, while Gothic interiors are illuminated by sunlight transformed through stained glass into a myriad of mysterious prismatic colors. The interior masses and voids become activated and etherealized by the directional flow of light, and material and immaterial elements fuse into a glowing harmonious whole.

Sculpture of Chartres Cathedral

As important to the medieval mind as the structure of the cathedral itself was the choice and location of the sculptural and pictorial representations that were to give the church its significance and meaning. In a Romanesque monastic church, these were found in the carved tympanums over the narthex portals, on the capitals of the columns throughout the interior, and in wall paintings, especially in the apsidal end. Since such representations were designed for those leading cloistered lives, they were placed inside, and the variety and subtlety of their subjects make it clear they were meant to be pondered upon and carefully studied.

Gothic sculpture was more popularly oriented and faced the outside world, where it clustered around and over the porches and entrance portals to form an integral part of the architectural design. Both the large number of figures and the quality of their execution testify to the importance of sculpture

in the art of the period. The exterior of Chartres has more than 2000 carved figures, which are about evenly distributed among the west façade and the north and south porches of the transepts.

Gothic sculpture, like the Romanesque, was done by itinerant craftsmen who gathered wherever a church was being built. From the enormous productivity of the period, it seems clear that the ranks of these craftsmen must have been numerous, and that the strokes of the sculptor's chisel on stone must have been a familiar sound. Gothic sculptors had the advantage of excellent stone models to follow, where their Romanesque predecessors had had to translate the lines of illuminated manuscripts into the stone medium. While Romanesque sculptors thought more in linear terms (see Figs. 141, 154), their Gothic counterparts were more concerned with carving in depth; and the placement of the Gothic sculpture out of doors also made the play of light and shade more important. While the technique of the Gothic sculptor undoubtedly was superior, the iconography had become standardized in this time and did not allow quite so much imaginative freedom as the Romanesque sculptor had enjoyed. Both Romanesque and Gothic sculpture, however, shows the unevenness of workmanship associated with "school sculpture," because some freelance carvers were more skillful than others.

The profusion of sculpture in a Gothic cathedral might lead to considerable confusion were it not for the close relationship of the sculptured forms to the architectural framework. The Gothic structure was so complete, so overwhelming, that no amount of decorative license would have been able to overshadow it. Nevertheless, the Gothic carvers had no intentions of going their separate ways, and their work was always conceived and executed in terms of the architectural frame of reference. Even so, the enormous number of examples would be bewildering were it not for some attempt to unify the iconography. Since it is a people's church, the cathedral could not follow so consistent a system as that of an abbey, which was designed for a small group of people following a common ideal of life. Instead of single unified compositions, therefore, the designer of the Gothic cathedral sought to provide something for every level of taste.

A Gothic cathedral, with the all-embracing activities it housed and the all-encompassing subject matter of its sculpture and stained glass, has often been likened to a *summa,* a comprehensive summary of law, philosophy, and theology written by medieval scholars. Cathedrals have also been described as the Bible in stone and glass, or the books of the illiterate; but they should not be overlooked as visual encyclopedias for the educated as well.

Iconography

The key to the iconography of Chartres is the encyclopedic character of medieval thought as found in the *Speculum Majus* of the French Dominican scholar Vincent of Beauvais, who divided all learning into Mirrors of Nature, Instruction, History, and Morality. The Mirror of Nature is seen in the plant and animal forms that are represented in comprehensive fashion. Instruction is present in the personifications of the seven liberal arts and the branches of learning taught in the universities. History is found in the story of humanity from Adam and Eve to the Last Judgment. Finally, Morality can be seen in the figures depicting virtue and vice, the wise and foolish virgins, the saved and the damned in the Last Judgment, and in the hovering saints and angels and fleeing gargoyles and devils.

There is also a recognizable sequence of presentation. The beginning is on the west façade, where the story of Christ from His ancestors to His ascension is told. The middle is on the north porch, where the history of Mary is traced along Old Testament lines from the creation of Adam to her death and heavenly coronation. And the end is on the south porch, which takes up the drama of redemption from the New Testament, through the work of the Church, its saints, popes, abbots, and bishops, to the climax of the final day of the universe at the Last Judgment.

Each of the three porches has some seven hundred carved figures clustered in the three tympanums over the portals, the archivolts that frame them, and the columns below and galleries above. In addition to the scriptural scenes and lives of the saints, the designers found a place for ancient lore and contemporary history, for prophecy and fact, for fabulous animals and the latest scientific knowledge, for portraits of princes and those of merchants, for beautiful angels and grotesque gargoyles (some of which function as water spouts to drain the roof, others as decorative motifs symbolizing demons fleeing from the sacred precincts of the church).

The iconography at Chartres stems from three principal sources: the dedication of the cathedral to Our Lady, a church privilege that was shared with such other Notre Dame cathedrals as those at Paris, Rheims, Rouen, and Amiens; the presence of a cathedral school, an important center of learning, for Mary was also the patroness of the liberal arts; and the preferences of such patrons as the royal family, lesser nobility, and local guilds who donated assorted representations.

It must also be borne in mind that sacred and secular elements in a medieval town and manor were so closely interwoven that every spiritual manifestation had a worldly counterpart. So the cathedral, as the court of Mary, Queen of Heaven, had to surpass in magnificence the grandeur that surrounded any mere earthly queen. Gothic chivalry and courtliness were rapidly replacing the might-makes-right code of Romanesque feudalism. And just as the clergy sang the praises of Notre Dame, so the knights of the castles praised their ladies in particular and Our Lady in general. The high place of womanhood in secular circles is thus the courtly parallel of the religious cult of the Virgin.

In the poetry of the time, a knight's lady love is always the paragon of feminine virtue and charm. To woo and win her, he who aspired to her favor had to storm the fortress of her heart by techniques far more intricate and subtle than those needed to take a castle. When successful, he became the vassal of his mistress and she his liege lady to command him as she would. The concept of romantic love originated here in the Gothic period and came to full flower in the complex code of chivalry. With its exaltation of the position of women and its concern with the defense of the weak against the strong, chivalry established the Western code of manners that has remained the ideal well into modern times.

West Façade

The sculptures and doorways of the west façade at Chartres are called the Royal Portal (Fig. 182). The central tympanum encloses the figure of Christ in Majesty surrounded by the four symbolic beasts of the Evangelists and the twenty-four elders of the Apocalypse. The tympanum over the left portal depicts the close of Christ's days on earth and His ascension. On the right is the tympanum of the Virgin Portal (Fig. 183), depicting the beginning of the Savior's earthly life.

In the simplest terms, the story is told in three rising panels. Starting in the lower left is the Annunciation, with just the figures of the Angel Gabriel and Mary. The next pair shows the Visitation. The Nativity is in the center. The shepherds in the midst of their sheep are coming from the right for the Adoration, just as their successors came in from the fields near Chartres to worship at Mary's shrine. The middle panel depicts the presentation of the young Jesus in the temple. His position on the altar foreshadows His later sacrifice. Friends approach from both sides bearing gifts. In the top panel, the Virgin sits crowned and enthroned, holding her Divine Son and attended by a pair of archangels. She is shown frontally as a queen accepting the homage of the humble, who enter her court through the portal below.

Seven Liberal Arts   Of great interest are the figures in the archivolts that frame the tympanum.

above: 182. Royal Portal, west façade, Chartres Cathedral. Right, Virgin Portal. c. 1145–70.

right: 183. *Life of the Virgin Mary,* tympanum of Virgin Portal, west façade, Chartres Cathedral. c. 1145–70.

These symbolize Mary's attributes. Like Athena of old, the Virgin was the patroness of the arts and sciences. The German philospher Albertus Magnus in his *Mariale* declared that the Virgin was perfect in the arts; and in his *Summa,* the Italian theologian Thomas Aquinas included among his propositions the question of "Whether the Blessed Virgin Mary possessed perfectly the seven liberal arts"—which, of course, was triumphantly affirmed. These representations are also reminders that this was an age which produced great scholars, and that intellectual understanding as well as faith was now one of the paths to salvation. The fact that Chartres was the location of one of the great cathedral schools is also brought out. Before the founding of the University of Paris, it shared with Rheims the distinction of being one of the best-known centers of learning in Europe.

The curriculum of the cathedral school was, of course, the seven liberal arts. These were divided into the *trivium,* which dealt with the science of words in the three subjects of grammar, rhetoric, and dialectic (logic), and into the higher faculty of the *quadrivium,* which was concerned with the science of numbers through the study of arithmetic, geometry, astronomy, and music.

On the archivolt, these seven arts are symbolized abstractly by female figures somewhat akin to the ancient Muses, while below them are found their most famous human representatives. Beginning with the lower left corner of the outside archivolt, Aristotle is seen dipping his pen into the inkwell. Above him is the thoughtful figure of Dialectic. In one hand she holds a dragon-headed serpent symbolizing subtlety of thought, and in the other the torch of knowledge. Then comes Cicero as the great orator, and over him the figure of Rhetoric making a characteristic oratorical gesture. The next pair are Euclid and Geometry, both of whom are deep in their calculations. In the same band, moving now from the top

184–185. Details, Virgin Portal tympanum, west façade, Chartres Cathedral. c. 1145–70.

downward are Arithmetic and probably Boethius. Below them is the stargazing figure of Astronomy, who holds a bushel basket which signifies the relationship of her science to the calendar, so important in a farming district like Chartres. Ptolemy, to whom the medievalists ascribed the invention of the calendar and clock, is her human representative.

The figures on the lowest level are Grammar and Donatus, the ancient Roman grammarian. Grammar (Fig. 184) holds an open book in one hand and the disciplinary switch in the other over two young pupils, one laughing and pulling the other's hair.

The last pair in the series of seven are adjacent to those in the inner archivolt. Below is Pythagoras, the reputed founder of music theory, who is shown writing in medieval fashion with a desk over his knees. Above him is the figure of Music (Fig. 185) surrounded by instruments. At her back is a monochord, used to calculate musical intervals and to determine accuracy of pitch. On her lap is a psaltery. On the wall hangs a three-stringed viol. She is striking the set of three chime bells, an allusion to the Pythagorean discovery of the mathematical ratios of the perfect intervals—the octave, the fifth, and the fourth. Both Gerbert of Rheims and his pupil Bishop Fulbert of Chartres are known to have taken an active interest not only in the theory of music but in its performance as well. The two figures, showing Pythagoras as the thinker and Music as the per-

former, signify that Chartres was an important center for theoretical and practical aspects of music.

North and South Porches

Far more elaborate in scope and less restrained in decorative detail than the west façade is the incomparable north porch. With its three portals it stretches out to a width of 120 feet (36.6 meters), thus spanning the transept completely. A gift of the royal family of France, its construction and decoration extended from the reign of Louis VIII and the regency of his queen, Blanche of Castile, through that of their son St. Louis (Louis IX), or roughly the first three quarters of the 13th century. The north porch is dedicated to the Virgin and expands the theme of the Virgin Portal on the west façade to encyclopedic proportions. Her history from the annunciation and nativity through the childhood of Jesus is found on the left portal. The scenes of her death and assumption are depicted on the lintel over the central door, while those of her enthronement and coronation are in the tympanum above.

Mary's attributes are revealed in the archivolts through series after series of cyclical representations, such as those of the fourteen heavenly beatitudes and twelve feminine personifications of the active and contemplative life. Especially fine is the single figure of her mother, St. Anne, holding the infant Mary in her arms (Fig. 186), which adorns the *trumeau,* the post or pillar, that supports the lintel and tympanum of the central portal. From the harmonious lines of the folds of her drapery to the dignified and matronly face, the work is one of the most satisfying realizations of the mature Gothic sculptural style.

It will be noted from the contours of the south porch (Fig. 180) that the arches of the portals are now more highly pointed, and their enclosure by triangular gables further emphasizes their verticality. The deep recession of the porch allows for a much greater play of light and shade in the statuary that covers every available space from the bases of the columns to the peak of the gable.

The figures on both the north and south porches, in comparison with the earlier ones on the west façade, have bodies more naturally proportioned; their postures show greater variety and informality; and their facial expressions have far more mobility. The representations of plants and animals are considerably closer to nature; and in comparison with the impersonality of those on the west front, many of the human figures are so individualized that they seem like portraits of living persons. In the change of style, however, something of the previous symbolic meaning and monumentality has been lost as well as the closer identity with architecture.

186. *St. Anne with the Virgin,* trumeau of center portal, north porch, Chartres Cathedral. c. 1250.

The Stained Glass of Chartres

Time has taken its inevitable toll of the exterior sculptures of Chartres. The flow of carved lines remains, and the varied play of light and shade relieves the present browns and grays. But only traces of the original colors and gilt are left to remind the observer that here was once a feast of color with an effect that can now only be imagined. In the interior, however, where the stained glass remains undimmed, the full color of medieval pageantry still exists. The wealth of pure color in the 175 surviving glass panels hypnotizes the senses. Through the medium of multicolored light something of the emotional exaltation that inspired medieval people to create such a temple to the Queen of Heaven can still be felt.

Here, as elsewhere, the structural and decorative elements are closely tied together. Just as with the sculpture, the glass does not exist separately but only as a related part of the whole. The designer was always aware of the size, proportion, and placement of the window in relation to the architectural setting.

Glass is not usually thought of as a building material until the 19th and 20th centuries, but in medieval times and later it did have to fill a large architectural void while taking into account the pressure of wind and weather. This the designer accomplished mainly by dividing the space geometrically into smaller parts by use of *mullions,* the vertical posts that divide the windows; by stone tracery to frame smaller glass panels, as in the great rose windows; by parallel iron bars across the open expanse; and, more minutely, by the fine strips of lead that hold the small pieces of glass in place.

While Chartres must divide architectural and sculptural honors with its neighboring cities, the town was especially well known as the center of glass making, and with the highest achievements of its glaziers exemplified in their own cathedral, Chartres is unsurpassed in this respect. The great variety of jewel-like color was achieved chemically by the addition of certain minerals to the glass while it was in a molten state. When cool, the sheets were cut into smaller sections, and the designer fitted these into a previously prepared outline. Pieces of various sizes next were joined together by lead strips. Details, such as the features in the faces, were then applied in the form of metal oxides and made permanent by firing in a kiln. Finally, the individual panels making up the pattern of the whole window were fastened to the iron bars already imbedded in the masonry. When seen against the light the glass appears translucent, while the lead and iron become opaque black lines that outline the figures and separate the colors to prevent blurring when at a distance.

The artists of stained glass shared with mosaicists and manuscript illuminators a distinct preference for two-dimensional designs. The dignified formality of their figures and the abstract patterns of the borders blended their work admirably into the architectural setting. By thus avoiding any hint of naturalistic effects, such as landscape backgrounds, and by concentrating on patterns of pure color and geometrical forms, they helped to promote the illusion of infinite space.

Iconography and Donors

The iconographical plan of the glass at Chartres, like that of the exterior sculptures, is held together mainly by the dedication of the church as a shrine of the Virgin Mary. There is never any doubt on the part of those who enter that they are in the presence of the Queen of Heaven, who sits enthroned in majesty in the central panel of the apse over the high altar. Grouped around her in neighboring panels are the archangels, saints, and prophets, emblems of the noble donors, and symbols of the craftsmen and tradespeople, almost 4000 figures in all, who honor her and make up her court. Below, on her feast days, were the crowds of living pilgrims who gathered in the nave and chapels, aspiring to enter her eternal presence one day as they had entered her shrine.

187. *Bakers,* detail of stained glass window, Chartres Cathedral. c. 1250.

the donor; with a guild, the "signature" took the form of a craftsman engaged in some typical phase of work. In the windows of Chartres some nineteen different guilds are shown including that of the bakers (Fig. 187).

Rose Windows

The great rose window of the west façade dates from the early 13th century and thus is contemporary with the majority of examples in the rest of the church. The three lancets below it, however, like the portals and surrounding masonry on the exterior, originally were part of the previous church. Besides being the earliest of all the windows, they are, possibly, also the best. Their origin has been traced to the school that did the windows for Suger's church at St. Denis, and their work was on the whole much finer-grained and more jewel-like, with infinite care lavished on the geometrical and arabesque patterns in the borders. They are dominated by their vibrant blue background, while the figures and abstract patterns have been done in several shades of red, emerald green, yellow, sapphire, and white. Also dating from before the fire of 1194 is the central section of the regal and glowing panel known as *Notre Dame de Belle Verrière,* or "Our Lady of the Beautiful Window" (Fig. 188).

The great rose window of the north transept (Fig. 189), like the sculpture on the porch outside, glorifies the Virgin Mary. Together with its lancets, the composition shares with the other glass of the 13th century a preference for red backgrounds instead of the earlier blue. Also, the individual panes are larger, and the borders are more conventionalized. Its greatest effect comes from the large splashes of warm color that contrast with the cool tones of the lancets of the west façade.

In the Gothic period the art of stained glass replaced the mosaics and mural paintings of the early Christian and Romanesque churches, and is the ultimate stage in the etherealization of interior space. Because it gives form and meaning to light, the art of the glazier is perhaps better adapted to the expression of transcendental concepts than any other artistic medium.

By the transformation of raw sunlight into a spectrum of brilliant prismatic color, the architect gained complete control over interior lighting. It could be caused to flow in any manner the architect willed. This material control over an immaterial medium could then be placed at the disposal of the architects and iconographers to shape light to their structural, pictorial, and expressive needs.

Something of the ecstasy felt by medieval men and women in the contemplation of the precious

An interesting commentary on the changing social conditions of the 13th century can be read in the records of the donors of the windows. In the lowest part of each one is a "signature" indicating the individual, family, or group who bore the great expense of the glass. Only a royal purse was equal to a large rose window, as evidenced by the fleur-de-lys insignia so prominent in the north rose (see Fig. 189). Within the means of members of the aristocracy and the Church hierarchy, such as bishops and canons, were the lancet windows of the nave and choir. The status and prosperity of the medieval guilds of craftsmen and merchants, however, was such that the vast majority of the windows were donated by them.

While the royal family of France and the Duke of Brittany were content with windows in the transepts, the most prominent windows of all, the 47-foot (14.3-meter) high center lancets of the apse, were given by the guilds. The one over the high altar, toward which all eyes are drawn, was the gift of the bakers. Each guild had a patron saint, and a window under a guild's patronage was concerned with the life and miracles of its special saint. In the case of the nobility, the family coat of arms was sufficient to identify

188. *Notre Dame de Belle Verrière.* 12th century. Stained glass window. Chartres Cathedral.

189. North rose window, Chartres Cathedral. 1223–26. Diameter 44' (13.41 m).

stones that adorned the altar and the jeweled glass of the windows is expressed in the following passage by Abbot Suger:

> Thus, when—out of my delight in the beauty of the house of God—the loveliness of the many-colored gems has called me away from eternal cares, and worthy meditation has induced me to reflect, transferring that which is material to that which is immaterial, on the diversity of the sacred virtues: then it seems to me that I see myself dwelling, as it were, in some strange region of the universe which neither exists entirely in the slime of the earth nor entirely in the purity of Heaven; and that, by the grace of God, I can be transported from this inferior to that higher world in an anagogical manner.

Music

Massive and magnificent as the Gothic cathedral is, it can be considered the highest achievement of its time only if associated with the various activities it was designed to house. Most important, of course, is the liturgy. As the enclosed space increased, the cathedral grew into a vast auditorium that hummed with collective voices at communal prayer, resounded with readings and the spoken word from the pulpit, and reverberated with the chanting of solo and choral song from the choir.

The Île-de-France, site of the most significant developments in architecture of the 12th and 13th centuries, was also the scene of the most important musical innovations of the Gothic period. Specifically, these were the more sophisticated practices of *polyphonic,* or "many-voiced," music and their relation with the still universally practiced *monophonic,* or unison, art of Gregorian Chant. Singing in parts was of northern origin in contrast to the prevailing Mediterranean style of singing in unison, and part singing in folk music apparently predates by several centuries its incorporation into church music. Just as the Gothic cathedral was the culmination in the long process of reconciling the northern urge for verticality with the southern horizontal basilica form, so Gothic music was the union of the northern tradition of many-voiced singing with the southern one-voice tradition to form a new church music.

School of Chartres

The role of Chartres in these developments is obscure. The English prelate John of Salisbury, master of the cathedral school when the symbolic figure of Music was done for the west façade (Fig. 185), is known to have approved the theoretical study of music as a part of the *quadrivium* as heartily as he disapproved of certain innovations in the music performed by the choir there. Scholarly discussions about the mathematical ratios of musical intervals had been going on ever since antiquity, and such abstract problems as how the music of the spheres or an angelic choir would sound had been on the academic agenda ever since Boethius' time.

It is therefore probable that at this time the greater progress was being made in the field of practical music which John so despised. According to the English historian William of Malmesbury, who died about 1142, Chartres was celebrated for its "many musical modulations," and one of the greatest 13th-century musical theorists, Franco of Cologne, is supposed to have been educated at Chartres. Documents and surviving manuscripts, however, indicate that the greatest forward strides in practical music making were being made in the Cathedral School of Paris, known after 1163 as the School of Notre Dame.

School of Notre Dame in Paris

It has already been noted that in the construction of the first Gothic church the builder of St. Denis brought together many principles that had been developed separately elsewhere and for the first time used them in a systematic whole. The same was true of music, and Paris as the growing capital of the French kingdom was the logical place for the pieces to be fitted into a whole. The *contrapuntal,* or polyphonic, forms and textures developed in such monasteries as Cluny and in such cathedral schools as Rheims and Chartres, as well as the tradition of folk singing in several parts, were organized systematically for the first time at the School of Notre Dame in Paris. Again, as in the case of architecture, the man and the time can be fixed with certainty. The first great monument of Gothic music was the *Magnus Liber Organi* by Leonin, dating from c. 1163. As its name implies, it was a great book bringing together a collection of music in two parts, arranged cyclically so as to provide appropriate music for all the feast days and seasons of the calendar year.

Tenor, or Cantus Firmus   In the traditional rendering of the Gregorian Chant, some parts were sung by a soloist and answered responsorially by a

Mira Lege (12th-century descant)   (after Coussemaker)

chorus singing in unison. In the Gothic period, the choir still chanted in the way it had done for centuries, but the solo parts began to be performed simultaneously by two or more individual singers. Notre Dame in Paris, for example, employed four such singers. The distinction between solo voice and choir hence was replaced by the opposition of a group of individual singers and a massed chorus. With several skilled soloists available, the way was open for an art of much greater complexity than had ever been developed before.

Since the music, however, was still intended for church performance, it was required that one of the traditional sacred melodies be used. A special part called the *tenor,* a term derived from the Latin *tenere,* meaning "to hold," was reserved for it. This melody was also known as the *cantus firmus,* or "fixed song," implying that it could not be changed. The development of Gothic music was that of taking this *cantus firmus* as an established basis, and adding one by one the voices called in ascending order, the *duplum, triplum,* and *quadruplum.* Since these voices were superimposed one above the other, a definite concept of verticality is implied, which contrasted strongly with the horizontal succession of tones that characterized the older monophonic chant.

The earliest forms of Gothic polyphony are almost as rigid in their way as the old parallel organum of the Romanesque period, but they are based on the new principle of *punctus contra punctum,* literally "note against note," or point counter point. *Mira Lege* (above) illustrates one of the strictest applications of this idea. The Gregorian melody is in the lower part, while the counterpoint above moves as much in opposition to it as possible. Though parallel movement is not against the rule, and from time to time does occur, contrary motion is preferred. A treatise written at the beginning of the 12th century declares: "If the main voice is ascending, the accompanying part should descend, and vice versa." The name given to this newly created melodic line was the *discantus,* or "descant," referring to the practice of singing against the established melody, a practice that has continued in religious and secular music ever since.

Two-Part Motet   In addition to such examples, Leonin's *Magnus Liber* contains another type of

Organum Duplum (c. 1175)   (in Leonin's style)

Triplum (13th century)   (in Perotin's style;
after Rokseth)

counterpoint known as *organum duplum* (above, top). The Gregorian *cantus firmus* is found in the lower voice, but the individual tones are stretched out to extraordinary lengths. The descanting, or duplum, voice moves now in free counterpoint consisting of ornate melismas over what has in effect become a relatively fixed base.

The greater melodic and rhythmic freedom that the descant assumed called for expert solo singers, and much of the descanting of Gothic times is known to have been improvised. The practice of such a freely flowing melodic line over a relatively fixed bass points to a possible origin in one of the old types of folk singing. Survivals are found in the instrumental music of the Scottish bagpipers, where such a tune as "The Campbells Are Coming" is heard over a droning bass note.

In performance, the slowly moving tenor, or *cantus firmus,* may have been sung by the choir, while the soloist sang his freely moving duplum part over it; or the tenor may have been played on the organ, as the instrument is known to have been in use at this time. The organ keyboard was a 13th-century Gothic innovation, and the many manuscript illustrations from the period point to the wide usage of organs. The term "organ point," furthermore, continues to be used to refer to a musical passage in which the bass tone remains fixed, while the other parts move freely over it.

Three-Part Motet   The next most significant development was the addition of a third part above the other two, which was known as the *triplum,* and

from which the term "treble" is derived. This step is associated with the name of the first practicing musician in history to have the quality of greatness attached to his name. He was Magister Perotinus Magnus, or Master Perotin the Great, active in Paris in the late 12th and probably in the early 13th century. In his revision of the work of his predecessor Leonin, Perotin moved away from polyphonic improvisational practices toward an art based on stricter melodic control and clearer rhythmic definition. By thus achieving a surer command of his materials, and evolving a logical technique for manipulating them, he was able to add a third voice to the original two (see left), and in two known instances there is even a fourth part.

The three-part motet, like its predecessors, still had its *cantus firmus* in the tenor, which was the lowest part and held the *mot,* or "word," from which the term *motet* is probably derived. Over it the contrapuntal voices wove a web of two different strands, singing their independent melodic lines. In the hands of Perotin the three-part motet became the most favored and characteristic practice of 13th-century Gothic music.

Besides achieving ever-greater melodic independence, the two contrapuntal voices even had their own separate texts. A three-part motet thus had three distinct sets of words—the tenor, with its traditional line, and usually two contemporary hymnlike verses over and above it—which were sung simultaneously. Intended as they were for church performance, the words customarily were in Latin. However, around the middle of the 13th century, it was not uncommon for one of the voices to have its verses in French.

With the entrance of the *vernacular,* or local, language came also popular melodies. So above the stately tenor, it was possible to have a hymn to the Virgin in Latin and a secular love song in French going on at the same time. By the simple expedient of replacing the sacred melodies with secular tunes, a fully developed musical art independent of the Church was not only possible but by the end of the 13th century had become an accomplished fact.

Gothic music exists in such close unity with other manifestations of the Gothic style that it can scarcely be understood as a thing apart. The subjects of the new hymns, especially those with the words of St. Bernard and the melodies of Adam of St. Victor, were mainly devoted to the Virgin, as were most of the cathedrals and the iconography of the sculpture and stained glass. Instead of a monolithic choir chanting in unison or in parallel organum, Gothic listeners now heard a small group of professional singers. In the case of a three-part motet, they could choose, according to their temperament or mood, to follow either the solemn traditional melody, the Latin commentary above it, or the French triplum in their own everyday mode of speech. This allowance for diversity of musical taste is a part of the general shift from the homogeneity of monastic life in the abbey to the heterogeneity of city life, of which the cathedral is the expression. The new melodic, rhythmic, and textual variety implies a congregation made up of people from all walks of life, just as had been the case with the diversified imagery of the sculpture and stained glass.

Since the individual voices were superimposed one above the other, a concept of verticality, similar to the architectural developments, is realized. The ear, like the eye, needs fixed points to measure rises and falls. In the *Mira Lege* example (p. 167), the intervals of the lower part established the point over which the descant moved in contrary motion. In the case of the *organum duplum* (p. 168), it was the long sustained tone in the tenor against which the soaring upward and plunging downward movement of the melody could be heard.

In addition to this linear impulse, all types of counterpoint achieve a sense of rhythmical progress by having a relatively static, or stable, point against which the more rapid movement of the other voices can be measured. Together with the several opposing melodies, the clash of dissonant intervals, the simultaneous singing of separate texts, as well as the progress of several independent rhythms, Gothic music was able to build a sense of mounting tension that set it apart as a distinctive new style.

Ideas

In the century between the dedication of the great Romanesque abbey church at Cluny (1095) and the beginning of Chartres cathedral (1194), much more than a change in artistic styles had occurred. A mighty shift in social and political institutions and in basic modes of thought had taken place. The resulting changes in church, secular, and artistic life brought into the open sharp divisions of opinion. Old conflicts, long restrained by the power of the medieval divinely ordered social structure, now burst into flames, and new ones broke out, fanned by the breath of new voices clamoring to be heard. Intellectual disputes grew hot and bitter as emotional tensions deepened.

In this critical situation, rational processes of scholastic philosophy were brought to bear on these divisive forces, and the Gothic is best understood as a clashing and dissonant style in which opposite elements were maintained momentarily in a state of uneasy equilibrium. With the eventual dissolution of the Gothic synthesis in the following century, the basic oppositions, or the dualism, became so impossible to reconcile that they led in some cases to the battlefield, in others to schisms, or divisions, within the Church, and generally to growing philosophical and artistic conflicts.

Gothic Dualism

Politically, the age-old struggle of Church and state, evident in Romanesque times in the endless quarrels between popes and Holy Roman emperors, now shaped up as the conflict between traditional ecclesiastical authority and the growing power of northern European kingdoms, especially France and England. Simultaneously came the beginning of a split between the internationalism of the Church and Holy Roman Empire and rising nationalism that produced centuries of rivalry between the south and north for the domination of Europe.

The prevailing monastic and feudal organizations of Romanesque times had tended to separate society into widely scattered units of cloister and manor, thereby isolating many of the causes of social strains. But as the towns began to grow into cities, the different elements were brought together in a common center where confrontation made problems more immediate.

Tensions mounted between the landed aristocrats on the one hand and the volatile urban groups on the other, between the monastic orders and the growing secular clergy. And towns witnessed at close range the bitter rivalries between abbot and bishop, lord and burgher, clergy and laity.

For the common people there was always the contrast between the squalor in which they existed and the luxury of their lords, bishops, and abbots; between the poverty of their daily lives and promises of heavenly glory in the beyond; between the strife of their world and the visions of serenity and peace in Paradise.

Gothic Dualism and the Arts　The arts were torn between expressing the aspirations of this world and those of the next, and artists between accepting a relatively anonymous status in the service of God and competing actively with their fellows in search of worldly recognition. Instead of the comparative unity of artistic patronage in the aristocratically oriented Romanesque period, patronage in the city was now divided between the aristocrats and clergy on the one hand and the increasingly important middle class and guilds on the other. The rising power of the middle class is well illustrated by such dwelling places as one of the surviving Gothic half-timbered houses at Rouen (Fig. 190) and the splendid residence of the banker Jacques Coeur at Bourges (Fig. 191).

left: 190. Gothic half-timbered house, Rouen. 15th century.
right: 191. Courtyard, house of Jacques Coeur, Bourges. 1443–51.

In architecture, be it the interior or exterior of the Gothic cathedral, there is an opposition between the masses and voids and an interplay of thrust and counterthrust, and of attraction and repulsion that awaken dead weights into dynamic forces.

In sculpture, the conflict of the particular and universal is seen in the remarkable feeling for human individuality in some of the separate figures. It is apparant as well in the iconographic necessity of molding them into the dignified impersonality required of a row of prophets and saints.

In literature, the opposition between Latin and the vernacular languages becomes as evident as the growing distinction between the sacred and secular musical styles. Within the province of the tonal art are found such external disparities as the fruitless academic discussions about the hypothetical nature of the music of the spheres and the increasing importance of the actual sounds heard in the choirs of the churches; the abstract study of theoretical acoustics in the universities and the practical art of writing and making music.

In music also there are such internal differences as the singing of monophonic choruses alternately with groups singing polyphonically, the contrast between voices and instruments, the flow of horizontally moving melodic lines versus their simultaneous vertical aspects, the opposition of consonance and dissonance, and the rhythmical contrast between the independent voices within a polyphonic motet, line against line, *cantus* versus *discantus.* In short, Gothic music displays all the inherent oppositions of an art based on the principle of point counter point.

The Scholastic Synthesis

In the face of so many differences, it seems only a step short of the miraculous that the Gothic style was able to effect a synthesis at all. Such dualities, however, generated the need for some sort of coexistence. That this was achieved is yet another proof of the remarkable intellectual ingenuity and creative vitality of the Gothic period. The method for achieving this coexistence was devised by scholasticism: a kind of pro-and-con dialogue followed by a resolution. The results of this dialectic shaped up in the form of the Gothic monarchy, university, encyclopedia, *summa,* and cathedral.

On entering Chartres Cathedral through the Virgin Portal, the worshiper was reminded by the personification of the seven liberal arts that faith needed to be enlightened by reason and knowledge. Architecture had to be a kind of logic in stone; sculpture and glass had to be encyclopedic in scope; and music had to be a form of mathematics in sound. All experience, in fact, had to be interpreted intellectually rather than emotionally, as in the Romanesque.

To the scholastic philosopher, God, as the Creator of a world based on principles of reason, was approachable through the logical power of the mind. Hence the key to understanding of the universe was in the exercise of the rational faculties. Philosophical truth or artistic value was determined by how well an idea fitted a logically ordered system.

Abelard's *Sic et Non* (*Pro and Con*) was an early manifesto of Gothic dualistic thinking. With unprecedented daring, Abelard posed one pertinent question after another, then lined up unquestionable authorities from the Scriptures and Church fathers for and against. His purpose was to bring out into the open some of the wide cleavages of thought among sanctioned authorities, and he made no attempt at reconciling them.

Aquinas' Summa　The scholastic successors of Abelard debated whether ultimate truth was to be found through faith or reason, blind acceptance of hallowed authorities or evidence of the senses, universals or particulars, causes or effects, theses or antitheses, determinism or freedom of the will, intuition or reason. Thomas Aquinas and his fellow scholastics found the answer in the dialectical method, or logical method of argument. Aquinas' synthesis, as found in his *Summa Theologiae* (*Summation of Theology*), was a comprehensive attempt to bring together all Christian articles of faith in a rational system. Abelard's pros and cons, and the divergent views of the previous 1000 years of speculation, were reconciled by a subtlety of intellect that has never been surpassed.

Such a *summa* was as intricately constructed as a Gothic cathedral and had to embrace the totality of a subject, systematically divided into propositions and subpropositions, with inclusions deduced from major and minor premises. Every logical proposition was fitted exactly into place like each stone in a Gothic vault. If one of the premises were disproved, the whole structure would fall like an arch without its necessary keystone.

Aesthetics and Number Theory　From Aquinas' highly rationalistic viewpoint followed the scholastic definition of beauty, which, according to St. Thomas, rested on the criteria of completeness, proportion, harmony, and clarity—because, he said, the mind needed order and demanded unity above all other considerations. Mathematical calculation and symbolism therefore played an important part in the thought of the time, though it was sometimes more closely allied with the sort of Pythagorean number-magic now associated with numerology than with the modern sense. The number 3 was especially favored because of its association with the Trinity; 4, to a lesser extent because it signified the material elements of fire, air, earth, and water; 7, as the sum of the two, indicated a human being, whose dual nature was composed of both spirit and matter; and the product of these numbers pointed to such groups as the 12 apostles, 12 lesser prophets, and so on.

Since the sacred number was 3, it was used by most of the overall formal divisions. The encyclopedias and the *summas* have three divisions each; the façades of cathedrals have three portals, and the sculptural tympanums above, three rising bands. Naves have a main and two side aisles; vertically, they ascend in the triple division of nave arcade, triforium gallery, and clerestory; and in the clerestory, each bay at Chartres had two lancets and one rose window, and so on. The triple rhyming plan of the Latin poetry as in the *Dies Irae* (p. 185) and in the *terza rima* that Dante wrote in Italian (see p. 186) will serve as literary examples. In music, Gothic composers favored the three-part motet and *ternary,* or three-part, rhythm which was called *tempus perfectum* because of its Trinity symbolism. They considered binary rhythms too worldly to be used.

In the cathedral schools and later in the universities, music was studied mainly as a branch of mathematics. Bishop Fulbert of Chartres emphasized theory in the training of singers, saying that without it "the songs are worthless." His view was generally held throughout the Gothic period. As one theorist put it, a singer who is ignorant of theory is like "a drunkard who, while he is able to find his home, is completely ignorant of the way that took him home." Mathematical considerations, in fact, led composers to emphasize the perfect intervals of the octave, fifth, and fourth for theoretical reasons more than for the agreeableness of sound. The tendency was to suppress sensuous beauty of tone and emphasize the mathematical, theoretical, and symbolic aspects of the musician's art.

Broader Resolutions　The rise of national monarchies in France and England began to limit the international authority of the papacy, as well as to curb the provincial powers of the feudal lords domestically by increasing centralization of civil authority. In England, a political resolution between king and nobles, and between nobles and commoners, was made in the Magna Charta that became the basis for parliamentary government. In France, the establishment of a working relationship between the king and the urban middle class accomplished a similar purpose. King Louis IX of France was skillful enough to strengthen his own kingdom, while maintaining such good relations with the popes that he became a saint. In the cities the guilds brought patrons and craftsmen together; meanwhile, the system of apprenticeships and examinations ensured a high standard of quality and workmanship.

The undertaking of the fantastic Crusades was found to be a way of uniting many opposing European factions in a cause against a common enemy. The code of chivalry was an attempt to reconcile the opposition between idealistic love and the gratification of the senses, and, more broadly, to establish a standard of behavior between strong and weak, lord and peasant, rich and poor, oppressor and oppressed.

192. Salisbury Cathedral. 1220–58. Length 473′ (144.17 m), width 230′ (70.1 m), height of spire 404′ (123.14 m).

The Gothic universities were set up as institutions to bring together all the diverse disciplines and controversial personalities and to fit all the various intellectual activities into a single universal framework. Scholasticism became the common mode of thought, and its dialectic the common method of solving intellectual problems.

The structural uniformity of Gothic vaulting and buttressing was, in effect, the Gothic builder's answer to Romanesque experimentalism. Ample allowance for urban diversity was made in the iconography of the individual cathedral and in the differences of cathedrals from town to town, and from country to country, where each was distinctive (Fig. 192).

Both internally and externally, Gothic architecture tried to synthesize the building with the space surrounding it. Externally, the eye follows the numerous rising vertical lines to the spires and pinnacles and then to the sky. Inside, the experience is similar; the vertical lines rise to the window levels and from these through the glass to the space beyond. In contrast to the monastic church that was based on the notion of excluding the outside world, the Gothic cathedral attempted an architectural union of the inner and outer world as the exterior and interior flowed together through the glass-curtained walls. The thrust and counterthrust of the interior vaulting was paralleled on the outside by that of pier and flying buttress; the sculptural embellishments of the exterior were repeated in the ico-nography of the glass in the interior. Through the medium of stained glass, the iconographers endowed light with meaning by transforming physical light into metaphysical illumination.

The various European languages and dialects found a place for themselves in secular literature, but Latin was championed by the Church and universities as the universal language of scholarship. In music, Latin and the language spoken by the common people were reconciled in the multiple texts of the motet. When only one language was used, the same form provided a highly ingenious method by which an authoritative text was sung, while at the same time one or more running commentaries upon it could be presented. Gothic music also represented a synthesis of theory and practice functioning together as equals. Through all these separate manifestations the Gothic spirit was revealed, whether in the systematic logic of St. Thomas, in the heightened sense of time achieved by the musicians, or the visual aspirations and linear tensions of the builders.

No one of these resolutions was in any sense final, and the Gothic style must, in the last analysis, be viewed as a dynamic process rather than an end result. By contrast, a Greek temple or even a Romanesque abbey is a completed whole, and in both the observer's eye eventually can come to rest. The appeal of the Gothic lies in the very restlessness that prevents this sense of completion. The observer is caught and swept up in the general stream of movement and from the initial impulse gets the desire to continue it. The completion, however, can only be in the imagination. There were, in fact, no finished cathedrals. Each lacked something, from a set of spires in some cases to a nave as at Beauvais. Vincent's encyclopedia and Thomas Aquinas' *Summa* were likewise never completed.

Gothic unity is therefore to be found mainly in such methods and procedures as its dialectic in philosophy, structural principles in architecture, and techniques of writing in literature and music. No more effective processes could have been devised to deal with the specific inconsistencies with which the Gothic mind had to contend. They were, in fact, the only ways to reconcile the seemingly irreconcilable, to arrive at the irrational by ingenious rational arguments, and to achieve the utmost in immateriality through material manifestations.

The object of Gothic thought was thus to work out a method for comprehending the incomprehensible, for pondering on the imponderables, for dividing the indivisible. Gothic art as a whole was designed to bridge the impossible gap between matter and spirit, mass and void, natural and supernatural, inspiration and aspiration, the finite and the infinite.

THE RENAISSANCE

The fertile period known as the Renaissance embraced several major movements and new directions. Among them were the advancement of humanistic and scientific knowledge, an amazing outburst of productivity in the arts, the rise of the Reformation, the discovery of new worlds through navigation, and the growth of cities and national states.

The humanistic scholars saw the Renaissance as an intellectual awakening after a long medieval winter. They searched the monasteries for neglected volumes, collected libraries, and studied the Greco-Roman classics from a new viewpoint. After the fall of Constantinople many Greek scholars found refuge in Italy. They brought with them their learning and ancient manuscripts.

The humanists were inspired by classical models and the rediscovery of the joys and beauties of the natural world. Pico della Mirandola reaffirmed the ancient belief that "nothing is more wonderful than man." He placed emphasis on the individual as "the intermediary between creatures, the intimate of higher beings and the king of lower beings, the interpreter of nature by the sharpness of his senses, by the questing curiosity of his reason, and by the light of his intelligence. . . ."

The discovery of movable type made books more readily available and aided the spread of knowledge. It has been estimated, for instance, that in the 50 years after Gutenberg published his Bible, more books were printed than had been copied by hand in the preceding 1000 years.

More broadly, humanism promoted a revival of interest in the affairs of the everyday world, reasserted the faith of men and women in themselves, and reinforced the role of individuals in all spheres. Poets, writers, dramatists, visual artists, and musicians flourished. Architects were inspired by the geometrical clarity and harmonious proportions of the Roman style. Sculptors and painters studied geometry, optics, and anatomy so as to represent the world in three dimensions as the eye beholds it and to render images of the human body more naturalistically. Women enjoyed a higher place in Renaissance society. Such forceful figures as Queen Elizabeth in England, Catherine de' Medici as regent in France, Beatrice and Isabella d'Este and Caterina Sforza in Italy were important patrons of the arts as well as rulers.

In northern Europe, Renaissance humanism expressed itself less in terms of the revival of antiquity than in scientific observation and careful study of natural phenomena. In the arts this new spirit meant a shift away from medieval symbolism and heavenly visions toward a more careful description and more accurate representation of forms as seen in the natural world. In science this led, among other developments, to the speculations of Copernicus. He literally turned the world inside out by theorizing that the sun was the center of a vast solar system and that the earth was but one of the planets revolving around it.

Galileo and his fellow astronomers set their telescopes to scan the skies and to gather proof of the Copernican theory. In his book *The Starry Messenger*, Galileo said that he had seen "stars in myriads, which have never been seen before." He also discovered four of Jupiter's moons and was the first to publish maps of the earth's moon. His discoveries, however, conflicted with the established position of the Church in heavenly matters. As a result, he was tried before the Inquisition court and ordered to recant his teachings and writings.

The position of the Church as a powerful political force and as an institution increasingly concerned with worldly affairs came in for close scrutiny. The abuses among the clergy in amassing land and money laid the basis for the Reformation, as did the greater interest of the popes in winning victories on the battlefield than in caring for human souls. The reformers rejected the central authority of the Church and the mediation of the priesthood. They held that individuals by reading the Scriptures could interpret the word of God for themselves and arrive at truths independent of traditional religious doctrines.

Erasmus' book *In Praise of Folly* ridiculed the system of monasticism, the pretensions of popes, bishops, university professors, and all who supported what he held to be the outmoded doctrines of the Church. Martin Luther, a German Augustinian monk and professor of theology, led a revolt against such worldly practices as the selling of indulgences in return for the forgiveness of sins. When excommunicated by Pope Leo X in 1520, he publicly burned the papal document that censured him and set the German Reformation in motion. Europe was soon divided into two opposing camps. Italy, France, Spain, Portugal, southern Germany, and Austria remained loyal to Rome. Northern Germany, England, parts of Switzerland, and the Scandinavian countries supported the Reformation.

The age of exploration further broadened the Renaissance world view. The Portuguese navigator Dias reached the southern tip of Africa, and a decade later his compatriot Vasco da Gama made the first journey by sea to India. Columbus discovered America; Magellan led the first voyage around the world. Then Cortez explored and won Mexico, and his fellow Spaniard Pizarro conquered Peru. Meanwhile the English, French, and Dutch were settling along the Atlantic coast of North America.

In the Renaissance the merchant and artisan classes rose to challenge the entrenched position of the landed nobility. This progress of the new urban middle class was fortified by the expansion of trade in the wake of the geographical explorations and by a broader spread of political power among city officials and councils. Some merchant princes became important patrons of the arts and letters. Kings, particularly in England and France, found it advantageous to make alliances with the growing middle class in the cities against their mutual foe, the landed nobility. As a result stronger national states began to develop.

All in all, with these momentous developments in knowledge, thought, science, religion, exploration, statecraft, and the arts, the Renaissance was truly a rebirth for humanity at the dawn of the modern era.

9
The Early Italian Renaissance Style

Italian Panorama, 14th Century

The oppositions that the Gothic 13th century had managed to maintain in a state of uneasy equilibrium by the application of scholastic logic and strict structurality broke out in the 14th century into open conflicts. Like a stormy landscape, Italy was by turns chilled by the winds of a waning medieval winter and warmed by the first breaths of a waxing Renaissance spring.

Gothic cathedrals were still being built in the north, while the sleeping beauty of classical art was being awakened in the south. Thunderous threats of fire and brimstone and fear of the Lord were hurled from church pulpits one day, to be followed the next by comforting Franciscan parables and assurance of divine love and mercy. Professors in universities still argued with the icy logic of scholastic philosophy, while the followers of St. Francis were persuading people by simple human truths. Some painters designed images of doomsday filled with warring angels and demons, while others portrayed biblical stories as seen through the eyes of simple folk. And people wondered whether the world they lived in was a moral trap set by the devil to ensnare the unwary or a pleasant place a loving Creator designed for them to enjoy.

For a drama of such sweeping scope, no single city or center could serve as the stage. All Europe, in fact, was the theater for this many-faceted performance in which people and their arts were in a state of creative ferment. The old Ghibelline and Guelph wars, which had started as a struggle between the forces loyal to the Holy Roman Empire and the supporters of the popes, assumed a new shape in the 14th century. People were moving from the country to the towns, where the entrenched landowning aristocrats rallied around the Ghibelline banner, and the growing ranks of merchants and craft guilds raised the Guelph flag.

The new Franciscan and Dominican orders of monks rarely kept to their cloisters but took to the highways and byways as preachers to all who would gather and listen. Internal Church dissensions were such that even the popes had fled their hereditary seat in Rome to hold court in widely scattered residences, most notably at Avignon in southern France. Writers, such as Dante and Petrarch, became exiles from their native cities, and their words were written during extended stays in half a dozen centers. Like them, the great painters were journeymen, traveling to wherever their work called them. Giotto, the leader of the Florentine school, did fresco cycles that occupied him several years each in Rome, Assisi, and Padua as well as in his home city. Simone Martini of Siena was active in Pisa and Naples before he painted a chapel in St. Francis' church at Assisi. Then he spent his last years at the papal court in France at Avignon.

The great sculptors of Pisa worked also in Siena, Florence, Padua, and Arezzo. Musicians, likewise, sought their fortunes at various courts, with French and Flemish influences and musical forms dominating the Italian musical scene. Artistic modes in general showed wide variation. Local styles sprang up in such centers as Venice, Pisa, Siena, and Florence, while an international style took shape in southern France at Avignon, where the papal court attracted the best talents from every country.

CHRONOLOGY
Italy, Late 13th and 14th Centuries

GENERAL EVENTS		
	1140	Guelph and Ghibelline wars began
1182–	1226	St. Francis of Assisi; 1210 founded Franciscan order (confirmed by pope, 1223); 1225 wrote *Canticle of the Sun;* 1228 declared saint
1198–	1216	Innocent III, pope; Church reached pinnacle of power
1228–	1253	Basilica of St. Francis built at Assisi
	1229	Thomas of Celano's *Life of St. Francis*
	c.1260	Pulpit in Pisa Baptistry finished by Nicola Pisano
	1262	St. Bonaventura's *Life of St. Francis*
1278–	1283	Campo Santo at Pisa built by Giovanni di Simone
c.1296–	1300	Frescoes on life of St. Francis painted at Assisi
c.1305–	1309	Giotto painted frescoes on history of the Virgin at Padua
1308–	1311	Duccio painted Maestà altarpiece, Siena Cathedral
1309–	1376	Popes at Avignon
1314–	1321	*Divine Comedy* written by Dante Alighieri

	1316	*Ars Nova,* musical treatise, by Philippe de Vitry
	c.1320	Giotto painted Bardi Chapel frescoes in Santa Croce, Florence
	1322	*Little Flowers of St. Francis*
1330–	1339	Bronze doors of Baptistry at Florence cast by Andrea Pisano
	c.1334	Andrea Pisano and Giotto collaborated on sculpture for Florence Campanile
	1348	Black Death swept Europe
1348–	1352	*Decameron* written by Boccaccio
	c.1350	*Triumph of Death* painted in Campo Santo at Pisa by Traini
	c.1354	*Triumph of Death* written by Petrarch
1378–	1417	Great Schism between rival popes

PHILOSOPHERS		
c.1214–	1294	Roger Bacon, Franciscan monk and scientist
c.1225–	1274	Thomas Aquinas, scholastic philosopher

c.1270–	1347	William of Occam, Franciscan monk and nominalist philosopher

PAINTERS		
1240–c.1302		Giovanni Cimabue
c.1255–	1319	Duccio di Buoninsegna
c.1266–c.1336		Giotto di Bondone
c.1285–	1344	Simone Martini
1305–	1348	Pietro Lorenzetti active
1321–	1363	Francesco Traini active
1323–	1348	Ambrogio Lorenzetti active

SCULPTORS		
c.1205–	1278	Nicola (d'Apulia) Pisano
c.1250–c.1317		Giovanni Pisano
c.1270–	1349	Andrea Pisano

WRITERS		
1265–	1321	Dante Alighieri
1304–	1374	Petrarch (Francesco Petrarca)
1312–	1353	Giovanni Boccaccio

MUSICIANS		
c.1200–c.1255		Thomas of Celano
	1306	Jacopone da Todi died
1291–	1361	Philippe de Vitry
1325–	1397	Francesco Landini, organist-composer at Florence

In this era of change, the little village of Assisi in the Umbrian hills of central Italy became more representative than a large center like Rome. A town of such small size would, of course, have been too insignificant to support a major art movement, and no important artist could have survived in this provincial location had Assisi not been the birthplace of one of the most beloved medieval saints. Consequently, after the completion in the mid-13th century of Assisi's great pilgrimage basilica, many of the outstanding artists of the age came to decorate its walls.

The town of Assisi was built upon a rocky hill in the midst of a countryside both gentle and lush. A truly mountainous terrain might have nourished a rugged spirit capable of bringing down some new commandments from above, but the gentle rolling green hills instead brought forth the most humble of Christian saints. A large city might have produced a great organizer, capable of moving the minds of the many with clever speeches to bring about a new social order. Francis of Assisi, however, recognized the dangers of bombastic oratory and the short-lived nature of all forms of social organization. He accomplished his mission with the sweet persuasion of simple parables and the eloquence of his own exemplary life.

While the mature life of St. Francis fell within the 13th century, the collection of tales that made him a living legend, as well as the full development of the Franciscan movement, belongs to the 14th. The clergy who received their training in the universities and the scholarly orders of monks had never influenced a broad segment of society. The Franciscans, however, found a way into the hearts and minds of the multitudes by preaching to them in their own language and in the simplest terms, and Franciscan voices were heard more often in village squares than in the pulpits of the churches.

The essence of the Franciscan idea is contained in the mystical marriage of the saint to Lady Poverty, the subject of one of the Assisi frescoes. When a young man had approached Christ and asked what he should do in order to have eternal life, the answer came, ". . . go and sell that thou hast, and give to the poor, and thou shalt have treasure in heaven: and come and follow me" (Matt. 19:21). St. Francis took this commandment literally, and in his last will and testament described his early life and that of his first followers. "They contented themselves," he wrote, "with a tunic, patched within and without, with the cord and breeches, and we desired to have nothing more. . . . We loved to live in poor and abandoned churches, and we were ignorant and submissive to all." He then asked his followers to "appropriate nothing to themselves, neither a house, nor a place, nor anything; but as pilgrims and strangers in this world, in poverty and humility serving God, they shall confidently go seeking for alms."

The Basilica of St. Francis at Assisi

Had St. Francis' vow of complete poverty been followed strictly, no great art movement would have developed at Assisi. A building program involved the accumulation and expenditure of large sums, and immediately after Francis' death this matter created dissension among those who had been closest to him. Brother Elias wanted to build a great church as a fitting monument to his friend and master, while others felt that Francis should be honored by the closest possible adherence to his simple life pattern. The monument Brother Elias had in mind would take a vast treasure to erect, and many of his fellow friars were shocked when Elias set up a marble vase to collect offerings from pilgrims who came to Assisi to honor Francis. Yet only two years later, at the very time he was made saint, a great basilica and monastery was begun on the hill where St. Francis had wished to be buried.

Taking advantage of the natural contours of the site, the architects designed a structure that included two churches, a large one above for pilgrims and a smaller one below for the Franciscan monks. In spite

193. Nave, Upper Church of St. Francis, Assisi. 1228–53.

of their comparatively large size, both churches are without side aisles, having just central naves terminating beyond transepts in apses. The large interior areas are spanned by spacious quadripartite ribbed vaults, which are partially supported by rows of columns set against the walls. Italian Gothic, contrary to the northern style, did not accent well-lighted interiors in which the walls were almost completely replaced with stained glass windows. The southern sun made shade more welcome, and the interiors took on the character of cool retreats from the burning brightness of the world outside.

The absence of a nave arcade and side aisles, and the small number of stained glass windows, allowed ample wall space in both the upper and lower churches at Assisi for the brightly colored fresco paintings that cover them. Lighted principally by the clerestory, the walls of the upper church glow in the dim interior with a mild inner light all their own, illuminated as they are by scenes from the life of St. Francis. More than anything else, it is these murals that bring the twin churches their most special distinction, and the names of the artists who worked on them read like a roster of the great painters of the period: Cimabue and Giotto of Florence and Simone Martini and Pietro Lorenzetti of the Sienese school.

The Life of St. Francis in Fresco

On the walls of the nave of the upper church at Assisi are the series of frescoes on the life of St. Francis that tradition attributes to Giotto (Fig. 193). His actual role as principal painter or designer is still a matter of scholarly debate. The date generally

the entire wall with a layer of rough plaster and allowing it to dry thoroughly, the artist makes a *cartoon,* a preliminary drawing in charcoal, on the surface. Then, taking an area that can be finished in a single day, the artist smooths on a thin layer of wet plaster and may retrace the original drawing. Next, earth pigments (colors) are mixed with water, combined with white of egg as a binder, and applied directly to the fresh plaster—hence the term *fresco.*

The pigments and wet plaster combine chemically to produce a surface as permanent as that of any medium in painting. Artists sometimes paint over the surface after it is dry, but this repainting usually flakes off in time. If corrections are necessary, the entire section must be knocked out and redone. Fresco, then, is a medium that does not encourage overly subtle types of expression; and it is best adapted to a certain boldness of design and simplicity of composition. The emotional depth, the communicative value, and the masterly execution of Giotto's cycles rank them among the highest achievements in world art.

Assisi and Padua Series

The first two panels of the series at Assisi are worthy of Giotto himself, but since Giotto worked with a group of assistants, it is impossible to be completely certain these are actually his work. On the right, after one passes through the entrance portals, is the *Miracle of the Spring* (Fig. 194), while on the left is the well-known *Sermon to the Birds.* The order of the scenes is psychological rather than chronological. These two were placed on either side of the entrance probably to impress pilgrims at the outset with the most popular Franciscan legends—those showing the saint ministering to the poor and humble on one side, and his kinship with all God's creatures, including his brothers the birds, on the other.

The literary source for the *Miracle of the Spring* is in the *Legend of the Three Companions,* which tells of Francis' journey to the monastery of Monte La Verna. A fellow friar, a peasant, and his donkey accompanied him, but the way was steep and the day hot. Overcome by thirst, the peasant cried out for water. Kneeling in prayer, the saint turned to him saying, "Hasten to that rock and thou shalt find a living water which in pity Christ has sent thee from the stone to drink." Pilgrims entering the church were thirsty for spiritual refreshment, and the placement of this picture assured them that they had arrived at a spiritual spring.

assigned to the work is the four-year span just before the jubilee year of 1300. Knowing that more pilgrims than ever before would be traveling to Rome for the celebrations, the artists at Assisi made every effort to cover the bare walls of the upper church in time. The frescoes for the friars' own lower church had to wait until the mid-14th century for completion.

Giotto, like other master artists of his period, had learned to work in a variety of techniques. In addition to frescoes, he did mosaics, painted altarpieces in tempera on wood, and was a sculptor. Several years before his death, he was named the chief architect of Florence, and in this capacity he designed the *campanile,* or bell tower, of the cathedral (see Fig. 207), still popularly called "Giotto's Tower." Some of the sculptured reliefs on the ground-floor level may have been his, and others were presumably carried out from his designs by Andrea Pisano. Giotto's greatest fame, however, rests most securely on the three fresco cycles in Assisi, Padua, and Florence.

The fresco medium calls for the rapid and sure strokes of a steady hand and for designs that harmonize with the architectural scheme and awaken walls into a vibrant and colorful life. After first covering

195. Giotto.
Pietà (*Lamentation*).
1305–06. Fresco,
7′7″ × 7′9″ (2.31 × 2.36 m)
Arena Chapel, Padua.

The composition is as simple as it is masterly. St. Francis is the focal center of two crisscrossing diagonal lines like the letter X. The descending light from the rocky peak in the upper right reveals the contours of the mountain in a series of planes. It reaches its greatest intensity in its union with St. Francis' halo, diminishing in his shadow where his two companions and the donkey stand. The dark mountain at the upper left moves downward toward the shadowy figure of the drinking peasant at the lower right, as if to say he is still in spiritual darkness. But since St. Francis is also on this diagonal line, the way to enlightenment is suggested.

Giotto's marvelous mountains are found in such other of his major compositions as *Joachim Returning to the Sheepfold* (see Fig. 206), the *Flight into Egypt,* and the great *Pietà* (Fig. 195), all in the Arena Chapel at Padua. Structurally, the mountains advance and recede to form niches for his figures, and their hardness and heaviness are complementary to the compassion and expressiveness of his human beings. The mountains, or architectural backgrounds, do not exist in their own right but become volumes and masses in Giotto's pictorial designs as well as inanimate extensions of human nature. Giotto's spatial proportions, furthermore, are psychologically rather than actually correct. Human beings, in keeping with their greater expressive importance, loom large against their mountain backgrounds; and his scattered trees are simply spatial accents.

Perhaps the most dramatic of the series is *St. Francis Renouncing His Father* (Fig. 196) after a controversy involving worldly goods. In his haste to abandon the material world, Francis casts off his garments and stands naked before the townspeople saying, "Until this hour I have called thee my father upon earth; from henceforth, I may say confidently, my Father who art in Heaven, in whose hands I have laid up all my treasure, all my trust, and all my hope." The bishop covers Francis with his own cloak and receives him into the Church.

The expressions of the various figures as revealed in their gestures and facial expressions make this fresco an interesting study of human attitudes. The angry father has to be physically restrained from violence by a fellow townsman, yet his face shows the puzzled concern of a parent who cannot understand his son's actions. His counterpart on the other side is the bishop, who becomes the new father of the saint in the Church. Disliking such a scene, his glance shows both embarrassment and sympathy. These opposing figures are supported respectively by the group of townspeople behind which is an apartment house and by the clergymen behind whom are church buildings. An interesting pictorial geometry is used to unify the picture and resolve the tension. The two opposing groups, symbolizing material pur-

suits and spiritual aspirations, become the base of a triangle. Between them the hand of St. Francis points upward toward the apex where the hand of God is coming through the clouds.

Giotto's Late Style

A notable example of Giotto's late style is found in the *Death of St. Francis* (Fig. 197), the climax of a series of seven he did twenty years later for the Church of Santa Croce in Florence. The stationary horizontal lines of the reclining body are relieved by the varied gestures of the surrounding groups, and with one exception all eyes concentrate on the head of St. Francis. The architectural framework echoes the arrangement of the figures, with the horizontal line of the wall paralleling the body of St. Francis and the vertical lines, those of the standing figures. Within this setting a sense of depth is conveyed by color. The ermine collar and red robe of the figure kneeling at the saint's right hand project him into the foreground; the neutral grays and browns of the habits of the monks in back of the bier place them in the middle ground; and the deep blue sky recedes into the background.

Here again Giotto uses a triangular pattern in telling his story. According to St. Bonaventura's biography, at the moment of Francis' death one of

left: 196. Giotto (?). *St. Francis Renouncing His Father.* c. 1296–1300. Fresco. Upper Church of St. Francis, Assisi.

below: 197. Giotto. *Death of St. Francis* (without 19th-century restorations). c 1318–20. Fresco. Bardi Chapel, Church of Santa Croce, Florence.

right: 198. Nicola Pisano. *Annunciation and Nativity,* detail of pulpit. 1259–60. Marble. Baptistry, Pisa.

below: 199. Giovanni Pisano. *Nativity and Annunciation to the Shepherds,* detail of pulpit. 1302–10. Marble. Pisa Cathedral.

the brothers beheld a vision of the saint's "soul under the likeness of a star exceeding bright borne on a dazzling cloudlet over many waters mounting in a straight curve unto Heaven. . . ." In the fresco, the sides of the triangle are the line carried upward from the saint's head by the gesture of the disciple who sees the vision and the line formed by the inclining crucifix that meet at the apex where the heavenward journey is seen. Giotto thus ties the story content, emotional situation, and dramatic tension into a tight whole in his pictorial structure.

Before and After the Black Death

All went well in Italy during the first third of the 14th century. Townspeople prospered, life was good, the arts flourished. Beginning in 1340, however, a series of disasters befell Italy, starting with local crop failures and continuing with the miseries of famine and disease. The climax came in an outbreak of bubonic plague in the catastrophic year of 1348. In this so-called Black Death, more than half the populations of such cities as Florence, Siena, and Pisa perished. A chronicler of Siena, after burying five of his children, said quite simply: "No one wept for the dead, because everyone expected death himself."

An event so catastrophic, and one that spread over the entire European continent, was bound to have a deep effect upon social and cultural trends. Many survivors found themselves suddenly made poor or, through unexpected inheritances, vastly enriched. Thousands of residents in the relatively safe countryside flocked into the cities to take the place of those who had died. The lives of individuals underwent radical changes that quickened their normal instincts. For some, it was the "eat, drink, and be merry" philosophy, exemplified in Boccaccio's *Decameron;* for others, it was moral self-accusation and repentance, as seen in the purgatorial vision of the same author's later *Corbaccio.*

Driven by fear and a sense of guilt, people felt that something had gone disastrously wrong and that the Black Death, like the biblical plagues of old, must have been sent by an angry God to chastise humanity and turn it from its wicked ways. Both Boccaccio and Petrarch in the literary world turned to this view after their earlier, more worldly writings, and what was true of literature was true also of painting.

Sculpture at Pisa

Giovanni Pisano and his father Nicola were the two outstanding sculptors of their time. Nicola Pisano, also known as Nicola d'Apulia from his southern Italian origin, designed a handsome pulpit with six religious panels for the Baptistry at Pisa, and some years later Giovanni did one for the cathedral. The panels of both depict scenes from the New Testament. The differing attitudes of the father's generation and of the son's are revealed when panels dealing with the same subject are compared. Together, their work represents the trend of sculpture before the Black Death.

Nicola's panel of the *Annunciation and Nativity* (Fig. 198) clearly was influenced by the relief sculpture he knew so well from his formative years spent near Rome (see Figs. 85, 104, 105, 109). The Virgin appears as a dignified Roman matron reclining in a characteristic classical pose. The angel at the left in

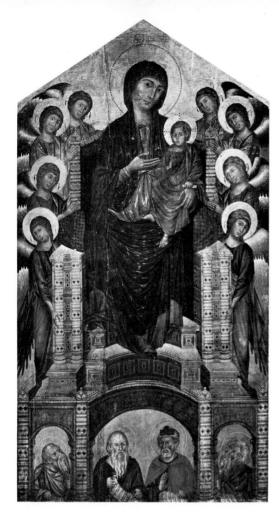

200. Cimabue. *Madonna Enthroned*. 1270–85. Tempera on wood, 12′6″ × 7′4″ (3.81 × 2.24 m). Uffizi. Florence.

the Annunciation section is seen against a classical temple and is dressed in a Roman toga, as are many of the other figures. Nicola employs the old simultaneous mode of narration, with the Virgin making three appearances on the same panel. The relief as a whole projects a mood of monumental calm.

Giovanni's work, as seen in his *Nativity and Annunciation to the Shepherds* (Fig. 199), moved away from his father's classicism into the French Gothic orbit. His figures are smaller in scale and more naturally proportioned to their surrounding space. Greater animation and agitation of line replace the serene repose of his father's style. The work of both father and son, however, has a sense of human warmth that closely resembles the spirit of Giotto's frescoes on the life of St. Francis.

Sienese and Florentine Schools of Painting

Nearby Siena, prior to the Black Death, was also enjoying a period of prosperity. Unlike its rival city Florence, which was a Guelph stronghold where power was held by the guilds and rich merchants,

Siena was a faithful Ghibelline town dominated by the landed aristocracy. These oppositions led Florence in a progressive direction and kept Siena as a stronghold of tradition. Cimabue, the leading Florentine artist of the late 13th century who brought the Gothic style to its peak in his city, was succeeded by the formidable figure of Giotto, whose painting points clearly to the coming Renaissance. In Siena, however, the great Duccio was followed by Simone Martini and the Lorenzetti brothers, who continued in the Byzantine tradition that had been introduced into Italy via such centers as Ravenna and Venice many centuries earlier. Despite this traditionalism, the Sienese school poured enough late Gothic wine into the old medieval wineskins to bring about a brilliant, but final, flowering of Italo-Byzantine painting.

Four altarpieces for Florentine churches—similar in purpose, theme, and form but different in style—will illustrate this painterly trend. Cimabue's *Madonna Enthroned* (Fig. 200), designed for the high altar of Santa Trinità, has all the feeling of medieval majesty and monumentality. Gothic verticality governs the two-story composition with four solemn prophets below displaying their scrolls and the ascending ranks of the eight angels above. The Madonna sits frontally on a solid architectural throne of complexly inlaid wood. Her dark blue mantle and rose-red robe are flecked with highlights of gold that combine with the rich folds to create a rhythmic linear pattern. The Christ Child conforms to the theological image of the miniature patriarch born knowing all things.

Duccio's altarpiece called the *"Rucellai" Madonna* (Fig. 201), from the Church of Santa Maria Novella, is in a lighter, more buoyant and decorative vein. While Duccio undoubtedly knew Cimabue's monumental style, his kneeling angels are airier, as if gently settling down after a heavenly flight. The folds of the background drapery, liberal use of gold, Byzantine richness of line, surpassing delicacy of the zigzag edges of the Madonna's robe, slight off-center angle of the throne, gauzy drapery of the Child whose mantle has casually slipped down—all achieve a maximum of grace and elegance.

The new direction of the early Renaissance, however, is manifest in Giotto's *Madonna Enthroned* (Fig. 202), painted for the Church of Ognissanti about twenty years later than those of Cimabue and Duccio. Two angels kneel in the foreground, while the angels of the heavenly choir are placed one in front of the other so as to expand the sense of space and to create a recession in depth toward the back row where six grave saints are depicted. The draw-

above left: 201. Duccio.
"Rucellai" Madonna. 1285.
Tempera on wood,
14′9″ × 9′6″ (4.5 × 2.9 m).
Uffizi, Florence.

above right: 202. Giotto.
Madonna Enthroned. c. 1310.
Tempera on wood,
10′8″ × 6′8″ (3.25 × 2.03 m).
Uffizi, Florence.

right: 203.
Simone Martini. *Annunciation*
(saints in side panels
by Lippo Memmi). 1333.
Tempera on wood,
8′8″ × 10′ (2.64 × 3.05 m).
Uffizi, Florence.

204. Francesco Traini. *Triumph of Death,* detail. c. 1350 (partially destroyed 1944). Fresco. Campo Santo, Pisa.

ing is simplified, thus parting company with its predecessors. Among other differences, the Madonna's gaze meets that of her beholders, her figure is heavier, the breasts prominent, the Child in a more natural posture, and the Madonna's robe is modeled in light and shadow to delineate the flesh beneath.

In the *Annunciation* (Fig. 203) by Duccio's Sienese disciple and Giotto's contemporary Simone Martini, aristocratic aloofness prevails. The Gothic setting is courtly with the elegant vase of lilies and the regal Madonna draped in a French-style blue gown rendered in pigment made from the powdered semiprecious blue stone lapis lazuli. Disturbed in her reading by the sudden appearance of the Archangel Gabriel, his robes and wings aflutter, the startled Virgin recoils in fear and astonishment as she hears the words that appear in relief: "Hail Mary . . . the Lord is with thee." The composition is a masterly combination of vivid colors and curvilinear design as revealed in the folds of the costumes, the vase of flowers, the spiraling columns, and the arched niches that frame the figures.

Reaction to the Plague

As a result of the Black Death of 1348, Sienese art declined. The reaction to the great plague is well illustrated in the series of frescoes on the inner walls

of the Campo Santo at Pisa. The theme is the Last Judgment, and Traini's *Triumph of Death* (Fig. 204) took its name from a poem by Petrarch. While no cause-and-effect relationship between picture and poem can be proved, both were reactions to the plague, both shared common attitudes of the time, and both were based on a similar theme.

Triumph of Death is a grandiose statement, with so much detail crowded into every bit of space that something in it was bound to appeal to everybody. Like the sermons of the time, each part warned of the closeness of death, the terrors of hell if the soul were claimed by the devil, or the bliss of being carried off by the angels.

In Traini's fresco a group of mounted nobles are shown equipped for the hunt, but instead of the quarry they are pursuing, they find only the prey of death. Inside the three open coffins serpents are consuming the corpses of the onetime great of the earth. Petrarch also speaks of death as the great leveler when he notes in his poem that neither "the Popes, Emperors, nor Kings, no enseigns wore of their past hight but naked show'd and poor," and then asks, "Where be their riches, where their precious gems? Their miters, scepters, robes and diadems?" Nearby is a bearded Anchorite monk unfolding a prophetic scroll that warns them to repent before it is too late. The only relief from this scene of horror and desolation is found in the upper left where some monks are gathered around a chapel busying themselves with the usual monastic duties. Apparently only those who renounce the world can find relief from its general turmoil and terror of death.

Music and Literature

The contrast between the gloomy, threatening medieval world view and the kind, joyful Franciscan spirit is illustrated by two 13th-century hymns. The facts behind their composition alone are sufficient to point out the split in thought of the period. The *Dies Irae,* which so admirably reflects the prevailing medieval spirit, was written by the great Latin stylist Thomas of Celano a few years before he met St. Francis and became one of his friars. The second, the *Canticle of the Sun,* is by St. Francis himself. Thomas of Celano entered the Franciscan order about the year 1215, enjoyed the friendship of St. Francis for several years, and was entrusted by Pope Gregory IX with the official biography that was written shortly after Francis was declared saint in 1228.

The Dies Irae

In the triple stanzas and 57 lines of the *Dies Irae,* the medieval Latin poetic style reaches a high point. Its content invokes the vision of the final dissolution of the universe, the sounding of the angelic trumpets calling forth the dead from their tombs, and the overwhelming majesty of the coming of Christ as king to judge the living and the dead. The grandeur of its language and the perfection of its poetic form are in every way equal to this solemn and awesome theme. The images and moods run from anger and terror to hope and bliss before coming to a close with a final plea for eternal rest. A sampling of its vivid verses can be gained from the following stanzas:

> Day of Wrath! O day of mourning!
> See fulfilled the prophets' warning,
> Heaven and earth in ashes burning!
>
> Wondrous sound the trumpet flingeth;
> Through earth's sepulchres it ringeth;
> All before the Throne it bringeth.
>
> Guilty, now I pour my moaning,
> All my shame with anguish owning;
> Spare, O God, Thy suppliant groaning!
>
> While the wicked are confounded,
> Doomed to flames of woe unbounded,
> Call me, with Thy saints surrounded.

Although the colorful language and verbal rhythms of the Latin original have a music all their own, the *Dies Irae* is inseparable from a melodic

Dies Irae
(sequence, early 13th century)   Thomas of Celano

Di - es i - rae, di - es il - la Sol - vet saec - lum
Quan - tus tre - mor est fu - tu - rus, Quan - do ju - dex

in fa - vil - la, Te - ste Da - vid cum Si - byl - la.
est ven - tu - rus, Cunc - ta stri - cte dis - cus - su - rus.

setting in the mixed Dorian mode (above). Both the poem and its melody found their way into the liturgy as an important hymn in the requiem mass for the dead. Later this melody was to become famous as a symbol of medieval hellfire and brimstone in the 19th-century romantic movement (see pp. 372–373).

Lauds and the Canticle of the Sun

The most characteristic Franciscan contribution to poetry and music is found in a body of informal hymns called *laudi spirituali*—songs of praise or, simply, "lauds"—traceable directly to St. Francis and his immediate circle. The practice of spontaneous hymn singing continued from his time onward and in the 14th century was firmly established as the most popular form of religious music.

In music, as in his religious work, St. Francis drew together the sacred, courtly, and popular traditions. The lauds were thus a poetic bridge between the traditional music of the Church, the music of the castle, and the music of the streets. The words always had a religious theme. Often they were mere variations of psalms and prayers sung to popular airs. Above all, they were music and poetry that the people could both sing and feel with their hearts.

Contrapuntal choral music, whether it was in the form of a church motet or a secular madrigal, was a sophisticated musical medium that needed the voices of skilled professionals. By contrast, the lauds were folklike in spirit, simple and direct in their appeal, and sung either as solos or jointly with others in unison. Just as the highly trained monastic choir was characteristic of the Cluniac movement and the contrapuntal chorus the musical counterpart of the northern Gothic spirit, the lauds became the special and characteristic expression of the Franciscans.

The *Canticle of the Sun,* by St. Francis, is at once the most sublime of all the lauds as well as the most original. The legend goes that when St. Francis was recovering from an illness in a hut outside the convent of St. Clare, the nuns heard from his lips this rapturous new song. The informality, even casualness, of its composition and its rambling rhythms and rhymes make it as simple and unaffected in its form as the Umbrian dialect in which it is written. Sincerity and deep human feeling dominate the unequal stanzas of St. Francis' songs of praise, rather than any attempt at learned communication or poetic elegance.

> O most high, almighty, good Lord God, to Thee belong praise, glory, honor, and all blessing!
>
> Praised be my Lord God with all his creatures, and especially our brother the sun, who brings us the day and who brings us the light; fair is he and shines with very great splendor; O Lord, he signifies to us Thee!
>
> Praised be my Lord for our sister the moon, and for the stars, the which He has set clear and lovely in heaven.
>
> Praised be my Lord for our sister water, who is very serviceable unto us and humble and precious and clean.
>
> Praised be my Lord for our brother fire, through whom thou givest us light in the darkness; and he is bright and pleasant and very mighty and strong.

While the original melody of the *Canticle of the Sun* is now lost forever, countless lauds do survive, some of which date back to shortly after St. Francis' time. A Franciscan monk by the name of Jacopone da Todi, who died in 1306, was one of the greatest writers of lauds. His most famous hymn is the *Stabat Mater Dolorosa,* which was officially incorporated in the liturgy in the 18th century to be sung for the Feast of the Seven Sorrows. This remarkable man, like St. Francis before him, was of Umbrian origin, and, after a succession of such diverse careers as lawyer, hermit, and Franciscan preacher, he turned poet and composer. His hymns readily found their way into the texts of the early miracle plays, which dramatized episodes in the life of a miracle-working saint or martyr, and his music became the foundation of the laudistic tradition. The example (above, right) is a part of one of his lauds. Its emotional intensity and stylistic character mark it as typical of the early Franciscan movement.

Dante's Divine Comedy

In the early years of the 14th century, a synthesis of diverse philosophical, political, and religious world views was achieved by Dante Alighieri in his *Divine Comedy*—at once the greatest book of the medieval past and a prophecy of Renaissance things to come. In one stroke, Dante established Italian spoken by the common people as a modern literary language and endowed his country with its most enduring literary masterpiece. The *Divine Comedy* is not only

Lauda (late 13th century)

Jacopone da Todi
(after Liuzzi)

O Chri-sto' ni-po-ten-te, Do-ve sie-te in-vi-a-to, Che si po-ve-ra-men-te Gi-te pel-le-gri-na-to?

a synthesis of scholastic and Franciscan philosophies but of the whole thought of the medieval period and of Greco-Roman antiquity as its author knew it. Classical figures, such as Aristotle, Vergil, Ovid, and Cicero, rub shoulders across its pages with Boethius, St. Thomas Aquinas, St. Francis, and Giotto who, as tradition has it, portrayed Dante in a *Paradiso* of his own painted in the Chapel of the Bargello at Florence (Fig. 205).

The form of the poem is heavily loaded with medieval mathematical symbolism, the mystical number 3 serving as a kind of trinitarian motif. Each stanza has three verses; the rhyming scheme is the melodious *terza rima—aba, bcb,* etc.; one time after another, Dante is terrified by three animals; in each case he is saved by the mediation of three holy women; he is piloted on his travels by three guides.

The whole poem is divided into three parts—Hell, Purgatory, and Heaven; each section contains 33 cantos, the number of Christ's years on earth; and, finally, the introductory canto, added to the three times 33 others, brings the total to an even 100, that number having the quality of wholeness.

In spite of the heavy burden of number theory and other scholastic baggage—discussions of the laws of planetary motion, civil and church law, medieval science, dialectical argumentation, and allegorical meanings, such as that of Vergil representing reason and Beatrice inspiration—Dante is far from a traditional scholastic thinker. If he were, he would have written a treatise in the learned Latin instead of a poem in Tuscan Italian. No scholarly discussion ever began with the announcement: "The style is careless and humble, because it is in the vulgar tongue, in which even housewives hold converse."

The revolutionary nature of this linguistic departure is almost impossible for the modern reader to understand, for in Dante's time literature was a possession of the learned few who had an adequate knowledge of Latin. All those who read poetry, philosophy, or history in effect had to do so in a foreign language. But even to an Italian, Dante's progress through the Inferno, Purgatory, and Paradise is not an easy one to follow. The path is hard and rough, and its obscurity comes from the doubts and conflicts that clouded the time. Since lecturers in Italian universities offered commentaries on it soon after the

205. Giotto (?). *Portrait of Dante,* detail of fresco.
c. 1325. Chapel of Palazzo del Podestà, Bargello, Florence.

poet's death, the *Divine Comedy* must also have been difficult for those close to Dante's own time. Nevertheless, Dante, like Giotto, possessed the gift of making his characters live by just a few deft strokes. Like St. Francis', his allegories are not mere riddles for the learned but lively tales for the untutored.

Dante has a true musician's ear for sound, and his verses have a music all their own. He also has the expert painter's eye for the smallest details of appearances, and his images are a feast for the inner eye of the imagination as well. One instance of this imagery is his sensitivity to the medium of light. Primarily it is a spiritual light that concerns him, but he conjures up its vision in familiar everyday impressions filtered through the mind's eye of a great poet. He sings of sunlight, firelight, starlight; the sparkle of precious stones; the gleaming rays of a lamp in the darkness; the translucent effects of light filtered through water, glass, and jewels; rainbows and the colored reflections from clouds; the ruddy glow of infernal flames and the pure unearthly radiance of Paradise; the light of the human eye and that of the halos surrounding the heads of the saints. Finally, soaring toward the firmament, each of the three sections of the poem closes on the word "stars."

While the *Divine Comedy* is subtitled the *Vision of Dante Alighieri,* and the scene is laid in Hell, Purgatory, and Paradise, Dante's vision is not concerned only with life after death. By inference, he is describing the spiritual course of human life from birth in original sin through the purgation process of experience to a knowledge of ideal goodness. This dynamic spiritual journey is full of unmedieval emotions.

After plunging into the bowels of the earth, Dante makes an upward ascent through the infernal regions on the back of Satan to the mountain of Purgatory, and, finally, into the metaphysical strato-

sphere of the various stages of Heaven. Civilization likewise, as Dante saw it, had struggled upward from the pagan world of Greece and Rome to the divinely ordered social structure of the medieval world, which had rested on an all-powerful Church and its secular counterpart, the Holy Roman Empire. It is a vertical and dynamic concept representing the ascent of humanity from the depths to the heights, from darkness into the light.

Ideas

Italy in the 14th century had one foot in the Middle Ages and the other in the Renaissance. The opposing world views are reflected in a number of situations. Among them are the great Church schism, the social struggle between the old landed aristocracy and the growing cities, the incompatibility of Gothic architecture and the sunny landscape of Italy, the presence of medieval devils and genuine human types in Giotto's frescoes, the opposing visions of the Inferno and Paradise in Dante's *Divine Comedy,* and the attitudes expressed in poetry and painting before and after the Black Death.

The backward and forward directions are illustrated also in the struggle within the minds and consciences of individual persons. The life of St. Francis, to cite one example, combined an otherworldly self-denial with an obvious worldly love of natural beauty. Fire for him was not created so much for roasting the souls of sinners in Hell as to give light in the darkness and warmth on a cold night.

The Romanesque St. Peter Damian had said: "The world is so filthy with vices the holy mind is befouled by even thinking of it." In contrast, the Gothic encyclopedist Vincent of Beauvais exclaimed: "How great is even the humblest beauty of this world!" St. Francis in his *Canticle of the Sun* found evidence of God's goodness everywhere—in the radiance of the sun, in the eternal miracle of springtime. He saw all nature as a revelation of divinity and his thought foreshadowed a departure from the divisive medieval dualism based on opposition of flesh and spirit. After a lifetime of self-denial and self-inflicted pain, he humbly begged pardon of his brother the body for the suffering he had caused it to endure.

The 14th century thus straddles the medieval and the Renaissance worlds. Looking backward, it represents a culmination of certain aspects of later medievalism; looking forward, it anticipates many of the ideas of the Renaissance. The breakdown of medieval symbolism is seen in the growth of naturalism in painting, and the shift from an otherworldly focus to one on this world is apparent in the rise of humanitarianism. It is important, however, to distinguish between the 14th-century naturalism, which is largely an outgrowth of late Gothic ideas, and its more scientific equivalent in the 15th century, between Franciscan humanitarianism and the classically oriented humanism of the later Renaissance.

Late Medieval Naturalism

The abstractions of the scholastic mind found a new challenge in the down-to-earth reasoning of the philosophers who called themselves *nominalists*. Late scholasticism had, in fact, become more and more a strained exercise in logical gymnastics. Its forms all too often disregarded the real world and the facts necessary to give substance to thought.

On their road to knowledge the nominalists simply turned the scholastic ways upside down. They insisted that generalities must be built from the bottom up, first by gathering the data and sorting out particular things and events, then by putting like with like. Only in this way, they said, was it possible to classify things and give a *name* to those that grouped themselves together (hence the term "nominalists"). The question was whether to start with an assumption determined beforehand and then look for the supporting data as did the scholastic thinkers, or whether to assemble the facts first. These two methods approximate the difference between deductive and inductive thought, the latter leading to the experimental method of modern science.

The nominalist viewpoint, as it gained a foothold, weakened medieval authoritarianism, in which the word of Aristotle and the Church fathers was accepted without question. Correspondingly, it initiated the modern practice of finding facts from firsthand observation. Particular things became more important than universal forms. A plant, now, was a vegetable or flower that grew in a garden rather than the manifestation of a universal idea of a plant existing in the mind of God.

The result of this new mental orientation was a renewed interest in a tangible reality that would have as important consequences in art as it did in the realm of scientific inquiry. In the next century, it was to lead to the representation of figures in natural surroundings, the rendering of the body with anatomical accuracy, the modeling of figures three-dimensionally by means of light and shadow, and the working out of laws of linear perspective for foreground and background effects.

While opposing systems of logic were being argued in the universities, the friars of St. Francis were bringing his message to town and country folk. With them, religious devotion became a voluntary, spontaneous relationship between human beings and God rather than an imposed obligation, an act based on love rather than on fear. The Franciscans also sought to establish a common bond between individuals, whatever their station in life, and their neighbors, thus implementing the golden rule, "Love thy neighbor as thyself." This was an important shift from the vertical feudal organization of society, in which individuals were related to those above and below them by a hierarchical authority, to a horizontally oriented ethical relationship that bound people to their fellows.

Nominalism and the Arts   St. Francis saw evidence of God's love in everything, from the fruits and flowers of the earth to the winds and the clouds in the sky—a concept that was to have great consequences for the course of art. The birds to which St. Francis preached, for instance, were the birds that were heard chirping and singing every day, not the symbolic dove of the Holy Spirit or the apocalyptical eagle of St. John.

While this tendency toward naturalism was already noticeable in the 13th-century sculpture of Chartres and elsewhere, it became widespread in the 14th century. As this view of the natural world gained ascendance over the supernatural, based as it was on concrete observation rather than on metaphysical speculation, it released the visual arts from the perplexing problems of how to represent the unseen. The love of St. Francis for his fellows and for such simple things as grass and trees, which could be represented as seen in nature, opened up new vistas for artists to explore.

St. Francis' message was taught in parables and simple images of life that all could understand, and Giotto succeeded in translating these into pictorial form. In this favorable naturalistic climate, he found his balance between the abstract and the concrete, between divine essence and human reality.

Giotto, by refraining from placing his accent on symbolism, moved away from medieval mysticism and in his pictures portrayed understandable human situations. To him, the saints were not remote ethereal spirits but human beings, who felt all the usual emotions from joy to despair—just as did the people in the Italian towns he knew so well. Now that he no longer had to be concerned mainly with allegories but could reproduce the world of objects and actions as he saw it, a new pathway was opened.

Even his contemporaries could see that Giotto was blazing new trails. Yet their admiration for his faithfulness to nature must be measured by the art that had preceded his time rather than by 15th-century or later standards. While Giotto undoubtedly showed a love of nature as such, he never accented it to the point where it might weaken his primary emphasis. His interest was less in nature for its own sake than in its meaning in the lives of his subjects.

In viewing a picture by Giotto, one does well to begin with his people and be concerned only secondarily with their natural surroundings, because his pictures are in psychological rather than in linear perspective. His subjects seem to create their own environment by their expressive attitudes and dramatic placement. While his work shows an increasing concern with problems of natural space, this space then becomes less important than his expressive intentions. His use of color and shading gives his human figures the sense of depth and volume that brings them to life. In this way, both human nature and nature as such achieve an intimate and distinctive identity in Giotto's art.

Franciscan Humanitarianism

Long before, Cluny had changed the character of monasticism by uniting cloistered life with feudalism. Now the new orientation of the Franciscan order was no less revolutionary. St. Francis did not confine his monks in cloisters but sent them forth as fishers of men. The idea of evangelical poverty, humility, and love for humanity expressed through living and working with simple people resulted in a union with, rather than a withdrawal from, society. The Franciscans did not avoid the world so much as they avoided worldly pursuits. As the English writer G. K. Chesterton has remarked, what St. Benedict had stored, St. Francis scattered. The Cluniacs were, in the proper sense of the word, an order—that is, their discipline required a strict hierarchical organization. The Franciscans by contrast were, in every sense of the word, a movement.

The icy intellectualism of the medieval universities was bound to thaw in the warmth of Franciscan emotionalism. Self-denial held little appeal for an increasingly prosperous urban middle class. The mathematical elegance of Gothic structures began to yield to more informal types of buildings. The logical linear patterns of the surviving Byzantine pictorial style gave way to the expressive warmth of Giotto's figures, and the empty, stylized faces of Byzantine saints pale in the light of the human tenderness found in a smiling mouth or tearful eye in a Giotto picture. The formal architectural sculpture and abstract patterns of Gothic stained glass were replaced by the colorful informality of mural paintings in fresco. St. Francis in his music, as in his religious work, drew the sacred and popular traditions closer together, and in the lauds, he encouraged people to sing. He gave people a music to feel in their hearts without having to understand it with their brains.

Humanitarianism and the Arts   When Dante declared that Giotto's fame outshone that of

206. Giotto. *Joachim Returning to the Sheepfold.* 1305-06. Fresco. Arena Chapel, Padua.

Cimabue, and when Boccaccio proclaimed that Giotto revived painting after it had "been in the grave" for centuries, they were recognizing in his art a new spirit and style. These are also apparent in the *Decameron,* which mocks the manners and ways of Gothic knights, abbots, and monks and the outmoded feudal ideal to which they clung.

The new feeling was also apparent in music. In France, Philippe de Vitry published a musical treatise in 1316 with the title *Ars Nova,* or *New Art,* which he opposed to the *ars antiqua,* or "old art," of the Gothic 13th century. He was the ardent champion of bringing some lively new dancelike rhythms into church music. His book gained such popularity that it brought down upon it the anger of conservative Church leaders in the form of a papal criticism issued by Pope John XXII in 1325.

A new spirit of freedom was in the air, a freedom from tradition. St. Francis earlier had struck out in a new religious direction, and Giotto, by translating the saint's life into pictures, avoided the traditional biblical subjects and their traditional stylized treatment. Actually he was working on an almost contemporary subject as well as rendering it in a new manner. Giotto did subjects that came within the iconographical tradition, such as *Joachim Returning to the Sheepfold* (Fig. 206) and the *Pietà* (Fig. 195), or *Lamentation,* far more dramatically than before. In general, his figures moved about in the space he created for them with greater suppleness than in earlier pictures. His world was marked by a new, warm, and compatible relationship between human beings, their natural environment, and their God.

Representations of Christ as an infant in arms began to replace the mature image in divine majesty of the Gothic period. Along with the growing interest in the cycle of Christ's infancy, legends of Mary's life became increasingly prominent. The emotional element in the Passion was largely conveyed through compassion for the Virgin as the mother of sorrows. This was as true for Giotto's cycle in Padua as it was for Jacopone da Todi's *Stabat Mater Dolorosa.*

The adoption of the language of ordinary people in literature, the informal treatment of fresco painting, and the folk spirit in the music—all make it apparent that works of art were being addressed to a new group of patrons. Furthermore, one of Giotto's recorded sayings reveals the artist's new conception of himself. Each man, he said, "should save his soul as best he can. As for me, I intend to serve painting in my own way and only so far as it serves me, for the sake of the lovely moments it gives at the price of an agreeable fatigue." Even the Black Death had some beneficial effects for the artists after Giotto's time, because the younger masters could assert their independence and develop new ideas and techniques with fewer restrictions from conservative guilds.

Survival of Classicism   What appears to be a renewed interest in classical antiquity began to be seen, heard, and read in the works of the artists and writers of the 14th century. The panels of Nicola Pisano's pulpit show the classical Roman influence of such narrative reliefs as Trajan's Column (see Figs. 104, 105). However, what seems to be a revival of Roman classical forms is also something in the nature of a survival. For if Nicola's sculpture is placed chronologically after a group of French Gothic examples, it certainly seems to be closer to the art of ancient Rome than to the Gothic. But since Roman sculpture was present everywhere in Italy, any Italian sculptor with open eyes could not miss seeing it. Simple as it may sound, the explanation is a geographical rather than a chronological or psychological one—central Italy is closer to Rome than to northern France. Likewise, since Dante was writing an epic poem, the obvious model was Vergil's *Aeneid,* which had never ceased to be read.

While a growing consciousness of the classical in the works of Dante and his contemporaries is not to be overlooked, it must be seen from the 14th-century point of view as a continuation of a cultural tradition rather than as a sudden rebirth of classicism. The influence of the classic authors and classical art had never been quite so neglected or dead as many historians have supposed. Vergil, Cicero, and certain works of Aristotle were as widely read and written about in medieval times as they were in the 14th and 15th centuries.

This is not to deny that a new spirit of curiosity enlivened the search, begun by Petrarch and Boccaccio, in monastic libraries for manuscripts by other Greek and Roman authors than those who bore the sacred approval of Church tradition. This probing also went hand in hand with the discovery in Rome of some long-buried antique sculpture and with the study of Roman building methods.

Even though Petrarch amid much classical fanfare was crowned in Rome with the laurel wreath, that ancient token of immortal fame, and even though he wrote his cycle of Triumphs with the Roman triumphal arch form in mind, it is doubtful that he or Dante or Boccaccio did more than bring the ancient world a little closer to their own time. They certainly had no such admiration for pagan antiquity for its own sake as did the 15th-century Florentines. Even though Giotto spent some time in Rome, the joyous humanistic spirit that permeates his work is much closer to the new Franciscan outlook and the continuous tradition of Roman relief sculpture and fresco painting than to any conscious reappraisal of classical culture as such. It is necessary, then, to disassociate the spontaneous 14th-century Franciscan humanitarianism from the more self-conscious revival of antiquity for its own sake that characterized developments in 15th-century Florentine and early 16th-century Roman humanism.

The 14th-century conflict of opposing ideas and forward-backward trends has variously been termed the post-Gothic, proto-Renaissance, or pre-Renaissance period. But any period that contains the magic names of St. Francis, Dante, Petrarch, Boccaccio, Giotto, Duccio, and Simone Martini and that shows such a high degree of originality and creativity can well stand on its own rather than be a postlude or a prelude to another. In style as well as ideas it is indeed the Early Renaissance.

10
The Florentine Renaissance Style

Florence, 15th Century

Colorful festivals were the delight of all Florentines, but March 25, 1436, was a special occasion that would linger long in the memory of these prosperous and pleasure-loving people. The dedication of Florence's newly completed cathedral (Fig. 207) brought together an unprecedented number of Church dignitaries, statesmen, and diplomats, and in their wake were famous artists, poets, scholars, and musicians. The white-robed Pope Eugene IV, crowned with the triple tiara, attended by 7 cardinals in bright red and no less than 37 bishops and archbishops in purple vestments, made a triumphal progress through the banner-lined streets, accompanied by city officials and heads of the guilds with their honor guards.

Appropriately enough, the cathedral was christened Santa Maria del Fiore ("St. Mary of the Flower"), since Florence (derived from *flora*) was indeed the city of flowers. March 25 was also the Feast of the Annunciation, the beginning of new life nine months before Christ's birth, and both the Annunciation and Nativity were favorite subjects of Florentine art.

Brunelleschi's Dome

The eyes and thoughts of all Florentines that day were directed upward to the mighty *cupola,* or dome, that crowned the crossing of their cathedral and gave their city its characteristic profile. Though begun in the late 13th century, the building's construction had long been delayed because no architect possessed the necessary knowledge to dome such an enormous, gaping, 140-foot (42.7-meter)-wide octagonal space (Fig. 208).

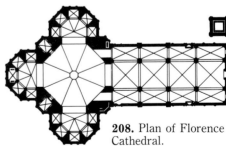

208. Plan of Florence Cathedral.

left: **207.** Florence Cathedral group. Cathedral begun by Arnolfo di Cambio, 1296; dome by Filippo Brunelleschi, 1420–36; present façade 1875–87. Length of cathedral 508′ (154.84 m), height of dome 367′ (111.86 m). Campanile begun 1334 by Giotto, continued by Andrea Pisano, 1336–48; height 269′ (81.99 m). Baptistry (lower right) 1060–1150.

CHRONOLOGY
15th-Century Florence

GENERAL EVENTS

1401	Competition for Florence Baptistry north doors
1403–1424	Ghiberti worked on Florence Baptistry north doors
1406	Pisa under Florentine rule
1421	Giovanni de' Medici elected magistrate
1425–1452	Ghiberti worked on Florence Baptistry east doors
c.1429	Pazzi Chapel begun by Brunelleschi
1434	Pro-Medici government elected; Cosimo de' Medici (1389–1464) began rule
1434–1444	Pope Eugene IV resided in Florence
1436	Florence Cathedral dedicated (begun 1298; dome by Brunelleschi, 1420–36)
1439–1442	Council of Florence brought nominal union of Eastern and Western Churches
1444–1459	Medici-Riccardi Palace built by Michelozzo
1447	Parentucelli, Florentine humanist, elected Pope Nicholas V
1464–1469	Piero de' Medici ruled after Cosimo's death
1469–1492	Lorenzo de' Medici ruled
1476	*Portinari Altarpiece* by van der Goes of Flanders brought to Florence
1478	Pazzi family led unsuccessful revolt against Medici; Giuliano de' Medici assassinated; Lorenzo consolidated political power
c.1480	Heinrich Isaac succeeded Squarcialupi as organist at cathedral; court composer to Lorenzo
1482	Marsilio Ficino's translations of Plato's dialogues printed
c.1485	Alberti's treatise *On Architecture* printed; *On Painting* (1436), *On Sculpture* (1464) printed c. 1485
1489	Savonarola (1452–98) preached moral reform. Michelangelo apprenticed to Ghirlandaio
c.1490	Aldine Press founded in Venice began publishing works of Plato and Aristotle
1492	Lorenzo de' Medici died
1494	Medici exiled from Florence; government dominated by Savonarola
1497	Burning of books, pictures, "vanities"
1498	Savonarola burned at stake

ARCHITECTS

1377–1446	Filippo Brunelleschi
1391–1473	Michelozzo di Bartolommeo
1404–1472	Leone Battista Alberti

PAINTERS

1387–1455	Fra Angelico
1397–1475	Paolo Uccello
c.1400–1461	Domenico Veneziano
1401–1428	Masaccio
c.1406–1469	Filippo Lippi
c.1416–1492	Piero della Francesca
1420–1497	Benozzo Gozzoli
1423–1457	Andrea del Castagno
c.1429–1498	Antonio Pollaiuolo
1444–1510	Sandro Botticelli
1449–1494	Domenico Ghirlandaio
1452–1519	Leonardo da Vinci
1458–1504	Filippino Lippi

SCULPTORS

1371–1438	Jacopo della Quercia
1378–1455	Lorenzo Ghiberti
1386–1466	Donatello
1400–1482	Luca della Robbia
c.1429–1498	Antonio Pollaiuolo
1435–1488	Andrea del Verrocchio
1475–1564	Michelangelo Buonarroti

MUSICIANS

1400–1474	Guillaume Dufay
1430–1495	Jean de Ockeghem
1436–1475	Antonio Squarcialupi
c.1450–1517	Heinrich Isaac
1450–1505	Jacob Obrecht
c.1460–1521	Josquin des Prez

WRITERS AND PHILOSOPHERS

1304–1374	Petrarch (Francesco Petrarca)
1313–1375	Giovanni Boccaccio
1433–1499	Marsilio Ficino
1449–1492	Lorenzo de' Medici
1454–1494	Angelo Poliziano
1463–1494	Pico della Mirandola
1469–1527	Niccolò Machiavelli
1478–1529	Baldassare Castiglione

Filippo Brunelleschi, however, after studying the Pantheon and other ancient monuments in Rome, had returned and undertaken the gigantic task now at the point of completion. Starting at a level some 180 feet (54.9 meters) above ground, he sent eight massive ribs soaring skyward from the angles of the supporting octagon to a point almost 100 feet (30.5 meters) higher where they converged at the base of a lantern tower. Concealing them from external view, he added two minor radial ribs between each major rib, twenty-four in all, to make his inner shell. Reinforcing these by wooden beams and iron clasps at key points, he then had the necessary support for the masonry of his inner and outer shells. The structure is, in effect, an eight-sided Gothic vault. But by concealing the functional elements and shaping a smooth external silhouette, Brunelleschi crossed the bridge into Renaissance architecture.

Opposite the façade of the cathedral is the old Romanesque baptistry (Fig. 207, lower right), which was feeling new Renaissance life with Ghiberti's gilded bronze doors. Already in place were the handsome north doors, and the sculptor was well on his way to completing the east doors (Fig. 209), which Michelangelo was later to hail as worthy of being the "Gates of Paradise." Helping him cast these doors in his workshop at various times were the architect Michelozzo, the sculptor Donatello, and the painters Paolo Uccello and Benozzo Gozzoli. Donatello, at the same time, was working on a series of statues of prophets for niches on the exterior of both the cathedral and the campanile, traditionally known as "Giotto's Tower."

In Pope Eugene's company were some of the leading Florentine humanists, including the artist-scholar Leone Battista Alberti, who had just completed his book *On Painting* and was at work on his influential study *On Architecture*. On hand to provide music for the occasion was the papal choir, whose ranks included the foremost musician of his generation, Guillaume Dufay, who composed the commemorative motet for the occasion. Antonio Squarcialupi,

209. Lorenzo Ghiberti. "Gates of Paradise," east doors of Baptistry, Florence. 1425–52. Gilt bronze, height 18′6″ (5.64 m).

regular organist of the cathedral and private master of music in the Medici household, is thought to have composed the solemn high mass.

According to an eyewitness, the magnificent papal procession was preceded by a great band of wind players, "each carrying his instrument in hand, and arrayed in gorgeous cloth of gold garments." After them came the choirs that "sang at times with such mighty harmonies that the songs seemed . . . to be coming from the angels themselves."

The Florentine City-State

Lining the streets for the grand procession and crowding their way into the vast nave of the cathedral were the colorfully costumed citizens of this prosperous Tuscan town. In contrast with northern countries, city life in this region had come of age. At a time when many feudal aristocrats still lived in their cold fortresslike castles, the Florentine patrician families lived in a style that could well have been the envy of kings.

The working members of the population belonged to the various guilds and trade organizations, the most important of which were those dealing with the carding, weaving, and dyeing of wool and silk for the famous Florentine textile industry. Metalcrafts and stonework followed in importance, and so on down to the butchers and bakers. The masters of the principal guilds were the influential citizens from whose ranks the members of the Signory, or city council, were chosen and from which the merchant and banking families emerged.

The most renowned of these families were the Medici, whose head at this time was Cosimo. By a combination of political understanding and keen financial ability, he dominated the government of the city. Knowing his fellow townspeople's passion for equality, Cosimo never assumed a title or other outward sign of authority. Instead, he was the political boss, ruling from behind the scenes with the support of the guilds, which knew that a stable government and peaceful relations with their neighbors (see map, p. 213) were the best safeguards of their prosperity.

The Medici were also the papal bankers who received on deposit Church funds from England, France, and Flanders. From their branch offices in London, Lyon, and Antwerp, they lent this money at fantastic rates of interest to foreign heads of state. With the papal revenues, they also bought English wool, had it processed in the Netherlands, shipped it to Florence to be woven into fine fabrics, and exported these at a handsome profit. It was Cosimo who made the florin the soundest currency in Europe. But political power and high finance were not the only pursuits of this ambitious banker.

Cosimo's other accomplishments were unusual for a Renaissance merchant capitalist. As a serious student of Plato, he became one of the founders of the Neoplatonic Academy, an institution that had enormous intellectual influence. From all the parts of Europe where his financial interests extended, he commissioned works of art. At home he gathered a library of rare manuscripts for study and translation.

Through Cosimo's generosity, a group of Dominican monks had just moved into the monastery of San Marco, which was being rebuilt for them by his personal architect Michelozzo. Among the monks was Fra Angelico, whom Cosimo encouraged to decorate the monastery walls with his famous frescoes. Although Masaccio, one of the century's most original painters, had been dead for six years, Filippo Lippi, the future teacher of Botticelli, was active and looking to Cosimo for commissions. Cosimo took Donatello's advice, collected antique statuary, placed it in his gardens, and encouraged young sculptors to work there. Small wonder, then, that the Signory voted him the posthumous title *Pater Patriae*—"Father of His Country."

Dufay's Dedicatory Motet

For such solemn ceremonies as dedications and coronations, it was the custom to perform a motet especially written for the occasion. Dufay, a musician educated in the Burgundian French tradition, had been a member of the papal choir since 1428 and had composed such an occasional motet for the ceremonies at the conclusion of peace between Pope Eugene and the Emperor Sigismund in 1433. The motet, coming as it does outside the normal liturgical music of the mass, lent itself well to the purposes of an occasional piece that could be composed for a specific ceremony to a text which contained topical allusions, and other references to the day, place, and occasion for which it was written. The words in this case begin: *Nuper rosarum flores ex dono pontificis*—"Flower of roses, gift of the pontiff." The cathedral is referred to as this "most spacious temple," and Brunelleschi's dome is praised as a "mighty artifice," a "marvel of art." The text appropriately concludes with a supplication to the Virgin Mary on behalf of the people of Florence: "O Virgin, the glory of virgins, thy devoted people of Florence beseech thee that he who prays . . . may deserve to receive thy gracious benefits. . . ."

Since such motets were composed for official occasions, their style tended toward traditional practices rather than experimentation. Dufay therefore built his formal structure on the severe principles developed by the 14th-century French composers. Such a method is governed by certain rules of musical logic, and the forms are built of sections that are unified by the use of identical rhythmic relationships but not necessarily the same melodic patterns. Such music was never intended primarily to please the ear or stir the emotions but to mirror the hidden harmonies of the universe and thus to constitute a worthy offering to its Creator. In Dufay's conception, however, the universe is no mere structure but is populated with shapely melodies, warm harmonic colors, and a variety of rhythmic forms.

This dedicatory scene of Santa Maria del Fiore has often been cited, both by those who witnessed it and by later historians, as the beginning of a new era. There was, of course, a new spirit in the air, but at the same time it was never clearer that no sharp break with the medieval past was being made. The cathedral was late Gothic in style; the dome was constructed by Gothic vaulting methods; and the dedicatory motet was late Gothic in form.

The Italian Gothic, however, had never had either the dynamic verticality or the aspiring force of its northern counterpart. Brunelleschi's dome was, to be sure, the first of such magnitude to be constructed since antiquity, but smaller domes over the crossing were not unusual in Tuscany. But while the construction of Brunelleschi's dome fell within the scope of the Gothic, the new emphasis was on smoother lines and the shapeliness of the external silhouette.

Dufay's motet, for its part, showed an increasing secular feeling in church music, since the composer was apparently much less concerned with making a pious setting of his text than he was with making his formal proportions fit smoothly into his musical structure. While such mental gymnastics were late

Gothic in conception, the Italian sense of melodic contour, the increased emphasis on secular two-beat time, the softening of the dissonant passing tones, and the pliancy of the contrapuntal texture all point in the direction of the Renaissance. Dufay's special contribution was in clothing the austere skeletal structure of such a composition with smooth melodic lines and a fluency of sound that made it a joy to the ear as well as to the mind.

Pazzi Chapel and Medici-Riccardi Palace

Impressive as is the immense cupola of Florence's cathedral, the new architectural spirit is more readily grasped in Brunelleschi's smaller Pazzi Chapel (Fig. 210). Here, in a building of small proportions, the architect could give his full attention to design without having to be absorbed in complex construction problems (Fig. 211).

The fruits of his studies of ancient Roman buildings are more in evidence here, and the break with the Gothic tradition is complete. The harmonious spacing of the columns of the porch, the treatment of the walls as flat surfaces, and the balance of horizontal and vertical elements make Brunelleschi's design the prototype of the Renaissance architectural style. The entablature, above the columns and below the roof, gives still further evidence of the classical influence. The curved pattern above comes directly from ancient Roman sarcophagi, while the elegant carving of the Corinthian capitals, the Composite pilasters, and other design details reveal Brunelleschi's early training as a silversmith as well as his study of authentic Roman originals.

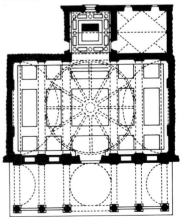

left: 210. Filippo Brunelleschi. Façade, Pazzi Chapel, Cloister of Church of Santa Croce, Florence. c. 1429–33.

below: 211. Plan of Pazzi Chapel.

The interior bears out the promise of the façade and shows a Roman classical concern with the logical molding of interior space (Fig. 212). Lacking Gothic mystery and indefiniteness, the pilastered walls give a cool, crisp impression. Frames of dark-colored stone divide the surfaces into geometric forms easily understood by the eye. Mystery and infinity have yielded to geometrical clarity. The rectangular room is covered by barrel vaults, with a low dome on pendentives (see Fig. 123) rising in the center at the point of intersection. Somewhat hesitantly to be sure, this interior indicated a new concept of space without, however, realizing its full implications. The clear-cut simplicity of its design made the Pazzi Chapel a highly influential model throughout the Renaissance, and the unity of its centralized organization under a dome became the point of departure for the church plans of Alberti, Bramante, and Michelangelo.

When Cosimo de' Medici decided to build himself a new house, he is said to have rejected a magnificent plan submitted by Brunelleschi, with the observation that envy was a plant that should not be watered. For the Medici-Riccardi Palace (Fig. 213) he chose instead a less pretentious design submitted by Brunelleschi's disciple Michelozzo. (The palace has a dual name because it was acquired in the 17th century by the Riccardi family.)

As the palace design materialized, the building turned out to be an appropriately solid structure, eminently suited to the taste of a man of such considerable substance as Cosimo. As a type, such buildings were actually a continuation, rather than a revival, of the multistoried Roman city apartment house. Here the dominance of solid mass over the space allowed for the windows, plus the heavily rusticated masonry of the first story (many of the rough-cut stones protrude more than a foot) still has something of the forbidding aspect of a medieval fortress. But as the eye moves upward, the second and third floors present an increasingly urbane appearance. The accent on horizontal lines, seen in the molding strips that separate the three stories and in the boldly projecting cornice at the roof level, are quite unmedieval. A classical allusion can be seen in the semicircular arches that frame the windows (the pediments over those on the lower story are a somewhat later addition). Details, such as the colonnettes of the windows on the second and third floors as well as the egg-and-dart pattern and the dentil range that appear in the cornice frieze, just under the roof, are definitely Renaissance in style.

Cosimo's sense of modesty stopped with the palace's exterior; inside the doors everything was on a princely scale. With the frescoes of Benozzo Gozzoli and an altarpiece by Filippo Lippi decorating its

top: 212. Filippo Brunelleschi. Interior, Pazzi Chapel, Cloister of Church of Santa Croce, Florence. c. 1429–33. Length 59′9″ (18.21 m), width 35′8″ (10.87 m).

above: 213. Michelozzo. Façade, Medici-Riccardi Palace, Florence. 1444–59. Length 225′ (68.58 m), height 80′ (24.38 m).

second-floor chapel, easel paintings by Uccello and Botticelli hanging on salon walls, antique and contemporary bronze and marble statues standing in the courtyard and gardens, collections of ancient and medieval carved gems and coins in its cabinets, and precious metal vessels and figurines standing on its tables, and priceless manuscripts including the works of Dante, Petrarch, and Boccaccio in its library, the Medici-Riccardi Palace was, in fact, one of the first and richest museums in Europe.

Sculpture

Ghiberti versus Brunelleschi

In the year 1401, the Signory of Florence together with the Guild of Merchants had held a competition to determine who should be awarded the contract for the projected north doors of the baptistry. Like the earlier pair by Andrea Pisano, the material was to be bronze, and the individual panels were to be enclosed in the *quatrefoil,* or four-lobed, pattern. The subject, for the purpose of the contest, was to be the Sacrifice of Isaac. Some half-dozen sculptors were invited to submit models, among them Brunelleschi and Lorenzo Ghiberti.

Both men were in their early twenties and were skilled workers in metal and members in good standing of the Goldsmiths' Guild; however, a comparison of their panels reveals many significant differences of viewpoint and technique (Figs. 214, 215).

Brunelleschi's composition shows the influence of Gothic verticality in the way the design is built in three rising planes. Ghiberti's composition is almost horizontal, and his two scenes are divided diagonally by a mountain in the manner of Giotto. Brunelleschi's panel is crowded, and his figures spill out over their frame. Ghiberti's is uncluttered, and all his figures and details converge toward a center of interest in the upper right formed by the heads of the principal figures. Brunelleschi accents dramatic tension, with Abraham seizing the screaming Isaac by the neck and the angel staying his hand at the last moment. Ghiberti sacrifices intensity for poise and decorative elegance. Brunelleschi shapes Isaac's awkward body with Gothic angularity. Ghiberti models it with the smooth lines and impersonal grace of a Hellenistic statue. (Ghiberti's *Commentaries* mention the discovery near Florence of the torso of an ancient classical statue on which he modeled his Isaac.) Finally, Brunelleschi cast his relief in separate sections, mounting these on the bronze background plate. Ghiberti, with greater technical command, cast his in a single mold.

left: 214. Filippo Brunelleschi. *Sacrifice of Isaac.* 1401. Gilt bronze, 21 × 17½″ (53 × 44 cm) without peripheral molding. National Museum, Florence.

right: 215. Lorenzo Ghiberti. *Sacrifice of Isaac.* 1401. Gilt bronze, 21 × 17½″ (53 × 44 cm). National Museum, Florence.

216. Lorenzo Ghiberti. *Story of Adam and Eve,* detail of east doors, Baptistry, Florence. c. 1435. Gilt bronze, 31¼" (79 cm) square.

The decision in Ghiberti's favor showed the way the aesthetic winds were blowing in 1401. Ghiberti then set to work on the 20 panels of the north doors, which were to occupy the major part of his time for the next 24 years, while Brunelleschi, accompanied by his friend the sculptor Donatello, traveled to Rome to study architecture.

Ghiberti's East Doors

Ghiberti's north doors were no sooner in place than he was commissioned, this time without competition, to execute another set. The famous east doors (Fig. 209), on which he worked from 1425 to 1452, tell their own tale. The Gothic quatrefoil frames of the competition panels were now a thing of the past, and, while his north doors were conceived in terms of their architectural function, the east doors served largely as a convenient framework for decoration. They even disregard techniques appropriate to the three-dimensional medium of relief sculpture and become like pictures painted in gilded bronze.

Ghiberti attempts daring perspectives far in advance of the painting of the period. Some figures, such as those in the center panel of the left door, are in such high relief as to be almost completely in the round. In the Adam and Eve panel at the top of the left door (Fig. 216), he uses three receding planes. The high relief in the lower foreground is used to tell of the creation of Adam (left) and Eve (center) and the expulsion (right) in the present tense. The immediate past is seen in the half relief of the middle ground showing the Garden of Eden. And in the low

relief of the background God and his accompanying cloud of angels seem to be dissolving into the thin air of the remote past.

On either side of the pictorial panels, Ghiberti included a series of full-length figurines that alternate with heads that recall Roman portrait busts. Hebrew prophets on the outer sides are set opposite pagan sibyls, all of whom were supposed to have foretold the coming of Christ. The figure beside the second panel from the top on the right door is that of the biblical strong man Samson, but his stance and musculature are those of a Hellenistic Hercules. Ghiberti mentions in his *Commentaries* how he sought to imitate nature in the manner of the ancient Greeks when molding the plant and animal forms of these door frames.

The care and delicate craftsmanship Ghiberti lavished on these and other details make the east doors a high point in the metalworker's art. Ghiberti, as was said, belonged to the Goldsmiths' Guild, and its influence is felt in many aspects of Florentine art. It is to be seen not only in such door moldings but in pulpits, wall panels, window brackets, columns, pilasters, cornices—all of which were executed with a wealth of fine detail lovingly dwelt upon.

Donatello

Donatello's personality and career contrast strongly with Ghiberti's. A man of fiery temperament and bold imagination, Donatello scorned the fussy details which allied Ghiberti's work with that of the jeweler. His sculpture has a rugged grandeur that makes Ghiberti's appear precious by comparison. While Ghiberti studied local examples of antique sculpture and read Vitruvius' books, Donatello journeyed to Rome with Brunelleschi to see the finest surviving classical statuary.

While Ghiberti remained a specialist in bronze, Donatello was at home with all materials—marble, wood, painted terra-cotta, gilded bronze. He was equally comfortable in all mediums—relief and in the round, small scale and heroic size, architectural embellishment and independent figure—and in all subjects—sacred and secular, historical scene and portraiture. While Ghiberti had a single style, Donatello had many. His power of epic expression, enormous energies, passion, and impetuosity make him the representative sculptor of his period and the immediate artistic ancestor of Michelangelo.

The *Prophet* (Fig. 217), also known as *Lo Zuccone,* which means "pumpkin head" or "baldpate," is one of a series of marble statues that Donatello was commissioned to do for the Florence Cathedral and its campanile in 1424. Designed for a third-story niche of the campanile, it was intended to be seen about 55 feet (16.8 meters) above ground level. The deep-cut drapery and lines of the face consequently took into account this angle of vision and lighting. By the boniness of the huge frame, the powerful musculature of the arms, the convulsive gesture of the right wrist, the tension of the muscles of the neck, and the intensity of the face, Donatello sought to produce a powerfully expressive rather than a handsome figure.

Donatello is representing an Old Testament prophet (either Habakkuk or Jeremiah). The figure is full of inner fire and fear of the Lord, a seer capable of fasting in the desert, dwelling alone on a mountaintop, or passionately preaching to an unheeding multitude from his niche and urging them to repent. The classical influence is seen in the drapery, an adaptation of the toga, and in the rugged features and baldness, which recall realistic Roman portraiture. With *Lo Zuccone,* Donatello created a unique figure of strong individuality, not one of the traditional iconographical types. The nickname given the statue shows that it was accepted as such.

In his bronze *David* (Fig. 218), Donatello works in a more lyrical vein. As a figure meant to be seen from all angles, the *David* is definitely a departure from the Gothic tradition of sculpture in niches and as architectural embellishment. As the first life-size bronze nude in the round since antiquity, it marks the revival of classical nude statuary.

David stands alone in the confident attitude of the victor over the vanquished, a sword in his right hand, a stone in his left. The serenity of the classical profile and the stance and modeling of the youthful body show Hellenistic influence. A local touch is provided by the Tuscan shepherd's hat, which throws the smooth, delicate-featured face into strong shadow and serves to accent the somewhat gawky lines of the adolescent body. The opposite end of Donatello's emotional range is seen in the ghostly *Repentant Magdalene* (Fig. 219). The emaciated, cadaverous

left: **217.** Donatello. *Prophet (Lo Zuccone),* from campanile, Florence Cathedral. 1423–25. Marble, height 6′5″ (1.96 m). Original in Cathedral Museum, Florence.

right: **218.** Donatello. *David.* c. 1430–32. Bronze, height 5′2¼″ (1.58 m). National Museum, Florence.

far right: **219.** Donatello. *Repentant Magdalene.* 1454–55. Wood, height 6′2″ (1.88 m). Baptistry, Florence.

figure stood in the Florence Baptistry as a reminder to the participants in the baptismal ceremony of the original sin that is washed away, and of the universal presence of death among the living.

Pollaiuolo
and Verrocchio

Quite another attitude is revealed in the work of the next generation, of which Antonio Pollaiuolo and Andrea del Verrocchio are the leading exponents. The work of Pollaiuolo is dominated by scientific curiosity, especially in regard to human anatomy. (He is known to have dissected corpses in order to study the muscle and bone structure at first hand.) Trained with his brothers in his father's goldsmith shop, he specialized in such muscular figures as the bronze *Hercules Strangling Antaeus* (Fig. 220), of which he made both painted and sculptural versions.

The legends of the strong man of antiquity were excellent subjects that permitted the artist to bring out the musculature of the male figure in action. In this instance, Hercules overcomes his enemy, the Lybian giant, by raising him off the earth which is the source of his strength while Antaeus struggles desperately to release the stranglehold Hercules has upon him. The muscles in Hercules' legs as they bear the weight of both bodies should be noted. Pollaiuolo also painted a series of pictures on the Labors of Hercules. Like his work in bronze, they are studies of muscular tension, full of athletic energy and quite unrelieved by gracefulness.

Verrocchio, a contemporary of Pollaiuolo, was the official sculptor of the Medici. For this powerful and prolific family he designed everything—tournament trophies, parade gear, portraits, and tombs.

Like Pollaiuolo, Verrocchio was also a painter at a time when sculpture led the field in experiments with perspective, anatomy, and light and shadow. Unlike the classical orientation of Ghiberti and Donatello, Pollaiuolo and Verrocchio were primarily scientifically minded, and it was in Verrocchio's workshop that Leonardo da Vinci got his training. It was Leonardo who carried on the searching scientific curiosity of his master, while it remained for Michelangelo, under the stimulus of Donatello's art, to carry on the humanistic ideal into the next century.

above right: 220. Antonio Pollaiuolo.
Hercules Strangling Antaeus.
c. 1475. Bronze, height 17¾″ (40 cm).
National Museum, Florence.

right: 221. Masaccio.
Expulsion from the Garden. c. 1427.
Fresco, 6′6″ × 2′9″ (1.98 × .84 m). Brancacci Chapel,
Church of Santa Maria del Carmine, Florence.

Painting

Masaccio

With Brunelleschi and Donatello, the third member of the trio of early 15th-century innovators was Masaccio, the only one born within the century. The importance of his series of frescoes in the Brancacci Chapel of the Church of Santa Maria del Carmine can hardly be overestimated. In the *Expulsion from the Garden* (Fig. 221), he chose one of the few subjects in the iconographical tradition in which the nude human body could be portrayed in churches without raising ecclesiastical eyebrows.

By defining the source of light as coming diagonally from the right and by having Adam and Eve approach it, Masaccio was able to represent them as casting natural shadows. In addition, by surrounding his figures with light and air, by relating them to the space they occupy, by modeling them in light and shadow like a sculptor would so that they appear as if seen in the round with all the weight and volume of living forms, Masaccio achieved one of the great innovations in painting—*atmospheric perspective.*

Masaccio, moreover, was well aware of the drama of the situation. The full force of this first moral crisis in human history is expressed by the body alone with almost no reliance on surrounding details. Eve, aware of her nakedness, cries aloud, while Adam, ashamed to face the light, expresses his remorse by covering his face. Even the avenging angel who drives them out of the garden reflects the tragedy of the fall from grace by an expression of human concern and compassion. The curved line of Adam's right leg was apparently so drawn to show the hurried motion of the expulsion; but the proportions of his arms, and the drawing of Eve's lower hand, are anatomically incorrect. Such flaws, however, are minor in comparison with the momentous step in painting that puts figures in an entirely new relationship to their spatial environment.

The *Tribute Money* (Fig. 222), another of the Brancacci Chapel frescoes, illustrates still further the principle of atmospheric perspective. The figures are well modeled in light and shade and each occupies his appointed space in the front and middle planes with ease and assurance. Approached by the tax collector, Peter and his fellow Apostles question the propriety of Christian believers paying tribute to the Roman authorities, whereupon Jesus responds, "Render therefore unto Caesar the things that are Caesar's; and unto God the things that are God's" (Matt. 22:21). Jesus then tells Peter that the first fish he catches will have a coin in its mouth. The old simultaneous mode of presentation is employed with St. Peter appearing first in the center, then at the left fishing, and finally at the right paying the debt. Masaccio's premature death at the age of twenty-seven prevented a more complete realization of his discoveries.

Fra Angelico

Spiritually, Fra Angelico was in many respects a late Gothic artist, who never painted anything but reli-

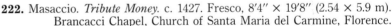

222. Masaccio. *Tribute Money.* c. 1427. Fresco, 8'4" × 19'8" (2.54 × 5.9 m). Brancacci Chapel, Church of Santa Maria del Carmine, Florence.

gious subjects. While he dwelt lovingly on the older forms, he did, however, often treat them within the new frame of reference. The *Annunciation* (Fig. 223) that he painted for the upper corridor of his own monastery of San Marco is a remarkable blend of these old and new elements.

A mystic by temperament, Fra Angelico found angels as real as his fellow human beings. But while he always paints with the deepest religious sentiment, his figures in this case appear within the new conception of space. The perspective and the 15th-century architectural details are so exact that the event could well be taking place in a corner of the San Marco cloister that Michelozzo recently had rebuilt. Furthermore, the native Tuscan flowers seen in the garden are observed well enough to satisfy a botanical expert. The lighting, however, is far from the natural illumination of Masaccio. Fra Angelico makes it seem that the figure of Gabriel and the serene purity of Mary are beheld as if in a vision.

left: **223.** Fra Angelico. *Annunciation.* c. 1445–50. Fresco, 7′6″ × 10′5″ (2.29 × 3.18 m). Monastery of San Marco, Florence.

below: **224.** Benozzo Gozzoli. *Journey of the Magi,* detail. c. 1459–63. Fresco, length 12′4¼″ (3.77 m). Chapel, Medici-Riccardi Palace, Florence.

225. Fra Filippo Lippi. *Nativity.* c. 1459. Tempera on wood, 4'2" × 3'10" (1.27 × 1.17 m). State Museums, West Berlin.

Benozzo Gozzoli and Fra Filippo Lippi

Unlike the eyes of Fra Angelico, those of his favorite pupil Benozzo Gozzoli were focused firmly on this world. With Cosimo's son Piero as his patron, Benozzo painted the *Journey of the Magi,* a favorite subject for pomp and pageantry. Here, his talents were more than equal to their task—a fresco cycle on three walls of the chapel in the Medici Palace.

In the detail (Fig. 224), a richly costumed young Wise Man sits astride his splendid horse. At the head of the retinue that follows in his wake Benozzo portrays three generations of the Medici family. At the far right, Piero de' Medici (in profile) appears at the head of the procession. Displayed on the lower part of the harness of his white horse is the motto *Semper* ("Forever"), a part of the Medici coat of arms, each letter being in the center of one of the jeweled rings that make a continuous chain. Beside him is the elderly Cosimo (also in profile) on a gray mule with a black groom at his side. The youthful Giuliano and his older brother, the future Lorenzo the Magnificent, are at the extreme left. Bringing up the rear are various intimates and retainers of the Medici court, with the artist himself in the second row back identified by a cap band that reads *Opus Benotii* ("Work of Benozzo"). Other faces may represent the philosopher Pico della Mirandola, the poet Poliziano, and Fra Angelico.

The procession winds around through the mountains and valleys of the lovely Tuscan landscape punctuated by tall parasol pines and needle cypresses. It terminates at the fourth wall of the chapel where Fra Filippo Lippi's altarpiece, the *Nativity* (Fig. 225) could be seen. His Madonnas are slim and

226. Paolo Uccello. *Battle of San Romano.* c. 1455. Tempera on wood, 6′ × 10′5″ (1.83 × 3.18 m). Uffizi, Florence.

girlish, his babies plump and childlike, his saints kindly and paternal. The linear emphasis of Lippi's drawing, softened by his lush palette of pastel hues, had a decisive influence on the art of his pupil Botticelli. In this *Nativity,* the pictorial space is divided symmetrically by the Trinity with God the Father imparting a blessing on His Son through the descending rays of the Holy Spirit. The rays find an earthly echo in the vertical lines of the tree trunks that rise by steps in the background, thus creating niches for the figures of the Madonna, St. John, and St. Joseph.

Paolo Uccello

To decorate one of the rooms of the Medici Palace, Cosimo called upon Paolo Uccello. As a student of spatial science, Uccello was trying to solve the problem of *linear perspective*—the formula of arranging lines on a two-dimensional surface so that they converge at a vanishing point on the horizon and promote the illusion of recession in depth. One of his three scenes depicting the *Battle of San Romano* (Fig. 226), a skirmish of 1432 in which the Florentines put the Sienese army to flight, shows his pioneering effort in applying Euclidean geometry to pictorial mechanics.

As a scientific experiment, Uccello lays his lances and banners out on the ground as if on a chessboard. He was evidently so absorbed with his lines that his bloodless battle is staged more in the manner of a dress parade than a clashing conflict. He also did not

develop the element of light and shade, so that his merry-go-roundlike horses, despite the variety of their postures, remain as flat as cardboard. For all this intellectual effort, the solution of the linear problem eluded him, and in this respect he was always a pupil and never a master.

Piero della Francesca

Present in Florence during the 1440s was Piero della Francesca. As an assistant to Domenico Veneziano, he absorbed the richness of Venetian color. Studying Masaccio, he learned about atmospheric perspective and how to model figures in light and shade. Associating with Ghiberti, Brunelleschi, Alberti, and Paolo Uccello, he eventually became a master of linear perspective and later wrote an essay on the subject.

Piero's *Resurrection* (Fig. 227), painted for the chapel of the town hall of his native Umbrian town of Borgo San Sepolcro, is one of his most sophisticated works. His geometrical clarity of design is seen at once in the compact pyramidal composition that builds up from the sleeping soldiers (the second from the left is generally thought to be a self-portrait) and sarcophagus to the figure of Christ modeled like a classical statue and holding the triumphant banner.

Color contrasts, as well as light and shade, play important roles both in the pictorial mechanics and in the symbolism of this *Resurrection.* The somber tones of the soldiers' costumes are offset by the radiant pink of Christ's robe. Furthermore, the dark-clad soldiers, paralleled by the shadowy earth, set up an alternating rhythm with the glowing figure of Jesus against the Easter dawn. The barren earth on the left yields to the springtime rebirth of the fields on the right. The effect of the brightening sky above, together with the radiant spirit of Christ with His piercing, almost hypnotic gaze, is reflected in the disturbed soldiers below, who, though still asleep, are just beginning to be aware of the dawn.

Botticelli

Painting in the first part of the 15th century had to reckon with many different trends and diverse personalities. Sandro Botticelli, however, rose above the majority of his contemporaries. He became the most representative artist of the humanistic thought that dominated the latter half of the century.

Botticelli enjoyed the patronage of the Medici family, and in his *Adoration of the Magi* (Fig. 228) he portrays the clan as had his predecessor Benozzo Gozzoli (Fig. 224). Among the admirably arranged figures, one finds the elderly Cosimo kneeling at the feet of the Christ Child. Also kneeling are his two sons Piero and Giovanni. To their right, standing against the ruined wall, is the profiled figure of Giuliano, the handsome grandson of Cosimo and the younger brother of Lorenzo the Magnificent, who is to be found in the extreme left foreground. His opposite number at the right usually is identified as Botticelli himself. Though the coloring is bright—ranging

above: 227. Piero della Francesca. *Resurrection.* c. 1460. Fresco, 9'6" × 8'4" (2.9 × 2.54 m). Gallery, Palazzo del Commune, Borgo San Sepolcro.

left: 228. Sandro Botticelli. *Adoration of the Magi.* c. 1475. Tempera on wood, 3'7½" × 4'4¾" (1.1 × 1.34 m). Uffizi, Florence

from the cool sky blue of the Virgin's robe and the dark green and gold embroidery of Cosimo's costume to the ermine-lined crimson cloak of the kneeling Piero and the bright orange of Botticelli's mantle—it falls into a harmonious pattern. Attention should also be called to the classical touch provided by the Roman ruin in the left background.

Botticelli was not a popular painter of pageants like Benozzo Gozzoli and his contemporary Ghirlandaio but a member of the sophisticated group of humanists who gathered around his Medici patrons. In this circle, which included the poet Angelo Poliziano and the philosophers Marsilio Ficino and Pico della Mirandola, as well as Lorenzo the Magnifi-cent and his cousin Pierfrancesco di Lorenzo de' Medici, classical myths were constantly discussed and interpreted. The dialogues of Plato, the *Enneads* of the Roman philosopher Plotinus, and Greek musical theory were all thoroughly explored. With the Florentine interest in the pictorial arts, the ancient references to sculpture and painting were not neglected. This neopagan atmosphere with Christian parallels is seen in many of Botticelli's paintings.

Venus and Mars (Fig. 229) is one of Botticelli's allegorical pictures inspired by the humanistic speculations of the Florentine Neoplatonists. Commissioned apparently for a marriage in the famous Vespucci family, the unusual shape of the panel suggests

above: 229. Sandro Botticelli. *Venus and Mars.* c. 1485. Oil on wood, 2'2¾″ × 5'7¾″ (.68 × 1.72 m). National Gallery, London (reproduced by courtesy of the Trustees).

left: 230. Sandro Botticelli. *Birth of Venus.* c. 1480. Tempera on canvas, 6'7″ × 9'2″ (2.01 × 2.79 m). Uffizi, Florence.

231. Jan van Eyck.
Giovanni Arnolfini and His Wife. 1434.
Oil on wood, 33 × 22½″ (84 × 57 cm).
National Gallery, London
(reproduced by courtesy of the Trustees).

that its model was a classical sarcophagus (see Figs. 109, 131) and that it was intended either for a wedding chest or a bed board. Venus and Mars were, of course, the mythological lovers of antiquity. Marsilio Ficino, in his commentary on Plato's *Symposium,* mentioned that "Mars is outstanding in strength among planets because he makes men stronger, but Venus masters him. . . ."

The wealthy Vespucci family, close associates of the Medici, numbered several celebrated members, among them Simonetta Cattaneo, wife of one Marco Vespucci, and Amerigo Vespucci, the Florentine geographer and explorer whose claim that he had discovered an unknown continent gave his name to the New World. The fair Simonetta was elevated into a Platonic personification of ideal beauty and goodness. As such she was enshrined by Poliziano and Lorenzo the Magnificent in a poetic niche, much as Beatrice had been by Dante, and Laura by Petrarch. She is also thought to have inspired the ideal Venus type in many of Botticelli's masterpieces.

In the *Birth of Venus* (Fig. 230), a celebrated masterpiece, Botticelli depicts the goddess vividly as she floats across the green sea on a pink shell gently blown by Zephyrs, personifications of gentle breezes. On the shore ready to clothe her in a flowery mantle is one of the *Horae,* or "Hours." The coloring of the picture is as cool as called for by a classical subject. The fluttering drapery of the side figures creates a sense of lightness and movement and leads the eye toward the head of Venus, which is surrounded by an aura of golden hair. The clarity of outline, the ballet-like choreography of lines, the pattern of linear rhythms recall the technique of relief sculpture.

Medici Patronage in Bruges

Jan van Eyck   Medici patronage reached out beyond Florence to all the European centers where the family had branch banks—Milan, Venice, Lyon, London, and especially Bruges, where two Medici representatives figured prominently in Flemish

232. Hugo van der Goes. *Portinari Altarpiece.* c. 1476. Oil on wood, 9′2½″ × 21′8½″ (2.81 × 6.62 m). Uffizi, Florence.

painting. *Giovanni Arnolfini and His Wife* (Fig. 231) by Jan van Eyck is a master portrait of the shrewd, calculating Medici banker. Bright light bathes the entire space and illuminates every object evenly and naturally. Each detail is described with the keenest observation from the more subdued tones and textures of the wooden floor and shoes, the furry dog, and the cloth of costumes and bed to the higher gloss of the metal chandelier and the mirror. The mirror is itself a picture in miniature reflecting the wedding certificate and a self-portrait of the artist as witness to the ceremony.

Hugo van der Goes   In the latter half of the 15th century, Tommaso Portinari, another Medici representative in Bruges, commissioned an altarpiece for the hospital of Santa Maria Nuova in Florence (Fig. 232). Hugo van der Goes, the artistic heir of van Eyck, painted the donor, his wife and children, and their patron saints, Thomas and Margaret, in the wings of the three-paneled picture, or *triptych.*

In the central panel, depicting the Adoration of the Shepherds, one sees the same close observation of naturalistic detail as van Eyck's—from the weather-beaten faces of the shepherds to the brocaded cloth of the angels' robes. But van der Goes is also concerned with symbolism—the harp in the tympanum of the background building indicates that Mary and the Child stem from the house of David; the sheaf of wheat signifies Bethlehem; and the flowers, the future sorrows of Mary. The artist also makes use of some spatial distortion to achieve expressive effect— the floor tipping slightly upward to project the figures forward; the relative sizes of the figures in rela-

tion to the picture plane, with Joseph, Mary, and the shepherds in the middle ground looming larger than the angels in the foreground.

The arrival of this triptych in Florence in 1476 created a sensation, for it provided the first opportunity local painters had to observe a large-scale product by one of their northern contemporaries. Clearly it influenced Ghirlandaio and Botticelli. Their special interest was in the new *oil medium* perfected by Jan van Eyck. In Italy, such panels traditionally were done with water-soluble pigments to obtain colors in the process known as *tempera.* The Flemish painters, however, were now using oil to suspend pigments. The boards on which they painted were first treated with a fine white plaster or cementlike substance called *gesso,* and on this a *cartoon,* or a full-scale sketch, of the picture was drawn with ink and modeled in light and shade.

After the painting had been made in opaque oil colors, a translucent glaze with varnishlike brightness was then applied. This glaze, also in an oil medium, could be worked with the brush to give lustrous effects, so that the colors seemed to glow from within the picture. Gradually, the deeper colors and brilliant enamel-like finish of this oil medium supplanted the brighter-colored but duller surfaces of Italian tempera painting.

Poetry and Music
Lorenzo as Poet and Patron

The principal poets of the Florentine Renaissance were Lorenzo de' Medici and Poliziano. Lorenzo's title *Il Magnifico,* in retrospect, seems fitting in recognition of his activities as poet, humanist, philosopher, discoverer of genius, patron of the arts and sciences, and adviser to writers, sculptors, painters, and musicians.

Under the wise guidance of his grandfather Cosimo, *Pater Patriae,* Lorenzo had been educated by Pico della Mirandola and other Latin and Greek scholars of the highest repute to be the type of philosopher-ruler that Plato had described in his *Republic.* Social conditions, however, had changed considerably since Cosimo's time, and while his grandfather had been a banker with intellectual and artistic tastes, Lorenzo became a prince whose power rested on philosophical prestige and leadership in matters of taste as well as on his banking fortune.

Lorenzo maintained embassies at all the principal courts to which he made loans. He was willing to finance foreign conflicts, provided he saw a substantial profit for himself, but he preferred to fight his own wars with words. By having the services of the greatest humanists under his command, he never ran out of ammunition in the form of elegantly turned phrases, veiled threats, and verbal thunderbolts.

Changes in the status of the arts had also come about as the 15th century progressed. In the early decades Ghiberti had been employed by the Signory, and his work was intended for public view. Later the major commissions came from a few wealthy families. Under Lorenzo the arts took on a more courtly character, and the audiences grew correspondingly smaller and more elite. Some painters were able to remain outside the charmed circle and to make careers depicting social scenes of births and marriages for an upper middle-class clientele. Botticelli's pictures, however, were mainly for the humanistic intellectuals of the time.

Carnival Songs   Lorenzo himself, though the leader of this exclusive group, had the instincts of a popular ruler and did not neglect the common touch. He participated actively in the Florentine festivals by composing new verses for the traditional folk tunes, by encouraging others in his circle to do the same, and by holding competitions among composers for better musical settings of the songs.

Lorenzo thus gave new impetus to popular literature in the native dialect. In a commentary on four of his own sonnets, he went to considerable lengths to defend the expressive possibilities of Tuscan Italian. After comparing it with Hebrew, Greek, and Latin, he found that its harmoniousness and sweetness outdid all the others. While he continued to write sophisticated sonnets, Lorenzo also wrote popular verses that have, in addition to their beauty and literary polish, all the spontaneous freshness, humor,

and charm of folk poetry. In some of his pastoral poems he even uses the rustic dialogue of true country folk. Few poets could rival the lyricism of his *canti carnascialeschi,* or "carnival songs," one of which contains the oft-quoted lines:

> *Quanto è bella giovinezza,*
> *Che si fugge tuttavia!*
> *Chi vuol esser lieto, sia:*
> *Di doman non c' è certezza.*

> Fair is youth and free of sorrow,
> Yet how soon its joys we bury!
> Let who would be, now be merry:
> Sure is no one of tomorrow.

In order to flourish, popular poetry needed appropriate musical settings. A young man of eighteen, Lorenzo was in search of a composer to set his lyrics, and a letter he wrote in 1467 requests the "venerable Gugliemo Dufay," who by this time was approaching seventy, to compose music for his verses. This was the same Guillaume Dufay who some thirty years earlier had composed the dedicatory motet for the cathedral.

Collaboration with Heinrich Isaac   Popular music making in Florence and other Italian cities was as much a part of the good life as any of the other arts. But it was mainly an art of performance, and little music was ever written down. When the time came to appoint a successor to Squarcialupi as private master of music in the Medici household after his death in 1475, Lorenzo's choice fell on Heinrich Isaac, a native of Flanders and a rapid and productive composer. Florence immediately became a second home to this truly cosmopolitan figure, and native Italian idioms soon were combined with those of his own background and training.

Isaac's duties included those of organist and choirmaster at the Florence Cathedral as well as at the Medici Palace, where Lorenzo is known to have had no less than five organs. Together with the poet Angelo Poliziano, he was also the teacher of Lorenzo's sons, one of whom was destined to be the music- and art-loving Pope Leo X. But most important, Isaac collaborated with Lorenzo on the songs written for popular festivals. He thus became co-creator of one of the popular kinds of secular music that eventually led to the 16th-century *madrigal.* The madrigal was a popular type of vocal chamber music in the polyphonic style, usually of amorous character and designed for home entertainment.

Dufay's settings of Lorenzo's verses are now lost, but many by Isaac still exist. In one of these, he shows the tendency away from complex counterpoint and toward simple harmonic, or chordal, texture. Its

Un di lieto   Lorenzo de' Medici and Heinrich Isaac

style is that of a Florentine *frottola,* a carnival song for dancing as well as singing, and its lilting rhythm freely shifts its meter. As the setting stands (above), it could be performed by a three-part chorus. It could also be performed as a solo song with the two lower parts taken by the lute or two viols or other instruments, or as a vocal duet with the soprano and either one of the two other voices.

The collaboration of Lorenzo and Isaac thus resulted in both a meeting of minds and a merging of poetic and musical forms. Lorenzo's verses were a union of the courtly *ballata* and popular poetry, while Isaac succeeded in Italianizing the Burgundian *chanson,* or "song." Italianizing in this case means simplifying, omitting all artificiality, and enlivening a rather stiff form with the graceful Florentine folk melodies and rhythm. It can be seen that such a movement worked both ways by raising the level of popular poetry on the one hand, and at the same time giving new life to more sophisticated poetic and musical forms by contact with popular idioms.

Ideas

The dominating ideas of the Florentine Renaissance cluster around three concepts—classical humanism, scientific naturalism, and Renaissance individualism. In their broadest meaning, humanism, naturalism, and individualism were far from new. When classical humanism took shape in Italy, it was very likely as much a survival from ancient times—for Roman architecture and sculpture were always present on Italian territory—as a true revival in the sense of a reinterpretation and new adaptation of the older Greco-Roman forms.

Naturalism, in the sense of faithfulness to nature, appears in a well-developed form both in the northern Gothic sculpture and in the poetry of St. Francis, who had died as long before as 1226. By the 14th century, representations of humans and nature alike had pretty well lost their value as otherworldly symbols. But rather than being content with describing the world as seen by the eye alone, Florentine 15th-century naturalism took a noticeably scientific turn. Careful observation of natural events and the will to reproduce objects as the eye sees them was evidence of an empirical attitude; dissection of corpses in

order to see the structure of the human body revealed a spirit of free inquiry; and the study of mathematics so as to put objects into proper perspective involved a new concept of space. Clearly a new scientific spirit was now afoot.

While individualism as such is practically universal, the distinctive feature of its Florentine expression was that conditions in this small city-state were almost ideal for artists to come into immediate and fruitful contact with their patrons and audience. Competition was keen; desire for personal fame was intense; and a high regard for personality is seen in the portraiture, biographies, and autobiographies.

Humanism in the humanitarian Franciscan sense was a carryover from the 13th and 14th centuries. Naturalism stemmed from late Gothic times. And some form of individualism is always present in any period. It should therefore be clear that the Florentine Renaissance was characterized by no sharp division from the past, and that its special flavor lies in the quality of its humanism, in the tendency of its naturalism, and in its particular regard for the nature of its individualism.

Classical Humanism

The term *Renaissance,* implying as it does a "rebirth," is a source of some confusion. To the early 16th-century historians, it meant an awakening to the values of ancient classical arts and letters after the long medieval night. But just what, if anything, was *reborn* has never been satisfactorily explained. Since all the principal ideas were present in the Gothic period, one might do better to speak of the maturing of certain tendencies present in late medieval times. Yet there was a specific drive that gave an extraordinary stimulus and color to the creative life and thought of this small Tuscan city-state in the 15th century. It is important to discover what it was, and what it was not, that gave humanism in Florence its special flavor.

Though Florentine humanism evolved from the Franciscan spirit, it did take on a consciously classical coloration. Here again, however, a word of caution is necessary when speaking of a "rebirth" of the spirit of antiquity. In Italy, much more than in northern Europe, the classical tradition had been more or less continuous. Roman remains were everywhere in evidence. Many Roman arches, aqueducts, bridges, and roads were still in use, while fragments of ancient buildings were reused as building materials.

In the late 13th century, Nicola Pisano's sculptural models were the Roman remains he saw all around him, and by the 15th century the revival of the classical male nude as an instrument of expression is seen in the work of Ghiberti, Donatello,

233. Michelangelo. *David.* 1501-04.
Marble, height 18′ (5.49 m). Academy, Florence.

Pollaiuolo, and Verrocchio. At the beginning of the
16th century Michelangelo had developed such a
formidable sculptural technique that his *David*
(Fig. 233) not only rivaled the work of such ancient
sculptors as Praxiteles (see Fig. 50), but surpassed it.

Aristotle was still the official philosopher of the
Church, and ancient musical theory continued to be
studied. What was new to Florence was the study of
the Greek language, the setting up of Ciceronian
rather than medieval Latin as a standard, and a
passionate interest in Plato. In spite of a certain
concern for antique books and works of art, however,
the net result was less a revival of things past than a
step forward. It was a search for past examples to
justify new practices.

Much has been said also about the pagan aspect
of this interest in antiquity. Here again it was less
anti-Christian than appears on the surface. Florentine Neoplatonism was certainly antischolastic, but it
was mainly a substitution of the authority of Plato
for that of Aristotle. Marsilio Ficino, as the high
priest of the movement, in his interpretation of the
Republic and *Laws,* speaks of Plato as the Athenian
"Moses." He is also known to have added "Saint"
Socrates to his litany and to have burned a candle
before the bust of Plato. In this light, his thought
appears more as a reinterpretation of Christianity in
Platonic terms than paganism as such.

Meanwhile the Church under the Renaissance
popes was taking on a distinctly worldly character
and seemed to be more concerned with political and
financial affairs than with spiritual power. Abuses by
the clergy brought opposition in Florence as well as
elsewhere, and it was to become one of the causes of
the Reformation. Lorenzo, however, as papal banker
and a father who chose the Church for his son
Giovanni's career, was not so much a religious skep-
tic as he was a political realist. It is also important to
keep in mind that the Florentine humanists were a
small learned band whose Platonic arguments have
made much more noise in the corridors of history
than they did in their own time. Actually, the Florentine humanists never had, nor did they seek, a large
audience. In the first quarter of the following century, however, they had the international forum of
Rome. The artistic expression of Neoplatonism came
to its climax there in the works of Michelangelo.
So, a full discussion of this elitist movement—which
must include the art of Botticelli and Raphael, the
patronage of Julius II and the Medici popes Leo X
and Clement VII, and the Neoplatonic philosophers—will have to await the chapter that follows.

Scientific Naturalism

The two basic directions taken by the naturalism of
the 15th century led to a new experimental attitude
and a new concept of space. A close partnership
between art and science developed, with architects
becoming mathematicians, sculptors anatomists,
painters geometricians, and musicians acousticians.

The spirit of free inquiry was by no means confined to the arts alone. It penetrated all the progressive aspects of the life of the time from a reexamination of the forms of secular government to
Machiavelli's observations on how people behave in a
certain given set of political circumstances. This
searching curiosity reached its full fruition in the
early years of the 16th century in Machiavelli's political handbook *The Prince,* and in the same author's
attempt to apply the Thucydidean method of rational

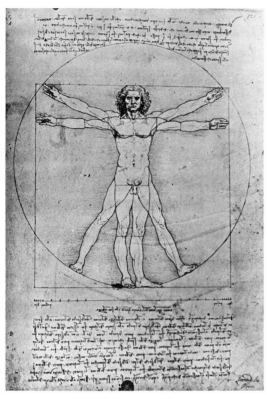

above: 234. Leonardo da Vinci.
Study of Human Proportions according to Vitruvius.
c. 1485–90. Pen and ink, 13½ × 9¾″ (34 × 25 cm).
Academy, Venice.

below: 235. Leonardo da Vinci.
Adoration of the Magi, detail. 1481–82.
Tempera on wood, entire work
7′11⅝″ × 8′⅞″ (2.43 × 2.46 m). Uffizi, Florence.

historical analysis in his *History of Florence.* The scientific observations in Leonardo's notebooks, which cover everything from astronomy to hydraulics, show an equally pronounced searching curiosity.

Well within the 15th century, however, the same spirit manifested itself. Ghiberti's *Commentaries* took up the mathematical proportions of the human body as the basis of its beauty, and he wrote the first essay in Italian on optics. Brunelleschi, as a diligent student of the ancient Roman architect Vitruvius, was concerned with the mathematical proportions of his buildings. Alberti, in his books on painting, sculpture, and architecture, stressed the study of mathematics as the underlying principle of all the arts.

The sculptors and painters who followed the leadership of Antonio Pollaiuolo and Verrocchio were animated by the desire to express the structural forms of the body beneath its external appearance. Their anatomical studies opened the way to the modeling of the movements and gestures of the human body (Fig. 234). The result was the reaffirmation of the expressive power of the nude.

In painting, naturalism meant a more faithful representation of the world of appearances, one based on detailed and accurate observation. Even Fra Angelico showed an interest in the exact reproduction of Tuscan botanical specimens in the garden of his *Annunciation* (Fig. 223). Botticelli, too, under the influence of Pollaiuolo and Verrocchio, combined objective techniques with imaginative subjects.

The culmination of this line of thought was reached in Verrocchio's pupil Leonardo da Vinci, who considered painting a science and sculpture a mechanical art. Leonardo's scientific probing went beyond the physical and anatomical into the metaphysical and psychological aspects of human nature. A detail from his early, unfinished *Adoration of the Magi* (Fig. 235), for instance, reveals through agitated gestures and puzzled facial expressions the bewilderment and emotional turmoil of the Wise Men as they try to comprehend the miraculous meaning of the Messiah's coming.

In music there was a continued interest in Greek theory, coupled, however, with attempts to experiment with acoustical problems. The compositions of Dufay and others of the northern school were characterized by extreme learning. For instance, mathematical laws were strictly applied to such aspects of composition as rhythmical progressions, formal proportions, and the development of technical devices.

Highly dramatic was the conquest of geographical space that began with the voyages of Columbus, leading to the development of trade routes and commerce and the tapping of new and distant sources of wealth. In architecture, this breakthrough in space is reflected in the raising of Brunelleschi's cupola al-

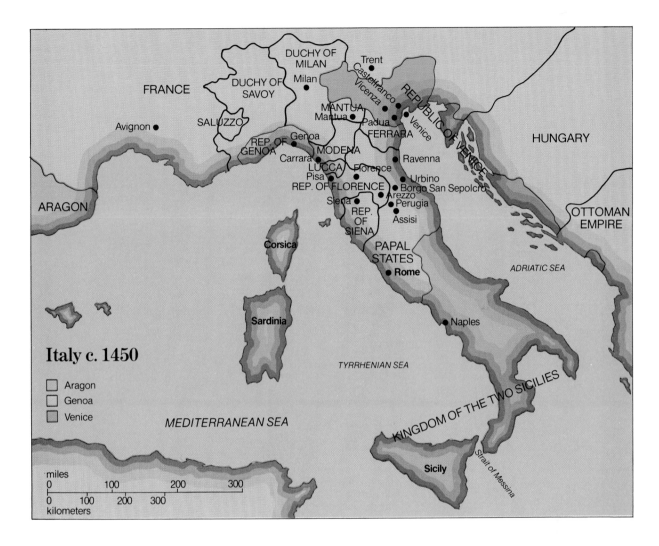

Italy c. 1450

- Aragon
- Genoa
- Venice

most 370 feet (112.7 meters) into the air. In painting, it is seen in a number of advances. Among them are the placing of figures in a more normal relationship to the space they occupy, and the use of landscape settings. Others are Masaccio's development of atmospheric perspective, in which figures are modeled in light and shade, and the working out of rules for linear perspective whereby the illusion of depth on a two-dimensional surface is achieved by defining a point at which lines converge. *Foreshortening,* the reduction in the size of figures and objects in direct ratio to their distance from the picture plane, is yet another.

Since the subject matter of medieval art was drawn from the otherworld, it fell outside the scope of naturalistic representation and had to be shown symbolically. Art now entered a new phase of self-awareness as Renaissance artists began to think less in terms of allegory, symbolism, and moral lessons and more in terms of aesthetic problems, modes of presentation, and pictorial mechanics. In medieval music, the emphasis had been on perfect intervals and mathematical rhythmic ratios in order to please the ear of God. Renaissance musicians now reversed the process by concentrating on sounds that would delight the human ear. The new spirit was also heard in the extension of the range of musical instruments in both higher and lower registers, to broaden the scope of tonal space. Thus, the development of pleasant harmonic textures, the softening of dissonances, and the writing of singable melodies and danceable rhythms are all related developments giving style to the period.

In this trend toward scientific naturalism, the arts of painting and sculpture became firmly allied with geometrical and scientific laws, a union that lasted until 20th-century expressionism and abstract art. The 15th-century Florentine artists literally reveled in the perspective, optical, and anatomical discoveries of their day. And when all the basic research,

236. Perugino. *Christ Delivering Keys of the Kingdom to St. Peter.* 1481–83. Fresco, 11 × 18′ (3.35 × 5.49 m). Sistine Chapel, Vatican, Rome.

experiments, and discoveries had been made, it was left for their successors—Leonardo da Vinci, Michelangelo, and Raphael—to explore their full expressive possibilities.

Renaissance Individualism

In the Renaissance, the desire for personal prestige through art became of prime importance. Wealthy families and individuals commissioned artists to build memorial churches and chapels as well as do statues and paintings. The high regard for individual personality is also mirrored in the number and quality of portraits painted at this time. Since artists were so eagerly sought after, their social status rose accordingly, and sculptors and painters became important personalities in their own right.

The religious nature of the vast majority of the works of art has already been pointed out, but personal patronage was in the ascendancy. Brunelleschi built the Pazzi Chapel, Masolino and Masaccio decorated the Brancacci Chapel, and Benozzo Gozzoli and Fra Filippo Lippi did the paintings for the Medici Chapel, all on commission from private donors as memorials to themselves and their families. San Lorenzo, the parish church of the Medici, was rebuilt and redecorated by Brunelleschi and Donatello—but

the money came from Cosimo and not from the Church. Fra Angelico decorated the corridors of the monastery of San Marco, which was under the protection of the Medici family, and Squarcialupi and Isaac were on the payroll of the Medici when they played the organ in the cathedral, in a church, or in the family palace. Piousness and the desire for spiritual salvation were not the only motives for such generosity. A knowledge that the donor's present and future fame depended on building monuments and choosing artists to decorate them was all-important.

In addition to the circumstances of patronage, certain technical considerations within the arts themselves point in the same individualistic direction. The development of perspective drawing, for example, implied that the subject in the picture—whether a Madonna, a saint, or an angel—was definitely placed in this world rather than symbolically in the next. Hence the figure was more on a basis of equality with the observer. The unification of space by having all the lines converge at one point on the horizon tended to flatter the spectator. By clear organization of lines and planes, linear perspective assumes that everything is seen from a single optical vantage point (Fig. 236). While the point of view is actually that of the artist, it is made to seem as if it were also that of the observer. By closing the form, the artist further implies that nothing of importance lies outside the painting, and the whole of the picture can then be taken in at a glance. Since nothing, then, is beyond the grasp of the viewer, and all can be understood with relatively little effort, the eye and mind of the onlooker are reassured.

The central-type church that Alberti, Bramante, and, later, Michelangelo and Palladio preferred to design, in which the space is unified under a dome, is the architectural expression of the same idea. The Gothic cathedral purposely led the eye and imagination outward into the infinite beyond, while the central-type church revolves around the individual. Standing under the cupola, the observer is aware that the axis of the building is not objectively outside or beyond but subjectively within. The observer is, for the moment, the center of the architectural space. The center of the universe exists not at some remote point beyond the horizon but within the viewer.

Human figures, whether rendered as prophets or portraits, tended to become more personal and individual. Each statue by Donatello, be it *Lo Zuccone* (Fig. 217) or the *David* (Fig. 218), was an individual person who made a powerful, unique impression. Even Fra Angelico's Madonna was a personality more than an abstraction, and his figure of the Angel Gabriel possessed genuine human dignity. Whether the medium was marble, terra-cotta, paint, words, or tones, there was evidence of the new value placed on human individuality. Whether the picture was a disguised family group, as Botticelli's *Adoration of the Magi* (Fig. 228), or a personal portrait, as Verrocchio's bust of Lorenzo, the figures were authentic personages rather than stylized abstractions; even though Lorenzo de' Medici was the most powerful political figure of Florence, Verrocchio saw him as a man, not as an institution.

The higher social status given to Florentine artists was evident in the inclusion of self-portraits in such paintings as that of Benozzo Gozzoli in his *Journey of the Magi* (Fig. 224) and the prominent position Botticelli allowed himself in his *Adoration of the Magi.* Ghiberti's personal reminiscences in his *Commentaries* were probably the first autobiography of an artist in history. His inclusion of the lives and legends of his famous 14th-century predecessors were the first biographies of individual artists. He also included a self-portrait in one of the round medallions in the center of his famous doors (Fig. 209).

Signatures of artists on their works became the rule, not the exception. The culmination came when Michelangelo realized that his work was so highly individual that he no longer needed to sign it. The desire for personal fame grew to such an extent that Benvenuto Cellini no longer was content to let his works speak for him but wrote a lengthy autobiography filled with self-praise. The painter Giorgio Vasari likewise took up the pen to record the lives of the artists he knew personally and by reputation. More broadly, such works as Pico della Mirandola's essay on the *Dignity of Man,* Machiavelli's *The Prince,* and Castiglione's *The Courtier* were written to enhance the intellectual, political, and social status of humanity in general and the scholar, politician, courtier, and artist in particular.

In late medieval and early Renaissance times, artists were content with their status as craftsmen. They were trained as apprentices to grind pigments, carve wooden chests, make engravings, and prepare wall surfaces for frescoes as well as to carve marble reliefs and paint pictures. In the late 15th and early 16th centuries, however, it was not enough for artists to create works of art. They had to know the theory of art and the place of art and the artist in the intellectual atmosphere of their period.

The quality most admired in Renaissance times was *virtù* (the word comes closer in the modern sense to "virtuoso" than "virtuous"). *Virtù* revealed itself in the boundless vitality and extraordinary ability that led to the achievements of a Lorenzo the Magnificent or the breathtaking conceptions of a Michelangelo. With *virtù,* Renaissance artists could no longer be satisfied with a single specialty but sought to become universal in ability. Brunelleschi was a goldsmith, sculptor, engineer, and mathematician as well as one of the leading lights of Renaissance architecture. Alberti was an athlete, horseman, brilliant wit, Latin stylist, mathematician, architect, musician, playwright, and founder of Renaissance theory of art. With Leonardo Renaissance universality reached its peak, for it is more difficult to find a field in which he was not proficient than one in which he excelled.

From Lorenzo's time through the early 16th century, the greatest artists were intellectuals. Alberti was a scholar-architect who wrote books on the subject, designed buildings on paper, and left the actual construction to a master mason. Botticelli associated with writers and worked elaborate allegories into his pictures. Leonardo da Vinci thought sculpture inferior to painting because of the physical labor involved, and in his later years devoted himself more to science than to painting. Bramante and Raphael were to be artist-scholars as well as architects and painters. Michelangelo hated the workshop, even though the realization of his grandiose designs depended on the work of many hands. He was to become the ideal of the modern individualistic artist, consciously an intellectual, dealing with popes and princes as equals, insisting that he painted with his brains not with his hands, and rejecting all offers of noble titles. When people began calling him "the divine," the cycle was complete.

11
The Roman Renaissance Style

Rome, Early 16th Century

On April 18, 1506, when the foundation stone of the new Basilica of St. Peter was laid (Fig. 237), Rome was well on its way to becoming the undisputed artistic and intellectual capital of the Western world. Pope Julius II was gathering about him the foremost living artists in all fields, and together they continued the transformation of the Eternal City from its medieval past into the brilliant Rome of today.

Donato Bramante, originally from Umbria but educated in Lombardy, was the architect at work on the plans for the new St. Peter's, the central church of the Christian world. Michelangelo Buonarroti from Florence was collecting the marble for a monumental tomb for Julius and was about to begin the painting of the Sistine ceiling. Raffaelo (Raphael) Sanzio from Umbria would soon be summoned from Florence to decorate the rooms of the Vatican Palace. The Florentine Andrea Sansovino was carving a cardinal's tomb in one of Julius II's favorite Roman churches, Santa Maria del Popolo, where the Umbrian Pinturicchio was covering its choir vaults with a series of frescoes. The singer-composer Josquin des Prez, already a member of the papal choir for eight years, had left to become choirmaster to the king of France.

The papal court under Julius II and his successor Leo X was such a powerful magnet that for three years the three greatest figures of the Renaissance—Leonardo da Vinci, Michelangelo, and Raphael—found themselves at the Vatican. In 1517, however,

237. St. Peter's Basilica and the Vatican, Rome. Apse and dome by Michelangelo, 1547-64; dome completed by Giacomo della Porta, 1588-92; nave and façade by Carlo Maderno, 1601-26; colonnades by Gianlorenzo Bernini, 1656-63. Height of façade 147′ (44.81 m), width 374′ (114 m).

the aged Leonardo abandoned the artistic field of honor there to join the court of Francis I of France.

The flight of the Medici from Florence in 1494 had signaled a general exodus of artists. Many found temporary havens in the ducal courts of Italy, but the magnet of attraction proved to be the papal court at Rome. Hence, during the days of the two great Renaissance popes, Julius II and Leo X, the cultural capital shifted from Florence to Rome. And, since Leonardo, Andrea Sansovino, Michelangelo, and Pope Leo were from Florence, and since Bramante and Raphael had absorbed the Florentine style and ideas in extended visits there, the cultural continuity was unbroken. It was, in fact, like a smooth transplantation from the confines of a nursery to an open field—a move that led artists to branch out from local styles into the universal air of Rome.

Such projects as the building of the world's largest church, the construction of Julius II's tomb, the painting of the Sistine ceiling, and the Vatican Palace murals could be found only in Rome. Nowhere else were monuments of such proportions or commissions of such magnitude possible. In Rome also resided the cardinals, who maintained palaces that rivaled the brilliance of the papal court.

The interest in antiquity had animated many other Italian centers, but when the Renaissance got under way in Rome, it was, so to speak, on home soil. When antique statues were excavated elsewhere, they caused a considerable stir. In Rome, however, many of the ancient monuments were still standing, and when the archaeological shovels probed the proper places, a veritable treasure trove was waiting. One by one the *Apollo Belvedere* (see Fig. 84), the *Venus of the Vatican,* and the *Laocoön Group* (see Fig. 81) came to light to stimulate the work of Michelangelo and other sculptors. The frescoes from Nero's Domus Aureus and the Baths of Titus provided the first important specimens of ancient painting. While the art of painting on fresh plaster had never died out, these ancient Roman fragments gave fresco painting a new importance.

Julius II had received most of his training in diplomacy and statecraft from his uncle Pope Sixtus IV. Fortunately, a passionate love of the arts was included in this education. It was Sixtus who had built the chapel that has subsequently carried his name, and who had installed there the group of papal singers that have ever since been known as the *Cappella Sistina,* or "Sistine Chapel Choir." It remained for Julius to establish a chorus to perform in St. Peter's—one that still bears his name, the *Cappella Giulia,* or "Julian Choir." This latter group corresponded to the ancient Schola Cantorum and prepared the singers for the Sistine Choir. Both have always received strong papal support.

Essentially a man of action, Julius II was an expert with the soldier's sword as well as the bishop's staff. He met his age on its own terms, and the spectacle of the Pope riding a fiery horse into the smoke of battle had a remarkably demoralizing effect on his enemies. As one of the principal architects of the modern papacy, he also saw the need of a setting on a scale with the importance of the Church founded by St. Peter and made it a matter of policy to command artists as well as soldiers. At the end of his career, Julius II became the subject of one of Raphael's most penetrating portraits (Fig. 238).

When Leo X ascended the papal throne, one of the sayings went: "Venus has had her day, and Mars his, now comes the turn of Minerva." Venus symbolized the reign of the Borgia pope, Alexander VI; Mars, of course, referred to Julius II; and Minerva, the Roman equivalent of Athena, was Leo. As the son of Lorenzo the Magnificent, he brought with him to Rome the intellectual spirit of Florence, that latterday Athens. Michelangelo, whom Leo had known

238. Raphael. *Julius II.* 1511–12.
Oil on wood, 42½ × 31½″ (108 × 80 cm).
National Gallery, London
(reproduced by courtesy of the Trustees).

CHRONOLOGY
Late 15th- and Early 16th-Century Rome

GENERAL EVENTS		
1471–1527	Roman Renaissance art and humanism at climax	
1471–1484	Sixtus IV (della Rovere), pope	
1473–1480	Sistine Chapel built	
1481–1482	Sistine Chapel side-wall frescoes painted by Rosselli, Ghirlandaio, Botticelli, Perugino, Signorelli, Pinturicchio, Piero di Cosimo	
1484–1492	Innocent VIII (Cibò), pope	
1486–1492	Josquin des Prez in Sistine Chapel Choir	
1492–1503	Alexander VI (Borgia), pope	
1493–1506	Ancient Roman frescoes and statues uncovered: *Apollo Belvedere, Laocoön Group*	
1496–1501	Michelangelo in Rome, working on *Bacchus* and *Pietà*	
1503–1513	Julius II (della Rovere), pope	
1505	Michelangelo began Julius II's tomb	
1506	New Basilica of St. Peter begun by Bramante; Old St. Peter's razed	
1508–1512	Michelangelo painted Sistine Chapel ceiling. Raphael painted frescoes in Vatican Palace	
1512	Cappella Giulia Choir founded	
1513–1516	Leonardo da Vinci in Rome	

1513–1521	Leo X (de' Medici), pope	
1515	Ariosto wrote *Orlando Furioso* (*Madness of Roland*)	
1517	Protestant Reformation began in Germany with Luther's 95 Theses	
1521	Luther excommunicated	
1523–1534	Clement VII (de' Medici), pope	
1523	Michelangelo worked on Medici tombs in Florence	
1527	Rome sacked by Emperor Charles V; Clement VII imprisoned	
1528	Castiglione's *The Courtier* published	
1532	Machiavelli's *The Prince* published	
1534–1549	Paul III (Farnese), pope	
1534	Church of England separated from Rome. Reaction to Renaissance humanism began	
1535–1541	Michelangelo painted *Last Judgment* in Sistine Chapel	
1542	Michelangelo painted frescoes in Pauline Chapel	
1547	Michelangelo named architect of St. Peter's	
1550	Vasari's *Lives of the Most Eminent Painters, Sculptors, and Architects* published	

c.1550	Philippe de Monte in Rome; published first book of madrigals 1554	
1551	Orlando di Lasso in Rome	
1564	Michelangelo died	
ARCHITECTS		
c.1444–1514	Donato Bramante	
1475–1564	Michelangelo Buonarroti	
1556–1629	Carlo Maderno	
SCULPTORS		
1460–1529	Andrea Sansovino	
1475–1564	Michelangelo Buonarroti	
1500–1571	Benvenuto Cellini	
c.1524–1608	Giovanni da Bologna	
PAINTERS		
c.1441–1523	Luca Signorelli	
c.1450–1523	Perugino	
1452–1519	Leonardo da Vinci	
1454–1513	Bernardino Pinturicchio	
1475–1564	Michelangelo Buonarroti	
1483–1520	Raphael Sanzio	
WRITERS		
1474–1533	Ludovico Ariosto	
1478–1529	Baldassare Castiglione	
1483–1531	Martin Luther	
1511–1574	Giorgio Vasari	
1544–1595	Torquato Tasso	
1548–1600	Giordano Bruno	
MUSICIANS		
c.1445–1521	Josquin des Prez	
c.1521–1603	Philippe de Monte	
1525–1594	Giovanni da Palestrina	
c.1532–1594	Orlando di Lasso	

since his childhood at the Medici palace, was unfortunately bound by the terms of his contract to serve the heirs of Pope Julius, but the suave and worldly Raphael was available—and more congenial to the personal taste of Pope Leo than the gruff titan Michelangelo. Once again Raphael served as papal portraitist in an unusually fine study (Fig. 239).

Heinrich Isaac, Leo's old music teacher, wrote the six-part motet that commemorated his accession, and Isaac's pupil became one of the most liberal of all Renaissance patrons of music. Other princes of Europe had difficulty in keeping their best musicians, because the Pope's love of the tonal art was so well known. Leo collected lute and viol players, organists, and the finest singers; chamber music was avidly cultivated at the papal palace; and a wind ensemble performed at papal dinners. Leo's encouragement of music to the point of putting it on a par with literary pursuits caused considerable murmurings among poets and writers. As a competent composer in his own right, he knew the art from the inside as few patrons have ever known it. As a philosopher, writer, and collector, his patronage, like that of his father, was accompanied by an active participation in many of the pursuits that he sponsored. The Renaissance historian Jacob Burkhardt wrote that Rome "possessed in the unique court of Leo X a society to which the history of the world offers no parallel."

Sculpture: Michelangelo

Despite his many masterpieces in other media, Michelangelo always thought of himself first and foremost as a sculptor. Other projects were undertaken reluctantly. On the contract for the painting of the Sistine Chapel ceiling, for example, he pointedly signed *Michelangelo scultore*—"Michelangelo the sculptor"—as a protest. His first visit to Rome at the age of 21 coincided with the discovery of some ancient statuary, including the *Apollo Belvedere* (see Fig. 84), that proved a powerful stimulant to his own productivity. His most important statues from this early period illustrate the conflicting pagan and Christian ideals that were to affect his aesthetic thought throughout a long career.

The Pietà

The *Pietà* (Fig. 240), now in St. Peter's, was commissioned in 1498 by Cardinal Villiers, the French am-

above: 239. Raphael.
Leo X with Two Cardinals.
c. 1518. Oil on wood,
5′5⅝″ × 3′8⅞″ (1.54 × 1.14 m).
Uffizi, Florence.

left: 240. Michelangelo. *Pietà.* 1498–99.
Marble, height 5′9″ (1.75 m).
St. Peter's, Vatican, Rome.

bassador to the Vatican. Its beauty of execution, delicacy of detail, and poignancy of expression reveal that Michelangelo was still under the spell of the Florentine Renaissance. Its pyramidal composition follows a type worked out by Piero della Francesca (see Fig. 227) and by Leonardo da Vinci, as exemplified in his drawing for *Madonna and Child with St. Anne* (Fig. 241). Michelangelo uses the voluminous folds of the Virgin's drapery as the base of the pyramid and her head as the apex.

The figure of Christ is cast in the perfect form of a Greek god, while the Madonna, though overwhelmed by grief, maintains a classical composure. No tears, no outcry, no gesture mar this conception of Mary as the matronly mother of sorrows. Yet Michelangelo allows himself many liberties with the proportions of his figures in order to heighten their expressive effect and enhance the harmony of his design. The excessive drapery exists to increase the number of folds and sweeping lines. The horizontal body of Christ is far shorter than the vertical Madonna, but the disproportion serves to make the composition more compact. The triangular shape, as a self-sufficient form, holds the attention within the composition and makes unnecessary such external considerations as niches or architectural backgrounds. As such, the *Pietà* is a sculptural declaration of independence, and it bears the distinction of being the only work Michelangelo ever signed.

Tomb of Julius II

After finishing the *Pietà,* Michelangelo went home to Florence, where he worked on the *Bruges Madonna* and the *David* (Fig. 233). In 1505, however, he was summoned back to Rome by the lordly Julius to discuss a project for a colossal tomb. In the original conception of this gigantic composition, the artist's imagination for once met its match in his patron's ambitions. Julius' monument was conceived as a small temple within the great new temple—St. Peter's—that was being built. It was to rise pyramidally from a massive quadrangular base visible from all four sides, and it was to include more than forty statues (Fig. 242).

When Julius died in 1513, only a few parts of the project had been finished, and a new contract with his heirs had to be negotiated. Further revisions were made later, each reducing the proportions of the project and eliminating more of the unfinished statues. In its final form of 1545, the great temple had shrunk to the relatively modest wall tomb now in the aisle of the Church of San Pietro in Vincoli.

Tombs of the popes, like the triple tiaras with which they were crowned, were traditionally in three rising zones, symbolizing earthly existence, death, and salvation. For the original project, Michelangelo translated these divisions into Neoplatonic terms

above: 241. Leonardo da Vinci. Cartoon for *Madonna and Child with St. Anne.* 1497-99. Charcoal and white chalk on paper, 4'6¾" × 3'3¾" (1.39 × 1.01 m). National Gallery, London (reproduced by courtesy of the Trustees).

left: 242. Michelangelo. *Projected Tomb of Julius II.* Drawing. Uffizi, Florence.

representing the successive stages of the liberation of the soul from its bodily prison. For the final project, the monument lapsed into more traditional stages. In the original scheme, the lowest level was to have figures symbolizing those who are crushed by the burden of life and those who rise above the bonds of matter (Fig. 242). This idea was retained in some of the later revisions, and six of the so-called Slaves or Captives and one so-called Victory survive in various stages of completion.

On the second level of the original project were to have been placed heroic figures of the leaders of humanity, those individuals who pointed the way toward the divine goal of reunion with God. Moses and St. Paul were to represent the old and new law, while Rachel and Leah would personify the active and contemplative ways of life. Of these, only the Moses was finished by Michelangelo himself.

The three figures that date from the years 1513 to 1516, when Leo X was pope, are the two "Slaves" now in the Louvre and the *Moses*. The *"Bound Slave"* (Fig. 243) is the more nearly finished of the two, and it seems to represent a sleeping adolescent tormented by a dream rather than the "dying captive" it is sometimes called. The imprisoned soul, tortured by the memory of its divine origin, has found momentary peace in sleep. The cloth bands by which the figure is bound are only symbolic, since Michelangelo is not concerned with the external aspect of captivity but rather with the internal torment. It is the tragedy of the human race, limited by time but troubled by the knowledge of eternity; mortal but with a vision of immortality; bound by the weight of the body yet dreaming of a boundless freedom.

This tragedy of the tomb was understood only too well by Michelangelo himself, who had the conception of his great project in mind but was doomed to see only a few fragments of his dream completed. Figures such as the "Slaves" and the "Victory" that he planned were associated with the triumphal arches as well as with the mausoleums and sarcophagi of ancient Rome. The similarity between the *"Bound Slave"* (Fig. 243) and the younger son in the 2nd century B.C. *Laocoön Group* (Fig. 81) has aptly been pointed out.

The Platonic idea of the human soul confined in the bonds of flesh was continued in a later version of the tomb (Fig. 244). The imprisonment of the spirit

above: 243. Michelangelo. *"Bound Slave."* 1513–16. Marble, height 7'5" (2.26 m). Louvre, Paris.

left: 244. Michelangelo. *"Boboli Captive."* c. 1530–34. Marble, height 7'6½" (2.3 m). Academy, Florence.

by matter in these "Captives" is all but complete. Unconscious, locked in their stone wombs, they struggle and writhe to emerge from their material bondage. Their unfinished state gives an interesting glimpse into Michelangelo's methods, which were similar to those of relief sculpture. The statue to Michelangelo was a potential form hidden in the block of marble awaiting the hand of the master sculptor in order to be born. "The greatest artist has no single concept which a rough marble block does not contain already in its core. . . ," wrote Michelangelo in a sonnet. The artist-creator, he continues, must discover, "concealed in the hard marble of the North, the living figure one has to bring forth. (The less of stone remains, the more that grows.)" The Neoplatonic implication is that the soul is still entombed in the body and can only be perfected into pure being by the hand of a higher creative power.

Moses (Fig. 245) is the only statue completed entirely by Michelangelo's hand to find its place in

245. Michelangelo. *Moses.* 1513–15. Marble, height 8'4" (2.54 m). San Pietro in Vincoli, Rome.

the finished tomb. Both Julius II and Michelangelo possessed the quality of *terribilità,* or "awesomeness," that is embodied in this figure. Julius was known as *il papa terribile,* meaning the "forceful" or "powerful pope," imbued with the fear of the Lord. Michelangelo conceived his *Moses* as the personification of a powerful will, and partially as an idealized portrait of the determined Julius who, as the formulator of a code of Church laws, had something in common with the ancient Hebrew lawgiver. Moses is further portrayed as the personification of the elemental forces. He is the human volcano about to erupt with righteous wrath, the calm before a storm of moral indignation, the dead center of a hurricane of emotional fury, the author of those thunderous "Thou Shalt Nots" of the Ten Commandments, the man capable of ascending Mt. Sinai to talk with God and coming back down to review all humanity from the seat of judgment. The smoldering agitation revealed through the drapery, the powerful musculature of the arms, the dominating intelligence of the face, the fiery mood, and the twisting of the body in the act of rising are characteristic of Michelangelo's style. An interesting detail is the carved irises of the eyes, found earlier in his *David* (see Fig. 233), which Michelangelo did to express a look of fixed determination. When he wanted to convey the qualities of dreaminess, gentleness, and resignation, as in his Madonnas, he left the eyes untouched.

Michelangelo worked at the time when many of the most outstanding examples of antique statuary were being unearthed and admired. Inevitably this led to critical comparisons. Michelangelo, like the Greco-Roman artists, saw men and women as the lords of creation, but their natural environment was always a matter of indifference to him. His early art especially was an affirmation of the supreme place of humanity in the universal scheme of things. That world was populated by godlike beings at the peak of their physical power, full of vitality, creatively active, and affirmatively self-confident.

As Michelangelo's art matured, his men and women were beset with quite unclassical tensions, doubts, and conflicts. Unlike the statues of antiquity, his figures, when they come to grips with fate, are armed with mental and moral powers that imply the hope of ultimate victory. Having thus surpassed the art of the ancients as well as that of his own time, not only by his technical mastery but by his expressive power, he came to be regarded by his contemporaries with awe. Vasari, his biographer, wrote: "The man who bears the palm of all the ages, transcending and eclipsing all the rest, is the divine M. Buonarroti, who is supreme not in one art only but in all three at once." History has since had no reason to reverse this judgment.

Painting

Michelangelo's Sistine Ceiling Frescoes

When Michelangelo fled from Rome because of numerous frustrations with plans for Julius II's tomb, the Pope resorted to every means from force to diplomacy to get him to return. Knowing he had a restless genius on his hands, Julius conceived some interim projects to keep Michelangelo busy until all the problems with his tomb were solved. Thinking it soon to be done, he set Michelangelo to painting the Sistine Chapel ceiling.

The building itself, the roof of which can be seen paralleling the nave on the right of St. Peter's in Figure 237, was built by and named for Julius' uncle, Pope Sixtus IV, as the private chapel of the popes. The interior consists of a single rectangular room 44 by 132 feet (13.4 by 40.2 meters) (Fig. 246). Around the walls were frescoes painted by the foremost 15th-century artists, including the Florentines Ghirlandaio (who was one of Michelangelo's teachers), Botticelli, and Perugino (see Fig. 236), teacher of Raphael. Above the frescoes were six windows in the side walls, and overhead was a barrel-vaulted ceiling 68 feet (20.7 meters) above the floor with 700 square yards (585.3 square meters) of surface stretching before Michelangelo.

The entire Sistine ceiling was conceived as an organic composition motivated by a single unifying philosophical as well as artistic design (Fig. 247). The iconography is a fusion of traditional Hebrew-Christian theology and Neoplatonic philosophy that Michelangelo knew from his days in the Medici household. The space is divided into geometrical

above: **246.** Sistine Chapel, view toward Michelangelo's *Last Judgment* over the altar. 1473–80. Height of ceiling 68′ (20.73 m). Vatican, Rome.

below: **247.** Michelangelo. Ceiling, Sistine Chapel. 1508–12. Fresco, 44 × 128′ (13.41 × 39.01 m). Vatican, Rome.

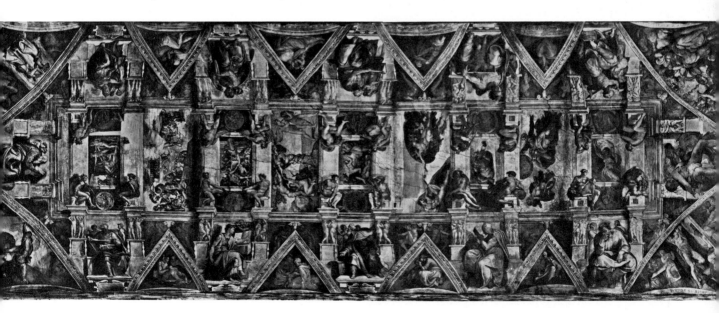

forms, such as the triangle, circle, and square, which were regarded in Plato's philosophy as the eternal forms that furnish clues to the true nature of the universe. Next is a three-way division into zones in which the varying intensity of the lighting plays a part. The lowest and darkest zone consists of eight concave, triangular-shaped spaces above the windows and four corner, pendentive-shaped spaces. The intermediate zone includes all the surrounding space except that given to the nine center panels, which in turn form the third and brightest zone.

Symbolically these divisions correspond to the three Platonic stages—the world of matter, the world of becoming, and the world of being. Analogies to such triple divisions run as an undercurrent through all aspects of Plato's thought. Plato divided society, for instance, into three classes: workers, free citizens, and philosophers, which he symbolized by the metals brass, silver, and gold. Each stratum had its characteristic goal: the love of gain, the development of ambition, and the pursuit of truth. Learning was similarly broken down into the three stages of ignorance, opinion, and knowledge. Plato's theory of the human soul was also tripartite in nature, consisting of the appetitive, emotional, and rational faculties, located in the abdomen, breast, and head, respectively. Of these only the rational or intellective part could aspire to immortality.

Michelangelo placed uninspired men and women on the lower level. In the intermediate area are the inspired Old Testament prophets and pagan sibyls, who have knowledge of the divine and act as intermediaries between humanity and God. In the central section are the panels that tell the story of men and women in their direct relationship to God. They are seen through the architectural divisions as if taking place beyond on a more cosmic plane.

Lower and Intermediate Area   The eight border triangles tell the dismal tale of humanity without vision, who, as St. Luke says, "sit in darkness and in the shadow of death," awaiting the light that will come when the Savior is born. In the four corners are the heroic men and women whose active deeds secured temporary deliverance for their people: David's slaying of Goliath, Judith's beheading of Holofernes, Haman's punishment through Esther, and Moses' transformation of his rod into a serpent that devoured the similarly transformed rods of the Egyptian priests.

This serves as an introduction to the representations of the seven Hebrew prophets, who alternate with five pagan sibyls like a chorus prophesying salvation. As intermediaries between the human and divine spheres, they are placed in a zone where the lighting approaches that of the central panels.

The *Delphic Sibyl* is the first of the series (Fig. 248). In the Greek tradition and in Plato, she was the priestess of Apollo at Delphi. In Vergil's *Aeneid,* Book VI, she is described as a young woman possessed by the spirit of prophecy. In the grip of divine fury, she turns her head toward the voice of her inspiration. Though clothed in Greek garments, her beauty recalls that of Michelangelo's early Madonnas.

Above each of the prophets and sibyls and framing the central panels are *ignudi,* or "nude youths," as seen in Figure 251. In the Christian tradition, these figures would have been represented as angels. In the Platonic theory, however, they personify the rational faculties of the sibyls and prophets by which they rise to the contemplation of divine truth, and by which they are able to bridge the gap between the physical and spiritual, or earthly and heavenly, regions. Thus, all the prophets and sibyls have a single figure below to denote the body, a pair of nudes behind them to signify the will, and a heroic *ignudo* to personify the immortal soul. These three levels correspond to Plato's tripartite conception of the soul—the appetitive, the emotional, and the intellective faculties. These symbolic figures also serve to soften the contours of the architectural design.

Center Panels   In the center panels of the Sistine Chapel ceiling, instead of starting at the beginning and proceeding chronologically as in Genesis, Mi-

248. Michelangelo. *Delphic Sibyl,* detail of Sistine Chapel ceiling. 1509. Fresco. Vatican, Rome.

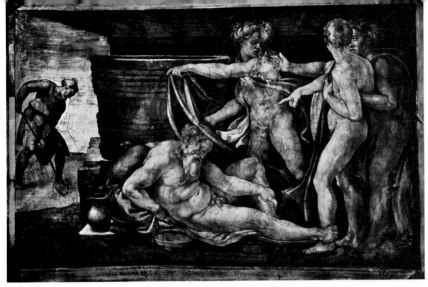

left: 249. Michelangelo.
Drunkenness of Noah,
detail of Sistine Chapel ceiling.
1508-09. Fresco. Vatican, Rome.

below: 250. Michelangelo.
Creation of Adam,
detail of Sistine Chapel ceiling.
1511. Fresco. Vatican, Rome.

chelangelo conceives the story of creation in reverse order, or as the Platonic ascent of humanity from its lowest estate back to its divine origin. In this return to God, the soul in its bodily prison gradually becomes aware of God and moves from finiteness to infinity, from material bondage to spiritual freedom. Immortality, in this sense, is not the reward for a passive and pious existence but the result of a tremendous effort of the soul struggling out of the darkness of ignorance into the light of truth.

The first of the histories in the nine central panels is the *Drunkenness of Noah* (Fig. 249). As in the "Slave" figures of the Julius monument, the picture of Noah shows a mortal man in his most abysmal condition, the victim of bodily appetites. Noah's servitude is symbolized at the left, where he is seen tilling the parched soil. He is still strong physically, but his spirit is overwhelmed by the flesh. His sons, young adolescents in their physical prime, do not seem to be discovering their father's nakedness, as related in the Bible, but the tragic fate of all mortals, who must work, grow old, and die. Noah's reclining posture recalls that of the ancient Roman river gods, and in this case the head has sunk forward on his chest in what seems to be a premonition of death. After this picture of Noah as the prisoner of his own baser nature, the next panel represents the *Deluge,* which shows the plight of men and women when beset by the elemental forces of nature beyond their control. In the third panel, *Noah's Sacrifice,* human dependence on God is implied for the first time.

The *Fall and Expulsion from Paradise* follows next. Then the last five panels are concerned with various aspects of God's nature. In the *Creation of Eve* He appears as a paternal figure closed within the folds of His mantle. In the *Creation of Adam* (Fig.

The Roman Renaissance Style **225**

250), God is seen in the skies, His mantle surrounding Him like a cloud, as He moves toward the earth and the inert body of Adam. The creative force is here the divine fire that flashes like lightning from the cloud to the earth. Adam's body is one with the rock on which he lies, not unlike the unfinished "Slaves" of the Julius tomb. In keeping with the Platonic idea of life as a burden and imprisonment, Adam is awakening to life reluctantly rather than eagerly. With His other arm, God embraces Eve, who again resembles Michelangelo's Madonna types, and who looks with fear and awe on this act of creation. God's fingers point to the coming Christ Child, while behind Him are the heads of unborn future generations of humanity.

In the *Creation of the Sun and Moon* (see Fig. 6), the figure of God becomes a personification of the creative principle, while in *God Dividing the Light from Darkness* (Fig. 251), the final panel of the series, the climax and the realm of pure being are attained. Here is clarity coming out of chaos, order from the void, existence from nothingness. Light here is the symbol for enlightenment and the knowledge that gives freedom from the darkness of ignorance and bondage. Only through the light of wisdom can an individual attain the highest human and divine status. "You shall know the truth and the truth shall make you free," say the Scriptures; "Know thyself," the Delphic oracle told Socrates.

The conception of God has progressed from the paternal human figure of the *Creation of Eve* to a cosmic spirit in the intervening panels, and now to a swirling abstraction in the realm of pure being. The Neoplatonic goal of the union of the soul with God has been achieved by the gradual progress from the bondage of blind humanity, through the prophetic visions of the seers, and, finally, by ascending the ladder of the histories into the pure light of knowledge, to the point of dissolving into the freedom of infinity. In the words of Pico della Mirandola, the human being "withdraws into the center of his own oneness, his spirit made one with God."

The weight of expression, story content, and philosophical meaning is carried entirely by Michelangelo's placement and treatment of the more than three hundred human figures in a seemingly infinite variety of postures.

Though he later returned to the Sistine Chapel to paint the *Last Judgment* on the altar wall (Fig. 290) and worked on another group for the Pauline Chapel in the Vatican, Michelangelo never recaptured the optimism and creative force of the earlier series.

Raphael's Vatican Murals

At the same time that Michelangelo was painting the Sistine ceiling, Raphael, a younger contemporary, was at work on the murals of the Vatican Palace. In *School of Athens* (Fig. 252), Raphael presents such a complete visual philosophy that it places him, along with Michelangelo, in the select ranks of artist-scholars. Raphael's fresco is full of intellectual as well as pictorial complexities. Yet by the expanding space of the setting and the skillful arrangement of the figures, as well as their relationships to each other and the architecture, it is clear and uncluttered. As members of a philosophical circle intent on reconciling the views of Plato and Aristotle, Raphael and his friends held that any point in Plato could be translated into a proposition of Aristotle and vice versa—the principal difference being that Plato wrote in poetic images, while Aristotle used the language of rational analysis. The two philosophers, "who agree in substance while they disagree in words," are placed on either side of the central axis of the fresco with the vanishing point between them. The book Plato holds in his hands is his *Timaeus,* and he points skyward to indicate his idealistic world view. Aristotle carries his *Ethics* and indicates by his earthward gesture his greater concern with the real world.

In the spacious hall, which recalls the Roman poet Lucretius' remark on "temples raised by philos-

251. Michelangelo.
God Dividing the Light from Darkness,
detail of Sistine Chapel ceiling. 1511.
Fresco. Vatican, Rome.

252. Raphael. *School of Athens.* 1510–11. Fresco, 26 × 18′ (7.92 × 5.49 m). Stanza della Segnatura, Vatican, Rome.

ophy," the various schools of thought argue or ponder the ideas put forth by the two central figures. On Plato's side a niche contains a statue of Apollo, patron of poetry. On Aristotle's side is one of Athena, goddess of reason. This division of the central figures balances the entire picture, with the metaphysical philosophers ranked on Plato's side and the physical scientists pursuing their researches on Aristotle's.

Spreading outward are groups corresponding to the separate schools of thought within the two major divisions, and which carry the various arguments to their logical conclusion. The figure of Plato is thought to be an idealized portrait of Leonardo da Vinci. In the group at the lower right Raphael portrayed his architect friend Bramante as Archimedes demonstrating on his slate a geometrical proposition. At the extreme right, Raphael paints a self-portrait in profile next to his friend the painter Sodoma.

In *School of Athens* as a whole, Raphael captured the intellectual atmosphere and the zest with which Renaissance ideas were argued. By his grouping and placement of figures, and by their attitudes, attributes, and gestures, he provides a far clearer commentary on the complex thought of his time than did the more complex and lengthy philosophical treatises of the period. To paint such metaphysical abstraction at all, and clothe them with plastic form, is a triumph of clear thinking and logical organization. Posterity is fortunate to have this summation of Renaissance humanism as seen through the eyes of such a profound artist as was Raphael.

The Dome of St. Peter's

The foundations of the new St. Peter's (Fig. 237) had been laid as early as 1506, when Michelangelo was starting plans for Pope Julius' tomb. Comparatively little progress had been made in the stormy years that followed, in spite of the succession of brilliant architects. Michelangelo favored the centralized church plans of Brunelleschi and Alberti just as his predecessor Bramante had done. The latter's design, however, was to have culminated in a low dome,

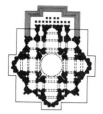

253. Michelangelo.
Plan of St. Peter's.

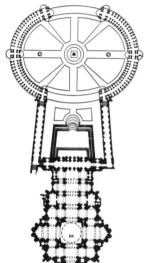

above: 254. Michelangelo.
Apse and dome,
St. Peter's. Begun 1547.
Height of dome
452′ (137.77 m).

left: 255. St. Peter's.
Plan of present complex.

modeled after that of the Pantheon but with a series of columns at the base and a lantern tower on top.

Michelangelo accepted Bramante's Greek-cross ground plan with a few alterations of his own (Fig. 253), but he projected a loftier dome rising over the lengendary site of St. Peter's tomb. This cupola was to be of such monumental proportions that it would unify not only the interior spaces and exterior masses of the building but would serve also as the climax of the liturgical, religious, and artistic forces of the Catholic world and as a symbol of Christendom.

Michelangelo's first problem was an engineering one—to find out if the masonry was strong enough to support such a dome. It was not, and he had to reinforce the four main piers until each was a massive 60 feet (18.3 meters) square. Pendentives became the means by which the square understructure was encircled, and then the cylindrical drum was ready to rise. Meanwhile he made a large model of the dome itself, so that it could be built by others in case of his death. All the preparatory work was thus completed, and Michelangelo lived just long enough to see the drum finished. The dome (Fig. 254) was completed after his death by two of his associates without substantial alterations.

If not for the aftermath of the Council of Trent and the Counter-Reformation, Michelangelo's centralized church might also have been finished. The new spirit of conservatism, however, frowned on anything that might be considered a pagan form, and a reactionary wave was started in favor of a return to the traditional Latin-cross plan. In the early 17th century, then, Carlo Maderno undertook the lengthening of the nave and the design of the façade (Figs. 237, 255).

Liturgically, the new nave provided more space for the grandiose processions. Practically, it afforded room for larger congregations. Historically, it absorbed all the area formerly occupied by Constantine's basilica, demolished to make way for the new structure. Aesthetically, however, the proportions suffered and the climactic effect of the great dome was lessened. The scale of the interior, however, had been set by Michelangelo's huge piers beneath the dome, and Maderno had to continue the same proportions. The vaulting thus rises a little over 150 feet (45.7 meters) above the pavement, while the enormous interior covers more than 25,000 square yards (20,903 square meters) in area.

The exterior of the church Michelangelo planned can best be seen from the apse, and the interior from beneath the dome where it appears as the compact unified structure he wanted. From the apse of the completed church (Fig. 254), where the lengthened nave does not detract, the effect is still substantially as Michelangelo intended it to be. From this vantage point the building itself appears as a great podium for the support of the vast superstructure; and from the ground level to the base of the dome there is a rise of about 250 feet (76 meters). The cupola then continues upward to the top of the lantern tower, where an ultimate height of 452 feet (137.8 meters) above the ground level is attained.

Coming as it did with the spread of the Counter-Reformation and the commercial exploitation and colonization of the New World, St. Peter's and its great dome had enormous influence on future church architecture (see Figs. 357–360). It also had a large influence on such secular structures as the Capitol in Washington, D.C., and on a number of the American state capitols.

Josquin des Prez and the Sistine Chapel Choir

A Florentine literary historian in a book on Dante published in 1567 wrote:

> I am well aware that in his day Ockeghem was as it were the first to rediscover music, then as good as dead, just as Donatello discovered sculpture in his; and that of Josquin, Ockeghem's pupil, one might say that he was a natural prodigy in music, just as our own Michelangelo Buonarroti has been in architecture, painting, and sculpture; for just as Josquin has still to be surpassed in his compositions, so Michelangelo stands alone and without a peer among all who have practiced his arts; and the one and the other have opened the eyes of all who delight in these arts, now and in the future.

Josquin des Prez, to whom he referred, was thus still regarded almost half a century after his death as a figure comparable to that of Michelangelo. A Florentine could bestow no higher praise. This opinion, moreover, was also held by musicians. The distinguished theorist Glareanus wrote that the work of Josquin des Prez was "the perfect art to which nothing can be added, after which nothing but decline can be expected."

The so-called *ars perfecta,* or "perfect art," rested on the typical Renaissance historical assumption of the great development of the arts in antiquity, which had been lost in medieval days and subsequently rediscovered in the then-modern times. The previously given quotation is a critical application of this doctrine of regained perfection to the art of music.

Italians, whether at home or abroad, took the greatest pride in the achievements of their own architects, sculptors, and painters, but universally they acknowledged the supremacy of the northern composers. The spread of the northern polyphonic art dated from the time the popes had become acquainted with it at Avignon. Later, it led to the establishment of the *Cappella Sistina* in 1473, which

was dominated by Flemish, Burgundian, and French musicians, whose influence from there spread over the entire Christian world. From this time forward, the mastery of these artists in contrapuntal writing became the standard of perfection.

Under Pope Sixtus IV, church music had moved from its status as the modest servant of the liturgy to a position of major importance. The grandeur of the Roman liturgical displays called for music of comparable magnificence. Owing to the prevailing taste of the time, musicians from the great singing centers of Antwerp, Liège, and Cambrai thus flocked to Rome to seek their fortunes. The highest honor of all was an appointment to the Sistine Choir, whose privilege it was to perform on the occasions when the pope himself officiated.

Membership in the Sistine Choir was highly selective, totaling from 16 to 24 singers except during the time of the musical Leo, who increased it to 36. These singers were divided into four parts: boy sopranos, male altos, tenors, and basses. Normally they sang *a cappella*—that is, "in the chapel manner" without instrumental accompaniment—a practice that was exceptional rather than usual at the time.

The quality of this choir can be deduced from the list of distinguished men who made their reputations in its ranks. In the archives are numerous masses, motets, and psalm settings composed by Josquin des Prez during his service there from 1486 to 1494. Palestrina, who studied Josquin's contrapuntal technique, became a member in 1551 and later brought the organization to a pinnacle of technical perfection.

In Josquin's compositions, the stark, barren intervals of Gothic polyphony and all traces of harshness in the harmonies are eliminated. He allows dissonances to occur only on weak beats or as suspensions on the stronger ones. His rhythms and forms are based on strict symmetry and mathematically regular proportions. His writing is characterized by the usual northern fondness for imitation of a melody by successive voice parts, in the manner of a *canon,* and other complicated contrapuntal constructions. Such devices, however, are managed with complete mastery, and his tremendous technique in composition never intrudes upon the expressive content.

Josquin was at home in all Renaissance musical forms, excelling perhaps in his motets and in his solo and choral songs. In Rome, where his unique abilities were combined with the warmth and liquid smoothness of Italian lyricism, Josquin mellowed in his music until it achieved a style of incomparable beauty, formal clarity, and the purest expressivity.

Josquin's four-part motet *Ave Maria* will serve as an admirable illustration of his art. Like Michelangelo's early *Pietà* (Fig. 240), it is in a perfectly self-contained form, emotionally restrained, and full of luxuriantly flowing lines. Even such a short excerpt as that reproduced (right) shows his love of canonic imitation between the voices and the smoothness of contour that comes with stepwise melodic motion. These imitations can be seen when the melody in the top line is imitated exactly a fifth below by the next lower line. Later the same thing occurs beginning with the words *Nostra fuit* and also with those starting *Ut lucifer lux.*

Josquin treats all four voices with balanced impartiality but prefers to group them in pairs, as in this example, in order to achieve a transparency of texture and purity of sound. Darker sides of Josquin's emotional spectrum can be found in his requiem masses and in his setting of the psalm *De Profundis.*

Later periods saw in Michelangelo both a summing up of the Renaissance and the beginning of the baroque style. Josquin's place was more limited. While he enjoyed universal acclaim as the greatest musical mind of the early 16th century, the very perfection of his art implied that it was on the verge of becoming archaic. Josquin's mantle was inherited by a number of composers in the succeeding generation, who carried his art to its logical conclusion. Palestrina's music is, perhaps, better adapted to religious purposes, though he remains Josquin's inferior in invention, inspiration, and depth of expression. Victoria carried the style to Spain, William Byrd to England; and through Philippe de Monte and Orlando di Lasso, it spread throughout France and Germany. In the 17th century, though the art was still studied, it became known as the "antique style" in contrast to the baroque music, which was called the "modern style." Within its limitations the art has never been surpassed. Even today it is considered the ideal for church music.

Ideas: Humanism

Revival of Classical Forms

Florentine humanism and its Roman aftermath were motivated by a reappraisal of the values of Greco-Roman antiquity, by an attempt to reconcile pagan forms with Christian practices, by a desire to reinstate the philosophy of Plato and reinterpret that of Aristotle, and, above all, by a rediscovery of this world and human values. Renaissance humanists were not primarily religious- or scientific-minded. They tended to substitute the authority of respected classical writers for that of the Bible and Church dogma. In looking forward, they found more convenient and convincing precedents in the civilizations of Greece and Rome than in the immediate medieval past. Lorenzo de' Medici, for instance, saw a new orientation for secular government in Plato's *Repub-*

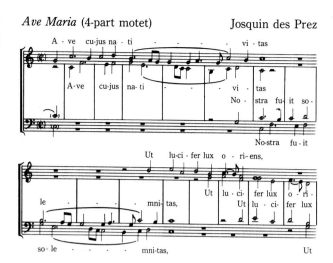

Ave Maria (4-part motet)　　　Josquin des Prez

lic. Machiavelli found a new method for writing history in Thucydides. And Bramante made a new adaptation of the Greco-Roman temple for Christian worship.

Bramante's Tempietto (Fig. 256) was a conscious revival of the rounded commemorative structures of antiquity (see Figs. 100–102, 108). This temple in miniature, coming as it did at the outset of the 16th century, became the architectural manifesto of the Roman Renaissance, just as Brunelleschi's Pazzi Chapel (see Figs. 210–212) had been in the 15th-century Florentine Renaissance. Placed in the cloistered courtyard of the Church of San Pietro in Montorio, the little temple rests on the site where St. Peter is supposed to have been crucified.

For his architectural order Bramante chose the simple yet monumental Doric order. He held to the classical principle of the module whereby all parts of the building are either multiples or fractions of the basic unit of measure. He also promoted the feeling of balance and proportion by making the height and width of the lower floor equal to that of the upper story. Spare of ornament, the only formal decorative element is in the Doric frieze with the regular triglyphs alternating with metopes that employ a shell motif.

Above all, Bramante wished to demonstrate the cohesiveness and compactness of the centralized plan under the unifying crown of a cupola. Later, when Pope Julius entrusted him with the design of the new St. Peter's, Bramante had his chance to build on a monumental scale. Here again he turned to antiquity for inspiration and is reputed to have declared: "I shall place the Pantheon on top of the Basilica of Constantine."

The humanists preferred purer versions of classical art forms to the adaptations that had been made in the thousand-year period between the fall of Rome and their own time. The members of the Florentine humanistic circle learned to read and speak ancient Greek under native tutors. Ficino translated the dialogues of Plato, while Poliziano translated Homer from the original Greek into Italian and wrote essays in Latin on Greek poetic and musical theory. Other scholars catalogued and edited books for the Medici library, while Squarcialupi compiled the musical compositions of the preceding century.

The interest in cataloguing, editing, translating, and commenting was pursued with such enthusiasm that it all but blotted out the production of live literature. The Latin of Renaissance scholars was Ciceronian rather than medieval Latin, which they considered corrupt. The architects read Vitruvius and preferred central-type churches modeled on the Pantheon to the rectangular basilica form that had been evolved over the centuries. They revived the classical orders and architectural proportions in a more authentic form. Decorative motifs were derived directly from ancient sarcophagi, reliefs, and carved gems. Sculptors reaffirmed the possibilities of the nude, and with Michelangelo it became the chief expressive vehicle of his art. Painters, lacking major models from antiquity, used mythological subjects and the literary descriptions of ancient works.

Musicians reinterpreted Greek musical thought, and some actually made attempts to put into practice the theories expounded by Euclid's musical essay. The Greek assertion that art imitates nature was universally acknowledged, but in architecture and music this had to be applied in the general sense of nature as an orderly and regular system conforming to mathematical proportions and laws. Josquin des Prez was hailed as a modern Orpheus who had regained the lost perfect art of the ancients—though the Greeks would have been bewildered by his musical style. Josquin's less enthusiastic admirers pointed out that the trees and stones still showed some reluctance to follow him as they had not in the case of the original Orpheus. His art, however, like that of Michelangelo, was thought by the humanists to be a path back to a classical paradise.

Pagan versus Christian Ideals

Both Botticelli and Michelangelo set out to produce works in the Neoplatonic spirit. The literary ancestry of Botticelli's *Allegory of Spring* (*Primavera*), *Birth of Venus* (see Fig. 230), and *Venus and Mars* (see Fig. 229) has been traced through the poetry of his contemporary Poliziano back to the Roman poets Lucretius and Horace. Their philosophical ancestor, however, is the Plato of the *Symposium,* which deals with the nature of love and beauty. Human beings, according to Plato's theory, have drunk of the waters of oblivion and forgotten their divine origin. Falling in love with a beautiful person reminds them of their natural affinity for beauty. From physical attraction and fleeting loveliness, they are led to thoughts of the lasting beauty of truth and, finally, to the contemplation of the eternal verities of absolute beauty, truth, and goodness. Venus is, of course, the image of this transcendent beauty, and the way to approach it is through love. The eternal feminine, as Goethe later said in *Faust,* draws us ever onward.

Michelangelo's Plato, however, was the Plato of the *Timaeus,* which dwells on the creation of the world, the spiritual nature of the human soul, and the return to God. Unlike Botticelli, who had a fragile dream of beauty, Michelangelo had a vigorous vision of the creative process itself. When Botticelli came under the influence of the fiery moralist Savonarola with his resurgence of medievalism, he repented of his paganism and painted only religious pictures.

Botticelli never tried to combine his paganism and Christianity as did Michelangelo, and for him

256. Donato Bramante.
Tempietto, San Pietro in Montorio, Rome. 1504.
Marble; height 46′ (14.02 m),
diameter of colonnade 29′ (8.84 m).

The Roman Renaissance Style **231**

above: **257.** Leonardo da Vinci. *Last Supper.*
1495–98. Fresco, 14′5″ × 28¼″ (4.39 × 8.54 m).
Santa Maria della Grazie, Milan.

below: **258.** Leonardo da Vinci.
Drawing of flying apparatus (helicopter),
from Manuscript B. c. 1485–90.
Bibliothèque de l'Institut de France, Paris.

they remained in separate compartments and on an either/or basis. Michelangelo, however, had the mind to assimilate Platonic abstractions, the overwhelming urge to express his ideas, and the technical equipment to translate them into dramatic visual form. But the voice of Savonarola spoke loudly to him, too, and in his rugged mind Michelangelo was destined to wrestle with the two essentially irreconcilable philosophies for the rest of his life. Leonardo da Vinci, by contrast, kept the religious themes of his painting (Fig. 257) and his scientific inquiries (Fig. 258) in separate intellectual compartments.

Michelangelo's Madonnas reveal the unity between mortal beauty and eternal beauty; his *Moses* (Fig. 245) links human moral power with eternal goodness; and his organic compositions connect the truth of historical time with eternal truth. His triple divisions symbolizing the stages of the soul as it progresses from its bodily tomb to its liberation and reunion with God are a constantly recurring preoccupation. Even in the abstract architectural forms of St. Peter's this concern with the progress of the soul is apparent. The pilasters, like imprisoned columns, are the "slaves" held down by the weight of the heavy burden they must carry. Overhead soars the lofty dome in the geometrical perfection of the circular form, symbolizing the paradise that humanity has lost and must somehow regain. The whole building is thus conceived as an organic system of upward pressures and tensions, reaching its highest point in a cupola that ascends toward the divine realm and finally dissolves into the freedom of infinity.

IV
THE
BAROQUE
PERIOD

The baroque period was one of restless oppositions, violent clashes, and vast expansion. It was an age of reason when the mind and imagination opened up new worlds of scientific knowledge and artistic creativity. It was an era of religious reorientation, with Europe split between loyalty to Roman Catholicism and to various forms of Protestantism. It was an age of empire building with European countries staking out new overseas territories. It was also a time of absolutism, with the consolidation of political power leading to strong centralized states.

The French philosopher René Descartes laid the cornerstone of the Age of Reason with the declaration, "I think, therefore I am." His skeptical attitude is revealed in his remark that the only thing that cannot be doubted is doubt itself. His method is described in his equally apt statement that only the things the mind perceives clearly and distinctly are true. Descartes' thought led to the picture of a materialistic, mechanistic, predictable universe.

Other scientists added to the list of discoveries. Isaac Newton's speculations on celestial mechanics led to the formulation of the laws of universal gravitation. Baron Leibniz devised the infinitesimal, or differential, calculus, a mathematics capable of dealing with infinity and with a universe in constant motion. Robert Boyle's book *The Sceptical Chymist* set forth the laws that became the basis for modern chemistry. And William Harvey's researches into the functions of the heart and circulation of the blood began modern medicine.

This brave new world of matter in motion was not born without a continued challenge from religious sources. Roman Catholicism first met the Protestant threat by an inner reform of its own, the Counter-Reformation. At the Council of Trent the basic doctrines of the Church were reaffirmed, the clergy rededicated themselves to religious work, and the Index of books that good Catholics were forbidden to read was compiled. Earlier the Universal Inquisition had been set up to weed out beliefs thought contrary to Church doctrine and to punish the guilty.

New religious orders were also founded. A former Spanish soldier, Ignatius Loyola, organized the Society of Jesus, a militant organization that fought Protestantism, carried on missionary work all over the world, and established schools with new methods of study. The Spanish mystic

Teresa of Avila reorganized the Carmelite order of nuns. The Roman social worker Philip Neri and his Oratorian Fathers brought religious inspiration and instruction to the poor and oppressed people of the cities.

In the wake of the great navigators and explorers, western European kingdoms established vast world empires. Spanish America included the entire west and southeast coasts of South America, all of Central America, and parts of North America. Spain also claimed island possessions all over the globe, notably the Philippines, named after King Philip II. With the gold and silver of the New World pouring into its treasury, Spain became for a time the richest nation on earth.

Portuguese possessions included Brazil, settlements all along the west and east coasts of Africa, and others as far as India and China. The Dutch turned their eyes to Asia, establishing the Dutch East India Company with rights to trade in the silks and spices of the Orient and to rule territories that included Ceylon, the Malay Peninsula, and Indonesia. The French created colonies and trading posts in Canada and the St. Lawrence and Mississippi valleys. The latter, including all the middle part of what is now the United States down to New Orleans, was named Louisiana after Louis XIV. The English, meanwhile, laid claim to all of northern Canada around Hudson Bay and Newfoundland, as well as to the east coast of North America from Maine to Virginia, where the thirteen original colonies were founded.

Politically, Europe was divided by the rivalries of ruling families and the competition of strong national states. Charles I of Spain was elected Charles V of the Holy Roman Empire in 1519. This brought Spain, Flanders, Holland, the Germanies, and Austria under a single powerful ruler. He also inherited the great Spanish empire. Charles V tried to contain Protestantism and at the same time quarreled with the pope. He blocked the advances of the Ottoman Turks in eastern Europe and the Balkans, and checked French ambitions in Italy, which was hopelessly divided into small city-states and rival provinces. With the exception of Venice, all Italy was brought under Spanish dominion. After Charles V's reign his brother became ruler of the Germanies and Austria, while his son Philip II succeeded as king of Spain, Flanders, Holland, and the overseas territories.

In France the kings had gained control of the army and expelled the English. Louis XIII's astute prime minister, Cardinal Richelieu, and his successor under Louis XIV, Cardinal Mazarin, consolidated the absolute monarchy and created a powerful centralized state. After the horrors of the Thirty Years' War, France became the dominant European power.

England had prospered under the Tudors, but when Queen Elizabeth's successors began moving toward a more absolute monarchy in the manner of France and Spain, a bitter struggle with Parliament ensued. After Charles I had governed alone for eleven years, he was confronted with a civil war, and was captured, tried, and beheaded. The civil war and the Puritan Revolution swept Oliver Cromwell into power. After his death, the British genius for compromise once again came to the fore, and the Restoration under the more limited monarchy of Charles II allowed for representative government and political freedom.

Despite its turbulence and turmoil, the baroque period was a favorable climate for the arts. Grandeur and magnificence were the order of the day. Emperors, kings, popes, and princes vied with one another to attract great artists to their courts. Immense building programs were undertaken, and large commissions were forthcoming. The arts were, in general, caught up in the service of Church and state and were involved in the creation of the myths of the miraculous and the majestic.

12
Venetian Renaissance, Mannerism, and Early Baroque

Venice, 16th Century

A glimpse of Venice as it was at the threshold of the 16th century can be seen through the eyes of the painter Gentile Bellini. His faithful reporting in *Procession in St. Mark's Square* (Fig. 259) is so accurate that architectural historians can make reconstructions of buildings long since destroyed; that researchers can study the mosaics and sculptures of St. Mark's Basilica as they were before later restorations; that historians of liturgy, musical performances, and costume find it prime source material.

When compared with the forthcoming flights of mannerist and early baroque imagination, the stateliness and stability of Bellini's painting are all the more striking. Hence, its subject matter, story content, mode of representation, formal organization, and the circumstances of its commission reveal much about the life of Venice and the unique developments in the arts during a period of transition.

St. Mark's Basilica at once proclaims Venice the meeting place of Orient and Occident, of East and West. Begun in the 10th century, it is the product of centuries of community effort. Indeed, an early law

259. Gentile Bellini. *Procession in St. Mark's Square.* 1496. Oil on canvas, 12 × 24′ (3.66 × 7.32 m). Academy, Venice.

CHRONOLOGY
16th-Century Venice

GENERAL EVENTS

1453	Turks conquered Constantinople; Venetian commerce challenged
1492	Geographical discoveries by Spanish and Portuguese navigators weakened Venetian maritime trade
1495	Aldine Press began publishing inexpensive editions of Greco-Roman classics
1501	*Odhecaton,* anthology of vocal and instrumental works by Josquin des Prez, Obrecht, Isaac, and others printed in Venice by Petrucci
1517	Protestant Reformation began
1527–1562	Willaert choirmaster of St. Mark's
1536	Library of St. Mark built by Sansovino
1540	Loggietta at base of campanile built by Sansovino
1545–1563	Council of Trent initiated Counter-Reformation
1549	Basilica at Vicenza built by Palladio
1550	Villa Rotonda near Vicenza begun by Palladio
1565	Church of San Giorgio Maggiore, Venice, built by Palladio
1570	Palladio published *Four Books of Architecture*
1571	Naval Battle of Lepanto; Venice and Spain defeated Turks
1573	Veronese called before Inquisition
1576–1578	Church of Il Redentore, Venice, built by Palladio
1579–1580	Olympic Theater, Vicenza, built by Palladio
1584	Procuratie Nuove, continuation of Sansovino's design of St. Mark's Library built by Scamozzi
1585–1612	Giovanni Gabrieli choirmaster of St. Mark's
1589	Olympic Theater, Vicenza, dedicated with performance of Sophocles' *Oedipus* (music by A. Gabrieli)
1613–1643	Monteverdi choirmaster of St. Mark's
1631	Santa Maria della Salute begun

ARCHITECTS

1486–1570	Jacopo Sansovino
1508–1580	Andrea Palladio
1552–1616	Vincenzo Scamozzi
1604–1675	Baldassare Longhena

PAINTERS

1429–1507	Gentile Bellini
c.1430–1516	Giovanni Bellini
c.1455–c.1526	Vittore Carpaccio
c.1490–1576	Titian (Tiziano Vecelli)
c.1470–1528	Matthias Grünewald
1471–1528	Albrecht Dürer
1478–1510	Giorgione
1510–1592	Jacopo Bassano
1518–1594	Jacopo Tintoretto
1528–1588	Paolo Veronese

MUSICIANS

c.1480–1562	Adrian Willaert
1510–1586	Andrea Gabrieli
1516–1565	Cipriano de Rore
1517–1590	Gioseffo Zarlino
1557–1612	Giovanni Gabrieli
1567–1643	Claudio Monteverdi
1602–1676	Francesco Cavalli

MANNERISTS

c.1492–1546	Giulio Romano
1494–1540	Rosso Fiorentino
1494–1556	Jacopo Pontormo
1500–1571	Benvenuto Cellini
1503–1540	Francesco Parmigianino
1503–1572	Agnolo Bronzino
1511–1574	Giorgio Vasari
1529–1600	Giovanni da Bologna
c.1540–1609	Federigo Zuccaro
1555–1619	Ludovico Carracci
1560–1609	Annibale Carracci

required every Venetian ship to bring back materials for the construction or decoration of the church. As a result, fragments from every Mediterranean country can be found somewhere in its fabric—from the Greco-Roman bronze horses of the first century A.D. over the central portal (Fig. 260), the Alexandrian many-colored marble columns and Greek alabaster windows, to the present-day changes. The plan is that of a Greek cross with smaller domes covering each of the four wings and a large cupola 42 feet (12.7 meters) in diameter at the center.

Above the narthex entrance, stretching the full width of the façade, is an open gallery on which, in Bellini's picture, several people can be seen. Above the gallery is a row of five graceful 13th-century Gothic gables that frame the upper tier of mosaics. On the crest of the central gable is the winged lion of St. Mark, placed here to honor the city's patron saint.

To the right is a corner of the Doge's Palace where the doge—the chief official of Venice—and his guests are seated on the second-story arcade. This striking variation of a Gothic town hall rises in two stories of open pointed arches surmounted by a third story notable for its diamond-shaped design in bright pink marble tiling. Across the square on the left is the old library from which many spectators are watching the activities. This building with its curious chimney pots also dates from medieval times.

More remarkable than its architecture, however, is the institution of the library itself. Venice treasured the great collections of books that had been left her by the poet Petrarch, the Greek scholar Cardinal Bessarion, and other donors, because in this watery city the danger of fire was less than elsewhere. In addition to these collections, the library housed all the specimens of the city's elegant printing and bookmaking industry. These included fine but inexpensive editions of classics published here for the first time by the famous Aldine Press, and which gave such great momentum to the spread of learning throughout the educated world. In the 16th century, these collections were transferred to the handsome building across the square designed by Sansovino especially to house them (Fig. 261).

In the procession scene, a feeling of open public life and freedom of social movement can be sensed in both the participants and the bystanders. The independence of Venice and the prosperity of her citizenry were due in many respects to the city's unusual situation. Built on a group of island lagoons at the head of the Adriatic Sea, Venice was truly what a Florentine poet described as "a city in the water without walls."

Secure from attack by land and by sea as a result of its possessing the largest navy then in existence, Venice carried on an active commerce between East and West that afforded her citizens a manner of life unrivaled in its time for comfort and luxury. Without the ups and downs of other medieval and Renaissance cities, such as Pisa and Siena with their brief periods of glory, Venice developed slowly and consistently from the glow of its Byzantine dawn, through a Renaissance high noon and a brief thunderstorm of mannerism, to its florid baroque sunset.

Here lived no literary giant such as Dante, no merchant prince with the vision of a Lorenzo, no political philosopher of the quality of Machiavelli, no thundering religious reformer like Savonarola. In fact, without great writers and poets, without eminent individual art patrons, without inspired religious leaders—in short, without experiencing the heights and depths of the human spirit known in Florence or Rome—Venice built up in its architecture, painting, and music a culture uniquely its own.

The fall of Constantinople to the Turks in 1453 and the rising power of the Ottoman Empire spelled competition for Venice's commercial empire, and naval warfare had already begun. While Venice had given birth to one great explorer, Marco Polo, the voyages of the 16th-century Spanish, Portuguese, Dutch, and English navigators were being exploited to enrich rival countries, thereby upsetting the tradi-

tional economy in which Venice had flourished. Mainland Italy was soon to become a battleground in the European power struggle between the Holy Roman Empire and France. Charles V, Titian's great patron, became emperor in 1519, and in addition to Spain his dominions included Holland, Flanders, Germany, and Austria. Francis I of France, feeling his country caught in a giant squeeze play, tried to fortify his position by invading Italy. But one by one each Italian kingdom, principality, dukedom, and republic fell instead to Charles V. Finally, by sacking and pillaging Rome itself with his ruthless mercenaries and imprisoning Pope Clement VII, Charles achieved the surrender of the papacy.

The religious crisis brought on by opposing forces of the Reformation and Counter-Reformation likewise unsettled Venice's trade and cultural relations with northern Europe. Though the Universal Inquisition—that fearsome inquiry into the consciences and conduct of Christians in Roman Catholic countries to determine their total loyalty to the Church—was felt more mildly in Venice than elsewhere, Roman Catholic censorship of printed matter and assertion of the clergy's control of art proved more than a threat to Venice's publishing industry and artistic freedom. Venetians, to be sure, were no strangers to insecurity as fabulous fortunes were made overnight when their ships came in, while financial ruin and debtor's prison followed shipwrecks, seizure by pirates, or sinkings in naval battles.

This Pandora's box of troubles created a crisis in the literal sense of a split, with East and West divided—the Ottoman Turkish Empire on one side and an alliance of Christian European states on the other; with the Christian world itself torn apart by the Reformation and the Counter-Reformation; with Italy under siege by both the Holy Roman Emperor and the

260. Four horses of Greek origin. 1st century A.D. Gilt bronze, life-size. St. Mark's Basilica, Venice.

261. Jacopo Sansovino, Library of St. Mark, Venice. Begun 1536. Length 290′ (88.39 m), height 60′ (18.29 m).

king of France. Such a critical state, with its inner anxieties and complicated contradictions, was bound to find expression in the arts.

One road out of the crisis was to lead to a freezing of Renaissance convention, formal logic, and balanced symmetry in a conservative academic *mannerism*—art "in the manner" of the great masters of the immediate past, such as Michelangelo and Raphael. The other was to lead to the search for a new style in a free mannerism with its deliberate violations of Renaissance proportions, its experimental forms, its whimsical eccentricities, its unresolved tensions, and its restless imbalances. A reconciliation of these opposites was eventually to resolve itself into the synthesis of the baroque style in the 17th century.

Architecture

Sansovino

As did all the other arts, Venetian architecture reached out toward new forms. Although begun as early as 1536 and still within the Renaissance tradition, the Library of St. Mark by Jacopo Sansovino already had enough new ideas to qualify it as a transition to the coming baroque style (Fig. 261). Standing out from the façade are the decorative details the Venetians loved. Instead of the flat surfaces of a Renaissance façade with a rusticated ground floor (see Fig. 213), Sansovino has an open arcade, paralleled above by the deeply indented windows.

This projection in depth creates an effective play of light and shadow, an element normally associated more with sculpture and painting than with architecture. The dignified arcade of the lower story serves as a base for the increasingly rich adornment of the upper parts. The deeply arched windows of the second

floor are unified by the regularity of the Ionic columns, while the poses of the sculptured nudes in the spandrels provide variety. Above runs a frieze of cherubs in high relief holding garlands that alternate with small, deep-set windows. Over this rises a *balustrade,* a row of short posts topped by a rail, that goes all the way around the roof and supports a row of statues silhouetted against the skyline.

Palladio

Sansovino's designs influenced Andrea Palladio, the greatest architect associated with the Venetian style. As the author of the highly influential *Four Books of Architecture,* first published in Venice in 1570, Palladio has left a detailed discussion of his philosophy. In the preface to this work, Palladio paid eloquent tribute to his ancient Roman guide Vitruvius, whose writings stimulated his study of the classical buildings in Rome. "Finding that they deserved a much more diligent Observation than I thought at first Sight," he noted, "I began with the utmost Accuracy to measure every minutest part by itself."

Palladio's ideas thus were based on a thorough study of traditional design. He also saluted his immediate predecessor Sansovino, whose Library he praised as "perhaps the most sumptuous and the most beautiful edifice . . . since the time of the Ancients."

Villa Rotonda   Palladio's architecture can be studied more fully in nearby Vicenza, then a part of the Venetian Republic's holdings on the mainland. Just outside Vicenza is the Villa Rotonda (Fig. 262), a country house in the grand style and the prototype of many later buildings. The plan is a cube enclosing a cylindrical core with a low saucer dome (Fig. 263).

On four sides grand flights of steps lead to Ionic porches that project 14 feet (4.3 meters) forward and are 40 feet (12.2 meters) wide. The pediments are those of a classical temple, with statues on either side and above. Each porch provides entrance into the imposing round reception room that gives the villa the name *rotonda.* This central salon is as high as the house itself and rises to the cupola above. Alcoves left over from the parts between the round central hall and the square sides of the building allow space for four winding staircases and for no less than 32 rooms in the adjoining corners—all excellently lighted both from the outside and from the eight round windows at the base of the cupola.

At the corners of the main floor are four large reception rooms, each 20 by 30 feet (6.1 by 9.1 meters), and four smaller ones—eight in all on this floor alone. Below, a basement includes storerooms, servants' quarters, and kitchens. Palladio's achievement here is a house that is spacious but simple in plan.

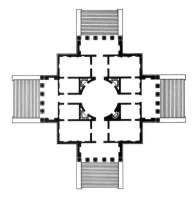

above: 263. Andrea Palladio. Plan of Villa Rotonda.

262. Andrea Palladio. Villa Rotonda, Vicenza. Begun 1550. 80′ (24.38 m) square, height of dome 70′ (21.34 m).

Church of Il Redentore When advancing years limited Sansovino's activities, Palladio was called to Venice to construct several buildings, among them the Church of Il Redentore (Fig. 264), or "the Redeemer." Palladio set himself the problem of reconciling the Greco-Roman temple with the traditional oblong Christian basilica plan (Fig. 265). Since a classical temple is of uniform height with a simple shed roof, and a Christian basilica has a Latin-cross ground plan with a central nave rising high above two side aisles, his solution shows great ingenuity.

The central part of the façade of Il Redentore becomes the portico of a classical temple complete

left: 265. Andrea Palladio. Plan of I1 Redentore.

below: 266. Andrea Palladio. Interior, I1 Redentore, Venice. 1576–92.

264. Andrea Palladio. I1 Redentore, Venice. 1576–92.

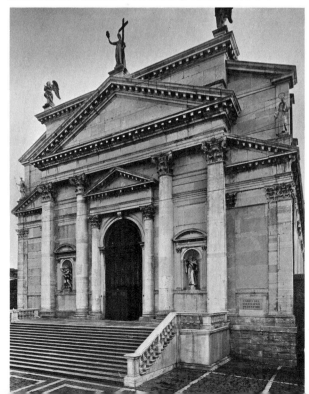

267. Andrea Palladio.
Interior, Olympic Theater, Vicenza.
1580–84.

with columns and pediment to face the high central nave within, while the acute angles of a fragmentary second pediment face the side aisles. The pediment idea is repeated in the small triangle above the entrance and in the side angles at the roof level, to make in all two complete and two incomplete pediments. This *broken-pediment* motif was later incorporated into the baroque vocabulary. To create the feeling of deep space, Palladio alternated square pilasters with round attached columns and arranged the pediments in a complex intersecting design.

The interior of Il Redentore is a model of geometrical clarity (Fig. 266). In order to create the impression of spatial depth, Palladio eliminated the traditional solid-walled apse that usually closes the space around the altar. In its place he used a semicircular open colonnade against clear glass windows. The effect is to lead the viewer's eye past the altar and on into the distance.

Olympic Theater The last building Palladio undertook was the Olympic Theater at Vicenza (Fig. 267). It was begun the year of his death and finished later from his designs by Scamozzi. An ingenious device to create the feeling of deep space is seen through the central arch from which actors made their entrances—a rising ramp flanked by building façades, which recedes only about 50 feet (15.2 meters) but creates the illusion of a long avenue leading to an open city square in the distance. Clearly inspired by ancient Roman amphitheaters, the Olympic has, in turn, been the inspiration for many later theaters, including one of London's largest, the Palladium.

Scamozzi, Romano, and Longhena

Scamozzi, the younger collaborator of both Sansovino and Palladio, was commissioned in 1584 to add a wing

to Sansovino's Library on the side toward St. Mark's Square (Fig. 268), to house the Procuratie Nuove, the new civic agencies. His design shows the usual Palladian sharp angularity, but he turned to Michelangelo for the alternation of semicircular and angular window brackets. A touch of manneristic whimsy is found in the insecurely perched nudes on top of the third-story window brackets.

Similar mannerist shock techniques are seen in the Palazzo del Tè (Fig. 269), or "Tea Palace," that Giulio Romano built for the ruling family of the neighboring duchy of Mantua. To enclose this small pleasure garden, he built a wall of heavily rusticated masonry much too massive for its function, and of Doric columns far larger than necessary to support the frieze. This dramatic overstatement, however, pales in comparison with the somewhat unnerving effect of the frieze itself, in which every third triglyph slips downward a notch, thus creating a syncopated visual rhythm.

It remained for Longhena in the early years of the 17th century to make the break from the brittle rectilinear style of Palladio and Scamozzi and carry Venetian architecture over into the exuberant baroque spirit with his Church of Santa Maria della Salute (Fig. 270). The ground plan is that of an octagon. The main entrance (right) is like a Roman triumphal arch with a classical triangular pediment rising above. Each of the other seven sides echoes this idea. Supporting the high-pitched dome are buttresses in the form of ornamental scrolls, a motif that was to achieve wide use throughout the baroque period. The elaborately decorated exterior is held together by the good composition of the design as a whole. This building was far more to the taste of the Venetians than the restrained and academic Palladian style, and it is one of the finest examples of the early baroque.

Palladio, however, emerges as the most influential architect of his period. His thought as he expressed it

in *Four Books of Architecture,* with their sketches and drawings, had an even wider influence in France, England, Ireland, and America than did his buildings. The English translation, published with notes by his disciple Inigo Jones, helped establish the Georgian tradition in both England (see Fig. 354) and America, where it was carried on by Thomas Jefferson. The latter's loyal Palladianism is seen in the designs he prepared for his residence at Monticello and the Rotunda of the University of Virginia (see Fig. 394), both of which are adaptations of the Villa Rotonda (Fig. 262). Jefferson also wanted to build the White House at Washington, D.C., on the same plan, but his proposal, submitted anonymously, was not the one chosen. However, even in its present form the White House has a typical Palladian design with a classical Ionic porch in the center and two equal wings spreading outward.

Painting

Venetian painting in the course of the 16th century displayed a wide range of styles—from the Renaissance work of Giorgione, with his partial emancipation from traditional subject matter and story content, to the mannerist paintings of Tintoretto and Veronese, with their illusionism and flights of imagination. Technically, Venetian painting is marked by the refinement and perfection of painting with oil on canvas, since the methods of tempera on wood panels and fresco were unsuited to the damp Venetian climate. Venetian painters also developed rich color palettes and used high intensities of light by which the principal figures are dramatically spotlighted and subordinate ones thrown into shadow.

270. Baldassare Longhena.
Santa Maria della Salute, Venice. 1631–56.
Length 200′ (60.96 m), width 155′ (47.24 m).

271. Giorgione. *Concert Champêtre (Pastoral Concert).* c. 1510. Oil on canvas, 3'7¼" × 4'6⅜" (1.1 × 1.38 m). Louvre, Paris.

above: 272. Giorgione. *Tempest.* c. 1505. Oil on canvas, 32¼ × 28¾" (82 × 73 cm). Academy, Venice.

right: 273. Titian. *Assumption of the Virgin.* 1516–18. Oil on canvas, 22'6" × 11'8" (6.86 × 3.56 m). Frari Church, Venice.

Giorgione

Giorgione's *Concert Champêtre* (Fig. 271), or *Pastoral Concert,* impresses with its spaciousness and its distribution of interest from foreground to background. The eye first is attracted to the four figures of the picture plane, then is led leisurely toward the middle ground where the shepherd is tending his flock, and finally comes to rest on the gleaming water of the distant horizon. This pastoral idyll, or interlude, is enlivened by several oppositions. Among them are the clothed male figures and female nudes; the pairing of the polished courtier and stately lady at the left with the rustic shepherd and shepherdess on the right; the attitudes of the two women—one intent upon her lover, the other turning away; and the lute symbolizing lyric poetry and the flute, pastoral poetry.

Giorgione's so-called *Tempest* (Fig. 272) is even less concerned with storytelling than *Concert Champêtre* and more with pictorial mechanics. The sunny foreground and human figures define the picture plane, while the eye is led in receding planes to deep space and the threatening sky in the distance. Stability is maintained by the careful balance of vertical (standing figure, broken columns, trees, buildings) and horizontal (unfinished wall, bridge) lines.

In both the *Pastoral Concert* and the *Tempest,* Giorgione creates a mood rather than tells a story, builds a picture rather than communicates specific meaning. A puzzle to his contemporaries who were accustomed to the usual iconographical subjects, Giorgione is understandable to the modern observer, who is used to separating subject matter from pictorial form and to seeing a picture as a composition complete within itself rather than as an illustration of a religious or literary theme.

Titian

The dynamic vertical movement of Titian's *Assumption of the Virgin* (Fig. 273) marks a definite departure from Renaissance calm and static monumentality. In this dramatic composition, heavenly and earthly spheres converge momentarily. Below, in deep shadow, are grouped the apostles, their arms raised toward the intermediate zone and the ascending Madonna, whose gesture, in turn, directs the eye to the dazzling brightness above. The upward motion then is arrested by the descending figure of God the Father surrounded by His angels. Linear movement and gradations of light, as well as transitions of color from somber shades to light pastel hues, are skillfully

275. Tintoretto. *Last Supper*. 1592–94.
Oil on canvas, 12′ × 18′8″ (3.66 × 5.69 m). San Giorgio Maggiore, Venice.

adapted by Titian to carry out his theme of the soaring human spirit triumphant over the gravitational pull of earthly considerations. Titian herewith created a new pictorial type that was to have a profound influence on the mannerist El Greco (Fig. 309), the baroque sculptor Bernini (Fig. 302), and a number of 17th-century painters.

Titian's sumptuous coloring also became the model for such later Venetians as Tintoretto, as well as for such baroque masters as Rubens and Velázquez. The extraordinary brilliance and bright tonality of the master's palette was startlingly revealed in the 1960s by the cleaning and restoration of the *Bacchus and Ariadne* in London's National Gallery (Fig. 274). Titian depicts the mythological incident of the god's return from India accompanied by his odd and mixed band of revelers. On seeing the lovelorn Ariadne, who has been deserted by Theseus, he leaps from his panther-drawn chariot, his pink drapery aflutter, to embrace her in wedlock.

Titian devises a slashing diagonal direction for the sharp downward plunge of Bacchus, a device to be copied often in the baroque period. A subtle touch of visual counterpoint can be seen in the sky, where the incident is reenacted by the clouds whose shapes echo the drapery and gestures of the principals, and where the starry crown of immortality awaits Ariadne.

In spite of Titian's compositional innovations and great influence on later periods, his art as a whole remains within the scope of the Renaissance. The painting of his younger colleague Tintoretto, however, crosses the stylistic bridge and penetrates deep into the expressive possibilities developed in Venetian mannerism.

Tintoretto

The drawing of Michelangelo and the color of Titian were the twin ideals of Tintoretto. His violent contrasts of light and dark; his off-center diagonal directions; his interplay of the natural and supernatural, earthly and unearthly light, human and divine figures; and his placement of principal figures on the edge of the action, from where he created lines that lead the eye in several different directions—all these elements combine to make his art both dynamic and dramatic.

In his *Last Supper* (Fig. 275), Tintoretto represents the miraculous moment when Jesus offers the bread and wine as the sacrificial body and blood of human redemption. To throw light on this unfathomable mystery of faith, Tintoretto bathes his canvas in a supernatural glow that seems to come partly from the figure of Christ and partly from the flickering flames of the oil lamp. The smoke is then transformed into an angelic choir hovering to form a burst of glorious light around the head of Christ. The drastic diagonals of the floor are paralleled by those of the table, but instead of directing the eye to the head of Christ, they lead to an indefinite point in the upper right and to space beyond the picture.

276. Paolo Veronese. *Marriage at Cana.* c. 1560. Oil on canvas, 21'10″ × 32'5″ (6.65 × 9.88 m). Louvre, Paris.

Veronese

Of all subjects, the most congenial to Veronese's art was festivity. Painted with the primary object of delighting the eye, his canvases nevertheless captured an important aspect of Venetian life—the pleasure and amusement of large social gatherings and the love of rich surroundings embellished with fruits, flowers, animals, furniture, draperies, and jesters.

Veronese seems never to have refused a commission to do a feast, and a note on the back of one of his drawings, believed to be in his own handwriting, bears this out.

> If I ever have time, I want to represent a sumptuous banquet in a superb hall, at which will be present the Virgin, the Saviour, and St. Joseph. They will be served by the most brilliant retinue of angels which one can imagine, busied in offering them the daintiest viands and an abundance of splendid fruit in dishes of silver and gold. Other angels will hand them precious wines in transparent crystal glasses and gilded goblets, in order to show with what zeal blessed spirits serve the Lord.

Marriage at Cana (Fig. 276) is truly a complete picture in that Veronese paints a historical-religious subject, includes portraiture, works in casual genre scenes, delights in still-life detail, and puts everything in an outdoor urban setting instead of in a landscape. The meaning of the picture, moreover, can be read on many different levels, from the surface to a deep allegorical interpretation. In his masterly representation of the world of appearances Veronese most completely expresses himself; in so doing, the Verona-born artist succeeds in being more Venetian than the Venetians. The scene, except for the central figures of Jesus and Mary, is that of a rich wedding feast, drawn from observation and imagination.

The guests are a portrait gallery of the great personages of the 16th century. The black-bearded groom, dressed in purple and gold and seated at the extreme left, is Alfonso d'Avalos, a contemporary Spanish nobleman. Next to him as the bride is Eleanor of Austria, sister of Charles V and in real life the second wife of Francis I of France. Other royal portraits include those of Francis I, Charles V, Suleiman I, sultan of Turkey, and Queen Mary of England. Monks, cardinals, and the artist's personal friends are also depicted.

The major interest in portraiture is concentrated on the orchestra in the center foreground, which is made up of the leading Venetian painters of the day. To the right, in this large canvas, the figure holding the cup in his left hand is the artist's brother Benedetto Cagliari, who collaborated with him by adding architectural backgrounds to this and other of Veronese's large paintings. Less important figures are everywhere. Above and behind Christ's head a butcher chops meat with a cleaver, while bustling servants prepare food or rush to and fro to serve it.

For unity in composition, Veronese's picture relies principally on the horizontal and vertical linear patterns beginning with the table, back through the balustrade and the rich Corinthian columns on either side, to the Sansovinian-Palladian architecture against the bright sky. The rigidity of such a plan is softened by the series of intricate curves that carry the eye to the head of Christ. A fine balance is contained in the opposition of the crowded scene below to the architectural order and spaciousness of the sky above.

Beyond its sumptuous surface, Veronese's *Marriage at Cana* probes for the deeper philosophical meaning of the miracle. The hourglass and musical score on the table were often used in Renaissance art as symbols of the passage of time. The painter-musicians, moreover, are to be interpreted as representations of the three ages of man, a traditional humanistic theme. In a period when great artists enjoyed the favors of princes—Titian, for instance, was ennobled by Emperor Charles V and highly honored by his son Philip II of Spain—famous painters would never have been depicted as mere public entertainers. The bearded Titian is portrayed as the dean of Venetian artists, clothed in a red damask robe and playing the bass viol; Veronese in a brilliant yellow cloak sits opposite, with Tintoretto whispering in his ear. Both are in their middle years and both are playing violas. The young flute player in back is thought to be Jacopo Bassano, placed behind the others since wind instruments had been ranked lower by Plato and Aristotle.

In Christian thought, the Marriage at Cana, the first of Christ's miracles in which water was changed to wine, is considered as a prophecy of the Last Supper, in which He changed the bread and wine into His body and blood to be shed for the forgiveness of sins. The scriptural passage describing the wedding feast reveals Jesus as being reluctant to comply with Mary's request, answering "mine hour is not yet come" (John 2:4). The picture on this level then becomes an allegory of time, which Plato had so eloquently described as being the moving image of eternity.

Another of Veronese's colossal canvases is the *Feast in the House of Levi,* painted as a Last Supper for a Venetian monastery (Fig. 277). Questions were soon raised, however, about the propriety of its content. By tradition a *Last Supper* portrayed only Christ and the twelve apostles, but Veronese had included some fifty figures, and this departure from tradition brought him before the Inquisition.

In one of the most remarkable documents in the history of painting—a summary of the painter's actual testimony—much about this picture in particular and about Veronese's conception of art in general is revealed. The inquisitors were disturbed not only by the number of figures but by the presence of a dog and cat, which Veronese had painted in the foreground. Even more disturbing was the inclusion of German soldiers sitting on the staircase at the very time when the Roman Catholic Church was experiencing a theological confrontation with the Lutheran Reformation in Germany.

Question. Did anyone commission you to paint Germans, buffoons, and similar things in that picture?

Answer. No, milords, but I received the commission to decorate the picture as I saw fit. It is large and, it seemed to me, it could hold many figures.

Q. Are not the decorations which you painters are accustomed to add to paintings or pictures supposed to be suitable and proper to the subject and the principal figures or are they just for pleasure—simply what comes to your imagination without any discretion or judiciousness?

277. Paolo Veronese. *Feast in the House of Levi.* 1573. Oil on canvas, 18'2" × 42' (5.54 × 12.8 m). Academy, Venice.

A. I paint pictures as I see fit and as well as my talent permits.

Q. Does it seem fitting at the Last Supper of the Lord to paint buffoons, drunkards, Germans, dwarfs and similar vulgarities?

A. No, milords.

Q. Do you not know that in Germany and in other places infected with heresy it is customary with various pictures full of scurrilousness and similar inventions to mock, vituperate, and scorn the things of the Holy Catholic Church in order to teach bad doctrines to foolish and ignorant people?

A. Yes, that is wrong; but I return to what I have said, that I am obliged to follow what my superiors have done.

Q. What have your superiors done? Have they perhaps done similar things?

A. Michelangelo in Rome in the Pontifical Chapel painted Our Lord, Jesus Christ, His Mother, St. John, St. Peter, and the Heavenly Host. These are all represented in the nude—even the Virgin Mary—and in poses with little reverence.*

The figures seated with Jesus at the damask-covered table should be the twelve apostles, but only two could be specifically identified by the artist—St. Peter, on His right, in robes of rose and gray, who according to the painter is "carving the lamb in order to pass it to the other end of the table"; and St. John, on His left. When questioned about the other figures, Veronese was evasive and pleaded that he could not recall them as he had "painted the picture some months ago." Since but ten months had passed, this was his way of avoiding explanation of the portraits of Titian and Michelangelo seated at the table under the left and right arches, respectively.

The verdict required Veronese to make certain changes in the picture. Rather than comply, he simply changed the title to *Feast in the House of Levi,* thereby placing it outside the iconographical tradition. The controversy with the Inquisition is a landmark in art history. By defending his work, Veronese raised aesthetic and formal values above those of subject matter.

Music

The high peak of Renaissance musical development was the polyphonic style of the Netherland composers. The general admiration for this art at the begin-

Literary Sources of Art History: An Anthology of Texts from Theophilus to Goethe, ed. Elizabeth G. Holt (copyright © 1947, 1975 by Princeton University Press), reprinted by permission of Princeton University Press.

ning of the 16th century was summed up by the Venetian ambassador to the court of Burgundy, who, in effect, said that three things were of the highest excellence: first, the finest, most exquisite linen of Holland; second, the tapestries of Brabant, most beautiful in design; and third, the music, which certainly could be said to be perfect. With such sentiments being expressed in official circles, it is not surprising to find that a Netherlander, Adrian Willaert, was appointed in 1527 to the highest musical position in Venice—choirmaster of St. Mark's.

Adoption of the northern musical idea is but another instance of the internationalism of the Venetians. Under Willaert, a leading representative of the polyphonic art, and his successors, Venice became a center of musical progress, while Rome remained the fortress of tradition. The measure of its religious freedom also predisposed Venice to new developments, and a number of new musical forms and radical changes of older ones were the results. In vocal music, this meant the development of the madrigal, the modification of the church motet, and the development of the *polychoral style* that made simultaneous use of two, three, and sometimes four choirs.

Instrumental music found new forms in the organ *intonazione* (short prelude), *ricercare* (contrapuntal composition), and *toccata* (brilliant showpiece) for keyboard solo, and in the *sinfonia,* and early *concertato* and *concerto* forms for orchestra. Here the Venetian school spoke in a new voice and in tones of individual character.

During the late 16th century, as it gradually lost favor, the old *ars perfecta* became known as the *stile antico* in contrast to the *stile moderno.* This "modern style" was associated in Venice with Giovanni Gabrieli and his organ music, early orchestral writing, and the development of the polychoral style. In Florence it was associated with Vincenzo Galilei, Peri, and Caccini and their solo songs and early opera experiments. In Rome, Frescobaldi and his virtuoso organ works were linked to the modern style. And in Mantua and Venice, Claudio Monteverdi, whose madrigals and operas became the cornerstone of baroque music, was another leader in this new style.

Gabrieli

The culmination of the musical development that Willaert began was reached in the work of Giovanni Gabrieli, who held the position of first organist at St. Mark's from the year 1585 until his death. His principal works were published under the title of *Symphoniae Sacrae* in 1597 and 1615.

The domed Greek-cross plan of St. Mark's, with its choir lofts placed in the transept wings, seems to

In ecclesiis (processional motet) Giovanni Gabrieli

have suggested some unusual acoustical possibilities to composers. When a choir is concentrated in the more compact space beyond the transept, as in the traditional Latin-cross church, the body of sound is more unified. When placed in two or more widely separated groups, as at St. Mark's, the interplay of sound led to experiments that resulted in the so-called polychoral style. In effect, it dissolved the traditional choruses and heralded a new development in the choral art.

These *chori spezzati*—literally, "broken choruses"—as they were called, added the element of spatial contrast to Venetian music, and new color effects were created. These included the echo device, so important in the entire baroque tradition; the alternation of two contrasting bodies of sound, such as chorus against chorus, single line versus a full choir, solo voice opposing full choir, instruments pitted against voices, and contrasting instrumental groups; the alternation of high and low voices; a soft level of sound alternated with a loud one; the fragmentary versus the continuous; and blocked chords contrasting with flowing counterpoint.

The resultant principle of duality, or opposing elements, is the basis for the *concertato* or *concerting* style, both words being derived from *concertare,* meaning "to compete with or to strive against." The

word appears in the title of some works Giovanni published jointly with his uncle Andrea Gabrieli in 1587: *Concerti . . . per voci et stromenti* ("Concertos . . . for voices and instruments"). The term later came to be widely used, with such titles as *Concerti Ecclesiastici* (*Church Concertos*) appearing frequently.

The motet *In ecclesiis* (left), written as the second part of the *Symphoniae Sacrae,* is an example of Gabrieli's mature style. Though the specific occasion for which it was intended is unknown, Gabrieli's motet is of the processional type and as such appropriate music for ceremonies similar to that depicted in Bellini's picture (Fig. 259). And the choirs he arranged in groups, as well as a brass ensemble, are similar to Bellini's details (Figs. 278, 279).

Since Bellini's setting was in St. Mark's Square, all the Venetian love of civic pomp and splendor are in evidence, and Gabrieli's music was in every respect quite able to fulfill the similar demands of any such later outdoor ceremony. His art was as typical of its time and place as that of his colleagues in other arts—Titian, Veronese, Sansovino, Palladio.

The Latin text of *In ecclesiis* reads like one of the Psalms of David. Together with a parenthetical English translation, it goes in part:

In ecclesiis benedicite Domino.
(Praise the Lord in the congregation.)
Alleluia, alleluia, alleluia.

In omni loco dominationis benedic, anima mea,
   Dominum.
(In every place of worship praise the Lord, O my
   soul.)
Alleluia, alleluia, alleluia.

In Deo, salutari mea et gloria mea.
Deus auxilium meum et spes mea in Deo est.
(In God, who is my salvation and glory,
my help, and my hope is in God.)
Alleluia, alleluia, alleluia.

. . . .
Deus, Deus, adjutor noster aeternam.
(O God, my God, our eternal judge.)
Alleluia, alleluia, alleluia.

The structure of Gabrieli's motet is based on the word *alleluia,* which functions as a *refrain,* or recurring section, and acts as a divider between the verses. The alleluias also are set in the more stationary triple meter suggesting a pause in the procession, while the stanzas have the more active beat of march time.

The work opens with the sopranos of Chorus I singing the first verse with organ accompaniment. The first *Alleluia* refrain (measures 6–12) is taken by the sopranos of Chorus I, all of Chorus II, and the organ (the numbering of the bars follows the edition published by G. Schirmer, Inc., New York). The tenors of Chorus I then sing the second verse with organ accompaniment (measures 13–31), while the *Alleluia* following this verse is the same as at first. Now come the blazing chords of the instrumental Sinfonia (32–43) with their strange, clashing dissonances. The third verse is sung in two-part counterpoint by the altos and tenors of Chorus I supported now by the six-part instrumental group without organ. The *Alleluia* after this verse (93–99) is taken by the same two voices of Chorus I, with the full Chorus II and organ but without the brass ensemble.The fifth verse is for full double choir, instruments, and organ, making a total of fourteen independent parts.

The gradual buildup of volume can be heard in the sequence of sopranos and full chorus; tenors and full chorus; the instrumental Sinfonia first alone, then in combination with tenors and altos; and the instrumental color against the chorus with organ support. The cumulative climax is then brought about by the final grandiose union of all vocal and instrumental forces, ending in a solid cadence radiating with musical color and producing the huge sonority necessary to bring the mighty work to its close. The magnificence of these massive sounds seems to fill the out-of-doors, just as it filled the vast interior of St. Mark's.

Giovanni Gabrieli's music foreshadows the baroque by setting up such oppositions as chorus against chorus, solo and choir, voices versus instruments, strings alternating with wind ensembles; the interplay of harmonic and contrapuntal textures; diatonic and chromatic harmony; the oppositions of soprano and bass lines, loud and soft dynamics; and the distinction of sacred and secular styles.

Monteverdi

While Gabrieli's vast tonal murals became the precedent for the later "colossal baroque," it remained for his great successor Claudio Monteverdi to probe the inner spirit of the new style. With Monteverdi in music, as with Longhena in architecture, the transition to the baroque is complete. Appointed master of music of the Most Serene Republic of Venice in 1613 after serving as court composer at Mantua for 23 years, Monteverdi achieved a working combination of Renaissance counterpoint and all the experimental techniques of his own time.

At Mantua, Monteverdi had already written his *Orfeo* (1607), the first full-length and complete opera in music history. At Venice, where the first public opera house was established in 1637, he continued with a series of lyrical dramas of which only the last two survive: *Return of Ulysses* (1641) and the *Coronation of Poppea* (1642). Both operas are heard today in concert performance and international opera houses with increasing frequency.

In addition, Monteverdi gave a new twist to the Renaissance *madrigal,* a type of nonchoral vocal music for two or more singers each of whom has a separate part. The madrigal with lyrics devoted to the delights of love and the beauties of nature reached a high point of popularity in 16th-century Italy and also in the England of Queen Elizabeth. With Monteverdi, however, the madrigal took on a special emotional and dramatic character that paralleled the developments in visual mannerism.

The new emotional orientation is stated in Monteverdi's *Eighth Book of Madrigals* (1638): "I have reflected that the principal passions or affections of our mind are three, namely, anger, moderation, and humility or supplication; so the best philosophers declare, and the very nature of our voice indicates this in having high, low, and middle registers. The art of music also points clearly to these three in its terms 'agitated,' 'soft,' and 'moderate' [*concitato, molle,* and *temperato*]." The collection has the significant subtitle, "Madrigals of War and Love," and

278–279. Gentile Bellini. Details of Figure 259.

278. *Brass Ensemble.*

279. *Choristers.*

Zefiro torna ("Return, O Zephyr")   Monteverdi

Monteverdi says he intends to depict anger, warfare, entreaty, and death as well as the accents of brave men engaged in battle. According to Monteverdi, vocal music of this type should be "a simulation of the passions of the words." Descriptive melodies in this *representative* style reflected the imagery of the poetic text. In Monteverdi's madrigal *Zefiro torna* ("Return, O Zephyr"), the word *l'onde* ("waves") is expressed by a rippling melody while *da monti e da valli ime e profonde* ("from mountains and valleys high and deep") is rendered by sharply rising and falling lines (see above).

Ideas: Mannerism

Venetian architecture, painting, and music—with their recurring themes, attitudes, qualities, shapes, and ideas—rise above a merely local style. All these are sufficiently representative not only to embrace a significant phase of mannerism but also to mark the beginning of baroque art.

Venetian space is never in repose but is restless and teeming with action. Sansovino's and Palladio's buildings, with their open *loggias*, or galleries, recessed entrances and windows, and pierced, deep-cut masonry, invite entrance. Inside, their spacious interiors allow for freedom of movement. Action is also felt in the lively contrasts of structural elements and decorative details, rectangularity side by side with roundness, and complete and broken intersecting pediments. Palladio's churches, with their open semicircular colonnades around the altar and windows in the apse, allow the eye to continue into deep space beyond. The reflection of façades in the rippling waters of the canals and the use of mirrored interior walls serve to activate the heavy masses of masonry and to increase the perception of light and space.

The breaking up of Renaissance unity in the composition of Venetian paintings is a similar instance in two dimensions. Dynamic, rather than stable, space is felt in the winged balance of opposite forms and figures on the picture plane and in the receding planes of a composition in depth that let the eye travel from foreground to middle ground and background with points of interest in each succeeding plane. Both devices can be seen in Giorgione's

Concert Champêtre (Fig. 271) and *Tempest* (Fig. 272). Similarly active space is achieved by the rising planes of a vertical organization, as in Titian's *Assumption* (Fig. 273); and by the wheel-like rotary movement Tintoretto sets up in his *Marriage of Bacchus and Ariadne* (Fig. 280). The diagonal accent is found in the slashing movement from upper right to lower left in Titian's *Bacchus and Ariadne* (Fig. 274). In the pictures of Tintoretto and Veronese, breaking up the unity of central perspective produces a fragmentation that leads the eye in several directions.

A similar expression is heard in music. In Gabrieli's "broken" choirs, parts of one group are contrasted with the full sound of a whole chorus, and the sequence of contrasting sound progressively builds up ever-larger volumes until the climax is reached in the union of them all. The tossing back and forth of contrasting, unequal sound masses in the concerting style; the alternation of loud and soft dynamic levels of opposing groups as well as in the Venetian echo effect; and the contrast of high and low parts—all intensify the motional and emotional effects of music.

While mannerism had its beginnings in Florence early in the 16th century and subsequently developed elsewhere, it was the Venetian adaptation of the style that was most speedily absorbed into the baroque.

Living in the shadow of such unrivaled masters of the immediate past as Leonardo da Vinci, Michelangelo, and Raphael created a dilemma for the younger generation of painters. Quite aware that a golden age had preceded them, and that there was no possibility of improving on the craftsmanship of their famous predecessors, these young artists found themselves at a crossroads. Following the old paths would mean selecting certain ideas and techniques of their predecessors and reducing them to workable formulas. Striking out in new directions would imply taking for granted such perfected technical achievements as linear and atmospheric perspective, mathematical principles of foreshortening, and correct rendering of anatomy and then deliberately breaking the rules with telling effect.

The first course meant working "in the manner" of the giants of the past, and academies sprang up to transmit the traditional techniques to young artists. The second course led to bold, dramatic departures from precedent. It was this revolutionary aspect that loyal followers of the Renaissance saw as the collapse of an ideal order and the adoption of an "affected manner" by highly individual artists.

Either of the two courses eventually led in new directions, and some present-day historians separate the period of about 1520 to 1600 from the dying Renaissance and the baroque that was being born. To distinguish and characterize much of the art of these years, they propose a period and style called *man-*

280. Tintoretto. *Marriage of Bacchus and Ariadne.* 1577–88. Oil on canvas, 4′9″ × 5′5″ (1.45 × 1.65 m). Doge's Palace, Venice.

nerism. Since mannerism was born of crisis, it is a style facing in two different directions. The more conservative artists linked themselves with tradition and can be classified as *academic mannerists;* the more daring group can be termed *free mannerists.*

Academic Mannerism

When Vasari, the disciple of Michelangelo, used the term *de maniera,* he meant working in the manner of Leonardo, Michelangelo, and Raphael. By reducing their art to a system of rules, he could work fast and efficiently. His fondest boast was that while it took Michelangelo six years to finish one work, he could do six works in one year.

The experimental stage was over; the era of fulfillment was at hand, an era not of eccentric genius or soul-searching prophecy, only competent craft. Such was the course taken by Vasari, Palladio, and Veronese. Vasari, in Florence, was instrumental in founding an Academy of Design in 1561. At Bologna in 1585, the Carracci family established an institute with the significant word *academy* in its name, and courses in art theory and practice was offered.

Such academic mannerist artists did not go to nature for their models as Leonardo had done but studied masterpieces with the thought of mastering systematically the artistic vocabularies of the late Renaissance giants. Art, in other words, did not hold up a mirror to nature but rather to art. At the lowest level, this implied well-schooled technicians and a style based on conventions—a free borrowing and reassembling without the birth pangs of the original creative synthesis. At its highest, this approach could lead to virtuosity of execution. In no way did it rule out that intangible essence—inspiration.

With Palladio, academic mannerism came to terms with the classical orders of his ancient Roman guide Vitruvius. By adapting Roman architectural forms to his contemporary needs, he held in check the Venetian love of lavishness and curbed the excesses of overdecoration. Veronese, by the symmetry of his designs, his closed forms, and the organizing function of his architectural backgrounds, was able to handle large crowds and bustling movement without injury to his pictorial unity. And while Gabrieli's music broke up the unity of the Renaissance choir—encompassing and increasing the scope of musical space—his support of the traditional Renaissance polyphony kept his work under strict control.

Free Mannerism

Mannerism also included the "mannered" art of highly individual artists who, in their revolt against Renaissance ideals, cultivated eccentricity and rev-

281. Benvenuto Cellini. Saltcellar of Francis I. 1539–43. Gold, 10¼ × 13″ (26 × 33 cm). Kunsthistorisches Museum, Vienna.

are uncomfortably superimposed on each other; how St. Anne supports the weight of the Madonna and what they are sitting on is left to the imagination. In the black terror and bleak despair of Michelangelo's *Last Judgment* (see Fig. 290), clarity of space no longer exists—there are crowded parts and bare spaces; the size of figures is out of proportion; and one cannot even be sure who are the saved and who the damned.

The exception in the High Renaissance, however, became the rule under mannerism, which quickly, though briefly, emerged as an international style. Such Florentine mannerists as Rosso Fiorentino and Benvenuto Cellini (Fig. 281) were summoned to Paris to become court artists of Francis I, and Raphael's pupil Giulio Romano was the official architect of the Duke of Mantua (Fig. 269).

In spite of their desire to dazzle and their whimsically contrived tricks, these men had no intention to deceive, since their art was addressed to the sophisticated few. Only those well aware of the rules could enjoy the witty turns and startling twists by which they were broken. This courtly phase of the mannerist style, however, was too much restricted to a single class and too refined and self-conscious in its aestheticism to endure long. In the more sophisticated, middle-class atmosphere of Venice, where the group patronage of special citizen organizations broadened its base, mannerism gained vitality and vigor. It was these aspects that were transmitted to the baroque.

Venice the Crossroads

Venice during the 16th century was the stylistic clearinghouse for currents of thought flowing from the Italian South, the Mediterranean East, and the European North. Flemish and German merchants had trade connections and resident communities in the city of canals, while prosperous commerce was continuous. Equally active was the traffic in artists. Among others, the two greatest northern painters of their time made extensive visits to this mecca of the arts—Albrecht Dürer at the threshold of the 16th century and Peter Paul Rubens at the onset of the 17th century. The span marked the march from the Renaissance through mannerism to the baroque.

Dürer's Synthesis of North and South

Coming from the German city of Nuremberg, Dürer was destined to make a fruitful synthesis of northern aesthetic ideas with southern Renaissance theories and practice. Without for a moment sacrificing his own strong individuality, Dürer struck a balance in his art between the piety of Germanic puritanism and

eled in inner conflicts. This generation of painters could no longer be thrilled by the mathematics of linear perspective or by finding the proper size and relationship of figures to their surrounding space. Instead, they found excitement in breaking established rules with dash and daring and in violating Renaissance assumptions for the sheer shock effect.

Under such conditions, a number of changes occurred. Naturalism gave way to the free play of the imagination. Classical composure yielded to nervous movement. Clear definition of space became a jumble of picture planes crowded with twisted figures. Symmetry and focus on the central figure were replaced by off-balance diagonals that made it difficult to find the protagonist of the drama amid the numerous directional lines. Backgrounds no longer contained the picture but were vaguely defined or nonexistent. The norms of body proportion were distorted by the unnatural elongation of figures. *Chiaroscuro,* the art of light and shade, served no more to model figures but to create optical illusions, violent contrasts, and theatrical lighting effects. Finally, strong deep color and rich costumes faded to pastel hues and gauzy fluttering drapery. In short, the Renaissance dream of clarity and order became the mannerist nightmare of haunted space, art was in danger of becoming artifice, and the natural gave way to the artificial.

Some of these tendencies were already present in the High Renaissance. Giorgione's puzzling pictures that broke with the iconographical tradition confused his contemporaries. In Leonardo's *Madonna and Child with St. Anne* (see Fig. 241), the figures

left: **282.** Giovanni Bellini.
St. Jerome Reading. c. 1505.
Oil on wood, 19¼ × 15½″ (49 × 39 cm).
National Gallery of Art, Washington, D.C.
(Samuel H. Kress Collection).

below: **283.** Giovanni Bellini.
Madonna and Child. 1505.
Oil on wood, 19⅝ × 16⅛″ (50 × 41 cm).
Borghese Gallery, Rome.

the hedonism of Italian paganism, between northern severity and mystical soul-searching and southern freedom and rationality.

When the young Dürer first visited Venice in 1495, Gentile Bellini was working on his *Procession in St. Mark's Square* (Fig. 259). His brother Giovanni was doing a series of altarpieces for Venetian churches as well as teaching his pupils, among whom it is believed were Giorgione and Titian. Together this quartet of painters spoke to northerners in different accents, but for Dürer the most persuasive voice of all was that of Giovanni Bellini. Even on a later visit, the German master referred to Giovanni as "still the greatest painter in Venice."

The root of Giovanni Bellini's art was a harmonious, familial blend of his father Jacopo's Renaissance heritage and the special contributions of his brother Gentile and his brother-in-law Andrea Mantegna of Mantua. But the beautiful branches of this family tree were Giovanni's own paintings that embraced an emotional range from the silent suffering of his *Pietà,* through the melancholy meditations of saints and hermits (Fig. 282), to the lyrical grace and joyous maternity of his Madonnas (Fig. 283)—all set in po-

left: **284.** Albrecht Dürer. *Self-Portrait.* 1498.
Oil on wood. 20½ × 16⅛″ (52 × 41 cm).
Prado, Madrid.

below left: **285.** Albrecht Dürer. *Hercules at the Crossroads.*
c. 1498. Copperplate engraving, 12½ × 8¾″ (32 × 22 cm).
National Gallery of Art, Washington, D.C. (Rosenwald Collection).

below: **286.** Albrecht Dürer. *Madonna and Child
with a Multitude of Animals.* c. 1503.
Pen and ink with watercolor,
12⅝ × 9⅝″ (32 × 24 cm). Albertina, Vienna.

etic landscapes filled with the soft, mellow, golden
light that brought all of nature into a warmly glowing unity. The fruits of Giovanni's art nurtured the
development not only of his pupils and successors but
also that of Dürer.

In his *Self-Portrait* of 1498 (Fig. 284) Dürer divides his pictorial space so that the figure is seen
against a closed background on one side, while the
other suggests deeper space. This northern device
was also absorbed into the Venetian vocabulary as
seen in the works of Giovanni Bellini, Giorgione, and
Titian. Here Dürer reveals himself not as a craftsman and artist, but as a grave, confident young
master and a free Renaissance humanist.

287. Matthias Grünewald. *Crucifixion,* center panel of exterior of *Isenheim Altarpiece.* Completed 1515. Oil on wood, 8′9⅞″ × 10′7⅞″ (2.69 × 3.07 m). Musée d'Unterlinden, Colmar.

The dated inscription of this self-portrait bears the legend: "I made this according to my appearance when I was 26." The long curly hair and elegant costume are accents of visual enrichment, while the serious, searching expression provides a thoughtful note. Foreboding also is the landscape with its menacing mountains that loom over the fertile Italian plain in the foreground. For beyond these Alps lay Germany, which was facing a tortured century of peasant wars, internal dissents, and religious reformation as it sought to disentangle itself from the outmoded medievalism that had accumulated over centuries.

Hercules at the Crossroads (Fig. 285) is a highly personal statement that may mirror this young, artistic, and strong man's inner struggle between northern and southern crosscurrents. This copper engraving exemplifies the graphic arts (woodcuts, etchings, silverpoint) that occupied Dürer's attention throughout his creative career quite as much as did his painting. The traditional mythological legend tells of Hercules' choice between Virtue and Vice, lawful and licentious love. In this case, however, Virtue is no mere bland personification of the good life, but an irate Amazon taking up the cudgel to punish her adversary who, for her part, is actively engaged in amorous pursuits with a horned satyr. Hercules faces Virtue, but his position is quite ambivalent as he is looking at Vice while trying to stop the fight and subdue the too eager efforts of Virtue. The drawing of the Hercules clearly shows the influence of Pollaiuolo (see Fig. 220), whom Dürer greatly admired. It is interesting to note the two-way stream

of influence. While Dürer was absorbing the Venetian tradition, his own prints in turn had a notable effect on the work of the Florentine and Venetian mannerists.

Dürer's lifelong preoccupation with the accurate rendering of nature is seen in his *Madonna and Child with a Multitude of Animals* (Fig. 286). His beasts show no affinity with medieval bestiaries but are true-to-life animals from field and forest. Dürer's lambs leap and graze, his foxes stalk their prey, his birds take wing. Such minute and accurate observations were gained not only from his eager eye but also from the long and hard study of essays on geological formations, the structure of plants, and the anatomy of animals and birds.

Grünewald's Altarpiece: The Northern Spirit

The spirit of the North but dimly touched by the rays of the Italian Renaissance sun is marvelously realized in the *Isenheim Altarpiece* (Fig. 287) by Dürer's older contemporary, Matthias Grünewald. This masterpiece was painted for the monks of St. Anthony, a religious order that maintained hospitals for the needy, sick, and poor.

The work consists of a cycle of scenes painted on the front and back of two sets of folding panels, with immovable side wings, paired one behind the other. This intricate form shows a likeness to the northern art of the book, opening leaf after leaf to allow the stories of the Christian calendar to pass by in review. Earthly, heavenly, and infernal beings alike are present to worship, to witness, to horrify, to tempt. The moods run from the ecstatic joy of the music-making angels in the *Nativity* panel (Fig. 288) to the depths of despair in the *Temptation of St. Anthony* (Fig. 289), where the words of the suffering saint are inscribed on a scrap of paper at the lower right: "Where were You, good Jesus, where were You? Why did You not come to heal my wounds?" The details range from the Annunciation and Nativity, through the Passion and Entombment of Jesus, to the fantastic ordeals of St. Anthony, the legendary prophet of Christian monasticism.

The unusual and obscure iconography derives from a number of sources including the Scriptures, the mystical writings of St. Bridget of Sweden, and the pictures of Grünewald's contemporaries, not the least of whom was Dürer. The strange *Nativity* (Fig. 288) omits St. Joseph, the crib, the animals and shepherds. The *Crucifixion* scene (Fig. 287) includes St. John the Baptist, rare in this context. In this *Nativity* Mary appears twice, on the right as the more familiar Madonna with Child, and on the left kneeling in prayer in a Gothic templelike chapel, her head surrounded by heavenly light. Such a vision is described by St. Bridget in her *Revelations,* and the allusion also suggests the Magnificat in St. Luke (1:46–55) where the Virgin prays: "My soul doth magnify the Lord, and my spirit hath rejoiced in God

my Saviour." The images of the prophets, musicians, and the Venetian glass pitcher at her feet may point to the Revelation of St. John where the 24 elders of the Apocalypse appear with jars to symbolize their prayers and with musical instruments to signify their praises given to the Lord.

In the *Crucifixion* (Fig. 287) Grünewald depicts the Baptist on the right side of the cross, St. John the Evangelist on the left, and Sts. Sebastian and Anthony on the side wings. He thus includes the interceders for the principal maladies treated at the hospital: St. Sebastian for the plague, the two Johns for epilepsy and St. Anthony for St. Anthony's fire (often thought to be the feverish, infectious inflammation of the skin now known as erysipelas). No Italian harmony softens the grim agony of the crucified Christ. Festering sores and dried blood cover the ghastly green flesh. Such details are naturalistic, but the unnatural dimensions of the figures bear no relation to southern Renaissance practice. Is Grünewald following the medieval way of proportioning his figures according to their religious or dramatic importance? Compare the size of the kneeling Magdalene's hands with those of the Savior. Or is he emphasizing graphically the inscribed prophecy of the Baptist: "He must increase, but I must decrease" (John 3:30)? In either case he is sacrificing "correct" proportions for the sake of his design and expressive intent.

288. Matthias Grünewald. *Nativity,* center panel of front opening of *Isenheim Altarpiece.* Completed 1515. Oil on wood, 8'9⅞" × 10'⅞" (2.69 × 3.07 m). Musée d'Unterlinden. Colmar.

The *Temption of St. Anthony* (Fig. 289), with its ghoulish and monstrous apparitions, reminded the suffering patients of the horrible ordeals endured by their patron saint. With its all-encompassing range of human feeling, Grünewald's altarpiece becomes one of the most moving documents in art history. As such it is comparable in scope and magnitude to Michelangelo's Sistine ceiling (see Figs. 246–251), Raphael's frescoes in the Vatican (see Fig. 252) and Dürer's *Apocalypse* or *Passion* series, all of which were completed in the same decade.

Roads to the Baroque

From Venice, as well as from Rome and the centers where international mannerism flourished, the roads to the baroque fanned out in all directions. The thriving painting industry assured the circulation of Venetian ideas in every civilized country. The writings of Palladio, as translated in English with commentary by Inigo Jones, led to the architecture of Christopher Wren and the Georgian styles and from there to the colonial and federal styles in America. The printing of musical scores assured Venetian composers of general prominence. Venetian diplomacy, by avoiding commitments to either extreme, paved the way for the acceptance of certain aspects of the Venetian style in both Reformation and Counter-Reformation countries.

Venetian innovations in architecture and painting were eagerly adopted in the Church and court circles of Spain and France. Both the Church hierarchy and the aristocracy needed the impressive splendor of the arts to enhance their exalted positions. The more monumental the buildings, the more lavish the decorations, the more grandiose the musical entertainments, the better the arts served their purpose of impressiveness and magnificence. Hence, it was natural for both to seek out the richest expression of this ideal, which in Venice was to be found in abundance.

El Greco, after studying in Titian's workshop and absorbing Tintoretto's mannerism, found his way to Church and court circles in Spain, where his art made a deep impression. Rubens spent eight years in Italy, much of the time making copies of Titian's pictures, then took the Venetian techniques with him to his native Flanders and later France. Rubens and his pupil van Dyck, in turn, transmitted them to England, and eventually they reached America.

In the Counter-Reformation countries—Italy, Spain, France, and Austria—church music remained more constant to the Roman tradition, but Venetian music was readily accepted in secular circles. However, for the Reformation centers—Holland, Scandinavia, and northern Germany—the greater liturgical freedom of Venetian musical forms proved more

289. Matthias Grünewald. *Temptation of St. Anthony,* right panel of second opening of *Isenheim Altarpiece.* Completed 1515. Oil on wood, 8'9⅞" × 4'8¼" (2.69 × 1.43 m). Musée d'Unterlinden, Colmar.

adaptable to Protestant church purposes precisely because of their departure from Roman models.

Sweelinck, who studied the works of both Andrea Gabrieli and Zarlino, carried the Venetian keyboard style to Amsterdam, where his great reputation brought him organ students from Germany who later taught the generation of Pachelbel and Buxtehude, both major influences on the style of Bach and Handel. Cavalli, Monteverdi's successor at the Venetian opera, was called to Paris to write the music for the wedding festivities of Louis XIV. Heinrich Schütz, the greatest German composer before Johann Sebastian Bach and George Frederick Handel and another force in determining their art, was a pupil of both Giovanni Gabrieli and Monteverdi. In sum, the Venetian style became a part of the basic vocabulary of the baroque artistic language.

13
The Counter-Reformation Baroque Style

Rome, Late 16th and Early 17th Centuries

The catastrophic events that shook Rome and all Europe in the course of the 16th century awakened the Eternal City from its Renaissance dream of harmony and confronted it with the stark reality of contradiction and conflict. Subsequently, every aspect of life—religious, scientific, political, social, economic, and aesthetic—was destined then to undergo reexamination and radical change. A succession of disturbing visitors proved to be forerunners of developments to come. Martin Luther had been in Rome at the turn of the century, and his observations had added fuel to the fire of his moral indignation. The reform movement he initiated, along with Zwingli and John Calvin, was to split the unity of the Universal Church and divide Europe into Reformation and Counter-Reformation camps.

The next visitor, the Holy Roman Emperor Charles V, was even less welcome. Previously, the voyages of the great navigators and the exploits of the colonizers who followed in their wake had brought most of North, Central, and South America under the Spanish crown. With the monopoly of the spice trade of the Orient and with the gold and silver mines of the New World pouring fabulous riches into its treasury, Spain was rapidly becoming the most powerful country in the world. By a combination of heredity, marriage, and high finance, Charles I of Spain had become Charles V of the Holy Roman Empire. With Holland and Flanders, the Germanies, and Austria firmly in his grasp, the ambitious Emperor turned his attention next to Italy. One by one, the formerly independent Italian duchies and city-states came under his domination. Opposition from any quarter was intolerable, and in 1527 His Catholic Majesty's mercenaries marched on Rome, sacking and plundering. Eight days later the great city was a smoking ruin, the Vatican a barracks, St. Peter's a stable, and Pope Clement VII a prisoner at Castel Sant' Angelo (see Fig. 108).

Thereafter, the papacy had no choice but to submit to Spanish policy; a Spanish viceroy ruled in Naples, and a Spanish government was installed in Milan. Through the Gonzagas in Mantua, the Estes in Ferrara, and the Medici in Florence, the Spaniards controlled all important centers; and with Spanish rule came Spanish austerity and religiosity, etiquette and courtly elegance.

Another visitor to Rome was the astronomer Copernicus, whose book *On The Revolution of the Planets in Their Orbits* was destined to change the conception of the cosmos from an earth-centered to a sun-centered world. A shock reaction followed as Renaissance people began to realize they inhabited a minor planet whirling through space, and that they were no longer at the center of creation. Later, when his observations tended to prove the Copernican theory, Galileo was tried for heresy, sentenced to prison, and released only when he disavowed his teachings and writings. The combined effect of these and other scientific discoveries began to weaken the belief in miracles and divine intervention in human affairs.

Then came the theologians, during the sessions of the Council of Trent that undertook the reform of the Church from within. When the test came, many changes occurred: Bold humanistic thinking was transformed into violent reaction. Neoplatonic philosophy was succeeded by a return to Aristotelian scholasticism. The distant but seductive voices of pagan antiquity were drowned out by the roar of rekindled medieval fire and brimstone. The reveling in sensuous beauty was followed by bitter self-reproach. Promises of liberal religious attitudes were broken by a return to strict Church doctrines. New access to literature and knowledge through the printing press and scientific discoveries was suppressed through the Universal Inquisition and the *Index Expurgatorius.* God appeared not as the Loving Father but as a terrifying Judge, Christ not as the Good Shepherd but as the Great Avenger.

The founders of the new Counter-Reformation religious orders, which were to shape the course of Roman Catholicism in the 17th century, were in Rome at various times. Philip Neri brought together, for informal meetings in his Congregation of the Oratory, people of all classes, from aristocrats to street urchins, and encouraged them to pray or preach as the spirit moved them. By dramatizing and setting to music familiar biblical stories and parables (the origin of the baroque oratorios), he generated a cheerful devotional spirit that stirred the hearts of the poor and humble.

Ignatius Loyola came from Spain to obtain papal sanction for his Society of Jesus, a militant order generally known as the "Jesuits" and dedicated to foreign missionary work, education, and active participation in worldly affairs. There were also the mystics Teresa of Avila and John of the Cross, whose abilities to combine the contemplative and active ways of life resulted in a significant literary expression of the period and in the reorganization and redirection of the Carmelite orders. In Rome too was Carlo Borromeo, the young energetic archbishop of Milan, who wrote manuals for architects and artists as well as for the students and teachers in the many seminaries he founded.

At a single grand ceremony in the newly completed Basilica of St. Peter on May 22, 1622, Ignatius Loyola, Francis Xavier, Teresa of Avila, and Philip Neri were canonized and admitted to the honors of the altar. Thereupon, the architects Giacomo Vignola, Giacomo della Porta, Carlo Maderno, Gianlorenzo Bernini, and Francesco Borromini were called upon to build churches and chapels dedicated to them.

In this floodtide of reform, the classical harmony, stability, and poise of Renaissance art were not hardy enough to survive, nor could the overrefined, overly dramatic art of mannerism adapt itself to the new religious climate. Gaiety gave way to sobriety, Venuses reverted to Virgins, Bacchuses and Apollos to bearded Christs. The organic form and unity of Michelangelo's Sistine ceiling was succeeded by the calculated shapelessness of his awesome *Last Judg-*

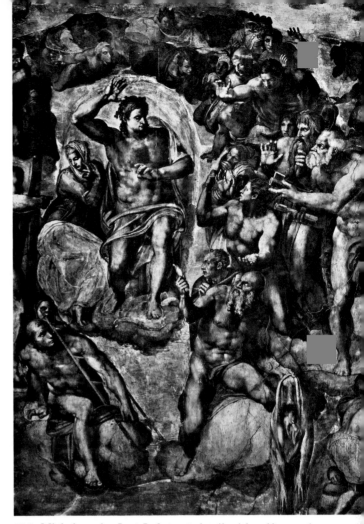

290. Michelangelo. *Last Judgment,* detail with self-portrait on flayed skin at lower right. 1534–41. Fresco, 48 × 44′ (14.63 × 13.41 m). Sistine Chapel, Vatican, Rome.

ment (Fig. 290, see also Fig. 246). Palestrina was conscience-stricken for having written madrigals and thenceforth wrote only masses. Under the rulings of the Council of Trent, Church art was firmly rewed to religion, and the clergy had to assume responsibility for the way artists treated religious subjects.

The lives and attitudes of Counter-Reformation artists were deeply affected by the new religious climate. Michelangelo's *Last Judgment* received censure because his Apollo-type Christ was unbearded and because such pagan classical details as Charon, the ghostly boatman rowing souls across the river Styx, had been included. Drapery was ordered to cover his "offending nudes," and only the timely intervention of a group of artists saved the *Last Judgment* from complete destruction.

Michelangelo became a recluse in his last years, gave up figurative art for the abstractions of architecture, and devoted himself to the building of St. Peter's, a project for which he would accept no

CHRONOLOGY
Rome and Spain, 16th and Early 17th Centuries

GENERAL EVENTS: ROME

1527	Charles V's mercenaries sacked Rome. Protestant Reformation in progress under Luther in Germany, Zwingli and Calvin in Switzerland. Reaction to Renaissance humanism began.
1534	Counter-Reformation began
1540	Society of Jesus (Jesuit order) founded by Ignatius Loyola
1542	Universal Inquisition established
1543	Copernicus' *De Revolutionibus Orbium Coelestium* published. Censorship of printed matter began
1545	Council of Trent (1545–63) undertook reform within Church; reaffirmed dogma
1547	Michelangelo named architect of St. Peter's
1555	Volterra ordered to paint drapery on "offending" nudes in Michelangelo's *Last Judgment*
c.1562	Teresa of Avila and John of the Cross reformed Carmelite orders
1575	Congregation of the Oratory (founded by Philip Neri) approved
1616	Galileo enjoined by pope not to "teach or defend" researches

confirming Copernican theory; called before Inquisition in 1633

1622	Canonization of Ignatius Loyola, Teresa of Avila, Philip Neri, Francis Xavier

GENERAL EVENTS: SPAIN

1474-1516	Ferdinand and Isabella reigned; West Indies discovered by Columbus (1492); South America (1498); expulsion of Moors and Jews from Spain
1516-1556	Charles I, king of Spain; became Holy Roman Emperor Charles V in 1519
1556-1598	Philip II, king of Spain; Spanish empire reached greatest extent
1561	Madrid chosen as capital
1563-1584	Escorial Palace built
1583	Victoria published *Missarum Libri Duo,* books of masses dedicated to Philip II
1588	English navy sank Spanish armada
1598-1621	Philip III, king of Spain; decline of Spanish power
1600	Victoria published collection of masses, motets, psalms, hymns, dedicated to Philip II
1604	Cervantes' *Don Quixote,* Part I, published in Madrid (Part II, 1615)

1621-1665	Philip IV, king of Spain
1623	Velázquez appointed court painter
1648	Treaty of Westphalia; Spanish power in Europe checked

ARCHITECTS AND SCULPTORS

? -1567	Juan Bautista de Toledo
1507-1573	Giacomo Vignola
1530-1597	Juan de Herrera
1531-1621	Juan Bautista Monegro
c.1540-1604	Giacomo della Porta
1556-1629	Carlo Maderno
c.1580-1648	Juan Gomez de Mora
1598-1680	Gianlorenzo Bernini
1599-1667	Francesco Borromini
1665-1725	José de Churriguera
c.1683-1742	Pedro de Ribera

PAINTERS

1498-1578	Giulio Clovio
c.1541-1614	El Greco (Domenicos Theotocopoulos)
1573-1610	Michelangelo Merisi da Caravaggio
1599-1660	Diego Velázquez
1617-1682	Bartolomé Murillo
1642-1709	Fra Andrea Pozzo

MUSICIANS

c.1500-1553	Cristobal Morales
c.1500-1566	Antonio de Cabezón
1524-1594	Giovanni da Palestrina
c.1548-1611	Tomás Luis de Victoria

WRITERS

1491-1556	Ignatius Loyola
1515-1582	Teresa of Avila
1538-1584	Charles Borromeo
1542-1591	John of the Cross
1547-1616	Miguel de Cervantes
1562-1635	Lope de Vega
1600-1681	Pedro Calderón

fee. In the privacy of his own studio, he worked periodically at sculpture and brooded over his last *Pietàs,* one of them intended for his own tomb. Palestrina was banished from his post as leader of the Sistine Choir because he refused to take the priestly vow of celibacy and give up his wife. Later he was reinstated and asked to reform Church music.

Gianlorenzo Bernini, busiest and most successful sculptor-architect of the Counter-Reformation baroque style, was closely associated with the Jesuits and regularly practiced St. Ignatius' *Spiritual Exercises.* Andrea Pozzo, who painted the illusionistic ceiling of the Church of Sant'Ignazio (Fig. 299), was a member of the Society of Jesus. El Greco, Spain's

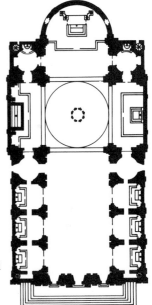

greatest representative of Counter-Reformation art, was a religious mystic in whose last visionary canvases physical matter practically ceases to exist. His tall, slender figures are more spirit than flesh, his settings more of the realm of heaven than of earth.

As matters shaped up, the Counter-Reformation baroque style had its beginning in Rome, where it reached its climax in the fifty-year period from about 1620 to 1670. Its consequences were felt simultaneously in Spain, the strong secular arm of the Church militant. Thereafter the style spread throughout the Roman Catholic countries of Europe and traveled with the missionary orders to the Americas and everywhere in the far-flung colonies established by Spain and Portugal.

Roman Counter-Reformation Art

Architecture

As the central monument of the Jesuit order, the Church of Il Gesù in Rome (Figs. 291–293) became the prototype for many Counter-Reformation churches (Figs. 294–296). Indeed, so many different versions and variants have since appeared that with justification it has been called the most influential church design of the past four centuries. Commissioned in 1564, Il Gesù combines classical motifs from the Renaissance heritage with some of the new elements that were to identify Counter-Reformation architecture. The heart of the structure—the domed

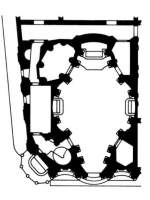

left: 294.
Francesco Borromini.
Façade, San Carlo
alle Quattro Fontane, Rome.
Begun 1635, façade 1667.
Length 52′ (15.86 m),
width 34′ (10.36 m),
width of façade 38′
(11.58 m).

right: 295.
Francesco Borromini.
Plan of San Carlo
alle Quattro Fontane.

crossing of the nave and the short transepts—is derived from Michelangelo's and Palladio's centralized plans, like those reproduced in Figures 253 and 263. But the short nave reaching forward from the crossing repeats the compromise achieved in St. Peter's when Bramante's and Michelangelo's plans were combined with the addition of Carlo Maderno's long nave, as seen in Figure 255. Giacomo Vignola's design for the façade, somewhat revised after his death by his successor Giacomo della Porta, recalls a Roman triumphal arch on the ground floor, but the lean-to roofing over the side chapels is masked with graceful scrolls that swirl upward toward the triangular templelike pediment.

Borromini's San Carlo alle Quattro Fontane (Fig. 294) is one of the most original expressions of the period. Turning to full advantage the small site at the intersection of two streets with a fountain at each of the four corners, the architect devised a plan that embraced a complex interplay of geometrical shapes. The plan is formed by two equal-sided triangles joined at their bases to make a diamond-shaped rhombus, which was then softened with curved lines (Fig. 295). The façade, with its walls rippling like a stage curtain, rises upward toward an oval dome. The inner surface of the dome is a geometrical triangle with its play of octagons and elongated hexagons that join to produce Greek crosses in the intervening spaces (Fig. 296). These shapes diminish in size toward the top to suggest greater height, though it is actually quite shallow. Partially concealed openings allow light to filter in and give the honeycomblike pattern a gleaming brightness. The façade (Fig. 294) is set into swaying motion by the alternating concave and convex walls and the flow of curved lines and forms, which allow a maximum play of light and shade over the irregular surface.

Painting and Sculpture

Of all the painters and sculptors active in post-Renaissance Rome, two tower above all the others—Caravaggio and Bernini. Taking his name from his

below: 296. Francesco Borromini. Interior of dome, San Carlo alle Quattro Fontane, Rome. c. 1638.

297. Caravaggio. *Calling of St. Matthew.* c. 1597–98. Oil on canvas, 11'1" × 11'5" (3.38 × 3.48 m). Contarelli Chapel, San Luigi dei Francesi, Rome.

native town, Caravaggio brought the northern Italian and Venetian tradition of free mannerism with him to Rome. The sculptor-architect-designer-painter Bernini, for his part, synthesized Renaissance, Michelangelesque, mannerist, and baroque elements and brought the baroque to its expressive climax in the Eternal City.

Restless and rebellious, Caravaggio was always at odds with society and his patrons, while Bernini, despite his passionate temperament, was nevertheless a polished courtier. "It is your good luck," Bernini was told by the newly elected Pope Urban VIII, "to see Maffeo Barberini pope; but we are even luckier that Cavaliere Bernini lives at the time of our pontificate." Caravaggio's life and career proved brief, solitary, and meteoric; Bernini's was long, social, and prodigiously productive. Both artists were destined to have far-reaching effects on future developments. Caravaggio with his bold chiaroscuro influenced later Italian and French baroque painters, as well as Rubens and Rembrandt. Bernini with his twisted columns and visionary illusionism had a major impact on baroque sculpture and architecture.

Caravaggio Caravaggio, who painted in Rome from about 1590 to 1606, scorned Renaissance correctness, dignity, and elegance and set out to depict religious subjects in a vivid, down-to-earth way. His *Calling of St. Matthew* (Fig. 297) shows the future Evangelist among a group at a public tavern. A significant darkness hovers over the table where tax money is being counted. As Jesus enters, a shaft of light illuminates the bearded face of St. Matthew and the faces of the young men in the center. As the light strikes each figure and object with varying degrees of intensity, it becomes the means by which Caravaggio penetrates the surface of events and reveals the inner spirit of the subjects he depicts. The *Calling of St. Matthew* was at first refused by the church for which it had been painted, because it showed the saint in a too-worldly situation, even though the story is told by the Evangelist himself.

In the *Conversion of St. Paul,* (Fig. 298) Caravaggio creates a blinding, lightninglike flash to highlight the saint's inner illumination. "And suddenly there shined round about him a light from heaven," reads the New Testament passage, "and he fell to earth, and heard a voice saying unto him, Saul, Saul, why persecutest thou me?" (Acts 9:4–5).

As observers behold St. Paul's prone body from an extremely foreshortened angle, with arms flung out as if to embrace the new light, they are caught up in the event and share the wonderment and concern of the attendant and the huge horse. One fascination of the picture is the way Caravaggio creates a tense vertical rhythm with the alternation of horse's shanks and human arms and legs. Manneristic freedom can be seen with the artist moving the head and shoulders of the groom over to the right. This keeps the design below undisturbed, but there is no natural way for the man's limbs to be joined to his trunk and shoulders. Pictorial construction for Caravaggio was the first consideration.

Caravaggio's efforts to create a truly popular religious art as seen through the eyes of the common people met with a mixed reception. Paradoxically, it was only the sophisticated few who grasped its originality and significance. Both the Roman priests and public preferred more conventional elegance and illusionism. It was the work of Pozzo and Bernini that this audience found more congenial to its taste.

Pozzo   Andrea Pozzo succeeded in capturing the new spirit in his extraordinary painting on the barrel-vaulted ceiling of the Church of Sant' Ignazio (Fig. 299), a sister church in Rome of Il Gesù (Fig. 293) and dedicated to the founder of the Jesuit order. Above the clerestory windows, the walls of the build-

left: 298. Caravaggio. *Conversion of St. Paul.* 1601-02. Oil on canvas, 7'6½" × 5'9" (2.3 × 1.75 m). Cerasi Chapel, Santa Maria del Popolo, Rome.

above: 299. Andrea Pozzo. *St. Ignatius in Glory.* c. 1691. Fresco, nave ceiling. Sant' Ignazio, Rome.

ing seem to soar upward so that the vaulting of the nave becomes that of heaven itself. In a series of remarkable foreshortenings, St. Ignatius, accompanied by a heavenly host, ascends in a winding spiral toward figures symbolizing the Trinity. Here all the lines converge, and beams of light radiate outward to illuminate the four corners of the world—personified by allegorical representations of Europe, Asia, Africa, and America—where missionary work of the Society of Jesus was carried on. Pozzo was also the author of a definitive book on perspective, in which he advised artists "to draw all points thereof to that true point, the Glory of God."

Bernini   In Gianlorenzo Bernini, the fiery and versatile architect, sculptor, and painter, the Roman Counter-Reformation baroque found its most representative and productive champion. Designer of the Piazza of St. Peter's that begins with the trapezoidal plaza in front of the basilica's façade and opens out into the mighty oval area framed by massive fourfold Doric colonnades (see Figs. 237, 255); sculptor of many of the basilica's chapels, notably the one in the apse containing the Chair of St. Peter; designer of such public monuments as the Fountain of Four Rivers in Piazza Navona (Fig. 300)—Bernini, even more than Michelangelo, is responsible for lifting the face of Rome and for giving the city the appearance it has today.

Of all Bernini's works, the Cornaro Chapel (Fig. 301), dedicated to the Spanish mystic St. Teresa, is most typical of this phase of the baroque. In the central sculptured group over the altar (Fig. 302), Bernini portrays the saint in a state of ecstasy, his source being Teresa's visionary writings. She describes the miraculous appearance of a bright angel holding a golden spear, which he has plunged into her heart, as follows:

above: **300.** Gianlorenzo Bernini. Fountain of Four Rivers, Piazza Navona, Rome. 1648–51.

below left: **301.** Anonymous. *Cornaro Chapel, Santa Maria della Vittoria, Rome.* c. 1644. Oil on canvas. Staatliches Museum, Schwerin, East Germany.

below: **302.** Gianlorenzo Bernini. *St. Teresa in Ecstasy.* 1645–52. Marble and gilt bronze, life-size. Cornaro Chapel, Santa Maria della Vittoria, Rome.

The dart wherewith He wounded me
Was all embarbed round with love
And thus my spirit came to be
One with its Maker, God above.

St. Teresa, as revealed by the fluctuating folds of her deep-cut drapery, seems to be rising and falling in sensuous rapture, and the angel (closely resembling Cupid with his dart) is about to pierce her heart. The polished white-marble group is framed by dark marble columns and set in a niche of many-colored marbles of brown, red, pink, green, and amber hues. Gleaming gilded bronze rays descend from above, and the whole is lighted magically by a concealed window glazed with yellow glass. On either side are groups in relief portraying members of the Cornaro family, donors of the chapel, who watch the miraculous proceedings as if from stage boxes at the theater.

The chapel begs the questions, "Is it architecture, sculpture, painting, stage design? Is it sculpture in the round, in relief?" The answer in each case must be "yes"—but combined not separated, in fusion not isolation. The sculpture group is surrounded by actual and illusionary architecture; the painted sky and the theatrical lighting form part of a single conception in which real and visionary elements blend into one, in which metal, marble, forms, colors, and light harmonize as a multimedia concert of the arts.

Spanish Counter-Reformation Art

The close alliance of Italy and Spain that had begun with the invasion of Charles V continued throughout the baroque period. Politically and economically the Spanish crown controlled all major Italian regions by viceroys and puppet regimes. Papal approval of the Jesuit order made the influence of its militant missionaries worldwide and brought sainthood to two of its Spanish founding members, Ignatius Loyola and Francis Xavier. And the words of two great Spaniards, St. Teresa of Avila and St. John of the Cross, perhaps most completely captured the Counter-Reformation spirit in literature and became the most widely read in the Roman Catholic world.

The personal tastes of that melancholy monarch Philip II, who succeeded his father Charles V, were austere to the point of severity. His worldly position and ambitions, however, made it necessary that he surround himself with sufficient magnificence to command awe and respect. To unify his kingdom, take local authority away from his feudal lords, and give himself all the power of an absolute monarch, Philip selected as his capital the then-obscure but centrally located town of Madrid. There, an enor-

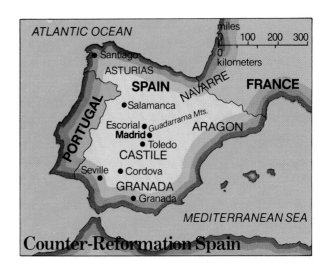

Counter-Reformation Spain

mous building program had to be undertaken to house the court and provide city palaces for the aristocracy (see map above).

With the riches of the Old World and the unlimited resources of the New at his command, Philip summoned the leading artists of Europe to help build and embellish his chosen capital, and his ambassadors were under instruction to buy any available masterpiece of painting and sculpture. While they remained in their native cities, Titian and other Italian artists continued to paint for Philip as they had for his father. But Domenicos Theotocopoulos, the Greek-born artist who had been trained in the Venetian mannerist style and had studied the work of Michelangelo and Raphael in Rome, settled in Spain, where he became known as the foreigner El Greco ("the Greek"). The Spanish composer Victoria, though he was fully established in Rome, dedicated a book of masses to Philip in the hope of receiving a court commission. Attracted by the glitter of Spanish gold, other artists from all parts of Europe, known and unknown, flocked to Madrid in search of fame and fortune. Thus, while Spain's power and prestige were to decline in the 17th century, the precedent set by Charles V and Philip II as patrons of the arts was continued by Philip III and Philip IV to round out a full century of brilliant artistic activity.

Architecture

The Escorial Bound by the terms of his father's will to build Charles V a tomb, bound by his own solemn oath to found a monastery dedicated to the Spanish martyr St. Lawrence, on whose day he gained his great military victory over the French, and bound also by his intense religious fervor and his consciousness of his royal position, Philip II envi-

303. Juan Bautista de Toledo and Juan de Herrera. Escorial Palace, near Madrid. 1553–84. Engraving after Herrera.

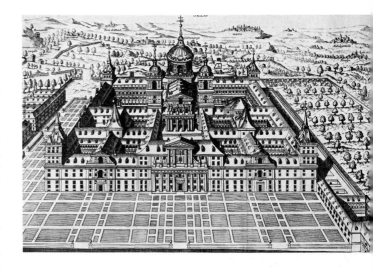

sioned a vast architectural project that would coordinate these different objectives and resolve some of his own inner conflicts. As the plan matured in the King's mind, this monument was to be at once a temple to God, a mausoleum for his ancestors and descendants, a national archive of arts and letters, a dwelling place for the monks of St. Jerome, a college and seminary, a place of pilgrimage with a lodging for strangers, a royal residence, and, in general, a symbol of the glory of the Spanish monarchy.

A site in the barren foothills of the Guadarrama Mountains about 30 miles (48 kilometers) from Madrid was chosen for the undertaking, which took its name from the nearby village of Escorial. The original plans were drawn up by Juan Bautista de Toledo, who had studied with Jacopo Sansovino and Palladio in Venice and worked on St. Peter's in Rome under the direction of Michelangelo. After his death, the work was completed by Juan Bautista's collaborator, Juan de Herrera.

According to Philip's instructions, the monument had to embody the ideals of "nobility without arrogance, majesty without ostentation." As it stands, the Escorial is a vast quadrangle of almost 500,000 square feet (46,500 square meters), which is subdivided into a symmetrical system of courts and cloisters (Fig. 303). The form symbolically refers to the gridiron on which St. Lawrence was roasted alive. The corner towers can be said to represent the legs of the iron grill, while the palace, which projects from the east end, forms its handle. Elsewhere in the building the grill is widely used as a decorative motif.

The Escorial strikes a note of gloomy grandeur and stark magnificence in keeping at once with the Spanish spirit as well as with the somber personality

of Philip II. Each side presents a long expanse of wall, entirely lacking in decoration, its monotony broken only by the endless rows of windows (Fig. 304). The principal entrance (Fig. 303), which is found on the west front, is carried out in the strict Doric order with only the royal coat of arms and a colossal statue of St. Lawrence holding his gridiron to relieve the general austerity. The portal leads into the Patio of the Kings, which takes its name from the statues of David, Solomon, and the other kings of Israel over the entrance to the imposing church which occupies the central place in the design.

Much of the Escorial's area is devoted to the monastery and seminary of the Order of St. Jerome. The heart of this section is the handsomely designed, spacious, double-decked cloister known as the Court of the Evangelists (Fig. 305). The walk below is again in the Doric order with its simple frieze punctuated by the rhythmical triglyphs. Still more space for monastic meditations is provided by the Ionic

304. Escorial Palace, side view.

305. Juan de Herrera.
Court of Evangelists, Escorial Palace. 1563–84.
Length 210′ (64.01 m), width 207′ (63.09 m).

gallery, which, in turn, is topped by a balustrade in the Palladian manner. In the center of the cloister is a small structure of richly colored marble that functions as an echo of the great dome of the church which soars above it. Statues by Monegro of each of the four Evangelists look outward from their niches toward their respective pools, watered from spouts in the forms of the symbolic evangelical beasts.

In the palace section of the Escorial are the reception halls, the impressive galleries, and the state dining rooms that go with the grandeur of the proud Spanish monarchy. The only departure from the air of splendor is the monastic simplicity of Philip's own apartment. Elsewhere there are the quarters of the courtiers and the secretaries of state, lodgings for ambassadors, and apartments for members of the royal family. To awe friends and warn foes, pictures

306. Juan Gomez de Mora.
Façade, La Clérica (left). 1617. Casa de las Conchas ("House of Shells"), right. 1514. Salamanca.

307. José de Churriguera.
Altarpiece, San Esteban, Salamanca. 1693.

of Spain's sea and land victories line the walls of the ambassadorial waiting rooms. Other halls are hung with rich Flemish tapestries depicting biblical, mythological, and literary subjects. The picture galleries contained a vast number of the paintings that were purchased so liberally over the centuries by the Spanish kings.

The Escorial, by reaching out to bring all the functions of an absolute monarch within a single structure, is baroque in the grandeur of its conception. However, the restraint of Philip's taste, as well as the discipline of his architects, kept the urge to decorate well within academic bounds. Exercising the privilege of an absolute monarch, Philip insisted on the right to pass on the suitability and style of every public building that was undertaken during his reign. Herrera, as the court architect, was commissioned to inspect all such plans and, as a consequence, became an artistic dictator who enforced the severe tastes of his royal master on the nation.

Plateresque and Churrigueresque Styles   Not until after Philip's death did Spain have the freedom to develop the richly elaborated style that is now such a prominent feature of its large cities. Indeed, some of the florid baroque's emotional enthusiasm and excesses came as a direct reaction to the formal severity of Philip's time. Daring designs, fantastic forms, curved lines, the spiral twist of corkscrew columns replaced the austere façades and classical orders enforced by Herrera.

Architectural developments at Salamanca and Madrid will dramatize the situation. The Casa de las Conchas (Fig. 306, right), or "House of the Shells," is a Renaissance structure built in 1514, well before Philip's time. It nevertheless shows the tendency toward applied decoration that was popularly known as the *plateresque* style, a name derived from the Spanish word *platero,* or "silversmith."

Across the street is the church of the Jesuit college of La Clérica (Fig. 306, left), which was begun after the period of Philip and Herrera. The lower part dates from the early 17th century and was designed by Juan Gomez de Mora. Even though it still adheres nominally to the classical orders, the decorative urge is seen clearly in the attached Composite columns and in the baroque frieze above them, as well as in many of the other details. The towers and gable belong to the latter part of the 17th century and were executed by Churriguera, whose name is associated with the more ornate aspects of Spanish baroque, the *Churrigueresque* style.

Churriguera's ornate altarpiece for the Church of San Esteban is an architectural-sculptural-pictorial extravaganza (Fig. 307). More than 90 feet (27.4 meters) high, it combines the Composite order (see p. 77, Fig. 86) with gilded and garlanded twisted columns, set at various depths, that wriggle and writhe upward in rhythmic spirals.

Painting

El Greco   While the Escorial was still under construction, Philip II commissioned El Greco to paint an altarpiece for the Chapel of St. Maurice. The subject of El Greco's early masterpiece, the *Martyrdom of St. Maurice and Theban Legion* (Fig. 308), is typical of the Counter-Reformation in that it has to do with the dilemma of the individual who is caught between conflicting loyalties. St. Maurice, the figure in the right foreground, was the commander of the Theban Legion, a unit of Christians serving in the Roman imperial army. An order has just arrived commanding all members of the unit to acknowledge the traditional Roman deities—Jupiter, Juno, and Minerva—or be put to death. In the expressive gestures of their hands, St. Maurice and his staff officers reveal their positions. Christ, it is true, has approved by his own

308. El Greco. *Martyrdom of St. Maurice and Theban Legion.* 1581–84. Oil on canvas, 14'6" × 9'10" (4.42 × 3 m). Escorial Palace.

309. El Greco. *Assumption of the Virgin.*
c. 1577. Oil on canvas,
13′2″ × 7′6″ (4.01 × 2.29 m).
Art Institute of Chicago.

are drawn into the center of a Dantesque spiritual whirlwind that bears them aloft. The eye is led upward by the constantly increasing light and the transition of color from the darker hues below to the vaporous pink and white clouds above. There a visionary vista in the heavens is beheld, where some of the angelic figures hover and hold crowns for those who suffer and die below, while others produce the sounds of celestial harmony.

Despite the grimness of the subject, the light, transparent palette that El Greco employs gives the work an almost festive air, with the rose-colored banners, steel blue and lemon yellow costumes set against a background of silvery gray. The originality of the work, with its daring color dissonances and the lavish use of costly ultramarine blue, lost for El Greco the favor of King Philip, whose tastes ran to the more conservative Italian style. El Greco made only one other attempt to interest the royal patron: a study for a picture that the artist later called the *Dream of Philip II.* The commission for its execution, however, never came.

If the doors to the Escorial were closed, the gates to Toledo, the seat of the archbishop primate, always remained open to El Greco. His reputation there had been securely established by the series of paintings he had done for the Church of San Domingo el Antiguo. Most renowned of these was the *Assumption of the Virgin* for the high altar (Fig. 309).

El Greco's model for the *Assumption* was the picture Titian had painted on the same subject some sixty years earlier (see Fig. 273). El Greco's version, however, reveals the baroque preference for open space, while Titian contains all action within his picture. By dividing his composition into three planes, Titian starts a vertical ascending motion in the lower two but arrests it by the descending figure of God above. By combining the acute receding diagonal lines of the apostles, El Greco in his *Assumption* forms a conelike base from which the Madonna soars aloft in a spiraling movement that leads the eye upward out of the picture into the open space above.

Also for Toledo, El Greco painted his masterpiece, the *Burial of Count Orgaz* (Fig. 310), for his own parish church of San Tomé. The count, who rebuilt and endowed the church, was legendarily honored in 1323 by the miraculous appearance of St. Stephen and St. Augustine, who gently lower him into his tomb which is just below the picture. The vivid earthly and visionary heavenly spheres are separated by the flickering torches and swirling draperies as

example the rendering unto Caesar the material things that are Caesar's, but the worship of false idols is another matter. The line is thus clearly drawn, and a choice has to be made between duty to the state and duty to the Church, between the earthly city and the city of God. St. Maurice points upward, indicating his decision.

El Greco's spiral composition is well adapted to convey the tension between the material and spiritual realms, the natural and supernatural, the earthly and heavenly. It can be sensed in the twitching muscles, flamelike fingers, taut faces, and swirling upward motion of the composition itself. In snakelike fashion, it winds around to the left middle ground where St. Maurice is seen again, this time giving comfort to the men as they await their turn for beheading. The tempo is increased toward the background where the nude figures of the soldiers seem already to have parted company with bodiliness and

310. El Greco.
Burial of Count Orgaz.
1586. Oil on canvas,
16′ × 11′10″ (4.88 × 3.61 m).
San Tomé, Toledo, Spain.

the soul of the Count is borne heavenward on angelic wings to be received by the radiant figure of Christ.

The row of mourners includes portraits of the Toledo clergy and gentry, among them a self-portrait of the artist with his hand raised directly above the head of St. Stephen. A note of subtle humor is struck in the portrait of El Greco's eight-year-old son Jorge Manuel as the attendant in the lower left. The boy points to the encircled white-and-gold rose embroidered on St. Stephen's vestment—the circle being the symbol of immortality, the rose of love. On his son's pocket handkerchief El Greco signed in Greek: "Domenicos Theotocopoulos made me, 1578." However, the date is not that of the picture but of his son's birth.

The driving out of the money changers from the temple is the only incident in the Gospels where Christ assumes an attitude of righteous anger and the only time when He resorted to physical action

and bodily punishment. Consequently, the subject had been rare in Christian iconography. It was revived during the Counter-Reformation when the Roman Catholic Church was undergoing just such a purge. El Greco painted no less than six versions of this theme.

In *Expulsion from the Temple* (Fig. 311) Christ appears in the role of the refining fire as prophesied by Isaiah, and His mood of fiery anger is reflected in El Greco's clashing colors of crimson red, pink, orange, and greenish yellow. While Christ's gesture indicates violence, His face is serene in the knowledge that what He does is for the good of those whom He punishes. The atmosphere recalls that of a Last Judgment with the figure of Christ separating the two groups. The side toward which His lash is directed is full of turbulence and confusion as the traders cringe under the accusing eye, yet try to save their wares. On the other side, all is calm as the

right: **311.** El Greco. *Expulsion from the Temple.* c. 1572–74. Oil on canvas, 4'8" × 4'11" (1.42 × 1.5 m). Minneapolis Institute of Arts (Dunwoody Fund).

below: **312.** Diego Velázquez. *Water Carrier of Seville.* c. 1619–21. Oil on canvas, 41½ × 31½" (105 × 80 cm). Wellington Museum, London (Crown Copyright reserved).

disciples ponder the meaning of the event. The four heads in the lower right acknowledge El Greco's debt to his predecessors Titian, Michelangelo, Giulio Clovio, and Raphael, whom he greatly admired.

Velázquez   Spain's other great baroque master, Diego Velázquez, had spent his early years in his native Seville painting genre pictures such as the well-known *Water Carrier of Seville* (Fig. 312). Less than a decade after El Greco's death, the new monarch Philip IV appointed Velázquez his court painter. Velázquez' art, consequently, comes within the category of the aristocratic baroque, which is treated in the next chapter, but as a complete contrast to El Greco and as an equally great contribution to the high Spanish period, it is more appropriately discussed here.

While El Greco concerned himself almost exclusively with religious subjects, Velázquez, with few exceptions, painted scenes of courtly life. In contrast to El Greco's personal involvement in his pictorial content, Velázquez sees his world with cool detachment and an objective eye. His work is admirably summed up in his masterpiece *Las Meninas,* or the *Maids of Honor* (Fig. 313). With it, the painter combines the formality of a royal group portrait with the informality of a more casual genre scene in his studio. In the picture attention is about evenly distributed among the various groups. In the foreground, the Infanta Margarita, dressed in a gown of white

313. Diego Velázquez. *Las Meninas (Maids of Honor).* 1656. Oil on canvas, 10'5¼" × 9'¾" (3.18 × 2.76 m). Prado, Madrid.

satin, is standing in the center. On the left, a maid of honor is offering her a drink from a red cup on a gold tray. At the right is a group made up of a second maid of honor and two of the court dwarfs, one of whom is poking the sleepy dog with his foot.

In the middle ground, on the left, is Velázquez himself wearing the cross of the Order of Santiago, which was conferred on him by his friend and patron, the King. He stands before a canvas which, by reason of its large dimensions, seems to be *Las Meninas* itself. He is looking at King Philip IV and Queen Mariana, whose faces are reflected in the mirror at the back of the room. As a balance for his own figure, Velázquez paints the conversing lady-in-waiting and courtier in the right middle ground. In the rear of the room, a court attendant stands in the open doorway pulling back a curtain, possibly to adjust the light.

Velázquez is a virtuoso in the handling of space and light. With the utmost precision, he has organized the picture into a series of receding planes, and by so doing, he gives the figures their spatial relationships. The first plane is in front of the picture itself where the King and Queen and, by inference, the observer are standing. Next comes that in which the principal group stands in the light of the window at the right, which again is outside the picture but which provides the brilliant illumination that falls on the blond hair of the princess. The light here is balanced by that from the door at the rear, which defines the plane in the background. In between is the intermediate plane with the figures of Velázquez and the atttendants, who are shown in more subdued light. Five receding planes can thus be distinguished. Otherwise the space is broken up geometrically into a pattern of rectangles, such as the floor, ceiling, the easel, the pictures hanging on the wall, the mirror, and the door at the back.

In such a precise analytical study of space and light, which lacks both the spiritual mysticism of El Greco and the worldly grandeur of the Venetian painters, the baroque qualities are not immediately apparent. Velázquez, however, is a master of external rather than internal vision, and therefore his baroque qualities are found in such things as the intricate play of light and shadow, the complex spatial arrangements, the fact that much lies outside the picture space itself, and the subtle relationships of the subjects to each other. Proof of the latter is the fact that Velázquez experts still cannot agree on what is actually going on. Is Velázquez painting the King and Queen, and have the Infanta and her ladies wandered in to look around? Or is Velázquez looking into a mirror as he paints the Infanta, and have her parents dropped in to watch the proceedings?

Just as Spanish architecture showed a reaction when the restraints of the earlier period were lifted, Spanish painting moved away from the austerity and intensity of the previous century. No painter could sustain the spiritual insight and emotional power of El Greco. The relaxation into sentimentality is clearly seen in Murillo's *Immaculate Conception* (Fig. 314). The subject was in particular favor with the Spanish church, and Murillo and his workshop are known to have turned out some twenty versions of it. According to Roman Catholic belief, Mary was conceived miraculously without original sin. Artistically she is represented as in St. John's vision: "And there appeared a great wonder in heaven; a woman clothed with the sun, and the moon under her feet, and upon her head a crown of twelve stars" (Rev. 12:1). In this instance she is borne aloft by cherubs holding the lily, rose, olive branch, and palm leaf—symbols of purity, love, peace, and martyrdom respectively.

Music

The Roman urge for reform predisposed Church music to look more to the past than the future, to traditional rather than experimental forms. "The Antiphonals, Graduals, and Psalters have been filled to overflowing with barbarisms, obscurities, contrarieties, and superfluities as the result of clumsiness or negligence or even wickedness of the composers, scribes, and printers," reads the papal brief authorizing Giovanni da Palestrina to undertake the reform of Church music along lines laid down by the Council of Trent. An ardent advocate of the Flemish contrapuntal style of Josquin des Prez and Heinrich Isaac, Palestrina, together with his great contemporaries Orlando di Lasso and Tomás Luis de Victoria, brought that art to its final fruition.

Palestrina's prayers in song achieved a fluidity and transparency of texture, a balance of melody and harmony, a spiritual and organic unity worthy of the closing years of the *ars perfecta,* or "perfect art." The music of his younger colleague Victoria, however, has a darker mood, a brooding emotional fervor, and a deeper concern with the dramatic meaning of his texts. After serving thirty years as a chaplain, singer, and composer in the German College in Rome, an institution founded by his fellow Spaniard Ignatius Loyola, Victoria returned to his native country as choirmaster in court circles.

The music at the court of Philip II, like the architecture, painting, and sculpture, was religiously oriented, and the records of the period, as well as the design of the church at the Escorial, testify to the important place given the tonal art there. The choir at the Escorial was established even before the whole building was completed and in 1586 numbered in its ranks 150 monks. The choir section of the church is

314. Bartolomé Murillo. *Immaculate Conception.* c. 1666–70. Oil on canvas, 6'9" × 4'8⅝" (2.06 × 1.44 m). Prado, Madrid.

O vos omnes (4-part motet)   Tomás Luis de Victoria

Si est do-lor do - lor si - mi-lis

divided into two parts, since Philip's musical preferences were for the Venetian double-choral style he had heard in his youth. Besides the two organs in the choir, there are two others on either side of the nave, both large double-manual concert instruments of Flemish manufacture, 50 feet (15.2 meters) wide and 40 feet (12.2 meters) high. The same maker also built three portable organs for processions, which were placed in the galleries, thus making it possible on high feast days to hear seven organs pealing forth.

Victoria's settings of the *Offices for Holy Week* have become an established tradition for performance in the Sistine Chapel. One of these is the four-part motet *O vos omnes,* the text of which comes from Jeremiah and the mood of which is one of lamentation. The passage above shows the characteristic grieving motif in the descending tenor voice in measure 4, as well as the dissonance created by the dip of the minor second by the same voice in measure 5, to intensify the word *dolor,* or "sorrow."

Victoria never wrote a single note of secular music. As he stated in one of his dedications, he was led by some inner impulse to devote himself solely to church music. In his motets and masses, he even avoided the secular *cantus firmus* themes that were customarily employed by his contemporaries. Instead, he chose his motifs and melodies from his own religious works or from the traditional plainsong. In later compositions after his return to Spain, Victoria's work took on an even greater passion and intensity. With its religious ardor and devotional spirit, his music rises in its way to the same heights of mystical grandeur as the writings of St. Teresa of Avila, the architecture of Herrera, and the pictures of El Greco.

Ideas: Militant Mysticism

The Counter-Reformation was accompanied by a vigorous reassertion of the mystical world view. In keeping with the spirit of the times, however, it was a practical mysticism of this world as well as the next, a realistic blending of the active as well as contemplative life, a religious experience not limited to future saints but broadened to include all those faithful to the Church as the mystical body of Christ.

The new mysticism was socially oriented to enlist laity as well as clergy, those active in worldly affairs

as well as those behind convent walls. It was a rekindling of the fires of faith at a time when the foundations of faith were threatened by new scientific discoveries; a call to arms for all those willing to fight for their convictions in a war to the finish against doctrines the Roman Catholic Church considered to be heresy; a military mysticism of a Church militant on the march.

The enemy was made up of the various Protestant movements at home; the pagan religions of Africa, Asia, and the Americas abroad; the materialistic world view that went with growing nationalism and colonial expansion; and the forces of rationalism unleashed by free scientific inquiry.

The Counter-Reformation was just as much a reassertion of spiritual and moral values in the face of growing scientific materialism as it was an anti-Protestant movement. The Church plainly saw that if the mechanical image of the world as "matter in motion" were generally accepted, the belief in miracles would be undermined, the notion of divine intervention in worldly affairs would be destroyed, and the sense of mystery would be drained out of the cosmos.

The new psychology was not so much concerned with abstract theological notions as with concrete religious experience through vivid imagery. The mysticism of St. Teresa and St. John of the Cross differed from medieval mysticism in its rational control and written documentation of each stage of the soul's ascent from the depths of temptation and sin to the ecstasy of union with the divine.

St. Ignatius and the Jesuits

The most typical expression of the Church militant, however, was the Society of Jesus, founded by that soldier and man of action St. Ignatius Loyola. His Jesuits helped adapt Church doctrine to modern conditions, faced the moral and political realities of the century, and took an active part in education, public affairs, as well as missionary work. Under the director general, a Jesuit enlisted as a "warrior of God under the banner of the Cross" and stood ready to go for the "propagation of the faith to the Turks or other infidels even in India or to heretics, schismatics or some of the faithful." The whole world, for missionary purposes, was divided into Jesuit provinces, and the priestly army of occupation followed in the wake of the navigators and colonizers.

The spiritual side of the Jesuit military organization is reflected in St. Ignatius' *Spiritual Exercises,* a precise, disciplined exploration of the mysteries of faith through the medium of the senses. As part of the Jesuit system of education, St. Ignatius worked out a four-week series of meditations leading to a

315. Mexico City Cathedral. 1656–71.

cleansing and purifying of the soul. All faculties are brought into play so that the experience becomes a vividly personal one.

Sin is the subject of the first week, and its consequences are felt through each of the senses in turn. In the "Torment of Sight," the student visualizes the terrible words engraved on the gates of Hell—*Ever, Never*—and sees the flames spring up around. In the "Torment of Sound," the sinner listens to the groans of millions of the damned, the howls of demons, the crackle of flames that devour the victims. With the "Torment of Smell," he or she is reminded that the bodies of the doomed retain in Hell the corruption of the grave. Their "stink shall come up out of their carcases," prophesied Isaiah (Isa. 34:3). For the "Torment of Taste," the condemned shall suffer hunger like dogs; "they shall eat every man the flesh of his own arm" (Isa. 9:20), and their wine shall be the "poison of dragons, and the cruel venom of asps" (Deut. 32:33). And in the "Torment of Touch," the damned will be enveloped in flames that boil the blood in the veins and the marrow in the bones but do not consume the victim. Both flames and flesh are forever renewed so that pain is eternal.

In the final phases, the progress leads up to the suffering, resurrection, and the ascension of Christ, and it closes with the contemplation of heavenly bliss. By proclaiming that human beings could influence their own spiritual destiny, Jesuit optimism held a ready appeal for people of action.

Mysticism and the Arts

Such a strong accent on sense experience as the means to excite religious feeling was bound to find expression in the arts. Through architectural, sculptural, pictorial, literary, and musical illusions, miracles and transcendental ideas could be made to seem real to the senses, and the mystical world view could be reasserted through aesthetic imagery. The increasing complexity of life, the rapid growth of new knowledge, the deepening of psychological insights—all shaped the course of baroque art. As religious, social, and economic pressures mounted, people were increasingly inclined to resolve their insecurities by turning to the cults of visionary saints or to the power of the absolute state. Artists were enthusiastically enlisted to enhance the power and glory of both Church and state. Counter-Reformation churches were spacious, light, and cheerful; and visual artists, dramatists, and composers joined forces to make them like theaters where a concert of the arts played a prelude to future heavenly bliss.

Renaissance clarity of definition and the division of space into clearly understood patterns gave way to an intricate baroque geometry that took fluidity of movement into account. Neat Renaissance lines, circles, triangles, and rectangles became the intertwining spirals, curves, ovals, elongated diamond shapes, rhombuses, and irregular polygons of the baroque. With Borromini, horizontal and vertical surfaces were set into waves of rippling rhythms; balance and symmetry yielded to restless, unsettled movement; walls were molded sculpturally, surfaces were treated with a rich play of color, light, and shadow. Pictures escaped from their vertical walls and settled upon spherical triangular pendentives and spandrels, concave and convex moldings, and the inner surfaces of ceilings, vaults, and domes.

With Pozzo's paintings, solid walls, vaulted ceilings, and domes dissolved into cloudy, illusionistic vistas of the great beyond. With Bernini, marble saints and angels floated freely in space. With El Greco, bodily being almost ceased to exist, and his figures are more spirit than flesh, his landscape backgrounds more heavenly than earthly. St. Teresa recorded and published her ecstatic visions in sparkling Spanish prose and poetry so that a wide public could experience them by proxy. Palestrina and Victoria illuminated the hymns of the liturgical year with the clarity of their counterpoint, and their melodies made them glow with new meaning.

By adopting the baroque style as their own and helping shape the artistic vocabulary of the time, the Jesuits not only brought baroque art down from the exclusive aristocratic level but carried the new ideas with them wherever they went, thus broadening the baroque into an international style. Counter-Reformation baroque churches are found as far afield as Mexico (Fig. 315), South America, and the Philippines. The extraordinary vigor of the Church militant thus succeeded in tapping new spiritual sources and vitalizing Roman Catholicism to such an extent that it re-emerged as a popular religious movement.

14
The Aristocratic Baroque Style

France in the Time of Louis XIV

Everything about Louis XIV suggested grandeur. His concept of kingship assured him the title *le grand roi,* or "great king," his code of etiquette created the grand manner and made him in every sense the *grand seigneur,* or "great gentleman," and his reign gave his century the name *le grand siècle,* or "great century." At the time of his portrait by Hyacinthe Rigaud in 1701 (Fig. 316), Louis had been king in name for well over half a century and a king in fact for a full forty of those years. Dressed in his ermine-lined coronation robes, with the collar of the Grand Master of the Order of the Holy Spirit draped about his regal neck, Louis XIV might actually be uttering the words for which he was so famous: *L'Etat c'est moi*—"I am the state." Since he was in fact the personification of France, his portrait, appropriately, was that of an institution; his figure was as much a pillar holding up the state as is the column that supports the building in the background. Pompous and pretentious though the portrait may be, it formed part of the illusionism of a period that strove to make such abstractions as the divine right of kings, absolutism, and the politically centralized state seem real to the senses.

The success of this system of centralization is seen in the list of positive accomplishments of Louis XIV's reign. In the course of his kingship the feudal power of the provincial nobles was broken, the Church became a part of the state instead of the state a part of the Church, Paris became the intellectual and artistic capital of the world, and France attained the dominant position among European nations. For

316. Hyacinthe Rigaud. *Louis XIV.* 1701. Oil on canvas, 9'1½" × 6'2⅝" (2.78 × 1.9 m). Louvre, Paris.

CHRONOLOGY
17th-Century France

GENERAL EVENTS	
1598–1610	Henry IV, king of France
1610–1643	Louis XIII, king of France with his mother Maria de' Medici (1573–1642) as regent during his minority
1615–1624	Luxembourg Palace built for Queen Mother by Salomon de Brosse
1618–1648	Thirty Years' War. Spain and Austria defeated, France became dominant European nation
1621	Rubens commissioned to paint murals in Luxembourg Palace
1624–1642	Cardinal Richelieu (1585–1642), prime minister
1635	French Academy of Language and Literature established
1636	Mersenne's *Treatise on Universal Harmony* published
1640	Poussin returned from Rome to decorate the Louvre Palace
1643–1661	Cardinal Mazarin (1602–61), prime minister
1643–1715	Louis XIV, king of France; ruled without prime minister from 1661

1648	Royal Academy of Painting and Sculpture founded
1661–1688	Versailles Palace built by Le Vau and Mansart; chapel added 1699–1708
1665–1683	Colbert (1619–83), minister of finance
1665	Bernini came to Paris to rebuild the Louvre Palace. French Academy in Rome established
1666	Academy of Sciences established
1667–1674	East façade of the Louvre Palace built by Perrault
1669	Royal Academy of Music (Paris Opera) established under Lully
1671	Academy of Architecture established
1674	*Alceste,* lyrical tragedy by Quinault and Lully, performed at Versailles. Boileau's *Art of Poetry* published
1683	Government and ministries of France installed at Versailles

ARCHITECTS	
1552–1626	Salomon de Brosse
1598–1680	Gianlorenzo Bernini
1612–1670	Louis Le Vau
1613–1688	Claude Perrault
1613–1700	André Le Nôtre
1646–1708	J. Hardouin-Mansart

PAINTERS	
1577–1640	Peter Paul Rubens
1594–1665	Nicolas Poussin
1600–1682	Claude Lorrain (Claude Gellée)
1619–1690	Charles Lebrun
1659–1743	Hyacinthe Rigaud

WRITERS AND PHILOSOPHERS	
1596–1650	René Descartes
1606–1684	Pierre Corneille
1621–1695	Jean de La Fontaine
1622–1673	Molière (J. B. Poquelin)
1623–1662	Blaise Pascal
1635–1688	Philippe Quinault
1636–1711	Nicolas Boileau
1639–1699	Jean Racine

SCULPTORS	
1598–1680	Gianlorenzo Bernini
1622–1694	Pierre Puget
1628–1715	François Girardon
1640–1720	Antoine Coysevox

MUSICIANS	
1602–1676	Francesco Cavalli, Venetian opera composer
c.1602–1672	Jacques de Chambonniéres, organist and clavecinist
1632–1687	Jean Baptiste Lully
1668–1733	François Couperin le Grand, clavecinist
1683–1764	Jean Philippe Rameau

the arts, the alliance with absolutism meant that they were of value as instruments of propaganda, as factors in the assertion of national power and prestige, and as the means of glorifying the state, impressing visiting dignitaries, and stimulating export trade. All this led, of course, to the concept of art as an aid to the cult of majesty and as the creator of the myth that by divine right the king could do no wrong.

With the King as principal patron, art inevitably became a department of the government, and Louis was surrounded with a system of cultural satellites each of whom was supreme in a specific field. The foundation of the Academy of Language and Literature in 1635, the Royal Academy of Painting and Sculpture in 1648, and the others which followed made it possible for Boileau to dominate the field of letters, Lebrun the visual arts, and Lully music.

Absolutism also meant standardization, since no artist could receive commissions or employment except through official channels. Louis, however, knew what he was about, and in an address to the Academy he once remarked: "Gentlemen, I entrust to you the most precious thing on earth, my fame." Consequently, he defended his writers and artists, supported them generously, and above all exercised that most noble trait any patron can possess—good taste.

The outward and visible sign of this absolutism was to be seen in the dramatization of the personal

317. Claude Perrault. East façade, Louvre, Paris. 1667–70. Length 570′ (173.74 m), height 90′ (27.43 m).

and social life of this *Roi Soleil,* or "Sun King." The adoption of the sun as his symbol was natural enough, and such motifs as the sunburst were widely used in the decor of his palaces. As patron of the arts, Louis could identify himself freely with Apollo, the sun god, who was also the Olympian protector of the Muses. In the morning, when it was time for the Sun King to rise and shine, the *lever du roi* was as dazzling in its way as a second sunrise. This special dawn was accompanied by a cloud of attendants who flocked into the royal bedchamber precisely at 8 A.M. in order to hand the King the various parts of his royal apparel. A similarly colorful ceremony accompanied the *coucher du roi,* when the Sun King in a golden glow of candlelight finally set at 10 P.M.

Louis' life was one continuous pageant in which each hour had its appropriate activity, costume, cast, and audience. Less frequent events, such as a christening, a wedding, or a coronation, had their special ceremonies. Even the royal births called for an audience so as to assure the country of the legitimacy of any future sovereign. In the present day of dull cabinet officers and drab parliamentary bodies, it is difficult to imagine the overwhelming effect of the formal pomp and circumstance surrounding an absolute monarch's court. If his peers and subjects beheld a sufficiently majestic spectacle, a ruler apparently could get away with anything.

Throughout a reign of 72 years, Louis XIV played the leading role in this constant court drama with all the effortless technique and perfect self-assurance of an accomplished actor. Such a great actor needed, of course, a great audience; and such a dramatic spectacle demanded an appropriate stage setting. Architects therefore were called upon to plan the endless series of connecting salons as impressive backdrops for the triumphal entries. Landscape designers were summoned to fashion the grand avenues for the open-air processions. Painters were commissioned to decorate the ceilings with pink clouds and classical

deities so that the monarch could descend the long flights of stairs as if from the Olympian skies. Musicians, too, were brought in to sound the ruffles and flourishes that accompanied the grand entrances.

It was thus no accident that the Louvre and Versailles palaces resembled vast theaters, that the paintings and tapestries of Lebrun seemed like curtains and backdrops, and that Bernini's, Puget's, and Coysevox's sculptural adornments took on the aspect of stage props. Nor was it by chance that the most important literary expression should be the tragedies of Racine and the comedies of Molière, and that the characteristic musical forms should be Lully's court ballets and operas.

Architecture

Louvre Palace

In 1665, at the insistence of his minister Colbert, Louis XIV requested the pope to permit his principal architect Gianlorenzo Bernini to come to Paris to supervise the rebuilding of the Louvre Palace. When he arrived on French soil, Bernini was received with all the honor due him as the ranking artist of his day. The design he made for the Louvre was radical in many ways. It would have required the replacement of the existing parts of the building by a grandiose baroque city palace of the Italian type. Colbert admitted that Bernini's palace was truly grand in style, but it left the King housed no better than before.

After a round of festivities, Bernini returned to Rome. His plan was scrapped, and a French architect, Claude Perrault, was appointed to finish the job. This little episode proved to be a turning point in cultural history. It marked the weakening of Italian artistic influence in France. It also indicated that Louis XIV had plans of his own.

Perrault's façade (Fig. 317) incorporated some parts of Bernini's project, such as the flat roof con-

left: **318.** Versailles Palace,
aerial view. 1661–88.
Width of palace 1935′
(589.79 m).

below left: **319.** Louis le Vau
and Jules Hardouin-Mansart.
Garden façade,
Versailles Palace. 1669–85.

cealed behind a Palladian balustrade and the long straight front with the wings extending toward the side instead of projecting forward to enclose a court in the traditional French manner. Perrault's own contributions can be seen in the solid ground floor, which is relieved only by the series of windows. This story functions as a platform for the classically proportioned Corinthian colonnade, with its rhythmic row of paired columns marching majestically across the broad expanse of the façade. The space between the colonnade and the wall of the building allows for the rich play of light and shadow that was so much a part of the baroque ideal. The frieze of garlands adds an ornate touch, while the central pediment as well as the classical orders of the columns and pilasters act as a restraining influence.

320. Jules Hardouin-Mansart
and Charles Lebrun.
Hall of Mirrors,
Versailles Palace. Begun 1676.
Length 240′ (73.15 m),
width 34′ (10.36 m),
height 43′ (13.11 m).

280   The Baroque Period

Versailles Palace

Even before Bernini came to Paris and long before the Louvre was completed, Louis XIV had conceived the idea of a royal residence outside Paris where he could escape from the restrictions of the city, take nature into partnership, and design a new way of life. Colbert, who felt that a king's place was in his capital, advised against it, and Louis allowed the Louvre to be completed as a gesture to Paris. But his real capital was destined to be Versailles. This project was sufficiently awesome to serve as a symbol of the supremacy of the young absolute monarch. With such a center he could assert his power over rival nations, the landed aristocracy of his own country, the parliament, the provincial governments, the town councils, and the middle-class merchants. Away from Paris there would be a minimum of distraction and a maximum of concentration on his own person. In a wooded site almost half the size of Paris, which belonged entirely to the crown, everything could be planned from the beginning, and a completely new manner of living could be organized.

The grand axis, or main line of direction, of the Versailles Palace starts with the Avenue de Paris (Fig. 318, top right), continues through the center of the palace building itself, and runs along the grand canal toward the horizon, where it trails off into infinity. As the avenue enters the palace grounds, the barracks for the honor guard, coach houses, stables, kennels, and orangeries are found on either side. The latter building caused an ambassador from a foreign country to remark that Louis XIV must indeed be the most magnificent of beings since he had a palace for his orange trees more beautiful than the residences of other monarchs.

The wide avenue narrows progressively with the parade grounds toward the marble court of honor (see Fig. 331), above which is found the heart of the plan—the state bedroom of Louis XIV. The whole grand design is so logical, so symmetrical, that it becomes a study in absolute space composition. It makes Versailles an all-embracing universal structure which incorporates a vast segment of external as well as internal space. No one building or any part of it is a law unto itself, and together they are inconceivable without their natural environment. The gardens, parks, avenues, and radiating pathways are just as much an essential part of the whole as the halls, salons, and corridors of the palace itself.

Jules Hardouin-Mansart was the architect of the two wings that extend the main building to a width

of over a quarter of a mile (about half a kilometer) (Fig. 318). His design is noteworthy for the horizontal accent attained by the uniform level of the roof line, broken only by the roof of the chapel, which was added in the early 18th century. The simplicity and elegance of these long, straight lines, in contrast to the irregular profile of a medieval building, proclaim the new feeling for space. From every room vistas of the garden are a part of the interior design and tell of a new awareness of nature. A detail of the garden façade (Fig. 319) reveals how freely Mansart treated the classical orders, and how the levels become increasingly ornate from the podiumlike base below to the attic and balustrade with its file of silhouetted statuary. As a whole the building is a commanding example of baroque luxuriance and grandeur modified by Palladian discretion and restraint.

Some of the interior rooms have been preserved or restored in the style of Louis XIV. The grandest room of the palace is the famous Hall of Mirrors stretching across the main axis of the building and looking out toward the spacious gardens (Fig. 320). Designed by Mansart and decorated by Lebrun, it was the scene of the most important state ceremonies and a kind of glorification of the absolute monarchy. Corinthian pilasters of green marble support the ornate vault that is covered with paintings by Lebrun and inscriptions by Boileau and Racine—all to the greater glorification of the Sun King.

The gardens, which were laid out by André Le Nôtre, are not just a frame for the buildings but are part of the whole spatial design (Fig. 321). Their

321. André Le Nôtre.
Plan of Gardens of Versailles. 1662–88.

formality and geometrical organization symbolized human dominance over nature, but with the idea of embracing nature rather than keeping it at arm's length. The square pools across the garden side, so liberally populated with goldfish and swans, reflect the contours of the building like an external echo of the mirrored chambers within. The statues of river gods and nymphs at the angles, designed by Lebrun, personify the rivers and streams of France.

The gardens and park form a logical system of terraces, broad avenues, and pathways radiating outward from clearings. They are lavishly embellished by fountains, pools, canals, pavilions, and grottos, all of which are richly decorated with statuary. More than 1200 fountains were installed by skilled engineers of waterworks, and with their jets spouting water into the air in many patterns, they were marvels of their craft. Each had its name, and each was adorned with an appropriate sculptural group.

The Versailles Palace, in the broader political sense, was not so much a monument to the vanity of Louis XIV as it was a symbol of the absolute monarchy and the outstanding example of aristocratic baroque architecture. It represented a movement away from a feudal, decentralized government toward a modern, centralized state. As a vast advertising project it was also a highly influential factor in the international diplomacy of the time. By urbanizing the country aristocracy and promoting court activities, Versailles built up for the arts a larger and more knowledgeable audience. It assured the shift of the artistic center of gravity from Italy to France. The French court was also a center of style and dress, and as a school for the training of craftsmen, it assured France leadership in fashion and elegance.

By combining all the activities of a court into a single structure, Versailles pointed the way toward the concept of architecture as a means of creating a new pattern of life. The design of Versailles also became a model for later city planning. A large housing development the size of a town was constructed so as to envelop rather than escape from nature. Details of Le Nôtre's garden plan, such as the radiating pathways, were the acknowledged basis for the laying out of new sections of Paris; and the city plan of Washington, D.C., for instance, was a direct descendant of the parks of Versailles. Modern city planners and housing developers have hailed Versailles as the origin of the contemporary ideal of placing large residential units in close contact with nature. Finally, by starting with a grand design, Versailles pointed the way to the planning of whole cities from the start without the usual haphazard growth and change. In this light, Versailles is one of the earliest examples of modern urbanism and city planning on a large scale.

Sculpture

While Gianlorenzo Bernini was working on the Louvre plans, he was besieged by requests from would-be patrons to design everything from fountains for their gardens to tombs for their ancestors. The King as usual came first in such matters, and Bernini received a commission from Louis XIV for a portrait bust (Fig. 322). This minor by-product of the artist's visit to Paris ultimately turned out to be far more successful than his major mission.

Dispensing with the usual formal sittings, Bernini made rapid pencil sketches while Louis was playing tennis or presiding at cabinet meetings, so that he could observe his subject in action. He was convinced that movement was the medium that best defined the personality and brought out the unique characteristics of his subjects. The informal sketches were made, as he said, "to steep myself in, and imbue myself with, the King's features."

After Bernini had captured the individuality he was to portray, his next step was to decide on the general ideas—nobility, majesty, and the optimistic pride of youth. Here all the accessories, such as the costume, drapery, position of the head, and so on, would play their part. After the preliminaries were over and the particular as well as the general aspects

322. Gianlorenzo Bernini. *Louis XIV.* 1665. Marble, height 33⅛″ (84 cm). Versailles Palace.

were settled, the King sat thirteen times while Bernini made finishing touches directly on the marble.

Like most other works of the period, the bust has its allegorical meanings. Bernini noted in his conversations the resemblance of Louis XIV to Alexander the Great, whose face he knew from ancient coins. Courtly flattery was partially responsible, of course. Nevertheless, according to the conventions of the time, if the King were to appear as a military hero, it would be as a Roman emperor on horseback; if he were to be the *roi soleil,* it would be as Apollo. Since Bernini's intention here was to convey grandeur and majesty, Alexander, as the personification of kingly character, was the logical choice.

In addition to such portraits, Bernini's fame as a sculptor rested more broadly on religious statues, such as his *St. Teresa in Ecstasy* (see Fig. 302), on the many fountains he designed for Rome, and on mythological groups such as his *Apollo and Daphne* (Fig. 323), to embellish aristocratic residences.

This youthful work is full of motion and tense excitement. According to the myth, Apollo, as the patron of the Muses, was in pursuit of ideal beauty, symbolized here by the nymph Daphne. The sculptor chose to make permanent the pregnant moment from which the previous and forthcoming action may be perceived. As Daphne flees from Apollo's ardent embrace, she cries aloud to the gods, who hear her plea and change her into a laurel tree. Though root-bound and with bark already enclosing her limbs, she seems to be in quivering motion. The diagonal line from Apollo's hand to Daphne's leafy fingers leads the eye upward and outward.

The complex surfaces of the sculpture are handled so as to give maximum play to light and shadow. Bernini has carefully carved the various textures, such as the smooth flesh, flowing drapery, floating hair, the bark, leaves, and branches, in keeping with his objective of painting in marble. But above all the sculptor has accomplished his express intention, which was to achieve emotion and movement at all costs and to make marble seem to float in space.

The Versailles gardens provided French sculptors with an inexhaustible outlet for their wares. Many went to Italy to copy such admired antiques as the *Laocoön Group* (see Fig. 81). These replicas were then sent back and placed on pedestals along the various walks at Versailles. Other sculptors, like Girardon, made variants of Bernini's fountains and incorporated the movement of the water into their designs as he had done. Most of the statuary at Versailles, however, is effective mainly as part of the general setting, and only a few works have survived the test of time to emerge as individual masterpieces.

Notable among these sculptures were such works of Pierre Puget as his *Milo of Crotona* (Fig. 324). This

above: **323.** Gianlorenzo Bernini. *Apollo and Daphne.* 1622–25. Marble, life-size. Borghese Gallery, Rome.

below: **324.** Pierre Puget. *Milo of Crotona.* 1671–83. Marble; height 8'10½" (2.71 m), width 4'7" (1.4 m). Louvre, Paris.

statue shows the ancient Olympic wrestling champion, who had challenged Apollo himself to a match. He was, of course, given the punishment due a mortal who dares to compete with a god—death.

Painting

Patronage of the arts on a lavish and international scale had been a royal privilege ever since the time of Francis I. The procession of major figures to the French court beginning in the 16th century with Leonardo da Vinci and Benvenuto Cellini had never ceased. Foremost among the newcomers was that great internationally celebrated Fleming, Peter Paul Rubens. Though loyal to Flanders and Antwerp, where he maintained his studio, Rubens had studied the works of Titian and Tintoretto in Venice as well as those of Michelangelo and Raphael in Rome. Never lacking aristocratic favor, he passed long periods in Spain and, particularly, in Italy at Mantua.

325. Peter Paul Rubens. *Henry IV Receiving the Portrait of Maria de' Medici.* 1622-25. Oil on canvas, 13′ × 9′8″ (3.96 × 2.95 m). Louvre, Paris.

Rubens

During the reign of Louis XIII, when the Luxembourg Palace was being completed for the Queen Mother Maria de' Medici, her expressed desire was for a painter who could decorate the walls of its Festival Gallery in a manner matching the Italian baroque style of its architecture. Maria's career as Henry IV's queen and as Louis XIII's regent was as lacking in luster as her own mediocre talents could possibly have made it. Nevertheless, as the direct descendant of Lorenzo the Magnificent, she seemed to sense that the immortal reputations of princes often depended more on their choice of artists than on their skill in statecraft. Maria's choice for the Festival Gallery murals was Rubens.

Rubens' cycle of 21 large canvases gave the needed imaginary glorification to Maria's unimaginative life. The success of this visual biography, however, belonged more truly to the man who painted it than to the lady who lived it. The remarkable thing was how Rubens could exercise so much individual freedom within the limits of courtly officialdom and succeed so well in pleasing both himself and his royal mistress.

In Rubens' grandiose conception, the ancient gods had deserted the lofty regions of Mt. Olympus and taken up their abode in the vastly more stimulating atmosphere of Paris. Even before Maria's birth, Juno and Jupiter had persuaded the Three Fates to spin a brilliant web of destiny for her. The governess who taught her to read was none other than Minerva, while her music teacher was Apollo himself. Her mythical eloquence came from the lips of Mercury, and every possible feminine fascination was given to her by the Three Graces.

When Maria reached grace and beauty, the Capitoline Triad themselves—Jupiter, Juno, and Minerva—presided over the scene of *Henry IV Receiving the Portrait of Maria de' Medici* (Fig. 325). Minerva, as goddess of peace and war, whispers words of wisdom into the King's ear. An amusing touch is provided by the cupids who playfully try to lift the heavy helmet and shield of the monarch's armor. The celestial scene above assures everyone concerned that marriages are indeed made in heaven, where Jupiter and his eagle and Juno with her peacocks are seen bestowing their Olympian blessing.

The baroque ideal of richness and lavishness is seen once again in a picture from Rubens' later years, the *Garden of Love* (Fig. 326). The actual setting for this allegory was the garden of his magnificent home at Antwerp, and the ornate doorway in the background still exists. The scene of amorous revelry unfolds in a diagonal line beginning with the chubby cherub in the lower left. Rubens himself is

326. Peter Paul Rubens. *Garden of Love.* c. 1632–34. Oil on canvas, 6′6″ × 9′3½″ (1.98 × 2.83 m). Prado, Madrid.

seen urging his second wife, Helena Fourment, who appeared in so many of his later pictures, to join the others in the garden of love. The rest of the picture expands in a series of spirals mounting upward toward the figure of Venus who, as a part of the fountain, presides over the festivities. The use of large areas of strong primary colors—reds, blues, yellows—enlivens the scene and strengthens the pictorial structure.

Rubens succeeded in combining the rich color of Titian and the dramatic tension of Tintoretto with an unbounded energy and physical power of his own. His conceptions have something of the heroic sweep of Michelangelo, though they lack the latter's thoughtfulness and restraint. His complex organization of space and freedom of movement recall El Greco, but his figures are as round and robust as the latter's were tall and thin. His success in religious pictures, hunting scenes, and landscapes, as well as the mythological paintings that suited his temperament so well, shows the enormous sweep of his pictorial powers. For sheer imaginative invention and brilliant handling of the brush he has rarely, if ever, been equaled.

Poussin

While Rubens was executing his murals for the Festival Hall, an obscure French painter named Nicolas Poussin, who had been working on minor decorations, left the Luxembourg Palace for the less confining atmosphere of Rome. There he soon built a solid reputation that came to the attention of Cardinal Richelieu, who bought many of Poussin's paintings and determined to bring the artist back to Paris. In 1640, Poussin did return to decorate the Grand Gallery of the Louvre—and receive from Louis XIII a shower of favors and the much desired title of First Painter to the King. The inevitable courtly intrigues that followed such marked attention made Poussin so miserable that after two years he returned to Rome. There he acted as the artistic ambassador of France and supervised the French painters sent under government subsidies to study and copy Italian masterpieces for the decoration of the Louvre. And there, for the rest of his life, Poussin had the freedom to pursue his classical studies, the independence to work out his own principles and ideals, and the time to paint pictures ranging from mythological and

left: **327.** Peter Paul Rubens.
Rape of Daughters of Leucippus.
c. 1618. Oil on canvas, 7′3″ × 6′10″
(2.21 × 2.08 m).
Alte Pinakothek, Munich.

below: **328.** Nicolas Poussin.
Rape of Sabine Women. c. 1636–37.
Oil on canvas, 5′1″ × 6′10½″
(1.55 × 2.1 m).
Metropolitan Museum of Art, New York
(Harris Brisbane Dick Fund, 1946).

329. Nicolas Poussin.
Et in Arcadia Ego
(*I Too Once Dwelled in Arcady*).
1638–39. Oil on canvas,
$33\frac{1}{2} \times 47\frac{5}{8}''$ (85 × 121 cm).
Louvre, Paris.

religious subjects to historical canvases and architectural landscapes.

Two truly superb paintings depicting similar violent and passionate themes (Figs. 327, 328) provide a lively comparison of the differences in temperament between Rubens and his younger French colleague. Poussin's scene (Fig. 328) refers to the legendary founding of Rome according to the historians Livy and Plutarch. Romulus, having been unsuccessful in negotiating marriages for his warriors, has arranged a religious celebration with games and festivities as a plan to bring families from the neighboring town of Sabina to the Roman Forum. For Rubens (Fig. 327), the affair is one of robust personal passion in which Castor and Pollux "fairly dived into the sea of female flesh that splashed and wildly undulated around them," as the English writer Aldous Huxley put it.

The more studious Poussin, in his efforts to re-create the classical past, turned to Roman museums for models of many of his figures, and to Vitruvius for his architectural setting. Romulus, from his position of prominence on the porch of the temple at the left, is giving the prearranged signal of unfolding his mantle, whereupon every Roman seizes a Sabine maiden and makes off with her. Though the subject is one of passion and violence, Poussin manages to balance his picture by a careful arrangement of opposites. The anger of the outraged victims contrasts with the impressive calm of Romulus and his attendants; for, as a ruler, Romulus knows that the future of his city rests on the foundation of families, and that here the end justifies the means. The turbulent human action is counterbalanced also by the ordered repose of the architectural and landscape back-

ground. The smooth marblelike flesh of the women contrasts with the bulging muscles beneath the bronzed skins of the Romans, and the contours of the figures generally are as clearly defined as if they had been chiseled out of stone.

Poussin's obsession with antique sculpture is readily seen when the group in the right foreground is compared with the Hellenistic *Gaul and His Wife* (see Fig. 67). Poussin's male figure is an exact copy of the ancient statue, but the position of the left arm and right hand are reconstructions as he thought they ought to be. While such direct copies are comparatively rare, this group reveals the close study the artist made of ancient architecture and statuary in Rome's libraries and museums. The building at the right, for instance, is taken from a description of a Roman basilica in Vitruvius' book on architecture. Both the reconstruction of the statue and the shape of the basilica turn out to be quite wrong in the light of later, more exact archaeology.

Et in Arcadia Ego (Fig. 329) shows Poussin in a quieter and more lyrical mood. The rustic figures of the shepherds might well have stepped out of one of Vergil's pastoral poems, while the shepherdess could be the tragic Muse in one of Corneille's dramas. As they trace out the letters of the Latin inscription on the sarcophagus, "I Too Once Dwelled in Arcady," their mood becomes thoughtful. That the shepherd in the tomb once lived and loved as they do casts a spell of gentle melancholy over the group. In this meditative study in the composition of space, the female figure parallels the trunk of the tree to define the vertical axis, while the arm of the shepherd on the left rests on the tomb to supply the horizontal bal-

330. Claude Lorrain.
Disembarkation of Cleopatra at Tarsus.
c. 1647. Oil on canvas,
3'10¾" × 5'6½" (1.19 × 1.69 m).
Louvre, Paris.

ance. Each gesture, each line, follows inevitably from this initial spatial statement with all the cool logic of a geometrical theorem.

The subject is obviously a sympathetic one to Poussin, for he had found his own Arcadia in Italy and took a lifelong delight in the monuments of antiquity and the voices from the past that spoke through just such inscriptions. Like the ancients, he tried to conduct his own search for truth and beauty in a stately tempo and with a graceful gesture. Like them, too, he sought for the permanent in the momentary, the type in the individual, the universal in the particular, and the one in the many.

Claude Lorrain

Claude Gellée, better known as Claude Lorrain, like his countryman Poussin, also preferred life in Italy to that in his native France. His lifelong interest was landscape, but the convention of the time demanded that pictures contain personages and also have titles. Claude solved the problem by painting his landscapes, letting his assistants put in a few incidental figures, and giving the pictures obscure names, such as *Embarkation of the Queen of Sheba, Expulsion of Hagar,* or *David at the Cave of Adullam*—subjects no other artist had ever painted. With tongue in cheek, he once remarked that he sold his figures and gave away his landscapes.

Harbor scenes like the one entitled *Disembarkation of Cleopatra at Tarsus* (Fig. 330) were his special delight. In them, he could concentrate on limitless space and the soft atmospheric effect of sunlight on misty air. His usual procedure was to balance his compositions on either side of the foreground with buildings or trees, which are treated in considerable

detail. Then the eye is drawn deeper into the intervening space with long vistas over land or sea toward the indefinite horizon. Formal values based on geometrical principles dominate.

The stylistic differences of Rubens and Poussin admirably illustrate the free and academic sides of the baroque coin. Both painters were well versed in the classics, both reflected the spirit of the Counter-Reformation, and both in their way represented the aristocratic tradition. But while Rubens' emotionalism knew no bounds, Poussin remained aloof and reserved; while Rubens cast restraint to the winds and filled his pictures with violent movement, Poussin was quietly pursuing his formal values; while Rubens' figures are soft and fleshy, Poussin's are hard and statuesque; while Rubens sweeps up his spectators in the tidal wave of his volcanic energy, Poussin encourages quiet meditation. The Academy's championship of Poussin made clear the distinction between academic and free baroque. In the late 17th and 18th centuries, painters were divided into camps labeling themselves either "Poussinist" or "Rubenist," and well into the 19th century echoes were still to be heard in the controversy of classic versus romantic.

Music

The musical and dramatic productions at the court of Louis XIV were as lavish in scale as the other arts. Three groups of musicians were maintained, the first of which was the *chambre* group, which included the famous *Vingt-quatre Violons* ("Twenty-four String Players"), the first permanent orchestra in Europe. This was the string ensemble that played for balls, dinners, concerts, and the opera. Lutenists and keyboard players also were found in this group. Next came the *chapelle,* the chorus that sang for religious services, and the organists. The *Grande Écurie,* or military band, formed the third category, which consisted mainly of the wind ensemble, available for parades, outdoor festivities, and hunting parties.

Lully and French Opera

During Louis' youthful years his Italian prime minister Cardinal Mazarin sought to bring the new Italian opera, "the spectacle of princes" as it was known, into French courtly life. Cavalli, the pupil and successor of Monteverdi, who had brought the Venetian lyric drama to a high point of development, was invited to Paris in 1660 to write and produce an opera. It met with a mixed reception, but two years later Cavalli was again on hand to write another, this time for Louis' wedding celebration. Another challenge to the court ballet came from Molière, who united the elements of comedy, music, and the dance into a form he called *comédie-ballet.* The best known of these is the popular *Le Bourgeois Gentilhomme* (*The Would-be Gentleman*), which was first performed at the court in 1670.

The ever-resourceful Jean Baptiste Lully, however, was biding his time on the sidelines until he could spring some surprises of his own. A Florentine by birth and French by education, he was fiddling away at the early age of seventeen as a violinist in the *Vingt-quatre Violons.* When Cavalli produced his two operas, it was Lully who wrote the ballet sequences that, incidentally, proved more popular than the operas themselves. It was Lully again who collaborated with Molière by supplying the musical portions of the *comédie-ballets.* And when the right moment arrived, it was Lully who came up with a French form of opera that he called *tragédie lyrique,* or "lyrical tragedy."

One of the earliest of these operas was the performance of *Alceste* in the Marble Court at Versailles on July 4, 1674 (Fig. 331). With a genius for organization, Lully used the *Vingt-quatre Violons* as the nucleus of his orchestra, supplementing them with wind instruments from the *Grande Ecurie* for fanfares as well as for the hunting, battle, and climactic transformation scenes. The *chapelle* was also drafted into the operatic service for the choruses, and the generous dance sequences that Lully included assured the ballet group plenty of activity. Lully could have commanded the services of the great dramatist Racine for the texts, but he deliberately chose Quinault, a poet of less distinction, who could be counted upon not to claim too much credit.

Form The form of lyrical tragedies crystallized early and changed little in the following years. Each begins with an instrumental number of the type known as the "French overture." The first part is a march with dotted notes, massive sonorities, resolving dissonances as in the first example on page 290. The second half is livelier and contrapuntal.

Next came the prologue, and that of *Alceste* is quite typical. The setting is the garden of the Tuileries, the palace in Paris that was still the official royal residence at this time, where the Nymph of the Seine is discovered. Singing her lines in *recitative* style, she makes some topical references to the current war in flowery and mythological terms. (Recitative is a kind of free vocal delivery of lines that sets the scene, describes the action, or carries on the dialogue. It is usually sung to the accompaniment of a keyboard instrument supported by a string bass. Recitative is opposed to the more formally organized and melodic *arias* or *airs* that are accompanied by the orchestra.)

Glory now enters to the tune of a triumphal march, and a duet and solo are then sung. The two are joined eventually by a chorus of water nymphs and pastoral divinities, whose songs and dances give

331. Louis Le Vau. Marble Court, Versailles Palace. Engraving by Lepautre showing a performance of Lully's *Alceste,* 1674. Metropolitan Museum of Art, New York (Harris Brisbane Dick Fund, 1930).

assurance that France will be ever victorious under the leadership of a great hero, whose identity is never for a moment in doubt. The overture is repeated, and the five acts of a classical tragedy follow with much the same formal pattern as the prologue.

Style Two excerpts from Act III, scene 5 of *Alceste* will illustrate Lully's style. After the death of Alceste, a long instrumental *ritornel* provides the pompous funereal strains for the entrance of the mourning chorus. One of the grief-stricken women approaches, indicating sorrow by her gestures and facial expressions. Her air (right) is in the recitative style, which Jean Jacques Rousseau considered Lully's chief "title to glory." The composer always insisted that the music and all other elements of the opera were the servants of drama and poetry, and he counseled singers to follow the noble and expansive intonations of the actors trained by Racine. Thus, a Lully air is never so set as an Italian aria but follows the elastic, fluid speech rhythms and the natural recitation of French baroque poetry and prose. The mourning chorus takes up where the air leaves off with a variant of the opening ritornel, and the scene closes with a long passage alternately for orchestra and chorus based on a continuation of the ritornel.

Since the hero was so closely identified with the monarch, a tragic ending was quite impossible. A *deus ex machina*—usually Apollo, Mercury or Minerva—descended just when all seemed darkest. After everything had been put right, the final act brought the tragedy to a glorious conclusion.

The Academy of Music

By exploiting the success of his operas and through clever diplomatic strategy, Lully became by royal warrant the founder and head of the *Académie Royale de Musique.* With the substitution of the word *Nationale* for *Royale,* this is still the official title of the Paris grand opera company. With incredible energy, this musical monopolist of the regime produced an opera every year. In addition to writing the score, he conducted the orchestra, trained the choir, coached the singers and dancers, and directed the staging.

Lully ruled his musical and dramatic forces with the iron hand of an absolutist, allowing nothing arbitrary or whimsical to creep in anywhere. As a consequence, he developed the best-disciplined group of singers, dancers, and instrumentalists in Europe. Their fame spread far and wide, and from accounts of that time his orchestra was especially noted for the purity of its intonation, uniform bowing of the strings, accuracy of tempo and measure, and the elegance of its trills and melodic ornaments that were compared to the "sparkling of precious stones."

Alceste (ritornel, Act III, scene 5)   Jean-Baptiste Lully

Alceste (air, Act III, scene 5)   Jean-Baptiste Lully

La mort, la mort bar - ba - reDe - truit au - jourd'huy   mille ap - pas.

Practically singlehanded, Lully unified the ballet and founded French opera. His standardization of the sequence of dances became known as the "French suite," his form of the overture was called the "French overture," and his organization of the opera remained standard practice for almost two centuries. Even though Quinault wrote the texts, Lully's operas may be considered the musical reflection of Racine's tragedies. In them are found the same observance of classical rules of drama, the same dignified prosody, the same polished correctness.

The limitations of Lully's operas were the inevitable outgrowth of the circumstances of their creation. By being addressed so exclusively to a single social group, they neglected to provide the more resonant human sounding board needed for survival in the repertory. Like Poussin's paintings, Lully's operas remained aloof, restrained, and aristocratic. The concept of opera, however, by its combination of elevated language, emotional appeal, sonorous splendor, majestic movement, and visual elegance, emerges as one of the most magnificent creations of the baroque era.

Ideas

The many aspects of the aristocratic baroque style revolve mainly around two distinct but interrelated ideas—absolutism and academicism.

Absolutism

The concept of the modern unified state, which first emerged in the Spain of Philip II, was adapted to French political purposes by Cardinal Richelieu and ultimately reached its triumphant realization under Louis XIV. "It is the respect which absolute power demands, that none should question when a king commands," was the way Corneille stated the doctrine in 1637 in his heroic drama *The Cid.* As the

332. Jean Baptiste Martin. *Promenade of Louis XIV in the Gardens at Versailles,* detail. c. 1705. Oil on canvas, entire work 7'3¾" × 6'1⅜" (2.25 × 1.88 m). Grand Trianon, Versailles.

principal personification of monarchical absolutism and the centralized state, Louis XIV, the Sun King, assumed the authority to replace natural and human disorderliness with a reasonable facsimile of cosmic law and order. All human and social activities came under his protectorship, and by taking the arts under his paternal wing, he saw that they served the cult of majesty. Versailles became the symbol of absolutism, the seat of absolute monarchy, and the personal glorification of the King.

Unification of the Arts   Just as political absolutism meant the unification of all social and governmental institutions under one head, its aesthetic counterpart implied the bringing together of all the separate arts into a single rational plan. While Louis' reign produced some buildings, statuary, paintings, literature, and music that command attention in their own right, they spoke out most impressively in their combined forms.

It is impossible to think of Versailles except as a combination of all art forms woven together into a unified pattern and as a reflection of the life and institutions of the absolute monarchy. The parks, gardens, fountains, statuary, buildings, courtyards, halls, murals, tapestries, furnishings, and recreational activities are all parts of a single coordinated design (Fig. 332). As such, Versailles accomplished the daring feat of unifying all visible space and all units of time into a spatial-temporal setting for the aristocratic way of life. Indoor and outdoor space are inseparable; even music and the theater went outdoors. Sculpture was an embellishment of the landscape; painting was allied with interior design; comedy with ballet; and tragedy with opera.

All the arts, in fact, were mirrored in the operatic form with its literary lyricism, orchestral rhetoric, dramatic recitation, instrumental interludes, statuesque dancing, architectural stage settings, mechanical marvels, and picturesque posturings. In Lully's hands opera became a kind of microcosm of court life, an absolute art form in which all the separate parts related closely to the whole.

The spirit of absolutism was also directly revealed in the drama surrounding the life of the monarch. All the arts took the cue, became theatrical, and sought to surprise and astonish. The purely human element was buried under an avalanche of palatial scenery, pompous wigs, props, and protocol.

Only in Molière's satires, La Fontaine's fables, and the secret memoirs of the period is it possible to catch glimpses of a more truthful version of the actualities behind the scenes of courtly life. Otherwise the architecture of Versailles, the statuary of Bernini and Coysevox (Fig. 333), the murals of Lebrun, the tragedies of Racine, and the operas of Lully were all designed to promote the illusion that Louis XIV and his courtiers were beings of heroic stature, powerful will, and grandiose utterance.

333. Jules Hardouin-Mansart and Charles Lebrun. Salon de la Guerre, Versailles Palace. Begun 1678. Relief of Louis XIV on horseback by Antoine Coysevox.

Academicism

While the academic movement began formally with the first French academy during the reign of Louis XIII, it was not until later in the century that the implications of academicism were completely realized and its force fully mobilized. Both Louis XIV and his minister Colbert believed that art was much too important to be left exclusively in the hands of artists. The various academies, therefore, became branches of the government and the arts a part of the civil service. An administrative organization was instituted, topped by the King and director through professors, members, and associates, to the students. Approved principles were taught, and theoretical and practical knowledge communicated by lectures, demonstrations, and discussions.

Boileau as the head of the Academy of Language and Literature, Lebrun of the Academy of Painting and Sculpture, Mansart of the Academy of Architecture, and Lully of the Academy of Music were subject directly to the King and were absolute dictators in their respective fields. As such, they were the principal advisers to the King and his ministers, and, in turn, they were responsible for carrying out the royal will. Control of patronage was centered in their hands. Theirs was the final word in determining who would receive commissions, appointments, titles, licenses, degrees, pensions, prizes, entrance to art schools, and the privilege of exhibiting in the salons.

The academies were thus the means of transmitting the absolute idea to the aesthetic sphere. Academicism invariably implied an authoritarian principle, whereby regularly constituted judges of taste placed their stamp of approval on the products in the various art media. These interpreters of the official point of view inevitably tended to become highly conservative.

Aristocratic baroque art was the superpersonal expression of a class whose code of behavior was based on etiquette, politeness, and cultivation of good taste. All personal feeling, whimsy, and eccentricity had to yield to self-discipline, sophistication, correctness, and accepted standards of good form. The academies were therefore charged with the making of aesthetic definitions, artistic codes, and technical formulas valid for their respective fields. They functioned as a kind of board of directors who decided what was best for the stockholders. They had, moreover, the power to enforce their decisions, which meant that academicism could, at best, establish and maintain a high level of creative quality and, at worst, degenerate into conventionalism and downright regimentation.

One example will show how academicism worked. Under Lebrun, the Academy of Painting and Sculpture favored the restrained style of Poussin over the passionate emotionalism of Rubens. It thereby set up an academic subdivision of the baroque style as opposed to the expression of the free baroque. Many reasons for the choice can, of course, be advanced. Poussin's pictorialism, for instance, may—quickly and easily—be reduced to a system of formal values based on geometrical principles. Rubens' style, however, is so personal, fiery, sensuous, and violently emotional that it always remains a bit beyond the grasp. Academicism in this case was trying to tame baroque enthusiasm and reduce it to formulas and rules. Nothing eccentric, nothing unpredictable was allowed to creep in and destroy the general impression of orderliness. The Academy always remained somewhat skeptical of emotion and color, since neither was subject to scientific laws.

The pictorial standards of the Academy were therefore based on formal purity, clear mathematical relationships, logical definition, and rational analysis. These were the qualities that brought academic art the designation of *classic,* a term that was defined at the time as "belonging to the highest class" and hence approved as a model. Since similar standards were generally to be found in Roman antiquity, classic and Roman art became accepted models.

French academicism was from the start an unqualified practical success. Under the academies, the artistic dominance of Europe passed from Italy to France where it has effectively remained up to recent times. The hundreds of skilled artists and artisans who were trained on the vast projects of Louis XIV became the founders and teachers of a tradition of high technical excellence. French painting alone, to use the most obvious example, continued its unbroken supremacy until the 20th century.

In Spain, by way of contrast, the only successor to El Greco, Velázquez, and Murillo was the lonely figure of Goya. In Flanders there were no outstanding followers of Rubens and van Dyck except Watteau, who made his entire career in France. In Holland there was no one to take up where Rembrandt and Vermeer had left off until Van Gogh in the late 19th century.

In France, however, painting continued on a high level throughout the 18th and 19th centuries; and, by setting high technical standards, academicism was a determining force even in nonacademic circles. The work of Perrault and Mansart in architecture, Boileau in criticism, Molière in comedy, Racine in tragedy, and Lully in opera was also absorbed directly into a tradition that succeeded in setting up measuring rods of symmetry, order, regularity, dignity, reserve, and clarity. To this day these measures still have a certain validity even if only as points of departure.

15
The Bourgeois Baroque Style

Amsterdam, 17th Century

If visitors to 17th-century Amsterdam— or any of the other sturdy Dutch towns for that matter—looked about for triumphal arches, pretentious palaces, or military monuments, they were doomed to disappointment. In fact, if there was anything grand at all about life in Holland and Flanders, it was its complete commonplaceness.

After they had achieved their cherished independence by winning back their country town by town and province by province from the grasp of the Spanish despots, the people organized their government with a minimum of unity and a maximum of diversity. They had no intention of substituting one brand of tyranny for another, much less a domestic variety; and so the land became the United Provinces under a *stadtholder,* or "governor." Let their English rivals call them the "united bogs"; their muddy swamps and marshlands were poor things, but at least they were their own (see map, p. 307).

The Dutch wars of independence, geographical isolation, constant struggle against the steady advances of the sea, harsh climate, seafaring economy, Calvinist Protestantism, and individualistic temperaments conspired with all the other circumstances of Dutch life to focus the center of interest in the home. A Dutch home was not even a castle; it was just a solid, comfortable, plain brick house. Instead of the cult of majesty, there was the cult of the home.

When Jakob van Ruisdael painted the *Quay at Amsterdam* (Fig. 334), he was showing more than just a view of the old fish market at the end of the broad canal known as the Damrak. In this local

334. Jakob van Ruisdael. *Quay at Amsterdam.* c. 1670. Oil on canvas, 20¾ × 26″ (53 × 66 cm). Frick Collection, New York (copyright).

CHRONOLOGY
17th-Century Holland

GENERAL EVENTS

1517	Protestant Reformation began in Germany
1535	*Institution of Christian Religion* published by John Calvin (1509–64); Dutch Reformed Church established later along Calvinist lines
1566	Revolt of Netherlands against Spain began
1575	University of Leyden, first Dutch university, founded by William the Silent, prince of Orange
1602	Dutch East India Company organized
1609	Holland and Flanders given virtual independence in truce with Spain
1618–1648	Thirty Years' War; full independence given to Holland under Treaty of Westphalia (1648)
1621	Dutch West India Company founded
1624	*Tablatura Nova* by Samuel Scheidt
1629–1648	René Descartes resided in Holland
1630–1687	Limited public art patronage dispensed through Constantijn Huygens
1631	Rembrandt settled in Amsterdam
1637	*Discourse on Method* published in Leyden by Descartes
1642	Dutch explorer Tasman discovered New Zealand
1644	*Principles of Philosophy* published by Descartes in Amsterdam
1648	Independence of Netherlands recognized by Treaty of Westphalia
1652–1674	Anglo-Dutch commercial wars
1670	Spinoza published *Tractatus Theologica-Politicus*

PAINTERS

c.1580–1666	Frans Hals
1606–1669	Rembrandt van Rijn
c.1617–1681	Gerhardt Terborch
c.1628–1682	Jakob van Ruisdael
c.1629–1679	Jan Steen
c.1629–1683	Pieter de Hooch
1632–1675	Jan Vermeer van Delft

PHILOSOPHERS AND SCIENTISTS

1467–1536	Desiderius Erasmus
1583–1645	Hugo Grotius, founder of international law
1596–1650	René Descartes
1629–1695	Christian Huygens
1632–1677	Baruch Spinoza

WRITERS

1587–1679	Joost van den Vondel, Dutch dramatist, author of *Lucifer,* poem similar to Milton's *Paradise Lost*
1596–1687	Constantijn Huygens, poet, humanist, diplomat

MUSICIANS

1562–1621	Jan Pieterszoon Sweelinck

English School

c.1542–1623	William Byrd
c.1562–1628	John Bull, organist at Antwerp (1617–28), friend of Sweelinck
c.1562–1638	Francis Pilkington, author, *First Booke of Ayres*
c.1576–1643	Henry Peacham, author of *Compleat Gentleman,* teacher and composer
1583–1625	Orlando Gibbons.

German School

1585–1672	Heinrich Schütz
1587–1654	Samuel Scheidt, pupil of Sweelinck
1596–1663	Heinrich Scheidemann, pupil of Sweelinck
1623–1722	J. A. Reinken, successor of Scheidemann at Hamburg, and influencer of J. S. Bach
1685–1750	Johann Sebastian Bach
1685–1759	George Frederick Handel

variant of the international academic style (compare with Fig. 330), he was in fact picturing the bourgeois, or middle class, way of life in a scene where thrifty housewives were gathering up provisions for their dinner tables; where a part of the fishing fleet that gave the Dutch a monopoly of the pickled and salted herring industry was moored; where, lying at anchor in the distance, were some of the merchant vessels that helped the Dutch create an efficient modern commerce by sailing the seven seas, trading their clay pipes, glazed tiles, Delft pottery.

In such a situation, some families inevitably accumulated more than others, and by means of the wealth that was concentrated in their hands, they became a ruling class. These so-called regent families were the ones from whose ranks the members of the town councils and mayors were selected. They were, however, an upper-middle-class group rather than an aristocracy, and there was safety in their numbers. Their power, together with that of the professional and merchant societies known as "guilds," depended upon exercising a maximum of local authority.

This decentralization favored the growth of universities—those at Leyden and Utrecht became the most distinguished in Europe—and promoted the careers of such noted native humanists as Constantijn Huygens, friend and patron of Rembrandt, and Hugo Grotius, founder of the new discipline of international law. The freedom to think and work attracted such foreigners as the French philosopher René Descartes, who resided in Holland for almost twenty years, and the parents of Baruch Spinoza—one of the most profound human intellects of all time—who found refuge in Amsterdam after the persecution of the Jews had made life intolerable for them in their native Portugal.

The architectural expression of this bourgeois way of life is found in the various town halls, in such commercial structures as warehouses, counting-houses, and the market building, seen on the extreme right in Figure 334, and, above all, in the long rows of gabled brick houses like those seen on either side of the canal in the same picture. Dating from former times were such ecclesiastical buildings as the Oudekerk, or "Old Church," whose Gothic tower is silhouetted against the sky in the right background. Originally Roman Catholic, the building had been taken over by the Dutch Reformed Church after the Reformation.

As organized under the precepts of John Calvin, the Reformed Church held that religious truth was not the exclusive possession of any individual or any group, and that the word of God was available to all without the mediation of priestly authority. Through the development of the printing press, every family could have its own Bible, and the high degree of literacy meant almost everyone could read it.

As in government, the Dutch people were wary of authority in religion; and as confirmed Protestants, they took rather literally the words of Christ to go into their closets and pray. Thus, through family devotions, hymn singing, and Bible reading, much of the important religious activity took place in the home. According to the teaching of Calvin, the reason for going to church was to hear a sermon and sing the praises of the Lord. No architectural embellishments, statuary, paintings, and professional choirs or orchestras should distract the worshipers' attention. Since commissions no longer came from Church and aristocratic sources, artists had to seek an outlet for their work in family circles.

The prosperous Dutch families fortunately felt the need of an art that would reflect their healthy materialism and reveal their outlook, their institutions, and their country just as they were—solid, matter-of-fact, and without airs. In this happy state of affairs, patronage was spread on a sufficiently broad basis so that almost every home had at least a small collection of pictures.

Dutch art avoided the *history* paintings of heroic battle scenes and grandiose mythological allegories with complex symbolism that were so popular at the courts of Spain and France. They did, however, favor biblical subjects. *Landscape* had a strong attraction, since the Dutch had fought for every bit of their soil,

335. Jan Jansz. van de Velde. *Still Life: Fruit Piece.* 1657. Oil on wood, 15 × 12¾″ (38 × 32 cm). Frans Hals Museum, Haarlem.

and paintings of their fields, mills, and cottages appealed to their sense of ownership. *Genre scenes* were likewise popular, because such casualness and informality harmonized with their domestic surroundings.

The severe simplicity of *still-life* compositions also found favor, since quiet arrangements of fruit, flowers, oysters, herrings, ceramics, and textiles were visible evidences of the good life (Fig. 335). Because of their respect for commercial enterprise the Dutch liked *corporation pictures,* where they were depicted among their fellow directors or board members in a group portrait designed to perpetuate their memory on the walls of some guild hall, professional society, officers' club, or charitable trust. Above all, the Dutch burgher wanted family *portraits* for his living room. These might be commemorative pictures of such family festivals as christenings and weddings; paintings of quiet interiors with his wife or daughter dutifully doing some household chore or, if one of them showed special talent, perhaps playing a musical instrument; and for himself, he liked to be portrayed at his work, surrounded by the familiar objects of his worldly position (Fig. 336).

Under Calvinistic austerity, the only professional musicians to survive were the church organists, the hired groups of singers and instrumentalists who performed for weddings, banquets, and parades, and the band of music teachers who taught the younger members of the family to sing and to play the lute (see Fig. 344), viols, and keyboard instruments, such as the virginal and spinet (see Fig. 350). Music, therefore, like all the other aspects of Dutch life, was centered largely in the home. During the Renaissance, Holland and Flanders had dominated European music with the polyphonic glories of their distinguished composers. Only one musical genius of universal stature was left in the Amsterdam of the early 17th century: Jan Pieterszoon Sweelinck, whose career brought to a brilliant close the radiant chapter of Dutch music that had dominated the Renaissance.

All the arts were thus centered in the home. The simple and unpretentious Dutch dwelling with its polished tiled floors, tidy interiors, and window boxes for the tulips was the modest framework for this bourgeois way of life. Unless ceramics are included, there was little sculpture other than a few figurines on the mantelpiece and an occasional statuette. The primary aesthetic pleasures of the Dutch were their domestic pictures and music making, while such objects as their Delft pottery jugs, tablecloths, laces, and draperies enriched their world of qualities.

The reality of daily life was made up of the routine of the business establishment, the marketplace, and the household. It was a reality of simple truths in which nothing was too small to be overlooked. All things, even the most insignificant, were considered to be gifts of God. As such, they were studied in the Holland of the 17th century in the smallest detail.

Painting

Rembrandt

Towering above all other Dutch painters, because of the breadth of his vision, the power of his characterizations, and the uncompromising integrity of his ideals, stands the figure of Rembrandt van Rijn in lonely prominence. Like his contemporaries, Rembrandt painted portraits, genre scenes, historical subjects, and landscapes, but unlike them he refused to specialize and succeeded magnificently in all. Fur-

above: 336. Rembrandt.
Jan Uytenbogaert, Receiver General
(The Goldweigher). 1639.
Etching, 9¾ × 8″ (25 × 20 cm).
Rijksprentenkabinet,
Rijksmuseum, Amsterdam.

right: 337. Rembrandt.
Dr. Tulp's Anatomy Lesson. 1632.
Oil on canvas, 5′3⅜″ × 7′1¼″
(1.61 × 2.17 m).
Mauritshuis, The Hague.

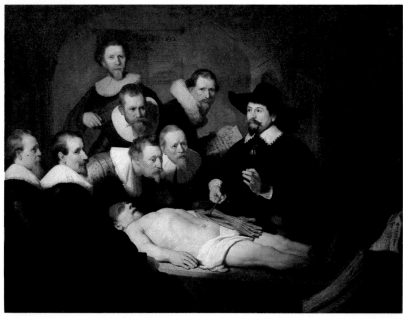

thermore, he brought a new psychological depth to his portraiture, an unaccustomed liveliness to his genre scenes, a greater dramatic intensity to his religious pictures, and a broader sweep to his landscapes than had been achieved before in the northern tradition.

Above all, Rembrandt's discoveries of the power of light, in all its varying degrees, to illuminate character both from without and from within, to define space by varying degrees of brightness, and to give life to that space by the flowing movement of shadows identify him as a prime mover in the establishment of the northern baroque pictorial style. Rembrandt's art as a whole shows a steady growth from his early to his late years in the capacity to penetrate appearances, to discover and reveal the spiritual forces that lie beneath.

Soon after he settled in Amsterdam, the 26-year-old painter received his first important assignment from the local Guild of Surgeons and Physicians. The result was *Dr. Tulp's Anatomy Lesson* (Fig. 337), a composition that combines group portraiture of the so-called corporation type with the anatomy pictures of the medieval and Renaissance tradition. The subjects in this case were the heads of the guild and other prominent citizens, whose names are recorded on the sheet of paper held by the figure in the center.

In his painting, Rembrandt's grouping of figures and placement of the heads on different levels give a certain freedom and informality to the composition. By the use of light, the artist develops the essential drama of the situation, and by the expression on each of the faces shows reactions that vary from intense concentration to casual indifference. The fullest light is focused on the corpse and on the hands of Dr. Nicholas Tulp, the professor of anatomy who is giving the lecture. The large open book at the feet of the corpse is quite possibly a recent edition of Vesalius' *Anatomy.* This universally recognized authority was the work of the Dutch scientist Andries van Wesel (1514–1564), who had taught and held just such demonstrations at the University of Padua. Since Dr. Tulp styled himself *Vesalius redivivus* ("Vesalius revived"), the reference is appropriate. In sum, Rembrandt's dramatization of the spirit of scientific inquiry is a vivid product of a period that has been aptly called the Age of Observation.

Exactly a decade elapsed between the *Anatomy Lesson* and the *Sortie of Captain Banning Cocq's Company of the Civic Guard* (Fig. 338), Rembrandt's

338. Rembrandt. *Sortie of Captain Banning Cocq's Company of the Civic Guard.* 1642. Oil on canvas, 12'2" × 14'7" (3.71 × 4.45 m). Rijksmuseum, Amsterdam.

339. Rembrandt.
Christ Healing the Sick
(*Hundred Guilder Print*). c. 1649.
Etching, $10\frac{7}{8} \times 15\frac{3}{8}''$ (28 × 39 cm).
Metropolitan Museum of Art, New York
(H. O. Havemeyer Collection, 1929).

masterpiece of the corporation type. Group portraits of such military units that had fought against the Spaniards were common enough at the time to have the designation "musketeer pictures." Once their original purpose in the struggle for independence was gone, many of these companies continued as parts of the civic guard and as officers' clubs, available as the occasion warranted for anything from emergency duty to a parade. By 1642, most members had become prosperous shopkeepers, who hugely enjoyed dressing up now and then in their dashing uniforms, polishing their shooting irons, and posing as warriors in processions or civic celebrations.

In "musketeer pictures," these military units were usually shown in convivial situations, such as gathered around a banquet table. However, in order to get life and movement into his picture, Rembrandt discarded this rather stilted pose and chose to show Captain Cocq's company in action, as if responding to a call to duty. The life-size figures are therefore seen moving out of the city gate.

Popularly known as *The Night Watch,* the painting, thanks to a thorough cleaning, has proved to be a "Day Watch" instead. Its varnish that had darkened in the course of time and its placement over a large fireplace were responsible for the general gloom. Now the free flow of light can be seen moving throughout the whole composition, filling every corner with dynamic gradations from dark to bright.

The light is most intense in the center, where Captain Cocq is explaining the plans to his lieutenant, whose uniform catches the rays of the morning sun. As a counterbalance, Rembrandt places the whimsical figure of a young girl in gleaming cream-colored satin at the captain's other side. Strung from her belt are a powder horn and a white cockerel, possibly a pun by Rembrandt on the captain's name. The shadow of Captain Cocq's hand falling across the lieutenant's uniform defines the source of light that, in turn, blends together and relates all the other figures to the central pair by the intensity with which it illuminates them. Such skill in the handling of light and shadow was one of Rembrandt's unique achievements and was evident also in his prints.

The etching *Christ Healing the Sick* (Fig. 339), familiarly known as the *Hundred Guilder Print,* is an example of Rembrandt's several hundred works in what was then a popular medium in the visual arts. Financially, the relatively modest price of an etching assured Rembrandt of some income—and a fairly wide distribution of his work—at those times when his paintings piled up unsold in his studio. (The price in the case of this etching was a record high rather than a rule.)

Technically, the *etching* medium gave Rembrandt the opportunity to explore the qualities of light in simple line patterns independent of colors. By scratching a coated metal plate with a sharp, penlike stylus, an artist makes a linear pattern that is etched, or bitten, into the metal upon being plunged into an acid solution. When the coating is removed and the plate inked, an etching is made by transferring the inked impression on the metal plate to paper. In this example, the gradations of light and dark run from such inky blackness as that behind the figure of Christ to the whiteness of the untouched paper, like that of the large rock in the extreme left. Rembrandt's true artistic stature is revealed in the way his art scales the heights of moral grandeur within severe limitations. The expressive power of this print is as great as the medium is small.

Rembrandt was brought up in a family of Anabaptists who tried to live according to strict biblical teachings. His religious subjects are seen from a Protestant point of view and, as such, show an intimate personal knowledge of the Scriptures. Since he was not painting for churches, and thus was under no compulsion to conform to the usual iconographical tradition of Madonnas and Child, Crucifixions, and so on, he was free to develop new themes and new points of view. Much of the intimacy and effectiveness of such free works is due to the fact that they were not conceived as public showpieces. Rembrandt also loved to explore the Amsterdam ghetto and found subjects for his art among the descendants of the people who created the Old Testament.

Self-Portraits   Rembrandt is known to have painted at least 62 self-portraits, surely a record number. The motivation, however, came more from a strong tendency to look inward than from personal vanity. Besides, no model was more quickly available. Extending from young manhood to his last year, his likenesses of himself read like a pictorial autobiography. After successfully establishing himself in Amsterdam and after his marriage to Saskia van Uylenburch, daughter of a wealthy family, Rem-

brandt enjoyed a period of material prosperity. In cavalier costume and enthusiastic mood, he paints himself with his young wife sitting on his knee as he lifts his glass in a toast (Fig. 340).

From 1640 on, Rembrandt sustained a series of tragedies, beginning with his mother's death, which was followed two years later by that of Saskia shortly after the birth of their son Titus. By 1650 artistic tastes had changed, but Rembrandt firmly followed his own genius, making no bow to fickle fashions.

The penetrating look in the self-image reproduced in Figure 341, glowing with an internal light, peers into the depths of his own character and seems to be asking, "Which way now?" From this time onward, Rembrandt realized more and more that his mission was to explore the world of the imagination and leave the world of appearances to others. Consequently, his face shows the serenity of a man who, having chosen his course, knows there is no longer any turning back.

left: **340.** Rembrandt. *Self-Portrait with Saskia.*
c. 1634. Oil on canvas,
5′3½″ × 4′3½″ (1.61 × 1.31 m).
Gemäldegalerie, Dresden.

above: **341.** Rembrandt. *Self-Portrait.* 1650.
Oil on canvas, 34¾ × 28″ (88 × 71 cm).
National Gallery of Art, Washington, D.C.
(Widener Collection, 1942).

left: 342. Rembrandt. *Self-Portrait.* 1656-58. Oil on wood, 20 × 16″ (51 × 41 cm). Kunsthistorisches Museum, Vienna.

right: 343. Rembrandt. *Old Self-Portrait.* 1669. Oil on canvas, 23¼ × 20¾″ (59 × 53 cm). Mauritshuis, The Hague.

Financial troubles increased as debts piled up, and from 1656 to 1660 the artist went through bankruptcy. His fine house with its furnishings, his personal collections of paintings, prints, armor, and artistic props all were sold to satisfy creditors. At this point (Fig. 342), the searching gaze of the glowing eyes begins to turn inward in self-appraisal as he forthrightly evaluates his moral and artistic progress. The last years were saddened by the deaths of his faithful friend and housekeeper Hendrickje Stoeffels (1662) and his son Titus (1668). Still working continuously, Rembrandt in his last self-portrait shows the familiar face marked by illness and resignation but still full of the deep human compassion that characterized his life and art (Fig. 343).

Hals, de Hooch, and Ruisdael

Between the polar extremes of the introspective Rembrandt and the calculated detachment of his younger colleague Vermeer (see Figs. 347–350) is the range of subjects and moods projected by their contemporaries. While Rembrandt sought to portray the spirit of the whole person, Frans Hals was content to capture human individuality in a fleeting glance or a casual gesture. In his early work he was more interested in appearances than essences. Later, when he came under the influence of Rembrandt's soul-searching, he gave up his vivid colors and light touch for somber hues and serious subjects. The infectious gaiety of his *Merry Lute Player* (Fig. 344) is typical of Hals' carefree early period. With mussed hair and

cap cocked at a jaunty angle, the subject might well be an entertainer at a public tavern. The way the glass of sparkling wine is held reveals the source of light, which strikes both face and instrument. In similar pictures the people of Hals' native Haarlem—quarreling fishwives, reveling officers, and tipsy merrymakers—live again with all their vitality.

Pieter de Hooch's *Mother and Child* (Fig. 345) is a quiet study of domestic life in a proper household. Like his fellow painters, de Hooch knew that light was the magnet which attracted the eye and that its vibrations gave such an interior its share of life and movement. But de Hooch works with a softer light that matches the calm of his subject matter. Sunlight streams inward from the open Dutch door at the back and the window at the upper right. By this means the artist separates his space into three receding planes; explores the contrasting textures of the tile flooring, transparent glass, varnished wood surfaces, soft textiles, and metallic brilliance of the copper bedwarmer; as well as reveals the figures of mother, daughter, and dog.

De Hooch's world is more stable than Rembrandt's, his figures less animated than Hals', and his pictorial geometry more casual than Vermeer's. Yet each of his interiors has the timeless essence of a still life, with figures and objects blending together to make a compositional whole.

Jakob van Ruisdael's somber study of a cemetery belongs to the category of the landscapes that meant so much to the Dutch people who had fought persistently for their country against the Spanish oppressors. While his *Quay at Amsterdam* (Fig. 334) is a forthright cityscape, exact in its descriptive detail, Ruisdael in the *Jewish Graveyard* (Fig. 346) seems to be searching for deeper symbolic values. The setting was the Jewish graveyard near the Oudekerk in Amsterdam, but to heighten the mood of his picture the painter invents many imaginary picturesque details that contribute here to the somber feelings, loneliness, and desolation of mortals when confronted with forces beyond their control. The abandoned ruins of the old castle and the skeletonlike trunks of two dead trees, which were not in the actual scene, unite with the white stone slabs of the tombs to haunt the picture with thoughts of death.

The inscriptions on the headstones—several of which are still there—remind the viewer that the religious toleration of the Netherlands made the country the haven for the Jewish refugees from the Spanish and Portuguese inquisitions. Ruisdael projects a depth of feeling as well as of space into this landscape. With the waterfall and knotted, twisted trees groping toward the threatening sky, he captures something of the sublimity of nature that sweeps mere mortals and all their works before it. His art with its flights of imagination, rugged grandeur, and eye for the picturesque anticipates certain similar aspects of 19th-century romanticism (see Figs. 8, 421, 422).

above left: 344. Frans Hals.
Merry Lute Player. c. 1627.
Oil on canvas, $35\frac{1}{2} \times 29\frac{1}{2}''$ (90×75 cm).
Private collection.

above right: 345. Pieter de Hooch.
Mother and Child. c. 1660.
Oil on canvas, $20\frac{3}{4} \times 24''$ (53×61 cm).
Rijksmuseum, Amsterdam.

left: 346. Jakob van Ruisdael.
Jewish Graveyard. c. 1660.
Oil on canvas, $4'8'' \times 6'2\frac{1}{4}''$ (1.42×1.89 m).
Detroit Institute of Arts.

347. Jan Vermeer. *View of Delft*.
c. 1658. Oil on canvas,
38¾ × 46¼″ (98 × 117 cm).
Mauritshuis, The Hague.

Vermeer

In his *View of Delft* (Fig. 347) Jan Vermeer van Delft painted the profile of his native city. From the people strolling in the lower left foreground, the artist carries the eye across the canal, along the line of commercial buildings and houses behind the city wall on the left, past the stone bridge in the center with the steeple of the church rising in the background, to the moored boats and drawbridge on the extreme right. Vermeer's unusual and inventive handling of pictorial space is seen in this horizontal sweep, which makes no attempt to draw the eye into the deep background space based on a single vanishing point.

The effectiveness of the *View of Delft* is greatly increased by the subtle treatment of light and color. As the sunshine filters through the broken clouds, the light falls unevenly over the landscape, varying from the shadowy foreground and the dull red of the brick buildings, through the flame and orange tones in the sunny distance, to the brilliant gleam of the church tower. More than half the area of the picture is given to the ever-changing Dutch sky, where patches of blue alternate with the silvery and leaden grays of the clouds, while the waters below reflect the mirror image of the town.

With utmost economy of means, Jan Vermeer also painted a group of interior scenes, such as *Officer and Laughing Girl* (Fig. 348). Here Vermeer's logical organization of rectangles and intersecting surfaces is somewhat softened by the importance given to the conversing couple. The daring camera-like perspective projects the figure of the officer forward and gives greater size to his large slouch hat and head than to the figure of the girl. His red coat and sash also contrast noticeably with the cooler colors of the girl's white cap, black and yellow bodice, and blue apron that allow her figure to recede. The map on the wall is painted with the greatest care in relation to the light and angle of the wall. Its Latin title is quite clear, and reads: "New and Accurate Map of all Holland and West Friesland." The warm, rich, natural light that streams in from the open window gives both unity and life to the severe division of planes. It bathes every object and fills every corner of the room, starting with the maximum intensity of the area around the source and tapering off by degrees into the cool bluish tones of the shadows in the lower right.

It may seem that Vermeer lets objects and situations speak for themselves, but many of his pictures have subtle symbolic meanings. *Artist in His Studio* (Fig. 349) is, to be sure, a self-portrait, and the studio is Vermeer's own. The lady, however, personifies fame, and the artist is starting his picture with her laurel wreath to indicate his pursuit of beauty and immortality. The trumpet, as if to sound a fanfare for a famous person, is one of Fame's attributes; and the book in her arm and the volumes and death mask on the table add a literary and sculptural dimension to this allegory of the arts.

The contrast between Rembrandt's restless, searching spirit and Vermeer's sober, objective detachment is fully as great as that between El Greco

and Velázquez, or Rubens and Poussin. Rembrandt's light is the glow of the burning human spirit, Vermeer's that from the open window. Rembrandt tries to penetrate the world of appearances, Vermeer is content with the visual image. With his warm personal quality, Rembrandt embraces humanity as completely as Vermeer, with his cool impersonality, encompasses space. Rembrandt is concerned at all times with moral beauty, Vermeer with physical perfection. Rembrandt's inner dramas need only the crescendo of a single color from deep brown to golden yellow or in an etching from black to white, while Vermeer's absence of drama demands the entire spectrum of colors.

Like a philosopher, Rembrandt lays the soul bare in his moving characterizations, while Vermeer, like a jeweler, delights the eye with his unique perception of the quality and texture of things. Thus, in Holland, as well as in both Spain and France, the 17th century, like a stormy March, had been swept in on the leonine gusts of the free florid baroque and had gone out on a gentle lamblike academic breeze.

above: 348. Jan Vermeer.
Officer and Laughing Girl. 1655–60.
Oil on canvas, 20 × 18″ (51 × 46 cm).
Frick Collection, New York (copyright).

right: 349. Jan Vermeer.
Artist in His Studio. c. 1665–70.
Oil on canvas, 4′4″ × 3′8″ (1.32 × 1.12 m).
Kunsthistorisches Museum, Vienna.

Music

Sweelinck

Jan Pieterszoon Sweelinck was the last great representative of that brilliant period when Dutch and Flemish composers dominated the European musical scene. Unlike Heinrich Isaac, Josquin des Prez, and so many of his earlier fellow composers, Sweelinck remained a lifelong resident of Amsterdam, where he held the post of organist at the Oudekerk for over forty years. Under the strict rules of Calvinism, church music consisted mainly of the congregational singing of psalms and hymns. The development of music as an art, then, would have been ruled out were it not for the fact that Dutch tradition favored the organ, and the organist was allowed to play preludes and postludes before and after the service. On special occasions, choral settings of the psalms with some elaboration were performed.

Sweelinck's viewpoint was international in scope. He knew the work of the great organists and choirmasters of Venice, including the Gabrielis, and was thoroughly familiar with the English keyboard school. His official title was Organist of Amsterdam, and as such his duties included the giving of public concerts. The Oudekerk, according to contemporary accounts, was always crowded on these occasions, and large audiences took delight in his improvisations and variations on sacred and secular themes; the baroque flourishes of his Venetian toccatas; his

fantasies "in the manner of an echo," a keyboard adaptation of the Venetian double-choral style; and the choral preludes and fugues that he built on Protestant hymn tunes.

The other public Dutch music was of the occasional type, given by choral groups and instrumental ensembles that, for a modest price, would furnish anything from the madrigals sung at weddings to the dances played at receptions. The home, however, was the center of the major part of the musical life of the time. Most of the surviving compositions from this period are found in the numerous manuscript copies that were made for home use. Printed scores, however, were obtainable from Venice and London, and early in the 17th century music printing began to flourish in Antwerp, Leyden, and Amsterdam. Holland also became noted as a center for the manufacture of musical instruments. The musical practices of the times can be vividly reconstructed by combining the surviving scores and musical instruments with the rich visual evidence in paintings of the period.

Vermeer's *Concert* (Fig. 350), for one, shows a typical musical situation in the home. The trio is made up of a young woman, who reads her song part from the score she holds in her hand; a seated man, who supplies the harmonic background on his theorbo, a type of lute; and a girl at the spinet, the winged version of the virginal, who plays the keyboard part. On the floor is a viola da gamba, somewhat like the modern cello. Had it a player, this instrument would duplicate the bass line of the keyboard part in a combination known as the *continuo*.

The widespread custom of domestic music making resulted in a large body of literature that was designed for the home rather than public performance. An example of this type of music is Francis Pilkington's "Now Peep, Boe Peep" (Fig. 351), a number from that composer's *First Booke of Ayres,* published in 1605. The score was arranged and printed so that the participants could be seated comfortably around a table. On the left side, the words and melody, in this case the soprano part, appear above the lute tablature. To their right sits the tenor opposite the alto, with the bass in between.

Sweelinck's fame attracted to Amsterdam students from all over northern Europe. Through them his influence spread, especially over the Protestant parts of Germany. His most noted pupil here was Samuel Scheidt of Halle, whose *Tablatura Nova,* published in 1624, did much to crystallize the German Protestant organ and choral style. In this book, all the technical procedures he had learned from

350. Jan Vermeer. *Concert.* c. 1660.
Oil on canvas, 28 × 24¾″ (71 × 63 cm).
Isabella Stewart Gardner Museum, Boston.

Sweelinck were brought together and worked out with characteristic Germanic thoroughness. Happily, however, they were coupled with a considerable degree of creative imagination as well as technical invention. In its pages are found compositions intended for home performance, mainly in the form of variations on popular songs and dances as well as harmonizations of Lutheran hymns with ornamental commentaries in the form of variations. Scheidt's work became a landmark in organ literature, since it brought together for the first time a collection of pieces admirably adapted for Protestant church purposes, and a number of musical models for other composers to follow. A direct line thus extended from Sweelinck, who coordinated the Venetian and English schools, through such pupils as Scheidt, who transmitted the tradition to northern Germany, where Johann Sebastian Bach and George Frederick Handel were born in the year 1685.

Bach

The warm, all-embracing art of Johann Sebastian Bach is deeply rooted in the soil of the German Reformation. Though he wrote chamber music, instrumental dance suites, and concertos for the pleasure of aristocratic patrons, and though he composed his monumental B-minor Mass for a Roman Catholic prince, the vast quantity of his artistic output consists of the cantatas, oratorios, and organ pieces he wrote for the faithful congregations of St. Thomas' Lutheran Church in Leipzig. While the Reformation put restrictions on the visual arts, and some rigorous sects even disapproved of professional musicians generally, the Lutherans in the main were far more liberal than the Calvinists concerning music.

The Reformation first found its musical voice in the simple, unadorned congregational *chorales,* or hymns, which were sung in family circles and schools as well as in churches. The chorale thus became the nucleus of its musical tradition, with such other expressions as organ choral preludes, cantatas, and oratorios growing around it. Martin Luther himself was thought to be the author of many of these chorales that had such influence. One of them, *A Mighty Fortress Is Our God,* has aptly been called the "Marseillaise of the Reformation."

Bach's duties included not only playing the organ, directing the choir, and on special occasions conducting the small orchestra, but also writing most of the music for church services. This meant a cantata for Sundays; large-scale oratorios for Christmas, Passion Week, and Easter; as well as occasional music for marriages, funerals, the installation of a pastor, important civic occasions, and the like. Bach's fertile musical imagination and inexhaustible industry led to his completing no less than five series of cantatas for each Sunday and feast day of the church calendar—some three hundred in all, of which about two hundred still exist.

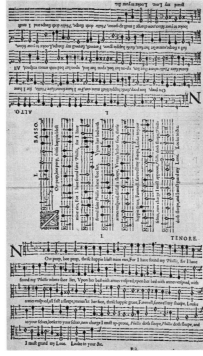

351. Francis Pilkington's *First Booke of Songs or Ayres of 4 Parts: With Tablature for Lute or Orpherian with violl de gamba.* London, 1605. Henry E. Huntington Library, San Marino, California.

Chorale from Cantata No. 140   Johann Sebastian Bach
(*Wachet auf, ruft uns die Stimme*)

Wa-chet auf! ruft uns die Stim me der Wach-ter sehr hoch
auf der Zin ne: wach' auf, du Stadt Je- ru - sa - lem!

The *cantata* is a form of incidental music for voices and instruments, woven directly into the Sunday service—the Protestant counterpart of the Roman Catholic sung mass. After the reading of the scriptural lesson the first half of the cantata was performed. Then came the sermon and the second half of the cantata, ending with the chorale, or hymn of the day, with the whole congregation participating. Just as the sermon was an interpretation of the Scriptures, the cantata was a musical commentary.

Awake, the Voice Is Calling (*Wachet auf, ruft uns die Stimme*), Bach's Cantata No. 140, written for the twenty-seventh Sunday after Trinity Sunday, will serve as a typical example. It is scored for solo soprano, tenor, and bass; four-part chorus; an orchestra of strings with the addition of two oboes, English horn, French horn; and a continuo consisting of the organ or harpsichord supported by a cello or double bass. The text has to do with the story of the Wise and Foolish Virgins. The Bride (the symbol of the Church and its congregation) is preparing for the coming of the Bridegroom (Jesus). The first five parts express longing, the last two fulfillment.

The sturdy chorale, the words of which give the cantata its name, provides the basic musical material and in whole or part is present in all sections of the cantata's fabric (see above). A short recitative follows for tenor with continuo accompaniment. This leads up to a duet for soprano and bass also with continuo accompaniment, but with the addition of an *obbligato,* or embellishing, part for solo violin that embroiders garlands around and over the voice parts. In the exact center of the design the chorale again appears—this time with the tenors carrying the melody, supported by the continuo below and the violins and violas above. This number is a typical *chorale prelude,* confirmed by Bach's own arrangement of it for organ solo. These organ compositions based on a chorale were played during the service and before

the chorale was sung by the congregation. Now follows another recitative written for bass voice, continuo, and strings. The next-to-last number is a duet for soprano and bass with oboe obbligato and continuo accompaniment. Finally comes the chorale once more, this time as a harmonized hymn in which the choir, orchestra, and congregation all join.

For the great church festivals Bach provided special music on a much larger scale. The tradition for such presentations goes all the way back to the mystery, miracle, and passion plays of the Middle Ages when, for instance, at Christmas time a manger scene, or *crèche,* was set up in the church for the reenactment of the story of the Nativity. In such a liturgical drama the choirboys would represent angels, adult choristers the shepherds, and members of the clergy Joseph and the Three Wise Men. Bach's famous 17th-century predecessor, Heinrich Schütz, wrote a notable example called the *Christmas Story;* and Bach himself composed a *Christmas Oratorio,* consisting of a series of six cantatas for weekly presentations during Advent, a period of anticipation beginning four weeks before Christmas, with the last one scheduled for the day after Christmas.

The Passion oratorios, similarly, grew out of the liturgical dramas performed during the week preceding Easter, particularly on Good Friday. They are the epic counterparts of the more lyrical and intimate Sunday cantatas. Here Bach again had, among others, the precedent of Schütz's *St. Matthew Passion.*

In keeping with established tradition, the scriptural passages in Bach's *St. Matthew Passion* are delivered by the Evangelist, who is represented by a tenor singing in recitative style. In the course of the work, the recitatives, solos, and ensembles represent the dramatic action, which is balanced by the more thoughtful choral sections. The solo passages thus represent individual reactions, while the chorus symbolizes at various times the crowd or mob, and ultimately the body of faithful Christians. The congregation joins in for the chorales. Thus they gain a sense of participation in the events in the life of the Lord. Bach's *St. Matthew Passion* and B-minor Mass represent his supreme achievement in choral music.

A certain domestic intimacy associated with family festivals characterizes the Protestant musical treatment of these biblical stories, so that the Christmas story and Passion become in turn the counterparts of the events in family life—birth, marriage, suffering, death. In Bach however, the Protestant Reformation reaches its highest musical fulfillment.

Ideas: Domesticity

The various aspects of the bourgeois baroque style find a common undercurrent in the idea of domesticity. Many related ideas, such as commercialism, Protestantism, antiauthoritarianism, nationalism, individualism, the passionate championship of individual rights and liberties, and the practical application of scientific discoveries, come together on this central concept. But the unity lies in the cult of the home. Bourgeois house comforts, for instance, were never so highly cultivated in the warmer, friendlier south, where recreational activity can occur in the open air. The northern climate, however, contributed to the concentration of family pleasures in the home.

The spirit of commerce led to navigational adventure on the high seas and to the exploration of distant lands. The conquests of the Dutch, however, were mainly those of the business people. Their empire was based on corporate enterprise, and their personal kingdoms were those of the banking houses and holding companies. Hard work and industriousness coupled with thrift led to a widespread accumulation of wealth in the hands of the middle class.

No riotous living or public displays of luxury were possible when the Protestant church permitted no embellishment in its buildings and no musical elaboration in its services. While both the Anglican and Lutheran reform movements preserved much of the beauty of the traditional Roman Catholic liturgy in a modified form, Calvinistic Protestantism was marked by its extreme austerity. A strict interpretation of Calvinism would lead directly to a gloomy form of asceticism, but the natural good sense and honest enjoyment of material pleasures saved the Dutch from the bleaker aspects of this doctrine. So the principal outlet for their prosperity and desire for aesthetic enjoyment was their homes.

Wealthy burghers, however, did not build palaces—though they certainly had the means to do so. They were content with comfortable houses that were functionally suited to their needs. Fighting the Spanish crown for their independence and resisting the growing menace of Louis XIV's absolute state made the Dutch look with disfavor on any form of courtly pomp and display.

The Protestant movement also fortified Dutch hostility to authority and intensified nationalist consciousness. Middle-class merchants particularly resented the draining off of their province's wealth in the direction of Rome. The resentment was equally strong against the secular arm of the Roman Catholic Church: the Holy Roman Empire. Protestantism thus took root and became identified in the Dutch mind with patriotism. Protection of their national rights and individual freedoms further focused attention on their homes, where they were lords.

Philosophy, social theory, and the natural sciences flourished in the Dutch universities. These intellectual pursuits theorized on the existence of an ordered and regulated universe in which everything could be measured and understood. Solid citizens instinctively distrusted the physical and emotional forces that could render their world chaotic and unpredictable. Hence, an ideal universe had considerable appeal for a middle class whose security and comforts could be perpetuated by it.

Descartes' rational theory of the universe, his equally rational psychology, and Spinoza's mathematically provable ethical system paralleled the concept of art as a form of reasoned organization. It took a Rembrandt, however, to illuminate this age of reason with an inner glow and to warm this rational world with the fire of human feeling.

Human anatomy was of consuming interest, and with Vesalius' *Anatomy* as a point of departure, dissection was carried over into other fields. Books had titles like *Anatomy of Melancholy, Anatomy of Wit, Anatomy of Abuses,* and *Anatomy of the World.*

In this Age of Observation, the restless human eye extended by the lens could explore many worlds, and more things were seen in heaven and earth than were ever dreamed of before. Optical instruments were developed by the skilled lens makers of Holland, whose ranks included Spinoza. An astronomical observatory was built at the University of Leyden, where the telescope could scan the skies. Conversely, the microscope opened up a new world in miniature.

Though their eyes were on the heavens, Dutch scientists did not neglect earthly applications of their discoveries. Astronomical calculations led to the discovery of triangulation and the spiral balance, both of vast value to navigation. The pendulum was applied to the keeping of time, and the pocket watch gave punctuality to daily life.

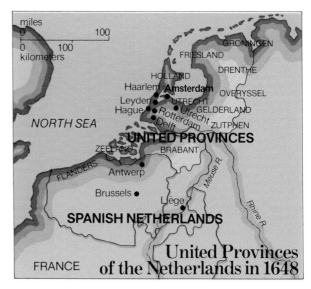

Domesticity and the Arts

The circumstances of the Dutch state of mind and material prosperity led to the placement of artistic patronage in the hands of a well-to-do middle class. Outside such necessary public buildings as the town halls, churches, and commercial structures, Dutch architecture was, for all intents and purposes, domestic architecture. Since the houses were about the same size as middle-class homes today, they provided neither room nor opportunity for monumental sculpture. The major domestic aesthetic expressions occurred, therefore, in painting and music, together with all the minor decorative arts that added to the comfort and beauty of the home.

Destined for living room walls, pictures were correspondingly smaller than those painted for palaces and public halls. There was a seemingly inexhaustible demand for pictures and the output was enormous. The number of professional artists multiplied with the demand and led to a corresponding degree of specialization. In portraiture there were the painters of the proper family types, of the drinkers in public taverns, and of corporation pictures. There were landscapists, seascapists, skyscapists, and even those whose specialty was cows. Painters also were drawn to the various social levels, with Jan Steen painting coarse tavern scenes and boisterous domestic interiors (Fig. 352); Frans Hals finding his subjects among fishwives and fruit peddlers; de Hooch and Vermeer depicting scenes in proper middle-class homes; and Terborch delighting in subtle narrative scenes (Fig. 353) and elegant society portraits.

The character of music was likewise molded by bourgeois patronage. In free cities, the organist and other municipal musicians were chosen by committees of the town councils, which supervised the musical life of the community as thoroughly as any of its other aspects. Auditions were held and competition encouraged. Public employment from the musician's point of view meant freedom from the arbitrary whims of a single aristocratic patron, and was generally preferred because of the security it implied. When the tastes of the many had to be taken into consideration, however, experimentation tended to be suppressed and standardization often was promoted. This was balanced to a great extent by the opportunities for music making in the home.

The home was thus the factor that determined the art forms and gave them such an intimate character and quality. Dutch domestic architecture, painting, and music were all designed to be lived with and enjoyed by middle-class people who frankly took delight in their physical comforts and the arts that enriched their lives.

Large canvases designed for altarpieces or to cover palace ceilings, colossal choral compositions for cathedrals, and operatic performances for palaces could produce grandiose utterances but had no place in the home. The more modest dimensions of a painting or an etching intended for the wall of a living room or of a chamber sonata or solo keyboard piece meant to be played in the same room encouraged a more intimate and personal form of communication.

The home was the dominant architectural form as well as the place where the pictures were hung, the books read, and the music played. In Holland and the northern countries generally, the baroque style was adapted both to Protestantism and to the tastes of the middle class. The bourgeois aspect of baroque art finds its unity in the cult of the home, and domesticity is the key to its understanding.

left: 352. Jan Steen. *Merry Family.* 1668. Oil on canvas, 3'7¼" × 4'7½" (1.1 × 1.41 m). Rijksmuseum, Amsterdam.
right: 353. Gerard Terborch. *Gallant Scene.* 1655. Oil on canvas, 27⅜ × 23⅜" (70 × 60 cm). State Museums, Berlin.

16
The Baroque Synthesis

London during the Restoration

That day in 1661, as Charles II made his triumphal progress to Westminster Abbey for his coronation, the sounds of Mr. Matthew Locke's march music for trombones and cornets mingled with the cordial cheers of Charles' subjects. They were the cheers of a people wearied by a generation of civil strife and the effort of conforming to the rigors of puritanical idealism. They were the cheers of a people who hoped and prayed that the Restoration would bring them peace and normalcy. They were the cheers of a people who did not know that in a few years a great number of them would die in an outbreak of the dreaded bubonic plague; that their city would be leveled by the Great Fire of London; and that the Restoration, which was supposed to be bringing back the old order, was actually ushering in the new.

The picture of a period populated by a merry monarch, libertine lords, loose ladies, and amorous adventurers has been painted all too often. That of a time which vibrated to the thunder of John Milton's poetry, spoke with the polished language of John Dryden, wondered at the mathematical cleverness of Isaac Newton's equations, marveled at the majesty of Christopher Wren's architecture, and heard the harmonies of Henry Purcell's music has received much less attention.

Even the Merry Monarch had a serious side, developed through the trials and tribulations of a troubled youth (during which his father's stormy reign had ended in Charles I's losing his head). Charles II was an amateur astronomer, whose enthu-siasm led to the founding of the Greenwich Observatory. He was also a patron of the theater, whose interest played an important role in the development of the Restoration drama; and of the arts, whose support of Christopher Wren caused an architectural rebirth in England. In addition, he was a music lover, who took pride now and then in lifting his voice in song in what has been described politely by his contemporaries as a "plump bass."

Thus, in 1661, Charles II's years of exile at Louis XIV's court were about to pay off handsomely, because in addition to some questionable absolutistic political ideas and some doubtful French courtly morals, he had brought back with him a goodly measure of Continental enthusiasm for the arts. During his reign, London was to become as much a cultural suburb of Versailles as the common sense of his subjects would bear.

London had caught a brief glimpse of Continental elegance under James I, Charles II's grandfather, who had commissioned Inigo Jones to build the Banqueting House at Whitehall (Fig. 354) as the first unit of a projected royal palace. Modeled on Palladian principles, this structure marked a departure in English architecture. When the great Peter Paul Rubens arrived in England on a diplomatic mission, he was persuaded by Charles I to paint the Banqueting House ceiling (Fig. 355). Anthony van Dyck, Rubens' most famous pupil, was appointed by Charles to paint a series of family portraits (Fig. 356). Now, with the restoration of the Stuart line under Charles II, the gates were about to be flung wide open.

Nicolas Lanier was dispatched to Italy to purchase pictures for the royal collections. William

CHRONOLOGY
17th-Century London

GENERAL EVENTS

1603–1625	James I (Stuart) reigned
1604	*Advancement of Learning* by Francis Bacon
1611	King James' authorized English translation of Bible completed
1619–1621	Banqueting House, Whitehall, built by Inigo Jones
1620	*Novum Organum* by Francis Bacon
1625–1649	Charles I reigned; after 1629 ruled without Parliament
1628	*Treatise on Terrestrial Magnetism and Electricity* by William Gilbert (1540–1603) published in English edition. Circulation of blood discovered by Harvey (1578–1657)
1642–1660	English Civil War
1643	Theaters closed by Parliament
1649	Charles I executed; England proclaimed Commonwealth
1651	*Leviathan* by Hobbes
1653–1658	Oliver Cromwell (1599–1658) ruled
1660	Restoration of monarchy
1660–1685	Charles II reigned
1661	*The Sceptical Chymist* by Robert Boyle (1627–91)
1662	Royal Society of London for Improving Natural Knowledge founded; Isaac Newton, Christopher Wren, Robert Boyle, John Dryden, charter members

1662	Christopher Wren appointed deputy surveyor-general to king; 1665 in Paris to observe remodeling of Louvre; met Bernini, Perrault, Mansart
1664–1665	Black Death (bubonic plague) swept London
1666	Great Fire of London
1667	*Paradise Lost* by Milton
1669	Wren appointed royal surveyor-general
1670	John Dryden named poet laureate and royal historian
1671–1680	St. Mary-le-Bow and other London parish churches built by Wren
1675–1710	St. Paul's Cathedral built
1678	*Pilgrim's Progress*, Part I, by Bunyan; Part II, 1684
1680	Purcell appointed organist at Westminster Abbey; named composer-in-ordinary to king (1683)
1682	*Venus and Adonis*, chamber opera by John Blow, performed at court
1685	*Albion and Albanius*, opera by Dryden and Purcell, performed in London
1685–1688	James II reigned
1687	*Mathematical Principles of Natural Philosophy* by Newton (1642–1727)
1688	Glorious Revolution; James II deposed; William of Orange and Mary (Stuart) became limited monarchs

1689–1702	William and Mary reigned
c.1689	*Dido and Aeneas*, opera, by Purcell
1690	Wing of Hampton Court Palace built by Wren; *Essay concerning Human Understanding* by John Locke
1691	*King Arthur . . . A Dramatick Opera* by Dryden and Purcell
1692	Nahum Tate named poet laureate
1704	*Opticks* by Newton
1722–1726	St. Martin-in-the-Fields built by Gibbs

WRITERS

1561–1626	Francis Bacon
1563–1593	Christopher Marlowe
1564–1616	William Shakespeare
1572–1631	John Donne
1573–1637	Ben Jonson
1588–1679	Thomas Hobbes
1608–1674	John Milton
1628–1688	John Bunyan
1631–1700	John Dryden
1632–1704	John Locke
1633–1703	Samuel Pepys
1652–1715	Nahum Tate

ARCHITECTS

1573–1652	Inigo Jones
1632–1723	Christopher Wren
1682–1754	James Gibbs

PAINTERS

1577–1640	Peter Paul Rubens
1599–1641	Anthony van Dyck

COMPOSERS

1606–1668	William Davenant
c.1647–1674	Pelham Humfrey
c.1648–1708	John Blow
1659–1695	Henry Purcell
1685–1759	George Frederick Handel

Davenant, who had been a guest in Paris of Charles and his mother and had closely observed Lully's musical methods, was summoned to become England's first opera manager. When the French opera composer Robert Cambert was ousted at home by the wily Lully, he found a ready welcome at the English court. Pelham Humfrey, a promising young composer of seventeen and later the teacher of Purcell, was sent to Paris by Charles to see how Lully managed his orchestra and ballet.

Since Louis XIV had his *Vingt-quatre Violons*, Charles II would have his Four-and-twenty Fiddles. When the monarch was looking around for a poet laureate, the choice fell to Dryden, who was most familiar with Boileau and the French baroque drama. And when Charles heard that King Louis and Colbert

left: **354.** Inigo Jones.
Banqueting House, Whitehall, London. 1619–22.
Length 120′ (36.58 m), height 75′ (22.86 m).

below: **355.** Inigo Jones.
Interior, Banqueting House, Whitehall, London.
Ceiling paintings by Peter Paul Rubens, 1629–34.

were getting ready to remodel the Louvre, he saw to it that Wren was on the spot to study the plans and to meet Bernini and Perrault.

London at the time of the Restoration had a character all its own. The city's population of merchants and clerks was independent of both clergy and monarchy. Living above their shops and countinghouses, this conservative middle class was driven by an "act of God" to change its city, when in 1666 a fire destroyed 13,000 houses, 400 streets, and 90 churches, according to Samuel Pepys, whose diaries describe daily life in London during this period. Before the

356. Anthony van Dyck.
Five Children of Charles I. 1637.
Oil on canvas,
5′4¼″ × 6′6¼″ (1.63 × 1.99 m).
Reproduced by permission of
the Lord Chamberlain's Office
(copyright reserved).

smoke cleared, Christopher Wren was sketching plans for the city's reconstruction. Even though his ideas were only partially achieved, they nonetheless determined later 17th-century London architecture and gave the city its superb skyline (see Fig. 364).

English Genius for Compromise

The collision between the substantial middle-class citizenry and their foreign-bred king brought further tangible proof of the English genius for compromise. The Stuarts from the beginning had tried to impose the Continental concept of absolutism on their reluctant subjects. The extremes of Charles I and his failure to come to terms with the middle-class merchants and their official body, the House of Commons, had brought about Cromwell's Commonwealth. The uncompromising Oliver Cromwell on his side had alienated the still-powerful aristocracy. Charles II had some success in trying to find a middle ground. His successor James II, however, again overstepped his authority, and it took still another revolution—this time the bloodless Glorious Revolution—to bring about the alliance between the king and the middle class under a limited monarchy.

Much the same struggle is mirrored in the arts. The French aristocratic baroque, just like the absolute monarchy, was too rich for the English diet. When it came time to build a new cathedral, Charles and his principal architect, Sir Christopher Wren, thought in terms of the richly embellished classical orders, the splendor and spaciousness of the Louvre and Versailles, and the central-type churches of Palladio and Michelangelo. The Church of England clergy and their parishioners, however, still thought of a cathedral as a tall, imposing Gothic structure. Wren wanted it to be crowned with a dome; the church leaders thought it should have a spire. So Wren built his dome and put a high lantern tower on top of it. Charles wanted the London parish churches to be free of Gothic gauntness and gloom, but the parishioners insisted on belfries with tall-spired steeples. So Wren gave them their steeples, but with classical geometrical flourishes.

A similar compromise was achieved in music. Charles wanted Lullian opera, but London theatergoers showed remarkable resistance toward sung recitative. So they got a hybrid form of spoken dialogue with songs and instrumental interludes inserted at intervals.

A comparison between the three great figures of the Restoration style—Wren, Dryden, and Purcell—can be illuminating. Each in his way was trying to bring his country up to date on the latest Continental developments, just as each was trying to inject something of the grandeur of the baroque style into an English art form. In order to do so, each was willing to make the necessary compromises to avoid parting company with English audiences.

When Wren was designing his preferred models on his drawing board, when Dryden was writing solely for a small circle of readers, and when Purcell was composing experimentally for amateurs, each could be as free as he chose. But when it came to building a cathedral, mounting a play, and composing music for the theater, many subtle and even drastic adjustments had to be made. Each man had sufficient mastery in his field and each was sufficiently versatile and inventive to make those adjustments. Each preferred and developed an aristocratic style but never neglected the common touch. Each, in his turn, had an influence that lasted well into the next century. Wren's buildings became the backbone of the Georgian style; Dryden's works, the background for 18th-century classicism in English literature; and Purcell's works were absorbed directly into the sacred and secular music of later generations.

With political authority divided between the monarch and Parliament, literary tastes between the classical and Elizabethan traditions, architectural ideas between the French baroque and English Gothic, and musical expression between the Continental developments and native preferences, the British genius for compromise was able to combine opposing elements into a whole. Remarkably, the British achieved a synthesis of aristocratic and middle-class institutions, Roman Catholicism and Protestantism, as well as the Continental and English traditions. Through the efforts and genius of three men—Wren in architecture, Dryden in literature, and Purcell in music—the Continental influences were merged with native traditions and transformed into a distinctive Restoration style.

Architecture

St. Paul's Cathedral

In the crypt beneath St. Paul's Cathedral in London a Latin inscription on a stone slab reads: "Beneath is laid the builder of this church and city, Christopher Wren, who lived more than 90 years, not for himself but for the good of the state. If you seek a monument, look around you." The most striking feature of St. Paul's (Fig. 357) is its structural unity, for this is the only major cathedral in Europe to be built by one architect, by one master mason, and during the episcopate of one bishop. In contrast, it took thirteen architects, twenty popes, and more than a century to build St. Peter's in Rome (Fig. 237). The last stone on the lantern tower above the dome of St. Paul's was

left: **357.** Christopher Wren. Façade, St. Paul's Cathedral, London, 1675–1710. Length 514′ (156.67 m), width 250′ (76.2 m), height of dome 366′ (111.56 m).

below: **358.** Plan, as executed, St. Paul's Cathedral.

put in place in 1710 by one of Wren's sons in the presence of the 78-year-old builder, and for another eight years Wren continued to supervise the completion of the last decorative details.

Even before the Great Fire, Wren was a member of a commission charged with the remodeling of Old St. Paul's. The plan had to be scrapped when a survey after the fire showed the building beyond repair. It was this that gave Wren his great opportunity.

Like Bramante and Michelangelo before him (see Fig. 253), Wren projected a spacious centralized area from which radiated subsidiary units of space. Like his famous predecessors, he too preferred a central-type church based on the Greek cross. In this way, a building of such monumental proportions could have both its exterior mass and interior space dominated by the all-embracing, unifying force of a dome. From a practical point of view, Wren was also aware that he was designing a Protestant cathedral which should permit as many people as possible to be within earshot of the pulpit so as to hear the sermon-centered service of the Anglican Church.

The conservative members of the clergy, with thoughts of the ancient Catholic processional liturgy in mind, wanted a long nave with aisles on either side. Wren, therefore, without sacrificing the heart of his plan, lengthened the edifice by adding an apse in the east and a domed *vestibule,* or lobby, with an extended porch in the west. His model, however, brought further objections from the clergy, necessitating still other revisions. All Wren's diplomacy, versatility, cleverness, and, above all, patience were called into play to create a workable compromise that would satisfy his difficult clients and yet save the essence of his cherished conception.

Wren gave the clergy their aisled nave and transepts and their deep choir, but he grouped these around the central plan of his original design (Fig. 358). In this way, he could still concentrate great space under the dome. Wren thus was actually building two churches, the clergy's and his own, a procedure that was bound to produce some architectural dissonances but for which he succeeded in finding a satisfactory if somewhat uneasy resolution in the cathedral that was finally completed.

Wren's practical problems with St. Paul's were as numerous as his difficulties with the authorities. For one thing, funds for construction were limited. For another, the site demanded engineering inventiveness, for as in much of London, solid ground was buried beneath 40 feet (12.2 meters) of clay and sand that could not bear too much weight. Furthermore, long before his cathedral was completed, Wren had had to abandon his hopes for an unobstructed view and a straight approach to his façade (Fig. 357) up Ludgate Hill on which St. Paul's rests. In the eagerness to rebuild after the fire, the vicinity had become a clutter of shops and houses, and it took the German air force in World War II to clear the land around the south side and the choir (Fig. 359).

359. St. Paul's Cathedral, from southeast.

Still another problem had developed when no quarry could supply stone of the necessary lengths for the great columns of his original façade. To solve this Wren had had to separate the façade into two separate stories of the Corinthian and Composite orders. His use of paired columns recalls Perrault's colonnade on the east front of the Louvre (see Fig. 317). The side *turrets,* or ornamental towers, were designed after 1700, and it is of more than passing interest that for some time one of them was left hollow except for a circular staircase for Wren and his fellow astronomers to use as an observatory.

The effect of Wren's preferred plan is felt most strongly in the rotunda beneath the dome (Fig. 360). Geometrically, the space is bounded by a gigantic octagon, accented at the angles by the eight piers on which the cupola rests. These are bridged over by a ring of connecting Roman triumphal arches, which, in turn, are crowned by the great dome, the culmination of the entire composition.

From this central area, the arches open outward into eight spatial subdivisions that give the interior such constant variety and interest. The centralization under the lofty dome, the complex divisions and subdivisions of space, the imaginative design and Roman detail reveal Wren's fondness for the baroque. The restraining influences of the conservative clergy, the lack of unlimited funds, and Wren's rationalistic viewpoint demonstrate his remarkable feat in making the style acceptable to British taste.

Wren's New Plan for London

Wren's plan for the rebuilding of London met with even stiffer resistance than his project for St. Paul's. It included the laying out of a series of new streets that extended outward starlike from central squares and that took the main traffic routes into consideration. Certain public buildings were to be situated on an axis involving the new cathedral and the Royal Exchange. The spires of the various parish churches were to point up the silhouette at certain points and lead up to the climax of St. Paul's dome.

The plan, if it had been carried out, would have gone far beyond that of Versailles. But Wren's king was not an absolute monarch with the power to condemn property and the money to buy it. Time also ran against Wren, because the shopkeepers throughout London were in a hurry to rebuild and start their business concerns again. About all he

360. Christopher Wren.
Rotunda, St. Paul's Cathedral.
Aquatint by Thomas Malton, 1798.

right: 361.
Christopher Wren.
St. Mary-le-Bow, London.
1671–80.
Total height 216'1"
(65.86 m),
steeple 104'6" (31.85 m).

far right: 362.
James Gibbs.
St. Martin-in-the-Fields,
London. 1721–26.

could rescue were the church steeples he was called upon to design.

As London's principal architect, Wren was commissioned to build more than fifty of these new parish churches. Discussions had to be held with the churchwardens on the problems and needs of each church. For monetary reasons the churches had to be modest affairs. Wren, in keeping with the spirit of the time, wanted to build them in the restrained baroque style based on the classical orders. His clients, however, still demanded the Gothic spires that not only had the force of symbols but the practical purpose of housing the bell tower, which was still a functional unit of a church. Wren's problem, therefore, was to balance the vertical tendency of the steeple with the horizontality of his classical temple façades—once more, the reconciliation of northern and southern building traditions. Wren's solution, among his

minor miracles, can only be understood through an actual example.

The steeple of St. Mary-le-Bow (Fig. 361), where the famous Bow Bells once rang out, shows the mathematician's obvious delight in a free play of geometrical forms. From a solid square base it moves through several circular phases and terminates finally in an octagonal pyramid. By the wise use of baroque scrolls and twists at various points, no hint of abruptness appears. Because the churches themselves would be hidden by the surrounding buildings, Wren lavished most of his skill on their spires.

The continuation of the Wren tradition into the next century is seen in James Gibbs' Church of St. Martin-in-the-Fields (Fig. 362). Wren had always planted his steeples firmly in the ground, so to speak, so that they seemed to grow in an organic relation to the whole composition. Gibbs' spire, by contrast,

The Baroque Synthesis **315**

appears to sprout unexpectedly out of the roof. The
memory of these churches and their steeples was
carried to the American colonies by the founding
fathers; and when they came to build their own
churches in new cities, it was to the designs of Wren
and Gibbs that they turned for their models.

Despite his many responsibilities, Wren found the
time to design some spacious and impressive houses
for well-to-do middle-class clients. During the reign
of William and Mary, he was also commissioned to
complete the unfinished Royal Hospital at Greenwich, begun earlier by Inigo Jones, and to add a new
wing for Hampton Court Palace. His patron, William
of Orange, remembered the good red brick of his
native Holland, while Wren recalled the grandeur of
the Louvre and Versailles palaces. Another of Wren's
famous compromises is found in his design for the

Fountain Court and the garden façade at Hampton
Court Palace (Fig. 363).

Thus it was that Wren, the professor of astronomy at London and Oxford, left off probing the mysteries of the heavens with his telescope and equations
and became the engineer and architect who penetrated that segment of the sky above London with
the majestic spires and domes that gave the city its
characteristic profile and skyline (Fig. 364).

Drama and Music

Dryden

On the gala occasion of the formal opening of the
King's Theatre in 1674, His Majesty and London's
most distinguished audience gathered there for the

evening's entertainment. John Dryden, that cold, aristocratic but brilliant author, took advantage of the situation offered by the prologue to express his sentiments in some well-chosen words:

'Twere folly now a stately pile to raise,
To build a playhouse while you throw down plays;
Whilst scenes, machines and empty Operas reign,
And for the Pencil you the Pen disdain;
While Troops of famished Frenchmen hither drive,
And laugh at those upon whose Alms they live:
Our English Authors vanish, and give place
To these new Conquerors of the Norman race.

Dryden was thus making the brave effort of a dedicated poet and playwright to stem the tide of foreign forms of opera, which, in his opinion, threatened to engulf reason with rhyme. Dryden, of course, felt that the dramatic logic of plot development would be arrested and overwhelmed by the music, and that the high art of poetry would have to yield to jingling rhymes for the convenience of singers. The course of events, however, was flowing far too strongly, and Dryden soon was collaborating with one of those fashionable Frenchmen and writing some fancy "scenes and machines" himself.

With all the adaptability of a thoroughly professional writer, Dryden honestly tried to squeeze some content into those "empty Operas." In his preface to *Albion and Albanius,* for instance, he was more than a little apologetic about having to write so as "to please the hearing rather than gratify the understanding"; and, he continued, "it appears, indeed, preposterous at first sight, that rhyme, on any consideration, should take the place of reason."

Purcell and English Opera

Meanwhile, Henry Purcell, England's greatest composer, was trying to bring some of the new Venetian and French techniques into an English form of opera. The London stage, however, was not yet ready for such Continental extravaganzas. To introduce and demonstrate the new style, he wrote and staged his miniature operatic masterpiece, *Dido and Aeneas,* for a school for young gentlewomen at Chelsea where he was music master. For the text he had to get along with a rather ordinary book by Nahum Tate, who later became poet laureate under William and Mary. The work is a true *chamber opera,* one designed for a limited space, restricted to a few characters, and employing a small orchestra. Though small in scale, it is large in emotional scope; and while it falls within the province of amateur performance, it is filled with the utmost musical sophistication.

Dido and Aeneas opens with a dignified overture in the Lully style, marked by the halting rhythms

Dido and Aeneas (recitative excerpts)   Henry Purcell

and constantly resolving chains of dissonances of a slow beginning, and the contrapuntal imitations of a lively conclusion. All the orchestral sections seem to have been scored only for strings with the usual keyboard support.

For his recitatives and airs, Purcell turns to the models developed by Monteverdi and his successor at the Venetian opera, Cavalli. Purcell makes particularly bold use of the "representative style," a type of word painting, by which the descriptive imagery of the text is reflected in the shape and turn of the melodic line (above). This can be illustrated by the first word in the opera, "Shake" (a), and the menacing movement of the line for "storms" (b). In a comment on Aeneas' parentage, the valor of his father Anchises is characterized by a warlike rhythm (c); while immediately afterward a modulation to the minor mode and a caressing melody express the sensuousness of Venus' charms (d). Also, when Aeneas' entrance is announced, Belinda's words take on the shape of a trumpet fanfare (e).

The airs show a considerable variety as to type. Dido's opening and closing songs are built over a short repeated bass pattern as in the Italian *ostinato aria.* The melody of "Oft She Visits" is written over a continuously flowing bass line in the manner of an Italian *continuo aria;* while the three-part melodic form of "Pursue Thy Conquest, Love," the final section of which repeats the beginning, identifies it as a *da capo aria.*

The emphasis on the choruses and dances is in the English court masque tradition, but both are handled by Purcell with a highly original blend of native and Continental elements. In the palace scenes, the courtiers function as a true Greek chorus by making solemn comments in unison on the action. The final number, "With Drooping Wings," is a typical French mourning chorus straight out of Lullian opera. The witches, however, sing in the English madrigal style with the amusing substitution of some malicious "Ho, ho, ho's" for the jollier "Fa la la's," to signify their sinister purposes.

Highly interesting is Purcell's introduction of a Venetian echo chorus in these solemn surroundings. While the witches sing "In Our Deep Vaulted Cell," an offstage chorus softly echoes "-ed cell." By thus increasing the perception of space. Purcell is able to

Dido and Aeneas   Henry Purcell
("When I Am Laid in Earth")

my fate, Re-mem-ber me, but ah!_____ for-get my_ fate!

add the necessary eerie touch as the witches start to prepare their mysterious charms. The spell is further carried out in the "Echo Dance of Furies," in which an offstage instrumental group echoes the principal orchestra with marked effect.

The dances show much of the same stylistic mixture as the choruses. Scene 1 concludes with the courtiers doing a "Triumphing Dance," which is a vigorous version of a Lully *chaconne,* a composition consisting of continuous variations on a short theme in slow triple meter, treated in this instance as a set of instrumental variations over a repeated ground bass. During Act III, when Aeneas is preparing to sail away from Carthage, Purcell paints a typical English seaport scene in which the swinging sailors' dances mingle with the salty comments of a chorus of common people. The angularity of such native rhythms as the hornpipe is a distinct contrast to the more formal *courantes* and chaconnes danced by the courtiers.

Purcell's logic and fine dramatic perception do not permit him to soften his opera toward the end by allowing a *deus ex machina* to bring it to a happy ending in the manner of the French court style of Lully. The human will when battling with the gods is always doomed, and the plot must move inevitably onward. The tragedy is therefore carried through to its predetermined conclusion with growing eloquence and mounting emotion.

As a consequence, "Dido's Farewell" (above) becomes one of the most moving moments in all music, combining as it does the most passionate feeling with the dignified restraint demanded of a tragic heroine out of Vergil's *Aeneid.* It is cast in the form of an ostinato aria with an obstinately repetitive bass pattern, which descends chromatically to the rhythm of the stately *passacaglia,* a dance tune similar to the

chaconne. Dido's inner struggle is expressed by the tension between the *obbligato,* or ornate melodic line, that she sings and the inflexible bass. She contends with this *ground bass* as with her tragic fate. Vainly she tries to bend it to her will, as seen in some of the asymmetrical diagonal shifts of her phrases off their center. In the end, however, she must resign herself to it while the orchestra carries the aria onward to its tragic conclusion.

Within the limitations of this short opera, which takes little more than an hour to perform, Purcell produced a major work of art. It reveals the sure touch of one who knows every aspect of the dramatic business. The extensive emotional range and the variety of technical devices are all the more astonishing in view of the few resources he had at his disposal. Purcell possesses, first of all, the rare power to create believable human characters by musical means, a gift he shares with Gluck and Mozart. He is also one of the few composers who know how to convert the dry academic techniques of counterpoint into lively dramatic devices, a characteristic he shares with Bach and Handel.

These traits can be illustrated in Dido's first air, "Ah, Belinda." Her melody is like a series of descending sighs over a ground bass that, like destiny, is relentless and unyielding. At the words "Peace and I are strangers grown," the parting of the two lovers' ways is depicted by a canon at the octave; and on the word "strangers," the predominant four-bar pattern begins to wander and is stretched out into five bars. Again, after Aeneas declares he will defy destiny itself in order to remain with Dido, the chorus makes contrapuntal comments that graphically give expression to their disturbed and conflicting emotions. When Purcell wants to depict the hustle and bustle around the departing ships in the scene at the dockside in Act III, the independent introduction in the form of a *fugue,* literally meaning "flight," with its imitative thematic entries and exits, humorously describes the coming and going of the people.

When such skillful means as these are combined with his deft handling of the orchestra, colorful use of chromaticism, and deep poetic feeling, they are sure to lead to significant ends—as indeed, in this case, they did.

Handel: Opera and Oratorio

Early in the 18th century another great composer, George Frederick Handel (Fig. 365), was to have a try at bringing English audiences around to the delights of Italian opera. In his native Germany, Handel had been music director at the court of the Elector of Hanover, who succeeded Queen Anne on the British throne as George I. Coming in the wake of the newly crowned king, his position in London was assured. Like Bach, Handel also wrote all forms of keyboard and chamber music, concertos, and other orchestral works. Vocal music took first place, however, as it did for all major baroque composers.

Italian opera was Handel's first love, but in spite of the beauty of such masterpieces as *Giulio Cesare* (*Julius Caesar*), these operas in Italian enjoyed only limited success in the London of their day. When that door was closed, Handel turned to large-scale oratorios with English texts. Like operas, oratorios had instrumental overtures and interludes, recitatives, solo arias, and choruses. However, they were usually presented in concert form without scenery, costumes, and dramatic action. Handel's oratorios were written to both sacred and secular texts and were primarily intended for public performances in theaters and large halls rather than in church. They were, in fact, promoted as "Grand Musical Entertainments." Such immortal works as *Semele,* the *Messiah,* and *Israel in Egypt* have won an assured place in the international repertory.

Handel's *Semele,* though technically described as a secular oratorio, is nonetheless an excellent example of his operatic writing. It has, moreover, the advantage of an English text of considerable literary quality by the distinguished playwright William Congreve. Act II opens with Juno venting her jealous fury in an impassioned recitative passage. Semele, by way of contrast, sings a serene solo aria, "Oh Sleep, Why Dost Thou Leave Me?" The eloquent melody rises over a lullabylike continuo accompaniment by harpsichord and cello revealing the sleepless state of a woman in love and longing for her lover—none other than the divine Jupiter himself. When Jupiter appears, their dialogue is carried on in a recitative that leads up to one of Handel's most eloquent arias, "Where'er You Walk."

After lavishing two such masterpieces on a single scene, Handel has still further lyrical surprises in store, such as Semele's aria, "Myself I Shall Adore." Semele's vanity, which is to be her downfall, has been cleverly prodded by Juno in disguise, and the aria is sung as she gazes fondly into her mirror. Handel chooses the *concerted aria,* in which the voice alternates with instruments for this situation, and Semele's reflection is graphically described by the violins, which reflect her phrases in echolike imitations of the vocal line. With his constant flow of melodic invention, and by matching such technical devices as the concerted aria with significant insights into human character, Handel succeeds in drawing dramatic sparks from the stately lines of Congreve's text and in writing convincingly for the lyric stage.

The inward direction and lyrical qualities of the *Messiah* contrast strongly with the sweep of such

365. Thomas Hudson.
George Frederick Handel. c. 1742.
Oil on canvas, 47⅛ × 39″ (121 × 100 cm).
City and University Library, Hamburg.

biblical epics as *Israel in Egypt.* In this mighty oratorio the chorus represents the collective image of the children of Israel and is both the dramatic protagonist as well as the group narrator. Free use is made of the *representative,* or word-painting, style, notably in such passages as those depicting the plagues. A leaping pattern that accompanies a solo aria, for instance, neatly describes the frogs mentioned in the text (No. 5).* Further graphic realism is found in the buzzing "Chorus of Flies" (No. 6), as well as in the "Hailstone Chorus" (No. 7). The mournful harmonies of "He Sent a Thick Darkness over the Land" (No. 8) paint a vivid picture of nightfall with the singers groping their way through a maze of remote harmonic centers; while the driving rhythms of "The Lord Is a Man of War" (No. 22) proceed in powerful, hammerlike strokes.

It is, of course, the chorus, not the solo aria, that dominates a Handel oratorio, and the power and breadth of the joyful sounds that make the most unforgettable impression.

---

*The numbers follow the order given in the Mendelssohn edition of the score published by G. Schirmer, Inc., New York.

Comparison with Bach   The two towering figures of the late baroque—Handel and Bach—invite comparison since, though they were fellow Germans and exact contemporaries, they were products of different social environments and different individual temperaments. Handel, for instance, was a sophisticated figure, at home in great capital cities. Bach, in spite of his formidable reputation, was content to pursue his career in German provincial centers. Bach's post at Leipzig was an important one, and Leipzig itself was a university town of some standing in Germany. But Handel in 18th-century London found himself in a city that competed with Paris for the position of the cultural and intellectual capital of Europe.

Handel, as a robust man of the world, had a straightforward, vigorous mind, while Bach was more disposed to brooding and self-searching contemplation. Handel was more concerned with the joy and beauty of this life, while Bach beheld blissful visions of ultimate truth in the next. Both were perceptive students of the Bible, but Handel favored the Old Testament and the inevitable victory of the righteous cause, while Bach preferred the New Testament and the problems of death and redemption. Handel, in his choral music, approached a text much more directly and concretely, while Bach's thought ran in a more abstract vein, even at times to the complete disregard of the text's metrical rhythm.

It has often been observed, too, that Handel was essentially a vocal composer, while Bach was primarily instrumentally minded. Both, however, were masters of external forms as well as inner expression,

366. Galileo Galilei. Telescopes. 1609. Museum of Science, Florence.

and in the end they must be considered complementary rather than contrasting figures. Both also, in any final evaluation, must be given equal importance in their respective spheres. Together these musical suns of the baroque period sum up two centuries of accumulated creative experience and expression.

Ideas: Baroque Rationalism

Stimulated by the explorations of navigators of the globe, the scanning of the skies by astronomers, and the advances of inventors, the baroque mind reassessed the world and the place of human beings in the universe. Galileo's telescopes (Fig. 366) confirmed Copernicus' theory of a solar system in which the earth revolved around the sun rather than vice versa. The concept of the unmoving Aristotelian universe thus had to yield to one that was full of whirling motion. Since the earth was no longer considered as a fixed point located at the nerve center of the cosmos, human beings could hardly be regarded any longer as the sole purpose of creation. It was some consolation, however, to know that this strange, new, moving universe at least was subject to mechanical and mathematical laws, and therefore to a considerable extent predictable. Copernicus and Kepler as well as the other scientists were convinced of its unity, proportion, and harmony; and the fact that the human mind had the privilege of probing into the secrets of nature—if the intellect proved equal to the task—was a great challenge.

The rationalism of the 17th century, then, was based on the view that the universe could at last be understood in logical, mathematical, and mechanical terms. As a philosophy and semireligion, this world view had far-reaching consequences by preparing for the theories of positivism and materialism, the doctrines of deism and atheism, and the mechanical and industrial revolutions.

While Greek rationalism had been based on the perception and measurement of a stable, immobile world, baroque rationalism had to come to terms with a dynamic universe. Scientific thought was concerned with movement in space and time. The need for a mathematics capable of understanding a world of matter in motion led Descartes to his analytical geometry, Pascal to a study of cycloid curves, and both Leibniz and Newton to the simultaneous but independent discovery of integral and differential calculus.

Baroque invention also led to refinements in navigation, to improvements in the telescope and microscope for the exploration of distant and extremely small regions of space, the barometer for the measurement of air pressure, the thermometer for the recording of temperature changes, and the anemometer for the calculation of the force of winds. Astronomers were occupied with the study of planetary motion; William Harvey discovered the circulation of the blood; and physicists were experimenting with thermodynamics and gravitation.

Newton's concern with mass, force, and momentum, his speculations on the principles of attraction and repulsion, and his calculations on earthly and heavenly mechanics led him to a monumental synthesis that he presented to the British Royal Society in 1686 and published in London a year later. Newton's *Principia* embraced a complete and systematic view of an orderly world based on mechanical principles, capable of mathematical proof, and evident by accurate prediction. His work was, in fact, a scientific *summa,* or summation, that established the intellectual architecture of the new view of the universe.

Such a changed world view was bound to have important consequences for the arts, which responded in this case with a ringing reassertion of human supremacy and a joyous acceptance of this new understanding of the universe. The application of rationalistic principles to aesthetic expression is by no means accidental or casual. Before he became an architect, Christopher Wren was a mechanical inventor, an experimental scientist, and a professor of astronomy at London and Oxford. As a founder of the Royal Society, he was in close contact with such men as Robert Boyle and Isaac Newton.

The fellows of the Royal Society appointed John Dryden to a committee the purpose of which was to study the English language with a view toward linguistic reforms. They recommended that English prose should have both purity and brevity, so that verbal communication could be brought as close to mathematical plainness and precision as possible. Dryden's embarrassment in writing an opera that was designed to please the ear rather than gratify the understanding was therefore quite understandable.

The music of Purcell and Handel was based on a system of complex contrapuntal principles and tonal logic in which given premises, such as sequences or repeated ground basses, are followed by predictable conclusions. Moreover, it is characterized by intellectual discipline, symmetry, clarity, and a sure sense of direction. Their forms are models of brevity in which each part has its place, no loose ends are left dangling, and the cadences bring everything to a positive finish.

Like Wren's architecture and Dryden's poetic drama, Purcell's and Handel's musical art reflects an assured self-confidence, an inventive spirit that gave birth to new forms, an exploration of novel optical and acoustical ideas, and a conviction that a work of art should be a reflection of an orderly and lawful universe.

Baroque Synthesis and Conclusion

While the baroque period is mainly centered in the 17th century, its extreme limits in time extend all the way from the mid-16th to the mid-18th centuries, from Michelangelo to Bach and Handel. During this span of time a number of crucial changes took place. The concept of the world had moved from an earth-centered to a sun-centered universe. Philosophical speculation had turned from a supernatural to a natural world view. The fundamental processes of thought had shifted from the acceptance of authority on faith to scientific experimentation. The unity of Christianity symbolized by one universal Church had been opposed by a number of Protestant sects. The theoretical political unity of the Holy Roman Empire had given way to the practical fact of a balance of power distributed among a family of nations.

The baroque period was one in which irresistible modern forces met immovable traditional objects. Out of all the theological conflicts, philosophical discussions, scientific arguments, social tensions, political strife, warfare, and artistic creation came both the baroque style and the modern age.

The baroque world was one in which oppositions that were impossible to reconcile had to find a way to coexist. The rise of rationalism was accompanied by the march of militant mysticism. The aristocratic cult of majesty was echoed by the bourgeois cult of domesticity. The internationalism of Roman Catholicism was in conflict with the nationalism of the Protestant sects. Religious orthodoxy had to contend with freedom of thought. The Jesuits brought all the arts into their churches, while Calvin did his best to exclude the arts as vanities. Philip II built a magnificent mausoleum and monastery, while Louis XIV erected a pleasure palace and theater. Charles I tried to force an absolute monarchy on England, and Cromwell's answer was a republican commonwealth. The printing press made books available, while suppression by censorship took them away. The boldest scientific thinking took place alongside a reassertion of the belief in miracles and a renewal of traditional religious beliefs. Newton's *Principia* and the final part of John Bunyan's *Pilgrim's Progress* appeared in London within two years of each other. The arts demonstrated similar oppositions. In Spain, the emotional involvement of El Greco was succeeded by the optical detachment of Velázquez. In France the spontaneity of Rubens was followed by the academic formalism of Poussin. In Holland, the broad humanity of Rembrandt led to the specialization and precision of Vermeer.

Such oppositions could hardly be expected to resolve themselves into a single uniform style. At

367. Antonio Gherardi. Cupola, Avila Chapel, Santa Maria in Trastevere, Rome. c. 1686.

their pictures and attempted to convey the impression of infinity through the bold use of light and exaggerated perspective effects. The Dutch landscapists tried to capture atmospheric perspective, and Rembrandt was concerned with the infinite gradations of light. Through use of illusionistic effects, ceilings of Counter-Reformation churches opened the skies and tried to promote the feeling of a world without end (see Fig. 299).

In music there was a corresponding expansion of tonal space. The organs and other keyboard instruments were built to include a wider range from bass to soprano. Both the wind and the stringed instruments were constructed in families, ranging all the way from what the English organist and composer Orlando Gibbons called the "Great Dooble Base" to the high soprano register of the violin. Louis XIV and Charles II incorporated this string family into groups of twenty-four players, thus increasing both resonance and volume of sound through the doubling process. The use of chromatic harmony with all the half-tone, or half-step, divisions of the octave was the internal extension of the same idea. Purcell's opposition of ground basses and soprano melodies emphasized the baroque love of a spacious distribution of resonances. His adoption of the Venetian double chorus and his dramatic use of the echo effect in *Dido and Aeneas* were still further evidence of the desire of baroque composers to increase the perception of space through sound.

Above all, the baroque universe was in ceaseless movement. Whether a rationalist thought of it in terms of whirling particles or a mystic as full of swirling spirits, both saw their world as a whirlpool of spheres and spirals making infinitely complex patterns of motion. Kepler's planets revolved in elliptical orbits. Counter-Reformation churches were built over undulating floor plans. Their walls rippled like stage curtains. The decorative lavishness of their façades further activated the heavy masses of masonry and increased their rhythmic pulsation. Under their domes terra-cotta angels flew in orbits. The unyielding stone of the statuary finally rose off the ground and melted into a myriad of fluid forms (Fig. 367). Paintings escaped from flat wall spaces and took flight to concave surfaces of the ceilings, where they could soar skyward and where more daring perspective effects were possible.

Baroque music also mirrored a moving universe. Its restless forms took on the color of this dynamic age, and its sound patterns floated freely through their tonal spaces freed from gravitational laws. No longer in bondage to religious ritual, to the dance, or to poetry, its emancipation was now complete. Of such ideas and materials was the image of this brave new baroque world constructed.

best, they could achieve a temporary resolution and a fusion of forms, such as those found in a Counter-Reformation church, the Versailles Palace, Rembrandt's visual dramatization of the Bible, and Purcell's operatic synthesis. In them, forceful striving and restless motion are more characteristic than calm and repose. Baroque art thus emerges from these tensions and speaks in eloquent accents of the expanding range of human activities, grandiose achievements, and a ceaseless search for more powerful means of expression.

Expansion of Space

The conflicts of the baroque world took place within a tremendously enlarged sense of space. The astronomers told of remote regions populated by an infinite number of stars. Pascal speculated on the mathematical implications of infinity. The gardens and avenues of Versailles were laid out in keeping with this vastly extended concept of space. The vistas led the eye toward the horizon and invited the imagination to continue beyond. The unification of the vast buildings and gardens there brought baroque society wholly within the scope of nature and declared it to be a part of the new measurable universe.

Wren's attempt to bring his cathedral, parish churches, and public buildings into one all-embracing scheme was also in keeping with this image of the comprehensive baroque universe. Painters likewise delighted in leading the eye outside

17
The 18th-Century Styles

18th-Century Panorama

The momentum of the baroque style was sufficient to propel it well into the 18th century. New social forces, new ideas, new aesthetic currents came together to bring about, in some cases, a meeting of the main baroque streams and, in others, the formation of new ones.

With the death of Louis XIV in 1715, the aristocratic baroque style moved into its final rococo phase. The regent for his young successor closed the majestic Versailles Palace and reestablished the royal residence in Paris. Artistic patronage was no longer the monopoly of the court, and the painter Watteau, arriving in Paris the same year the Sun King died, had to look for his patrons among a broad group drawn from both the nobility and the middle class. Throughout the century, the operas of Rameau, Gluck, and Mozart were composed for public opera houses where aristocrats rubbed shoulders with the bourgeoisie. The arts, in effect, moved out of the marble halls into the elegant salons (Fig. 368), where subtlety and charm were considered higher aesthetic virtues than impressiveness and grandeur.

The rococo, that late version of the aristocratic baroque style, was by no means confined to Paris. All European courts took on in some degree the character of cultural suburbs of Versailles. French fashions in architecture, painting, furniture, costume, and manners were echoed in such far-off corners as the courts of Catherine the Great of Russia and of Maria Theresa in Vienna. Whether a prince ruled a province in Poland or a duchy in Denmark, French was spoken in his household more naturally than the language of his native country. In Prussia, Frederick the Great built a rococo palace at Potsdam and called it *Sans-souci* ("Carefree"); the king of Saxony commissioned the jewel-like Zwinger pleasure pavilion in

368. Germain Boffrand. Salon de la Princesse, Hôtel de Soubise, Paris. c. 1740. Oval, 33 × 26′ (10.06 × 7.92 m).

CHRONOLOGY
18th Century

GENERAL EVENTS

1715	Louis XIV died
1715-1774	Louis XV, king of France
1724	Belvedere Palace, Vienna, finished; Hildebrandt architect
1726	*Gulliver's Travels* by Swift
1728	*Beggar's Opera* by John Gay (1685-1732) performed in London
1732	Hôtel de Soubise, Paris, begun; Boffrand, architect
1740-1780	Maria Theresa, empress of Austria
1740-1786	Frederick the Great, king of Prussia
1744	Schönbrunn Palace built in Vienna (begun in 1696 by Fischer von Erlach)
1748	*Spirit of Laws* by Condorcet. Excavations at Pompeii begun
1751-1772	*Encyclopédie,* or *A Classified Dictionary of the Sciences, Arts and Trades,* published by Diderot
1752	Pergolesi's *Serva Padrona* performed in Paris. *Guerre des Bouffons,* "war" in Paris over serious *versus* comic opera
1759	*Candide* by Voltaire
1762	*Social Contract* by Rousseau. Gluck's *Orpheus* performed in Vienna
1762-1768	Petit Trianon, Versailles, built by Louis XV for Mme. Dubarry; Gabriel, architect
1762-1796	Catherine the Great, empress of Russia

1774-1792	Louis XVI, king of France
1774	Gluck's *Orpheus* and *Iphigenia in Aulis* performed in Paris
1775	Beaumarchais' *Barber of Seville* presented in Paris
1776	American Declaration of Independence. *Storm and Stress,* play by Maximilian Klinger (1752-1831), gave name to art movement
1780-1790	Joseph II, emperor of Austria
1781	Mozart settled in Vienna. *Critique of Pure Reason* by Kant
1784	Beaumarchais' play *Marriage of Figaro* presented; 1786 Mozart's *Marriage of Figaro* performed in Vienna
1787	Mozart's *Don Giovanni* performed in Prague; in Vienna 1788
1789	French Revolution begun
1790	*Faust, A Fragment,* by Goethe published in Leipzig
1794	*Progress of the Human Spirit* by Condorcet
1797	*Sense and Sensibility* by Jane Austen; published in 1811

ARCHITECTS

1650-1723	Johann Fischer von Erlach
c.1660-1726	Jakob Prandtauer
1667-1754	Germain Boffrand
1668-1745	Lukas von Hildebrandt
1698-1782	Ange Jacques Gabriel

PAINTERS

1684-1721	Antoine Watteau
1697-1764	William Hogarth
1699-1779	J. B. S. Chardin
1703-1770	François Boucher
1725-1805	Jean Baptiste Greuze
1732-1806	Jean Honoré Fragonard
1775-1842	Élisabeth Vigée-Lebrun

SCULPTORS

1714-1785	Jean Baptiste Pigalle
1716-1791	Étienne Falconet
1738-1814	Clodion (Claude Michel)
1741-1828	Jean Antoine Houdon

COMPOSERS

1668-1733	François Couperin
1683-1764	Jean Philippe Rameau
1714-1787	Christoph Willibald von Gluck
1714-1788	C. P. E. Bach
1732-1809	Joseph Haydn
1756-1791	Wolfgang Amadeus Mozart

WRITERS AND PHILOSOPHERS

1667-1745	Jonathan Swift
1689-1761	Samuel Richardson
1694-1778	Voltaire (François Marie Arouet)
1698-1782	Pietro Metastasio
1707-1754	Henry Fielding
1712-1778	Jean Jacques Rousseau
1713-1784	Denis Diderot
1724-1804	Immanuel Kant
1728-1774	Oliver Goldsmith
1729-1781	Gotthold Ephraim Lessing
1732-1799	Caron de Beaumarchais
1744-1803	Johann Gottfried von Herder
1749-1832	Wolfgang von Goethe
1749-1838	Lorenzo da Ponte
1759-1805	Friedrich von Schiller
1775-1817	Jane Austen

Dresden; and the Prince-Bishop erected a handsome residence in Würzburg. Such French authors as Voltaire and Jean Jacques Rousseau found an international reading public; French dances dominated the balls and French plays the theaters.

In southern Germany and Austria, however, Italian influence was still strong. At the court in Vienna an Italian architect finished the Schönbrunn Palace for Maria Theresa; Italian paintings decorated its walls. Metastasio was the poet laureate, playwright, and opera librettist; and only plays and operas in Italian could be performed in the royal theaters. The missionary energy of the Jesuits working outward from Rome spread and popularized the religious counterpart of the aristocratic style throughout the Counter-Reformation countries.

Baroque rationalism had been the territory of a relatively few outstanding minds. In the 18th century, however, as the scientific knowledge of Newton and the social theories of John Locke became the common property of the educated classes, rationalism broadened into the movement known as the *Enlightenment,* a term—like the *rococo*—that generally refers to the period between 1715 and 1789. As the streams of rationalism and academicism met, the most characteristic expression of the Enlightenment became the 35-volume *Encyclopédie,* edited by Denis Diderot. In this *Classified Dictionary of the Sciences, Arts, and Trades,* some 180 outstanding minds collected and made available in clear language all the knowledge that had existed before only in difficult scientific studies.

While the fruits of rationalism became the common property of the middle class, *reason,* in the vocabulary of the 18th century, by no means implied only cold intellectuality. Reason was considered to be a mental faculty shared by all who chose to cultivate it. Among its implications were common sense, exercise of good judgment, and the development of taste—all of which were accompanied by a healthy involvement in active human pursuits.

As applied to the arts, reason meant the search for expressive forms and sentiments sufficiently universal and valid to be accepted by all who supported the principles of good taste and judgment. With the broadening of the bases of wealth and education, the middle class was able to rise and challenge the ancient authority and privileges of the aristocracy. Through the power of knowledge released by the Enlightenment, the age-old chains of superstition, intolerance, and fear began to be thrown off. The ideals of freedom championed by reasonable people were eventually written into the American Declaration of Independence and Bill of Rights and became the moving force behind the French Revolution. Increasingly, it was now the middle class who wrote and read the books, who constructed and lived in the buildings, who painted and bought the pictures, and who composed and listened to the music.

The philosophy of the Enlightenment did not, however, go unchallenged. Undercurrents of irrationalism were found in movements that anticipated 19th-century romanticism. Rousseau, for example, gave sensibility a deeper emotional tone, and in France generally *sensibilité* meant tugging at the heartstrings of readers, observers, and listeners. In Germany, emotionalism burst out in the more violent form of the so-called Storm-and-Stress movement that made a rather personal interpretation of Rousseau's initial statement in his *Social Contract:* "Man is born free, and everywhere he is in chains." Goethe's characterizations of Faust and Prometheus

and Mozart's Don Giovanni were independent human beings, who defied the gods of convention and demanded a range of inner and outer experience, even if they had to pay the penalty of eternal torment.

The truth such figures sought was one of feeling rather than logic, and their curiosity was boundless. By bursting the bonds of civilized restraints, they were in full rebellion against hereditary aristocratic privilege as well as stern middle-class morality. Their freedom was far from that of the Enlightenment. It was, in fact, an antirationalistic, antiuniversal, powerfully proindividualistic freedom that bordered on self-destruction and anarchy.

The 18th century as a whole was marked by a quickening of the pulse of human affairs. The flood of material from the printing presses alone made it all but impossible to keep up with the pace set in philosophy, literature, and music. The spread of wealth led to the development of urban centers and widespread building projects. Writers, painters, and musicians no longer aimed their output exclusively at one social group.

While it is often called the Age of Reason, the 18th century gave birth to some of the most bizarre and irrational beings, real or imaginary, ever conceived by the mind or imagination. The passionate disputes begun in the 17th century continued, but on the surface at least the divisions did not appear to be so sharp. The unresolvable oppositions of the baroque were softened in subtle satires, gentle ironies, witty verbal dueling, and nostalgic melancholies. What appeared as a period of comparative quiet, however, was but the calm before the storm, the prelude to a social explosion that brought the aristocratic rococo to a violent, revolutionary end, and hurled into the next century the forces of reason and emotion it had generated.

The Rococo

The word *rococo* apparently was a pun on *barocco,* the Italian word for "baroque," and on *rocailles* and *coquilles,* the French words for "rocks" and "shells," which were so widely used as decorative motifs in the rococo style. As such the rococo must be considered a modification or variation of the baroque rather than a style in opposition to baroque. Its effect is of a domesticated baroque, better suited to fashionable townhouses than palace halls, but used in both.

Architecture and the Decorative Arts

The rococo suited the intimate salon life of wit and subtle conversation. The style affected both the major art forms and the decorative arts. Typical of

above: **369.** Antoine Watteau.
Garden of Bacchus.
Engraving by Huquier, $10\frac{1}{4} \times 15''$ (26×38 cm).
Cooper-Hewitt Museum, Smithsonian Institution's
National Museum of Design, New York.

left: **370.** Salon, Hofburg Palace,
Vienna. c. 1760–80.

below: **371.** Lukas von Hildebrandt.
Detail of façade,
Belvedere Palace, Vienna. 1724.

the time is an engraved drawing by Watteau that
makes the shell a prominent motif (Fig. 369). Such a
design could have been applied to furniture, wall
paneling, stage curtains, ceramics, fabrics, and so on.
In relation to a Louis XIV interior (see Figs. 320,
333) the rococo rooms of Vienna's Hofburg Palace
(Fig. 370) are delicate, light, and charming. Monumentality, stateliness, and pompous purples are replaced by refinement, elegance, and pastel shades.

At the Belvedere Palace in Vienna, the decorative
impulse can be seen as the rococo bursts out-of-doors
into a lavish exterior design (Fig. 371). Details that
the French architects had for the most part confined
to interiors are found here on the garden façade of a
summer palace begun in 1713 by Lukas von Hildebrandt for Prince Eugene of Savoy. Palladian aca-

demic restraint has been cast to the winds. On either side of the windows, highly ornate double Composite pilasters can be found, and over the entrance struggling Atlaslike figures are grouped in balletlike formation. Otherwise the architectural orders as points of reference have all but disappeared. The sense of repose created by the triangular temple pediments and window brackets of the academic style has dissolved into flowing curves and broken rhythms.

The Counter-Reformation fusion of the arts in order to produce mystical-emotional excitement is well exemplified by the Benedictine abbey church at Melk, built in a commanding position on a rocky ledge overlooking the Danube (Fig. 372). In its colorful interior, designed by the Viennese theater architect Jakob Prandtauer, red marble columns and pi-

lasters rise upward toward the flowing lines, wavy curves, and visionary vistas of the heavens that enliven the vaulting. All the other decorative details combine to carry out this sense of heightened motion. A climax is reached in the choir loft and ceiling at the back (Fig. 373), where the tones of the organ mingle with the concealed chorus and float upward past the terra-cotta angels perching gracefully on stucco clouds to a point where the eye is lost in the vast atmospheric perspective of the painted vaulting.

Painting and Sculpture

The rococo painter without rival was Antoine Watteau. A quick comparison of the *Music Party* (Fig. 374), an example of his *fêtes galantes,* or "elegant entertainment" style, with the sensuous baroque *Garden of Love* by Rubens (see Fig. 326) reveals the hallmarks of the new style. The dimensions of the pictures alone tell their story, since Watteau did small easel paintings for the drawing room rather than murals for a grand gallery. Watteau, like Rubens, was Flemish, and he was an ardent admirer of the monumental art produced by his older countryman. In Watteau's pictures, however, Rubens' massive figures are reduced to graceful and slender proportions. They have animation, but Rubens' lusty revelers now dance the graceful minuet. With Watteau the effect is whimsical rather than monumental, and the mood spirited rather than sensuous.

In the *Music Party,* a group has gathered on a terrace for a pleasant afternoon of musical instruction. The cello has been laid aside, the score is still open, and the lady who has just had her lesson lets her elbow rest on her guitar. The music master is tuning his theorbo before beginning to play, and a soft mood of melancholy anticipation prevails.

375. François Boucher. *Toilet of Venus.* 1746. Oil on canvas, $42\frac{5}{8} \times 33\frac{1}{2}''$ (108 × 85 cm). Metropolitan Museum of Art, New York (bequest of William K. Vanderbilt, 1920).

Beginning as a genre painter specializing in scenes of Flemish village life, Watteau became associated in Paris with decorators and designers of theater scenery and took an interest in the world of elegance as found in the world of fashion. With extraordinary poetic intuition, he combined these elements to create a new style in which the fantasy of the stage and the reality of everyday life mixed to play out a comedy of love and desire.

The generation of Antoine Watteau was the first in over seventy years to experience life without the absolutist rule and style of grandiose public rhetoric upheld by Louis XIV. The averted gazes, turned backs, dreaminess, and personal isolation of Watteau's characters—like the theorbo player in the *Music Party* struggling alone to tune a temperamental instrument—suggest something of the loss of identity, the alienation, even anonymity felt by an aristocratic society no longer subject to the commands of a powerful authoritarian personality.

Sparkling with skillful brushwork, delicious in color, charming in imagery and conception Watteau's art achieved a freedom and fantasy new in Western painting. A deep poetic feeling, gentle irony, and the elusiveness of precious moments lifts these scenes of social frivolity to the level of great art. As in *Music Party,* misty, vaporous landscapes are important in conveying his subtle moods. Like characters in the pastoral novels of the time, ladies and lovers of equal elegance stroll through lush gardens like the Arcadian shepherds of old. Watteau handled such scenes with a characteristic lightness of touch and delicacy of sensation that set the tone for the later phases of the rococo style.

François Boucher, the favorite painter of Louis XV's mistress Madame de Pompadour, worked in a gayer vein than Watteau. The *Toilet of Venus* (Fig. 375) shows the 18th-century ideal of feminine charm in all its artificiality. Love is no longer the robust passion it was with Rubens but a sophisticated flirtation. Full, mature womanhood is replaced by slender girlish forms.

Jean Honoré Fragonard was Boucher's successor as the leading painter of the French rococo. *The Swing* (Fig. 376), which was commissioned by the young aristocrat shown in the lower left, portrays the frivolous, pleasure-seeking pursuits of his class. He has bribed the servant (lower right) to conceal him in the shrubbery while his lady love swings herself. As her skirts and petticoats billow on the breeze, her silken slipper flying off, the statue of Cupid enters the conspiracy by putting a finger to its lips. The artist's fine feeling for color and the masterly draftsmanship with which he handles his diagonal composition save the picture from the twin perils of overrefinement and triviality.

Much of the same spirit of elegance and charm animates the sculpture of Falconet and Clodion. Clay can be modeled quickly, and so terra-cotta, or ceramic, was a fine medium to capture the fleeting rhythms of Clodion's *Nymph and Satyr* (Fig. 377), a Bacchic dance honoring the god of wine and revelry. These rococo figurines based on classical themes were sometimes even franker in their eroticism than the paintings of the period.

The Bourgeois Influence

While the aristocrats were still powerful as leaders of fashion and judges of taste, their influence on the arts was lessening. Not only did wealth put the means of patronage in the pocket of a rising bourgeoisie, but education let the middle class speak increasingly in cultured accents. In France, many of Watteau's pictures were painted for bourgeois walls, and in England, the clientele for Hogarth's drawings and engravings came mostly from middle-class ranks. The vast majority of Voltaire's and Rousseau's readers were members of the middle class, while the novels of Richardson, Fielding, and Goldsmith were aimed at this growing reading public. Lessing's *Miss Sara Sampson* (1755) and Diderot's *The Natural Son* (1757) established the German and French bourgeois drama, respectively.

A similar shift occurred in music. The collective patronage of the concert hall replaced that of the restricted court circle. Instead of aiming to please one patron, the composer and performer now tried to win the favor of the many. Mozart, for one, felt strong enough to break with his tyrannical archbishop and strike out as an independent composer. It is far from an accident that his great opera *Don Giovanni* was commissioned for the municipality of Prague rather than for the royal capital of Vienna.

Painting

One of Watteau's most significant pictures (Fig. 378) was painted for a Paris art dealer by the name of Gersaint. The project was proposed by the artist himself who was dying of tuberculosis and wanted for a brief period, as he put it, "to get the stiffness out of my fingers." Watteau idealized his sponsor to the extent of showing him as the owner of a gallerylike showroom filled with the fashionable elite of Parisian society—though this was more wish fulfillment than reality. On the right, Gersaint is praising the virtues of a painting in the manner of Watteau to a lady and gentleman who view it through their lorgnettes. On the left, the picture being packed away is the portrait of Louis XIV. This implies farewell to the old regime and a salute both to the new age and style and to the name of Gersaint's shop, *Au Grand Monarque.* The scene (cut in half sometime after 1750) constitutes an elegant stage setting where real characters act out the drama of everyday life in 18th-century Paris.

Genre pictures with casual everyday subjects are among the 18th-century middle-class reactions to aristocratic posturing. As such they parallel those in Holland a century before (see Figs. 344–350). A master in this category was Chardin, whose sensitive painting revealed visual poetry in the lives of ordi-nary people going about their daily routines or in-dulging in quiet pleasures (Fig. 379). His many still-life compositions are glorifications of commonplace things familiar in every household—bottles, cups, jugs, kitchen utensils, fruit and vegetables for the dinner table (Fig. 380). But beyond Chardin's modest subject matter and deceptive simplicity, a thoughtful relationship between these objects is noticeable. By his careful arrangements, contrasts of textures, and subtle choice of colors, these became symbols of the good life. Chardin's geometrical clarity and pictorial harmony became the model for many modern mas-ters, notably Manet, Cézanne, and Matisse (see Figs. 430, 442, 461).

The English painter William Hogarth must be considered among the distinguished company of 18th-century social satirists. Like Swift's *Gulliver's Travels,* John Gay's *Beggar's Opera,* and Voltaire's *Candide,* Hogarth's series of six pictures entitled *Marriage à la Mode* was a merciless exposé of the conditions and customs of his time, modified by the saving grace of a brilliant wit. As Dickens and Zola, Goya and Daumier were to do in the less humorous 19th century, Hogarth dramatized the conditions he saw and issued a challenge to society to do some-thing about them. In this case it is the evil of putting human beings on the auction block of marriage.

378. Antoine Watteau. *Gersaint's Signboard.* 1720–21.
Oil on canvas, 5′3⅞″ × 10′1″ (1.62 × 3.07 m). State Museums, West Berlin.

left: **379.** Jean Baptiste Siméon Chardin.
Boy Spinning Top. 1741.
Oil on canvas, 26½ × 28¾″ (67 × 73 cm).
Louvre, Paris.

below: **380.** Jean Baptiste Siméon Chardin.
Still Life: Bowl of Plums. 1759.
Oil on canvas, 17¾ × 22½″ (45 × 57 cm).
Phillips Collection, Washington, D.C.

Hogarth's *Marriage Contract* (Fig. 381) introduces the characters as in the first scene of a play. The gouty nobleman points with pride to the family pedigree as he is about to sell his social standing in the person of his son to pay off the mortgage on his ancestral estate. The merchant, who is marrying off his daughter, carefully inspects the dowry settlement through his spectacles just as he would any other hard-driven bargain. The pawns in this game, the future bride and groom, sit with their backs to each other. The lawyer, Counselor Silvertongue, beginning a flirtation, flatters the future Lady Squanderfield, while her fiancé takes a pinch of snuff.

The other five scenes show the unhappy consequences of this loveless union as it progresses from boredom and frivolity to infidelities, a duel, and

The prints were widely sold by subscription, and this type of group patronage made them financially successful. Every detail in Hogarth's crowded rooms is a commentary on both the action and the taste of his time. Beyond their biting satire, his pictures became works of art by virtue of their superb draftsmanship and tight composition.

Sculpture

As might be expected, bourgeois sculptural expression was at home in the domain of portraiture. Houdon's fine feeling for characterization assures him a place among the foremost portraitists of Western art. His bust of Voltaire (Fig. 383) is one of several likenesses he did of the famous French philosopher and dramatist. By the tilt of the head and the humorous gleam of the eye, Houdon captures the amused look of the philosopher as he ponders and comments on the foibles and follies of his fellow mortals. To chisel a glance of amiable skepticism in marble is no small feat. Leaving a rough edge in the outline of the pupil of the eye, the artist is able to produce a special glint that gives just the desired effect. By such means Houdon achieved a speaking image in which, during a fleeting moment of animated conversation, the philosopher might just have coined one of his famous epigrams.

Houdon's subjects also included many Americans, including Thomas Jefferson, John Paul Jones, Robert Fulton, and Benjamin Franklin (Fig. 384), while he was ambassador to the court of Louis XVI. In 1785, on the invitation of Jefferson, he crossed the Atlantic with Franklin and spent several weeks at Mount Vernon making studies for the statue of George Washington now at the Virginia state capitol at Richmond.

The Mozartian Synthesis

Wolfgang Amadeus Mozart's most mature music was written during the last decade of his life as a resident of Vienna. While he continued to compose chamber music for aristocratic salons, an occasional chamber opera for the Schönbrunn Palace, and German comic operas for the popular musical theater, his art attains

death. In the *Countess' Levée* (Fig. 382), Lady Squanderfield entertains some of her fine-feathered friends as she makes her morning toilet. Counselor Silvertongue, now her lover, shows her tickets for a masked ball that evening, while an Italian barber dresses her hair, a servant passes cups of chocolate, a fencing master snores, a little black slave points gleefully to the horns of a doll (symbolic of a husband whose wife is unfaithful), and a fat singer and his lean flute-playing accompanist add to the general din. The singer may be Carestini, the famous castrato, who sang the female leads in Handel's Italian operas.

This and such other series as the *Harlot's Progress* and the *Rake's Progress* were first made as paintings and then copied in the form of copper engravings.

its most universal expression in the works he created for the public opera houses and concert halls, where nobles and commoners gathered together for their mutual recreation. It was here that Mozart's musical genius found its widest scope, here that he could explore the endless variety of tragic and comic situations that give his operas their boundless humanity, and here that his dramatic power could make its greatest impact. It is also these qualities that were carried over into the less direct and more abstract form of his symphonies and concertos and that give these compositions their dramatic intensity.

As a highly impressionable child, guided by an ambitious but wise father, Mozart had been piloted around the important musical centers, had met the most respected composers, and had absorbed all the current ideas. In London, he came under the sway of Johann Christian Bach, one of the sons of the productive Johann Sebastian. Mozart's generation had reacted to that of J. S. Bach and Handel much as the French painters had to Rubens and Lebrun. Consequently their music spoke in the gentler accents of the gallant style rather than in the muscular rhythms and massive sonorities of the baroque.

In Paris, Mozart was introduced to the rococo keyboard style, that art of the elegant trifle expressed in tinkling confections for the ear. There he also made his first contact with the operas of Gluck, from which he learned his deep regard for dramatic truth and elimination of everything except what was essential to the unfolding of the plot.

The Lyric Theater

In Italy, Mozart came to know the full beauty of the human voice and the persuasive quality of Latin lyricism. In Mannheim, he heard the finest orchestra in Europe and was struck by its dynamic *crescendos* and *diminuendos* (gradual, steady "increases" and "decreases" in loudness) as well as by the brilliance of its wind instruments. In Vienna, he learned from Joseph Haydn how to penetrate the soul of the orchestra and to explore the full expressive possibilities of the symphonic form. From firsthand contact he discovered the musical languages of the Neapolitan *opera seria* ("serious opera"), Pergolesi's *opera buffa* ("comic opera"), Rousseau's pastoral opera, and the German *Singspiel* ("musical comedy").

The spirit of the Enlightenment can be seen in the logical clarity and unified structure of Mozart's forms; his letters show his enthusiasm for Rousseauian naturalness; and from his knowledge of literature, the explosive energy of the Storm-and-Stress movement finds its way into his music. Indeed, everything in his epoch was processed in the laboratory of his brilliant mind, sifted through his creative

above right: 383. Jean Antoine Houdon.
Voltaire. 1781. Marble, height 20″ (51 cm).
Victoria & Albert Museum, London (Crown Copyright).

right: 384. Jean Antoine Houdon.
Benjamin Franklin. 1778.
Terra-cotta, height 16⅛″ (41 cm). Louvre Paris.

consciousness and eventually refined into pure musical gold. In opera, he found the form in which he could combine all these ideas and styles into one grand endlessly changing yet ordered pattern. For him the lyric theater was always his most natural medium of expression.

Mozart's power of characterization is akin to that of Shakespeare, though his dramas are made with musical materials. No composer understood better than Mozart that an opera is not a drama *with* music but a drama *in* music, or knew better that a character has no existence apart from the melody that is sung. The character simply *is* the melody. As the supreme musical dramatist, Mozart can awaken characters to life by a phrase or a rhythmical pattern, carry them through living situations by the direction of a melodic line, and develop the most complex interactions with the others in a scene by harmonic modulation and contrapuntal complexity.

Mozart's emotional range is enormous. Within a short span of time, Mozart can be both gay and profound, serene and agitated, cheerful and serious, calm and turbulent, ethical and diabolical. Yet all takes place within an ordered framework and nothing ever gets out of hand.

For example, Mozart's *Marriage of Figaro,* an adaptation of Beaumarchais' play, is really a vast human panorama in which all the characters, whether master or servant, noble or knave, appear as equal partners in the dance of life. Every possible amorous situation is explored with objectivity, psychological insight, good humor, and warm understanding. From Cherubino's adolescent awakening to the fascinations of the opposite sex and the mature love of Figaro and Susanna, he moves on to the Count and Countess as the unfaithful husband and neglected wife, and finally to a pair of scheming blackmailers. The situations meanwhile run a range from intrigue, flirtation, and lust to infidelity, forgiveness, and tender reconciliation. Much of Beaumarchais' political satire is missing, but every shade of human feeling is explored to the utmost.

Don Giovanni

For *Don Giovanni,* Mozart was fortunate in having the collaboration of Lorenzo da Ponte, a skillful writer and adapter with a real theatrical flair. On hand at the final rehearsals of this saga of the world's greatest lover, and helping put a few finishing touches on the text, was none other than Giacomo Casanova, a man who had done enough research on the subject to qualify him as an authority. The Don Juan story was far from new, and like the Faust legend, it went all the way back to the medieval morality drama.

Interpretations   Both the subject matter and Mozart's sparkling music led to the acceptance of *Don Giovanni* by the following generation as the ideal type of the romantic opera. In one of his late conversations, Goethe remarked rather ruefully that Mozart should have composed a *Faust.* What the great poet overlooked was that Mozart had already done so, since the Faustian concept completely parallels the character of Don Giovanni, who was a Mephistopheles and Faust rolled into one.

Stylistically, the opera embodies the spirit of the Storm-and-Stress drama and led directly to Spohr's opera *Faust,* E. T. A. Hoffmann's *Undine,* and Weber's *Der Freischütz.* The 19th century unfortunately burdened *Don Giovanni* with all kinds of interpretations. To the followers of the French Revolution, Don Giovanni was the dissolute nobleman bent like an archcriminal on bringing about the destruction of the moral law. If so, he was certainly the most beloved villain in all melodrama, with the sympathies of the audience enlisted for once on the side opposite law and order. The philosopher Kierkegaard regarded him as the incarnation of desire, which by its very nature can never admit of satisfaction. He thus became a superbeing, a Nietzschean *Übermensch* (literally, "overperson"), or personification of the Dionysian life force.

How then is it that in the opera each love affair either ends in frustration or leaves Don Giovanni in some ridiculous situation? To the classical enthusiasts, Don Giovanni was the mortal who dared to defy the very gods themselves and by so doing brought about his own destruction. To the romantics, he was the towering tragic hero who, like Faust, was the victim of his own unsatisfiable lusts. To others, he was the idealist always in pursuit of perfect beauty.

To find Mozart's real meaning, one must blow off the accumulation of 19th-century moral and philosophical dust and appraise it anew. Is it a tragedy or a comedy? Even today performances tend to emphasize one aspect or the other. Mozart's subtitle *dramma giocosa* ("comic drama") suggests a combination of both. In the thematic catalogue of his own works, he also refers to it as an "opera buffa in two acts." If one bears in mind that Mozart was entirely capable of leaving it as a subtle riddle, that his inspired music raises it to the status of a unique masterpiece, and that it was originally composed for a small theater, then the best approach to it might well be as a high-spirited 18th-century comedy of manners, in which Molièrian satire is mixed with some Storm-and-Stress demonic elements.

Plot and Characters   The pace of the opera is breathtaking. In the first scene alone there is an attempted rape, a challenge and duel, the dying gasps of an outraged father, blasphemy, the escape of the culprits, and oaths of vengeance. In all this the absolute dramatic center is Don Giovanni, who bursts the bonds of civilized restraint, defies all social conventions, sweeps aside every barrier in his way, and stands alone against the world. In the *Marriage of Figaro* all the characters interacted with each other; here the figures, like the spokes of a wheel, exist only in their relation to the hub, Don Giovanni himself. Opposite him are the three female leads, each of equal importance—Donna Anna, Donna Elvira, and the peasant girl Zerlina.

Chronologically, Donna Elvira comes first, since she has been seduced and deserted before the curtain rises. Hers is the fury of a woman scorned, joined with the desire to forgive and forget and to save Don Giovanni from damnation. Her character is most clearly revealed in Aria No. 8, *"In qual eccessi,"* where she advises the lightheaded young Zerlina of the pitfalls of life with the dashing Don. Mozart writes it as a typical baroque rage aria in the manner of Handel. By so doing, he implies that Elvira's moral sermons are old-fashioned and the dignified form makes it an effective contrast to the general frivolity.

The emotional life of Donna Anna, whose screams when Don Giovanni tries to seduce her are heard at the beginning of the opera, is no less complicated. Full of righteous wrath, possibly mixed with some unconscious admiration for Don Giovanni, and fixed with filial affection for her murdered father, she swears vengeance on his assassin. She is joined in this resolve by her gentlemanly fiancé, Don Ottavio. Together they constitute the serious couple usual in Italian opera buffa. Since Don Ottavio is the lonely champion of lawful love versus dissoluteness, he is bound to appear somewhat pale and conventional in these highly charged surroundings. His two tenor arias, *"Dalla sua pace"* and *"Il mio tesoro"* (Nos. 10B and 21), contain lovely lyricism but are not part of the main action. Donna Anna, on the contrary, rises to tragic stature in *"Or sai chi l'onore"* (Aria No. 10), where, outraged but also attracted to Don Giovanni, she intermingles hatred with passion.

Third in this list is the naïve but flirtatious Zerlina, torn between loyalty to her rustic bridegroom Masetto and the flattering attentions of the dashing Don. Zerlina and the Don's duet *'La ci darem la mano"* (No. 7) is a subtle piece of musical characterization in which the division of the melody between the voices and the subtle melodic variants point up their respective attitudes. The Don is tender, yet still the lordly aristocrat; Zerlina is feminine and doubtful of his intentions, but enjoying every moment. Later, the aria *"Vedrai carino"* (No. 18) reconciles Zerlina to her young peasant husband and reveals her maternal feelings toward him.

Don Giovanni   Wolfgang Amadeus Mozart
(dance scene, finale, Act I)

On the male side, Don Giovanni has no romantic competition, only a very substantial shadow in the form of Leporello, the comic servant who plays Sancho Panza to his Don Quixote. Leporello is a stock opera-buffa character, who expresses his rather earthy cynicism in some chattering patter songs based on a series of rapidly repeated syllables and notes. He introduces himself in the first aria of the opera; and in the famous "Catalogue Aria" (No. 4), he lists his master's amorous conquests in what must surely be the most hilarious set of statistics ever enumerated.

Finales to Acts I and II   The two scenes in which all the characters are on stage are the finales to Acts I and II. In the first, Don Giovanni is entertaining a lively peasant wedding party in the hope of winning the bride Zerlina for himself. Fine dramatic contrast is provided in Don Giovanni's gay drinking song (No. 11), which sparkles like the wine he is ordering, and the sullen resentment of Masetto when he senses that his bride's head is being turned by this glamorous member of the privileged class.

The scene reaches its brilliant climax when the dance music strikes up. There are no less than three instrumental groups on stage in addition to the main orchestra in the pit. Everyone at the time would have recognized this as a typical Viennese public ballroom scene for which Mozart frequently composed music. So that there would be dances that appealed to everybody, minuets were customarily played in one room, waltzes in another, and so on. Here the three groups also play different dances (above). The first group, consisting of two oboes, two horns, and strings, plays one of the best known minuets. On the repetition of the last part, the second stage orchestra, made up of violins and a bass, does a type of square dance known as a *contredanse;* while a third ensemble, also of stringed instruments, plays a type of old-fashioned German waltz known as a *Ländler*. An obvious separation of social levels is implied, with the masked figures of Donna Anna and Don Ottavio doing the aristocratic minuet; the peasants stamping out the vigorous, *Ländler*-like meter of the waltz, with strong accents on the first and third beats; while Don Giovanni and Zerlina meet on the middle-class ground of the bourgeois *contredanse*. Each social group is thus expressed through a characteristic rhythm. With the stage bands playing against the main orchestra below, all the plots and subplots boiling merrily away, and all the characters conversing and commenting on the action, the resulting rhythmic complexity and dramatic tension make this scene one of the major miracles of musical literature.

In the cemetery scene, which precedes the finale to Act II, Don Giovanni as a fugitive from justice is confronted with the equestrian statue of the Commendatore, Donna Anna's father, whom he has killed in the duel at the beginning of the opera. The ominous tones of the voice from the tomb reproach him for his wickedness; and Don Giovanni, always the courteous host, responds by inviting the statue to a midnight meal.

The final scene opens with the preparations for the banquet, while the trumpets and drums sound the proper note of aristocratic hospitality. Like all the nobles of his time, Don Giovanni has his own house orchestra standing by to play dinner music. This wind group plays snatches from two popular Italian operas by Mozart's rivals; and a delightful bit of humor is introduced when they quote the *"Non più andrai"* from his own *Marriage of Figaro,* which happened to be a hit tune of that season, not a classic as now.

Donna Elvira, ever the kill-joy, now enters to play her trump card, which is the announcement that she is returning to her convent where life under the veil will presumably be more peaceful. As she reaches the door, her shriek announces the arrival of the statue. With fatefully heavy footsteps, the monument sings a long melodic line as rigid in its way as rigor mortis itself, reinforced by the funereal sounds of the trombones, instruments which were then associated with solemn church festivals and burial services. The contrast between the living and the dead is brought out by the statue's stiff melody, around which all the other characters react in ways that vary from farce to tragedy.

When Don Giovanni takes the hand of his marble guest, the horror music that had been foreshadowed in the overture is heard. Strings play spine-tingling scale figures upward and downward, alternately soft and loud. Thunder roars, demons shout, and flames rise upward. The Don, unrepentant to the last, goes to his doom on a descending D-major scale. Breathlessly, the other characters arrive too late for the excitement but in time to sing a final quintet to these words: "Sinner, pause, and ponder well/Mark the end of Don Juan!/Are you going to Heaven or Hell?"

Ideas

The 18th-century styles either continued, modified, or departed from the high baroque. The shift of audience from a declining aristocracy to the rising bourgeoisie was speeded up, and the final phase of the aristocratic baroque style was reflected in the rococo. The continuation of 17th-century rationalism was found in the Enlightenment. Voices of a classical revival began to be heard. And new emotional outbursts were felt in the emphasis on sensibility and in the Storm-and-Stress movement. Besides neoclassicism, discussed in Chapter 18, the ideas that weave the arts of the 18th century into a meaningful pattern are the Enlightenment, the rococo, and the emotional reaction to them known as Storm and Stress.

The Enlightenment

The *Enlightenment* is a blanket term under which it is possible to group such tendencies as the inventive spirit, scientific inquiry, the encyclopedic movement, the optimistic world view, and the belief in progress. The thrust that the Enlightenment gave to scientific invention was applied by middle-class manufacturers and merchants to the production of wealth. Pure science and nature in this case were less important than technology and production.

The new social order is mirrored almost directly in the shift of artistic patronage in the direction of the middle-class audience. For the first time, it is possible to speak of the bourgeois novel and drama. Watteau painted one of his most important pictures for an art dealer; Chardin, Greuze, and Hogarth found their clientele among the same social segment. And Mozart, by turning the social tables upside down, making the Count the villain and the servant the hero, as in *Marriage of Figaro,* was certainly boosting the ego of the bourgeoisie and blasting the aristocracy.

The Enlightenment spirit of free scientific inquiry, which grew out of 17th-century rationalism, was so distinctly opposed to the clergy that it almost developed into a substitute religion. To the deists, God was a kind of cosmic clockmaker who created a mechanical universe, wound it up for all eternity, and let it go. The experimental method of science became the liturgy of this pseudoreligion, the encyclopedia its bible, nature its church, and all human beings of reason the congregation.

One of the most productive developments of this aspect of the Enlightenment was the encyclopedic movement. All the important intellects made their contributions to Diderot's *Encyclopédie,* with Voltaire writing the historical parts, Rousseau the sections on music, and so on.

The same intellectual spirit, though in different religious circumstances, is observable in the comprehensive musical output of J. S. Bach. In *The Art of Fugue* he applied the scientific method to musical composition. By keeping his themes constant, he carefully controlled the variables of form and thus systematized all possible fugal types. His existing cantatas add up to four for each Sunday of the year. His keyboard compositions were conceived encyclopedically and comprise examples in every possible form. His 48 preludes and fugues, known as *The Well-Tempered Clavier,* were written as a double cycle, two for each possible tonality; and his Brandenburg Concertos explore every possible instrumental combination. His entire works thus emerge as a comprehensive design consciously planned to survey and sum up all the musical practices known to him.

The Enlightenment image of the cool man of reason inhabiting a world governed by purely rational principles was the object of Voltaire's satirical pen in the novel *Candide.* While maintaining his strong belief that he lives in the Leibnizian "best of all possible worlds," the hero experiences every disaster known on the planet, including the great earthquake of Lisbon in 1745. The use of satire as a social weapon takes visual form in Hogarth's *Marriage à la Mode.* A certain amount of Voltairean skepticism can also be found in the character of Don Giovanni, who fears neither the supernatural nor the hereafter.

The Enlightenment was accompanied by a spirit of optimism and by a belief in progress and in human perfectibility. Theologically, the Hebraic and Christian viewpoints were based on the fall of humanity and the doctrine of original sin dating from the expulsion of Adam and Eve from the Garden of Eden. Philosophically, Plato's theory of knowledge was also founded on a doctrine of perfection prior to birth and the subsequent acquisition of knowledge by the process of remembrance. Humanists, such as Gibbon and Winckelmann, believed in the intellectual and artistic paradise of ancient Greece and Rome and as a consequence wrote books analyzing their declines and falls.

Without denying the greatness of Greece, the champions of the Enlightenment were well aware that they had gone far beyond classical science and believed that, if the rational processes could be properly applied, they would eventually surpass the ancients in all fields. Kant, for instance, enthusiastically hailed Rousseau as the Newton of the moral world, and Condorcet in his *Progress of the Human Spirit* listed the ten stages by which humanity had raised itself from ignorance and savagery to the threshold of perfection. Material progress was certainly an observable fact; and since nature held all the secrets that men and women needed to know, and reason could unlock them, eventually they could control their environment. If all mental and moral powers were used to their fullest extent, the argument ran, human development could go in one direction only, onward and upward.

The Rococo

The rococo is the last Western style that can lay claim to universality and the last to adhere strictly to the cult of charm and beauty. The sophisticated rococo (Fig. 385) reflects on an aristocracy that still

385. Giovanni Battista Tiepolo. *Apollo Presenting to Frederick Barbarossa His Bride, Beatrice of Burgundy.* 1751. Ceiling fresco. Kaisersaal, Episcopal Palace, Würzburg.

386. Élisabeth Vigée-Lebrun.
Marie Antoinette. 1778.
Oil on canvas,
36¾ × 30¼″ (93 × 77 cm).
Private collection, New York.

retained dominant control of artistic patronage. This was an international upper class who freely intermarried with the nobility of all parts of Europe, who spoke French and Italian better than the native tongues of their respective countries, who read French philosophers, attended French plays, and collected French art. This was, moreover, an educated group who cultivated wit, charm, social polish, and refinement of taste as a way of life. After the French Revolution and the Napoleonic wars, nationalism grew so strong that the arts appeared increasingly in local frames of reference.

Examples of the rococo are found wherever the aristocracy possessed the means to follow the fashionable style and where those who were Counter-Reformationists undertook the building of churches. The hallmarks of the style are found in the paintings of Watteau, Boucher, and Fragonard; in the sculptures of Falconet and Clodion; and in the light-hearted divertimentos and serenades that Haydn and Mozart wrote for chamber orchestra. Queen Marie Antoinette's favorite painter, Élisabeth Vigée-Lebrun catches the visual charm and delicacy of the rococo in a portrait of her friend and patron (Fig. 386). Noted for her keen psychological insight into the personalities of her subjects, Vigée-Lebrun was

elected to the exclusive French Academy, and after the Revolution of 1789 she achieved international acclaim for her elegant aristocratic portraits.

Storm and Stress

In the latter half of the 18th century, various irrational tendencies came about as reactions to both the rococo cult of the beautiful and the Enlightenment's emphasis on reason. As early as 1756, Burke's *Essay on the Sublime and the Beautiful* insisted that in literature and art there is an element more important then beauty. This is the *sublime,* which rises above mere beauty and can even admit of the ugly. "Whatever is fitted in any sort to excite the ideas of pain and danger," Burke said, "whatever is in any sort terrible, or conversant about terrible objects, is the source of the Sublime."

The free exercise of the emotions and the imagination, even if it meant experiencing the painful, the astonishing, the horrible, was therefore legitimate territory for art to explore. This idea led to a renewed interest in Shakespeare; reveled in Rousseau's descriptions of Alpine scenery, accompanied as they were by avalanches and storms; and delighted in the Rousseauian revolt against the artificial restraints of civilization.

This line of thought also constituted the background of the Storm-and-Stress movement in Germany. While the Enlightenment was trying to tame nature and bring it under human control, the *Sturm und Drang* authors were reveling in how nature imposed its obscure and mysterious will on humanity. In Goethe's early drama, Faust was the rebel against all accepted forms of wisdom, especially those arrived at through mathematical or scientific formulas. Both Faust and Don Giovanni were engaged in a quest for emotional truth and succeeded in unleashing the infernal forces that eventually consumed them.

The 18th century encompassed many major movements: the beginnings of the mechanical, industrial, and political revolutions; the decline of the aristocracy and the rise of the middle class; and the early phases of the neoclassical and romantic styles. Such were the social, intellectual, and emotional impulses that defined the horizon before which the panorama of the 18th-century arts unfolded.

V
THE REVOLUTIONARY PERIOD

The modern age was swept in on a tidal wave of revolution—industrial, social, political, technological, scientific, and cultural. Fundamental beliefs were washed away. Ideas of society, the processes of nature, and the structure of the universe were changed. In the age of reason, scientific knowledge had been greatly expanded but remained largely theoretical. When scientific principles were applied to practical problems, the invention of machinery revolutionized agriculture, manufacturing, communications, mining, and warfare, thus altering the entire picture of the Western world.

"Man is born free and is everywhere in chains," wrote Rousseau in the *Social Contract.* His slogan was echoed in the mid-19th century by the words of Karl Marx: "Workers of the world unite. You have nothing to lose but your chains." The fetters they meant were those of ignorance, superstition, poverty, and a social structure based on hereditary privilege, class distinction, and the divine right of kings. Rousseau and his fellow philosophers were heartened by events in the New World. The American colonies had shown that political freedom, religious toleration, and the goals of life, liberty, and the pursuit of happiness could coexist. By declaring and achieving independence, the American Revolution led the way. The French Revolution with its ideals of liberty, equality, and fraternity soon followed. When it failed to achieve Utopia, a counterrevolutionary reaction set in. Since then the political scene has been rife with a succession of limited monarchies, democratic republics, fascist and communist states, and military dictatorships.

Social and political revolutions have been mirrored in the underlying restlessness and aspirations of majorities, minorities, and other groups seeking expression. Nationalism—the belief that a state should be founded on the ethnic, cultural, and linguistic identity of its people rather than on royal dynasties, military conquests, or power politics—was of major importance. The emergence of new nations that began in the 19th century continues today, as does the clamor within established nations of the advocates of minority rights, including the women's and human rights movements, which one often forgets are not contemporary phenomena.

The great European powers had built empires out of colonial territories in Africa and Asia and developed them for the raw materials that fed their industrial machines. Competition for control over distant lands and peoples and the scramble for worldwide markets set the stage for the carnage of World War I. The Treaty of Versailles, which concluded the war, responded to nationalistic aspirations by creating a number of new European states out of the former Austro-Hungarian Empire, Germany, and Russia as well as redistributing their colonial possessions. This was followed by Marxist communism in Russia, fascism in Italy, and nazism in Germany.

The League of Nations, created by the Treaty of Versailles to counter rampant nationalism, proved ineffective in creating a new international order. This weakness and the same pressures that produced the first world war set the stage for the outbreak of World War II just twenty years later. The defeat of fascist Italy, nazi Germany, and imperial Japan brought about a world dominated by two superpowers, the USA and USSR. Although the creation of the United Nations and the establishment of the European Economic Community rekindled hope for a peaceful world order, the breakup of the great European empires and the rivalries of emerging states have led to more aggression, more wars, and more revolutions.

A swift sequence of inventions throughout the 19th century sped up the production and marketing of manufactured and raw goods. In the 20th century the natural outgrowths of this Industrial Revolution were the technological and electronic revolutions. Such initial advances as the railroad and the steamboat were followed by the automobile and airplane, which completely changed transportation. The harnessing of electricity, which had produced the telegraph, telephone, and radio, added totally new dimensions to communications through recordings, motion pictures, and television. Mass production, automation, laser beams, satellites, space exploration, and the development of the computer further changed the condition of human life.

Even more awesome than the consequences of the Industrial Revolution were the effects of the scientific revolution on the understanding of nature. Darwin in the mid-19th century had revolutionized biology by demonstrating that creation was a continuous evolutionary process in which plants and animals have changed over the ages. In the struggle for existence all species have the constant need to adapt to their environment, he wrote. Natural selection leads to the survival of the fittest.

In the 20th century Einstein's theory of relativity and the development of quantum theory produced a similar revolution in physics. Einstein's elegant equation $E = mc^2$—where E is energy, m is mass, and c^2 is the speed of light multiplied by itself—created the picture of the universe as a four-dimensional, space-time continuum. Space and time as separate absolutes were replaced by space-time in the light of relativity; light was joined to time, and time to space; likewise energy was joined to matter, matter to space, and space to gravitation.

This opened up a whole new concept of nature that holds not only for the starry cosmos but also for the ultimate tiny particles that are the basic building blocks of the universe. Like miniature solar systems, material particles are dissolved into events, events are related to each other in intervals, and all are contained in a relativistic space-time continuum. The basic material of the world, then, is not matter itself, since "matter" is simply a convenient way of grouping events that take place in a given field. The quantum physicists showed how these basic building blocks can be used to generate energy by splitting the nucleus of the atom into two relatively equal fragments (fission) or by combining two light nuclei to form a more massive nucleus (fusion).

Meanwhile artists were producing revolutions of their own. As in all previous periods the arts have reflected emotional and intellectual trends, allowed release from social stresses and strains, and continued to give voice to the eternal hopes and fears of humanity.

18 The Neoclassical Style

Paris, Early 19th Century

Some books, some archaeological discoveries, and some social upheavals brought to Paris many sweeping changes in social thought, in styles of art, and in forms of government during the latter part of the 18th and early part of the 19th century.

Stuart and Revett, two Englishmen who had visited Greece, published in 1762 *Antiquities of Athens,* which made a clear differentiation between Greek and Roman architecture. Two years later, Johann Joachim Winckelmann's highly influential *History of Ancient Art,* a landmark in art history, similarly distinguished between Greek and Roman sculpture. "The principal and universal characteristic of the masterpieces of Greek art is a noble simplicity and a quiet grandeur," he declared. "As the depth of the sea remains always at rest, however the surface may be agitated, so the expression in the figures of the Greeks reveals in the midst of passion a great and steadfast soul." The founder of classical archaeology, Winckelmann was portrayed in Rome, where the neoclassical style had its origins, by Angelica Kauffmann (Fig. 387). Later this Swiss-born and Italian-trained painter was to attain distinction as one of the major figures of neoclassicism and become one of the founding members of the Royal Academy of Arts in London.

Winckelmann's words provided the critics of the rococo style with the needed aesthetic ammunition to fire at Boucher and Fragonard because of the frivolous content of their paintings (see Figs. 375, 376). During revolutionary times, the voice of Diderot, moral philosopher and apostle of the Enlightenment, continued to be heard, especially his opinion that the

387. Angelica Kauffmann.
Johann Joachim Winckelmann. 1764.
Oil on canvas, $37\frac{7}{8} \times 27\frac{3}{4}''$ (97 × 71 cm).
Kunsthaus, Zürich.

CHRONOLOGY
Early 19th Century

function of art was to make "virtue adorable and vice repugnant."

Ancient Rome now became a symbol for the revolutionary protest. In politics, this at first meant a republican instead of a monarchical form of government. In religion, it was associated with a tolerant paganism as opposed to Christianity. (For a brief time, in fact, the Cathedral of Notre Dame in Paris was rededicated to the "Goddess of Reason.")

Heroism and self-sacrifice, rugged resolve and Spartan simplicity became hallmarks of the revolutionary spirit, and reflections of these qualities were easily found in Roman literature and art. The political writings of Cicero and Seneca were widely read and quoted to confirm the principle that sovereignty resided in the people and that government should be based on a voluntary agreement among citizens. Political pamphlets came to be studded with quotations from the Romans Tacitus, Sallust, and Horace, and the oratory of the period was modeled on that of Cicero.

The convention hall where the revolutionary legislators met was lined with laurel-crowned statues of Solon, Camillus, and other ancient statesmen, and in debates the speakers relied on apt phrases from Cicero to clinch important points. They referred to their followers as Brutuses and Catos and to their opponents as Catalines; their postures and gestures were studied imitations of Roman statues, and their oaths sworn on the head of Brutus or by the immortal gods.

Everyone who could read became biography-conscious and spoke like living characters out of

Plutarch's *Parallel Lives.* (On the day she murdered Marat, Charlotte Corday had spent her time reading Plutarch.) Never before had public personalities seemed so obviously to have walked straight out of books. Surely Oscar Wilde must have had this revolutionary period in mind when he wittily twisted the old Greek aesthetic doctrine by saying that nature, in this case human nature, is the imitation of art.

Many of the symbols of the French Revolution too were borrowed directly from the ancients. The cap of liberty was a copy of the Phrygian cap worn by the liberated slaves in Rome. The *fasces,* or bundle of sticks with the protruding ax tied together with a common bond, was once again the symbol of power.

When Napoleon Bonaparte rose to political power, he too shared the popular enthusiasm for all that was ancient. His chosen models were Alexander the Great and Julius Caesar, especially the latter since Caesar's career and Napoleon's had so many parallels. Napoleon became first a republican consul. Later he ruled France through a tribune. Then, after a plebiscite, he emerged as the modern embodiment of a Roman emperor. The *fasces* became his emblem of authority. The eagles of the old Roman legions he made into the insignia of the French battalions. Eventually he was crowned with the laurel wreath, that ancient symbol of immortal fame.

Such a manipulation of the forms and images of ancient glory had a vast appeal to this man of modest birth. Coming to power so soon after the end of an unpopular monarchy, Napoleon had to emphasize that many of the Roman emperors were of equally common backgrounds, and that the imperial toga had not necessarily been hereditary. But his hold on the people was indisputable and his elevation was made with full popular consent.

Napoleon's mission was to bring order to what had been political chaos and to consolidate the social gains that had been made. His meteoric career was the success story of the 19th century, embodying as it did the ideal of the liberated individual rising to leadership through personal efforts rather than by an accident of birth. In it, members of the society of his time who had only recently acquired wealth or power could find substance for their fondest materialistic daydreams. The truth was that now, with the reins of power in their hands, the middle class did not know quite how to manage them. Napoleon did.

Like its Roman model, Napoleon's empire was international in scope, and its intellectual and artistic life rose above national boundary lines. What Greece had been to Rome, Italy was now to France. Napoleon brought the Italian sculptor Canova to Paris for various commissions, and his musical preferences were for such composers as Paisiello and Spontini. His proclamation to the Italian people on the eve of his invasion of their country points up this internationalism. "We are the friends of all nations," he protested, perhaps too much, "especially the descendants of Brutus, the Scipios, and of the great men we have chosen for our own model." And he took frequent pains to point out that he was embarking on a cultural as well as a military mission. Here was no barbarian Attila the Hun storming the citadel, but a conqueror who came to sack Rome in the company of a group of art experts who were well aware of the value of everything they took.

A petition signed by all the important French artists actually had been sent to the Directory government in 1796, pointing out how much the Romans had become civilized by confiscating the art of ancient Greece and how France would likewise flourish by bringing original works to Paris to serve as models. While this returning Caesar brought back with him no human captives, his victory celebration was livened by the presence of such distinguished prisoners of war as the *Apollo Belvedere* (see Fig. 84), the paintings of Raphael, and the rare treasures he had taken from the Vatican and other Italian collections.

Architecture

With the reorganization of the government, the remaking of the constitution, and the rewriting of the laws on the model of the Roman Empire, Napoleon was determined that Paris should be replanned as a new Rome. He therefore undertook the ordering and commissioning of buildings with the same incredible vigor that marked his activities in other fields.

Paris, the New Rome

The heart of the new city was still to be the spacious center designed around the old Place Louis XV, which under the Directory had been renamed the Place de la Concorde (Fig. 388). Its axis began on the left bank of the Seine River with the old Palais Bourbon, now the Chamber of Deputies, which was to have its face lifted by a Corinthian colonnade. It continued across the river, by the bridge that had been begun in early revolutionary days (lower left), to the center of the Place, where some statuary was to cover the spot where the guillotine had done its grim work. The end of the axis was to be the unfinished Church of La Madeleine at the end of the Rue Royale, scheduled to be rebuilt in the form of a Roman temple (upper right).

To complete his scheme, Napoleon commissioned Percier and Fontaine, his favorite architects, to redesign the Rue de Rivoli, which intersected the axis at right angles and ran parallel to the Seine River (middle right). Elsewhere throughout Paris, triumphal

388. Place de la Concorde, Paris, aerial view.

above: **389.** Pierre Alexandre Vignon. La Madeleine, Paris. 1762–1829. Length 350′ (106.68 m), width 147′ (44.81 m), height of podium 23′ (58.42 m).

right: **390.** Plan of La Madeleine.

below: **391.** Interior, La Madeleine.

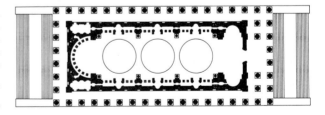

arches and monumental columns were to proclaim to the world the presence of a new Caesar and Trajan.

La Madeleine Napoleon showed his interest in these projects by frequently conferring with his architects and engineers, by visiting construction sites, and by dreaming up new ideas while on distant battlefields. It was in Poland that he signed the decree for the building of his Temple of Glory, La Madeleine (Fig. 389). According to his express wish, the unfinished church would be transformed and bear a dedicatory inscription: "From the Emperor to the soldiers of the Great Army." The building was not to look like a church but like such a temple as one would find in Athens or Rome.

For the Temple of Glory, Napoleon personally selected an architectural plan by Pierre Alexandre Vignon, because it fulfilled his conditions by looking sufficiently ancient and pagan. The building is indeed a Greco-Roman Corinthian temple, and, except for the sculptural details, it was completed according to Vignon's design (Fig. 390).

In the Roman manner, La Madeleine stands on a podium 23 feet (7 meters) high and is approached by a flight of steps in the front. Running completely around the building is a series of Corinthian columns about 63 feet (19.2 meters) in height, eighteen on each side, eight on each end, and an additional row of four in front that supports the cornice.

Since its rededication for religious purposes, this pagan temple of glory has had a large sculptural group by Lemaire on its pediment, representing the Last Judgment. In the center stands the figure of Christ, 17 feet (5.2 meters) high, with the repentant Mary Magdalene at His feet. To His left are allegorical figures representing envy, hypocrisy, and avarice, while on His right are an angel of mercy and personifications of faith, hope, charity, and innocence.

The interior cella of an ancient temple was never intended as a gathering place and always remained dark and mysterious. Hence, of necessity, Vignon had to depart from precedent and come up with something new. The surprise that awaits the visitor who passes through the massive bronze doors is complete, for the interior and exterior actually amount to two different buildings.

The aisleless nave is divided into three long bays and a choir (Fig. 391), which are not roofed in timber as in a Greek temple or vaulted in the Roman manner but are crowned with three low saucer-shaped domes on pendentives. The nave ends in a semicircular apse that is roofed over by a semidome. Chapels are located in the recesses created by the buttresses that support the domes, and two classical orders—the Corinthian and Ionic—form the basis of the decorative scheme.

Rich use is made of marble paneling, and the domes are coffered in the manner of the Roman Pantheon. What little light there is in this windowless interior comes from skylights at the tops of the domes, an idea derived from the Pantheon's oculus (see Fig. 101). The best that can be said about this method is that it keeps the exterior roof line intact. The exterior, as a study in classical design, has a certain dignity in its archaeological faithfulness to such older models as the Maison Carrée (see Fig. 93), but it excels them only in its larger proportions.

Napoleon's Arches of Triumph In 1806, after winning military victories in Germany and Austria, Napoleon entrusted to Percier and Fontaine the building of a triumphal arch. Now known as the Arc de Triomphe du Carrousel (Fig. 392), it was designed as a gate of honor to the Tuileries Palace. It turned out to be a rather slavish imitation of the Arch of Septimus Severus in Rome, though of more modest proportions. Standing on the platform above it, however, was one of Napoleon's proudest battle tro-

392. Charles Percier and Pierre F. L. Fontaine. Arc de Triomphe du Carrousel, Paris. 1806. Width 63'6" (19.35 m), height 48' (14.63 m).

phies—the group of four bronze horses taken from St. Mark's in Venice (Fig. 260). Owing to the shifting fortunes of war, Venice later got back the horses as a result of a peace treaty, and a triumphal chariot drawn by horses of a considerably later date was installed in their place to celebrate, somewhat ironically, the restoration of the Bourbons in the person of Louis XVIII. The face of the arch is decorated with rather undistinguished carvings in low relief depicting such scenes as the Battle of Austerlitz, the surrender of Ulm, the peace of Tilsit, and Napoleon's triumphal entries into Munich and Vienna.

When finished, the result was too meager to measure up to Napoleon's imperial ambitions, and so another and still grander arch was commissioned for the Place de l'Étoile, now renamed Place Charles de Gaulle. In this familiar Paris landmark, the architect Jean François Chalgrin achieved more life and elasticity by freely adapting rather than copying a known model. In it, French baroque precedents, Roman classical inspiration, and academic correctness of execution are combined in a harmonious manner. For his monumental effect, Chalgrin relied on bold proportions and a grand scale. Later, after Napoleonic times, the severity of the general outline was relieved by the skillful placement of high-relief sculptures by Cortot and Rude (see Fig. 409) on a scale comparable to the immense size of the arch.

Still not content, Napoleon ordered a monumental Doric column to be erected in the Place Vendôme (Fig. 393). In size and style of ornamentation, it was a conscious copy of Trajan's Column in Rome (see Fig. 91). The main difference was that its spiral reliefs were done on a bronze strip made from the guns and cannons captured from the defeated Prussian and Austrian armies. The sculpture recounts the story of the campaign of 1805 in scenes, such as Napoleon's address to his troops, the meeting of the three emperors, and the conquests of Istria and Dalmatia.

Classic Revivals Elsewhere

The wave of enthusiasm for classical architecture was by no means confined to Paris. Germany, England, and the United States had each experienced classic revivals in the 18th century. During the early 19th century, the Roman revival was strongest in the countries identified with Napoleon's Empire, while the Greek revival was accented in the anti-Napoleonic nations, notably England and Germany.

In England, such a public building as the British Museum was strongly Greek in character. In Berlin, an early example is the Brandenburg Gate, modeled after the Athenian Propylaea. In the United States,

above: 393. Charles Percier and Pierre F. L. Fontaine. Vendôme Column, Paris. 1810. Marble with bronze spiral frieze.

right: 394. Thomas Jefferson. Rotunda, University of Virginia, Charlottesville. 1819–26.

395. Jacques Louis David. *Oath of the Horatii.* 1784. Oil on canvas, 10'10" × 14' (3.3 × 4.27 m). Louvre, Paris.

the classical revival period corresponded generally to the federal style, which flourished from about 1785 to 1820. Buildings that show the Roman influence are the Virginia state capitol, which Thomas Jefferson designed after the Maison Carrée (Fig. 93), and the Rotunda (Fig. 394), the original library of the University of Virginia, which Jefferson modeled after the Pantheon in Rome (Fig. 100).

Painting

David and Neoclassicism

The most articulate artistic champion of this stern world of revolutionary fervor and ancient Roman heroism was destined to be Jacques Louis David, a painter whose temperament and technique were ideally suited to the spirit of the times. A reformer by nature and a classical enthusiast by nurture, David painted pictures the austerity of which was a conscious reaction to the rococo extravagances exemplified in the work of his great-uncle, Boucher (see Fig. 375). By virtue of his studies in Rome, David had absorbed all that was necessary for the exploitation of the classical enthusiasms of the readers of Plutarch's *Parallel Lives* and Winckelmann's *History of Ancient Art.* Harkening to Diderot and other earnest moralists, David never thought of a picture as a mere painting. It had to have a manifestolike message pointing to political and social action.

It was inevitable that the high moral purposes of the French Revolution would be reflected in art. Indeed, David's immediate success can be attributed to the fact that his style caught the same strong spirit that the revolutionists espoused. Bourgeois by birth and upbringing, David frankly addressed his art to the newly established middle-class social order.

Ancient Roman Subjects David's first great success was the *Oath of the Horatii* (Fig. 395), finished in Rome while Louis XVI was still on the French throne. The subject, one of the legends of the founding of the ancient Roman republic, was suggested by Corneille's ballet *Les Horaces* (*The Horatii*). The three arches of the severely simple setting separate the figures like niches for statuary. In the center stands Horatius Proclus dedicating the swords of his three sons, who swear to defend the Roman republic against the plotting Curatii, one of whom was the fiancé of their grief-stricken sister on the right. Baroque precedents can be cited for this important painting. "If I owe my subject to Corneille," said David, "I owe my picture to Poussin." Clarity of contour, sculpturesque sharpness of modeling, and harsh but clear handling of light and shadow characterize this stark but heroic canvas.

Over and beyond his work as a painter and the genuine value of his painting, David took on the role of power politician in the field of art with far-reaching effects. More academic than the former academi-

cians, he succeeded in laying the foundations of official art that endured for the rest of the 19th century. While his theories and subject matter are still a matter of controversy, David's craftsmanship was on a par with any of the master painters of the past, and many distinguished painters of the present have been well aware of his style and manner of execution. The technique of Salvador Dali and the 20th-century neo-classicism of Picasso, for instance, owe much to the cool objective art of their 19th-century predecessor.

David's picture of the *Lictors Bringing Back to Brutus the Bodies of His Sons* (Fig. 396) bears the date of the fateful year of 1789. It is both a reminder that his career began during the latter days of the monarchy and that he was attempting to continue the subject and substance of his earlier spectacular success, *Oath of the Horatii.* In it one finds the same stern spirit of self-sacrifice, the same severity of style that had appealed so much to the eyes that were weary of the fussy rococo, the same somber type of

setting that had interested those who were reading about the archaeological discoveries at Pompeii and Herculaneum. With remarkable boldness, David was able to flaunt the stern, do-or-die virtues of Roman republicanism right under the noses of his aristocratic patrons. These two pictures were not only the manifesto of a new style in art but of a new image of society as well. Their unparalleled success was due in no small measure to the fact that they appeared at precisely the right moment.

For his subject David again chose an incident from the days soon after the founding of the ancient Roman republic. Lucius Junius Brutus (foreground left), one of the consuls, had discovered that his own sons were involved in a plot to restore the recently overthrown monarchy. Having ordered their executions, he is shown as an isolated figure in the statuesque shadow of the goddess Roma. Behind him are the lictors, Roman officers, bearing the bodies of his sons, while a third group is formed by his grieving wife and daughters. Many who were living through the trying times of the Revolution could see something of themselves in that figure of stoic resolution, torn between his public duty to the state and his private grief.

Portraits In his portraiture, David reveals himself an expert judge of personality, and his viewers find in this category a certain relief from his more heroic efforts. A sensitive example is the unfinished portrait of *Madame Récamier* (Fig. 397), one of the most fascinating and intelligent women of the period. In her, David found a promising subject, who furnished her salon in the fashionable Pompeian style he had done so much to popularize. Here she reclines in the classical manner on an Empire chaise longue just as she might have done on the days she received her guests. Her white gown is draped with deep folds reminiscent of antique statuary. The only other pieces of furniture are the footstool and bronze lamp, which were drawn from Pompeian originals. The clarity with which David handles the outlines of the figure and the silhouette of the head combine with the austere setting for an orderly, elegant effect.

Napoleon's Coronation To commemorate his assuming the title of emperor, Napoleon in 1804 commissioned David, as First Painter, to execute four grandiose pictures. Since the Empire was destined to last but a decade, David had time to complete only two of them: *Le Sacre* (Fig. 398), or *The Corona-*

398. Jacques Louis David. *Le Sacre* (*The Coronation*). 1805–08. Oil on canvas, 20′ × 30′6½″ (6.1 × 9.31 m). Louvre, Paris.

tion, and the *Distribution of the Eagles,* those ancient standards of the Roman imperial legions that Napoleon had adopted as his own. Both were historical canvases in the grand tradition of Poussin and Lebrun (see Figs. 328, 320), but here David extended that type to include contemporary events.

Napoleon's coronation had taken place in the choir of the Cathedral of Notre Dame in Paris, where his decorators, Percier and Fontaine, had designed a special setting for the occasion. The ancient Gothic architecture had been camouflaged with imitation marble arches and pilasters that framed the boxes and galleries for distinguished guests. David originally proposed to paint the moment after Pope Pius VII had blessed the crown and Napoleon had taken it from the altar to place it on his own head. But the Emperor preferred the more gallant pose when he put the crown on the brow of his Empress.

Aside from this bit of incidental activity, David's painting amounts to a stately group portrait on a grand scale. As a piece of official art, the placement and attitude of every personage in it had to be passed on by the master of protocol and ratified by Napoleon himself, even to the inclusion of his mother who had made a particular point of being away from Paris that day. David, however, had been there and had made sketches on the spot. Yet, when he drew Pius VII with his hands resting on his knees as the artist had actually observed him, David was told by Napoleon that the successor of St. Peter had not come so far to do nothing. Consequently, David showed the Pope extending his hand in benediction.

In such circumstances, it is a minor miracle that David was able to get as much elasticity into the composition as he did. His achievement is all the more remarkable when one reflects how easily the whole thing could have become nothing more than a fancy-dress ball, with Napoleon as the middle-class messiah standing in the midst of the members of his family whom he had made kings, princes, cardinals, and so on. But David, by his masterly grouping, commanding postures, and sure handling of the wealth of detail, preserves the uncluttered spaciousness of the setting and the proportions of the whole. The scene also provided the painter of classical restraint with a chance to exploit the element of color, and David made rich but not lavish use of the medium. In all these ways the versatile David was able to adapt his art to Napoleon's dreams of imperial Roman grandeur.

The immense 20- by 30-foot (6- by 9-meter) canvas contains some 150 life-size portraits, and it took several years before each of these individuals had visited the church where David set up his studio to sit for his or her likeness. The group is made up mostly of marshals of the imperial army, maids of honor to the Empress, court chamberlains, and members of the diplomatic corps. The United States ambassador is included, but the English delegation is conspicuous by its absence. Napoleon's mother and other members of his family occupy the center box, while in the gallery above is a group of artists and intellectuals, including the composer Grétry. As a signature, David painted himself sitting and sketching, with his family, favorite pupils, and his teacher Vien.

The symbolism in *Le Sacre* calls for comment, because it underscores Napoleon's problem of holding a coronation that would not evoke the memories of the hated aristocracy and yet have an air of legitimacy, of striking a balance between the luxury and elegance of the old regime and the Spartan simplicity of the revolutionary period. This he had managed to achieve in the form of government when, figuratively speaking, he set ahead the hands of the clock of history to point to the hour of the prosperous Roman Empire instead of the austere Roman republic. It was this image that the pomp and circumstance of the coronation had to confirm.

In David's painting of the event the crimson coronation robes of the Emperor and Empress are embroidered all over with golden bees. Napoleon had chosen this symbol for the integrated state in which all members had their appointed place and worked for the good of the hive in order to produce the honey of prosperity. Elsewhere in the painting, the sheaves of wheat and horns of plenty are symbols of imperial abundance; palm branches and figures of victory symbolize triumph; and Napoleon's laurel-wreath crown is the ancient symbol of literary immortality.

The supreme symbol on the actual occasion was Napoleon's act of crowning himself. This gesture signified the break with the past and his derivation of authority from the people by a general election. By this dramatic touch, Napoleon also proclaimed the existence of the free individual who recognized no superior authority, and the fact that his political power was derived through his own efforts and those of the people, not from above. In the painting, however, this symbolism was transferred to Napoleon's act of crowning Josephine.

Goya's Opposition

No presentation of this revived Roman Empire that showed only the heroic attitudes of the conqueror would be complete. The sufferings of a subjugated people, which invariably follow in the wake of an invading army, found vivid expression in the scenes painted by Francisco Goya after the French campaign in Spain in 1808. His *Executions of the Third of May, 1808* (Fig. 399), which Goya finished some years later, accents the reverse side of the Napoleonic coin.

399. Francisco Goya. *Executions of the Third of May, 1808.* 1814–15. Oil on canvas, 8′9″ × 13′4″ (2.67 × 4.06 m). Prado, Madrid.

Goya saw nothing of the heroic aspect of warfare, only the desolation of his country and the accompanying horrors and bloodshed. In this picture, both the technique and the subject matter are quite antithetical to the cold and correct presentations of David. Goya, whose compassionate art was the very opposite of French neoclassicism, further explored the miseries that trail in war's wake in his cycle of 85 etchings, *Disasters of War.* Here, through his penetrating mind and biting wit, a carnival of fearful bestialities and demonic destruction is revealed.

Ingres and Academic Art

After David, the leading figure of the academic art world was his pupil, Jean Auguste Dominique Ingres. Like his teacher, Ingres realized the importance of championing the arts in official circles; eventually he became a senator of France. The Academy had been reestablished after Napoleon's downfall, and the idea of placing the official stamp of approval on writers and painters finds full expression in the *Apotheosis of Homer* (Fig. 400). Commissioned as a ceiling mural in

400. Jean Auguste Dominique Ingres. *Apotheosis of Homer.* 1827. Oil on canvas, 12′8″ × 16′10¾″ (3.86 × 5.15 m). Louvre, Paris.

The Neoclassical Style **351**

the newly established Charles X Museum in the Louvre, the painting is well adapted to its setting, impressive in content and in its large proportions.

Ingres treats his subject, the deification of Homer, as some supreme session of an academy of arts and letters for the immortals. In their midst sits the enthroned Homer, the father of poetry. Behind him is the façade of an Ionic temple. Winged Victory holds the laurel wreath above his brow; at his feet are the personifications of his brainchildren, the *Iliad* and the *Odyssey;* and about him are his successors who have carried the torch for poetry and art throughout the ages. In this exclusive society, Aeschylus is seen unfolding a scroll listing his tragedies; the poet Pindar holds up his lyre in tribute; Vergil and Dante (extreme left) represent epic poetry. Longinus is standing up for philosophy, Boileau for criticism. At the lower right Racine and Molière, in the courtly wigs of the time of Louis XIV, make an offering of tragic and comic masks; and Raphael, the profiled figure in the upper left, represents Renaissance painting. Below him in the foreground is Poussin, and behind him, Shakespeare.

Ingres' source seems to have been a Hellenistic relief, now in the British Museum, showing a simplified version of the same subject with allegorical representations of the *Iliad* and *Odyssey* as well as personifications of time and the muses of history, poetry, drama, and mythology. Ingres' great technical skill in drawing is seen in the sharply defined figures. Like his contemporaries, he accepted the Greek aesthetic of art as a representation of nature, with the reservation that it was the artist's function to endow nature with orderliness through the process of rearrangement and editorial selection. In this case, he builds his composition by means of precise lines, which he then organizes into a series of receding planes. Color for him, as for David, was secondary.

Sculpture: Canova

The sculptor Antonio Canova, who in his day enjoyed a reputation second to none, was summoned from Rome to Paris by Napoleon to execute statues of the Emperor and his family. Through his neoclassical eyes, the Italian artist saw Napoleon's mother as the matronly Agrippina of old, Napoleon's sister Pauline—not without some justification—as Venus Victorious (Fig. 401), and Napoleon himself, most obligingly, as a Roman emperor (Fig. 402).

Canova was accompanied to Paris by his brother, who recorded the conversations between artist and patron from which one learns that Napoleon had a few qualms about being portrayed, as the saying goes, in the "heroic altogether" and suggested an appropriate costume. To this Canova grandiosely replied: "We, like the poets, have our own language. If a poet introduced into a tragedy, phrases and idioms used habitually by the lower classes in the public streets, he would rightly be reprimanded. . . . We sculptors cannot clothe our statues in modern costumes without deserving a similar reproach."

The sculptor's arguments prevailed, and except for the suggestion of a toga draped over his shoulder, Napoleon stands there in all his marble glory, holding in his right hand an orb surmounted by winged Victory and in his left, a staff of authority in place of a scepter. The head is idealized but recognizable; the body with the shifting of the weight toward one side points directly to Praxitelean models (see Fig. 50).

The reclining statue of *Pauline Bonaparte as Venus* (Fig. 401) is another example of the use of a Hellenistic model, for Canova, like David, had come under the sway of Winckelmann. While it is almost an exact sculptural counterpart of David's *Madame Récamier* (Fig. 397), the statue conveys much less of the individuality of its subject than does the painting. Both Canova statues show how a sculptor, much more than a painter, was restricted in expression during this wave of classical enthusiasm.

While practically nothing of ancient painting was known to David, museums filled with well-preserved ancient statues offered themselves to Canova. Although the painter was free to create a new style, the sculptor had to conform to existing models. Like a good academician, Canova advised his students on a "scrupulous adherence to rules" and against "arbitrary and capricious errors."

Deviation from the "rules" was possible, however, when it could be justified on rational grounds. In Canova'a view, everything was defined by classical rules. Hence when he did a portrait of a contemporary figure, the body, its pose, and the drapery were taken directly from antique models, and the head was idealized just enough to fit the subject. In

403. Horatio Greenough. *George Washington.* 1832–41. Marble, height 11′4″ (3.45 m). National Collection of Fine Arts, Smithsonian Institution, Washington, D.C. (transfer from United States Capitol).

theory, Canova accepted the Greek idea of art as an imitation of nature, but in practice his art became an imitation of art. For his observations of human nature, he was content to look about the Vatican collections instead of studying people on the highways and byways. Furthermore, his constant self-conscious striving to create objects of art too often led to artificial works. In the mind and hands of a greater artist, Canova's view of art might possibly have produced more significant results. In his own case, however, it had a definitely repressive effect.

Because of the great demand for his work, Canova employed a large number of assistants in his studio. His huge output, plus the use of some modern devices and methods that were unknown to Praxiteles, gave his workshop something of the aspect of a factory. Among other things, he used chemical solutions to achieve the extraordinary smoothness of his surface textures, and he employed a pointing machine to make exact copies of ancient sculptures. Despite murmurs from less successful sculptors, nothing in Canova's lifetime diminished his glittering reputation. The many young Americans who were attracted to Rome by his fame returned from their studies to do things like the colossal statue of Washington as Zeus (Fig. 403) by

Horatio Greenough. It outgrew its intended setting in the Capitol and is now in the Smithsonian Institution.

The British Parliament invited Canova to London to evaluate the Parthenon sculptures before purchasing them from Lord Elgin (see Figs. 39, 44–46). One would have thought that, after feeling the full force of these originals, the Italian sculptor might have realized their superiority to his previous models. Instead, he smugly found in them the justification of his own life's work and seized the opportunity to point out how wrong his critics had been. He did show good judgment, however, in refusing to attempt a restoration. Canova also scored with his observations on the differences between the real Greek sculpture and the works designed for the Roman market.

Music

Napoleon as Patron

Musicians in Paris were as active as the architects and painters. Napoleon's attempts to win over the French artists and those of the conquered countries also extended into the field of music. "Among all the fine arts," he said, "music is the one which exercises the greatest influence upon the passions and is the one which the legislator should most encourage."

Napoleon's personal preferences leaned to the Italian vocal style, especially that of Paisiello, whose gentle lyricism was to his taste. It was Paisiello who received the commission to compose the triumphal *Te Deum* for the national celebration of the accord with the Vatican, and the appointment as first conductor of the Imperial Chapel Orchestra. A native French composer, Charles Alexandre Lesueur, was chosen to write the music for the coronation ceremonies and a successful opera on Macpherson's *Ossian,* one of Napoleon's favorite books.

The production that most closely caught the spirit of the new Empire, however, was Spontini's opera *La Vestale* (*The Vestal Virgin*). Appearing as it did in 1807 at the height of Napoleon's military successes, it had the necessary pomp and pageantry to whip public enthusiasm to a pitch of frenzy. It had the right Roman setting, and the spectacle of a vestal virgin's struggle between her desire for personal happiness and her vows of service to the state was sufficient to ensure more than a hundred performances in its first season in Paris. The plot stressed glory on the battlefield, and Spontini supplied the necessary triumphal marches. His music is full of the resounding brass and the trumpet's blare, singing in the grand style, and the sound of massive choruses. One of his contemporaries wrote that "his *forte* ["loud"] was a hurricane, his *piano* ["soft"] a breath, his *sforzando* ["sudden accent"] enough to wake the dead." It was none other than Berlioz who attributed to him the invention of the "colossal crescendo."

Beethoven: The Heroic Ideal

Unknown to Napoleon, the essence of the heroic ideal had been captured in musical form in Austria, one of the countries he had conquered. Ludwig van Beethoven's Third Symphony, which the composer entitled the *Eroica,* or *Heroic,* was never heard by the man whose career had suggested it; nor was it played in Paris until 1828, a quarter of a century after it was composed. Yet a French writer of later times, Romain Rolland, could declare with the full weight of history on his side: "Here is an Austerlitz of music, the conquest of an empire. And Beethoven's has endured longer than Napoleon's."

The original idea for this mighty work was apparently made on a visit to Vienna by Marshal Bernadotte, one of Napoleon's generals turned diplomat. He casually suggested that Beethoven write a work honoring Consul Bonaparte. Beethoven accepted the challenge, and after a period of four years of inspired effort the colossal symphony appeared bearing the desired dedication. But the year that the symphony was completed was the year in which Napoleon accepted the title of emperor. Beethoven, feeling that the former apostle of liberty had become both a traitor and a new tyrant, erased the name from the title page and inscribed it instead "to the memory of a great man."

That memory indeed had stirred Beethoven deeply, for from the days of his youth he had been a lifelong enthusiast for the ideals of liberty, equality, and fraternity. It was Napoleon's championing of these principles, his opposition to hereditary privilege, his will and ability to translate these ideals into action, that had moved Beethoven profoundly as it had so many other artists and writers of the time. The Third Symphony is not narrowly Napoleonic, but more generally an elaboration of the heroism of one who, for a time at least, rallied the progressive and freedom-loving people of all nations around his standard.

The music Beethoven wrote for the theater was invariably based on themes involving the quest for individual liberty and the cause of popular freedom. In his only opera, *Fidelio,* he insisted on a story that would reflect high moral purpose and steadfast resolve. In the fluid forms of his instrumental compositions, however, these ideals of liberty, equality, and fraternity reached their most abstract and universal expression. Beethoven used the power of his art to convey the spirit of these great human declarations.

Thus he illuminated the path of humanity toward its ultimate destiny of progress and perfectibility.

Through the *Eroica,* Beethoven was giving tangible shape to the goals of a large part of humanity during those stirring times. In it, he mirrored the titanic struggle between the opposing attitudes of submission and assertion, passivity and activity, acceptance and challenge. Through it, he gave flesh to the word of the triumph of spirit over matter, will over negation, and the victorious human drive against the forces of suppression.

Though the length of the symphony is unprecedented and the orchestra only somewhat expanded, Beethoven never fell into the trap that many of the French composers of the revolutionary period did when they equated colossal size with grandeur of expression. While the revolutionists wrote their choruses for 1000 voices, accompanied by cannons and three or four combined orchestras, he added just one horn to his usual brass section.

Beethoven clothed his ideas in rich folds of lustrous sound that grow out of the poetic idea itself. Furthermore, by raising the level of musical content and meaning, he succeeded in producing an organic work of art where others had failed. While the Third Symphony as a whole can be criticized on formal grounds and for a certain lack of unity in the four separate movements, the fiery spirit of creation when Beethoven was at the height of his mature powers has never been surpassed. The *Eroica* was as much a revolution in music as the American and French revolutions were in political thought and action.

The Promethean Idea   The *Eroica* might with equal justification be called the *Promethean* Symphony. It was none other than Prometheus who had taken the divine fire from the hearth of the gods on Mt. Olympus and brought it down to animate the bodies and souls of men and women and to release them from the bonds of ignorance. For fire brings warmth and light, and with the light comes enlightenment. Prometheus was adopted as the prime symbol of the Enlightenment in philosophy and social thought as well as in poetry, art, and drama. He represented for Beethoven—as for the poet Shelley—"the type of the highest perfection of moral and intellectual nature impelled by the purest and truest motives to the best and noblest ends."

Gradually a musical idea associated with Prometheus began to take shape in Beethoven's notebooks. It first saw the light as a simple popular dance tune, then in 1801 as a prominent number in his full-length ballet the *Creatures of Prometheus.* In 1802 it was used as a theme for an extended set of piano variations. In its most exalted form it became, at last, the basic material for the great finale of the *Eroica.* Here

Symphony No. 3   Ludwig van Beethoven
(finale: *Allegro molto,* bars 76–83)

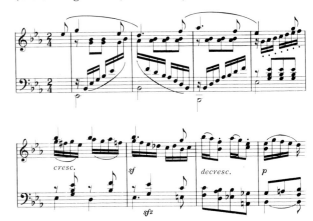

it is transformed into a monumental set of orchestral variations that become a veritable musical arch of triumph through which the image of a liberated humanity joyously passes by in review.

This last movement of the *Eroica* begins with a fiery plunging figure for strings, a motif taken from the ballet when Prometheus descends from Mt. Olympus, torch in hand. Then follows the so-called skeletal theme—the basis for the entire finale—derived from the lowest line of the Promethean dance.

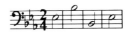

Starting on E flat, it rises five tones to the dominant note of B flat, descends an octave to the B flat below, then returns to the original E flat. In effect, this skeletal theme simply defines the tonal center of E-flat major with the empty upper and lower dominant limits of the tonality, or key center. This harmonic vacuum is gradually filled by the addition of a second, third, and fourth voice, while simultaneously the rhythmic divisions are quickened by similar subdivisions. Not until the 76th bar (top of page) is the Promethean melody joined to its previously heard skeletal bass.

The form of the finale is a series of variations unequal in length and strongly contrasted in style. What had before been a pleasant little dance tune now assumes the imposing shape of a triumphant melody. Beethoven, by his additive process, is able to build this melody into the cumulative structure he needs for his victory finale.

Some variations are aristocratic in sound, while others are rough and ready. Compare, for example, the elegant sonorities of bars 175–197 in the *Eroica* with the boisterous band music heard in bars 211–

255. A similar open-air episode to that heard in bars 211–255 occurs in the finale of the Ninth Symphony, where Beethoven inserts a popular "Turkish" march, scored in a striking manner for bassoons, horns, trombones, cymbals, triangle, and drums. Further contrasts in the *Eroica* finale can be heard in the fugal episodes (bars 117–174 and 226–348), which employ sophisticated contrapuntal devices, such as the inversion of the skeletal theme (277–280) and the sturdy German chorale (249–364) that begins at the point where the tempo is slackened to a more moderate *Poco andante* ("a little slower").

All this vast variety of forms—dances, songs, fugues, chorales—are arranged sequentially in the manner of a procession that eventually leads up to the rousing triumphant climax heard in bars 381–395. At this point, Beethoven throws in all his orchestral forces, including the brasses and drums, to bring about the image of ultimate achievement of the heroic idea. Afterward there remains only the quieter anticlimax (396–430), in which the whole awesome spectacle is contemplated retrospectively just before the fast, whirlwind *presto* that brings the movement to a triumphant close.

Earlier Movements of the Eroica　　The great opening movement is cast in *sonata form,* which might be described as a dramatic reconciliation of opposites, or, more technically, as a strategy of thematic and key relationships. Brought to perfection in the late 18th century by Haydn and Mozart, this balanced classical design, with its true Aristotelian beginning, middle, and end, unfolds with an opening section, called an *exposition.* This is followed by a central core, the *development,* and the work then concludes with a *recapitulation.* Optionally a prologue, or *introduction,* and an epilogue, or *coda,* may be added. The exposition presents an abstract dramatic encounter between a protagonist consisting of related motifs, themes, or subjects within a principal key center (the tonic) and an antagonist comprised of contrasting material in a different key center (the dominant, relative major or minor, and so on). Then follows the development, or working-out portion, in which the previously presented materials oppose or conflict and interact with one other. The subjects or themes may be broken up into fragments or segments, new tonal territories explored by modulating to new key centers close or remote, and themes combined in overlapping contrapuntal lines. Finally, the materials are reassembled in the recapitulation that reveals their altered character in a kind of dramatic reconciliation. Beethoven here projects a first movement on a heroic scale.

Each of the four movements in its way shattered precedent. The first is distinguished by its restless surging character and its enormous expansion of sonata form to include a development section of 245 bars. The mobilization of such forces, as well as the transformation of the coda into a terminal development of 140 measures, caused Romain Rolland to call it a "Grand Army of the soul, that will not stop until it has trampled on the whole earth."

A funeral march as the second movement of a symphony was another innovation, though Beethoven had included one in his earlier Piano Sonata, Op. 26, which bears the inscription "on the death of a hero." Its heroic proportions here, as well as its poetic conception as a glorification of the hero, link it with the first movement. While such a transformation scene is a fairly common idea for a painting, statue, poem, play, or opera, its use within the more abstract symphonic form is unique.

The effect of this funeral march is that of a glowing lamentation for the heroes who give up life itself so that the ideals for which they fought may live. It is, in this case, a collective rather than an individualized expression, though it emphasizes that every great human advance is accompanied by personal tragedy. The stately measured rhythms and muffled sonorities also reminded the listener of Beethoven's time that contemporary heroes, as well as such ancient ones as Socrates and Jesus, often suffered martyrdom at the hands of a society that did not understand them.

The title "Scherzo" over the third movement also appears for the first time in a formal symphony, though again it had been used earlier in piano sonatas and chamber music. Beethoven once more reveals himself a man of the revolutionary period by the substitution of this robust humor for the traditional minuet, but in such a grand design he hardly had any other alternative. Berlioz has referred to its energetic rhythms as a kind of play, "recalling that which the warriors of the *Iliad* celebrated round the tombs of their chiefs."

Then comes the great victory finale, which has already been described. The heroic image is later continued in the finales of the Fifth and Ninth symphonies. The amplification in these later works contributes to a more profound understanding of the earlier *Eroica.*

All three finales envision the emergence of a strong and free human society, and all three start with popular themes. In the *Eroica,* it is a modest little country dance; in the Fifth Symphony, a simple marching tune; and in the Ninth Symphony, an unpretentious hymn. One and all, they are built up to epic proportions. By the use of an immense variety of styles, episodic deviations, a wide range of keys, and shifting orchestral color, they become collective rather than individual expressions. Instead of being restricted to one side of life, they embrace a cross section of musical levels and reach out to include the entire human panorama.

The Archaeological Idea

The Napoleonic era was a mixture of forward and backward tendencies. At the very time when the social hopes of the revolutionary period were about to be realized in democratic forms, Europe was confronted with a militant revival of ancient Roman imperial authority. The 18th-century individualism that had led to the struggle for freedom was engulfed in a 19th-century regimentation, or uniformity, disguised as a movement to maintain the social gains that had been made. Revolutionary ideals were partially eclipsed by Napoleonic actualities; the desire for freedom collided with the need for order; the rights of individuals conflicted with the might of authority; and spiritual well-being was pitted against material considerations.

New scientific and technological advances competed for attention with revivals of ancient glories. Napoleon boasted of a new culture, yet he clothed it in a Roman toga. But the early 19th century was by no means unique in its revival of a bygone era. Every period in Western art since Greco-Roman days has revived classical ideas and motifs.

From the 1000-year span of Greco-Roman civilization, many choices have been made by succeeding centuries. Dramas and operas have been set in Athens, Sparta, the Alexandrian empire, the Roman republic, and the West and East Roman empires, and their characters have been lofty Olympian gods and rugged Roman heroes. Dramatists have chosen the Roman playwright Seneca as a model, as did Quinault and Racine in the baroque period. Shelley and Goethe, for their part, turned to the Athenian dramatists Aeschylus and Euripides. Architects in the 17th century, such as Bernini and Perrault, built then-modern palaces that they decorated with classical motifs, while the neoclassicists Vignon, Percier, and Fontaine constructed almost precise models of Greek and Roman temples. Forms of government, likewise, ranged from the democratic republic to the autocratic empire. Aside from the shape and spirit a revival assumes, it is largely a matter of selection from a wide choice of models.

Each period has tended to choose from the past those elements that harmonized with its specific ideals and goals. Florentine Renaissance humanists, in their reaction to medieval scholastic thought and the traditional Church interpretation of Aristotle, turned to the pagan beauties of antiquity in general and to the philosophy of Plato in particular. The Renaissance revival of classicism, however, was con-fined to a few intellectuals and artists. Neoclassicism, on the other hand, was mirrored in forms of government, became the officially approved art style, and rested on a base of broad popular acceptance. Baroque classical interests reflected an aristocratic image of society and were restricted to courtly circles. Again, Louis XIV and his associates identified themselves with the gods of Mt. Olympus, and their moral standards, like those of the ancient deities, were the ethics of a highly privileged class. Napoleonic neoclassicism, by contrast, was directed toward the middle class, which saw a comfortable image in the living standards of ancient Pompeii and Herculaneum but tempered luxury with the stricter moral standards of a revolutionary regime. The new interest in classical sculpture, architecture, and painting was also a bourgeois criticism of the artificiality and extravagance of courtly life as mirrored in the rococo. Without the moral overtones of this revived interest in the ancient world, the choice of conservative classical art forms would have been extremely odd for such a revolutionary period.

Faithfulness to Antique Models

The principal difference between early 19th-century artists and their predecessors was in the desire for faithfulness to antique models. Archaeological correctness was now possible, owing to a more detailed knowledge of the past. Winckelmann and his generation had made classical archaeology a science, and the excavations at Pompeii and Herculaneum had provided the material and stimulus for authenticity.

For neoclassical success, a building had to be archaeologically accurate. The Vendôme Column was planned as a replica of Trajan's Column, and the Arc du Carrousel preserved the proportions and shape of the Arch of Septimus Severus, even if reduced somewhat in size. When variations were made, as in the instance of the Arc de Triomphe and La Madeleine in Paris, the results were more interesting. The first two may be likened to a pair of competent academic theses, while the latter pair approximate the livelier style of good historical novels.

Archaeological correctness meant lifting an ancient building, which had been designed for quite a different purpose, out of its context, period, and century and putting it down bodily into another period where it had no practical reason for being. This would never have occurred in the rational Enlightenment period. While Palladio, Mansart, and Wren had been concerned with adapting classical principles and motifs to the needs of their times, Vignon, Percier, and Fontaine were busy trying to fit activities of the Napoleonic period into ancient Greek and Roman molds.

In poetry, a similar motivation can be found in the reforms of the poet-hero of the Revolution, André Chénier. They were based on his studies of the Latin and Greek originals. For the forms of his odes and elegies, his pastoral idylls and epics, he drew directly on Homer, Pindar, Vergil, and Horace. "Let us upon new thoughts write antique verses," he had declared; and to a considerable degree his enthusiasm helped him to carry out his announced objective.

Emancipation of Music

In this archaeological era, however, the musicians fared the best of all because they had no examples surviving from antiquity to emulate. An opera, to be sure, could get some authenticity into its plot, scenery and costumes; and such productions of 1807 as Persuis and Lesueur's *Triomphe de Trajan,* their *L'Inauguration du Temple de la Victoire,* and Spontini's *La Vestale* tried to make the grade in this respect. All this, however, was on the surface and could hardly be compared with the type of authenticity represented by the Vendôme Column or the Napoleonic arches of triumph.

Since the musicians had to evolve their own style, the music of the period has overshadowed the other contemporary arts and its vitality has given it a lasting general appeal. Just as the fussy rococo had brought about a countermovement in the prerevolutionary neoclassicism, so a reform in music had been carried out in the 18th century under Gluck. By reducing the number of characters in his operas, omitting complicated subplots, strengthening the role of the chorus, transferring much of the lyrical expression to the orchestra, writing simple unadorned melodies, and avoiding ornate coloratura cadenzas in the Italian style, Gluck had brought about a musical revolution similar to David's in painting and paved the way for a new style.

Gluck's ideas were based partially on a reinterpretation of Aristotle's *Poetics.* In his preface to *Alceste* (1767) he had stated that his music was designed to allow the drama to proceed "without interrupting the action or stifling it with a useless superfluity of ornaments." Echoing Winckelmann, he added that the great principles of beauty were "simplicity, truth and naturalness."

These principles found their ultimate expression in the sinewy music of Beethoven, who, by impatiently brushing aside ancient precedent, achieved an expressive style that was genuinely heroic and not merely theatrical.

Likewise, in the neoclassical style, a successful statue had to be accurate. And since so many antique models existed, the sculptors were limited in their creative freedom. Their desire for exactitude often led them to the point of absurdity (Fig. 403). They omitted carving the irises and pupils of the eyes and left them blank, because they did not know that the Greeks had painted in such details. The prevailing whiteness made their works resemble mortuary monuments, since they had overlooked the fact that the ancients had designed their statuary and friezes for the strong light and shadow of the open air and not for the dim interiors of museums. While Praxiteles and Michelangelo had turned marble into flesh, Canova and Thorvaldsen (Fig. 404) converted the living flesh of their models into cold stone.

Enthusiasm for antiquity sometimes led David into similar situations. For the heads of figures in his early pictures he used ancient Roman portrait busts instead of live models. In the baroque period, when Poussin and Claude Lorrain painted Rome, they did so usually in terms of picturesque ancient ruins, but David painted archaeological reconstructions. Madame Récamier was a 19th-century Parisian socialite, but David made her into a fancy-dress reincarnation of a Pompeian matron. David's reliance on lines and planes was often so strict that the effect of his paintings was almost as severe as that of relief sculpture. David was saved, however, from the major pitfalls of his architectural and sculptural colleagues because so few examples of ancient painting were known at the time. As a consequence, he was forced to divert his considerable talent as a painter to a new style.

19
The Romantic Style

Paris, 1830

Well before the romantic Revolution of July 1830, new ideas were stirring the minds and imaginations of the intellectuals and artists of Paris. In 1827, as the new movement was gaining momentum, Victor Hugo published his *Cromwell,* a drama with a preface that served as the manifesto of romanticism. Guizot was lecturing at the Sorbonne on the early history of France. François Rude, destined to be the principal sculptor of the period, returned from his Belgian exile. And the painter Delacroix wrote in his journal that when he went to the Odéon Theater to see Shakespeare's *Hamlet,* he met the writers Alexandre Dumas and Victor Hugo. The Ophelia in that production was Harriet Smithson, later to become the wife of the composer Hector Berlioz. Gérard de Nerval's translation of Goethe appeared that autumn and inspired Berlioz to compose *Eight Scenes from Faust,* which later reached popularity in the revision called the *Damnation of Faust.* Delacroix was already at work on his famous *Faust* lithographs to illustrate the 1828 edition of Goethe's drama.

All in all, the 1820s were an inspiring time, and when Théophile Gautier later came to write his history of romanticism, he looked back on his youthful years with nostalgia:

> What a marvelous time. Walter Scott was then in the flower of his success; one was initiated into the mysteries of Goethe's *Faust,* which as Madame de Staël said, contained everything. One discovered Shakespeare, and the poems of Lord Byron: *The Corsair; Lara; The Gaiour; Manfred; Beppo;* and *Don Juan* took us to the orient, which was not banal then as now. All was young, new, exotically colored, intoxicating, and strongly flavored. It turned our heads; it was as if we had entered into a strange new world.

Romanticism was swept in on a wave of political unrest culminating in the July Revolution of 1830. It was to be the dominant French style until the February Revolution of 1848.

Liberty Leading the People

Nowhere is there a better example of the mating of the artistic genius with the spirit of the time than in the life and work of Eugène Delacroix set in the Paris of 1830. His *Liberty Leading the People* brought those glorious July days to incandescent expression (Fig. 405). The canvas, in which he distilled the essence of that revolution, is dominated by the fiery allegorical figure of Liberty, here seen as the spirit of the French people whom she leads onward to triumph. No relaxed Mediterranean goddess but a virile, energetic reincarnation of the spirit of 1789, she has muscular arms strong enough to hold with ease both a bayoneted rifle and the tricolored banner of the republic. Though bare-breasted, she betrays no sign of softness or sensuality, and her powerful limbs stride over the street barricades as she leads her followers forward through the oncoming forces. While intended as an allegorical figure, she is treated by Delacroix as a living personality. Only the Phrygian cap and the almost-classic profile, serene in the face of danger, indicate her symbolic significance. She does not hover over the action on wings, as so many other artists depicted her; instead, with her feet on the ground, she is in the midst of the action.

Liberty's followers include both impulsive students and battle-scarred soldiers who have heeded her call rather than that of their reactionary king. The boy on the right is recruited from the Paris streets. Though too young to understand the events, he is there, a pistol in each hand.

CHRONOLOGY
Mid-19th Century

GENERAL EVENTS

1814	Fall of Napoleon. Restoration of the monarchy under Louis XVIII
1821	Napoleon died
1824	Louis XVIII succeeded by Charles X
1830	July Revolution overthrew old line of Bourbons. Louis Philippe began reign as limited monarch
1837	Commission for the Preservation of Historical Monuments founded by Louis Philippe
1840	Guizot, French historian and statesman, became prime minister
1848	February Revolution overthrew Louis Philippe's government. Second Republic proclaimed; Louis Napoleon, nephew of Napoleon I, elected president
1852	Louis Napoleon elected emperor; reigned as Napoleon III
1870	Napoleon III abdicated after unsuccessful conclusion of Franco-Prussian War. Third Republic proclaimed

ARCHITECTS

1726–1796	William Chambers
1748–1813	James Wyatt
1752–1835	John Nash
1790–1853	François Christian Gau
1795–1860	Charles Barry
1802–1878	Richard Upjohn
1814–1879	Eugène Viollet-le-Duc
1817–1885	Théodore Ballu
1818–1895	James Renwick
1824–1881	George Street

SCULPTORS

1784–1855	François Rude
1787–1843	Jean Pierre Cortot
1796–1875	Antoine Louis Barye

PAINTERS

1771–1835	Antoine Jean Gros
1775–1851	Joseph Mallord William Turner
1776–1837	John Constable
1780–1867	Jean Auguste Dominique Ingres
1791–1824	Théodore Géricault
1796–1875	Camille Corot
1798–1863	Eugène Delacroix
1808–1879	Honoré Daumier
1814–1875	François Millet

WRITERS

1717–1797	Horace Walpole
1749–1832	Johann Wolfgang von Goethe
1766–1817	Germaine de Staël
1768–1848	Chateaubriand
1771–1832	Walter Scott
1774–1843	Robert Southey
1783–1842	Stendhal (Henri Beyle)
1787–1874	François Guizot
1788–1824	Lord Byron
1788–1860	Arthur Schopenhauer
1792–1822	Percy Bysshe Shelley
1795–1821	John Keats
1797–1856	Heinrich Heine
1799–1850	Honoré de Balzac
1802–1870	Alexandre Dumas, Sr.
1802–1885	Victor Hugo
1803–1870	Prosper Mérimée
1804–1876	George Sand
1811–1872	Théophile Gautier

MUSICIANS

1782–1871	Daniel F. E. Auber
1782–1840	Niccolò Paganini
1784–1859	Ludwig Spohr
1786–1826	Carl Maria von Weber
1791–1864	Giacomo Meyerbeer
1803–1869	Hector Berlioz
1809–1847	Felix Mendelssohn
1810–1849	Frédéric Chopin
1810–1856	Robert Schumann
1811–1886	Franz Liszt
1813–1883	Richard Wagner
1813–1901	Giuseppe Verdi
1818–1893	Charles Gounod
1833–1897	Johannes Brahms
1838–1875	Georges Bizet

In the background are the remnants of the old guard from revolutionary days still carrying on the struggle. Two main social classes are represented—in the shadows on the extreme left, the man armed with a saber is obviously a working-class figure, while in front of him toward the center the more prominent figure in the fashionable frock coat, top hat, and sideburns is a bourgeois gentleman who has grabbed his musket and joined in the general confusion. It was his class that controlled the fighting and stamped its image on the new monarchy in the person of Louis Philippe, the "Citizen King."

Though the July Revolution was essentially a palace revolt replacing a reactionary Bourbon with his more liberal cousin, no aristocrats are represented as taking part. In the shadow below, the wounded and dying are strewn on the loose cobblestones looking toward Liberty, for she is both their inspiration and their reason for being. Through smoke at the right are the towers of Notre Dame.

Because of the contemporary frame of reference in which one recognizes the familiar shirts, blouses, trousers, rifles, pistols, and other 19th-century equipment, the picture sometimes has been called realistic. But, because the spirit of the work rises above the event itself, and because the artist has rendered feeling rather than actuality, the picture surely is in the romantic style. By infusing reality with the charge of an electric emotional attitude, Delacroix raises his picture to the level of an idealized though highly personal expression. As a consequence, all who see this painting seem to be experiencing the Revolution of July 1830 for themselves.

More eloquent than any page in a history book, the canvas has captured the feeling as well as the facts that make up the incident. It is as if all the noise had awakened Delacroix from his dreams of the past, and now suddenly wide awake, he has applied his expressive techniques consciously to one of the stirring happenings of his own time.

405. Eugène Delacroix. *Liberty Leading the People, 1830.* 1830. Oil on canvas, 8′6″ × 10′10″ (2.59 × 3.3 m). Louvre, Paris.

As always with Delacroix, color plays an important part in the communication of mood. Here, a striking instance of the use of color is seen in the way he takes the red, white, and blue of the banner (the symbol of patriotism) and merges them into the picture as a whole. The white central strip, signifying truth and purity, blends with the purifying smoke of battle. The blue, denoting freedom, matches the parts of the sky visible in the top corners through the smoke. The red in the flag high above balances the color of the blood of those below who have fallen for the ideal of liberty. Thus, the symbolism of the banner blends into the color scheme, and both combine with the dramatic lighting to define the emotional range. All these, in turn, expand the patriotic theme into a formal pictorial unity of intensity. With the purchase of this picture in the name of the state by the new bourgeois king at the time of its exhibition during the Salon of 1831, the seal of official approval was stamped on the romantic style.

Painting

Art and Literature

It was characteristic of romantic painting that Delacroix, its leading representative, should look to the fantasy of the literary world for the sources of his pictorial visions rather than to the world of everyday appearances. His choice of subjects as well as his treatment of them makes this immediately apparent. Such titles as the *Death of Sardanapalus, Mazeppa, Giaour and the Pasha,* and the *Shipwreck of Don Juan* all point to the germ of these French paintings in the poetic writings of the English noble Lord Byron. Delacroix's illustrations for Goethe's *Faust* won the complete admiration of none other than this most German of authors, who felt that for clarity and depth of insight they could not be surpassed (Figs. 406, 407, 415).

Delacroix's imagination had been haunted by *Faust* since he first saw it in London. In fact, in a

left: 406. Eugène Delacroix. *Mephistopheles Flying,* illustration for Goethe's *Faust.* 1828. Lithograph, 10¾ × 9" (27 × 23 cm). Metropolitan Museum of Art, New York (Rogers Fund, 1917).

above: 407. Eugène Delacroix. *Faust and Mephistopheles Galloping on the Witches' Sabbath,* illustration for Goethe's *Faust.* 1828. Lithograph, 8 × 11" (20 × 28 cm). Metropolitan Museum of Art, New York (Rogers Fund, 1917).

letter to a friend in Paris, he had commented particularly on its diabolical aspect. The lithographs, or prints, that eventually resulted show his mastery of illustration and prove Delacroix to have been adept in small works as well as large.

Despite his close kinship with Byron and Goethe, Delacroix was not always in sympathy with the work of his romantic Parisian contemporaries. In his diary he spoke of Meyerbeer's opera *Le Prophète* as "frightful" and referred to Berlioz and Hugo as those "so-called reformers." "The noise he makes is distracting," he wrote about Berlioz' music; "It is an heroic mess." Of all musicians he admired Mozart the most, and among his contemporaries only Chopin measured up to his standards.

Color and Emotion

Delacroix's color technique was a means of dramatizing his emotional and highly charged subject matter. For him, color was dominant over design. As he declared, "gray is the enemy of all painting . . . let us banish from our palette all earth colors . . . the greater the opposition in color, the greater the brilliance." His admitted models in painting were the heroic canvases of Rubens (see Figs. 325–327) and the dramatic pictures of Rembrandt, with their emphasis on the dynamics of light (see Figs. 337–339). Among his contemporaries he admired the mellow landscapes and subtle coloring of the English painter Constable (see Figs. 421, 422).

Delacroix's own art was built on principles of color, light, and emotion rather than on line, drawing, and form. This is nowhere better illustrated than

in his early masterpiece *Dante and Vergil in Hell* (Fig. 408), the first of his pictures to attract wide attention when it was exhibited in the Salon of 1822. The revival of Dante's *Divine Comedy* (see pp. 186–187) was another of the romantic literary enthusiasms. It was the *Inferno* part with its emphasis on tales of the demonic and macabre as well as on the tortures of the damned amid sulfurous fire and brimstone that held the greatest appeal.

Dante and Vergil in Hell

In the *Dante,* Delacroix enters the realm of pathos. The central figure is that of Vergil. In the crimson robe of a medieval Florentine crowned with the laurel wreath, he stands with dignified monumentality as a symbol of classic calm. On his left is Dante with a red hood on his head. In contrast to the serenity of his immortal companion, he is expressively human and emotionally involved with his grotesque and gruesome surroundings. He looks with terror on the damned who swirl about him.

The wake of the boat is filled with the writhing forms of the condemned, who hope eternally to reach the opposite shore by trying to attach themselves to the craft. One attempts to climb aboard, and the gnashing teeth of another bite into the edge of the boat, but in vain as they are plunged into the dark waters. Distress and despair are everywhere. On the right is Phlegyas, the ghostly boatman, seen from the rear as he strains at the rudder to guide the boat across the Styx River to the flaming shores of the city of Dis, visible in the distant background between the clouds of sulfurous fumes.

left: 408. Eugène Delacroix.
Dante and Vergil in Hell. 1822.
Oil on canvas, 6'1½" × 7'10½"
(1.87 × 2.4 m). Louvre, Paris.

below: 409. François Rude.
Departure of the Volunteers of 1792
(*La Marseillaise*). 1833–36.
Height 42' (12.8 m), width 26' (7.93 m).
Right stone relief,
Arc de Triomphe de l'Étoile, Paris.

When Delacroix was at work on it, he had a young friend read Dante's *Divine Comedy* to him and, as he says in his journal: "The best head in my Dante picture was swept in with the greatest speed and spirit while Pierret was reading me a canto from Dante which I knew already but to which he lent, by his accent, an energy that electrified me. That head is the one of the man behind the boat, facing you and trying to climb aboard, after throwing his arm over the gunwale." The particular passage that inflamed the artist's imagination and on which he built the picture is from the eighth book of the *Inferno*.

When first exhibited, the picture brought down storms of protest and critical abuse on Delacroix's head, which helped immeasurably to bring the young artist to critical attention. One defender of David's academic tradition called it a "splattering of color"; another critic thought Delacroix had "combined all the parts of the work in view of one emotion." While its expressive intensity was novel then, the work now easily falls into place as part of the macabre aspect of the romantic style. Even the nude figures, as muscular as those of Michelangelo and Rubens, function here more as color masses than as forms modeled three-dimensionally. As Delacroix once declared, color *is* painting, and his development of a color palette capable of arousing specific emotional reactions from his viewers was destined to have a far-reaching effect on later painting.

Sculpture: François Rude

The *Departure of the Volunteers of 1792* by François Rude (Fig. 409) is one of the dominating sculptural

410. François Rude.
Joan of Arc Listening to the Voices. 1845.
Marble, life-size. Musée de Dijon.

works of the romantic style. It achieved its stature by its impassioned expression and sustained heroic mood. Its prominent location on one side of the Arc de Triomphe in Paris assured it the largest possible audience. Sculptured in the boldest high relief, the dimensions of the composition alone—rising to a height of 42 feet (12.8 meters) and spreading to a width of 26 feet (7.9 meters)—make it of truly colossal proportions. The conception and commission of this work date from the wave of patriotic emotion associated with the Revolution of July 1830 and the memories that stirred of earlier struggles for freedom. This common source of inspiration was shared by both Delacroix and Rude, whose design certainly owes much to Delacroix's *Liberty Leading the People,* reproduced in Figure 405. It took Delacroix only a year to get his painting before the public, but a sculptural work of these proportions took Rude six years to complete.

The scene shown is that of a band of volunteers rallying to the defense of the newly established French Republic when it was threatened by foreign invasion in 1792. The five determined figures in the foreground are coming together to meet the common danger and are receiving mutual inspiration from the winged figure of Bellona, the Roman goddess of war, who hovers over them, urging them onward with the singing of *La Marseillaise.* A fine rhythmical mood is established by the compact grouping of the figures. It is reinforced by the repeated motifs of the legs that combine in a neat marchlike manner with the arms of the soldier stooping to tie his sandal. This rhythm serves to weld the composition together as a whole in the manner of a lively yet majestic march.

These representatives of the humanity so recently liberated by the French Revolution are self-motivated protectors of their newly won liberty, equality, and fraternity. The full force and power of four of the volunteers contrasts with the potential strength of the finely carved nude figure of the idealistic youth. The waning ability of the old man behind him is such that he can only point out the direction to the others and wave them on. The surging power of ideals held in common urges the volunteers onward with driving force and momentum.

Links with the Past

Because Rude designed the *Departure* for a Napoleonic arch of triumph, his motifs are of Roman origin. The soldiers are outfitted with Roman helmets and shields, though the coats of mail and weapons in the background recall those of the medieval period. The avoidance in the costumes and symbols of any contemporary reference in this representation of an event that had taken place less than a half-century before links the composition with the tendency to draw on the past for inspiration.

Popularly, and quite properly, called the *"Marseillaise* in stone," the *Departure* represents a most inventive sculptural use of a musical motif in suggesting the great revolutionary song, which serves to unify the patriotic spirit of the group. The anthem, with its stirring words "To arms, O citizens," was practically forgotten during the days of Napoleon's Empire, and under the Bourbon restoration it was, of course, officially banned. Credit for its rediscovery and revival goes to the composer Berlioz. Stirred to patriotic frenzy by the events of July 1830, though avoiding direct participation, this eccentric genius contented himself with scoring the song for double chorus and orchestra, asking "all who have voices, a heart, and blood in their veins" to join in.

In a later work, *Joan of Arc Listening to the Voices* (Fig. 410), Rude combines emotionalism and medieval subject matter. Executed originally in 1845 for the gardens of the Luxembourg Palace, the life-size statue represents the Maid of Orleans in peasant costume with a suit of armor at her side. In this way the sculptor indicated both her rural origin and her heroic mission. The mystic element is suggested as she lifts her hand to her ear in order to hear the angelic voices that guide her. By trying to capture the intangible sounds of these heavenly voices as Joan listens quiveringly with upraised head, Rude strains the marble medium to its expressive limits.

Rude, who had grown up in revolutionary times, was always thoroughly in sympathy with the liberal spirit. He accepted exile in Belgium in 1815 rather than live under a Bourbon ruler. Action was his aesthetic watchword. "The great thing for an artist," he once said, "is to *do*." Some critics find his *Departure of the Volunteers of 1792* overcrowded, overloaded, and unbalanced. Others feel that this crowding and imbalance are justified by the subject of a concerted uprising of the masses and that unity is achieved by the direction of its movement. Clearly it shows no will toward classical calm. Its sheer energy makes a clean break with academic tradition. By thus liberating sculpture from many outworn clichés, Rude revealed himself as a true romanticist.

Architecture

Romantic architecture received its initial thrust from the popularity in the late 18th century of the so-called Gothic novels. Romances and plays of this type published in England were variously entitled: *The Haunted Priory; The Horrid Mysteries; Banditti,* or *Love in a Labyrinth; Raymond and Agnes,* or *The Bleeding Nun of Lindenberg;* and Horace Walpole's famous *Castle of Otranto,* subtitled *A Gothic Tale.*

The settings for these stories were large baronial halls or decayed abbeys, liberally equipped with mysterious trapdoors, sliding panels, creaking gates, animated suits of armor, and ghostly voices emanating from ancient tombs. Such scenes served as backdrops for the injured innocence of fragile and helpless heroines and the fearless, if somewhat reckless, courage of dashing heroes. These tales played their part in the redefinition of the word *Gothic*—which Voltaire had called a fantastic compound of rudeness and filigree—into something more mystical, tinged with weirdness and bordering on the fantastic.

Gothic Revival in England

The imaginary castles of these novels first took on concrete form in England as the architectural whims of wealthy eccentrics. Walpole, the well-to-do son of a powerful prime minister, had indulged his fancy in a residence that gave its name to one aspect of the romantic style, "Strawberry Hill Gothick." William Beckford, whom Byron called "England's richest son," had the architect James Wyatt construct him a residence he called Fonthill Abbey (Fig. 411). Its

411. James Wyatt.
Fonthill Abbey (no longer standing),
Wiltshire. 1796–1807.
Height of tower 278′ (84.73 m).
Contemporary lithograph.

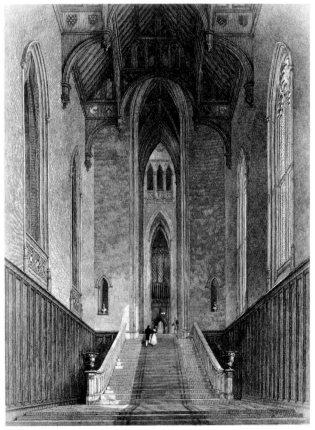

412. Interior, Fonthill Abbey. Length 25′ (7.62 m), width 35′ (10.67 m). Contemporary lithograph.

413. Charles Barry and A. W. N. Pugin. Houses of Parliament, London. 1840–60. Length 940' (286.51 m).

huge central tower rose over a spacious interior hall that was approached by a massive staircase (Fig. 412). The rest of the interior was a maze of long drafty corridors that provided the wall space for the proprietor's collections of pictures and tapestries as well as a suitable setting for his melancholy musings.

In his frenzy to have Fonthill Abbey completed, Beckford drove the workers day and night to the point where, in their haste, they neglected to provide an adequate foundation for the tower. Only a few years after its completion, the tower of Beckford's dream castle fell to the ground, taking most of the building with it. Since ruins were greatly admired as residences at the time, this catastrophe only served to enhance the abbey's picturesqueness.

In the early 1820's, Fonthill Abbey became so enormously popular that newspapers wrote of the "Fonthill mania." Visitors numbering up to five hundred a day made the pilgrimage to see it. Beckford's spectacular landscaping, which had involved transplanting over a million trees to create a picturesque setting, commanded the admiration of the painter Constable who lived nearby, as well as that of such poets as Lord Byron and Edgar Allan Poe.

The Gothic novel in literature and the Gothic revival in architecture steadily gained momentum. Jane Austen's *Northanger Abbey,* a delicious satire on the movement, was published just as Sir Walter Scott's historical novels were bringing their author such huge acclaim. Scott's novels were translated into French beginning about 1816. They, in turn, paved the way for the romances of Hugo and Dumas.

Among the surviving English architectural expressions of this literary phase are the Houses of Parliament (Fig. 413), begun by Sir Charles Barry in 1840 with the assistance of A. W. N. Pugin, and the New Law Courts by George Street, both of which are familiar landmarks in the London of today.

Gothic Revival in Germany and France

In Germany, as early as 1772, the young poet Goethe, under the guidance of his trusted university guide Gottfried von Herder, was writing praise of the builder of the Strasbourg Cathedral, Erwin von Steinbach. The book significantly was entitled *Von deutscher Baukunst* (*On German Architecture*). Later, Goethe placed his drama on the medieval Faust legend in a Gothic setting. In the 19th century, German literary interest in neomedievalism became the background for Richard Wagner's operas *Tannhäuser, Lohengrin,* and *Parsifal.* Wagner's most enthusiastic patron was King Ludwig II of Bavaria, who helped the composer build his opera house at Bayreuth.

Architectural energies in France at first were diverted toward the preservation of the many medieval monuments still in existence. Less than a year after the July Revolution, Victor Hugo had published his *Notre Dame de Paris* (known to the English-speaking world as *The Hunchback of Notre Dame*). The fact that the real hero of the novel is Paris' Gothic cathedral fanned into flames the popular enthusiasm for the restoration of churches, castles, and abbeys. Support for the reconstruction of Notre Dame was soon forthcoming in official circles from Guizot the historian, who was then prime minister. It was he who founded in 1837 the Commission for the Conservation of Historic Monuments.

In France, as previously in England and Germany, romantic architecture was associated with the upsurge of patriotic and nationalistic sentiment. It channeled French national energies into new flights of the imagination and provided French minds with an escape from recent dreams of Roman imperial glory that had turned into the nightmare of the Napoleonic defeat.

The precise scholarship of the French academic mind found a ready outlet in the establishment of the new science of medieval archaeology, which resulted in the restoration of such buildings as Ste. Chapelle and the Cathedral of Notre Dame in Paris. In his essay on medieval architecture, Eugène Viollet-le-Duc called attention to the engineering logic of medieval builders and demonstrated the organic unity of the Gothic structural system in which each stone played its part, and in which even the decorative details served useful purposes. That everything was necessary and nothing used merely for effect not only revised 19th-century architectural thought but also laid one of the bases for the 20th-century return to functional building.

Church of Ste. Clotilde   As comparative latecomers on the medieval revival scene, the French architects were in no hurry to leave their reconstructions and design new buildings. The advantage was theirs when they did so, however, because they could review all the previous experiments and avoid the follies and excesses that characterized the movement elsewhere. Though the Church of Ste. Clotilde (Fig. 414) was planned at the same time that Victor Hugo,

414. François Christian Gau and Théodore Ballu. Ste. Clotilde, Paris. 1846–57. Width 105′ (32 m), height 216′ (65.84 m).

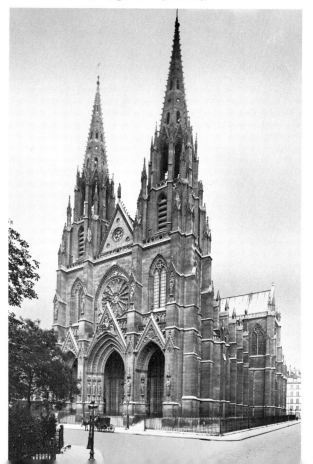

Delacroix, and Berlioz were active, it was not until 1846 that ground for it could be broken. Designed by François Christian Gau, a native of Cologne but a naturalized French citizen, the project was completed after his death by Théodore Ballu. Although built principally of white stone, Ste. Clotilde received the distinctive technical innovation of cast-iron girders added to the vaulting to assure strength and durability. The girders were disguised by blocks of stone, but the fact that a building of medieval design used materials developed by the 19th-century Industrial Revolution commanded great interest.

Based on Gothic models of the 14th century, the church has the usual features of a nave with side aisles, transept, choir, and apse with radiating chapels. The space of the richly ornamented façade is divided by four buttresses into three parts, each with an entrance portal. Those on the sides have tympanums showing in sculptured relief the martydom of St. Valéry and the baptism of Clovis. The approaches to the portals have niches containing standing figures of the Merovingian saints associated with the earliest history of French nationhood, including Ste. Clotilde, Clovis' queen, and Ste. Geneviève, patroness of Paris.

The interior is lighted by a clerestory with as many as sixty stained glass windows, which carry out the iconographical scheme promised by the sculptures of the façade. The representations tell the legendary stories of Ste. Clotilde and some of her contemporaries, St. Valéry, St. Martin of Tours, and St. Remi, as well as two of her children who were canonized, St. Cloud and Ste. Bathilde. The choir is the setting for a large organ with a case elaborately carved in the Gothic manner. Here the composer César Franck presided from the year 1872 until his death, performing his famous improvisations.

When the Church of Ste. Clotilde is compared with such original Gothic monuments as the cathedrals of Chartres (Fig. 173), Paris, and Rheims, it seems too consciously designed, overly symmetrical, and academically frigid. But when viewed in the context of its times and combined with the reflections of medieval fervor of Victor Hugo, the emotionalism of Rude's sculpture, the expressive color of Delacroix's painting, and the fantastic imagery of Berlioz' music, it catches some rays of their glowing warmth and becomes at once both their worthy architectural companion and an important incident in the unfolding of the romantic style.

Poetry: Victor Hugo

Of the three great literary figures who influenced the writings of Victor Hugo at this time, Dante and Shakespeare were out of the past, and only his elder contemporary Goethe came from his own time. These three writers, as he states in the preface to *Cromwell,* pointed out the sources of the grotesque elements that were to be found everywhere, "in the air, water, earth, fire those myriads of intermediate creatures which we find alive in the popular traditions of the middle ages; it is the grotesque which impels the ghastly antics of the witches' revels, which gives Satan his horns, his cloven feet and his bat's wings. It is the grotesque, still the grotesque, which now casts into the Christian hell the frightful faces which the severe genius of Dante and Milton will evoke. . . ."

Needless to say, understanding of Hugo's great predecessors involved a high degree of selectivity. It was the *Inferno* section that he extracted from Dante's *Divine Comedy.* His poem of 1837, written after a reading of Dante as the title—*Après une lecture de Dante*—states, closely parallels Delacroix's picture of Dante: "When the poet paints the image of hell," he wrote, "he paints that of his own life." Hugo sees Dante as surrounded by ghosts and specters, groping blindly through mysterious forests as weird forms block his dark path. Lost amid indecisive fogs, with each step he hears lamentations and the faint sounds of the grinding of white teeth in the black night. All the vices and scourges such as vengeance, famine, ambition, pride, and avarice darken the scene still more. Farther on, the souls of those who have tasted the poison of cowardice, fear, and treason mingle with the grimacing masks of those whom hatred has consumed. The only light amid this general gloom is the voice of the eternal artist, Vergil, who calls, "Continue onward."

In Petrarch, it was the Triumph of Death that Hugo admired; in Boccaccio, the vivid descriptions of the black plague; in Shakespeare, the macabre scenes from *Hamlet* and the boiling and bubbling of the witches' cauldron in *Macbeth;* and in Goethe's *Faust,* the descriptions of the Walpurgis Night. Collectively, these constitute a carnival of the macabre.

Rondo of the Witches' Sabbath

Hugo's transition to the new psychology is apparent as early as 1826. At this time he brought out a new edition of his *Odes* to which he added fifteen *Ballades,* with the fourteenth entitled *La Ronde du Sabbat,* or "Rondo of the Witches' Sabbath." This new outlook he explains in his introduction. The odes, he writes, included his purely religious inspirations and personal expression, which were cast in classical meters. Those with the title of "ballad" have a more imaginative character, and include pictorial fantasies, dreams, and legends of superstition. The latter came to him, he continues, under the inspiration of medieval troubadours, especially those Christian rhapsodies of epic nature that were chanted by minstrels to the accompaniment of their harps as they wandered from castle to castle.

"Witches' Sabbath" begins with a description of a Gothic church at midnight; the clock in the belfry tolls twelve, and the witching hour begins. Strange lights flash, the holy water begins to boil in the fonts. Shrieks and howls are heard, as from all directions come those who answer Satan's call—ghosts, dragons, vampires, ghouls, monsters, and the souls of the damned from their fresh-emptied tombs. While Satan sings a black mass, an imp reads the Gospel, and the whole fantastic congregation performs a wild dance.

> All in unison moving with swift-circling feet
> While Satan keeps time with his crozier's beat,
> And their steps shake the arches colossal and high,
> Disturbing the dead in their tombs close by.

The last two lines serve as a refrain and are repeated after each of the ten verses, two of which will suffice as examples.

> Come, he-goats profane,
> Come, lizards and snails,
> Come, serpents with scales,
> So fragile and frail.
> Burst into the fane!
> Let discord take wing,
> With melodious swing,
> Come, enter the ring,
> And repeat the refrain.

> And their steps shake the arches colossal and high,
> Disturbing the dead in their tombs close by.

> From his tomb with sad moans
> Each false monk to his stall
> Glides, concealed in his pall,
> That robe fatal to all,
> Which burns into his bones.
> Now a black priest draws nigh,
> With a flame he doth fly
> On the altar on high
> He the curst fire enthrones.

> The dawn whitens the arches colossal and gray,
> And drives all the devilish revellers away;
> The dead monks retire to their graves 'neath the halls,
> And veil their cold faces behind their dark palls.

For his introduction and refrain Hugo uses a dual rhyming scheme, *aa, bb, cc,* and so on. That of the intervening verses, however, is based on a variant of an old medieval triple-rhyming pattern recalling that of the 13th-century *Dies Irae* (p. 185), which was an important part of the requiem mass for the dead. The first, fifth, and ninth lines rhyme, while two groups of triple rhyme are placed between them to make a

415. Eugène Delacroix. *Margaret in Church,* illustration for Goethe's *Faust.* 1828. Lithograph, 10½ × 8¾″ (27 × 22 cm). Metropolitan Museum of Art, New York (Rogers Fund, 1917).

language and the outstanding literary figures, he was never a prime mover or noted for his originality. Highly skilled as a manipulator of symbols and a master of poetic forms, he was able to give clear expression to the changing voices of his time. Yet, in spite of all this verbal facility and the uniformly high quality of his output, he never succeeded in producing a poetic masterpiece that stood out above all others. In his work all the ideas of his time are mirrored in his unparalleled use of language, and his voice is as typical as any within this period.

The brief but pungent reply of a modern critic pretty well sums it up. When asked whom he considered the greatest French poet of the 19th century, he answered, "Unfortunately, Victor Hugo."

Music: Hector Berlioz

The salons of Paris during the days of the romantic dawn were populated with poets, playwrights, journalists, critics, architects, painters, sculptors, musicians, and utopian political reformers without number. Heinrich Heine, poet and journalist from north Germany, Chopin from Poland, Liszt from Hungary—all mixed freely with such homegrown artists and intellectuals as Victor Hugo, Théophile Gautier, Lamartine, Chateaubriand, de Musset, Dumas, George Sand, and others. Social philosophers like Lamennais, Proudhon, Auguste Comte, and Saint-Simon, gave a political tinge to aesthetic debates.

In the supercharged atmosphere of the Paris salons Hector Berlioz must have appeared as an authentic apparition, embodying in the flesh the wildest romantic dreams and nightmares. One contemporary described him as a young man trembling with passion, whose large umbrella of hair projected like a movable awning over the beak of a bird of prey. The German composer Robert Schumann saw him as a "shaggy monster with ravenous eyes"; his personality as that of a "raging bacchant"; and spoke of his effect on the society of his times as being "the terror of the Philistines." The suave and polished Felix Mendelssohn, on the other hand, found his French colleague completely exasperating, and he continually reproached Berlioz because, with all his strenuous efforts to go stark raving mad, he never once really succeeded.

In one striking personality, Berlioz combined qualities that made him a great composer, the ranking orchestral conductor of his day, a brilliant journalist, and an autobiographer. As a conductor, the painter Gustave Doré caricatured him as the mad musician (Fig. 416). At the first performance of one of his overtures, when the orchestra failed to give him the effect he demanded, he burst into tears, tore his hair, and fell sobbing on the kettledrums.

pattern of *a, bbb, a, ccc, a.* The *Dies Irae* had made an earlier appearance in the church scene of Goethe's *Faust,* where Margaret, aware of her doom, hears the chorus intone the awesome lines (Fig. 415).

Both the technique and imagery of Hugo's ballad are related to the fantastic sections of *Faust,* and both poems, in turn, have a common ancestor in the witches' scene from Shakespeare's *Macbeth.* The similarity of metrical plan and black-magic imagery is unmistakable. One finds the same rhythmic language that is designed to charm the ear and stimulate the imagination rather than make logical sense, especially in the Walpurgis Night scene from *Faust.* The scene is filled with witches riding he-goats and giant owls; the earth crawls with salamanders and coiling snakes; while bats fly around and glittering fireflies provide the illumination. As Mephistopheles describes the ghostly dance, all manner of gruesome and awesome night creatures

> . . . crowd and jostle, whirl, and flutter!
> They whisper, babble, twirl, and splutter!
> They glimmer, sparkle, stink, and flare—
> A true witch-element! Beware!

The sources of Hugo's inspiration are thus clear, but while he must be counted among the masters of

416. Gustave Doré. *Berlioz Conducting Massed Choirs.*
19th-century caricature.

Berlioz' *Memoirs* are stylistically a literary achievement of the first magnitude. From this lively source one gathers that Berlioz' development proceeded in a series of emotional shocks which he received from his first contacts with the literature and music of his time. One after the other, the fires of his explosive imagination were ignited by Goethe's *Faust,* which resulted in his oratorio the *Damnation of Faust;* by the poetry of Byron, which became the symphony for viola and orchestra, *Harold in Italy;* and by Dante's *Divine Comedy,* which was the inspiration for his great *Requiem.*

In music the shocks were provided first by Gluck, then Weber. He had scarcely recovered from these two, he said, when he "beheld Beethoven's giant form looming over the horizon. The shock was almost as great as that I had received from Shakespeare, and a new world of music was revealed to me by the musician, just as a new universe of poetry had been opened to me by the poet." It was, of course, the Beethoven of the *Eroica, Pastoral,* and Ninth symphonies. To a milder extent, the literary figures of Vergil, Walter Scott, and Victor Hugo made up the more distant claps of thunder in his creative brainstorms.

Berlioz even insisted on actually living out his enthusiasms to an alarmingly realistic degree. He fell violently in love with the Irish actress who was play-

ing the feminine leads in the Shakespearean troupe that was so successful in the Paris season of 1827. After a desperate romance that led both to the brink of suicide, he finally married the beautiful feminine package whom he thought of as Juliet and Ophelia wrapped up in one. When his wife turned out to be merely the actress Miss Harriet Smithson, now Madame H. Berlioz, he wrote with extreme anguish to a friend: "She's an ordinary woman."

The cold dawn of disillusionment brought years of personal misery, compensated for by some happier results on the musical side. For all his external flightiness, his literary, musical, and human loves were completely enduring, and he carried them with him to the end of his life. There one finds him still musing on the "mild, affable, and accessible" figure of Vergil; on Shakespeare, "that mighty, indifferent man, impassable as a mirror"; on Beethoven, "contemptuous and uncouth, yet gifted with such profound sensibility"; and on Gluck, "the superb."

Program Music: Fantastic Symphony

Berlioz' autobiographical *Fantastic* Symphony, first performed in the year 1830, contains a complex of many ideas he gathered from the musical and literary atmosphere that surrounded him. Its subtitle, "Episodes in the Life of an Artist," tells the listener that it is a program symphony based on a story. In the detailed programmatic notes he wrote for this work it is clear that he took the idea of poisoning by opium in the first movement, called "Reveries—Passions," from De Quincey's *Confessions of an English Opium Eater,* which had recently appeared.

The musical form of this movement, with its slow *Largo* introduction and the vigorous *Allegro agitato e appassionato assai* continuation, is in the symphonic tradition of Beethoven. Its principal claim to technical originality is the use of an *idée fixe,* or "fixed idea" (opposite, above), by which Berlioz conveys the notion of his beloved who is present and colors his every thought. The changing shape of the theme on its appearance in each of the movements fulfills a dual purpose. It provides an apearance of unity in the sequence of mood pieces, and it expresses, by its mutations, the necessary dramatic progress. The theme is varied in each of its reappearances and provides the listener with the necessary continuity to build up the image of a dramatic character through the associative process. All evidence, however, points to the fact that Berlioz' programmatic notes were written later than most of the music, which apparently was conceived for quite another purpose.

Gérard de Nerval's prose translation of Goethe's *Faust* had appeared late in the year 1827 and was the

Fantastic Symphony   Hector Berlioz
(*idée fixe*—"fixed idea," or leading melody)

direct inspiration for Berlioz' *Eight Scenes from Faust*. Since most of the movements of the *Fantastic* Symphony were being written at the same time, this alone would indicate a connection in the creative process. Berlioz was among the earliest to attempt a realization of Goethe's great drama in music. An opera by Spohr had appeared in 1816, but the well-known one by Gounod came many years later. A secular oratorio by Schumann, a *Faust* Symphony by Liszt, and a *Faust* Overture by Wagner are but a few of the many subsequent works on this theme.

The subject of Faust was in the wind, and the stages of London, Paris, and other Continental cities rang with the echoes of the many versions of this subject in dramatic and ballet form. The Paris Opera alone had accepted no less than three *librettos*, or texts, that were waiting to be commissioned. It is known that Berlioz was angling for one of these, and this fact further fortifies the case for the common source of inspiration for the *Damnation of Faust* and the *Fantastic* Symphony. Since the desired commission was not forthcoming, those parts projected for a Faust ballet became instead the movements of the *Fantastic* Symphony.

The reveries and passions of the first movement are certainly Faustian in a general, if not specific, sense. Every Faust ballet of the time contained a gay dance sequence for the "Auerbach's Cellar" scene, and the second movement of the *Fantastic* Symphony, called "A Ball," was probably first written for "Auerbach's Cellar." The external and internal storms of the third movement, the "Scenes in the Country," bring out the good as well as the evil aspects of the Faustian conception of nature. The closest correspondence, however, comes in the climactic final movements.

The fourth movement, the grim "March to the Scaffold," was probably composed first as the execution scene where Margaret pays the penalty for the double crime of killing her mother and child. In the symphony it becomes a musical nightmare of the first order in which the hero (autobiographically, Berlioz himself) marches to his own doom.

As other writers have pointed out, this scene may well have been suggested to Berlioz by the unfortunate execution of the gifted young poet André Chénier, who met death on the guillotine under Robespierre and thus became the martyred poet of the Revolution. In the final bars of this movement, the fixed melodic idea is sounded in the high, piercing register of the clarinet. It is suddenly cut off to suggest the fall of the blade and the beheading of the hero. After a dull thud and roll of the drums, the crowds roar their bloodthirsty approval of the execution now accomplished.

Witches' Sabbath Movement   The last movements of both the *Eight Scenes from Faust* and the *Fantastic* Symphony have to do with the triumph of the exultant diabolical forces as they claim the souls of their victims. The endings to Berlioz' early works are often the most wild and dissonant parts. No anticlimactic calms after the storms, no carefully planned resolutions, no safe havens after the shipwrecks. The symphony ends with a diabolical "Dream of a Witches' Sabbath," just as *Harold in Italy* ends with an "Orgy of the Brigands."

The grisly scene here is both the climax and the unresolved end. This is the movement that most fully justifies the title *Fantastic*. It is divided into three distinct sections. The first is introductory and begins with wild shrieks for the piccolo, flute, and oboe, accompanied by the ominous roll of the kettledrums in bars 7 and 8. This is echoed softly by the muted horns in bars 9 and 10 to suggest distance. After a repetition, the tempo changes from a leisurely *Larghetto* to a brisk *Allegro* and the *idée fixe* is heard in bars 21 through 28.

The ghostly appearance of the fixed melodic idea associated with Berlioz' beloved in this final movement undoubtedly was derived from the witches' kitchen scene from Goethe's drama. Faust has gone to the kitchen to have his form changed from that of old age back to young and lusty manhood, and the conjuring up of the image of Margaret is a part of the process. It is also related to the Walpurgis Night scene, where Margaret again appears.

Surely it is a novel notion that Berlioz' heroine, exemplified in previous versions of her theme as the embodiment of desirability, should now appear at the witches' sabbath. Was she a witch all along and disguised only in the hero's imagination in desirable human form? Or is this merely another manifestation of her "bewitching" power? The entrance at this point of his beloved on her broomstick, accompanied by a pandemonium of sulfurous sounds, is therefore somewhat unexpected. The hero, obviously Berlioz, gives a shriek of horror (29–39) as he listens to her modulate from the previously chaste C major to the more lurid key of E flat. Her instrumental coloration, while still that of the pale-sounding clarinet, descends now in pitch to a new low and more sensuous register. After this shocking revelation, she executes a few capers and subsides for the moment as the introduction concludes with bar 101.

The second section of the final movement is labeled *Lontano* ("in the distance") and begins with the tolling of the chimes recalling the opening lines of Hugo's ballad. After this signal for the unleashing of the infernal forces, the foreboding *Dies Irae* is solemnly intoned, first by the brass instruments in unison octaves. In bars 127–146, it is in dotted half-notes. Next, in bars 147–157, the rhythm is quickened into dotted quarters. Then it becomes syncopated in triplet eighths (157–162) and ends with an abrupt upward swish of the C scale.

With the appearance in off-beat syncopations and in such sacrilegious surroundings of this ancient Gothic liturgical melody, a solemn part of the old Roman Catholic requiem mass, Berlioz fulfills the promise of his program that he will compose a "burlesque parody" on the *Dies Irae* (see p. 185). Besides serving Berlioz as a symbol conjuring up all the fire-and-brimstone aspects of medieval Christianity, it also introduces at this point a form of macabre humor. This parody of a sacred melody caused considerable comment at the time. Schumann attributed it to romantic irony, one of the few forms of humor tolerated in a style practiced by artists who took life and themselves with deadly seriousness. Another explanation, however, seems more logical. It is to be found by applying a remark that Hugo made in the preface to *Cromwell*. "When Dante had finished his terrible Inferno," he wrote, "and naught remained save to give his work a name, the unerring instinct of his genius showed him that the multiform poem was an emanation of the drama, not of the epic; and on the front of that gigantic monument, he wrote with his pen of bronze: Divina Commedia." Thus, if Dante was justified in conceiving his *Inferno* as a comedy, though a divine one, then Berlioz could include the *Dies Irae* in this context. Even the devil is conceded to be a clever theologian, and in Goethe's drama he is found in the sacred precincts of the church, whispering in Margaret's ear as she listens to the choir chant the *Dies Irae* (Fig. 415).

The title of the third and final section of the fifth movement of Berlioz' Symphony, which begins with bar 241, is "Rondo of the Witches' Sabbath," the neomedieval, bloodcurdling, black-mass ballad published by Victor Hugo in 1826. It is also the subject of one of Goya's paintings, *Witches' Sabbath* (Fig. 417). A dance fragment hinted at previously now becomes the "Rondo of the Sabbath" theme and a four-bar phrase forming a fugue subject. The first entrance is for the cellos and double basses (241–244). This is followed by the violas (248–251). Next enter the first violins fortified by the bassoons (255–258). The final entrance is scored for woodwinds and horns.

These successive entries, each with a different instrumental combination, mark Berlioz' departure from the academic tradition of the linear fugue. Here he introduces the element of instrumental coloration into the usually austere fugal exposition. Other color combinations follow with melodic and chromatic variants of the subject in a fugal development that has won the composer wide admiration. It must be noted that when Berlioz is writing his wildest and most fantastic images, his mind is always fully in command. At the climax of such a work as this, he writes a fugue without either violating the rules or sacrificing his expressive intentions.

After the fugue on the dance theme has come to its climax with the entire string section playing an extension of the subject (407–413), the *Dies Irae* makes a reappearance, and the two themes are woven together with great skill from bar 414 to the end. Some of Berlioz' enthusiastic admirers have called this contrapuntal section a "double fugue." There is only one fugue, however, with the *Dies Irae* melody running concurrently. With the final blood-curdling shrieks and flying images, a composer, quite probably for the first time in music history, has written a fugue that vividly fulfills its literal meaning—that is, a flight.

417. Francisco Goya. *Witches' Sabbath.* c. 1819–23. Oil on canvas, 4'7⅛" × 14'4½" (1.4 × 4.38 m). Prado, Madrid.

Influence of Berlioz

After the *Fantastic* Symphony, the use of the *Dies Irae* became a symbol of the macabre, and it has been used countless times since. Liszt's *Totentanz* for piano and orchestra is a set of variations on it. It appears again in Gustav Mahler's Second Symphony and in some of Rachmaninoff's variations on a theme of Paganini. With this final movement, Berlioz also established a style that brought the demonic element—and a chain of harmonic and psychological dissonances—into music to stay. Both Moussorgsky's *Night on Bald Mountain* and Saint-Saëns' *Danse Macabre* are cut from the same cloth. One writer has even called this movement of Berlioz' the first piece of Russian music. Some of the wilder moments written by Stravinsky for his *Firebird* and *Rite of Spring* would certainly seem to bear this out.

Berlioz was one of the first composers to build up his musical forms by the use of tone color. The only way to understand his music is to hear it in all the full richness of its instrumental sound, because his scores can never be transcribed successfully for piano or any other instrumental medium. In addition to the incomparable richness of his orchestral palette, the sheer quantitative weight he added to the orchestras of his day is nothing short of spectacular. Seldom composing in any but the largest forms, he delighted in the use of orchestral and choral combinations of extraordinary complexity. To assemble all the necessary forces for a Berlioz performance is always a challenge, and the demands his works make on the performers are considerable.

In his gigantic *Requiem,* for instance, the composer employs an immense principal orchestra, a chorus of five hundred, a tenor soloist, and four huge brass bands. The latter were placed facing the four points of the compass, so as to suggest vast space and to enhance the acoustical effect made by the bands when they sound the call for Judgment Day. All this, plus such additional effects as a battery of sixteen kettledrums, caused the newspapers to comment the day following the first performance that Paris had not heard such sound since the fall of the Bastille.

There was always something of the conqueror about Berlioz as he marshaled his orchestral forces in such a composition. Each orchestra had its own conductor, and the choruses were signaled by commanders of lesser rank, with all of them taking their cues from the supreme commander himself, who appeared in the role of a musical Napoleon.

Berlioz was the first of the great orchestra conductors and the original model of the great maestros of today. No wonder his contemporaries did not know how to take him and found both his personality and his compositions somewhat difficult to absorb. He always reminded them of something monstrous. Heinrich Heine characterized him in the following way. "Here is the wingbeat that reveals no ordinary songbird," he wrote; "it is that of a colossal nightingale, a lark the size of an eagle, such as must have existed in the primeval world."

Ideas

The dynamics of the revolutionary period, with its social, political, and industrial upheavals, confronted artists with the image of a rapidly changing world. The shift of responsibility and wealth from the aristocracy to the middle class brought about a corresponding change in the patrons for whom the buildings were built, the statues carved, the pictures painted, and the music composed. No longer were the arts produced only for a small sophisticated group of aristocrats. Instead, they were addressed to a larger and more anonymous public, mainly bourgeois.

Discriminating taste, subtlety, and intellectual grasp of complex forms could not be expected in such audiences. Artists now had to charm, arouse, and astonish. An architect could no longer count on one patron for a single monumental project but had to cater to many clients with smaller buildings.

The consequences in the arts were profound and far-reaching. Artistic media were brought closer together, and painting and music in particular became allied with literature for poetic allusions and programmatic interpretations. Color in painting, as well as tone color in instrumentation, became important in the vocabulary of romanticism. It was not sufficient, moreover, for an artist to be a fine craftsman. It was necessary now to be a great personality and champion epic causes as well. Above all, perhaps, romanticism involved the psychology of escapism from an increasingly industrialized and mechanized world. The mainstream of romantic ideas, then, flowed from the closer alliance of the arts, colorism, individualism, and nationalism to the various escapes: revivals of the past, back to nature, and exoticism.

Alliance of the Arts and Color

Painters and sculptors began to work in a greater variety of forms than before, while poets and musicians likewise revealed the breaking up of their world view by writing shorter works and generally showing an inability to conceive or present their world as a systematic whole. Even when such a composer as Berlioz did write symphonies, the results were no longer the all-embracing universal structures of Beethoven but sequences of genre pieces strung together by a literary program or some recurrent motif that give them a semblance of unity.

New also was the idea that an artistic work was not a self-contained whole but something that shared many relationships internally as well as externally with other works of art. This idea began with the attempts by certain individual artists to overcome many of the arbitrary limitations and technical rules of their separate crafts. The literature of the period was filled with musical references, and musicians for their part were drawing on literature with full force for their program pieces. The architects were called upon to build dream castles out of the novels of Walpole, Scott, and Hugo; and it is difficult to think of Delacroix's painting or Berlioz' music without Vergil, Dante, Shakespeare, Goethe, and Byron.

The effect on music was a host of new and hybrid forms, such as the program symphony and the symphonic poem. The tonal art had been associated from its beginning with words, and program music was by no means an invention of the 19th century. No other period, however, built an entire style on this mixture.

There is also a considerable distinction between the setting of words to music, as in a song, or the musical dramatization of a play, as in an opera, and basing a purely instrumental form on the spirit of a poem or the sequential arrangements of episodes taken from a novel. Berlioz wrote overtures not only to operas but to such novels as Scott's *Waverly* and *Rob Roy*. Mendelssohn wrote *Songs without Words* for the piano leaving the imagination to supply the text, and Berlioz' *Fantastic* Symphony and *Harold in Italy* became operas without words. In such later works as the "dramatic symphony" *Romeo and Juliet* and the "dramatic legend" *Damnation of Faust,* both of which are scored for soloists and chorus as well as orchestra, he was, in effect, writing concert operas in which the costumes and scenery are left to the listener's imagination. This tendency continued until it reached a climax in Richard Wagner's music dramas, which he conceived as *Gesamtkunstwerke*—that is, complete or "total works of art."

Among the important innovations of the time was an increasing emphasis on color in the various artistic media, both for its own sake and for its capacity to convey symbolic meaning. For the painters and sculptors, color was associated with epic scenes and local color. Poetry began to depend on the sounds of words and their appeal to the senses more than to the mind. Hugo's "Witches' Sabbath" with its patterns of repeated sounds and colors would be practically meaningless if this literary tone color were omitted.

For Delacroix, color, more than line or composition, was the dimension on which he depended for intensity of expression. "When the tones are right," Delacroix wrote in his journal of 1847, "the lines take care of themselves." Berlioz can be understood only when his musical ideas are heard in the original instrumentation. He is a composer who defies transcription. If the English horn solo in the "Scenes in the Country," the third movement of the *Fantastic* Symphony, were to be played by a flute or clarinet, Berlioz' expressive intention would vanish instantly. Such an example reveals the extent to which Berlioz relied on the tone color of specific instruments. In his hands instrumentation becomes a musical dimension in itself, capable of carrying its own expressive weight independent of melody and rhythm. Both Delacroix and Berlioz based their styles on color.

Romantic Individualism and Nationalism

The romantic period was also the age of the emancipation of the individual and the era of the great individual who attained the heights by personal efforts. Napoleon had stamped his image on his age with his supremacy in the realm of military glory and statecraft. He thus gave rise to the idea of similar dominating figures in the smaller worlds of letters, painting, sculpture, architecture, and music.

Artists vied with each other for the top rung of the ladder in their respective fields. For sheer technique in letters it would be difficult to surpass Victor Hugo, who could write with mastery in any style. Viollet-le-Duc and other architects could duplicate any building in the history of architecture; and the names of such bravura composer-performers as the violinist Paganini and the pianist Liszt are legendary.

All this was, perhaps, a positive assertion of the diminishing self in the face of a growing organization of society under collective control. Each work of art was associated with the personality of a distinctive individual. It was no longer enough for an artist to be a master of a craft, no matter how high the degree of skill; the artist had also to be a great personality, a prophet, a leader. It was consequently an age of autobiography, confessions, memoirs, portraiture, and the dramatic stroke. The will to biography, the necessity of living a "life," often took so much time that it was actually a handicap to artistic production. More than in any other period there was an obligation to be a distinctive personality.

The place of the artist in society had been a matter of vital concern to such artists as David and Beethoven, who combined the moralistic fervor of revolutionary thought with a sense of social responsibility. David's championship of the cause of art in the French legislature, and Beethoven's behavior toward his patrons as their social equal, reveal both men as modern artists who placed the aristocracy of genius on a higher plane than that of birth.

The great individual, however, could not exist in a social or political vacuum. Byron, Delacroix, and others felt compelled to bend their energies and talents to the cause of liberating the oppressed Greek people from the Turkish tyrant's yoke.

Lord Byron's meteoric career in life and literature became at once the living symbol of romantic melancholy as well as the personification of freedom and political liberalism. He first visited Athens in 1809 and immediately identified himself with the goals of Greek independence. On that first visit he translated the famous ancient Greek war song, giving it a contemporary twist by substituting Turkey for the old Persian enemy:

> Sons of the Greeks! let us go
> In arms against the foe. . . .
>
> Then manfully despising
>   The Turkish tyrant's yoke,
> Let your country see you rising,
>   And all her chains are broke.

In a more melodious and lyrical vein he penned the lovely lines:

> Maid of Athens, ere we part,
> Give, oh give me back my heart!
> Or, since that has left my breast,
> Keep it now and take the rest!

In 1823 while residing in Italy, Byron joined the London Greek Committee in furthering the cause of Greek independence. He then chartered the ship *Hercules,* financing the campaign partly with his own fortune, and sailed to Missolonghi in western Greece, where he died of a fever in 1824 while trying to bring the feuding factions together.

Eugène Delacroix was a constant reader of Byron. As he remarks in his journal, "To set fire to yourself, remember certain passages from Byron." His *Massacre at Chios* (Fig. 418) was inspired by one of the most gory episodes in that messy war. In a naval battle off the shores of Chios, the Greeks had set fire to the Turkish flagship, burning the crew and a detachment of soldiers to death. As an act of reprisal the Turks rounded up 20,000 completely innocent bystanders on the island, burned their town, slaughtered most of them and sold the rest into slavery. This senseless incident inflamed the sympathies of all European countries. Delacroix's painting reflected this wave of emotion while it was still fresh.

The canvas is cast in the heroic mold, almost 14 feet (4.2 meters) high and over 11 feet (3.3 meters) wide. All the foreground and middle-distance figures are life-size. The full title is *Scenes of the Massacre at Chios: Greek Families Awaiting Death or Slavery.* Théophile Gautier commented on the "feverish convulsive drawing and the violent coloring." These

418. Eugène Delacroix. *Massacre at Chios.* 1824. Oil on canvas, 13′7″ × 11′10″ (4.19 × 3.64 m). Louvre, Paris.

were the very qualities that inflamed Delacroix's critics, who dubbed it "The Massacre of Painting." Particularly apparent is the sensuous treatment of the women's bodies, especially the bound figure in the right middle ground. This softness makes for a strong contrast with the force, muscularity, and cruelty seen in the face and form of the Turkish officer. Eloquent also is the sense of defeat, apprehension, and despair written on the grandmotherly face of the woman in the foreground. The distant background contributes to the sense of doom with the smoking town and the threatening sky.

Whether an artist's self-image was phrased in classical terms as a Prometheus or in the medieval vocabulary as a knight championing the weak against the strong was not too important. Simply a geographical sounding board, local color, and a language suited to the creative medium were all that the artist needed. Some could find it in folk tales and ballads of a particular locale; others in collections and variations of Spanish epics, Scottish ballads, German fairy tales; still others in the writing of Italian symphonies, Hungarian rhapsodies, and Polish mazurkas. In this light, nationalism, like the medieval revival, was a northern declaration of cultural independence from the

Mediterranean tradition, tied up in the immediate sense in England and Germany with opposition to Napoleon. Berlioz' nationalism is expressed in a more subtle way, but his operas without words, concert operas, and music dramas were as distinct a departure from the prevailing Italian operatic tradition as were those of Weber in Germany.

Escapism

During the romantic period there was a growing gulf between the realities of the early industrial age and the escapist tendencies in the arts. In recognition of the new technologies a Polytechnical School had been established in 1794 by the revolutionary government. Napoleon, however, yielded to the advice of David and others and allowed the establishment of a separate School of Fine Arts in 1806.

By thus educating engineers in one school and architects in another, the construction techniques of building tended to be divorced from the stylistic aspects of architecture. When the architects did begin using cast iron and other industrial materials, it was to build dream castles and neomedieval cathedrals. Likewise, when musicians began to write for the improved horns and trombones, it was to sound the call of Judgment Day and introduce a rain of neomedieval fire and brimstone into their symphonies. The full significance of the Industrial Revolution remained for a later age to exploit.

The American and French revolutions, which had at first held out such high hopes and promised the imminent liberation of humanity, were followed by a reaction bordering on pessimism when the results did not live up to the overly optimistic expectations. Then when the Revolution of July 1830 had overthrown the last of the old line of Bourbons, the French middle class was finally confronted by a king cast in its own image.

As the merchants and shopkeepers beheld King Louis Philippe in his frock coat, umbrella in hand, walking down the boulevard to the Stock Exchange they were somewhat dismayed to find that their monarch was—like themselves—stouter of figure than of heart and—again like themselves—engaged in the pursuit of causes more materialistic than ideal. A bit appalled at what they saw, is it any wonder that they sought psychological compensation in dreams of the more dashing royal personalities of the past, whose recklessness consisted of more hazardous adventures than buying and selling shares on the stock exchange? How could King Louis Philippe, living in a palace complete with the comforts of modern plumbing, compare with Joan of Arc's prince, who lived dangerously while being pursued by his pitiless enemies from one damp and drafty castle to another?

The activities of Darwin's earthworms, for instance, were infinitely more useful than the spectacle of one of Delacroix's lions in mortal combat with a stallion. But how could the worms capture the popular imagination as the lions did? A highly productive factory or an ingenious city sewer system made infinitely duller pictures and poetry than Oriental harems and the palm-lined shores of the Ganges River.

While willing to use the fruits of the Industrial Revolution as aids in the production and distribution of their artistic wares, the artists of the time were quite convinced that the new technologies were not making their world more beautiful. Thus, the gulf between usefulness and beauty widened. Refusing to reconcile themselves to reality, the artists sought ever-more-fanciful ways to avoid the issue. Certainly they knew what was going on in their world. As intellectuals, they were better educated and informed than similar groups in other times had been.

When employing their escape mechanisms, artists were fully aware of what they were escaping from. "Any time but now, and any place but here" became the battle cry of romanticism. The yearning for past periods—whether ancient Greco-Roman or medieval—was expressed in the various revivals. Since the classic and medieval revivals were accepted as official styles, and since they lingered longer than other aspects of romanticism, they have been dwelt upon in these pages at greater length. But the fuller vocabulary of romantic escapism included the "back to nature" movement and exoticism, with its fantasies of far-off places.

Revivals of the Past   Neoclassicism had been the earliest of the revivals of the past, and the passion for precision soon had divided it into separate Greek and Roman revival movements. Through historical novels and romantic imaginations, interest in medieval times was awakened; and as medieval scholars extended their studies, artists delved deeper into the Middle Ages. Revivals of Gothic, Romanesque, and Byzantine styles followed next. The romantic love for times past was then expanded into admiration for the Renaissance and baroque periods. The Library of Ste. Geneviève in Paris (see Figs. 447, 448) and the Boston Public Library, in their exteriors at least, were revivals of Renaissance architecture. The Paris Opera, begun in 1861, revived Louis XIV's Versailles. Wagner composed the opera *Rienzi* after a novel by the Englishman Bulwer-Lytton about a ruler of the Roman Renaissance. Mendelssohn rediscovered the greatness of Bach's choral music and in 1829 conducted the first performance of the *St. Matthew Passion* since the composer's death.

In retrospect, the 19th-century separation of the arts into classic and romantic camps has been resolved, because both now are seen as component parts of the same broader revival idea. The artists who lived on into the post-Napoleonic period drew their inspiration from Greco-Roman or medieval times with equal ease. John Nash, for example, built himself a neoclassical townhouse in London and a romantic Gothic castle in the country. Rude made statues of Roman nymphs and of Joan of Arc (Fig. 410). Ingres painted the *Apotheosis of Homer* (see Fig. 400) and later a picture of the Maid of Orleans. Keats wrote "Ode on a Grecian Urn" and also "The Eve of St. Agnes." Victor Hugo included neoclassical odes in the same volume with his medieval ballads. Berlioz admired Vergil as well as Dante and wrote *The Trojans,* an opera based on the *Aeneid.*

After neoclassicism and romanticism had run their courses, the revival idea led, in the later 19th century, to a broad *eclecticism,* or choosing at will from a variety of sources. In the arts this allowed an architect to build in any past style, a painter to do a portrait or historical canvas in the manner of Titian or Rubens, a poet to employ any form of metrical organization with ease, and a composer to pull out at will a Renaissance or baroque stop on the organ.

England and Germany both claimed the Gothic style as their own. To them it was a conscious departure from the Greco-Roman ideals of antiquity as well as their rebirth in the Renaissance, baroque, and neoclassical styles. In England especially, the Gothic revival was bound up closely with the wave of prosperity caused by a great industrial expansion, a glowing national pride, and a reaction against the Napoleonic empire that had threatened their own. A reassertion of the separation of the Church of England from Rome took shape in the Oxford movement. It demanded the turning away from Greco-Roman architectural forms as essentially pagan, and the restoring of medieval liturgies that, in turn, needed appropriate architectural settings.

In Germany, the Gothic revival took the form of a vision of past national glory associated with Charlemagne, whom the Germans adopted as their national hero *Karl der Grosse.* The relative security and fame of Germany under the rule of the Holy Roman Empire had continued intermittently up to the reign in the 16th century of the Hapsburg Charles V, the last of the powerful emperors. The past thus played an important role in the 19th-century revival of German power, based as it was on the memory of an empire dominated by the north. Stung into action by its abolition under Napoleon, German nationalism fermented during the 19th century until it matured into the heady wine of Bismarck's statesmanship, the aroma of which reminded Teutonic experts of the heroic bouquet of such ancient vintages as those of Attila, Alaric, and Frederick Barbarossa.

From the Renaissance on through the aristocratic baroque tradition and the 18th century, French art was closely bound to traditional Greco-Roman forms. During the Revolution of 1789 and its aftermath, a wave of opposition to the Roman Catholic clergy's interference in public affairs led to the actual destruction of some medieval buildings to protest against Church influence and herald the new freedom. The neoclassicism of Napoleon's Empire continued through the early years of the 19th century and, though weakened under the Bourbon restoration, had at least official approval right up to the Revolution of July 1830.

Underneath the political surface, however, the destruction of medieval monuments during the French Revolution had indirectly stimulated certain groups to preserve parts of these works in museums. When the glories of their own medieval past were brought to the attention of some of the French, at a time when the popular wave of neomedievalism was gathering momentum in England and Germany, there were bound to be consequences in France.

Unlike Protestant England and Germany, France had broken its ties with Roman Catholicism only briefly during the first wave of revolutionary fervor. Even Napoleon had found it politically convenient to make an accommodation with the Vatican and to be crowned in the sacred precincts of Notre Dame in Paris in the presence of the pope.

France had been the most powerful European country ever since the time of Louis XIV. Even when torn internally by the Revolution, France was able to hold its own against threats of foreign invasion as seen in Rude's *Departure of the Volunteers of 1792* (Fig. 409). Under Napoleon, French forces conquered the entire Continent. In all cases it was a France with imperial ambitions, and the symbols of empire and French supremacy had been found in the various forms of classicism associated with ancient glory. Very significantly, it was not until French national power had been thoroughly subdued under the coalition which defeated Napoleon in 1815 that the romantic style took a firm hold on the French mind and imagination. For the first time France began to look within and rediscover the roots of her nationhood in early medieval times. Even so, this interest in medievalism and romanticism lasted officially less than a generation—that is, between the revolutions of 1830 and 1848. Then, under the new Emperor Napoleon III, imperial ambitions rose up once more, and a later phase of neoclassicism became the official style.

The medieval revival is also found on the American scene. In New York the Gothic spires of Trinity Church rise among lower Broadway's skyscrapers. Two churches by Renwick furnish further exam-

above: **419.** James Renwick.
Grace Church, New York. 1845.

above right: **420.** Richard Mique.
Marie Antoinette's Cottage (*Le Hameau*),
Versailles. 1783–86.

right: **421.** John Constable.
Hay Wain. 1821. Oil on canvas,
4′2½″ × 6′1″ (1.28 × 1.85 m).
National Gallery, London
(reproduced by courtesy of the Trustees).

ples—Grace Church (Fig. 419) and St. Patrick's Cathedral, both dating from the mid-19th century. Many American colleges and universities, in their eagerness to be identified with ancient and honorable causes, were also built in the neomedieval style. And scattered throughout the country are half-timbered houses, castle residences, railroad stations, and other public buildings that show the wide influence of the medieval revival on American architecture.

Back to Nature   Rousseau had already sounded the call of "back to nature" in the late 18th century. By so doing, he challenged the elegant, civilized,

left: **422.** John Constable. *Salisbury Cathedral
from the Bishop's Garden.* 1826.
Oil on canvas, 35 × 44¼″ (89 × 112 cm).
Frick Collection, New York (copyright).

aristocratic image with his projection of the noble savage type whose rustic charm was achieved by shunning society and communing with nature.

For his own part, Rousseau was perfectly willing to be received in courtly circles, and his rustic little opera *Le Devin du Village* (*The Village Soothsayer*) was performed for Louis XVI at Versailles with great success. His ideas were partly responsible for the country cottage, complete with a dairy and mill, that Queen Marie Antoinette had built for herself amid the formal gardens of Versailles (Fig. 420).

The back-to-nature idea took root and became one of the more popular 19th-century escape mechanisms with that segment of the population which lived in cities and dreamed of an idyllic country life they had no intention of living. These people delighted, however, in reading poetry full of nature imagery as well as folk ballads and fairy tales. They hung landscapes by Corot and the now all-too-familiar peasant scenes of Millet on the walls of their apartments and townhouses. Beethoven's *Pastoral* Symphony and Wagner's *Forest Murmurs,* as well as dozens of piano pieces and songs, sounded the proper rustic note in music.

Weber's opera *Der Freischütz,* which had been the success of the 1826 season in Paris, brought out some of the darker aspects of nature. In it, much is made of the sinister powers of the night, and the forces over which it rules are effectively presented in the eerie "Wolf's Glen" scene. Nature, here, as well as in Goethe's *Faust,* exposed its terrifying as well as its inspiring aspects. Both works unleashed awesome elemental forces as well as powers of a magical and fantastic character.

Outstanding among landscapists was John Constable with his quiet studies of the English countryside, such as *Hay Wain* (Fig. 421) and *Salisbury Cathedral from the Bishop's Garden* (Fig. 422). In comparison with the formal French landscapes of Claude Lorrain that Constable admired (see Fig. 330), the composition of *Salisbury Cathedral* is as relaxed and informal as an English garden.

Constable's major pictorial interests were in capturing unpredictable and fleeting changes of atmosphere; the infinitely varied intensities of light on clear, showery, or foggy days; sunshine filtered through translucent green leaves; and the changing reflections of the many-colored sky and passing clouds on water. To capture these effects Constable made numerous oil sketches in the open air and later finished his pictures in his studio. When his paintings were exhibited in Paris, their freshness, warmth, and spontaneity created a considerable stir. Delacroix admired Constable's bold use of color. His descriptive powers and technical innovations had an important influence on the later impressionists.

In contrast to Constable's aim of accurate depiction of natural phenomena, the works of J. M. W. Turner, also English and a contemporary of Constable, were poetic invocations and emotionalized experiences tinged with a haunting romantic melancholy. In his early pictures Turner started with variations on the landscapes and seascapes of Claude Lorrain, whom he admired above all artists. His style, however, gradually turned away from history painting to more visual effects, while his grays and browns yielded to soft, pastel hues and sparkling, rainbow-like yellow and orange tonalities. As the titles of his paintings would imply, Turner sought to capture on canvas some of the elemental forces of nature—*Snowstorm: Hannibal and His Army Crossing the Alps; Shade and Darkness: The Evening of the Deluge; Wreck of a Transport Ship; Fire at Sea.*

In one of Turner's late works, *Rain, Steam, and Speed: The Great Western Railway* (Fig. 423) the viewer feels the impact of headlong movement in the Edinburgh express as it crosses a bridge in a driving storm. The rabbit racing ahead of the crack train symbolizes both speed and the romantic's vision of modern technology as a threat to nature and the organic fundamentals of life. Amid the swirling, spiraling storm of wind and rain, the engine's firebox glows with hot, flamelike color, which contrasts with the dark blue of the passenger cars and the flecks of light blue in the sky. Constable once criticized Turner for his "airy visions painted with tinted steam." But in retrospect, Turner's glowing canvases, many-colored light, and ethereal atmospheric effects proclaim him one of the most daring colorists in the history of painting. He pioneered the pathway leading to the use of light and color as a language for conveying mood and emotion.

Exoticism   The exotic perfumes of the Orient also were wafted into the nostrils and fancies of romantic patrons, intellectuals, and artists. While shrewd business leaders were opening up new foreign markets, and missionaries were going forth from Europe to try to bridge the Christian and pagan worlds, artists busied themselves capturing the popular imagination with scenes of exotic mysteries associated with far-off lands and peoples.

As early as 1759, Arthur Murphy in the prologue of a play called *Orphans of China* had proclaimed: "Enough of Greece and Rome: Th'exhausted store of either nation now can charm no more." So the Oriental world was added to the imaginative repertory, and its changing image in one guise or another has been mirrored in the arts up to the present time. Reflections of this early phase can be found in such operas as Gluck's *The Unforeseen Meeting* or *The Pilgrims to Mecca* (1764) and Mozart's *Abduction from the Seraglio* (1785), with its setting in a Turkish harem, and in William Beckford's Oriental novel *Vathek* (1786).

Kew Gardens, a public park in London, was studded with fanciful structures revealing a wide imaginative range. Some paths led to little rococo pavilions, others to Greek temples or Gothic chapels. Among them were a Moslem mosque, a Moorish palace, and a house of Confucius. A pagoda, built by the Palladian architect William Chambers, is the only one of these fancies that has survived.

Only a short time later, Napoleon was fighting his Battle of the Pyramids (1798). In England, a tale entitled *Thalabor the Destroyer* (1799) by Robert Southey included chapters called "The Desert Circle" and "Life in an Arab Tent." Drawing rooms were hung with wallpapers depicting scenes of mandarin China, and hostesses were pouring tea at Chinese Chippendale tables. The Prince Regent of England, like Kubla Khan in Coleridge's poem, did,

A stately pleasure-dome decree:
Where Alph, the sacred river, ran
Through caverns measureless to man
Down to the sunless sea.

Less poetically though no less fancifully, this was the Royal Pavilion (Fig. 424) the Prince Regent commissioned his architect to build at his favorite seaside resort of Brighton. John Nash, who had previously built an exotic country house for a gentleman who had lived in India, came up with an Arabian Nights extravaganza in a style that was then referred to as "Indian Gothic." The exterior is an exotic fantasy of minarets and cupolas, pinnacles and pagodas, all constructed over cast-iron frames. A domed ceiling painted like a spreading palm tree covers the dining hall (Fig. 425). Water-lily chandeliers suspended from the cast-iron claws of scaly dragons, lotus-blossom lamps, Oriental lacquerware, and Chinese Chippendale furniture complete the decor.

Schopenhauer's *World as Will and Idea,* based on the Oriental philosophy of the denial of the will, appeared in 1819. In a revolt against the academic rationalism and scientific naturalism of his time, Schopenhauer turned to Oriental mysticism. He thought the individual could achieve inner peace, harmony with society, and ultimate release into infinity by renouncing personal ambitions and materialistic pursuits. Richard Wagner reflects this idea at the end of *Tristan and Isolde,* when the unhappy

heroine, following her lover's death, aspires to the ecstatic bliss of Nirvana by surrendering her tortured personal will to the cosmic rhythms of the universe.

The colorful Japanese prints that found their way to Europe after Admiral Perry's voyage of 1852–1854 had an important effect on painting. Gautier published a popular book called *L'Orient* in 1860, which was based on his travels. At this same time, Delacroix was painting one of his last pictures, *The Lion Hunt,* which vividly portrayed the violent struggle of men and horses against the unbridled ferocity of wild animals. Gounod's opera *The Queen of Sheba* was produced in 1862 at about the same time Ingres was finishing his fleshscape *The Turkish Bath* (Fig. 426).

The search for exotic settings eventually reached its climax in two of the greatest works of the lyrical stage—Verdi's *Aïda,* written in 1871 for the Cairo Opera in celebration of the opening of the Suez Canal, and Bizet's *Carmen,* which, based on a short story by Prosper Mérimée, was first performed in 1875. Toward the end of the century exoticism began to pall, and the realistic novelist Zola made fun of his romantic colleague Gautier because "he needed a camel and four dirty Bedouins to tickle his brains into creative activity."

opposite: 423. Joseph Mallord William Turner. *Rain, Steam, and Speed: The Great Western Railway.* 1844. Oil on canvas, 35½ × 47⅝″ (90 × 121 cm). National Gallery, London (reproduced by courtesy of the Trustees).

top: 424. John Nash. Royal Pavilion, Brighton. 1815–21. Lithograph. Metropolitan Museum of Art, New York (Harris Brisbane Dick Fund, 1941).

above: 425. John Nash. Dining Hall, Royal Pavilion, Brighton. 1815–21. Lithograph. Metropolitan Museum of Art, New York (Harris Brisbane Dick Fund, 1941).

right: 426. Jean Auguste Dominique Ingres. *The Turkish Bath.* c. 1852–63. Oil on canvas, diameter 42½″ (108 cm). Louvre, Paris.

20

The Realistic
and Impressionistic
Styles

Paris, Late 19th Century

While neoclassicism and romanticism were dominated by flights from reality, realism and impressionism tried to come to terms with the contemporary world. One measure of the force of social progress is the rapid rise and overthrow of the various forms of government in France during the period from 1789 to 1852. Between the absolute monarchy of Louis XVI and the Empire of Napoleon III, Paris experienced a revolutionary reign of terror, a republic, the Napoleonic Empire, a royal restoration, a constitutional monarchy, and a socialist commune.

While these upheavals were making headlines, even more powerful and extreme changes were put into motion by the Industrial Revolution. The growth of factories employing the new machine methods of production meant the shift from a farming to an industrial economy and the migration of large numbers of people from the country to the cities. While 18th-century workers had been able to weigh the tangible produce of their farms or take satisfaction in the completion of a handmade pair of shoes, their 19th-century counterparts exchanged the intangible elements of time and labor for an uncertain living.

The application of modern scientific knowledge to industrial progress opened up many possibilities in the arts. Such new materials as cast iron aided the rapid construction of buildings and furnished the means whereby complicated decorative devices, formerly made painstakingly by hand, could be produced in quantity quickly and cheaply to satisfy the demand for the practical or the picturesque.

Painting, likewise, was indebted to modern science for the development of chemical pigments. Syn-thetic products began to replace the old earth pigments and ground minerals and often resulted in greater brilliancy and intensity than the genuine product. Low-cost reproductions, such as the lithograph and other prints, made possible a wider distribution for pictures and a new public.

The facilities provided by the mechanical printing press brought about the mass distribution of newspapers, novels, and sheet music. The musical world was additionally affected by the use of cast-iron instead of wooden frames for pianos. This meant that pianists could have larger and more durable instruments as well as ones that stayed in tune over longer periods of time. Also, the invention of new valve mechanisms for brass instruments and the comparative standardization of their manufacture gave composers a reasonable assurance of getting the complex instrumental effects they now demanded in their orchestrations.

Not only did the application of scientific knowledge to industrial progress open many possibilities, but from the mid-19th century onward it raised many questions as well. Governments were seeking constitutional formulas that would strike a just balance between social rights and material progress. Religious denominations were trying to reconcile time-honored scriptural truths with the new scientific knowledge. Social theories were concerned with how political liberalism could evolve side by side with traditional religious views. And philosophies were attempting a new resolution between the fixed absolutes of idealism and the dynamic thought underlying the theories of evolution.

Architects, too, were wondering how their work could still remain in the realm of the fine arts and yet

427. Honoré Daumier.
Third-Class Carriage. c. 1862.
Watercolor on paper,
8 × 11⅝″ (20 × 30 cm).
Walters Art Gallery, Baltimore.

make use of the new materials and technological methods they now commanded. Sculptors, such as Rodin, were asking whether the traditional mythological and historical themes could be replaced by more contemporary subjects. The realistic and impressionistic painters were seeking a formula for incorporating into the accepted framework of pictorial art the new physical discoveries concerning the nature of light and its perception by the human eye.

Likewise, novelists, such as Zola, were trying to establish an alliance between scientific and literary methods. Poets and playwrights, such as Mallarmé and Maeterlinck, were looking for a middle ground between the realities of the revolutionary age and the traditional limitations of poetic expression. And composers, such as Debussy, tried to harmonize the new discoveries involving the physics of sound with accepted concepts of tonality and musical form.

Governments and rulers settled down from high-flown heroics and theatrical displays into the drab but necessary routine of bureaucratic officialdom. The energies of artists were diverted from historical and exotic subjects into everyday life and seemingly trivial occurrences. The novels of Balzac and Dickens were concerned with social comment and criticism, as was the art of Honoré Daumier. The people of Daumier's Paris live on in such genre works as *Third-Class Carriage* (Fig. 427), where the artist's sense of social criticism is softened and his deep understanding and human compassion comes to the fore. Ugliness, violence, and shock techniques, however, were intended to arouse but not to insult, offend, or alienate potential patrons.

Some artists, though, found life so disillusioning that art became the sole compensation for the miseries of their existence. These painters and poets eventually cut their ties with their potential middle-class patrons altogether. They retreated into a private world of art, where the painters produced pictures for a limited audience of other painters of similar persuasion and the poets put down their inspirations principally for the eyes and ears of other poets. They thus led the insecure lives of an underprivileged social group and often banded together in desperate little societies within society.

All these new developments tended to turn artists toward the new world of the great city for their material and inspiration. The artificial replaced the natural, and urban entertainments eclipsed the delights of nature. The usual was dominant over the unusual, and the realistic here-and-now was in ascendance over the romantic there-and-then.

Painting

Realism

About the middle of the 19th century, the most important younger painters rejected romantic flights of the imagination and academic glorification of the heroic past. Those who styled themselves "realists" defined painting as a physical language and ruled out the metaphysical and invisible. The saints and miracles of the 19th century, according to them, were mines, machines, and railroad stations.

Courbet In the vanguard of the realists was Gustave Courbet. With a keen eye and a desire to record accurately what he saw about him, Courbet consciously set out to build an art on commonplace scenes. His painting was concerned with the present,

CHRONOLOGY
Late 19th Century

GENERAL EVENTS

1830–1848	Louis Philippe, constitutional king
1837–1901	Victoria, queen of England
1839	Daguerre and Niépce published findings on photography; daguerreotype process resulted
1848	February Revolution; Louis Philippe overthrown. Second French Republic proclaimed. *Communist Manifesto* issued by Marx and Engels
1851	Great Exhibition of All Nations in London; Crystal Palace by Paxton was one of buildings. Louis Napoleon, president of Second Republic, made *coup d'état*, became dictator
1852–1870	Louis Napoleon reigned as Emperor Napoleon III
1853	Admiral Perry opened Japan
1856–1866	*Physiological Optics* published by Helmholtz (1821–94); *On the Sensation of Tone as a Physiological Basis for the Theory of Music* published 1863
1857	*Les Fleurs du Mal (Flowers of Evil)* published by Baudelaire
1858–1868	Bibliothèque Nationale built by Labrouste

1859	*Origin of Species* published by Darwin
1863	*Life of Jesus* published by Renan
1870–1871	Franco-Prussian War; Napoleon III abdicated; Third French Republic established; Germany united as empire
1871	*Descent of Man* published by Darwin
1874	First impressionist exhibit held
1889	*La Grande Exposition Universelle* held in Paris; Eiffel Tower was one of buildings
1892	*Pelléas et Mélisande* by Maeterlinck presented in Paris
1896	*Matter and Memory* published by Bergson; *Creative Evolution* published in 1907
1902	Debussy's opera on Maeterlinck's *Pelléas et Mélisande* produced in Paris

PAINTERS

1808–1879	Honoré Daumier
1819–1877	Gustave Courbet
1832–1883	Édouard Manet
1834–1903	James A. McNeill Whistler
1834–1917	Edgar Degas
1839–1906	Paul Cézanne
1840–1926	Claude Monet
1841–1919	Pierre Auguste Renoir
1841–1895	Berthe Morisot
1844–1926	Mary Cassatt
1848–1903	Paul Gauguin
1853–1890	Vincent van Gogh
1859–1891	Georges Seurat

1864–1901	Henri de Toulouse-Lautrec
1864–1927	Paul Sérusier

SCULPTORS

1827–1875	Jean Baptiste Carpeaux
1840–1917	Auguste Rodin

ARCHITECTS

1801–1865	Joseph Paxton
1801–1875	Henri Labrouste
1809–1891	Georges Eugène Haussmann
1832–1923	Gustave Eiffel

MUSICIANS

1813–1883	Richard Wagner
1822–1890	César Franck
1833–1897	Johannes Brahms
1835–1921	Camille Saint-Saëns
1838–1875	Georges Bizet
1842–1912	Jules Massenet
1845–1924	Gabriel Fauré
1860–1956	Gustave Charpentier
1862–1918	Claude Debussy
1875–1937	Maurice Ravel

WRITERS AND PHILOSOPHERS

1798–1857	Auguste Comte
1799–1850	Honoré de Balzac
1809–1865	Pierre Joseph Proudhon
1812–1870	Charles Dickens
1820–1903	Herbert Spencer
1821–1867	Charles Baudelaire
1821–1880	Gustave Flaubert
1828–1906	Henrik Ibsen
1840–1902	Emile Zola
1842–1898	Stéphane Mallarmé
1844–1900	Friedrich Nietzsche
1850–1893	Guy de Maupassant
1859–1941	Henri Bergson
1862–1949	Maurice Maeterlinck
1870–1925	Pierre Louÿs
1871–1922	Marcel Proust

not the past; with the momentary, not the permanent; with bodies, not souls; with the material, not the spiritual. His nudes were no nymphs or goddesses; they were but models who posed in his studio.

The villagers attending the *Burial at Ornans* (Fig. 428) are there out of a sense of duty. The priest routinely reads the committal service, and the gravedigger casually waits to complete his job. No one betrays any great grief, and the skull and bone at the grave's edge add a realistic rather than a macabre touch. Courbet, however, sometimes became almost as passionate about the ugly as his predecessors had

been about the beautiful. Both Courbet and Édouard Manet, who came under his influence, were sometimes seduced, despite themselves, into a strong emotional interest in their subject matter.

Impressionism

The artists who followed Courbet sought for even greater closeness to nature in order to develop an art based on immediacy of expression. They took their easels out of doors and tried to do as much of their painting on the spot as possible rather than to work in their studios from sketches. They were against painting a picture that carried any moral, any message, or any literary associations and they cultivated indifference toward pictorial content.

Optical realism was pursued to the point of separating visual experience from memory and avoiding any associations the mind normally calls into play. In 1874, Claude Monet exhibited a picture called *Impression—Sunrise,* which gave the new movement its name. At first, *impressionism* was picked up as a term of critical derision. The word has remained, and it does have a certain appropriateness, implying the unfinished, the incomplete, an affair of the moment, an act of instantaneous vision, a sensation rather than a perception.

It is impossible, of course, to confirm any claim of a direct cause-and-effect relationship between science and art in this period or any formal connection between optical physics and painting. It is equally impossible to state that painters were unaware of or indifferent to such things as the invention of the camera, the scientific discoveries about the nature of light, and the new knowledge about the physiology of the eye. Joint researches of the painter Daguerre and the scientist Niépce on the making of photographic images on prepared metal plates, which resulted in the *daguerreotype* process, had been published as early as 1839. The revelation that visual imagery was primarily dependent on extremely fine gradations of light intensities was bound to have an effect on painting. Physicists, including Helmholtz, made discoveries about the component prismatic parts of white light, and pointed out that the sensation of color has more to do with a reaction in the retina of the eye than with objects themselves. The color wheel also demonstrated that two separate hues of a wheel at rest are fused by the eye into a third hue when the wheel is in rapid motion. And when all the colors of the spectrum are rotated, the eye sees them as tending toward white.

Painters also did some speculation of their own on the nature of the visual experience. Form and space, they reasoned, are not actually seen but implied from varying intensities of light and color. Objects are not so much things in themselves as they are agents for the absorption and refraction of light. Hard outlines, indeed lines themselves, do not exist in nature. Shadows, they maintained, are not black but tend to take on a color complementary to that of the objects that cast them. The concern of the painter, they concluded, should therefore be with light and color more than with objects and substances.

A painting, according to the impressionists, should consist of a breakdown of sunlight into its component parts, and brilliance should be achieved by the use of the primary colors that make up the spectrum. Instead of greens mixed by the painter on the palette, separate dabs of yellow and blue should be placed close together and the mixing left to the spectator's eye. What seems confusion at close range is clarified at the proper distance. By thus trying to increase the brightness of their canvases so as to convey the illusion of sunlight sifted through a prism, they achieved a veritable carnival of color in which the eye seems to join in a dance of vibrating light intensities. As a result of this reexamination of their technical means, the impressionists discovered a new method of visual representation.

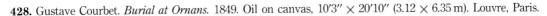

428. Gustave Courbet. *Burial at Ornans.* 1849. Oil on canvas, 10'3" × 20'10" (3.12 × 6.35 m). Louvre, Paris.

429. Édouard Manet.
*Rue Mosnier, Decorated
with Flags on June 30, 1878.*
1878. Oil on canvas,
$25\frac{1}{2} \times 31\frac{1}{2}''$ (65 × 80 cm).
Collection
Mr. and Mrs. Paul Mellon.

Manet Édouard Manet painted *Rue Mosnier, Decorated with Flags on June 30, 1878* (Fig. 429), late in life with the impressionistic theory in mind. In it, he builds a cityscape out of a pattern of interrelated planes. By his subtle use of color intensities more than by linear perspective, he achieves the effect of recession and depth. In other versions of this scene, he painted some road menders in the foreground, and his choice of such a casual street scene is in keeping with the general preference for subjects that can be taken in at a glance rather than those that must be studied carefully and in detail. It also exemplifies the conscious cultivation of the accidental—the random scene in which emotional involvement with the subject is impossible.

Manet's last large-scale work, *Bar at the Folies-Bergère* (Fig. 430), is a technical tour de force of major magnitude. At first glance the viewer would seem to be the customer the barmaid is waiting to serve, but her client apparently is the top-hatted, goateed gentleman who is seen in mirror image behind the girl's reflection at the upper left. For correctness the barmaid would have to stand almost sidewise to cast such a reflection, but with poetic license Manet lets her face forward. The composition is tightly structured, with the double image of the patient waitress and the bottles of the stunning still life in the foreground defining the vertical rise, and with the marble counter at the picture plane, its reflected image behind, and the mirrored ledge of the balcony taking care of the horizontal balance.

The Bohemian scene is bathed in glaring gaslight, glints of which are caught by the crystal chandeliers, assorted bottles, the vase and compote dish, and the balcony scene reflected in the shimmering expanse of the mirror. Except for the barmaid, all the figures are suggested rather than defined. With a few bold strokes Manet creates girls with opera glasses, ladies in colorful costumes, bearded men in stovepipe hats, and above all captures an evening's mood.

Degas In the art of Edgar Degas the human figure was the focal center. Unlike Courbet and his contemporaries, Degas never painted a single landscape. Beginning as a realist like his friend Manet, he eventually moved toward the lighter tonality and more brilliant color palette of the impressionists, particularly in his famous studies of ballet dancers. However, his deliberate approach, emphasis on line, and carefully constructed compositions made his relationship to the impressionists a peripheral one.

Degas' command of line, meticulous draftsmanship, and accuracy of detail are all evident in the *Cotton Exchange* (Fig. 431). Degas' mother and her family were from New Orleans, and on an extended visit to his uncle and brothers who were in the cotton business there, he painted this tightly knit composition in depth. "Everything attracts me here," he wrote back to a Paris friend. "I look at everything. . . ." Note the figures framed by the open windows, and how all the other figures occupy an appointed place in relation to the receding planes. Each

430. Édouard Manet.
Bar at the Folies-Bergère.
1881–82. Oil on canvas,
$3'1\frac{1}{2}'' \times 4'3''$
($.95 \times 1.3$ m).
Courtauld Institute
Galleries, London.

figure is also a portrait study in itself. Some are intent on inspecting the cotton, others at their work, and still others in casual attitudes awaiting developments. Degas' keen eye always seems to catch the exact moment that reveals individual character and personality whether the individual is a casual stroller in a park, a dancer executing arabesques, or a merchant at work.

Renoir   Auguste Renoir, like Manet, was interested in casual, lighthearted scenes. Even before Manet painted his *Bar at the Folies-Bergère,* Renoir had done a similar scene set in a popular outdoor Paris café, *Le Moulin de la Galette* (Fig. 432), which had been first shown in the 1877 impressionist exhibit. The full force of impressionistic color is felt in the rainbow of brilliant hues, especially the varia-

431. Edgar Degas.
Cotton Exchange at New Orleans.
1873. Oil on canvas,
$28\frac{3}{8}'' \times 35\frac{3}{8}''$ (72×90 cm).
Musée des Beaux-Arts, Pau, France.

tions of blue, and the marvelous quality of filtered sunlight that Renoir had at his command. His obvious intention was to evoke the atmosphere of care-free gaiety and the whirling movement of dance, as well as to revel in a world of color and light.

Monet More than any other painter, Claude Monet was the central figure of impressionism. His picture the *Old St. Lazare Station* (Fig. 433) is among his most typical works. The rendering of the humid atmosphere, the mixture of steam and smoke, the hazy sunlight filtering from the open background and transparent roof, and the contrast between the open spaces and the closed forms of the engines and railroad cars are the things that concern him most. There is no hustle and bustle, no drama of arriving or departing people, no crowds or excitement, no interplay of people and machines, such as one might expect in such a setting. Instead, his figures merely file from the waiting room toward the train, and the

434. Claude Monet.
Pool of Water Lilies.
c. 1899. Oil on canvas,
35 × 39″ (89 × 99 cm).
Art Institute of Chicago.

working people go about their tasks in a matter-of-fact and unemotional way. The picture as it materializes therefore becomes an atmospheric study in blues and greens.

The full development of Monet's broken-color technique is seen more clearly in *Pool of Water Lilies* (Fig. 434), painted in the garden of his home at Giverny. Here he breaks light up into a spectrum of bright colors that forms shimmering patterns in and around the leaves and lilies. Water imagery repeatedly recurs in impressionistic painting. Its surface reflections, the perpetual play of changing light, make water ideal to convey the insubstantial, impermanent nature of visual experience. Figure 434 is one of many versions Monet painted of the same subject, and his method of work reveals that the objects he painted were of less concern than the light and atmosphere surrounding them.

In order to capture the moment he wanted, Monet would take up in a single day a succession of canvases—one showing the garden at dawn, another in full morning light, and a third in a late afternoon glow. The following morning he would take up the dawn scene where he had left off the day before and, when the light changed, set it aside for the next canvas, and so on. With scientific detachment, he tried to maintain the constancy of his subject matter by painting series of *Haystacks, Rouen Cathedral,* and *Old St. Lazare Station,* so as to focus the interest on the variables of light and atmosphere. Each version varies according to the season, day, or hour. Monet might even be called the "weather man" of painting

were it not that, in spite of himself, his genuine involvement with nature usually overcame his objective detachment. As Cézanne once remarked: "Monet, he's only an eye, but my God what an eye!"

Impressionism is clearly an art of urban people who see themselves in terms of a fast time pace, mounting tensions, and sudden change. Their fleeting lives are ruled by impermanent rather than permanent forces, and becoming is more real to them than being. Impressionistic painters purposely chose everyday subjects, such as street scenes, children at play, and life in a night café. When they did go to the country, it was to the suburbs in the manner of city folk on a holiday. As a result, the general effect of impressionist painting is bright, cheerful, and lighthearted.

Impressionistic artists were intoxicated by light rather than life, and they saw the world as a myriad of mirrors that refracted a constantly changing kaleidoscope of color and varying intensities of light. They lived, therefore, in a visual world of reflections rather than substances, and one in which visual values replaced tactile ones.

To reproduce the fleeting atmospheric effects the impressionists desired, they had to work directly from nature. This led to a speeding up in the process of painting to a point where working with oils approached the more rapid technique of watercolor. The criticism of hasty work and careless craftsmanship that the impressionists incurred from their contemporaries was sometimes quite justified. But when their intentions are fully taken into account, one

finds no lack of technical skill on the part of the style's most important practitioners. They wanted their paintings to seem spontaneous and to have an improvised, fragmentary look. Beauty, like color, they felt was in the eye of the beholder, not in the picture itself. They intended to paint not so much what is seen but how it is seen. Instead of formal composing, which implies a placing together, they sought to isolate one aspect of experience and explore it to the utmost. Their art therefore becomes one of analysis more than synthesis, sensation more than perception, sight more than insight. As such the cool objectivity of impressionism could be said to represent the triumph of technique over expression.

Postimpressionism

In their total immersion in the two-dimensional world of appearances, the impressionists consciously neglected the other dimensions of psychological depth and emotional involvement. As a consequence, they soon began to feel discontented under the arbitrary restrictions of such a limited theory. Nor were their audiences happy with the role of innocent bystander they had been assigned. Both artist and spectator had, in effect, resigned the active role for that of the aloof observer of life.

In scarcely more than a dozen years after Monet had shown his *Impression—Sunrise,* the movement had lost its momentum. Even though no one painted an *Impression—Sunset* to commemorate the event, impressionism in its original form was at an end, to all intents and purposes, with the last impressionist exhibit in 1886. Many of the discoveries that had been made, however, survived in variously modified forms in the work of the postimpressionist painters.

Seurat and Cassatt *Sunday Afternoon on the Island of La Grande Jatte* (Fig. 435) by Georges Seurat shows how the impressionistic theory was carried to a logical, almost mathematical, conclusion. Light, shadow, and color are still the major concerns, and the subject is also that of an urban scene, this time of a relaxed group of middle-class Parisians on a Sunday outing. Instead of informal casual arrangements, however, everything here seems as set as an old-fashioned family portrait. Instead of misty indistinct forms, such details as a bustle, a parasol, or a stovepipe hat are as stylized and geometrical as in a Renaissance fresco.

opposite: **435.** Georges Seurat. *Sunday Afternoon on the Island of La Grande Jatte.* 1884–86. Oil on canvas, 6'9" × 10'6" (2.06 × 3.2 m). Art Institute of Chicago.

below: **436.** Mary Cassatt. *Boating Party.* 1893–94. Oil on canvas, 35½ × 46⅛" (90 × 117 cm). National Gallery of Art, Washington, D.C. (Chester Dale Collection).

right: **437.** Vincent van Gogh. *Starry Night.* 1889. Oil on canvas, 29 × 36½" (74 × 93 cm). Museum of Modern Art, New York (acquired through the Lillie P. Bliss Bequest).

Unlike the impressionists who improvised their pictures out of doors, Seurat carefully composed his large canvas in his studio over a period of years. Instead of hastily painted patches of broken color, Seurat worked out a system called *pointillism.* By this system thousands of dots of uniform size were applied to the canvas in such a calculated and painstaking way that the most subtle tints were brought under the painter's control. The picture, moreover, was divided into areas, and graduating shades blended tonalities into a total unity.

The work of the American-born and American-trained artist Mary Cassatt shows a similar turning away from the fleeting atmospheric effects of impressionism in order to achieve a pictoral art based on fine drawing and carefully controlled composition. After moving to Paris, she exhibited with the impressionists from 1879 to 1886. In her later period, however, such paintings as her *Boating Party* (Fig. 436) reveal how she retained the brilliance of impressionistic hues but, like Seurat, was searching for a more enduring and personally sensitive format.

Van Gogh and Gauguin It remained for the three great postimpressionist figures—Van Gogh, Gauguin, and Cézanne—to bring to fruition the full implications of the impressionistic breakthrough and to translate it into a far more expressive language. Vincent van Gogh's *Starry Night* (Fig. 437) demonstrates how colors can be used to achieve intensely expressive effects. The deep purple sky, the yellow light of the stars, the green upward-curling silhouette of the cypress tree all stem from impressionism. Broken color, however, has here become a myriad of swirling lines used as a means toward revealing an inner ecstatic vision.

Paul Gauguin's *Mahana No Atua* (Fig. 438), or *Day of the God,* also shows how the brilliant color of the impressionists can be adapted to make quiet, two-dimensional decorative designs. In 1888 the mature Gauguin expressed his theory of the correspondence between natural form and artistic feeling when, during an outdoor painting session in Brittany, he interrogated and advised a younger colleague, Paul Sérusier, in the following way: "How do you see that tree? . . . Is it quite green? Then put on green, the

finest green on your palette;—and that shadow, is it a bit blue? Don't be afraid to paint it as blue as possible." As Gauguin spoke, Sérusier worked through the exercise, using the purest of tube colors to create a brilliant little landscape on the back of a wooden cigar box cover. He called this remarkable painting *The Talisman* (Fig. 439).

The process Gauguin recommended was that of synthesizing the facts of nature with the artist's own aesthetic—the artist's sense of how and which lines, colors, shapes, and textures should be organized so as to have an intended effect. In an article published in 1890, Maurice Denis, a fellow student of Sérusier, formulated Gauguin's ideas into a formal statement that became fundamental to all understanding of abstraction in modern art: "... a picture—before being a war-horse, a nude woman, or some sort of anecdote—is essentially a surface covered with colors arranged in a certain order." In other words, form and design, much more than actual subject matter, would have the greatest potential for investing a picture with expressive content. Because they were willing to distort the image of nature so as to make each painting express the artist's feelings, Gauguin, Denis, Sérusier, and their associates considered themselves to be *symbolists*.

Cézanne In the 1870s, Paul Cézanne was using the prismatic color palette of the impressionists, but he soon discovered the expressive limitations of the theory. His solution for some of the pictorial problems it posed became a turning point in the history of painting. For him, the superficial beauty of impressionism did not provide the firm base on which to build a significant art. The delight in the transitory tended too much to exclude permanent values.

Instead of severing connections with the past, Cézanne said that he wanted "to make of impressionism something solid like the art of the museums." Poussin was the old master he chose to follow, and his expressed desire was to recreate Poussin in the light of nature. The cultivation of instantaneous vision, according to Cézanne, ruled out the participation of too many other important faculties. His pictures, unlike those of the impressionists, were not meant to be grasped immediately, and their meaning is never obvious. For Cézanne, painting should be not only an act of the eye but also of the mind. If painting aimed only at the senses, any deeper probing of human psychology would be eliminated. Light is important in itself, but it can also be used to achieve inner illumination. Color as such is paramount, but color is also a means of describing masses and volumes, revealing form, creating relationships, separating space into planes, and producing the illusion of projection and recession. Primary colors—red, yellow, and blue—produce brilliance, but careful mixtures can create a whole range of subtle effects.

Cézanne thus retained both light and color as the basis of his art, but not to the extent of eliminating the need for line and geometrical organization. Cézanne's interests are not so much in the specific as in the general. Analysis is necessary for simplification and to reduce a picture to its bare essentials, but for Cézanne composition and synthesis are still the primary processes of the pictorial art. His canvases therefore tend to be more austere than sensuous, more sinuous than lush. His pictures have order, repose, and a serene color harmony, yet they rise to high points of tension and grandeur.

The forms Cézanne chose were from his daily experience—apples, mountains, houses, trees—constants by which it is possible to measure the extent of his spiritual growth. "You must paint them to tame them," he once remarked. Mont Ste. Victoire, a rising rocky mass near his home in Aix-en-Provence, was for Cézanne a recurring motif, and it became a symbol of his ambitions.

The contrast of an early and a late version of Cézanne's favorite mountain provides an interesting index to his artistic growth. The first *Mont Ste. Victoire* (Fig. 440) dates between 1885 and 1887. Another version (Fig. 441) was done between 1904 and 1906. Both are landscapes organized into a pattern of planes by means of color. Both show his way of achieving perspective not by converging lines but by intersecting and overlapping planes of color. In the first version, there is a complementary balance between the vertical rise of the trees and the horizontal line of the viaduct. In the second, these details are omitted, and a balance is achieved between the dense green foliage of the lower foreground and the purple and light green jagged mass of the mountain in the background. In the earlier, the mountain descends in a series of gently sloping lines; in the latter, it plunges steeply downward. In the former, such de-

above: **440.** Paul Cézanne. *Mont Ste. Victoire.* 1885–87.
Oil on canvas, $25\frac{3}{8} \times 31\frac{7}{8}''$ (64 × 81 cm).
Metropolitan Museum of Art, New York (bequest of
Mrs. H. O. Havemeyer, 1929, the H. O. Havemeyer Collection).

below: **441.** Paul Cézanne. *Mont Ste. Victoire.* 1904–06.
Oil on canvas, $28\frac{7}{8} \times 36\frac{1}{4}''$ (73 × 92 cm).
Philadelphia Museum of Art (George W. Elkins Collection).

442. Paul Cézanne.
Basket of Apples. 1890–94.
Oil on canvas,
25¾ × 32″ (65 × 81 cm).
Art Institute of Chicago.

tails as the road, houses, and shrubs are quickly recognizable. In the latter, all is reduced to the barest essentials, and only such formal contours as the cones, cubes, and slanting surfaces remain. Both pictures, however, are landscapes interpreted by the same highly individual temperament. Both show Cézanne's desire to mold nature into a meaningful pattern in order to unite the inanimate world of things and the animate world of the human mind.

In such a still life as *Basket of Apples* (Fig. 442), Cézanne works in a more intimate vein. The search for pure formal values, however, still continues. In one of his letters, he remarked that nature reveals itself in the forms of the cylinder, the sphere, and the cone. Here his cylinders are the horizontally arranged biscuits, his spheres the apples, and his cone the vertically rising bottle. They are balanced in this case by the forward-tilting ellipse of the basket and the receding plane of the tabletop. An almost imperceptible feeling of diagonal motion is induced by the distribution of the fruit from the upper left to the lower right. This compositional momentum is brought to an equally imperceptible stop by means of the pear-shaped apple at the extreme right.

Cézanne brought a measure of form and stability into a visual world where everything was change and transition. If he succeeded only at times and failed at others, each result must be matched with the immensity of the task that he set for himself. Like all great masters, he realized in his mature years that he had made only a beginning, and he remarked that he would forever be the primitive of the method he himself discovered. This may be his historical posi-

tion, but his work may be said to bridge impressionism and modern abstract painting.

Sculpture: Rodin

Among the sculptural exhibits at the Paris Salon of 1877 was a statue of a nude youth entitled *The Bronze Age* (Fig. 443). Too lifelike, said the academic critics. Too good, thought his fellow sculptors as they started rumors that Auguste Rodin was trying to pass off a statue taken directly from plaster casts of a living model. In official quarters the gossip was given sufficient belief to cause the hasty withdrawal of the work. To refute one and all, Rodin had casts and photographs made of the model who had posed for him, and the following year, with official explanations and apologies *The Bronze Age* was again on exhibition. A short while later it was bought by the state for placement in the Luxembourg Gardens. Such was the gulf, however, between art and life, between a monument and a reality, that in academic circles a statue that looked too real, too lifelike or natural, was considered to be a disgrace.

Gates of Hell

Like his forward-looking contemporaries in other fields, Rodin had turned away from the heroic toward the natural. Although he admired Gothic sculpture and wrote a book about French cathedrals, his work contains few sermons in stone. Though he admired Dante and drew almost all his later subjects from an early project for the *Gates of Hell* (Fig. 444), his

above left: 443. Auguste Rodin. *The Bronze Age.* 1876.
Bronze, height 5'11" (1.8 m).
Minneapolis Institute of Arts (John R. Van Derlip Fund).

above: 444. Auguste Rodin. *Gates of Hell.* 1880–1917.
Bronze, height 18' (5.49 m), width 12' (3.66 m),
depth 2'9" (.84 m). Rodin Museum, Philadelphia.

left: 445. Auguste Rodin. *Three Shades.* 1880.
Bronze, height 6'3½" (1.92 m).
Permission of the Fine Arts Museums
of San Francisco.

conceptions show little of the escapism that motivated his immediate predecessors.

Intended as door panels for a projected building
to house the Paris Museum of Decorative Arts,
Rodin's gates had as their points of departure the
portals of the Florence Baptistry, notably Ghiberti's
Gates of Paradise (see Fig. 209), and the writhing
nudes of Michelangelo's *Last Judgment* (see Fig.
290). The literary source was an odd combination of
Dante and Baudelaire. "Dante is not only a visionary
but a sculptor," wrote Rodin. "His expression is lapi-

dary in the good sense of the word." By "lapidary"
Rodin implied that Dante's words and images were
carved as if on stone. Above the actual doors broods
the Michelangelesque figure of *The Thinker*—a man,
not Christ, is here to judge. Rodin's figures are bodies
not souls; his damned suffer more from sensuous
than spiritual longings.

Most details for *Gates of Hell* were worked out
between 1880 and 1887, except for readjustments
that went on until 1917. *The Thinker,* Rodin's best-
known work, and *Three Shades* (Fig. 445), *Adam,* and

446. Auguste Rodin. *Hand of God.* 1898. Marble, height 29″ (74 cm). Rodin Museum, Paris.

Eve, three of Rodin's later large-scale sculptures, were derived from the original germ of his inspiration for the *Gates of Hell.*

Rodin and His Materials

Not only did Rodin prefer the natural over the heroic, but he always acknowledged his material frankly, seeking neither to disguise it nor escape from it. In many of his works there is the feeling that his figures are just emerging out of their original state.

For Rodin, the process of forming supersedes that of form itself. The *Hand of God* (Fig. 446) exemplifies this, both in the method of execution and in the subject itself. Out of an indefinite mass of uncut stone, symbolic of the formless void, the hand of the Creator arises. Divine power over all things is suggested by the scale of the hand in relation to that of the human figures emerging from a lump of uncarved marble. The significance of the work was caught by the philosopher Henri Bergson, author of *Creative Evolution,* who called it "the fleeting moment of creation, which never stops." It is the implication that nothing is ever quite complete, that everything takes place in the flow of time, that matter is the womb which is continuously giving birth, that creation is never-ending—in short, the acceptance of the theory and philosophy of evolution—which gives Rodin's conception its daring quality.

This is not, however, the mighty Michelangelesque struggle of mortals against their material bonds. Rather it is a sensuous love of material as such, a reveling in the flesh or stone, and a desire to explore all its possibilities and potentialities. If Michelangelo left his figures incomplete and still dominated by their material medium, it was largely because circumstances prevented his finishing them. With Rodin, the incompleteness is a conscious and calculated part of his expressive design. Like the symbolist poets, the novelist Proust, and the dramatist Maeterlinck, Rodin went one step beyond mere description. For Rodin, as for his literary contemporaries, events were nothing in themselves. Only when conjured up later in memory did they acquire the necessary subjective coloration; and only then, paradoxically, could the artist treat them with the needed objective detachment.

Rodin always preferred to work from a memory image rather than directly from a model in the flesh. When he did work with a model, it was usually to make a quick sketch, a wash drawing, or an impression in wax or soft clay. He could then allow his figures to take plastic shape in this preliminary stage at the moment of inspiration and thus to promote the feeling that they were products of improvisation. The process of transferring his figures into marble or bronze was left until the forms had been refined in memory and had assumed a more subjective and personal quality. Through memory and by looking inward Rodin was able to give his compositions broader meaning; and by the addition of psychological depth, he gave his art the substance and quality to raise it well above the world of appearances.

Architecture

Throughout the 19th century there was a sharp division of thought about the work of an architect. Was the architect primarily an artist or a builder? A designer or engineer? Should the architect be concerned more with decoration or with structure? Was the architect's place in a studio making drawings or in the field working with materials?

The champions of the viewpoint that the architect was primarily a fine artist achieved such facility that at practically a moment's notice they could produce on their drawing boards a design based on any known building from the past. Late in the century, all the historical styles had been so carefully catalogued and documented that the range of choices was almost unlimited. What had begun as the revival of special periods now included them all.

The term for such a freedom of choice is *eclecticism,* and if a name is to be chosen for the architectural style of the period this is the only one possible. The sole limitation on this eclecticism was the generally accepted appropriateness of the styles of certain periods to special situations. The classical was considered best for commemorative buildings and monuments, but classicism now could be anything from Mycenaean Greek to late imperial Roman. Medieval

above: 447. Henri Labrouste. Library of Ste. Geneviève, University of Paris (the Sorbonne). 1843–50. Length 336′ (102.41 m).

right: 448. Henri Labrouste. Reading Room, Library of Ste. Geneviève, University of Paris (the Sorbonne). 1843–50. Length 330′ (100.58 m), width 60′ (18.29 m), height 42′ (12.80 m).

was the preference for churches, but this might mean Byzantine, Romanesque, early or late Gothic. For public buildings, Renaissance was thought to be the most suitable choice.

The industrial age, however, had produced new methods and materials that opened up novel possibilities. The potentialities of cast iron, for example, had been perceived by engineers and industrialists long before architects began to speculate on its creative applications to their art. The structural use of iron actually dates from the latter part of the 18th century, although at first it was found in bridges, cotton mills, and other functional buildings, where it usually was combined with brick, stone, or timber or else used as a substitute for one or more of them. Nevertheless, the first steps toward a revolution in the art of building had been taken.

The 19th century was eventually to see the spanning of broader widths, the enclosure of more cubic space, and projections toward greater heights than had hitherto been thought possible. The new materials and structural principles were both a threat and a challenge to the traditional pictorial designers, and the more they were used in building plans, the more progressive architecture became.

Labrouste's Libraries

It has already been noted how iron columns and girders had been used quite openly by John Nash in the exotic Royal Pavilion (see Figs. 424, 425) at Brighton, marking one of the first instances of their use in a large residential building. In Paris, François Gau had used iron girders masked with stone facings to reinforce his Church of Ste. Clotilde (see Fig. 414).

Now Henri Labrouste, with an even more penetrating insight into the possibilities of the new material at his command, went one step farther in his Library of Ste. Geneviève (Fig. 447). A first glance at its exterior reveals simply a well-executed Renaissance-revival building—as such it is indebted to a 15th-century Italian church in Rimini designed by Alberti—with the usual festoons of garlands adorning the space above its row of windows. A closer inspection, however, shows that the ground floor is conceived as a solid space, while the bold arcade of windows above gives promise of light and air within. Since the building is a library, there is a working relationship between the closed storage space for the books below and the open reading room above. This is as far as the exterior goes toward a unity of means and ends, however. The stone on the outside gives no hint that the interior is constructed of iron.

By utilizing the strength of metal, Labrouste was able to replace the massive masonry ordinarily required for such a large reading room (Fig. 448) and at the same time provide for a maximum of open space and brilliant illumination. The room is vaulted with two series of arches made of cast iron, supported by tall, thin, fluted cast-iron columns, which form two parallel barrel vaults. An open leafy pattern related to the classical acanthus motif is used as a decorative motif, and the vaults are supported by tall, thin, fluted Corinthian colonnettes, also made of iron. Labrouste thus managed his material so that he brought out its full structural possibilities. But by allowing his iron colonnettes to assume a form associated with carved stone, he compromised with tradition and let the expressive potentialities lag somewhat behind.

What Labrouste began in the Library of Ste. Geneviève, he brought to a brilliant fulfillment in his later masterwork, the Bibliothèque Nationale, the National Library of France (Fig. 449). This storage space for books is conceived as the very heart of the library. It is now brought out into the open alongside the reading room itself. Though closed to the public, a full view of it is possible through a glass-enclosed archway. All superfluous ornamentation is omitted in favor of the function for which it was designed. Except for the bookcases and the glass ceiling, everything is of cast iron.

By dividing his space into five stories, four above and one below the ground level, Labrouste provided for the housing of about a million volumes. The floors are of open grillwork, which permits a free flow of light to reach all levels. Frequent stairways provide rapid communication between floors, and the strategically placed bridges allow freedom of access between the two wings. As a composition, they present a pleasing visual pattern of vertical and horizontal intersecting planes. In both these libraries, it is evident that Labrouste had taken a bold stride toward the realization of the potentialities of the modern materials. His work as a whole is a contribution to the development of a new architecture.

Paxton's Crystal Palace

The same year that Labrouste was completing his first library, a new and original structure was going up in London that made no pretensions of being either a Roman bath or a Renaissance palace. The London *Times* referred to it as "Mr. Paxton's monstrous greenhouse"; and, to be sure, it was conceived and carried out by a landscape gardener skilled in the construction of conservatories and nurseries.

449. Henri Labrouste. Stacks, National Library, Paris. 1858–68.

The occasion was the Great Exhibition of the Works of Industry of All Nations, where the latest mechanical inventions as well as raw materials were to be brought together with the finished products of industry. Machinery of all sorts was to take its place beside the manufactured arts and crafts that were being turned out by the new factories. The Crystal Palace (Fig. 450) that Joseph Paxton constructed to house the exposition was destined to eclipse the exhibits themselves and to occupy a unique place in the history of modern architecture. His light and airy structure was rectangular in shape, 408 feet (124 meters) in width and—with a neat bit of symbolism to coincide with the year of the exhibition—1851 feet (564.2 meters) in length. It rose by means of a skeleton of cast-iron girders and wrought-iron trusses and supports, all bolted together with mathematical precision. Its walls and roof enclosed 33 million cubic feet (9.3 million cubic meters) of space.

The rapidity of the construction of the Crystal Palace was no less remarkable than its form. Previously, the whole structure had been accurately analyzed into a large number of prefabricated parts. So well planned was it that 18,000 panes of glass were put in place by 80 workers in one week. Begun the end of September 1850, it was easily ready for the grand opening, May 1, 1851.

Contrary to expectations, the Crystal Palace turned out to be a thing of surprising beauty and brilliance, as inexpensive in its construction as it was daring in its use of materials. No applied decoration of any sort marred the forthright character of the exterior. And while the iron columns of the interior paid lip service to their classical ancestors, the enormous scale made such details incidental.

At the inauguration ceremonies (Fig. 451), Albert, the Prince Consort, stood by a crystal fountain and restated the purpose of the exhibition: to present "a living picture of the point of development at which the whole of mankind had arrived, . . . and a new starting point from which all nations will be able to direct their further exertions." Nothing seemed impossible to the machine age, and the engineers were indeed the prophets of the new order. Everything now seemed set for the Victorians to step out of their self-created pseudo-Gothic gloom into the new shining age of industrial prosperity. Paxton and his greenhouse, however, had to wait more than half a century before the architects caught up with them.

Literature and Music
Realism and Naturalism

The desire on the part of writers to come to terms with their own world rather than to explore the

left: 450. Joseph Paxton.
Crystal Palace, London.
1851. Cast iron and glass,
width 1851' (564.18 m).
Lithograph.

below: 451. Joseph Paxton.
Foreign Pavilion,
Crystal Palace,
London. 1851. Lithograph.

avenues of escape was responsible for the literary movements known as *realism* and *naturalism.* In some cases, writers cultivated a kinship with the scientific materialism that dominated the thought of the period following the February Revolution of 1848. In others, notably with Zola and Ibsen, they allied themselves with sociology and wrote their novels and plays much as a social worker might handle a case history.

Somewhat earlier, Balzac had proved himself far too sophisticated a writer to see much in the medieval period beyond ignorance, poverty, and rustic village life and was able to write glowingly of the beauty of factories and big cities. The subject matter of his novels was drawn from the complex moral and psychological trials of middle-class life in the large urban centers. This did not imply complete acceptance of the bourgeois image; in fact, it often meant violent opposition to middle-class values.

Attitudes toward their writing varied with the temperaments of individual writers. Flaubert, for one, felt compelled to withdraw from life in order to describe it with the necessary objectivity. He was convinced that such scientific detachment alone qualified the artist as well as the scientist. Zola, on the other hand, could not write without a passionate self-identification with the oppressed subjects of his novels. In the spirit of a reformer, he found it a necessity to bring social sores out into the sunlight of public exposure in order to effect their cure. With him, the novelist becomes a social-research worker, and the novel a documentary case history.

Symbolism

The art of the symbolist is one of the fleeting moment. Everything rushes past in an accelerated panorama, as if seen from a moving train. With the metaphor as a starting point, a symbolist prose poem flows by in a sequence of images that sweeps the reader along on a swift current of words that scarcely leaves time to ponder their meaning.

Like the impressionistic painters, the symbolists reveled in sense data, and, like the realistic novelists, they looked for their material among the seemingly trivial occurrences of daily life. But in their attempt to endow such happenings with profundity and deeper symbolism, they went one step beyond.

While the painters had found a new world in the physics of light, and the novelists another new world in the social sciences, the symbolists looked to the new discoveries in psychology. By purposefully leaving their poetry in an inconclusive and fragmentary state, they were making use of the psychological mechanism of reasoning from part to whole. Since the poets did not define the whole, the reader's imagination was allowed full interpretive power.

Just as the impressionist painters had left the mixing of color to the eye of the observer, and the relationship of the subject matter to the viewer's mind, so Mallarmé and the symbolists left the connection, order, and form of their verbal still lifes to be completed by the reader. They also found a new world to explore in "listening" to colors, "looking" at sounds, "savoring" perfumes, and in all such mixtures of separate sensations known to psychology as *synaesthesia.* This fusion of sensations by which the awakening of one sense impression sets up a chain reaction of others is vividly expressed in Baudelaire's "Correspondences," a poem from his *Flowers of Evil.*

> Like those deep echoes that meet from afar
> In a dark and profound harmony,
> As vast as night and clarity,
> So perfumes, colors, tones answer each other.
> There are perfumes fresh as children's flesh,
> Soft as oboes, green as meadows. . . .

By developing a hypersensitive tonal palette, Claude Debussy, like his symbolist colleagues, was able to sound a range of images from volatile perfumes (*Sounds and Perfumes Turn on the Evening Air*), fluid architecture (*Engulfed Cathedral*), sparkling seascapes (*La Mer*), exotic festivities (*Ibéria, Fêtes*) to gaudy fireworks (*Feux d'Artifice*). The symbolists pushed outward to the limits of perception in order to develop more delicate sensibilities and stimulate the capacities for new and peripheral experiences. They moved about in a twilight zone where sensation ends and thought begins. The very word *symbolism,* however, implies the images are revelations of something beyond sense data. And it is here that they parted company with the objectivity of the realists and impressionists.

Maeterlinck's Symbolist Drama   Maurice Maeterlinck made an interesting attempt to translate the aims of the symbolist poets into dramatic form. His *Pelléas et Mélisande,* a play first performed in 1892, brings about a synthesis of the material world and the world of the imagination. In it, he denies the importance of external events and explores the quiet vibrations of the soul. His symbols function as links between the visible and invisible, the momentary and the eternal. The tangible fragments of common experience, the seemingly trivial everyday occurrences, furnish clues to the more decisive stuff of life.

"Beneath all human thoughts, volitions, passions, actions," writes Maeterlinck in one of his essays, "there lies the vast ocean of the Unconscious, the unknown source of all that is good, true and beautiful. All that we know, think, feel, see and will are but bubbles on the surface of this vast sea." This sea, then, is the symbol of the absolute toward which all life is reaching, but which can never quite be grasped. What is seen and heard are only the ripples on the surface.

In his drama, the sea, the forest, the fountain, the bottomless well are the *dramatis personae* in a deeper sense than the human characters, who are but shadowy reflections of real people. In spite of the settings in which they appear, Maeterlinck's characters belong neither to the past nor to the future but hover in an extended now. They seem to have no existence in space, no volume, but exist more as creatures of duration. So little is acted out that what plot there is seems to unfold within the characters. One overhears rather than hears the dialogue, and, in the ordinary sense, so little happens that a kind of dramatic vacuum is created which can be filled only by the imaginations of the spectators. Just as the eye must mix the colors in an impressionistic painting, so the observers' imaginations in a Maeterlinck play must connect the metaphors, must unite the tableaux, the frozen depiction of scenes, into a flow of images, must fill each pregnant pause with projections from their own experience, and must supply the emotional depth to its surface play of symbols.

Debussy's Lyric Drama   Maeterlinck's good fortune was to find a composer who could fill his silences with the necessary vague sounds, who could give voice to the "murmur of eternity on the horizon," and who could write the music that provided the link from dream to dream. It was, indeed, as if the music of Debussy had been created for the very purpose of providing the tonal envelope to enclose Maeterlinck's "ominous silence of the soul."

Debussy was able to make the sea sing "the mysterious chant of the infinite." In his score, the references to the ocean on which all the characters are floating toward their unknown destinies are handled with special sensitivity. In one guise or another, its waters are present in practically every scene, either in the fragmentary form of a spring in the forest, a well in a courtyard, a fountain in a park, or the stagnant pools of underground caverns.

This ever-present water imagery is used as the symbol of the flowing, fleeting nature of experience. As an unstable medium without form of its own, it becomes the means of capturing vague atmospheric effects and reflecting subtle changes of mood. The course of Mélisande's life is conveyed by means of these changing waters. She comes from over the sea, is found by a dark pool in the forests, discovers her love for Pelléas at a fountain in the park, and as she dies, asks that the window be opened so that she can once more be with the sea.

Other symbols play their appointed parts. Mélisande weeps in the first scene over the loss of a golden crown, symbolic of her happier state of childhood innocence. Later when she tosses her wedding ring up and down beside the fountain, one knows that she is taking her marriage vows lightly. When it falls into a bottomless well and disappears, it means that her marriage has dissolved. Only the circles on the surface of the water remain, subtly rendered by

Pelléas et Mélisande (Act II, scene I)   Claude Debussy

Ce n'est plus el - le.   Elle est per - due... per - du - e!
'Tis not my ring.__   The ring is lost... 'Tis lost!

Il n'y a plus qu'un grand cercle sur l'eau...
Nought but a cir - cle of wa - ter re - mains...

Debussy in the musical example above. As the ripples expand they foretell developments to come.

Debussy's style first took shape in the songs he wrote on texts by the symbolist poets, but Maeterlinck's drama provided him with the necessary lyric material to ripen it into maturity. Like the poets, his methods were in many ways the opposite of conventional operatic techniques. He followed Wagner in giving the orchestra the main task of carrying on the sequence of the drama. As a result, his work became more of a symphonic poem with running commentary by the singers than a conventional opera.

With characteristic insight, Debussy saw that melody, in the sense of a set operatic aria, stopped rather than promoted the dramatic progress. "I wished—intended, in fact—that the action should never be arrested; that it should be continuous, uninterrupted," he commented. "Melody is, if I may say so, almost antilyric, and powerless to express the constant change of emotion or life. Melody is suitable only for song, which confirms a fixed sentiment."

In thus considering recitative as the most important element of the lyric drama, Debussy allies himself with his famous predecessors Lully and Rameau. But while their characters spoke in the stylized accents of baroque theatrical bombast, his speak in rhythmic flows of sound more closely approximating modern conversational French. "The characters in this drama endeavor to sing like real persons," the composer wrote; and by bringing their language closer to everyday speech, and allowing the flow of dramatic action to proceed without interruption, his opera is far more plausible than is common in such a

highly artificial medium. By using modes other than the traditional major and minor, Debussy's recitative takes on the flexible character of psalmodic chant. The rhythms are free, and the absence of regular accentuation allows the words to flow with elasticity.

Debussy's musical motifs parallel the literary symbols and are often just broken fragments of melody. They suggest rather than define atmospheric effects or are associated with the mood of a character. While used with greater subtlety, they nevertheless are much closer to Wagner's system of leitmotifs than Debussy was willing to admit.

The harmonic method Debussy uses likewise was well suited to rendering the ambiguities and obscurities of the symbolist poets. His key centers lose their boundaries; progressions move about freely in tonal space; everything is in a state of flux, always on its way but never quite arriving.

Debussy's sensitivity to the *timbre,* or distinctive quality, of sounds borders on the uncanny. He thought of Mélisande's voice as "soft and silky," and thus the woodwinds dominate the orchestral coloration with their peculiarly poignant and penetrating quality. Above all, performers must know how to make this intangible music live and breathe, how to render its rhythms with the proper elasticity, and how to fill its silences with meaning.

Debussy's evocation of Maeterlinck's pale, shadowy world is one of those rare instances of the indissoluble union of literature and music that make it impossible for later generations to think of them as separate entities. Debussy worked on *Pelléas* over a period of ten years and was constantly worrying about the audience reaction to his fragile lyric drama. Maeterlinck's play had not been a success, and in a letter dated August 1894, Debussy anxiously asks a friend, "How will the world get along with these two poor little beings?" In an obvious reference to the popularity of Zola's writing, he goes on to express his hatred of "crowds, universal suffrage, and tri-colored phrases." Contrary to Debussy's expectation, the opera ultimately was a success and is still performed. His elusive music proved its capacity to cast a spell over the most indifferent audiences.

Ideas

Any interpretation of the complex interplay of forces that underlies and motivates the diverse tendencies of the latter part of the 19th century faces the usual danger of oversimplification. Two of the most prominent ideas, however, are chosen principally because they provide significant insights into the relationship of the several arts. These are the influence of the scientific method on the arts and the interpretation of experience in terms of time.

Alliance of Art and Science

Artists in all fields were aware of the extraordinary success of the scientific method. Realism and impressionism brought a new objective attitude into the arts, together with an emphasis on the technical side of the crafts and a tendency for artists to become specialists pursuing a single aspect of their media.

Architects began to look toward engineers for the more advanced developments in building. A painting for an impressionist was a kind of experiment, an adventure in problem solving. Cézanne thought of each of his pictures as a type of visual-research problem. In sculpture, Rodin was seeking a new synthesis of matter and form. The literary realists were cultivating a scientific detachment in their writing and developing a technique that would enable them to record the details of their close observations of everyday life with accuracy and precision. Zola, by means of his experimental novel, introduced a modified social-scientific technique to fiction. In addition to his poetic dramas, Maeterlinck wrote popular nature studies, such as *Life of the Bee* and the *Magic of the Stars.* Debussy spoke about some of his compositions as his "latest discoveries in musical chemistry."

Many of the actual discoveries of scientific research opened up new vistas in the various arts. Experiments in optical physics revealed secrets of light and color that painters could explore. New chemical syntheses provided brighter pigments for their canvases. Increased knowledge of the physiology of the eye and the psychology of perception led to a reexamination of how observers look at a picture and what they perceive. New metal alloys and processes of casting were a boon to sculptors. The theories of evolution gave Rodin some poetic ideas on how form emerges from matter, the animate from the inanimate. Helmholtz' *On the Sensation of Tone as a Physiological Basis for the Theory of Music* stirred Debussy and other composers to speculate on the relation of tone to overtone and consonance to dissonance in their harmonic techniques.

The impressionistic painters were convinced that pictures were made from light and color, not line and form; the symbolists claimed that poetry was made with words, not ideas; and composers felt that music should be a play of varied sonorities rather than a means of evoking programmatic associations. By pursuing this general line of thought, artists made a number of discoveries. Monet revealed a new concept of light and color and their interdependence; Rodin, an atmospheric extension of solid three-dimensional form. The symbolists found a new world of poetry; Debussy, a new concept of sound. Paxton and Eiffel, by incorporating light and air into their designs, achieved a new relationship of inner and outer space.

This mechanistic phase, however, could lead just so far, and artists were soon trying to push beyond it into paths that would lead to deeper psychological insights. Each of the postimpressionists was probing to find how the new discoveries could be used as a means toward new modes of expression. Cézanne's path led into a new concept of pictorial geometry that became an important anticipation of 20th-century abstract art and the point of departure for cubism. Maeterlinck attempted to humanize science and describe it in poetical terms. In his case, the result was a kind of animism that brought such inanimate objects as trees, stones, and fountains to life, gave them speech and a soul life of their own. In an essay on the "Intelligence of Flowers," he tried to establish more sympathetic ties between people and nature. In his stage fantasy *The Bluebird,* Sugar and Bread are among the live characters. Cézanne also felt the living force of the objects he placed in his still lifes, and in a conversation with a friend remarked that there are people who say a sugar bowl has no soul, yet it changes every day.

The symbolists also tried to bring about a synthesis between the phenomenal world and that of the creative imagination. Their metaphors were material in the sense that they received expression through the senses, but they hinted at the existence of a more profound world of ideas and were definitely based on a view that life was something more than the sum of its molecular parts. Debussy, too, turned away from the physical elements of sound toward the deeper psychological implications of tonal symbolism.

Continuous Flux

The arts of the late 19th century were also bound together by their common tendency toward the interpretation of experience in terms of time. Progress was an idea that was carried over from the late 18th century. Material progress continued to be an indisputable fact, but what was rapidly becoming apparent was that it did not go hand in hand with political, moral, spiritual, and aesthetic progress.

With industrialization came a specialization in which people were concerned more with fragments than with wholes. Industrial workers were rapidly forfeiting to the machine their place as the primary productive unit. With this loss of control came a corresponding shift from a rational world view toward an increasingly irrational one. With industrialization also came a capitalistic economy in which the lives of workers were controlled by intangible forces beyond themselves.

Two centuries previously, the baroque mind had been shaken by the Copernican revolution in which the notion of a fixed earth in the center of the universe was replaced by that of a freely moving satellite around the sun. The late 19th-century mind was similarly rocked by the Darwinian and other evolutionary theories, which taught that creation was an ever-continuing process rather than an accomplished fact. As a result of such forces and ideas, the onward-and-upward notion of progress was revised downward to one of continuous flux and change.

The literary and visual realists concentrated on the momentary, the fragmentary, the everyday occurence. Even when they planned their works in more comprehensive schemes, the effect was more that of a broad cross section than a complete three-dimensional structure. For twenty years, Balzac worked on parts of his *Human Comedy,* Wagner on his Ring Cycle, Rodin on his *Gates of Hell,* and Proust on his *Remembrance of Things Past.* None, however, is a systematic, organic, or logical whole or a single perfected masterpiece. Instead of having an all-embracing unity, they are easily broken down into a collection of fragments, motifs, genre scenes, scraps, and pieces. The late 19th century produced no grandiose metaphysical systems, such as those of Aquinas, Leibniz, Kant, or Hegel, each of whom tried to encompass all experience in one universal structure.

Bergson's Theory of Time   The thinker who came the closest to making a clear picture of this turbulent age was the French philosopher Henri Bergson. His point of departure was a remark made by the pre-Socratic philosopher Heraclitus, who had said that one cannot step into the same river twice. Bergson cited Heraclitus in support of his theory that time was more real than space, that the many were closer to experience than the one, and that becoming was closer to reality than being.

Bergson was critical of the intellect because it tended to reduce reality to immobility. He therefore ranked intuition as a higher faculty than reason, because through it the perception of the flow of duration was possible, and through it static, immobile quantitative facts were animated into the dynamic qualitative values of motion and change.

Existence, according to Bergson, is never static. Rather, it is a transition between states and between moments of duration. Experience is thus durational, "a series of qualitative changes, which melt into and permeate one another, without precise outlines. . . ."

Art for Bergson is a force that frees the soul and through which one can grasp "certain rhythms of life and breath," which compel the individual "to fall in with it, like passersby who join in a dance. Thus they compel us to set in motion, in the depth of our being, some secret chord which was only waiting to thrill." Convinced that reality is mobility, tendency, or "incipient change of direction," Bergson thus felt that

looking at or listening to a work of art is perceiving the mobile qualities of the objects or sounds presented. The aesthetic experience is essentially an experience in time and involves an "anticipation of movement," which permits the spectator or auditor in various ways "to grasp the future in the present." His theory of art is based on what he calls his "spiritualistic materialism," by which finely perceived material activity awakens spiritual echoes. All is based on the "uniqueness of the movement"; and perception of the flow of time is the same as an awareness of the pulsation of life, something that is quite apart from the mechanical or lifeless matter.

Past, present, and future, in Bergson's thought, are molded into an organic whole as "when we recall the notes of a tune melting, so to speak, into one another." Time, therefore, is "the continuous progress of the past, which gnaws into the future and which swells as it advances." But Bergson's concept of time is not clock time with its divisions into seconds, minutes, and hours; nor is it concerned with the usual groupings of past, present, and future. These are just arbitrary conveniences, like the points on a clock past which the hands move. Time cannot be measured in such a quantitative way; it is a quality, not a substance.

Bergson and the Arts   The application of Bergson's theory of time to the arts of the late 19th century can be very illuminating. The philosopher often cited the motion picture as an example of what he meant by the perception of duration. The separate frames in a motion picture film are still; but when the series is run through the projector, the mind melts them together in a continuous flow, and they appear to be animated and alive. So also are the separate colors on an impressionistic canvas, the separate metaphors in a symbolist poem, the separate scenes in a Maeterlinck play, the separate chords in a Debussy progression molded by the mind into a continuum of time. In visual impressionism, the eye mixes the colors; in a symbolist poem, the mind supplies the connecting verbs for the so-called fragments; in a Maeterlinck play, the imagination gives the irrelevancies of speech and action a dramatic meaning; and in Debussy's music, the ear bridges over the silences.

In all the arts, this ceaseless flux leads toward the improvisatory, the consciously incomplete. Each work tries to be a product of inspiration rather than calculation. With the visual impressionists, all pictorial substance is broken down into an airy mixture of color sprays, fleeting shadows, and momentary moods. Cézanne sometimes paints so thinly that parts of the canvas are actually bare, and at other times the texture is so thin as to be almost transparent. Rodin likewise leaves parts of the stone surrounding his figures uncut. And it is by no means an accident that some of the most important buildings of the time were open to the air and sky and were conceived as temporary exposition structures, such as the Crystal Palace, the Gallery of Machines, and the Eiffel Tower. In *Pelléas et Mélisande,* the characters are only outlined or sketched, and what they really feel has to be inferred by the spectator. The imagination actually supplies the emotional depth to what is but a surface play of forms. In all instances the audience, through perception, imagination, and memory, participates in the creative act.

The sense of creating for the moment is well illustrated in the sketches, color lithographs, posters, and paintings of Henri de Toulouse-Lautrec. Amid the surface play of flickering gaslight in *At the Moulin Rouge* (Fig. 452), the artist has captured with sure, deft strokes the mood and character of his subject, which includes a self-portrait (the small bearded man in front of the tall top-hatted figure in the upper center).

Imagery of a more somber, psychologically probing type is found in the work of the Norwegian artist Edvard Munch, who participated in the Paris scene from 1889 to 1891. He there absorbed the vocabulary of postimpressionism and symbolism as found in the styles of Gauguin, Van Gogh, and Toulouse-Lautrec. Stark terror and nightmarish fears haunt such works as *The Cry* (Fig. 453). The lines radiating outward from the head of the hysterical figure seem to continue the piercing cry in an organic pattern of shattering shock waves. Munch's violent and despairing moods were destined to become one of the points of departure for 20th-century expressionism.

Both the awareness of science and the accentuation of the flow of time became important means by which the arts at the end of the 19th century established the basis for the transition to the various modern styles. Cézanne has with justification been called the first great modern master. The functional architecture of Labrouste, Paxton, and Eiffel has become the foundation stone of contemporary architecture. Rodin's convex and concave surfaces and his preoccupation with the atmospheric problems of light and shadow have led to important new developments in sculpture. The fragmentary style of the symbolists anticipated the "stream-of-consciousness" and other techniques of modern literature. And Debussy's concept of relative rather than absolute tonality, together with his harmonic experimentation, have pointed toward some of the significant musical developments of the 20th century.

left: 452. Henri de Toulouse-Lautrec. *At the Moulin Rouge.* 1892. Oil on canvas, $4'3\frac{3}{8}'' \times 4'7\frac{1}{2}''$ (1.23 × 1.4 m). Art Institute of Chicago (Helen Birch Bartlett Collection).

below: 453. Edvard Munch. *The Cry.* 1893. Lithograph on red paper. $14\frac{1}{2} \times 9\frac{7}{8}''$ (37 × 25 cm). Museum of Fine Arts, Boston (William Francis Warden Fund).

21
The 20th-Century Styles

The Age of Isms and Schisms

Wars, revolutions, social upheavals, displacement of peoples, computers and automation—all have proceeded at such a pace that 20th-century men and women have difficulty keeping up with themselves. While new means of communication and transportation have shrunk the globe, the vast expansion of knowledge has made it impossible for the mind's eye to view the world as a whole.

The completion of the Industrial Revolution, the progress of electronic technology, and the necessity for specialization have further fragmented the vision. Clashes and discord are more usual than concord; disunity is ascendant over unity; discontinuity is more familiar than continuity; and a multiverse has replaced the universe. Bombarded on all sides by the mass media of television, radio, motion pictures, newspapers, and magazines, the quest for meaning and reality becomes ever more difficult. People must decide whether to conform or reform, suppress or express themselves, look within or without for enlightenment, and make yet another attempt to close the widening gap between the actual and the ideal.

The 19th century, somehow, had been able to contain the forces of liberty and authority, democracy and dictatorship, individualism and collectivism, free enterprise and economic monopoly, scientific advances and traditional religious beliefs, freedom of thought and anti-intellectual tendencies. The 20th century, however, has seen these smoldering disputes break out into open conflict. The clashes of rival colonialisms were followed by revolutions in the wake of two world wars that brought communism to Russia, China, and eastern Europe; nazism to Germany and Austria; civil war, totalitarianism, and cold war to most of the world; and the rise of a host of new nations out of old colonial empires.

Revolutions and wars, however, are but one aspect of the human struggle; art movements are another. Above all the noise and confusion, the voice of the present century can be heard, for pens and paint brushes are also weapons in the struggle.

Since the arts are forms of action, artists as well as social reformers and revolutionaries shout their battle cries, issue their manifestoes, propose their cure-alls, and formulate their own isms and schisms. In the late 19th century such relatively simple aesthetic creeds as realism, naturalism, symbolism, and impressionism had their flocks of faithful followers. By comparison the 20th century has become an angry Tower of Babel in which such gospels as constructivism, dynamism, neoplasticism, orphism, productivism, purism, suprematism, and vorticism have been proclaimed. Still on the current scene are cubism, dadaism, social realism, and surrealism.

Too often the organized art movements of the 20th century have been so preoccupied with their doctrines that they have produced little significant art. Their principal purpose has been to provoke lively discussion, attract attention, and arrange for exhibits, concerts, and publications. The passions associated with these isms have usually generated more heat than light, more confusion than clarification. And the groups responsible have rarely spoken or written about them very sensibly. Often these isms and schisms have led to dead ends, sometimes to important breakthroughs. Ultimately, what matters is whether the pictures, pieces, or poems are worth looking at, listening to, or reading.

CHRONOLOGY
20th Century

In approaching the art of the 20th century, one has much to keep in mind. Modern art, like the art of the past, must be understood in terms of its own frame of reference and what the artist is trying to do. Contemporary artists may intend to delight or irritate, to arouse or denounce, to exhort or castigate, to surprise or excite, to soothe or shock. They may be trying deliberately to achieve disorder rather than order, chaos rather than a cosmos. The act of creating sometimes replaces the importance of the object created. Painters may plan their pictures as visual socks in the eye; composers may intend their music as assault and battery on the ear. Judging from the reactions to Picasso's early exhibits and the riot that greeted Stravinsky's *Rite of Spring* ballet, some artists have succeeded beyond their wildest expectations. Sheer shock values soon diminish, however, and artists have learned that they can blow Gabriel's trumpet of Judgment once, but not every day.

The tempo of change has been so swift that the 20th-century mind cannot keep pace with the scientists and artists. The span of time between innovations and their understanding and popular acceptance is often referred to as "cultural lag." Fashions, fads, and fancies succeed each other with bewildering speed. This season's "in group" is next year's outcast. Alongside the passing trends, however, are found the solid accomplishments of artists of major stature. The discoveries of Frank Lloyd Wright, Gropius, and Le Corbusier in architecture, of Picasso, Kandinsky, and Mondrian in painting, of Schoenberg and Stravinsky in music rank as major breakthroughs in the history of art. These artists now enjoy the status of old masters of modern art. The younger generation of artists, as well as their public, today are passing through a period of consolidation; they are extending the gains that have been made and preparing the ground for future discoveries.

Modern materials and methods opened up new possibilities in the arts. Ferroconcrete, structural steel, glass, and laminated wood have taken their place alongside bricks and mortar, while cantilevering has joined the post and lintel. With the growth of cities, modern architects have had to construct facilities ranging from airline terminals, suspension bridges, and low-cost public housing to such entirely new capital cities as Brasília and Chandigarh. Side by side with the steel-and-glass office buildings and urban-planning projects of the industrialized society, 20th-century architects have been called upon to build new churches and temples in daring designs.

Sculptors now use the welding torch to replace the traditional hammer, chisel, and metal-casting methods (Fig. 454). Laminated woods, sophisticated metal alloys, Plexiglas, polyester resins, neon tubes, and plastics have superseded the older marble and bronze. Kinetic devices, powered by motors and programmed by computers, now bring actual motion to sculpture, while formerly, except in cases of fountains, action could be implied only through muscular tension, a bodily stance, or directional orientation.

Painters now work on Masonite and plastic surfaces as well as in mixed media. New synthetic paints, acrylics, and various textural additives have supplanted the earth pigments and natural oils used for centuries. And a new pictorial category of ab-

454. Pablo Picasso. *Woman in the Garden.* 1929–30. Bronze, after welded iron; height 6'10¾" (2.1 m). Collection the artist's estate.

stract and fantastic pictures has been added to the traditional classifications of history paintings, genre scenes, portraiture, landscape, and still life.

455. Pablo Picasso.
Les Demoiselles d'Avignon. 1907.
Oil on canvas, 8′ × 7′8″ (2.44 × 2.34 m).
Museum of Modern Art, New York
(acquired through the Lillie P. Bliss Bequest).

The graphic arts have been expanded to include many new media, among them silk-screen printing and color photography. The arbitrary distinction between the so-called major and minor arts, fine arts and crafts, beauty and utility has narrowed to the point where architect and engineer, sculptor and furniture designer, a cathedral and a suspension bridge—once thought to be poles apart—have been brought together in the modern unity of form and

function. Drama has expanded from the live theater to include motion pictures and television, and new language concepts are explored with words used as syllabic sounds in an abstract poetry.

Expressionism and Abstractionism

Pablo Picasso's *Les Demoiselles d'Avignon* (Fig. 455) incorporated so many of the ideas of the early 20th century that it became a landmark of the modern-art movement. At the turn of the century Paris was alive with young artists, new notions, and stimulating exhibits. Picasso was impressed in turn by the great Cézanne retrospective of 1907; with a showing of pre-Roman Iberian sculpture which, as in most archaic art, represented the human body in angular geometrical patterns; and with expositions of African tribal sculpture. As a result he began to reexamine his pictorial approach, turned away from representational conventions toward tighter geometrical controls, and began to acquire African sculpture.

Les Demoiselles d'Avignon had begun as an allegory. A man seated amid fruit and women was to have been Vice, while his opposite number entering on the left holding a skull in her hand was to have been Virtue. Under the new influences, however, the original plan was abandoned, and the picture developed in another direction by blending the figures, the background drapery, and the still life below into an abstract design. The girl on the left who is pulling back some curtains became a series of overlapping planes and geometrically arranged contours. The head of the figure in the upper right resembles a mask from Itumba (see Fig. 12) in what remained at this time the colonial territory of the French Congo. while the head just below and the profile of the figure on the left also show African tribal influence. Picasso's preliminary drawings reveal his fascination with the oval-shaped heads, the long noses, small mouths, and angular bodies that characterize the sculpture of the Ivory Coast. The color, with its spectrumlike shading of bright hues one into another, contributes to the effect of an emotional crescendo, while the formal arrangement of the figures suggests the angular rhythms of a primitive dance.

Les Demoiselles is thus a pivotal picture. The heightened postimpressionistic colors combined with the violence and energy of primitive art make it a summary of the avant-garde Paris school of painting at the turn of the century. It also marks Picasso's intuitive invention of *cubism,* that most important step toward abstraction. When Georges Braque, one of the fauve painters, first saw *Les Demoiselles,* he perceived that both he and Picasso had been assimilating Cézanne's geometry of cones, spheres, and cylinders and his principles of construction. Over the next four years they worked out the rules of cubism.

In sorting out the developments in contemporary art, one has basically but two ways of looking at the world—from within or from without, subjectively or objectively, through emotion or through reason. These outlooks are by no means mutually exclusive, since mind is necessary for emotional awareness, and without emotional drive even the most rational proposition would be empty and devoid of meaning. For purposes of the present study the arts in which emotional considerations are dominant have been grouped under *expressionism;* those in which logical and analytical processes are uppermost are under *abstractionism.* Here a note of caution must be sounded, because all art is expressive to some degree, just as all art is abstract to a certain extent.

Expressionism looks within to a world of emotional and psychological states rather than without to a fluid world of fleeting realism, as with impressionism. In their eagerness to develop a style with greater emotional force, the expressionist artists turned away from naturalism. With Van Gogh and Gauguin as their point of departure, these painters distorted outlines, applied strong colors, and exaggerated forms to convey their intentions (see Figs. 437, 438). Expressionism in its limited sense applies to the pre-World War I period and to the German art movements known as *Die Brücke* ("The Bridge") and *Der Blaue Reiter* ("The Blue Rider"). A broader definition, however, includes parallel developments in all major centers where artists were concerned primarily with the emotional approach to art and with their passionate involvement in all phases of life.

Expressionists are fully conscious of the visible world, but they leave behind the classical idea of art as an imitation of nature. They close their eyes to explore the mind, spirit, and imagination. They would agree with Goethe's saying that feeling is all, and they welcomed Freud's delving into the subconscious, which revealed a new world of emotion in the dark drives, hidden terrors, and mysterious motivations underlying human behavior. The expressionists are well aware that they inhabit a number of complex overlapping worlds, and they know too that there are worlds to be explored which are not seen by the eye and which are not subject to logic.

Expressionistic pictures are in psychological rather than natural focus. They describe intangible worlds with new techniques and new symbols, discordant colors and distorted shapes. The clashing dissonances of expressionistic music are intended to arouse rather than soothe the listener, and expressionistic literature startles the reader with revelations of neurotic, psychical, often psychotic, states.

To describe their reactions to physical, psychical, and spiritual events, the expressionists alter, distort, and color their images according to the intensity of their feelings. Expressionism, then, may range from quiet nostalgic moods, through sudden shock reactions and hysterical outbursts, to screaming nightmares. The results of such excursions into the subconscious may be quite uneven, but the artists' passport to these nether regions is nonetheless valid. Among others, expressionism has embraced such movements as neoprimitivism, dadaism, surrealism, and social realism.

Abstractionism implies analyzing, deriving, detaching, selecting, simplifying, geometrizing, before distilling the essence from nature and sense experiences. The heat generated by the psychological and political revolutions of the 20th century was felt in expressionism, but the light of the new intellectual points of view is mirrored in abstractionism.

In previous centuries, a picture was a reflection, in one way or another, of the outside world. In 20th-century abstractionism, artists free themselves from the representational convention. Natural appearances play little part in their designs, which reduce a landscape to a system of geometrical shapes, patterns, lines, angles, and swirls of color. Choosing their pictorial content from nature, abstract artists eliminate the unimportant minor details of the observed world and refine the haphazardness of nature and ordinary visual experience. Their imagination and invention are concentrated on pictorial mechanics and the arrangement of patterns, shapes, textures, and colors. From the semiabstract cubist art, in which objects are still discernible, abstractionism moves toward nonobjectivism in which a work of art has no representational, literary, or associational meaning outside itself, and the picture becomes its own self-defining referent.

In the early years of the century, physicists were at work formulating a fundamental new view of the universe, which resulted in the concepts of space-time and relativity. In the arts, meanwhile, new ways of seeing and listening were also being worked out. In painting, for example, the cubist system of multiple visual viewpoints was explored, whereby several sides of an object could be presented at the same time. In sculpture, a new theory of volume was developed, whereby open holes or gaps in the surface suggested the interpenetration of several planes, and the existence of other sides and surfaces not immediately in view. In architecture, the international style, using steel and glass, incorporated in a structure the simultaneous experience of outer and inner space.

Similar developments occurred in literature and music, which found new ways of presenting materials in the time dimension. In literature, the stream-of-consciousness technique merged objective description and subjective flow of images. In music, the so-called atonal method of composition was formulated, by which fixed tonal centers were avoided in favor of a state of continuous flux and variation.

Such novel organizations of space and time demanded new ways of thinking about the world, new ways of looking at it, listening to it, and reading about it. Abstractionism includes such developments as cubism, futurism, the mechanical style, nonobjectivism, the twelve-tone method of musical composition, and the international style of architecture.

Neoprimitivism

As the first bonfire of 20th-century expressionism burst into flame, the spark that set fire to that movement called *neoprimitivism* was the 19th-century discovery of the native arts of the South Sea Islanders and the wood carvings of African tribes. As the term is used here, neoprimitivism is limited to the conscious adaptations by sophisticated artists of authentic specimens of Oceanic, African, and other native art.

Painting   The first major artist to employ exotic patterns and motifs in woodcuts and paintings had been Gauguin, and such pictures as his *Mahana No Atua* (see Fig. 438), painted during his extended stay in Tahiti, clearly reflect the native influence. Examples of Polynesian handcraft, such as oars, arrows, and harpoons, had been collected by traders on their voyages and were shown in the Paris expositions of 1878 and 1889. Later, when expeditions went to the interior of Africa, wooden objects carved by members of black tribes were brought back for display. The ethnological museums, founded in Paris and Dresden to house these collections, commanded considerable interest among scholars, artists, and the general public. Books on African sculpture appeared, and in 1890 James Frazer began publishing *The Golden Bough,* a twelve-volume digest of primitive customs, folklore, magical practices, and taboos.

Native art, with its complete denial of the notion of progress and its free geometrical distortions of the human figure, seemed to be the promise of a new beginning. Especially appealing was the animistic attitude of the tribal carvers, who divined the spirit of wood and stone and expressed it in the grains, textures, and shapes of their materials. German expressionists were fascinated by the strange, weird forms and nonintellectualism of African images. French artists, among them Matisse, found in their simplified geometrical forms a wealth of decorative motifs and a justification for their abstract designs.

above: **456.** Amedeo Modigliani. *Head.* c. 1913.
Stone, height 24¾″ (63 cm).
Tate Gallery, London
(reproduced by courtesy of the Trustees).

right: **457.** Amedeo Modigliani. *Yellow Sweater*
(*Portrait of Mme. Hébuterne*). 1919.
Oil on canvas, 39⅜ × 25½″ (100 × 65 cm).
Solomon R. Guggenheim Museum, New York.

Sculpture The impact of native art also affected the course of 20th-century sculpture. When the young painter Modigliani came to Paris in 1906, he fell so completely under the spell of African tribal sculpture than for a while he traded the brush for the chisel. One of these works, *Head* (Fig. 456), is in the same Ivory Coast style that Picasso had adopted. In his paintings, Modigliani later used similarly stylized oval faces and elongated shapes, such as those in *Yellow Sweater* (Fig. 457).

The sources of Henry Moore's powerful sculpture are prehistoric primordial forms, Stonehenge, ancient Etruscan tombs, pre-Columbian Mexican carvings, African and Oceanic art, the way wind and water shape trees and erode boulders, and, above all, his own fertility of formal invention. "Truth to material," Moore wrote, is "one of the first principles of art so clearly seen in primitive work. . . . The artist shows an instinctive understanding of his material, its right use and possibilities."

Moore's reclining figures are like mother earth or some fertility goddess of a forgotten cult. The curves and intricate windings rise above the human form and become a part of the heaving hills and plunging valleys of a rolling landscape. Many of Moore's figures are pierced by holes and hollows so that his sculpture has an interior as well as exterior existence. With the *Reclining Figure* at Lincoln Center (Fig. 458) in New York City, Moore expanded his

below: **458.** Henry Moore. *Reclining Figure.* 1964.
Bronze, 16 × 30 × 17′ (4.88 × 9.14 × 5.18 m).
Lincoln Center for the Performing Arts, New York.

holes by dividing the figure so he could metaphorically shape not only his monumental masses but also the space around and between. The two parts are related but separate with the head and body at one end and the legs at the other. "But between them," Moore remarked, "I am trying to make a kind of mixture of the human figure and of landscape."

The elemental simplicity of Constantin Brancusi's sculpture has its inspiration in the power of native forms and the bold innovations of the fauve painters. Brancusi's objective was to free sculpture from everything nonessential and get down to ultimate essences. One egg-shaped marble piece, for instance, is called *Beginning of the World*. Like the neoprimitives, he accepts his materials for what they are—marble for its smoothness and roughness, metal for its hardness or softness. Whatever the material, he tries to understand its nature and fulfill its potentialities without forcing it to simulate something else. "What is real," Brancusi once remarked, "is not the external form, but the essence of things."

In his *Bird in Space* (Fig. 459) Brancusi is dealing with a bronze that has such a high copper content it approaches the glossy brilliance of gold. By molding it into a graceful curvilinear form and giving it a high polish, he releases the metal medium into a form of energy. It is the abstraction of a movement, a feather in flight. Brancusi has sometimes tried to increase the sense of motion in sculpture by placing his figures on slowly rotating turntables.

Music Knowledge of non-European musical systems had likewise increased rapidly during the late 19th century. The orchestrations of Debussy and Ravel had been influenced by the strange and exotic gong sounds of the gamelan orchestras from Java, which both composers had heard at the International Exposition of 1889. By far the strongest of these new influences, however, was American jazz music, which had its beginning in New Orleans and Chicago and which was heard in Europe through the traveling bands. In *The Children's Corner* (1908), Debussy included a number called "Golliwog's Cake Walk." The title refers to a stage dance developed from the American black minstrel show and based on walking steps and figures involving a high prance. A golliwog was a grotesque black doll popular in comic strips.

Stravinsky (Fig. 460), whose music reflects many style trends, achieved the neoprimitive musical counterpart of Picasso's *Les Demoiselles d'Avignon* in

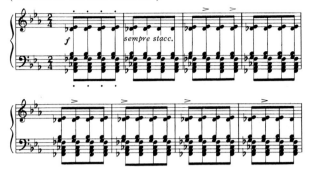

Rite of Spring   Igor Stravinsky
("Dance of the Adolescents")

the ballet *Rite of Spring,* which he wrote in Paris for the Diaghilev company in 1913. Subtitled *Scenes from Pagan Russia,* the opening "Dance of the Adolescents" (above) uses repetitive rhythms and syncopated accents somewhat like those of American jazz. The sharply angular melodies, the complex textures created by multiple rhythms, the brutal accentuations, and the geometrical movements of the dancers are a masterly realization of the spirit of savagery.

Jazz was born of the Afro-American union of the black people. They brought with them the African heritage of strong driving rhythms and choral singing. In America they encountered the Western harmonic and melodic traditions. This mixture of the memories of tribal ceremonies and more sophisticated musical conventions produced a music of such tremendous vitality that it swept all before it. Starting with the blues and ragtime in New Orleans, jazz spread to such centers as Chicago, St. Louis, and New York in the 1920s. With the various forms of rock, it now dominates popular music on both the national and international scene. So rich a source of expression was soon recognized by major composers. In Paris, Debussy, Ravel, and Darius Milhaud worked elements of jazz into their compositions. In the United States, George Gershwin, Aaron Copland, and Leonard Bernstein based a major part of their output on it. Today jazz has become an art form in its own right. As such, it is not only one of the most important contributions blacks have made to the arts, but also the unique American achievement in music.

Wild Beasts, the Bridge, Blue Rider, and Operatic Uproars

Expressionists deal with intensities of feeling rather than intensities of light. For them, the heat of creation supersedes the coldness of imitation. They present subjective reactions instead of representing objective realities and reassert the supremacy of the human imagination over the representation of nature. About the time Picasso was discovering tribal

sculpture, other groups were championing expressionism in painting as a reaction to the cool atmospheric effects and objectivity of impressionism.

Van Gogh had pointed the way with his frenzied canvases, passionate pictorial outbursts, saturated colors, and evangelical fervor. Such a painting as *Starry Night* (see Fig. 437), with the dark green flames of the cypress trees, rolling rhythms of the hills, and cosmic explosion of the Milky Way, was enough to set imaginations on fire. The barbaric splendor of Gauguin's color harmonies was seized upon as a useful means for producing lively emotional responses. The expressionists also looked more distantly at the luminous colors of medieval stained glass and the imaginative inventiveness of Romanesque sculpture. Native arts of Polynesia and Africa played their parts here too.

Fauvism   The violent color clashes and visual distortions of the French expressionistic painters earned for them the designation *les fauves* ("wild beasts"), from a chance remark by a critic at the 1905 Paris Autumn Salon who thought the room looked like a cage of wild animals. The early work of Matisse (Fig. 461), that most civilized of painters,

461. Henri Matisse. *Woman with Hat.* 1905. Oil on canvas, 32 × 23½″ (81 × 60 cm). Private collection.

462. Henri Matisse. *Blue Window.* 1911.
Oil on canvas, 4'3½" × 2'11⅝" (1.31 × .91 m).
Museum of Modern Art, New York (Abby Aldrich Rockefeller Fund).

414 The Revolutionary Period

463. Emil Nolde.
Dancing around the Golden Calf.
1910. Oil on canvas,
34¾ × 39½″ (88 × 100 cm).
Bavarian State Picture
Collection, Munich.

was so classified, though in retrospect it is difficult to understand why. If there was ever anything "wild" about Matisse, it was his reveling in brilliant color for its own sake, his resourcefulness of invention, and his quality of Oriental splendor, which made him a fauve but a fauve without ferocity.

The *Blue Window* (Fig. 462), which he painted in 1911, shows his concern with formal aesthetic problems, vibrant color harmonies, and arabesquelike decorative motifs. The picture is composed as an abstract still-life study merging subtly into a stylized landscape. The hatpins in the cushion on the left unite with the empty vase behind them; the flowers in the other vase grow into the foliage and the roof of the painter's studio outside; the Oriental idol in the center leads the eye to the vertical division of the casement window; while the lines formed by the contours of the lamp continue with those of the tree trunk in the garden. The bedroom table and its objects are thus united with the trees and sky beyond, and the interior and exterior elements become parts of one design. Depth and recession are suggested only by a slight lessening of the color intensities. In this picture, Matisse approached his dream of an "art of balance, of purity and serenity devoid of depressing subject matter."

For Matisse, expressionism did not apply to the content of his canvases or to the communication of an emotional message but rather to the entire formal management of his pictorial pattern. "Expression to my way of thinking," he once remarked, "does not consist of the passion mirrored upon a human face or betrayed by a violent gesture. The whole arrangement of my picture is expressive. . . ."

Die Brücke and Der Blaue Reiter Movements
German expressionism in the decade before World War I was mainly associated with two groups that developed simultaneously with the fauves: *Die Brücke* ("The Bridge") and *Der Blaue Reiter* ("The Blue Rider"). The Bridge was a loose association of Dresden painters who took this name because they wished to form links with all artists of the expressionistic persuasion, as well as a bridge toward the future. They acknowledged their debt to Van Gogh and Gauguin, but most especially to the Norwegian Edvard Munch (see Fig. 453).

Emil Nolde was among the most articulate members of Die Brücke, and *Dancing around the Golden Calf* (Fig. 463) was one of his many biblical subjects. Violent color dissonances of blood red and orange yellow plus distorted drawing carry his message of the primitive fury and demoniac energies of his tormented dancers.

Der Blaue Reiter was the title of a painting by Kandinsky that became the manifesto of the southern German expressionist movement. It was also the name of a book of 1912 edited by Franz Marc and Kandinsky that reproduced paintings shown at a Munich exhibit of the previous year. The volume included works by some of the French fauves and Paul Klee, in addition to those by Marc and Kandinsky. The book also contained articles on modern art, while the Viennese composer Arnold Schoenberg contributed a chapter on parallel expressionistic developments in music. Marc's art, as seen in his *Tower of Blue Horses* (Fig. 464), is one of pulsating rhythms, curvilinear design, and lyrical movement.

Kandinsky was an international figure, who first painted in his native Russia, worked in the post-impressionistic and fauve styles in Paris, and joined in founding the Blue Rider group in Munich. Works of his Blue Rider period, such as *Improvisation No. 30 (on a Warlike Theme)* (Fig. 465), still contained references to natural, human, and animal figures. In this instance, the artist mentions that he painted "subconsciously and in a state of strong tension" during 1913 when rumors of war were being heard. This, he added, explains the presence of the two cannons in the lower right and the explosive forms.

By eliminating objects and figures, dissolving material forms, and improvising according to his moods, Kandinsky reached the frontiers of nonobjective art and set the stage for the abstract expressionism of the 1940s and 1950s, in which painting is "liberated" from nature (see pp. 444–453). His *Picture with White Edge, No. 173* (Fig. 466) shows what he can express with lines, colors, and shapes. Commenting on his completely abstract paintings, Kandinsky stated that their content is "what the spectator *lives* or *feels* while under the effect of the *form and color combinations* of the picture"—which may or may not coincide with what the artist had in mind when he painted it.

Kandinsky, who published poetry, plays, and an autobiography, also recognized the affinity of his work to music. By his own account, he strove to reproduce on his canvases the "choir of colors which nature has so painfully thrust into my very soul," and he believed that a painting should be "an exact replica of some inner emotion." Works that required "an evenly sustained pitch of inner emotional uplift sometimes lasting for days" he called "compositions." Spontaneous shorter works, sketches, and watercolors that "do not last the span of a longer creative period" he termed "improvisations."

Musical Counterparts   Some of the earliest and most violent outbursts of musical expressionism are found in Richard Strauss' operas *Salome* (1905) and *Elektra* (1909), which he wrote in Munich while the Blue Rider movement was developing. Taking off

from Richard Wagner's *Tristan und Isolde,* Salome's "love death" is an operatic voyage into the realm of abnormal psychology. In *Salome,* Strauss lures his listeners with sensuous sounds and a rainbow of radiant orchestral colors, and then horrifies them with the gruesome spectacle of Salome's amorous soliloquy to the severed head of John the Baptist.

This simultaneous attraction and repulsion is bound to produce emotional excitement and elicit truly expressionistic reactions. The sensational nature of Oscar Wilde's play that Strauss adapted as his text, together with the famous "Dance of the Seven Veils," caused the opera to be banned in New York, Boston, and London. *Elektra* is a dramatically effective version of Sophocles' tragedy (as adapted by Hugo von Hofmannsthal) filled with emotional climaxes, piercing shrieks, and lurid orchestral sounds.

Arnold Schoenberg's expressionistic song cycle *Pierrot Lunaire* (1912) explores the weird world of Freudian symbolism, and in his monodrama of 1913 *Die Glückliche Hand* (*The Lucky Hand*) the dissonances of the musical score are reinforced by crescendos of colored psychedelic lights. Something of a high point is reached in Alban Berg's opera *Wozzeck* (1925), a musical dramatization of big-city low life, in which beggars, drunkards, and street girls pursue the murderer as he vainly tries to escape from his surroundings and himself.

While Wagner had worked up his climaxes over a considerable period of time, generally starting low in pitch and volume and mounting upward in an extended melodic, harmonic, and dynamic crescendo, Schoenberg and Berg compressed the process. Their music became all climax, with the extremes of low and high, soft and loud following each other suddenly by leaps instead of in a gradual progression. Dissonances with Wagner existed in chains of sequences that eventually were resolved. With Schoenberg and Berg, dissonance exists for its own sake with little or no relation to consonance, or resolution.

Cubism

Painting   Just as the discovery of the rules of linear perspective had revolutionized painting in the Florentine Renaissance, so *cubism* brought about a new way of looking at things in the 20th century. First worked out in painting, the consequences of cubism were echoed directly in sculpture and architecture, and indirectly in literature and music. A strong shove in the direction of abstraction had come from the large retrospective exhibit of Cézanne's painting held in Paris in 1907, where the young painters who saw it were struck by the artist's pictorial architecture. In the catalogue, they noted a quotation from a letter in which Cézanne remarked that

above: **464.** Franz Marc.
Tower of Blue Horses.
1912. Oil on canvas,
6′8″ × 4′3¼″ (2.03 × 1.3 m).
Formerly State Museums, Berlin.

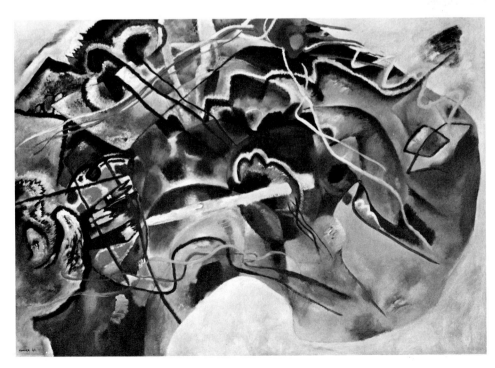

466. Wassily Kandinsky.
Picture with White Edge, No. 173.
1913. Oil on canvas,
4′7¾″ × 6′7″ (1.42 × 2.01 m).
Solomon R. Guggenheim Museum,
New York.

The 20th-Century Styles **417**

above left: 467. Georges Braque. *Oval Still Life (Le Violon).* 1914. Oil on canvas, 36⅜ × 24¾″ (92 × 63 cm). Museum of Modern Art, New York (gift of Advisory Committee).

above right: 468. Georges Braque. *The Portuguese.* 1911. Oil on canvas, 45⅞ × 32⅛″ (117 × 82 cm). Kunstmuseum, Basel.

natural objects can be reduced to the forms of the cylinder, the sphere, and the cone. Art, they reasoned, is not an imitation of nature in the usual sense but an imposition upon nature of geometrical forms derived from the human mind. As a result, cubist painting became a play of planes and angles on a flat surface. Cézanne's famous sentence, it should be pointed out, never mentioned cubes at all. His cylinders, spheres, and cones are rounded forms, presupposing curvilinear drawing; cubist drawing, on the contrary, is mainly angular and rectilinear.

The Renaissance ideal had been the complete description of a pictorial situation from a single point of view; another vantage point would imply another picture. The cubist theory of vision took into account the breaking up and discontinuity of the contemporary world view in which objects are perceived more hastily in parts rather than more leisurely as wholes.

The world, as a consequence, was seen fragmentarily and simultaneously from many points of view rather than entirely from a single viewpoint. In Picasso's *Demoiselles d'Avignon* (Fig. 455), for instance, the faces of the second and third figures from the left are seen frontally, while their noses appear in profile. Picasso and Braque, as the co-inventors of cubism, therefore undertook a new definition of pictorial space in which objects were represented simultaneously from many visual angles, in wholes or in parts, opaque and transparent. Just as the Crystal Palace (see Figs. 450, 451) had pointed the way to interpenetration of the inner and outer aspects of architectural space, so the art of the cubists undertook to move inside as well as outside an object, below and above it, in and around it.

The cubists also were convinced that pictorial space, limited as it is by the two dimensions of the flat canvas, was something quite apart from natural space. From the Renaissance onward, the accepted procedure had been to produce the illusion of three-dimensionality by some form of linear perspective derived from the principles of Euclidean geometry. Cubist painters, however, approached their canvases as architects in order to construct their pictures.

Instead of trying to create the illusion of depth, they built their pictures on the straight lines of the triangle and T-square by which they defined the planes of their surfaces.

The expression of volume, as achieved by the modeling of objects in light and shade, was also modified by the cubists, and so was the tactile feeling and structural solidity of Renaissance painting. Instead of representing objects in the round, the cubists analyzed them into their basic geometrical forms, broke them up into a series of planes, then collected, reassembled, and tilted them at will into a new but strictly pictorial pattern of interlocking, interpenetrating, and overlapping surfaces and planes.

Cubist color at the beginning was purposely confined to the rather neutral tones of gray, green, olive, and ochre. The emphasis was on design and texture, while unity was found in the picture itself rather than in the objects represented. The technique in its earliest stages can be observed in Figure 455 in the way Picasso renders the bodies of the figures on the extreme left and upper right.

Braque's *Oval Still Life* (Fig. 467) shows cubism in its more developed form after the rules had been worked out. Typical is its use of natural objects as a point of departure. Such still-life components as the table, violin, and sheet music are then broken up so that they can be reassembled in a design determined by the artist.

In their early doctrinaire stages, when the cubist painters were dogmatically trying to put their abstract doctrines into effect, cubist pictures tended to be rather cold, impersonal studies in abstract design (Fig. 468). However, modifications of this pure state began to appear, such as Picasso's *Three Musicians* (Fig. 469). The flat, two-dimensional arrangement is retained, but the bright coloration gives the canvas a gaiety not found earlier. The three masked figures sitting at a table are the same *commedia dell'arte* figures that regularly recur on Picasso's canvases, cubist or otherwise, and that come from his love of circus and theatrical performances in which clowns and other performers dress in gay carnival costumes. The figure on the left playing a violin is a Harlequin; the center one with the clarinet is a Pierrot; while the more solemn monk on the right plays what seems to be an accordion.

Sculpture   Picasso's *Woman's Head* (Fig. 470) is a translation of cubist principles into the three-dimensional medium of sculpture. It presents a geometrical analysis of the structure of the human face and emphasizes the most important planes and surfaces.

469. Pablo Picasso. *Three Musicians.* 1921.
Oil on canvas, 6'7" × 7'3¾" (2.01 × 2.23 m).
Museum of Modern Art, New York
(Mrs. Simon Guggenheim Fund).

above: 470. Pablo Picasso.
Woman's Head. c. 1909.
Bronze; height 16¼" (41 cm).
Albright-Knox Art Gallery, Buffalo.

By this process of disintegration, the head can be organized into a number of different facets, each of which can cast its own shadow and thus bring variety and a sense of movement to the composition.

The sculptures of Jacques Lipchitz are three-dimensional adaptations of cubism in its mature phase. The *Man with Mandolin* (Fig. 471) creates a repetitive pattern of rough stone textures, diagonal lines, tilted planes, irregular rectangles and triangles. From the side (Fig. 472), variants on the main theme appear, and curved shapes are accented to provide contrasts for the dominant straight lines of the design. In other works Lipchitz breaks down the traditional distinction between solids and voids, convex and concave surfaces, wholes and parts in intricate interlocking designs.

Music: Twelve-Tone System   The musical counterpart of this new concept of space is found in the breaking up of traditional tonality as well as in the search for new musical resources and mediums of expression. Stravinsky, as a strict follower of the principles of order, had said that "tonal elements become musical only by virtue of their being organized." The twelve-tone system of musical composition that Schoenberg evolved about 1915 was one of the stricter forms of tonal organization.

Schoenberg, who preferred to be called a constructor rather than a composer, begins a work by setting forth a basic row of twelve different tones.

This row can be played in normal order, upside down by melodic inversion, backward in retrograde motion, and upside down once more in retrograde inversion (see opposite, above). Furthermore, it can be presented successively in sequences or simultaneously as in the various styles of counterpoint. It can also be played in whole or in part simultaneously as in a chord or tone cluster, or it can be played serially, one note after another, as in a melody.

A row can be used either as a unit or it can be broken up into several shorter themes or motifs. It has been estimated that around half a billion different combinations are possible, which certainly is no limitation on its possibilities. The system provides the composer with a wealth of material as well as a certain freedom within an orderly framework. The twelve-tone method has generally been referred to as *atonality* (that is, without tonality), but Schoenberg preferred to call it simply a method of composing with twelve tones that are related only with one another. Tonality is thus relative rather than absolute, since there is no single tonal center. Tonality in the usual sense, however, is not excluded; rather, the system encompasses tonality and rises above it.

One of the most approachable works in the twelve-tone repertory is Alban Berg's Violin Concerto of 1935 (opposite, above). The row is a straight, ascending, vertical series without repetition that can easily be followed by the attentive ear. Skillfully contrived, the first six tones contain the four

right: 471. Jacques Lipchitz. *Man with Mandolin.* 1917. Stone, height 29¾″ (76 cm). Yale University Art Gallery, New Haven, Conn. (Collection Société Anonyme).

far right: 472. Jacques Lipchitz. *Man with Mandolin,* side view.

Violin Concerto (1935)   Alban Berg

triads of tonal music: notes one to three being the minor triad, two to four the augmented, three to five the major, four to six the diminished. A combination of four tones (one to four, two to five, and so on) forms types of seventh chords, while the top four notes make a series of whole tones resembling the scale favored by Debussy and the musical impressionists. Berg's tonal space thus includes traditional and impressionistic melody and harmony as a point of departure into nontonal or atonal music in which tones are relative only to each other rather than to a single tonal center.

Futurism and the Mechanical Style

The movement known as *futurism* was begun in Italy under the leadership of the poet and dramatist Filippo Tommaso Marinetti prior to World War I. Agreeing with Nietzsche, who said that history was the process by which the dead bury the living, Marinetti declared in his *Manifesto* of 1909 that futurism was being founded to "deliver Italy from its plague of professors, archaeologists, tourist guides and antique dealers."

The futurists wanted to destroy the museums, libraries, academies, and universities in order to make way for their particular wave of the future. "A roaring motorcar, which runs like a machine gun," they said, "is more beautiful than the winged Victory of Samothrace." Theirs was a vision of a state ruled by a mechanical superhuman mind, in which the people would be reduced to cogs in the gigantic wheel of a fully mechanized society.

Above all, the futurists projected an art for a fast-moving, machine-propelled age. They admired the motion, force, speed, and strength of mechanical forms, and in their pictures they wanted more than anything else to include the dynamic sensation of motion. A galloping horse, they said, has not four legs but twenty. Deriving his inspiration from automobiles, airplanes, trains, and machine guns, Severini painted *Armored Train* (Fig. 473) with its diagonal lines and plumes of smoke suggesting speed, while the gunfire adds the dimension of action.

Umberto Boccioni, the most distinguished futurist painter, was also the main sculptor of the group. His *Unique Forms of Continuity in Space* (Fig. 474)

above: 473. Gino Severini. *Armored Train.* 1915. Oil on canvas, 46 × 34½″ (177 × 88 cm). Richard S. Zeisler Collection, New York.

below: 474. Umberto Boccioni. *Unique Forms of Continuity in Space.* 1913. Bronze (cast 1931); height 43⅞″ (111 cm). Museum of Modern Art, New York (acquired through Lillie P. Bliss Bequest).

475. Fernand Léger. *The City.* 1919. Oil on canvas, 7'7" × 9'8½" (2.31 × 2.96 m). Philadelphia Museum of Art (A. E. Gallatin Collection).

captures the dynamics of motion in the agitated hurrying stride of a moving figure. The body itself is felt only in the implied massive muscular tensions. Boccioni's subject is not the figure, but speed as expressed in a continuum of swirling, spiraling lines and the rushing currents of air as the figure cuts its path through space.

Futurism was influential chiefly for its formation of the "mechanical style." By taking ideas from both the cubists and the futurists, Fernand Léger developed a style in which precise and neat parts all fit into an appointed place, as in *The City* (Fig. 475). Léger loved crankshafts, cylinder blocks, and pistons—all painted in gleaming primary colors. Taking Cézanne's statement about cylinders, spheres, and cones more literally than did the cubists, he drew curved forms and modeled them in light and dark. His is a world without sentiment, populated by robots whose parts are pure geometrical shapes. Human forms are introduced only for their "plastic value," and remain "purposely inexpressive." In 1924, Léger made an abstract film called *Ballet Mécanique,* in which machine forms replaced human beings and their activities.

The Musical Dimension Stravinsky, meanwhile, had composed a piece for player piano in 1917 entitled *Étude for Pianola,* and the French composer

Arthur Honegger, using the normal symphony orchestra, gave voice in 1924 to the triumphant song of the machine in a work called *Pacific 231.* Its name is a reference to that year's model of an American locomotive. The piece was designed to evoke the sounds of the railroad, complete with the powerful grinding of the wheels and the penetrating shriek of the steam whistle.

Perhaps the most successful musical realization of the mechanical style is found in the works of Edgar Varèse. Technically trained in two fields, Varèse was as much a physicist as a musician, and the titles of his works sound as if they came from a laboratory: *Intégrales, Density 2.15* (the specific gravity of the platinum of the flute for which it was composed), and *Ionization.* The last is constructed in a series of interlocking planes of sound that suggest, but are not directly imitative of, rhythms of modern city life. Varèse's expressed aim was to build a music that would face the realities of the industrial world rather than try to escape from it.

Dadaism and Surrealism

In their Paris exhibits of 1911 and 1912, the Italian Giorgio de Chirico and the Russian Marc Chagall anticipated the development of *dadaism* and *surrealism.* The latter term, in fact, was coined at that time by the French critic and playwright Guillaume Apollinaire to describe the dream fantasies, memory images, visual paradoxes, and assorted incongruities of their pictures. Chirico's dreamscape *Melancholy and Mystery of a Street* (Fig. 476) takes expressionism into an introspective world of free associations. "Everything," according to this artist, "has two aspects: the current aspect, which we see nearly always and which ordinary men see, and the ghostly and metaphysical aspect, which only rare individuals may see in moments of clairvoyance and metaphysical abstraction." His intention was to break down the barriers of childhood and adulthood, the sleeping and waking states, the unbelievable and the believable, the illogical and the logical, the fantastic and the familiar. *Melancholy and Mystery of a Street* is filled with an ominous silence and an all-pervading emptiness, made mysterious by deep perspective. Chirico's pictures are informed by Freudian psychology and furnished with sundials casting long shadows, arcaded galleries, empty vans, factories, and strange statues.

I and the Village (Fig. 477) grows out of Chagall's memories of Russia. In one of his childhood reveries he remembered the ceiling of his parents' crowded cottage suddenly becoming transparent. "Clouds and blue stars penetrated along with the smell of the fields, the stable and the roads," he writes, and "my head detaches itself gently from my body and weeps near the kitchen where fish is being prepared." In *I and the Village,* as in a rainbow-hued dream, one image is superimposed on another, the houses are topsy-turvy, the farmer going to the fields is right side up, the peasant woman upside down, and the cow seems to be experiencing a contented reverie about a milkmaid.

Dadaist Nonpictures Dadaism was the product of the disillusionment, defeatism, and insane butchery of World War I. Anguished artists felt that the civilization that had brought about such horrors should be swept away and a new beginning made. To christen their movement, these artists chose quite at random a childish word out of the French dictionary—*dada,* a child's vocalization signifying a hobbyhorse.

Dadaism, consequently, was a nihilistic movement, particularly distrustful of order and reason, a challenge to polite society and the establishment, a protest against all prevailing styles in art. It was, in

below: 476. Giorgio de Chirico.
Melancholy and Mystery of a Street. 1914.
Oil on canvas, 33½ × 27¼″ (85 × 69 cm).
Private collection.

right: 477. Marc Chagall. *I and the Village.* 1911.
Oil on canvas, 6′3⅝″ × 4′11⅝″ (1.92 × 1.51 m).
Museum of Modern Art, New York
(Mrs. Simon Guggenheim Fund).

L.H.O.O.Q.

left: 478. Marcel Duchamp. *L.H.O.O.Q.* 1919.
Rectified ready-made, pencil on reproduction of Leonardo's *Mona Lisa;*
7¾ × 4⅞″ (20 × 12 cm). Private collection.

above: 479. Salvador Dali. *Persistence of Memory.* 1931.
Oil on canvas, 9½ × 13″ (24 × 33 cm).
Museum of Modern Art, New York (anonymous gift).

fact, antiart (Fig. 478). Dada artists worked out an ism to end all isms, painted nonpictures compounded of the contents of wastebaskets, concocted nonsense for the sake of nonsense, wrote manifestoes against manifestoes, and their political expression was anarchy. Their bitter humor and attack on respected institutions, however, helped to explode hypocritical pomposities. Also, by reducing the role of art to absurdity, they cleared the air for the experiments and innovations of the postwar period. A brief movement, dadaism was absorbed into surrealism, which has appropriately been dubbed the "dadaism of the successful."

Psychic Automatism   The surrealist manifesto of 1924 proclaimed that the style was based on "pure psychic automatism by means of which one sets out to express, verbally, in writing or in any other manner, the real functioning of thought without any control by reason or any aesthetic or moral preoccupation." Surrealism, literally "superrealism," implies a greater reality underlying the world of appearances, an illogical, subconscious dream world beyond the logical, conscious, physical one. Members of the group believed in the superior reality of the dream to the waking state, of fantasy to reason, of the subconscious to the conscious. André Breton, author of the manifesto, also spoke of the "convulsive beauty" of dreams, and the surrealist poet Paul Éluard said, "a poem should be the debacle [or ruination] of the intellectual."

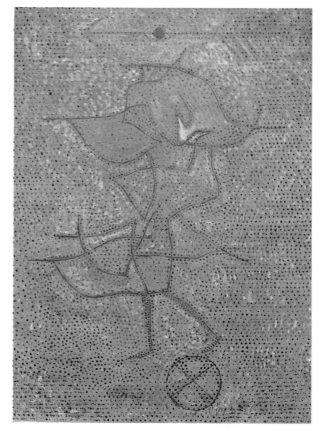

above: 480. Paul Klee. *Diana.* 1932.
Oil on wood, 31½ × 24″ (80 × 61 cm). Private collection.

481. Joan Miró. *Personages with Star.* 1933. Oil on canvas, 6′6¼″ × 8′1½″ (1.99 × 2.48 m). Art Institute of Chicago (gift of Mr. and Mrs. Maurice E. Culberg).

The painter Salvador Dali associated himself with the group in 1929 and became one of its leading advocates. He described his pictures as "handpainted dream photographs" and adorned them with symbols of various phobias, delusions, complexes, and other trappings of abnormal psychology. Like Chirico and Chagall, Dali was haunted by the mystery of time, and his *Persistence of Memory* (Fig. 479) suggests images of evolutionary, geological, and archaeological as well as dream time.

Today Paul Klee is generally accepted as one of the most significant pictorial talents of the 20th century. Such pictures as *Diana* (Fig. 480) have caused many to dismiss him with a shrug, a scoff, or a smile. His disarming childlike innocence, however, is a highly deceptive simplicity and usually masks infinitely subtle meaning. His inventiveness outdoes even Picasso. He can delight the eye, tickle the fancy, or repel the observer with images straight out of nightmares. *Apparatus for Magnetic Treatment of Plants, Twittering Machine, A Cookie Picture, Moonplay, Idol for Housecats, Child Consecrated to Suffering, A Phantom Breaks Up*—so the titles run.

The symbolism in Klee's *Diana* will show the extraordinary complexity of Klee's art. The title identifies the figure as the mythical goddess of the hunt, while the arrow is equipped magically with an eye to ensure unerring accuracy. The broken contours of Diana's body suggest hurried flight through space, and the wheel under the goddess' foot is derived from Romanesque sculpture where it signified

miraculous transportation. The color and surface treatment recall impressionism and Seurat's pointillism (see Fig. 435).

Klee consciously set out to look at the world through the eyes of a child in order to achieve a spontaneity untroubled by reason. "I want to be as though new-born, knowing nothing," as he put it. With Klee, as with Freud and St. Paul, the child was father of the man. By experimenting with hypnotic suggestion and *psychic automatism,* a technique that allowed the artist's hand to move spontaneously and at random, laying down on paper or canvas lines and patterns in no way formed by reason or logic, he gave his drawings the casual quality of doodles or the impulsiveness of improvisations. His mastery of line was so complete, however, that his work should never be confused with carelessness. By sticking mainly to small forms and to the techniques of watercolor and ink, pencil and crayon, he produced pictures with an element of genial humor that is notably missing in so much of modern art.

Joan Miró, like Klee, attempted an art of pure imagination existing outside logic or reason. In *Personages with Star* (Fig. 481) he used the technique of automatic drawing in a trancelike state and produced a painting that shows the influence of Kandinsky (Fig. 466). While much of surrealism is preoccupied with the morbid and the abnormal, Miró lightens his fantasies with whimsy. His pictures have such titles as *Persons Magnetized by the Stars Walking on the Music of a Furrowed Landscape.* They teem

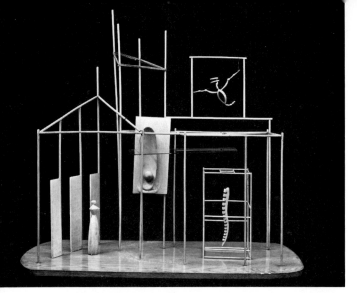

482. Alberto Giacometti. *Palace at 4 a.m.* 1932–33.
Wood, glass, wire, and string;
25 × 28¼ × 15¾″ (64 × 72 × 40 cm).
Museum of Modern Art, New York (purchase).

with abstract insects that buzz silently and geometrical worms that squirm statically.

Giacometti represents surrealism's sculptural dimension (see Fig. 3). His *Palace at 4 a.m.* (Fig. 482) uses a geometrical cagelike framework containing spectral and skeletal forms. The phantom figures in their interpenetrating open and closed spaces produce a haunting sensation of human isolation.

Literary and Musical Parallels   Significant parallels to surrealism in the fields of literature and music can be cited. For instance, James Joyce and Gertrude Stein tried to establish a method for automatic writing as a way to tap the reservoir of the subconscious mind. The result was the stream-of-consciousness technique, notably exemplified in Joyce's *Ulysses* (1922). In this work Joyce deals with the thoughts, feelings, and spiritual states of his characters without regard to logical argument or chronological or narrative sequence. His style has the timelessness of dreams.

The more irreverent and humorous tendencies of surrealist painting have their musical parallels in such compositions as Erik Satie's three piano pieces of 1913. Entitled *Desiccated Embryos,* they have sarcastic expression marks, such as that which calls upon the pianist to play a melody "like a nightingale with a toothache." There is also the biting satire of Prokofiev's fairy-tale opera *Love of Three Oranges* (1921) and the weird symbolism of Béla Bartók's legend-based opera *Bluebeard's Castle* (1922).

Paul Klee's world of childhood fantasy finds a charming lyrical counterpart in Maurice Ravel's opera *The Child and the Sorceries* (*L'Enfant et les Sortilèges*) of 1925. In Colette's text, a child breaks

some bric-a-brac and toys in a temper tantrum. In a dream sequence, the objects come to life to seek revenge. A Wedgewood teapot and a china cup, appropriately enough, carry on a conversation in broken English while dancing a fox-trot; a little old man pops up out of nowhere and sings multiplication tables and story problems with wrong answers; two cats sing a hilarious mewing duet; and all that is left of the torn picture of the fairy princess in the story book is "a golden hair and the debris of a dream." Ravel's clever orchestration adds whistles, wood blocks, and friction instruments such as cheese graters to the usual ones for a full range of effects.

Neoclassical Interlude

No century would be complete without its bow before the shrines of Greece and Rome. Just as the Renaissance and the 18th and 19th centuries did, so the 20th century also has its neoclassicism. While works with classical references abound in the present century, the neoclassic movement came into sharpest focus in the 1920s. The comparative calm before the storm of World War I had been broken by the emotional extremes of pictorial expressionism and such neoprimitive outbursts as Stravinsky's *Rite of Spring.* In the aftermath of war, order and clarity seemed more important than violent expression, as did the human figure, following the abstractions of cubism.

Multimedia Productions   In 1917, Picasso had made a trip to Italy where he was impressed by the Pompeian wall paintings and stimulated by meetings in Rome with Stravinsky and Sergei Diaghilev, who were there with the latter's Russian ballet company. One direct result was their three-way collaboration on a ballet with song called *Pulcinella,* which was first performed in Paris in 1920. Stravinsky's score was based on the form of the classical dance suite of the early 18th century with music adapted from Pergolesi. Picasso's costumes were designed in the manner of the stylized Pierrot and Harlequin *commedia dell'arte* figures, while his scenery included a backdrop filled with angular distortions showing a street in Naples with a view of the bay and a moonlit Mt. Vesuvius.

In 1922, an adaptation of Sophocles' *Antigone* by Jean Cocteau was mounted in Paris. Picasso designed the scenery and masks, while the incidental music for harp and oboe was supplied by Arthur Honegger. An opera called *The Eumenides* by Darius Milhaud, based on Paul Claudel's translation of the tragedy by Aeschylus, was written in the same year. *Mercury* was the title of still another ballet brought out by the Diaghilev company in 1924, with music by Erik Satie and costumes and scenery by Picasso.

Three years later, Stravinsky completed his opera-oratorio *Oedipus Rex.* Diaghilev again was the producer, and Jean Cocteau's text, based on Sophocles' tragedy, was translated into Latin so that it would be in a "petrified" language and thus reduced to mere syllabic material. The motionless stance of the actors was intended to make them as static as Greek columns, and the chorus was placed behind a low relief where only their heads were visible. Such collaborative productions continued occasionally throughout the 1930s when Stravinsky was found working with André Gide on a work for orchestra, chorus, and tenor called *Persephone* (1934).

Painting and Sculpture   Picasso's pictures in the 1920s, such as the *Three Graces* (Fig. 483), also reflect this neoclassicism and are characterized by elegance of line, sculpturesque modeling of bodies, and reduction of pictorial elements to the barest essentials. Others, like *Pipes of Pan* (Fig. 484), are beach scenes in which the figures appear statuesquely against geometrically organized backgrounds and chaste colors of white and blue.

While Picasso's painting took another turn after the *Three Graces,* his many book illustrations continued to show classical influences. Picasso had long admired the linear technique of Ingres (see Figs. 400, 426), and the incisive carvings of Greco-Roman sculptors. Even in such an austere medium as etching, his illustrations for a new edition of Ovid's *Metamorphoses* (1930) and for Gilbert Seldes' version of Aristophanes' *Lysistrata* (1934) show his capacity for effective expression with minimal means (Fig. 485).

In the neoclassical interlude, the statues of Maillol and Despiau reassert the expressive importance of

above: 483. Pablo Picasso. *Three Graces.* 1924. Oil and charcoal on canvas, 6'6⅞" × 4'11" (2 × 1.5 m). Collection the artist's estate.
below left: 484. Pablo Picasso. *Pipes of Pan.* 1923. Oil on canvas, 6'8½" × 5'8⅝" (2.04 × 1.74 m). Collection the artist's estate.
below right: 485. Pablo Picasso. *The Love of Jupiter and Semele,* Plate 6 for Ovid's *Metamorphoses* (Lausanne: Albert Skira, 1931). Etching, 12⅞" × 10⅛" (33 × 26 cm). Museum of Modern Art, New York (Louis E. Stern Collection).

the nude figure both in the round and in relief. Maillol's stable, calm figures are a welcome sight in an agitated century. His neoclassicism is creative not imitative, free not academic. The *Torso of Venus* (Fig. 486) with its Praxitelean curve and stance (see Fig. 56), its antiquity and modernity, achieves a quiet monumentality that is both universal and timeless.

The Literary Dimension One of the most consistent patterns of contemporary literature, especially in France, is the reinterpretation of Greek myths in highly sophisticated terms as a subtle device for pointing out modern moralistic or political parallels. This tendency runs regularly through the works of André Gide from his early *Prometheus Drops His Chains* (1899) to his autobiographical story *Theseus* (1946). It can also be found in Franz Werfel's antiwar play *The Trojan Women* (1914) and in Jean Paul Sartre's *The Flies* (1943). The latter was staged in Paris during the Nazi occupation, and the reference to the plague of flies that sucked Orestes' blood in Aristophanes' bitter comedy could have escaped no one.

Poets have sometimes found classical subjects a convenient way of leaving their works in a fragmentary state like antique ruins. Paul Ambroise Valéry's trilogy of 1922, for instance, contains a poem called *Fragments of Narcissus*. T. S. Eliot's *Sweeney Agonistes* (1932), in which the grandeur of the past is contrasted with the ordinariness of the present, likewise is incomplete and bears the subtitle *Fragments of an Aristophanic Melodrama*. Freud's use of the names of characters from Greek literature—Oedipus, Electra, Narcissus—as symbols of recurrent subconscious drives also found its way into literature.

James Joyce's novels *A Portrait of the Artist as a Young Man* (1916) and *Ulysses* (1922) use timeless classical myths as a way of placing characters in a broader human frame of reference, but the logic and clarity of Greek forms is consciously avoided. The author's admitted inspiration for *Ulysses* was Homer's *Odyssey*. With his adoption of the stream-of-consciousness technique, the classical molds became convenient devices to hold the hazy, dreamlike sequences in some semblance of unity. They also provide bewildered readers with a few recognizable straws to grasp when they begin to founder on the sea of such an unfamiliar style of writing.

The entire action of *Ulysses* occurs in Dublin in a single 24-hour period to preserve the classical unities of place and time. The plot concerns a wanderer who voyages through the terrors and temptations of the maze of Dublin's streets while on his way home to his wife and son. This is reminiscent of Odysseus' search for Penelope and Telemachus. In the larger sense, *Ulysses* is concerned with the human eternal search for a meaning for life. In Joyce's manuscript, the titles of chapters were based on quotations from the *Odyssey,* but these were omitted when it was printed. Most of the work is obscure, but the parallel with the heroic past helps to heighten the squalid picture of the present that the novelist paints.

Social Realism

Social realism represents the artist's protest against the intolerable conditions that beset humanity. In the tradition of Goya (Fig. 399), Hogarth (Figs. 381, 382), and Daumier (Fig. 427), many contemporary painters have championed the cause of the weak against the strong, the poor against the rich, the oppressed against their oppressors, of righteousness against human folly. They have explored the dregs of society, the human rubbish of skid row, and the ugliness of the lower depths, thus proving that the paint brush and the pen are often mightier than the sword.

This will be the last time, little father! (Fig. 487) is a print by Georges Rouault that depicts the heartbreaking farewell of a son as he leaves for war and almost certain death. Rouault's art is visionary, but his tragic clowns, comical lawyers, static acrobats, and active landscapes reveal his broad compassion for and passionate protests against human exploitation and degradation. His pictures often mirror the grimacing masks of those who presume to sit in judgment on their fellows, and the insensitive faces of people in positions of power who are indifferent to human suffering. His series of 100 etchings and aquatints for two projected portfolios entitled *Miserere* (*Have Mercy on Us*) and *Guerre* (*War*), with text by a literary friend, occupied him intermittently in the years following World War I. Though the portfolios as such were never published, 58 prints have

486. Aristide Maillol. *Torso of Venus.* 1925. Bronze, height 45″ (114 cm). Courtesy Galerie Dina Vierny, Paris.

been issued separately. The title page of the war volume in which Figure 487 was to have appeared reads: "They Have Ruined Even the Ruins."

José Clemente Orozco, one of the Mexican muralists deeply involved in his country's revolution, identified himself with the struggle of the illiterate masses as they tried to break the chains of their landowning and capitalist exploiters. His grim satire also extends to the academic community as pictured in *Gods of the Modern World* (Fig. 488). This macabre comment on the sterility of higher education depicts a skeleton giving birth, while one professor acts as a midwife and others witness the ghastly event.

The New York artist Ben Shahn was an ardent champion of minority groups and the eloquent portrayer of the anonymous city dweller who has lost the sense of community identity. The stark setting and grim faces of *Miners' Wives* (Fig. 489) express the anxiety, fear, and desolation of the families of men connected with a hazardous occupation. Humanity's inhumanity is the general theme, as Shahn pleads the cause of the victims of social injustice.

above: 487. Georges Rouault.
This will be the last time, little father!
Plate 36 of *Miserere* series. 1927.
Aquatint, drypoint, and roulette over
heliogravure, printed in black;
$23\frac{3}{8} \times 17''$ (59 × 43 cm).
Museum of Modern Art, New York
(gift of the artist).

above right: 488. José Clemente Orozco.
Gods of the Modern World. 1932–34. Fresco.
Dartmouth College, Hanover, N.H.
(by permission of the Trustees).

right: 489. Ben Shahn. *Miners' Wives.* 1948.
Egg tempera on board, 4 × 3′ (1.22 × .91 m).
Philadelphia Museum of Art
(gift of Wright S. Ludington).

429

Bitter satires on the junglelike conditions of urban life and the dismal effects of mass media on the popular mind preoccupy the English painter Francis Bacon. In his *Painting* (Fig. 490), subtitled *The Butcher,* he speaks with the vocabulary of expressionism and surrealism as he depicts his nightmarish apparition. Less bitter but nonetheless poignantly expressive are Andrew Wyeth's muted evocations of the social decay and unfulfilled aspirations of life on the American scene (Fig. 491).

Picasso's Guernica   Picasso's *Guernica* (Fig. 492) is at once the most monumental and comprehensive statement of social realism and a dramatic manifesto against the brutality of war. Picasso used a combination of expressionist and abstract techniques as a violent protest against a cruel and inhuman act by modern barbarians. What lighted the fuse that set off this pictorial explosion of death and terror was the first saturation air raid of the century. This horrible "experiment" by the German air force was carried out against the defenseless Basque town of Guernica and was an incident in General Franco's successful rebellion against the legally elected government of the Spanish Republic.

Picasso, a loyalist, was in Paris with the commission to paint a mural for the Spanish pavilion of the World's Fair of 1937. Just two days after the news of the bombing reached Paris, he began work. The huge canvas, accomplished in a matter of weeks, took up one wall of the Spanish pavilion, where it made an unforgettable impression on the thousands who saw it. The attention it attracted and the measure of understanding given to it have been altogether in proportion to the value of *Guernica* as one of the century's most important paintings.

Guernica, a picture in the great tradition of historical painting, is one of those rare incidents of the

490. Francis Bacon. *Painting* (*The Butcher*). 1946. Oil and tempera on canvas, 6′6″ × 4′4″ (1.98 × 1.32 m). Museum of Modern Art, New York (purchase).

491. Andrew Wyeth. *Mother Archie's Church.* 1945. Egg tempera on panel, 1′11″ × 4′ (.64 × 1.22 m). Addison Gallery of American Art, Phillips Academy, Andover, Mass.

right artist painting the right picture at the right time. Its purpose was frankly propagandistic; its intent, to horrify. But besides recalling the apocalyptic visions of Romanesque Last Judgments (see Fig. 154), it is a work of social protest in the manner of those 19th-century masters of irony Goya and Daumier. The principal action begins in the lower right, where a woman dashes forward, her hands in an attitude of despair. The triangular composition then mounts to its apex at the point where the lamp, the horse's head, and the eye of day (with the electric bulb of night as its pupil) come together. From this climax, the viewer's eye moves downward to the head of the dismembered warrior at the lower left.

According to Picasso, *Guernica* is allegorical, and he has explained some of the symbolism. The horse with the spear in its back, the inevitable victim of bullfights, signifies victimized humanity overwhelmed by brute force. The motif of the shrieking mouth is repeated in that of the screaming woman with her dead child at the left, the face of the soldier below, and the victim of the flames at the right. The bull, standing for brutality, is the only triumphant figure in this symbolic struggle between the forces of darkness and those of light, between barbarism and civilization. Above, an arm reaches forward to hold the lamp of truth over the whole gruesome scene. Amid the general havoc and gloom the artist sounds one soft note of optimism. Above the victim's severed arm and broken sword in the bottom center is a tiny plant in bloom to signify the force of renewal.

Guernica appeared at a time when many earlier pictorial experiments could be combined. It employs all the exaggerations, distortions, and shock techniques developed by expressionistic drawing, but it omits ghastly coloration in favor of the somber shades of mourning—black, white, and gradations of gray. The abstract design, the overlapping planes on a two-dimensional surface, and the absence of modeling all derive from cubism. So also does the simultaneous principle of the day-and-night symbol; the head of the bull, which is seen both from the front and the side at the same time; and the sensation of inner and outer space by which the observer is at once both inside and outside the burning buildings. The elongation of the heads to express headlong motion coincides with the photography of movement made with stroboscopic light. The screaming, nightmarish subject matter is derived from that of expressionism.

Picasso painted so rapidly and with such large output that he often had difficulty resisting the temptations of his own ready technique. Consequently, much of his work is uneven. Here, however, after making one hundred sketches, he worked in a disciplined and selective manner that shows him in complete command of his medium. Thus, his successful synthesis in *Guernica* of so many of these divergent 20th-century techniques, as well as the vivid dramatization of his subject, has given powerful expression to the chaos and conflicts of this century.

Nonobjectivism

Abstractionism was worked out to its logical geometrical conclusion by Piet Mondrian just as expressionism had reached its point of pure abstraction in the work of Kandinsky. The pictures of these two artists are, of course, poles apart. Both artists, however, are *nonobjective* in that they are nonfigurative and nonrepresentational and that the pictorial content of their canvases bears no reference to recogniz-

492. Pablo Picasso. *Guernica.* 1937.
Oil on canvas, 11'5½" × 25'5¾" (3.49 × 7.77 m).
On extended loan to Museum of Modern Art, New York, from the artist's estate.

able objects or to anything outside the actual pictures. All subject matter, all associational meanings, are carefully avoided. The picture with its lines, shapes, and colors is its own referent.

Mondrian's art, like Kandinsky's, evolved gradually from the concrete to the abstract. In his early years, Mondrian painted landscapes and quiet interior scenes in the tradition of his native Holland, and his later style, though completely abstract, owes much to the cool geometrical precision of his great predecessor Vermeer (see Figs. 347–350). Mondrian could well be describing his *New York City* (Fig. 493) when he wrote: "The new style will spring from the metropolis." He delighted in the crisscross patterns of city streets, architects' blueprints, gaunt structural steel skeletons of skyscrapers under construction, and simple faces of buildings of the international architectural style (see Figs. 500, 501).

The new art, he continued, would not be individual, but collective, impersonal, and international. All references to the "primitive animal nature of man" should be rigidly excluded in order to reveal "true human nature" through an art of "balance, unity, and stability." This objective he strove to realize by using "only a single neutral form: the rectangular

area in varying dimensions." His colors are likewise abstract—black lines of various widths against white backgrounds, relieved occasionally by a primary color "climax"—red, blue, or yellow—in as pure a state as possible.

In Mondrian's opinion, a work of art should be "constructed," and he approached a canvas with all the objectivity of a draftsman making a blueprint. The result of this pictorial engineering is the series of pure, two-dimensional studies of space for which he is best known. His visual patterns have a repose that is based on a precise balance of horizontal and vertical elements, and they are clean to the point of being antiseptic. His pictures are far more complex than they may seem to the casual eye. They have had a great influence on modern design, especially of advertising layouts, posters, and rugs.

Architecture

More than any of the other 20th-century arts, architecture has shown a greater sense of responsibility, and achieved a wider popular acceptance. A building, unlike a painting, has to stand up; unlike a sculptural group, it must fulfill some practical purpose. Experi-

493. Piet Mondrian *New York City*. 1942. Oil on canvas, 12 × 10′ (3.66 × 3.05 m). Courtesy Sidney Janis Gallery, New York.

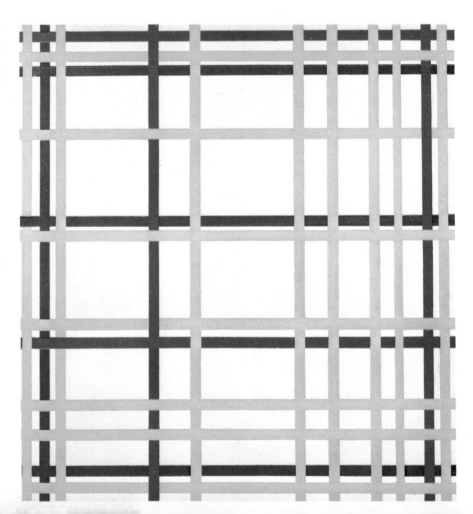

mental architecture is possible, but the discipline of sound engineering has kept architects from some of the wilder flights of fancy seen in painting, sculpture, literature, and music. Today's architect is no mere stonemason but an engineer of society, a philosopher, a poet and idealist, as well as a practical builder.

The needs of a complex, modern, urbanized society and the availability of new materials and structural methods have made a new architecture both possible and necessary. *Ferroconcrete,* or cement reinforced by embedding wire mesh or iron rods in it, leads the procession of new materials. It has the strength of both steel and stone without their weaknesses or expense; it can span broader spaces than can marble, and carry the weight of steel. The *cantilever*—the extension of a slab or beam horizontally into space beyond its supporting post—is an ancient principle that had to await ferroconcrete.

Frank Lloyd Wright on one side and Walter Gropius with Le Corbusier on the other were the leaders of two opposing schools of architectural thought. Wright spoke as a romantic in terms of the union of nature and human beings that could be realized through his "organic architecture." Gropius and Corbusier were champions of the international style and its emphasis on building for the machine age.

Organic Architecture: Sullivan and Wright

Louis Sullivan's slogan "form follows function" is subject to a variety of interpretations, but the line of thought it provoked led to an important reevaluation of architectural forms in relation to human activities. It also led to a reexamination of basic architectural methods, materials, and purposes. Sullivan's disciple Frank Lloyd Wright, and the architects identified with the international style, accepted the principle that stone should behave like stone, wood like wood, and steel like steel, and that the design should be modified by the materials used. Both also pointed to the absurdity of people catching trains in Roman baths, working in Renaissance office buildings, banking money in Doric temples, living in Tudor houses, and going to Gothic churches. The criterion for a successful building was no longer what it looked like, but how well it fulfilled its purpose.

The skyscraper, among the earliest and boldest instances of modern architecture, was made possible by steel-skeleton construction and the elevator. It came out of the American Middle West as an answer to the need for commercial centralization. In the hands of Louis Sullivan, who put up the Wainwright Building in St. Louis in 1891 (Fig. 494), the skyscraper was a "proud and soaring thing," reflecting the pride of business people in their work, as well as

above: **494.** Louis Sullivan. Wainwright Building, St. Louis. 1890–91.

below: **495.** Frank Lloyd Wright. Price Tower, Bartlesville, Okla. 1953.

496. Frank Lloyd Wright. "Falling Water" (Kaufmann House), Bear Run, Pa. 1936–37. Reinforced concrete and stone; depth 64′ (19.51), width 62′ (18.9 m).

nation. The principal drawback to skyscrapers, however, is their contribution to congestion. From a human standpoint, their value has thus far been less spectacular than their engineering.

Wright, picking up where Sullivan left off, saw both the advantages and drawbacks of the skyscraper. With characteristic romanticism, he spoke of his buildings in naturalistic terms. His eighteen-story skyscraper in Bartlesville, Oklahoma, has a "taproot" foundation, grows upward like a tree, with its floors and walls cantilevered outward like branches from its central trunk (Fig. 495).

Skyscrapers, Wright was convinced, did not belong in already congested cities but out in the open, where they could breathe and have room to cast decent shadows. Wright's philosophy of architecture was that of a liberating force, and his creative freedom allowed for decorative motifs to grow organically out of his basic designs, the relations of masses to voids, the arrangement of windows and doors, the colors and grains of wood, and the textures of stone. Through his masterly interrelations, space for living and working comes to life and breathes.

The architect, according to Frank Lloyd Wright, is the poet who imagines the ideal life and fashions the forms, shapes, and spaces that guide men and women to live it. His organic architecture was based on the unity of site, structure, and decoration, and the early houses he built in and around Chicago were his first claim to fame. For him a dwelling had to be a home for the human spirit as well as for the human body. A house, he thought, should express warmth, protection, and seclusion. The heart of the home,

according to Wright, is the hearth in the form of a central fireplace, and all the other rooms should be built around this. Interior space, moreover, should not confine but expand without interruption from the inside out to bring people closer to nature.

"Falling Water" (Fig. 496), which Wright built for Edgar J. Kaufmann at Bear Run, Pennsylvania, is an expressive combination of reinforced concrete material, cantilevered construction, and a dramatic site. The house comes close to realizing Wright's ideal of a structure growing organically out of its site.

In this case, Wright's client loved the waterfall and wanted to live near it. "Falling Water" therefore embraces both the stream and the waterfall. Wright accomplished this by means of the cantilevered slabs that project from the rock embankment on which they rest and which carry the living space outward over the water itself. The ledge of natural rock under the water is paralleled by the concrete shelf above, while the jutting slab on top is placed at right angles to repeat the direction of the moving water. The site as well as the building is a series of terraces reaching outward from a stone core.

The interior of "Falling Water" is one large room opening out onto the terraces and porches. The horizontal planes of these porches, in turn, are balanced by the vertical volumes of the fireplace. The local stone used in this chimney mass is related both in color and texture to the natural rock of the river bank. The cantilevering here allows the several stories the independence to develop their own fluid floor plans. As on the outside, the inside space radiates around the central core, with advancing and receding areas promoting what Wright called the "freedom of interior and exterior occupation."

Art Deco

Before Wright's organic architecture and the bland functionalism of the international style became widely accepted, the dominant approach of the 1920s and 1930s was what these architects labeled scornfully as "modernistic." In the 1970s this movement has become upgraded and is called *art deco*. The term derives from the title of a Paris exhibit of 1925, *Exposition des Arts Décoratifs.*

Art deco was a reflection of the jazz age of the roaring 1920s and more sober 1930s when it was the dominant style particularly in the United States. This was an art glorifying the machine and inspired by the speed of the automobile and airplane. It found expression in everything from soaring skyscrapers and luxury ocean liners, to streamlined statuettes, overstuffed furniture, jukebox designs, radio cabinets, toasters, and other kitchen gadgetry. Art deco was motivated by the vibrant energy released at the end of World War I, a faith in mechanized modernity, and a joy in such new materials as glass, aluminum, polished steel, and shiny chrome.

The most extravagant forms of art deco were found in the department stores and particularly in the movie houses of the period. These "people's palaces" were the stuff dreams were made on. Here could be found release from drudgery, boredom, and the humdrum activities of daily life. Audiences could revel in romances played by beautiful screen idols, hear the peals from the mighty Wurlitzer organs, and relax to the luxuriant sounds of real symphony orchestras that rose up on stage elevators as they played hit tunes from Broadway musicals.

The architecture of these theaters was eclecticism gone wild—fantastic mixtures inspired by the *Arabian Nights,* Persian gardens, Egyptian temples, and Chinese pagodas. There were imaginary recreations of King Solomon's temple, Babylonian towers, Moslem mosques with minarets, and jungle Mayan pyramids. All were designed for spectacular entertainment in delightfully gaudy interiors complete with spacious lobbies, winding staircases, grandiose murals, glittering chandeliers, and a general profusion of ornamentation defying description.

There were also the less ornate and more enduring architectural masterpieces such as the Chrysler Building (Fig. 497), long the symbol of New York City before the Empire State Building (also in art deco style) eclipsed it in height and size. It was finished in 1930 by its designer, William van Alen, who was called the "Ziegfeld of architecture." As the structure rises well over 1000 feet (304 meters), there is a pause at the thirtieth floor for a brick frieze featuring an abstract pattern that suggests automobiles with decorative hubcaps and huge winged radiator caps serving as gargoyles (Fig. 498). The culmination of the structure is the familiar stainless-steel sunburst tower, with its overlapping projections pierced by sharply pointed triangular windows, which terminates in a soaring cadmium-plated spire.

The rich art deco interior is equally remarkable with its three-story entrance hall leading to a triangular lobby of African marble with stainless-steel trim. Each detail participates in this exuberant design from the elevator doors (Fig. 499) to the marble

below: 497. William Van Alen. Chrysler Building, New York. 1930. Height 1048′ (319.43 m).

right: 498. Chrysler Building, detail of 30th-floor frieze.

below right: 499. Chrysler Building, elevator door.

floors. Even the elevator cabs with their inlaid wood and intricately detailed geometric patterns become perfectly appointed small art deco rooms.

There is now no doubt that art deco was the universally popular style of the time. Hence the heated attacks and harsh criticism heaped upon it by Wright and the architects of the international style. The major figures of this opposition—Wright, Gropius, Le Corbusier, and Miës van der Rohe—were also the leading intellectuals, social philosophers, and articulate critics for the attack. They fussed and fumed about what they saw as the bastard modernistic approach. The international stylists insisted on a functional and structural architecture free of decoration. They sniffed at art deco artists as embroiderers and lace makers and theorized that lack of decoration was a sign of spiritual strength. If there was to be decoration at all, it should not be applied to surfaces; rather, it must grow out of the materials and functions of the design itself.

In the 1970s, however, art deco has been favorably reappraised partly as a reaction to the endless spread of steel-and-glass boxes, nude buildings, and naked houses. Contemporary designers see that the urge for ornament is universal and cannot be repressed. They now ask, "Who is Walter Gropius to tell us that decoration is a crime and in bad taste?"

International Style: *Gropius and Le Corbusier*

The international style crystallized in Germany with the work of Walter Gropius and Ludwig Miës van der Rohe, in France with Le Corbusier, and in the Netherlands with J. J. P. Oud. When Gropius was commissioned to reorganize a German art school after World War I, he renamed it the *Bauhaus* ("Building Institute") and made it a technical school of design with special emphasis on the industrial arts and the study of modern materials and methods. For the plant he brought together the complex of studios, machine shops, administrative offices, and professors' houses into a single masterly group of interlocking and interrelated cubes. Smaller units had bland Mondrianlike façades; others, like the Machine Shop (Fig. 500), were open structures with glass-curtain walls.

As a champion of the international style, Gropius started with the open box as the basic unit of space, varied its volume, and grouped several in a related pattern of cubes. The Machine Shop shows how the building is treated as an open volume rather than as a closed mass. By the method of cantilevering, Gropius allowed the building to project several feet outward over its supporting piers. The horizontal emphasis thus established is then carried out in the concrete base and repeated at the roof level.

Between the parallel lines of the base and roof hang the glass-curtain walls that bear no structural weight. The transparency permits detail, such as the spiral staircase and the skeletal structure of the interior, to remain open and visible from the exterior. By thus allowing the interior and exterior of the building to be seen at the same time, Gropius achieved the architectural equivalent of the cubist painters, who presented simultaneously the front view and profile of a human face or several sides of an object. The Bauhaus group has proved to be one of the most influential buildings of its decade.

The Bauhaus exploration of materials and industrial processes led to many new approaches in printing, pottery, metalwork, weaving, and stagecraft. Students were taught never to forget the purposes their products were designed to serve. A chair, in other words, was made to sit in, a lamp to give efficient lighting. As a result, the Bauhaus became the fountainhead of the new industrial design. Such innovations as tubular steel chairs, indirect lighting fixtures, and streamlined appliances were accepted for mass production and are parts of every household today. In order to counterbalance the utilitarian side, however, Gropius added the painters Kandinsky, Klee, and Lyonel Feininger to his distinguished faculty to uphold the expressive and creative aspects of drawing and painting. Mondrian and the architect Miës van der Rohe also maintained close relations with the Bauhaus.

Le Corbusier, unlike Wright who had a naturalistic approach, thought of houses variously as machines for living, containers for families, extensions of public services. His commissions included a range from country villas to entire cities, private dwellings to apartment blocks, temporary exposition structures

500. Walter Gropius. Bauhaus Machine Shop, Dessau, Germany. 1925–26. Length 167′ (50.9 m), width 49′ (14.94 m).

501. Le Corbusier. L'Unité d'Habitation, Marseilles. 1947–52. Length 550′ (167.64 m), width 79′ (24.08 m), height 184′ (56.08 m).

to pilgrimage churches. For him, architecture was the masterly and magnificent play of masses brought together in the light. Cubes, cones, spheres, cylinders, pyramids, he said, are the great primary forms that reveal themselves in sun and shadow. While Wright's buildings expressed harmony with nature, Le Corbusier raised his structures on piers to assert the "independence of things human." Wright, rather tartly, called Le Corbusier's cubistic buildings "boxes on stilts."

Le Corbusier's L'Unité d'Habitation (Union for Living) is an apartment house in Marseilles that brings together in a single structure a community of 1600 persons with complete facilities for living, shopping, and recreation (Fig. 501). Remembering the dismal mass dwellings in Paris, which he called "disastrous architectural fortifications where thousands of families never see the sun," he set out to build apartments vibrating with color, light, and air.

To achieve his goal, Le Corbusier cantilevered a gigantic structure of rough-textured concrete over a double row of massive supports called pylons. The outside staircase is both functional and decorative in sculpturesque fashion. Set at an oblique angle to the horizontal axis, it relieves the rectangular masses with its rising motion.

The exterior is honeycombed with shallow balconies, which have sunbreaks tinted in many colors on the inner sides. These sunbreaks proved so effective in protecting the tall living rooms from the sun's glare that they have since become architectural clichés in warm climates. Each floor has duplex apartments served by a skip-stop elevator system. At the halfway point an entire floor is allotted to shops, while a day school for children, a gymnasium, and a theater are found at the roof level.

Ideas: Relativism

The only thing that is permanent is change. This seeming contradiction points at the very heart of 20th-century thought, whether expressed in philosophical, scientific, or aesthetic terms. No fixed unchanging absolute can possibly provide a satisfactory view of the moving world of today. Even the age-old principles of mathematics can no longer be regarded as eternal truths but, like art, as artificial expressions relative to the time and place of their creation. So also the firmest articles of religious faiths and political doctrines are subject to far more commentary and modification from time to time than their followers would care to admit.

The shift from a stable world order to the present dynamic view of the universe, which began with Copernicus and Galileo, has swept all before it. Those who believe in orderly progress toward a definable goal interpret this flux as some form of evolution. Those who accept it at face value, as most scientists do, believe simply in change. Both would agree with Nietzsche when he said that truth has never yet hung on the arm of an absolute; both must of necessity describe the world in relative terms.

In his observations of physical phenomena, Albert Einstein saw that, in a world where everything moves, any calculation or prediction, to be valid, must be based on the relative position of the observer. Newton's absolute space, which was immovable, and his absolute time, which flowed on uniformly—both of which were "unrelated to any outward circumstances"—had to be discarded and replaced by the theory of relativity. All space, in the modern view, is measured by mobility and change of relative position, and all time by the duration of movement in the space traveled across. The world becomes a space-time continuum; all matter, energy, and events are related in the four dimensions of space-time.

The study by anthropologists of the life and customs of primitive peoples has shown how ethical considerations are relative to tribal customs as well as social and economic conditions. In Tibet, a woman may have several husbands because one man may be too poor to support a wife. In Africa, some tribes permit a rich man to have as many wives as he can afford. The pragmatic philosophers William James and John Dewey took a long look at history and a wide view of the world and concluded that when an idea is effective, it must be true; when it ceases to work, its truth is no longer valid and another solution must be discovered.

Such a relative world, in which all things appear differently to each person and each group, depending on educational, geographical, historical, ethnic, and psychological backgrounds, can be understood only in terms of many frames of reference. Any absolutism—such a totalitarian society as Plato's *Republic,* a modern police state, or a military dictatorship—insists on a maximum of conformity in order to assure the stability of government. A relativism—such as that of a modern democracy—allows for many different human images.

This relative world, moreover, is populated by men and women who see themselves in multiple images and express themselves in many different styles. In it can be found Marx's proletarian person, speaking in some form of social protest and bent on bringing about the ultimate triumph of the working classes and masses. Darwin's jungle people are there, beating on their neoprimitive tom-toms and talking in existentialist vocabularies on the survival of the fittest. Nietzsche's *Übermensch,* or super being, who is determined to impose a mighty will on an unwilling world, has been thwarted in two brutal world wars.

The voices of Freud's psychological patients are heard, too, coming from couches and canvases as they try to share surrealistic nightmares with the world at large. Mechanical men and women, the spawn of the Industrial Revolution and the machine age, walk robotlike at large, thinking mechanistic thoughts in their electronic brains and expressing futuristic principles in their mechanical styles. There, too, is Einstein's relativist, who is drawing abstract pictures of the space-time world in slashing, angular lines that are organized by the many focal points of cubist perspective. Modern art as the mirror of this relativistic world therefore assumes multitudinous shapes in order to reflect the great number of human images.

Small wonder, then, that this world, which has produced scientists who analyze and synthesize and physicists who work with fission and fusion, has also given birth to revolutionists who want to destroy a social order so as to reconstruct it in a different way. Warring nations hope to break down one international order so as to build up a new balance of power. Idol smashers feel compelled to destroy certain images people live by so that they can remake the world in their own image. And there are the artists who distort tangible objects so as to reshape them into forms that exist exclusively in their imaginations and on their canvases.

Relativism and the Arts

In this relative world, therefore, the cubists disintegrate the objects in their paintings so that they can reintegrate them in patterns of their own choosing. Since each picture creates its own spatial relationships, space is relative to the mind and mood of the painter rather than an absolute as it is in Euclidean geometry.

It is both impossible and undesirable to make any precise analogy between cubist principles and the mathematics of space-time. A relationship, however unsystematic it may be, can nevertheless be found in the cubist concept of several viewpoints existing at the same time and showing objects from many sides at once. By representing bodies at rest or in successive stages of motion, a futurist or mechanical-style picture sets up a space-time continuum of its own. Similarly, Giorgio de Chirico in *The Disquieting Muses* (see Fig. 1) places classical statues in a space bounded by a medieval castle, a contemporary factory, and a futuristic tower in order to create an image of time in which past, present, and future coexist in an extended now.

In music, the experience of dissonance is freed from its dependence on consonance, so that it demands neither preparation, anticipation, nor resolution. The absolutes of tonality, rhythmical regularity, and musical form have yielded to a host of tonal relativisms. Instead of a single meter, a modern musical score can use sequences composed of many meters in which a measure of $4/8$ is succeeded by one of $7/8$, then $2/8$, $9/8$, and so on. The same principle can be used simultaneously with several rhythms going on at the same time, as in Stravinsky's *Rite of Spring.* This is called *polyrhythm.*

Instead of organizing a work around a single key center, some composers have employed two tonalities simultaneously in the technique known as *bitonality,* while others have gone one step farther into *polytonality.* This, in turn, led to Schoenberg's method of composing with twelve tones that are related not to a central tonality but only to one another. Within the internal organization of the work, the sequence of tones known as the row can be played forward or backward, normally or upside down, simultaneously as in a chord, or fragmented into shorter motifs. A given note cannot be repeated until all the other tones are heard. The twelve-tone method emphasizes change and discourages repetition. Its ideal is constant variation creating a continual and perpetual state of tonal flux.

In *Ulysses,* James Joyce found his answer by making a simultaneous cross section of the life of a city. In this mazelike literary space-time continuum, all events, whether memories of the past or premonitions of the future, flow together into a kind of extended present. As in a dream, there is no distinction between before and after. While the single day and night and city in which all takes place have some relation to the Greek unities of time, place, and action, there is no Aristotelian beginning, middle, or end to his structureless literary structure. Readers can begin at almost any place in the book, and the continuity will not be broken. The series of fleeting images are simply recorded, and the door to the dream world of free association of words and thoughts is left open for readers to supply the transitions between moods, the union of the fragments, and thus create their own relative order. Its end, therefore, is a conclusion in which nothing whatever is concluded.

Many of the forms of expressionism are also relative to the individual psychology of the artist, just as a Frank Lloyd Wright building is relative to the need of the human situation. Expressionism presupposes the free-associational techniques of psychological relativism. Somewhat like the romantic revolt of a century earlier, the expressionistic artist reasserts the primacy of the imagination over the intellect and takes flight from reality in order to find a superior reality in the world of mystery and fantasy. The tendency is anti-intellectual in the extreme, though the symbols and vocabulary are evolved by highly rationalistic procedures. The emotional content poured on their canvases, pages, and musical scores derives from a particular human imagination and hence is relative to the infinite number of unsolved conflicts and suppressed passions of many different private worlds.

Historical relativism has provided the modern artist with an unparalleled number of choices of styles and techniques from the past as well as the present. The artist of the 20th century is the heir of all the ages. A Picasso exhibit or a Stravinsky concert can present a bewildering assortment of styles. Picasso drew inspiration from ancient Iberian sculpture, African tribal masks, Romanesque wall frescoes, and medieval stained glass, as well as from contemporary sources. His paintings also include provocative variations on Velázquez' *Las Meninas,* Delacroix's *Pietà,* and other masterpieces that have caught his eye. His media may include pencil drawings, collages constructed of cloth and paper, ceramics, and woodcuts, as well as oils and watercolors. Sources for Stravinsky may include the free rhythms of Gregorian chant, the dissonant counterpoint of the 14th century, the operas of Mozart, or the multiple rhythms of African tribal music. To these masters, historical relativism provides a complete freedom of choice without the necessity of sacrificing either their originality or their principles.

Philosophers of history, such as Spengler and Toynbee, through their sweeping historical panoramas have shown that the past still exists within the living present. From the point of view of historical relativity, then, tradition is usually a more potent factor than innovation. At all times, including the present, evolution has been a more powerful force in the process of change than revolution.

Most 20th-century ideas and problems are variations on old themes that have bothered thinkers ever since the 5th century B.C. Those that in the past led to sharp dissonances have never been resolved. Instead, they have become outmoded, outgrown, temporarily forgotten, or they are bypassed, circumvented in one way or another, or made to assume new shapes and forms.

"Ideas have never conquered the world as ideas," as Romain Rolland remarked in his novel *Jean Christophe,* "but only by the force they represent. They do not grip men by their intellectual contents but by the radiant vitality which is given off from them at certain periods in history. . . . The loftiest and most sublime idea remains ineffective until the day when it becomes contagious, not by its own merits, but by the merits of the groups of men in whom it becomes incarnate by the transfusion of their blood." Guildenstern in Tom Stoppard's play *Rosenkrantz and Guildenstern Are Dead* (1967) expresses the same thought in different words: "There were always questions. To exchange one set for another is no very great matter."

More important than the solutions or lack of them have been the emotional forces these notions have generated and the good fruits they have yielded. All the workable ideas eventually have been embodied in the buildings people erect to house their activities, the statues and pictures that reflect their human images, the words that express their innermost thoughts, and the music that gives voice to their strivings and aspirations in a world that is forever changing, forever in flux.

22
Art Styles since 1945

Revolutions and Evolutions

Since 1945 and the end of World War II, the revolutionary spirit continues in full force—in science, industry, politics, and electronics, as well as in the arts. Rapid changes are occurring in religious beliefs, social structures, aesthetic values, morals, and manners. Gradually, social relativity and the pluralistic society are replacing the social absolute. Anthropologists are showing how relative are the behavioral patterns and moral values of today; psychologists are demonstrating the impossibility of drawing a fine line between the normal and the abnormal; and existentialists are shaking traditional Western concepts about the meaning and purposes of life and the existence of God.

Highly dramatic are the consequences of electronic communications via radio, television, satellite transmission, laser beam, tape recording, videotape, and color photography. The antennas and tentacles of the electronic media are heightening perceptions and psychologically extending the nervous systems of the new generation. Through electronic eyes people now watch the whole world, and the whole world is watching them. As a result the earth is like one great city in which each national unit functions as an ethnic minority inhabiting a neighborhood within a vast global complex.

Thus far, however, the process has produced more diversity than unity, more heat than light, as much conflict as understanding; but the possibilities for better or worse seem boundless. For instance, what has geographically and ethnologically condensed into a planetary city has also contracted in the temporal dimension. Through the easy access of books and recordings, the art, literature, and music of the past and present are now within the reach of everyone. Thus, knowledge and experience of the arts and the human past transform the present into an extended historical now.

In this larger context history shows that all revolutions are really evolutions. Like icebergs, the more sensational aspects of revolutionary change rise only about one-ninth above the surface. The true essence of change is to be found in the invisible, evolutionary portions that lie below. It is here that the continuity of ethical and aesthetic concepts is to be found.

The picture of the arts since 1945 is extremely complex, with trends toward fragmentation on one side and multimedia unification on the other. Some contemporary artists are showing considerable resistance to confinement as specialists working in a single medium. One might say that they are becoming ecumenical as they join hands to participate in multimedia events staged as theater productions, musicals, films, and happenings. Artists are also enlarging the integrity of the single medium to permit the inclusion of many processes and materials within a particular work. As a result, the former sharp distinctions between painting and sculpture, as well as architecture and sculpture, are breaking down. Eero Saarinen's Trans World Flight Center (Fig. 502), for instance, qualifies equally well as a massive piece of environmental sculpture and as a functional architectural work.

Developments in the theater dramatize the themes and attitudes found in all contemporary art expression. The new theater also reflects the multimedia trend by mixing elements of text, music,

502. Eero Saarinen. Trans World Flight Center, Kennedy International Airport, New York. 1962.

movement, mime, and motion picture techniques, all brought together in a group effort. Such experimental productions are often improvisatory, changing from one performance to another, and are informally organized as mosaics of impressions, sporadic snatches of emotion and experience.

"Action theater," as some of its manifestations in the late 1960s and early 1970s were called, is going increasingly in the direction of sound, light, pantomime, struggles, shouts, and cries, and doing it at the expense of text. In Julian Beck's *Paradise Now* contemporary characters in faded blue jeans and sweat shirts mix with such historical figures as Queen Elizabeth I, who appears as a rag doll, while Sophocles' Antigone has an altercation with Lady Macbeth as she walks on in a see-through nightgown. For Beck, all theater must grow out of the personal experience of the company. Spasms of kinetic energy are unleashed onstage as the characters grope and writhe. Rational dialogue gives way to groans and moans, hisses and screams. The picture of social organization this form of drama presents is that of a steaming jungle filled with sweating forms. The acropolis seems to have given way to the apocalypse.

Today the "theater of the absurd," or action theater, is becoming a thing of the past. Well-constructed plays are replacing the hectic improvisations, more lifelike naturalistic characters are supplanting the caricatures, and more logically motivated sequences are superseding the chaotic and unpredictable situations. Yet the exploration of chance and fantasy in the works of Samuel Beckett and Eugene Ionesco and their discovery of new patterns of experience still linger to color and enrich what is now called the "new naturalism."

In the modern theater, as in the other contemporary arts, the past is intimately interwoven with the present. The bare medieval stage without curtain or proscenium arch has its counterpart in the modern arrangement of theater-in-the-round. Members of the cast or stagehands shift all props in full view of the audience or when the lights are out. Too, a nonindividuality bordering on medieval anonymity seems to be favored in reaction against Renaissance individualism and the star system. For instance, several writers or even the actors themselves may collaborate on a sequence of scenes the end result of which can be distinguished only as a group effort. This parallels medieval anonymity, since miracle plays were also group productions, just as the cathedral sculptures emerged from schools of craftsmen and liturgical masses were written by several different composers. Not until the 14th century was an entire mass written by a single musician.

The explosive fragmentation in the arts that began with cubism has gone so far that artists no longer view life as a whole. The 18th century—which evolved the aristocratic palace and townhouse as a complete way of life, the rococo church as a *Gesamtkunstwerk* or "complete work of art," and the cyclically complete multimovement sonata-symphony form—was an age of enlightenment and reason in which society could perceive the world as a whole. Typical of the present age is the tendency to capitalize on the fragments, to zero in on a single aspect of visual, verbal, or musical activity.

Some composers, for instance, take their lead from the everyday experience of hearing sounds coming simultaneously from many sources. They can, for one, exploit the mixture of chance sounds

CHRONOLOGY
The Period since 1945

from ten transistor radios, all tuned in at once to different stations, with the performers manipulating the controls to raise and lower the volume at will. Other composers select the element of silence and achieve a degree of musical abstraction so that listeners can imagine what each one wants to hear.

Some contemporary canvases simply offer colors arranged on flat surfaces, which otherwise remain undefined by lines, geometrical shapes, or forms in the traditional sense. Other canvases are totally preoccupied with textures or, perhaps, a single color, as in color-field pictures painted all black or all red. Quite possibly the ultimate in abstraction has been achieved in a framed canvas presented with nothing at all on it. Here viewers feel what the artist experiences before beginning a work, and they can paint their own picture in their imaginations.

In the period since 1945 the philosophy of existentialism caught up with painting as it did with the theater of the absurd. Such neodada movements as pop art, which produced sculptured lipsticks two stories high and plastic hamburgers gigantic enough to fill a large room, tell of the essential absurdity of life. Just as in existentialism the act of living itself becomes the affirmation and meaning of life, so in one phase of contemporary art, the very act of painting becomes the work of art and its only meaning.

But just as the theater of the absurd has given way to the new naturalism, the human figure and recognizable objects are reappearing in painting. This trend, however, is far from a return to the past. Rather it is a rediscovery of certain basic aspects of human experience but seen in a new light.

The New York School

During the dark days of World War II, the United States continued to live up to its image as the melting pot. But this time it was a meeting and merging not so much of peoples as it was of personages and personalities. Prior to the American entry into the conflict, the great scientist Albert Einstein had come from Hitler's Germany, while Enrico Fermi arrived from Italy and Niels Bohr from Denmark. Together

1886–1969	Ludwig Miës van der Rohe
1891–1979	Pier Luigi Nervi
1892–1970	Richard Neutra
1895–	R. Buckminster Fuller
1901–1974	Louis I. Kahn
1902–	Marcel Breuer
1906–	Philip Johnson
1910–1961	Eero Saarinen
1917–	I. M. Pei
1918–	Joern Utzon
1925–	Robert Venturi
1931–	Denise Scott Brown
1933–	Richard Rogers
1937–	Renzo Piano

PAINTERS

1880–1966	Hans Hofmann
1887–1968	Marcel Duchamp
1888–1976	Josef Albers
1901–	Jean Dubuffet
1903–1970	Mark Rothko
1903–1974	Adolph Gottlieb
1904–1948	Arshile Gorky
1904–	Willem de Kooning
1904–	Clyfford Still
1905–1970	Barnett Newman
1908–	Lee Krasner
1910–	Francis Bacon
1910–1962	Franz Kline
1912–1956	Jackson Pollock
1912–1962	Morris Louis
1912–1963	William Baziotes
1913–1967	Ad Reinhardt

1915–	Robert Motherwell
1922–	Jules Olitski
1922–	Richard Diebenkorn
1923–	Roy Lichtenstein
1923–	Ellsworth Kelly
1924–	George Segal
1924–	Kenneth Noland
1925–	Robert Rauschenberg
1927–	Alfred Leslie
1927–	Philip Pearlstein
1928–	Helen Frankenthaler
1929–	Claes Oldenburg
1930–	Jasper Johns
1930–	Andy Warhol
1931–	Bridget Riley
1933–	James Rosenquist
1935–	Jim Dine
1936–	Frank Stella
1936–	Gregory Gillespie
1937–	David Hockney
1941–	Chuck Close
1941–	John de Andrea
1941–	Richard Estes

SCULPTORS

1898–1976	Alexander Calder
1900–	Louise Nevelson
1903–1975	Barbara Hepworth
1904–	Isamu Noguchi
1906–1965	David Smith
1912–	Nicolas Schöffer
1912–	Tony Smith
1914–	Bernard Rosenthal
1921–	Joseph Beuys

1922–	Howard Jones
1924–	Anthony Caro
1925–	Jean Tinguely
1925–	Duane Hanson
1927–	John Chamberlain
1928–	Donald Judd
1928–	Robert Smithson
1928–	Sol LeWitt
1931–	Robert Morris
1933–	Mark di Suvero
1935–	Carl André
1935–	Christo
1936–1970	Eva Hesse
1936–	Lucas Samaras
1939–	Richard Serra
1941–	Bruce Naumann
1945–	Joseph Kosuth

MUSICIANS

1896–	Virgil Thomson
1900–	Aaron Copland
1908–	Oliver Messiaen
1908–	Elliott Carter
1910–	Samuel Barber
1911–	Gian Carlo Menotti
1912–	John Cage
1913–1976	Benjamin Britten
1913–	Witold Lutoslawski
1916–	Milton Babbitt
1925–	Pierre Boulez
1926–	Hans Werner Henze
1928–	Karlheinz Stockhausen
1929–	George Crumb
1933–	Krzysztof Penderecki

they succeeded in splitting the atom and ushering in the nuclear age. Formerly of the Bauhaus in Germany, the renowned international-style architects Walter Gropius and Miës van der Rohe began to teach and build in the United States, while Eliel Saarinen and his son Eero migrated from Finland to make their careers on the Eastern Seaboard. Such literary figures as Thomas Mann and Aldous Huxley found Southern California a congenial place to live and write. The composers Igor Stravinsky, Arnold Schoenberg, and Darius Milhaud were also working and teaching in California, while Paul Hindemith joined the faculty of Yale University.

A similar emigration from Europe was seen among painters and sculptors. The outstanding nonobjective artist Piet Mondrian from Holland and the abstractionist Josef Albers, of the Bauhaus faculty, opened studios and began painting in New York. When the war clouds darkened and the Nazis occupied France, leading figures of the School of Paris also found in New York a sanctuary where they could live and work. These included the sculptor Jacques Lipchitz and such painters as Léger, Chagall, Dali, and Max Ernst.

Already established in New York since World War I was the great French dadaist Marcel Duchamp. In the 1920s and 1930s aspiring young American artists and musicians had sailed for Paris in the wake of writers Gertrude Stein, Ernest Hemingway, and Henry Miller and composers Virgil Thomson and Aaron Copland. Now a reverse migration changed the posture of American artists toward their Continental colleagues. In the early 1940s they stood squarely in the center of things.

When such eminent minds combined forces with their American counterparts they acted as catalytic agents that hurled the New York artists to the forefront. After 1945 and the war's end most of the Europeans returned to the Continent, but their mission had been accomplished. The School of Paris had lost its momentum, and most of the younger creative talents were to be found in New York. American artists were now free to accomplish their own creative synthesis of European styles.

For the first time in American history an international style originated on the American scene. New York (Fig. 503) became the worldwide capital of art and music, the achievements of the New York School were felt throughout the world, and abstract expressionism took its place in the history of art alongside impressionism, cubism, expressionism, and surrealism. It became the true heir and logical successor in this great evolutionary sequence of styles.

While major architectural developments depended on the expansion of American commerce and industry, painting and poetry belonged to the dispossessed few. Theirs were the voices of angry young men and women who had been confronted with the specter of the Great Depression at the beginning of their careers and the horror of war as they matured.

At first they had been sustained as artists only through the grace of government-sponsored projects. To relieve mass unemployment, President Franklin D. Roosevelt's New Deal included artists and musicians among those aided by the Works Progress Administration (WPA). These programs brought artists, writers, and composers together in group enterprises that gave them a modest living.

As they worked together creating murals for public buildings, plays for regional theaters, and music for ballet productions and symphonic ensembles, American artists found themselves lifted out of their individual isolation and their alienation from society. They formed friendships, developed a sense of community, and discussed philosophies of life and art in a way that could be translated into action.

The Depression years had produced an atmosphere of radical politics among intellectuals and artists at a time when the basic structures of government and social institutions were scrutinized and questioned in the light of their apparent collapse. In this context art tended toward social realism and to become an instrument of political propaganda for the exposure of poverty, hypocrisy, and injustice. It was to the credit of the abstract expressionists, who were nourished in this environment, that they sublimated their political revolt and transformed it into an aesthetic radicalism the purpose of which was to reexamine the basic assumptions and conventions of the American heritage. Although the dominant theme of American art in the 1930s had been social realism (see Fig. 489), such artists as the sculptor David Smith and the painters Willem de Kooning and Arshile Gorky possessed the vision and the daring to explore the aesthetic and expressive potential offered by cubism, expressionism, and surrealism.

Abstract Expressionism

The designation *New York School* was first coined to distinguish the younger generation of American painters and sculptors from the "School of Paris." The latter referred to the exceptional group of artists who lived and worked in Paris during the first four decades of the 20th century. Their brilliant innovations had made the French capital the center and symbol of achievement in high art. At first only the abstract expressionists were thought to constitute the New York School, but the meaning of the term has been widened to embrace all the styles whose development and acceptance have centered on New York since 1945.

503. Richard Estes. *Downtown.*
1978. Oil on canvas,
$4 \times 5'$ (1.22 × 1.52 m).
Collection Dr. Peter Ludwig,
Aachen, West Germany.

Just as the School of Paris had embraced the Spaniards Picasso, Juan Gris, and Joan Miró, the Italians Modigliani and Chirico, and the Russian Chagall, in addition to the Frenchmen Braque and Matisse, so also the New York School, which developed the abstract-expressionist style, comprised an international group. The German master Hans Hofmann was already in his fifties when he established an art school on West 8th Street. The Dutch-born Willem de Kooning had moved to New York in the late 1920s, as had Mark Rothko from Russia by way of Portland, Oregon, and Arshile Gorky from Turkish Armenia. Jackson Pollock had been born in Wyoming and raised in California and Franz Kline in the coal-mining country of Pennsylvania, while Robert Motherwell hailed from San Francisco, Clyfford Still from Spokane, Washington, and the sculptor David Smith from Indiana. Barnett Newman and Lee Krasner were the native New Yorkers in the group.

Once WPA projects fell casualty to the wartime budget, the artists all found themselves living on the ragged edge of poverty, even desperation, in the bare lofts and cold-water flats of the Greenwich Village section of lower Manhattan off Washington Square. Like Richard Estes' realistic cityscape (Fig. 503), theirs was not the prosperous, glittering New York of Wall Street, Madison Avenue, and the art galleries of the establishment on 57th Street. Alienation from American society, which they saw as a machine for brutality, was one of the common bonds linking their attitudes and giving them shape.

The focal point of these "loft rats" was the The Club, located at 35 East 8th Street, a local version of a Paris café where those who painted by day could talk to each other by night. In their vigorous arguments the members of the group often came to blows, but they all shared a common faith that art should be invested with powerful content and that the most powerful means for giving expression to that content lay in the possibilities of abstraction to reduce shapes and forms to their essence.

In 1943 Newman, Rothko, and Adolph Gottlieb—three member painters of the group—published a statement in the *New York Times* declaring that "there is no such thing as a good painting about nothing. . . . . the subject is crucial and only that subject matter is valid which is tragic and timeless." At the same time, they asserted that the "impact of elemental truth" called for the "simple expression of the complex thought, and the importance of the large shape because it has the impact of the unequivocal."

Of an evening at The Club, Hans Hofmann could be heard discussing the doctrine of abstraction. A naturalist or painter of physical life, he declared, could never become the creator of pictorial life. "You must give the most with the least," he taught, and "a

work of art can never be the imitation of life but only . . . the generation of life." On a Friday night the avant-garde composer John Cage might give "A Lecture on Nothing," or sit before a keyboard for four and a half minutes of silence. W. H. Auden, the British-born poet who had settled in New York in 1939, would drop in to discuss his *Age of Anxiety* or give voice to some of the pessimistic existentialist reflections that occupied him in those days.

The Welsh poet Dylan Thomas came to read his lyrics, and the restless Allen Ginsberg, poetic voice of the "beat" generation, would appear from time to time. There he read his poem *Howl,* a hymn of defeat, a hell of despair. But like a Jackson Pollock web of interpenetrating lines (see Fig. 506), *Howl* weaves a tapestry of images that captures the spirit of the seething metropolis:

> I saw the best minds of my generation destroyed by madness, starving hysterical naked, . . .
> who poverty and tatters and hollow-eyed and high sat up smoking in the supernatural darkness of cold-water flats floating across the tops of cities contemplating jazz, . . .
> who were expelled from the academies for crazy & publishing obscene odes on the windows of the skull, . . .
> . . . wine drunkenness over the roof tops, storefront boroughs of teahead joyride neon blinking traffic light, sun and moon and tree vibrations in the roaring winter dusks of Brooklyn, ashcan rantings and kind king light of mind, . . .
> who sank all night in submarine light of Bickford's floated out and sat through the stale beer afternoon in desolate Fugazzi's, listening to the crack of doom on the hydrogen jukebox,
> who talked continuously seventy hours from park to pad to bar to Bellevue to museum to the Brooklyn Bridge,
> a lost battalion of platonic conversationalists jumping down the stoops off fire escapes off windowsills off Empire State out of the moon. . . .*

The artists of the New York School did not think of themselves as a group with common ideals. The most that can be said for the unity of the school was that its members shared a range of attitudes, derived principally from the despair and anxiety of the times, from the opportunity for professional activity and cooperation afforded by the WPA, from the breakthrough in aesthetic form achieved by the cubists in their experiments with abstraction, and from the liberation of the subconscious attained among the surrealists using Freudian methods of analysis.

All the abstract expressionsts insisted on spontaneity, intensity of feeling, and a vast range of indi-

---

*From *Howl and Other Poems,* copyright © 1956, 1959 by Allen Ginsberg, reprinted by permission of City Lights Books.

504. Arshile Gorky.
The Liver Is the Cock's Comb.
1944. Oil on canvas,
6′ × 8′2″ (1.83 × 2.49 m).
Albright-Knox Art Gallery, Buffalo
(gift of Seymour H. Knox).

vidual choices, materials, and situations. In practice, after all the talking, the goal of these American artists became the realization of an entirely new pictorial style, one synthesized from cubism and surrealism and fully equal to these in ambition and accomplishment. Within this spectrum each remained an individual, each had access to an infinite set of options, each strained in a personal direction.

As the critic Harold Rosenberg noted, each was "fatally aware that only what he constructs for himself will ever be real to him." Or, as William Baziotes said, "[my paintings] are my mirrors. They tell me what I am like at the moment." For the New York School as for the existentialist thinkers, painting was being in nonbeing. Jean Paul Sartre expressed this view when he observed that "man first of all exists, encounters himself, surges up in the world—and defines himself afterward."

Origins and Derivations   From cubism the American artists learned the method of abstracting the essence from familiar shapes and forms. They also mastered the cubist techniques of analyzing and dissecting the subject matter of a painting in order to rearrange the parts into a satisfactory design for pictorial purposes. Like the cubists they frankly acknowledged the two-dimensionality and the shape of their canvases and made no attempt to create the illusion of deep space and fully rounded forms. As their teacher and guide Hans Hofmann put it, "The essence of pictorial space is flatness."

Surrealism likewise had a powerful effect on the New York group. European surrealists had discovered the free-association techniques of psychic au-

tomatism (see p. 424), the spontaneous and random quality of which appealed greatly to the New York group. As one of the group expressed it: "I want to keep a balance just on the edge of awareness, the narrow rim between the conscious and the subconscious, a balance between expanding and contracting, silence and sound." Once psychic automatism had released a free flow of creativity, the artist could work over, revise, and realize from the doodling some designs of a more controlled sort. Arshile Gorky's nightmarish picture *The Liver Is the Cock's Comb* (Fig. 504) illustrates this heritage from surrealism. In his gruesome painting the artist conjures up fantastic images of skeletal shapes jostling with imaginary creatures with sharp toothlike claws.

Psychic automatism gave priority to process, or the act of doing, over the logically worked out conceptions of form. In effect, it reversed the order of previous notions of abstract art, which were based on intellectually preconceived ideas before starting a

505. Jackson Pollock at work in his studio. 1950.

506. Jackson Pollock. *Lucifer.* 1947. Oil, enamel, and aluminum paint on canvas; 3'5" × 6'9" (1.04 × 2.06 m). Collection Mr. and Mrs. Harry W. Anderson, Atherton, Calif.

work. Once having accepted automatism as basic to the creative enterprise, the abstract expressionists converted it from the surrealist process of generating images to the act of painting itself. Thus they found a way of preserving freshness, of cultivating accidental dribbles and splashes for the evidence they offered of spontaneity and creative vigor.

Surrealism also pointed the way for the abstract expressionists to discover in the subconscious, the long-buried memory fragments of the innocent and primitive in modern men and women, the source of the free, the instinctual, and the fantastic in the human imagination. Surrealism thus indicated a technique for liberating the images trapped in the subconscious and making them available to the conscious mind of the artist for use as the vehicles of the artist's expressive intent. Then the abstract expressionists attempted to come to grips with the elemental, the profound, and universal aspects of human emotion. For this they needed to develop a visual language of signs and symbols to depict the pictorial equivalents of human experience, and in the process of artistic creation to find the metaphors for the myths of universal genesis, as did Barnett Newman in *Genesis—The Break* (see Fig. 5).

The abstract expressionists' view of painting as heroic gesture harks back to the sublime ideal of romanticism. Unlike the romanticists, however, they sought to create a poetic art in purely pictorial terms.

Action Painting Recognition of the abstract expressionists was slow in coming. Conservative art critics called their pictures "pots of paint flung in the face of the public." Even the avant-garde commercial

galleries hesitated to accept their paintings for exhibition. In 1943, however, Jackson Pollock's first one-man show in New York was an event that commanded international recognition and focused worldwide attention on himself and his fellow abstract expressionists. Pollock's explosive canvases revealed a teeming vitality, frenetic energy, and creative invention that heralded a new era in painting. He was the original "action painter" who spread his enormous canvases on the floor so as to feel closer to his painting (Fig. 505).

With commercial paints, house painter brushes, basting syringes and sticks and trowels he performed a kind of ritualistic oily ballet dance as he dripped, squirted, dribbled, and flung. His "poured paintings," as they have been called, had no predetermined pattern. They are simply energy made visible, a kind of trancelike pictorial choreography in which the spectator is invited to join in the dance. With *Lucifer* (Fig. 506), the viewer is irresistibly drawn into a web of

507. Detail of Figure 506.

nervous rhythms pulsating with dynamic energy, a perpetual motion of lines and colors, as might be compounded of such elemental forces of nature as air, fire, and water.

A closer look at Pollock's *Lucifer* (see detail, Fig. 507), reveals that the artist is a master of curvilinear drawing. He developed the pouring techniques so that he could achieve a kind of improvisational continuity of extended overlapping lines in the process of painting. This is something that cannot be done with the traditional way of handling the brush. In spite of the spontaneous and seemingly accidental quality, Pollock's battery of techniques is firmly controlled. He once insisted, "I can control the flow of paint. There is no accident." The result is an amazingly complex web of interwoven lines, colors, and motifs similar to musical counterpoint.

Neither Pollock nor his fellow abstract expressionists came as bursts from the blue, and no one was more aware of this than the painters themselves. Their stylistic synthesis, as previously discussed, had included elements derived from cubism, surrealism, and Kandinsky's passionate nonobjectivism. But there is a still larger and broader historical dimension. As early as 1756 the English prime minister and writer Edmund Burke had published his essay on the *Philosophical Enquiry into the Origins of Our Ideas of the Sublime and the Beautiful.* Beauty in the 18th-century sense was based on order, clarity, balance, elegance, and proportion. The sublime, however, could include fear-inspiring experiences; the magnificent, terrible, picturesque, and awesome; the horrendous forces of nature such as storms at sea and eruptions of volcanoes; and even the supernatural.

Around 1845, with the late pictures of the English painter J. M. W. Turner (see Fig. 423), one feels the same perpetual motion of blinding blizzards and wind-driven clouds, the same distillation of nature's most potent projections—energy, light, and motion—that characterize Pollock's paintings. As his contemporary the author William Hazlitt commented, Turner depicts "the elements of air, earth, and water. The artist delights to go back to the first chaos of the world or to that state of things when the waters were separating from the dry land, and light from darkness, but as yet no living thing nor tree bearing fruit was seen upon the face of the earth. All is without form and void."

The same thrust is carried into American art with the wider sweep of the romantic movement. Dating from about 1885, Albert Pinkham Ryder's *Jonah* (Fig. 508) seems to dissolve the material world into an ominous phosphorescent brightness. In his analysis of this picture, the art historian Robert Rosenblum observes that Ryder's conception merges the

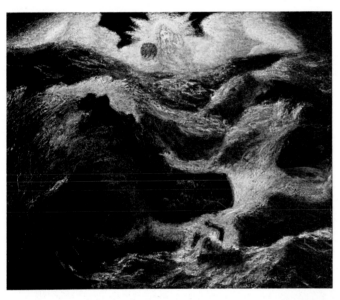

above: 508. Albert Pinkham Ryder. *Jonah.* c. 1885. Oil on canvas, 27¼ × 34⅜″ (69 × 87 cm). National Collection of Fine Arts, Smithsonian Institution, Washington, D.C. (gift of John Gellatly).

right: 509. Franz Kline. *Pennsylvania.* 1954. Oil on canvas, 3′11″ × 5′3″ (1.19 × 1.6 m). Courtesy the artist's estate.

"phenomena of sea, sky, moonlight with such aware-ness of their supernatural potential that he convinces us that a Biblical miracle could take place within the magical environment he usually creates in landscape alone."

Bringing together so many different and funda-mentally opposite elements—cubism and surrealism, form and content, reason and emotion, control and freedom, line and color, drawing and painting, figure and ground, abstraction and expression—and doing it on such a heroic scale and without identifiable sub-ject matter of any sort, Pollock achieved a balance so rare and exquisite that even he could not sustain the delicate poise for long. Eventually he chose to de-velop individually certain selected aspects of the totality present in his masterpieces. In just this way his followers carried modern art forward to new advances in aesthetic vision by basing their work on one feature or another of the complete statement made by Pollock in his most fertile and triumphant period, from 1948 through 1950.

Fundamental as color was to many of the ab-stract-expressionist group, black runs like a leitmotif through much abstract-expressionist painting. Scien-tifically, black is the total absorption or absence of light, which is the medium of color. Thus, by reduc-ing pigmentation to basic simplicity, black could be seen as a contribution to the quality of abstraction and as a speeding up of the painting process. For others, black played a symbolic role for moods of renunciation, grief, or despair.

Franz Kline, for instance, created angular black figures on white backgrounds. Many of his works seem like drawings blown up to the scale of large paintings. He reveled in the metallic skeletal forms so characteristic of the urban scene. *Pennsylvania* (Fig. 509) grows mysteriously in swift, sooty, ges-tural strokes like the structural stresses of opposing forces in the skeletons of iron bridges, railway trestles, and locomotive engines of the artist's coal-country origins. The image thus created is that of nostalgic, self-revealing memory.

Color-Field Painting   Pollock and Kline are often regarded as the representatives of "gestural abstrac-tion" within the New York group, while painters like Mark Rothko and Barnett Newman appear as "color abstractionists." A comparison of the Pollock and Kline works with Rothko's *Green and Maroon* (Fig. 510) or with Newman's *Vir Heroicus Sublimis* (Fig. 511) provides evidence of the reason for the distinc-tion. Kline's *Pennsylvania* with its blacks and whites reproduces quite well on the printed page. To a lesser extent Pollock's *Lucifer* (Fig. 506) with its accent on line would also survive in a black-and-white illustra-tion. The works of Rothko and Newman, however,

with their subtle and sensitive *saturations*—that is, purity, vividness, or intensity—of color would be lost and incomprehensible without their essential ele-ment. This fact emphasizes a fundamental division among the abstract expressionists, with the action painters appearing on one side and the *color-field* painters, or color abstractionists, on the other. The vigorous, muscular gestures of Pollock and Kline, for instance, have nothing to do with the delicate blend-ing processes used by Rothko and Newman.

Rothko's *Green and Maroon* (Fig. 510) consists of several irregular rectangles floating in an atmos-pheric blue space. The rectangles are of unequal size with unstable contours and are painted in luminous

510. Mark Rothko. *Green and Maroon*. 1953. Oil on canvas, 7'6¾" × 4'6½" (2.31 × 1.38 m). Phillips Collection, Washington, D.C.

above: **511.** Barnett Newman. *Vir Heroicus Sublimis.* 1950-51. Oil on canvas, 7'11⅜" × 17'9¼" (2.42 × 5.42 m). Museum of Modern Art, New York (gift of Mr. and Mrs. Ben Heller).
below: **512.** Adolph Gottlieb. *Forgotten Dream.* 1946. Oil on canvas, 24 × 30" (61 × 76 cm). Herbert F. Johnson Museum of Art, Cornell University, Ithaca, N.Y. (gift of Albert A. List).

hues brushed on with such delicacy that flickering light seems to radiate from the films of color. As the eye runs over the painterly edges of the rectangles the delicate harmonies of the colors set off vibrations that make the shapes appear to breathe and shimmer within the color-suffused space.

Newman carried abstraction still further into the form of densities and saturations of a single color.

Such pictures as *Vir Heroicus Sublimis* (Fig. 511), which might be translated as "Heroic Sublime Man," have but one vivid hue—in this case, red—expanding horizontally with syncopated interruptions by lean vertical bands. These march across the huge canvas like Giacometti's tall, thin figures (see Fig. 3). Newman dazzles the eyes of his viewers with sweeping sensuous color sensations. His vertical bands dominate his pictures with their nervous, vibrating contours. These "zips," as Newman called them, serve to "cut" the great field of absolute color and shock it into waves of visual energy that roll back and forth between the bands and the edges. This creates dynamic action in what otherwise seem a totally inert situation. These bands can also be read as abstract figures standing out against their color-field environment. In the way they parallel and echo the edges that fix the limit of Newman's canvases, they seem to be marking off pictures within pictures.

Both Pollock and Newman in their major pronouncements expanded the size of their paintings to immense proportions. They considered easel paintings of cabinet size to be a dying form. In their place they projected larger murals and environmental wall pictures so that the viewer could have a more complete sense of involvement. Smaller canvases, they reasoned, were of necessity seen in relation to their setting with other objects in the room, the texture and color of the walls against which they were hung, and in conjunction with other pictures on the same and surrounding walls. Large-scale murals, on the other hand, are more complete within themselves since they make their own environment. They can be

above: **513.** Lee Krasner. *Abstract No. 2.* 1948. Oil on canvas, 20½ × 23¼″ (52 × 59 cm). Courtesy the artist.

right: **514.** David Smith. *Cubi VI.* 1963. Stainless steel, height 9′10½″ (3.21 m). Billy Rose Art Garden, Israel Museum, Jerusalem (courtesy American Friends of the Israel Museum).

said to create space simply by occupying it, and the viewer is enveloped by the painting.

Adolph Gottlieb and Lee Krasner, on the other hand, worked on a smaller scale and tried to preserve the sense of intimacy in their personal statements. Both devised their own sets of symbols and images that seem to communicate in a pictographic language akin to the picture writing of ancient hieroglyphs. In *Forgotten Dream* (Fig. 512) Gottlieb, using a cubist grid, invents a kind of preconscious or subconscious set of symbols in the manner of surrealist automatism. But while Egyptian hieroglyphs can be deciphered and medieval motifs looked up in a dictionary of symbols, the pictographs in these pictures have no referent other than the painting itself or the subconscious mind of the artist himself. For her part, Krasner found her inspiration in Irish and Persian illuminated manuscripts. The study of Hebrew in her childhood, she says, also reinforced her concern and fascination with the curved lines of letter forms. Her *Abstract No. 2* (Fig. 513) is more abstract than Gottlieb's pictographs. As in a dream there is persistent repetition of an image with constant variations.

Sculptural Dimension   The sculptor David Smith was subject to the same forces that influenced the abstract-expressionist painters. He also associated intimately with the group, shared their goal of realiz-

ing new forms and a new style of abstraction and expression, and eventually became their sculptural counterpart. He began as a painting student at the Art Students' League of New York but switched in the early 1930s to sculpture after seeing reproductions of works by Picasso and others using what then constituted an inventive new technique of joining and welding metal pieces and parts into cubist assemblages (see Fig. 454). Smith was drawn to this technique in part because he had previously worked in automobile and locomotive factories where he had assembled and welded metal components.

Throughout his career Smith felt a great fascination for the basic quality of steel. "The metal," he wrote, "possesses little art history. What associations it has are those of this century: power, structure, movement, progress, suspension, destruction, brutality." Thus, Smith worked in the medium of constructed sculpture rather than in the traditional ones of carved stone and cast bronze. To have room for a machine-shop studio large enough to permit the construction of works on an architectural scale and ample environment for their display, Smith moved to a farm at Bolton Landing in upstate New York. There, he could achieve not only the epic scale of the *Cubi* works (Fig. 514) but also the perspective to conceptualize them within a series of related materials and forms.

Some of Smith's constructions retain the rough blackness of iron, others have been painted bright hues, while in the *Cubi* series Smith scored the stainless-steel surfaces of the geometric volumes to make them flash, dazzle, and all but dissolve in refracted sunlight. The sense of lightness this creates seems a contradiction of the heavy, solid appearance of the monumental forms, the mass of them raised aloft by cylinders and balanced there in dynamic majesty.

A master draftsman, who all his life drew from the model, Smith designed sculptures with such strong silhouettes and transparent interiors that they seem like "drawings-in-space"; in scale and proportion, they often relate to the human figure. The frontal views he designed also give many of the works a strong pictorial character. Smith possessed something of the surrealists' automatism in his astonishing ability to devise new forms. These frequently included standard industrial units or "found" objects from junkyards, which Smith transformed into artistic significance by making them integral with the whole of his design.

Smith's iron and steel constructions, like those in the *Cubi* series, create open and closed spaces that interpenetrate with their environment, defining space, movement, and color as they stand silhouetted against trees, buildings, or sky. Seeing symbol in structure, Smith wrote: "When one chooses a couple of old iron rings from the hub of a wagon, they are circles, they are suns; they all have the same radius; they all perform the same Euclidean relationships."

Success eventually came to the "loft rats," but after so much poverty, despair, and struggle, it seemed not a harbinger of the good life but the end of an epoch and the death of its heroes. Gorky committed suicide in 1948, and Pollock perished in an automobile acci-

515. Hans Hofmann.
Memoria in Aeternum. 1962.
Oil on canvas, 7' × 6⅛" (2.13 × 1.83 m).
Museum of Modern Art, New York
(gift of the artist).

516. Robert Rauschenberg.
Monogram. 1955–59.
Construction, 5′4½″ × 3′6″ × 5′3¼″
(1.64 × 1.07 × 1.61 m).
Moderna Museet, Stockholm.

dent in 1956, as did David Smith in 1965. Kline's untimely death occurred in 1962 at the age of 51, and Rothko killed himself in his studio in 1970.

It was the years 1947–1953 that saw the movement experience its most intense activity and dialogue and achieve the highest quality in innovation as well as in production. As late as 1951, however, the artists' state was so desperate for the want of recognition that a group calling themselves "the irascible eight," which included Pollock, Kline, Rothko, Newman, de Kooning, Hofmann, Motherwell, Gottlieb, and Reinhardt, picketed the Metropolitan Museum to demand the establishment of a department of American art. In the same year, the Museum of Modern Art recognized the movement with an exhibiton entitled "Abstract Painting and Sculpture in America."

Then about 1958 the prestige of the "heroic generation" soared when the museum circulated throughout Europe a comprehensive show of their work under the title "The New American Painting." This made abstract expressionism into an international style that transformed the character and appearance of new painting virtually all over the world.

In *Memoria in Aeternum* (Fig. 515), or *In Perpetual Memory,* Hans Hofmann, the old master of the style who survived many of his younger colleagues, paid tribute to the movement. Executed shortly after Kline's death, it is a melancholy picture of stark black-and-white contrasts, but one revealing the artist's astonishingly vigorous "push-pull" dynamic by which he caused painterly planes to achieve a daring structure of pictorial architecture.

The Aftermath

The emotional intensity, heroic ambitions, and personal preoccupations of the abstract expressionists proved impossible to sustain. By the early 1960s the momentum had slowed down and the younger generation of artists seemed to go off in all directions at once. Their reactions showed a trend toward lighter treatment and flashes of humor, chance rather than calculation, irreverence more than personal commitment, and more detached attitudes. The movements they engendered have variously been called neodadaism, pop art, conceptual art, op art, serialism, minimal art, kinetic art, and the new realism.

Neodada and Pop Art   The original dadaism (see pp. 422–424) had been a bitter expression born out of the disillusionment with the governments and society that had brought on the slaughter of World War I. Like the political anarchists, these artists wanted to destroy the accepted values in order to clear the way to reform. The neodadaists of the 1960s used the original vocabulary of the trivial and commonplace, and assemblages of debris from attics and junkyards. Missing, however, was the bitterness in the older fare, for both pop and neodadaism were nourished by a joyous acceptance of modern materialism and the flood of commercial material from the mass media.

While dada had been a desperately serious movement, neodada reveled in nonsense for its own sake and laughed with the world, not at it. As Robert Rauschenberg disarmingly remarked, he just wanted to live in the world, not reform it.

In Rauschenberg's *Monogram* (Fig. 516) it is apparent that pop art has allowed no boundary to separate art from life. Here is a hybrid form, an assemblage or "combine painting" in which the artist has incorporated such randomly chosen objects as a stuffed angora ram encircled by an automobile tire and other bits of debris that spill out to challenge the ambiguous spaces of abstract expressionism and literally close the gap between art and life. Completing the three-dimensional collage are photographs, cut-out letters, and colors applied with the painterly abandon inherited from the first generation of abstract expressionists. The real irony at the heart of pop works like *Monogram* is that however trite, commercial, debased, and nostalgic the contents, they have been composed, interpreted, and transformed by the means and standards of a living pictorial tradition. Despite the comic-strip, mass-media, or "cornball" imagery, the compositions of Rauschenberg and other artists of the pop movement relate less to these sources than to the art of Matisse, Picasso, and Léger.

From Rauschenberg's assemblages it is only a short step into the domain of junk sculpture and found art. John Chamberlain's *Silverheels* (Fig. 517) uses the crushed and compressed sheets of an actual automobile chassis caught momentarily at a point in the cycle between its original function and the junk-

517. John Chamberlain. *Silverheels.* 1963.
Welded auto metal,
46 × 41 × 36″ (117 × 104 × 91 cm).
Collection Mr. and Mrs. Leo Castelli, New York.

yard. Such art uses rusted machine discards, splintered wood, and industrial debris. It closely relates to the urban experience of throwaway materials.

With its accessible imagery, pop art at once celebrates and parodies the commonplaceness of a consumer society conspicuously dependent upon the supermarket, mass-media advertisements, billboards, and comic strips. The style was readily acceped as "fun art" by an international public, grateful at last to discover something so commonplace, so much a part of everyday experience.

So extensively did pop art offer easily recognizable subjects to which all could relate that art itself has now entered the mass market and become merchandise for popular consumption. There are Andy Warhol's still lifes filled with endlessly repeated soup cans and Coke bottles arranged as on supermarket shelves (Fig. 518), as well as Jasper Johns' shooting gallery targets, American flag, and numbers series and Roy Lichtenstein's comic-strip paintings. Allen Ginsberg's poetry captures the spirit of this phase of pop art in "A Supermarket in California":

> In my hungry fatigue, and shopping for images, I went into the neon fruit supermarket, dreaming of your enumerations!
> What peaches and what penumbras! wives in the avocados, babies in the tomatoes! And you, Garcia Lorca, what were you doing down by the watermellons? . . .
> I wandered in and out of the brilliant stacks of cans following you, and followed in my imagination by the store detective.
> We strode down the open corridors together in our solitary fancy tasting artichokes, possessing every frozen delicacy, and never passing the cashier.*

Rauschenberg and his fellow artists of pop and similar persuasions also joined in *happenings* comprised of improvisation, chance, and random activities. Happenings constitute a multimedia package in which spontaneous, unplanned audience participation plays a part. These events must, of course, be prepared to the extent of choosing the place and assembling the materials and personnel.

In a typical happening the designers create an environment of sights, sounds, smells, movement, and action. Several musical ensembles may be used at random—one playing classical repertory, another vintage jazz, and still another rock music. Clips of various moving pictures in no particular order might be shown on one wall and lantern slides in no discernible sequence projected onto a second, while on a third, psychedelic colors flash and twirl. Meanwhile, groups of dancers in bizarre costumes improvise

*From *Howl and Other Poems,* copyright © 1956, 1959 by Allen Ginsberg, reprinted by permission of City Lights Books.

steps and gestures, and athletes in track suits play games. Wind machines scatter confetti, a poet reads nonsense verse, a committed group stage a demonstration with placards and slogans, and an orator rants at the mob. As radio and television sets blare and vacuum cleaners roar, members of the audience contribute spontaneous reactions. Some might describe such events as action paintings in living motion, others as contrived chaos.

Conceptual and Op Art   As the term implies, *conceptual art* originates as an idea in the mind of the artist, materializes as a process, assumes whatever tangible shape it may, then disappears into memory or oblivion. The conceptualists question the nature of art as an object that can be bought, sold, or placed in a museum except temporarily. Conceptual art has produced body works, earth works, mere labels, and works consisting of such curious materials as grease, cheesecloth, cornflakes, blocks of ice, or just plain dirt. Removing them from galleries has meant scrubbing, sweeping, and shoveling. All that remains is the debris of a dream, a memory experience, and a documentary record in the form of videotapes or photographs. The art object itself, then, can only be found in a state of mind or in the activities involved.

Certain conceptualists like Christo do not offer objects for purchase and possession by collectors, but idea projects to be financed by patrons. Christo thinks on a stupendous scale, and his works include conceptions no one has ever conceived before. His projects show the effect of the imagination on the landscape and even the sea. *Valley Curtain,* for instance, stretched 1 million square feet (0.09 million square meters) of orange-colored fabric across the Grand Canyon. In 1974 his *Oceanfront* covered King's Beach Cove in Newport, Rhode Island, with 150,000 square feet (13,950 square meters) of polypropylene fabric floating on the surface of the sea.

Perhaps Christo's most spectacular work to date is his *Running Fence* (Fig. 519). It is something that might have been suggested by the Great Wall of China. After the conception came the arduous work of making sketches, drawings, and building the model. Specifications had to be drawn up and financial arrangements made. Then the steel poles, wire cables, and more than 2000 panels of white nylon fabric 18 feet (5.5 meters) high and 68 feet (20.6 meters) wide had to be assembled. As the process was set in motion people of all walks of life were drawn into Christo's orbit. Before getting the go-ahead rights there were the farmers who had to grant easements for their land; mayors, town counselors, highway authorities, and environmentalists had to be consulted for opinions and permissions; teams of workers and a corps of engineers had to be

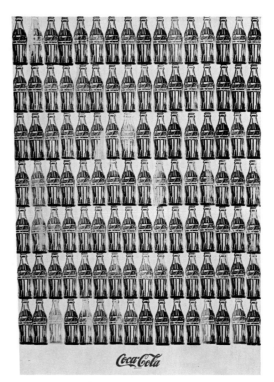

above: **518.** Andy Warhol. *Green Coca Cola Bottles.* 1962. Oil on canvas, 6′10¼″ × 4′9″ (2.1 × 1.45 m). Whitney Museum of American Art, New York (gift of the Friends of the Whitney Museum).

below: **519.** Christo. *Running Fence.* 1972–76. Nylon fabric and steel poles; height 18′ (5.49 m), length 24½ miles (39.43 km). Installed in Sonoma and Marin Counties, California, 1976, for two weeks.

520. Bridget Riley. *Current.* 1964.
Synthetic polymer paint on composition board,
4′10⅜″ (1.48 m) square.
Museum of Modern Art, New York (Philip Johnson Fund).

nirs. Christo's is a fun-and-games art, and he has aptly been called a manufacturer of memories.

Op art, or *optical art,* is yet another attempt to come to grips with the nature of the visual experience. It could be described as a type of action painting with the action taking place in the viewer's eye. Op artists have called their work, which developed out of geometrical abstraction and optical illusionism, "perpetual abstraction."

Bridget Riley's *Current* (Fig. 520) illustrates how stable lines seem to shift and deceive. Since it is impossible to apprehend the whole picture at once, different responses are induced as the eye moves over partial sectors of the surface so that the illusion of faster-slower and forward-backward movement occurs. The sense of perception is confused as eye and brain signals get their wires crossed. The viewer feels sensations varying from disorientation and discomfort to giddiness and exhilaration.

Optical artists are allied with mathematicians, physicists, and psychologists in their experimentations and explorations of optical phenomena. With op art seeing is deceiving instead of believing. Like the impressionists, optical artists are concerned primarily with the work of art as an act of the eye. However, unlike the impressionists, they avoid all association with the outside world and concentrate on the way the eye and brain respond to optical data. By activating the responsive eye, by the impact on perception of color dissonances and the manipulation of geometrical patterns, op art has produced startling effects that amount to a new way of seeing.

Serialism With *serialism* artistic enterprises are seen as aesthetic problems that admit of many different solutions. Such problems are pursued in a series, with each picture posing one possible solution. The lineage of serialism can be traced back to Monet, who in 1877 painted seven views of Paris' Old St. Lazare Railway Station (see Fig. 433). As he worked, the scene remained the same, but the atmosphere, light, steam, and color changed constantly, therefore appearing different in each painting. During the year 1891 Monet painted another series, the subject matter of which consisted of single and double haystacks in a field. On this occasion, he conceived the group as a whole so as to capture the variables of light and shadow, wind and weather, colors and hues, throughout the four seasons. Later, Monet rented a second-floor studio in Rouen, where he could face the intricately carved surface of the cathedral façade and paint it some twenty times.

Josef Albers, who worked in Germany along with Kandinsky and Klee at the Bauhaus and later in New York, extended this idea into the realm of abstraction (Figs. 521, 522). "In visual formation," this founder

hired; even the courts had to make rulings. All were involved in an ongoing artistic enterprise.

Running Fence eventually rose up from the sea north of San Francisco, meandered over farmlands like a white ribbon across the horizon for 24 miles (39.4 kilometers), only to disappear once more into the sea. Astonishingly it became a thing of beauty as the sheer white material caught sun and moonlight, the winds, and the tide's ebb and flow, while at the same time sending shock waves in all directions. People could see *Fence* by car from country roads and the coastal highway, in the fields on foot, and from the air by planes or helicopters. Reactions varied from controversy to astonishment, bewilderment to amusement, skepticism to admiration. It was also seen on all television news programs, covered by daily papers and news magazines. Angry and favorable letters to the editor were printed. Heated discussions were held. Once again everybody was asking the age-old question "Is it art?" only to find that the artist, as usual, had posed more questions than provided answers.

When *Fence* disappeared after its brief two-week lifespan, its memory continued to live on in conversation, verbal descriptions, photographs, drawings, documentation, critical reactions, and a few souve-

above right: 521. Josef Albers.
Homage to the Square: Early Diary.
1955. Oil on composition board,
15″ (38 cm) square.
Nebraska Art Association, Lincoln
(Thomas C. Woods Fund).

right: 522. Josef Albers.
Homage to the Square: Ascending.
1953. Oil on composition board,
43½″ (110 cm) square.
Whitney Museum
of American Art, New York.

of modern serialization declared, "there is no final solution, therefore I work in series." Serialism, moreover, can be apprehended fully only when all units in a series are beheld together in a room where they have a chance to reveal their relationships, where their reciprocal aspects can affect one another, and where their spacing against the surrounding walls plays a part as they form a continuum.

Serialism discards the idea of converging and compressing all ideas and elements into a single masterpiece. In serial painting there is no beginning, middle, or end, implying as this does the evolution and dramatic development of a single canvas. In the case of Monet, who can say which haystack or cathedral painting is the one and only great work? Serialism also moves away from the balanced simultaneity of cubism and extends the experience of space into an unfolding continuum, or, to put it in mathematical terms, into sets of continuous, independent variables.

Serialism, then, is a process, not a finality. Constant variation is the order of the day as each picture

above: 523. Frank Stella. *Tuftonboro I.* 1966. Synthetic polymer paint on canvas, 8′3″ × 9′1″ (2.51 × 2.77 m). Collection Mr. and Mrs. Victor W. Ganz, New York.

right: 524. Frank Stella. *Singerli Variation IV.* 1968. Fluorescent acrylic on canvas, diameter 10′ (3.05 m). Collection Mr. and Mrs. Burton Tremaine, Meriden, Conn.

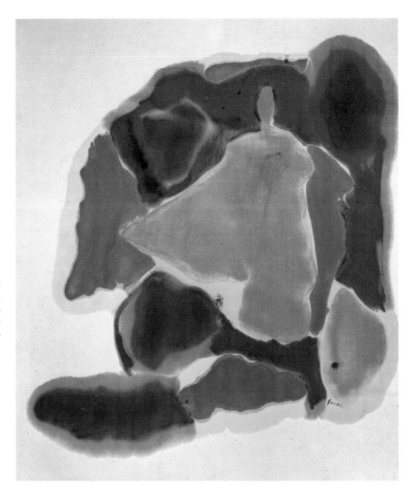

525. Helen Frankenthaler.
Formation. 1963.
Acrylic on canvas,
6′4″ × 5′5″ (1.93 × 1.65 m).
Collection Alexis Gregory, New York.

changes in size, structure, geometry, and shape. Or the shape itself can become the constant, while the color saturations, the densities of the paint, or the qualities of texture change. Or an element such as line can go through various vertical, horizontal, diagonal, or circular manipulations, always allowing for surprise or sport. An obvious analogy can be made with the theme-and-variation form in music. A more subtle one can be made with musical serialization, which emphasizes constant variation, as well as the process of thematic and rhythmic transformation, segmentation, fragmentation, and reassemblage and recombination of materials.

Frank Stella qualifies as both a serialist and minimalist and is a unique presence on the contemporary scene as well. In his *Tuftonboro* series he poses the question "Why do pictures have to be confined to any predetermined geometrical shape?" Everything is first reduced to the bare minimum of straight lines, severe geometrical forms, and strong colors. With *Tuftonboro I* (Fig. 523) the viewer is confronted with a slashing triangle that bursts the

bonds of its rectangular base. The pictorial situation is reinforced by the black ground that contrasts strongly with the bright colors.

In *Singerli Variation IV* (Fig. 524) Stella projects a circular space with a complex interplay of advancing warm colors and receding cool tones as the curvilinear bands weave in and out, over and under. The picture recalls some of the heraldic banners and intricate interlaced lettering found in medieval illuminated manuscripts.

Helen Frankenthaler, in contrast to the hard edges and severe geometry of Stella, adds yet another dimension to abstraction. She allows her colors—stained directly into raw canvas after the manner of Pollock—to assume free, shimmering shapes. She follows Pollock also in the technique of working a canvas that has been spread over the floor rather than set upon an easel or against a wall. In her *Formation* (Fig. 525) the result is a loose arrangement of lush colors washed in lyric abstraction across an open, generously scaled field. The thinness of the medium avoids the rich painterly surfaces of abstract expressionism and makes the hues seem filled with freshness and radiance.

Minimal and Kinetic Art   The implication behind *minimal art,* as the group in the 1960s called their work, is the reduction of sculpture to its irreducible minimum—a form, outline, or shape. Minimal artists were more concerned with the way their pieces created, enhanced, or blended into their architectural or urban environment than with the autonomy of their sculptural works as objects. The minimalist point of departure can be found in David Smith's late *Cubi* series (Fig. 514), but unlike Smith, the minimalists deemphasize personal involvement, expressive content, and hand welding in favor of fabricated impersonality. They also prefer "primary structures" (Figs. 526, 527)—basic geometric volumes so simple as to be redundant—over the planes typical of cubist-derived sculpture (see Figs. 470–472). Materials tend to be the industrial ones of galvanized iron, aluminum, stainless steel, laminated wood, fiberglass, and plastics.

The minimalists also employ industrial methods, drawing up plans and specifications and making a small model in painted wood. This then is turned over to an industrial shop for final execution. Like architects, they project their schemes on a huge scale for public sites and must await patrons with the capital to finance such enterprises. Before Tony

Smith could arrange for *Smoke* (Fig. 526) to be constructed in steel, he had it built in plywood for exhibition in a court at New York's Metropolitan Museum. Wandering in and out and through the work's huge arched forms and elemental shapes, the spectator is overwhelmed.

The minimalists shun the conception of sculpture as an isolated object. Their productions do not sit on pedestals; rather, they rest on the floor, stand against a wall, are suspended from the ceiling, or occupy a whole room. Better yet, they take to the out-of-doors, like Bernard Rosenthal's dramatically poised cube *Alamo* (Fig. 527), where they merge with the surrounding architectural space and become part of the total environment.

Many artists of the 1960s and 1970s have dematerialized their creations so that motion and colored light become the substance of the work of art. In this *kinetic art* sophisticated engineering and computer technology come into play. Leading the

below left: 526. Tony Smith. *Smoke.* 1967.
Plywood to be made into steel,
height 24′ (7.32 m).
Courtesy the artist.

below: 527. Bernard Rosenthal. *Alamo.* 1966.
Painted Cor-Ten steel, height 15′ (4.57 m).
Astor Place, New York.

left: 528. Marcel Duchamp. *Revolving Glass.* 1920.
Motorized optical device of five painted glass plates,
wood and metal braces, turning on a metal axis,
electrically operated; height 3′11½″ (1.21 m).
length 6′½″ (1.84 m). Yale University Art Gallery,
New Haven, Conn. (Collection Société Anonyme).

below: 529. Nicolas Schöffer. *Prisme Multiple with Lux 11.* 1960.
Mirror and stainless steel with motors and projectors;
height of *Prisme* 8′1½″ (2.5 m);
height of *Lux 11* 4′10½″ (1.5 m). Courtesy the artist.

way earlier in the century were Marcel Duchamp
with his primitive motorized works (Fig. 528) and
Alexander Calder with his mobiles animated by air
currents (see Fig. 554). Now with advancing electronic technology, light, action, and sound can be
combined in time-space creations that are variously
referred to as *kinetic, serially programmed,* or
luminist art.

Nicolas Schöffer uses computers to program his
creations in motion and light (Fig. 529) and employs
such terms as "spatiodynamics" and "luminiody-
namics" to discuss their alliance with science and
engineering. Others construct with gleaming metallic rods that whirl in fountainlike patterns whose
vibrations set up strange sound effects (Fig. 530).
Electromagnets can be programmed to sustain metal
objects in a pattern of attraction and repulsion.

The New Realism   The return of realism to the
scene in the 1970s has been hailed by some as going
back to the object, a return to the human figure, and
the triumph of common sense. Realism in various
guises and disguises, however, has been around ever
since the days of the cave artists. Realist easel paint-

530. Len Lye. *Fountain II.* 1963.
Steel rods and base, height 7′5½″ (2.27 m).
Tel Aviv Museum.

ing, in fact, is one of the oldest and grandest traditions in American art, as witnessed in *Old Models* (Fig. 531) by one of the old masters of the style, William Harnett. In the 20th century, realism has been all-pervasive by means of candid cameras, television, photojournalism, films, and theater.

The present generation of realist painters, however, refuses to yield naturalistic representational art to the photographers while at the same time it rejects the abstractionist notion that a picture has no referent beyond itself. The new realists are convinced that there is a world out there worth looking at and recording on canvas. This postabstractionist realism, however, does not shun the discoveries of the modern mode. It allows itself the choice of incorporating whatever devices may be relevant to its designs. The accent, in other words, is not on the subject or object portrayed, as in photography, or on the canvas as a flat surface, as in abstract art, but on the pictorial structure painted with all the refinements and sophistication possible.

It took both courage and self-confidence for an artist like Philip Pearlstein to paint the human figure (Fig. 532) in a style so long deplored and derided by abstractionist artists. He justifies his position persuasively:

> I have made a contribution to humanism in 20th-century painting—I rescued the human figure from its tormented, agonized condition given it by the expressionistic artists, and the cubist dissectors and distorters of the figure, and at the other extreme I have rescued it from the pornographers, and their easy exploitation of the figure for its sexual implications. I have presented the figure for itself, allowed it its own dignity as a form among other forms in nature.

above: 531. William Harnett. *Old Models.* 1892. Oil on canvas, 4′6″ × 2′4″ (1.37 × .71 m). Museum of Fine Arts, Boston (Charles Henry Hayden Fund).

right: 532. Philip Pearlstein. *Two Female Models in the Studio.* 1967. Oil on canvas, 4′2⅛″ × 5′1¼″ (1.27 × 1.53 m). Museum of Modern Art, New York (gift of Mr. and Mrs. Stephen B. Booke).

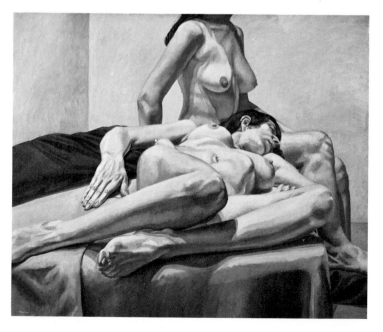

In his unblinking, up-close presentation of human flesh as it actually is—not the cosmetic counterfeits traditionally offered by both romantic and academic image makers—Pearlstein seems a literalist of the most blatant sort. But the viewer capable of absorbing the candor of this imagery may well succeed in granting to the human body its "dignity as a form among other forms in nature." The artist advances this cause by adopting a keen but unemotional attitude toward his subject—the studio model—and by cropping faces and heads so as to depersonalize the body. Simultaneously, however, Pearlstein is a man of his own time, and his interest in aesthetic form is no less committed than that of his abstractionist contemporaries.

Like his fellow artists Stella and Frankenthaler, Pearlstein is a cool rationalist who reacted against the reckless passion and formlessness of the gestural painters. Too, each painting represents for him both an intricate problem in composition and the resolution the artist has been able to bring to it. To dramatize his pictorial space, Pearlstein usually tilts his view down so as to bring images and background planes forward and align his figures with the picture plane. The harsh studio light he uses allows for little softening play of shadow. This cold, bright, artificial light is part of Pearlstein's cultivated detachment toward his subjects and paintings. By way of compensation color is brought into play, and a rich blend of hues provides a wide range of light and dark contrasting tones.

In Richard Estes' cityscapes such as *Downtown* (see Fig. 503) everything is sharply defined and crisply portrayed. They reveal an artist's reaction and commentary on the self-created urban environment people choose to live in. Through Estes' eyes people begin to see things they have not noticed before, and after they have seen Estes' pictures in a gallery, suddenly everything outside on the street begins to look to them like an Estes painting.

Estes works from photographs as raw material as his urban landscapes would be impossible to paint on the street itself. He does his own photography and develops the color prints himself. For *Downtown* he took over 75 exposures of the general view and details in various lighting and weather conditions. In the studio he produced a *photomontage,* or pasteup of photographic details, as a kind of working model. In the process, the photographic images were redrawn, positions of buildings and objects got shifted around, and the process of selection and elimination came into play so as to tighten up and clarify the composition. As he remarked in an interview: "I can select what to do or not to do from what's in the photograph. I can add or subtract from it. Every time I do something, it's a choice . . . it's a selection from the

533. Richard Estes. *Bus Window.* 1968–73.
Acrylic on canvas, 6 × 4′ (1.83 × 1.22 m).
Collection Mr. and Mrs. R. A. L. Ellis, Kansas City, Mo.

various aspects of reality." Then with his cool assured craftsmanship the final stage emerges with brilliant clarity and crisp definition.

In both *Downtown* and *Bus Window* (Fig. 533) reflections play a major role. Like mirrors they actually seem to double the pictorial space in a complex interplay of reality and reflection. By this means the viewer sees not only what occurs inside the picture plane with its recessions in depth, but also what goes on in front of the picture. This adds another plane and dimension to the picture space. With the interplay of plate-glass refractions everything seems doubled; for instance, one sees not only the interior of a building but its repetition with variants in mirror-image reflections as well.

In Estes' concentrated canvases his extremely careful rendering of detail and clarity of focus on objects both near and far spreads the interest equally over the entire picture surface. In such a complex work as *Bus Window* the diagonal alignment of the

534. Duane Hanson. *Man with Handcart.* 1975.
Polyester resin and fiberglass, polychromed in oil; life-size.
Collection Sydney and Frances Lewis, Richmond, Va.

street intersections, the system of angular lines, and
the reflections on the convex windshield produce a
pattern even more amazing and complex than anything found in cubism.

Duane Hanson provides the sculptural dimension
to the new realism. When seen in a gallery his figures mix right in with the crowd, and one can hardly
tell some of the spectators from the statues until they
move on. Returning to the street after seeing a
Duane Hanson show, one seems to see an animated
Hanson statue in every passerby.

Hanson's *Man with Handcart* (Fig. 534) is one of
his believable people. From the grave troubled face,
the weary posture with the sagging muscles, to the
scuffed worn-out shoes, it is a pathetic portrait of a
loser in the game of life. His *Supermarket Shopper*
(see Fig. 7) is a satire on overconsumption and what
is thought to be the good life. The shopper's cart is
piled up with TV dinners, prepared salads, cookies,
cans of Coke, and other assorted junk foods. It all
adds up to a devastating commentary on the conspicuous consumption in much of middle-class America.
Instead of living, Hanson's shopper is just existing,

rich enough to afford all the products television com-
mercials have sold her, yet a spiritual pauper.

Hanson uses live models and makes a flexible
mold of each section of the body—legs, torso, arms,
and head in turn. Then the parts are assembled and
shaped into the desired posture. Next, successive
layers of flesh-colored polyester resin are poured into
the negative mold, and it is reinforced with fiberglass. After the negative mold is removed, the positive mold is revealed and the needed repairs are
made. Then it is ready for painting and finishing.
Such details as wigs, clothes, eyeglasses, and accessories are all real. The resulting figures are so natural that they do everything but walk and breathe.
Hanson's work, however, is far from waxwork image
making. His figures are genuine human types shaped
by their environment, caught up in the web of their
social circumstances. It is illuminating to compare
Man with Handcart with the Hellenistic *Old Market
Woman* (see Fig. 82). Here are the same weary figures worn out by toil and trouble.

Hanson purposely picks ordinary, everyday people who live rather dull lives—working-class people,
the downtrodden, the commonplace. As he comments, "I prefer to stay away from unusual looking
people and try to produce a figure people can be
confronted with in their everyday lives." Yet he lifts
ordinary people to symbolic status. The honesty and
intensity he puts into his work brings both the absurd and serious aspects of life into focus. Hansen
obviously has a feeling of deep compassion and personal involvement in the lives of his fellow human
beings. Through them he is criticizing the social
circumstances that have brought them to their present plight. The range of his output spans social satire, the horrors of war, the forces that drive men and
women to desperate acts. His most recent work,
however, consists of penetrating studies of what urbanization, mechanization, and automation do to
individual human beings.

The new realism reaches into all categories except the fantastic inner world of dreams. A fine example of contemporary landscape painting is provided by Alfred Leslie's *View of the Connecticut
River as Seen from Mt. Holyoke* (see Fig. 9). For
sensitive portraiture, intensity, and probing self-analy-
sis, Gregory Gillespie's realistic *Self-Portrait* (Fig.
535) can compare with the best work of any age. In
his introspective gaze he is following the age-old
motto of Socrates, "Know thyself." For precedents
one would have to look at similar self-revelations by
Dürer (see Fig. 284), Caravaggio, Rembrandt (see
Figs. 340–343), and Van Gogh. This is not the cool
objectivity of Estes' photorealism, but rather a pene-
tration into the depths of one's being in the eternal
quest for self-knowledge.

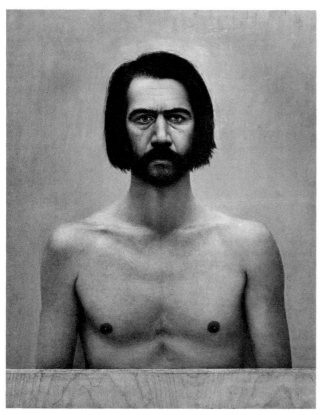

535. Gregory Gillespie. *Self-Portrait (Torso).* 1975. Oil and magna on wood, 30¼ × 24¾″ (77 × 63 cm). Collection Sydney and Frances Lewis, Richmond, Va.

Recent Musical Developments

Modern science has provided composers and audiences with a whole new world of sound. Instead of vibrations resulting from strings or columns of air as with traditional instruments, sound waves can now be produced by electronic oscillations. With the invention and development of electronically generated sound, the use and alteration of everyday sound data by tape recorder, the random choices of musical happenings, the management of mathematical-musical formulas via the computer, and the psychedelic manifestations in mixed media, there is a whole host of novel possibilities.

However, just because composers are inclined to experimentation does not necessarily mean that they are in the front of the procession, for experiments can lead to blind alleys and dead ends even more easily than to significant breakthroughs. And if such experiments do succeed in making major breakthroughs, the mere manipulation of new materials and ideas is not sufficient in itself to become the stuff of new art forms. For that it takes the appearance and efforts of a master composer, one able to control the new resources and shape them into the forms of a new creative synthesis.

So whether a composer moves in the direction of rigidly controlled serialism, employs electronic computerization, or adopts the tried-and-true traditions of selective eclecticism, only time can tell which road leads to the future. Historical experience reveals that these seemingly new phenomena are actually variants and extensions of age-old principles and basic human urges. Viewed in this objective light, the events of the last quarter of the 20th century will in all likelihood exhibit about the same mixture of old, new, and experimental elements, of conservative, liberal, and progressive directions, of past, present, and future trends as those to be encountered at any historical cross section of time.

Concrete music is the term used to identify one aspect of contemporary composition. It involves using the tape recorder to capture everyday sounds and manipulate them on magnetic tape. The procedure might be compared with the way Robert Rauschenberg puts together one of his assemblages (Fig. 516). The artist selects some random objects—Coke bottles, a birdcage, bedsprings, old newspaper clippings—and then combines them into a three-dimensional collage, even painting some sections.

The composer of *concrete music* finds sounds and noises all around—the clanking of trash cans, the whine of jet engines, the roar of city traffic, the sirens of fire trucks. Once recorded, these environmental sounds can be edited, the sequence controlled, and the tape run at varying speeds, spliced or scrambled, and played backward. The material can also be filtered by eliminating overtones, with feedback added or subtracted, and certain sounds may be isolated, fragmented, and broken down into separate components. The possibilities are far-ranging.

Another and more sophisticated approach is found in sounds artificially produced by means of the *synthesizer* used in combination with a *computer.* By converting sound waves, with their elements of pitch, dynamics, duration, and tone color, into digits or a number series, the synthesizer-computer can then be programmed to produce a tape capable of being played back on a tape recorder. There are also portable synthesizers suitable for use in live performance.

Composers who have mastered the techniques of computer sound generation can now dispense with conventional instruments and live musicians, if they wish, and use tapes or disks to distribute their works directly to the listener. The process of producing a musical work on tape is like that of the graphic arts, in which the artist creates a master plate of an etching or lithograph.

Many composers from Gluck to Stravinsky have protested bitterly against singers, instrumentalists, and conductors who take liberties with their scores in live performances. Thus, in one instance the composer runs the risk of having the purposes of a work altered by the interpreter, but in the other the composer loses the spontaneity of a live performance and the creative insights that a skilled and responsible performer can bring to music.

Some composers have found a middle ground by combining electronically produced material with live musical situations. It is also possible to write a symphony in which electronic sound becomes one of the sections of the symphony orchestra, or compose a concerto for synthesizer or tape recorder and orchestra. Whatever the case, it should be stressed that the medium is not the music. Computer-synthesizers, to be sure, are far more complex than pianos, violins, or even the symphony orchestra. But ultimately they are only instruments, the means to an end.

Electronically minded composers can work in any style they may desire. History, however, establishes that each breakthrough must evolve its own vocabularies and exploit areas idiomatic and unique to the properties of the particular medium. Eventually composers must summon the whole of their creative imagination in order to produce valid tonal continuums interesting and significant enough to establish contact with the listener.

Whether the musical process is improvisatory, as with concrete music and chance happenings, or rationally controlled, as with computerization, ample precedents in the musical past can be cited. Random fancy, for instance, is apparently as old as music itself. If the 20th-century composer seems to stress chance, the procedure is not essentially different from the vocal improvisations made in medieval times on old Gregorian tunes, an organist inventing variants on Protestant hymns, Bach writing out his free toccatas and fantasies, or a virtuoso instrumentalist ad-libbing cadenzas in a classical concerto.

Freedom and strictness, however, are neither mutually nor musically exclusive, and the wise composer maintains both options separately or in combination. The work of Karlheinz Stockhausen and John Cage, both prominent figures on the international musical scene, reveal some of the possibilities of this mode of music making.

When today's mathematically minded composer turns to the computer, the process may differ in kind but not in spirit from certain musical methods of the past. The mathematical basis for music, for instance, has been known ever since Pythagoras discovered the ratios of the musical intervals in the late 6th century B.C. (see p. 45). Some medieval composers accelerated or slowed down the note values of melodies and thereby expanded or contracted the rhythmic ratios of their motets. In his thirty variations on a theme, the famous *"Goldberg" Variations,* Bach in every third variation (the third, sixth, ninth, and so on) devised a series of canons, or exact imitations, from the unison, or same note, to the ninth.

In the earlier 20th century Schoenberg and Berg employed rigorous serial techniques with the tone rows and their segments appearing straightforward, in inversion, in retrograde, and in retrograde inversion (see pp. 420–421). The musical thought of Milton Babbitt illustrates this approach, while a string quartet by Elliott Carter exemplifies the continuity of the classical tradition.

Karlheinz Stockhausen

Now perhaps the outstanding representative of electronic composition, Karlheinz Stockhausen is one of a group associated with the Studio for Electronic Music, a subsidiary of the West German Radio at Cologne. Chance elements in his music are controlled so as to bring new forms into being—forms that grow out of the musical material.

Stockhausen began by working with "sine-wave tones," pure sounds stripped of their overtones, and then synthesizing them into a new and inventive sound spectrum. This implies the rearrangement and alteration of fundamental acoustical elements for the purpose of forming new textures and densities that become the building blocks of sound structures. This early phase of Stockhausen's work may be heard in *Study I* and *Study II* that date from 1953.

In *Gesang der Jünglinge* (*Song of the Boys in the Fiery Furnace*) of 1956 Stockhausen intended to bring the human voice into a working relationship with electronic sounds. He chose the text from Chapter 3 of the book of Daniel. The story, dating from the Babylonian captivity, is that of the men cast into the fiery furnace by Nebuchadnezzar whose golden statue they refused to worship. The materials are the vowels and consonants sung and spoken by a boy soprano, then pulverized into an impressionistic mist of pointillistic sounds and superimposed on electronically generated sound mixtures of varying density.

The vocal fragments in this work seem to float in and out, creating an effect that is airy, spacious, and transparent. Occasionally the listener hears intelligible words, but more often the vocal part comes across as pure sound. The work was conceived and recorded before stereophonic sound became widely available. Thus, Stockhausen prepared it to be heard in a large round room where five speakers could throw the tonal materials back and forth and around the listener, so as to envelop and surround the audience with sound waves moving through space.

Method of Composition   Despite his invention of ingenious notational symbols for scoring electronic sounds, Stockhausen, in his more recent work, has parted company with a written score in favor of composing directly on tape. The genesis of such a composition is to fix the limits of the time dimension arbitrarily to, say, twenty or forty minutes and do perhaps a dozen "takes." Then the composer, like a film director, edits and chooses what will eventually become the final version.

For this style Stockhausen has evolved a complicated technique in which he may use players to produce short motifs, often in the extreme registers of their instruments. Also, in the manner of the theater of the absurd, the composer can call on them to improvise a sequence of grunts and groans, shrieks and squawks, hisses and sighs.

Each instrumentalist in such a composition session has a contact microphone connected to a central control panel. Here sits Stockhausen (Fig. 536), like the conductor of old; but instead of a baton, he has a complex of electronic devices called "sine-wave generators," "potentiometers," and "ring modulators." In a series of takes he develops the final composition. Developing, according to Stockhausen, means that the sounds are "spread, condensed, extended, shortened, differently colored, more or less articulated, transposed, modulated, multiplied, synchronized."

This approach is illustrated in *Opus 1970.* Each of the four players is provided with a previously prepared tape consisting of various fragments of Beethoven's piano sonatas, symphonies, the violin concerto, and some vocal music. The tapes play continuously, but the player may turn the loudspeakers up or down at will. All the while Stockhausen sits at his controls filtering, altering, changing the speed, blending the timbres, so as to achieve the effects and shapes he desires.

The listener's impression is that of an electronic soundscape in which Beethoven's music is reduced to fine particles, reassembled, and cubistically combined into a sequence of tantalizing, wispy fragments. Occasionally the synthesizer may pick up a Beethovenian theme or line and carry on an inventive dialogue with it. Stockhausen says his intention is not to interpret, but "to hear familiar, old, performed musical material with new ears, to penetrate and transform it with a musical consciousness of today." To some, the result may sound like confusion confounded, a mixture of serenity and hysteria. For others it may accomplish what the composer hoped it would—that is, put Beethoven's music in a new relationship with the contemporary scene. In all events, it must be conceded that Stockhausen is a major musical mind, a composer of invention and ingenu-

536. Karlheinz Stockhausen during a performance of his *Mikrophonie I.*
Courtesy Westdeutscher Rundfunk Köln.

ity, a craftsman who manipulates and arranges his materials with a sure hand.

John Cage

From the 1930s through the 1970s, John Cage has invariably proved a provocative, often articulate leader for avant-garde experimental developments. Nowadays he is most closely identified with the kind of chance techniques and musical happenings commonly referred to as *aleatory music.* The word "aleatory" derives from the Latin *alea,* meaning "dice," and John Cage believes in rolling the musical dice, tossing tonal coins, and accepting whatever comes up at random in the world of sound.

Cage's announced objective is to bring about a "revolution in the nature of musical experience." It could be said that the concern of earlier Western music with the nature and reconciliation of the opposites of dissonance and consonance eventually led to the present complete liberation of dissonance. Should this be true, Cage shares with other contemporary composers the problem of synthesizing musical sounds and noise. An early 20th-century composer much admired by Cage is Erik Satie (see p. 426), who once declared himself ambitious to invent a music that would be like the furniture—a music partaking of the noises of the environment, one capable of softening the sounds of knives and forks at dinner and of filling the silences in conversation.

Cage's revolt is against the extreme ordering and ultracontrolled conditions of such music as twelve-tone serialism, in which a precise reason exists for the placement of each note. So he conceives his own music as an experimental activity that creates conditions in which nothing is foreseen. He would free sounds from any preset formal continuity. Composer-critic Virgil Thompson finds in Cage a "healthy lawlessness," and he hears Cage's music as a "collage of noises" that produces a "homogenized chaos" carrying "no program, no plot, no reminders of the history of beauty, and no personal statement."

Listener Participation   According to Cage, music should give people a feeling that they are doing something rather than having something done to them. Listeners, he believes, should experience involvement, and the music should afford them "the opportunity to have experiences they would not otherwise have had."

One phase of Cage's work (1967–1969) is heard in *HPSCHD* (computerese for "harpsichord," since the computer was not programmed to accommodate words of more than 6 letters). He and his colleague Lejaren Hiller "scored" the work for from 1 to 7 harpsichordists playing simultaneously and at random various compositions or fragments (chosen individually by each harpsichordist) from the music of Bach, Mozart, and Beethoven, as well as from jazz and blues. They play against a background of from 1 to 51 computer-generated sound tapes superimposed on each other in random montage structures.

When first presented at the University of Illinois, the performance, complete with a light show that included 64 projectors, lasted well over four hours. It is now available in condensed form as a publication and recording, the latter timed for a little over twenty minutes. The 51 sound tapes were programmed to produce a composite of tones and silences based on a series of equal-tempered scales by dividing the octave into equal steps varying from 5 to 56 tones. The sequences then appear as an intermixture of "successive events, melodic 'goals' (without cadence) and types (diatonic, chromatic, chordal arpeggiation), volume, and dynamics. . . ."

The hi-fi operator and the listener are also invited to get into the act as the composers provide a computer printout for playback control. At five-second intervals, the operator can change the volume and alternate the treble and bass controls. The operator also is directed to switch the stereo channels from left to right as well as to combine both together. The home listener's stereo set thus becomes a basic part of the composition.

Cage's pieces avoid the conventional sense of a beginning or an end. At a given point one begins to hear sounds, and after a while one does not. By avoiding repetition, Cage causes his works to seem endlessly repetitious. Some listeners thus may agree with Virgil Thompson that there is no need for playing any of Cage's recordings for longer than five minutes, "since we know that it will not be going any deeper into an emotion already depicted as static. Nor will it be following nature's way by developing an organic structure."

In coming to terms with the realities of musical experience, Cage's chance happenings and aleatory ramblings are essentially denied the moment they appear as recordings. He declares, with justification, that a composition played for a second time is something quite other than it was, and that a "recording of such a work has no more value than a postcard; it provides a knowledge of something that happened, whereas the action was a non-knowledge of something that had not yet happened." At one of his lectures Cage summarized himself as follows: "I have nothing to say and I am saying it, and that is poetry."

Milton Babbitt

Milton Babbitt's taking-off point was Schoenberg's twelve-tone method, but he extends serialism to include rhythm, dynamics, tone color, and speed, as well as pitch, harmony, and counterpoint. The computer is a natural instrument for Babbitt. He thinks with it and through it. With the computer, sounds can be superimposed; retrograde progressions become available by reversing the numbers; and all manner of speed changes, including rhythmic augmentation (expansion), diminution (contraction), and fluctuations (shifts) of tempo can be programmed.

The serialization of rhythm, for instance, involves ordering duration values in a graduated scale. Various rhythmic patterns and variants can then be programmed by multiplying or fractionalizing a proportional mathematical series. It could be a simple arithmetical progression such as 1, 2, 3, 4, 5, 6; or something more complex like 1, 2, 3, 5, 8, 13. Dynamic values—levels of soft and loud, fade-outs and fade-ins—may also be rotated in series.

The digital synthesizer (Fig. 537), in contrast to the limitations of conventional musical instruments, has the capability to control a limitless supply of musical and nonmusical sounds. With so vast a range of sonorities available to it, the computer can be programmed to perform as a composing machine. As such it can construct self-generated works or become the partner of a human composer.

Babbitt's *Vision and Prayer* (1961) for soprano and synthesizer merges the nonelectronic and electronic worlds of sound with a soprano singing live along with a tape produced by the computer (in this case the RCA Mark II Electronic Sound Synthesizer that fills an entire room at the Columbia-Princeton Electronic Music Center). The text by Dylan Thomas is sung by the soprano in wide-skipping intervals,

537. RCA Electronic Sound Synthesizer, Columbia-Princeton Electronic Music Center, New York.

I turn the corner of prayer and burn
In a blessing of the sudden
Sun. In the name of the damned
I would turn back and run
To the hidden land
But the loud sun
Christens down
The sky.
I
Am found.
O let him
Scald me and drown
Me in his world's wound.
His lightning answers my
Cry. My voice burns in his hand.
Now I am lost in the blinding
One. The sun roars at the prayer's end.*

while the computer's tape deals with the tone quality and the structure of the poem.

It is not surprising that Babbitt was attracted to a poem like Dylan Thomas' *Vision and Prayer*. It is a well-known anthology piece, an impressive vision that reads with a sense of verbal grandeur. Yet it is a serial poem, the length of the lines predetermined by the number of syllables that, according to the series, it must possess. The number series 1 to 9 yields on the printed page two visual designs, each with seventeen lines. The first design (for the first six stanzas) proceeds on the basis of one syllable for the first line, two for the second, three for the third, and so on up to nine syllables for the ninth line. The series then moves in retrograde. The tenth line has eight syllables, the eleventh has seven, and so on until at the seventeenth line one arrives again at a one-syllable word. This progression—1, 2, 3, 4, 5, 6, 7, 8, 9, 8, 7, 6, 5, 4, 3, 2, 1—yields a diamond-shaped stanza. For the second set of six stanzas, the syllables per line follow the progression 9, 8, 7, 6, 5, 4, 3, 2, 1, 2, 3, 4, 5, 6, 7, 8, 9, which produces on the page two triangles linked at their common apex (line 9). The first and last stanzas follow:

Who
Are you
Who is born
In the next room
So loud to my own
That I can hear the womb
Opening and the dark run
Over the ghost and the dropped son
Behind the wall thin as a wren's bone?
In the birth bloody room unknown
To the burn and turn of time
And the heart print of man
Bows no baptism
But dark alone
Blessing on
The wild
Child.

Babbitt's aesthetic stance rests upon an appeal to intellectual rigor as the basis for the putting together (that is, the composing) of a piece of music. It is a view that makes no concession to immediate popular understanding. As he himself has said, "the composer's first obligation is to his art, to the evolution of music and the advancement of musical concepts."

Elliott Carter

Igor Stravinsky once remarked that a new work by Elliot Carter was an event awaited in the musical world by all concerned with the serious music of the present time. Carter's String Quartet No. 1 (1951) received first prize in the prestigious *Concours International de Quatuor* (International Quartet Competition) of 1953 in Liège, Belgium. His String Quartet No. 2 (1959) has won several awards—the Pulitzer Prize for Music (1960), the New York Music Critics' Circle Award (1960), and the International Rostrum of Composers Award (UNESCO) in Paris (1961). His superb Double Concerto for Piano, Harpsichord, and Small Orchestra was hailed by Stravinsky as a masterpiece. It is worth adding that the acclaim and the awards have been richly deserved.

Nourished on traditional techniques as well as on Schoenberg's twelve-tone method, Carter also found inspiration in the idealism of Charles Ives, the old master of American music whom he knew as friend and neighbor. Carter has said that for him music must have "an audible order that can be distinguished, remembered, and followed." He also points out that his compositions are no longer built on themes or tone rows. Instead, the building blocks of his musical structures can just as well be "tone color, a chord, or a texture."

*From *The Poems of Dylan Thomas,* copyright 1946 by New Directions Publishing Corporation, reprinted by permission of New Directions Publishing Corporation, J. M. Dent & Sons Ltd., and the Trustees for the Copyrights of the late Dylan Thomas.

"I like music to be beautiful, ordered, and expressive of the more important aspects of life," Carter has observed. "The idea of my music, if it can be considered apart from its expressive and communicative character (which I doubt), could be said to be a constantly evolving series of shapes, like the patterns of choreography." Indeed, it is to Carter's remarkable rhythmic invention and unique command of the time experience that listeners must first look.

"Metrical modulation," as Carter calls it, is central to his thought. This is a rhythmic phenomenon in which tempos fluctuate in the different instrumental parts, and the rhythmic and metrical values are lengthened and shortened in a kind of neomedieval version of rigorously controlled motet construction. In earlier times, however, such rhythmic complexities involved simple augmentation and diminution, as when, for example, the basic unit is in quarter notes and the variants appear in halves or eighths. Carter's technique, however, is much more subtle and involves exact timing by the metronome, with the proportions—to cite the case of the Adagio of his Cello Concerto—set at seven to six as the eighth notes broaden from seventy per minute to sixty.

In Carter's pieces constant variety rather than repetition thus prevails in a kind of tidal motion of ebbs and flows, with constantly changing pulsations brought about by the overlapping of speeds in the various parts. Carter has said that he thinks of a work as "one large motion including many inner ones. The motion is often circular, in that there is a recall or return of the beginning. Within this, events emerge and disappear, usually affording hints or pretexts for succeeding ones."

Second String Quartet   "I regard my scores as scenarios—auditory scenarios—for performers to act out with their instruments, dramatizing the players as individuals and as participants in the ensemble," says Carter in his comments on the String Quartet No. 2. "To me the special teamwork of group playing is very wonderful and moving, and this feeling is always an important consideration in my chamber music." In this quartet Carter sets himself the problem of how a player can remain an individual while forming part of a group—just as in society.

A string quartet, the composer points out, has four instruments all very much alike in sound, "so in my Second Quartet, I had the idea of composing a piece for string quartet which would be, so to speak, a 'non-string quartet,' one in which the instruments were separate in sound and character. This involved composing parts that were much more highly differentiated in pitch, rhythm, and tessitura [range] than those of the Double Concerto because of the similarity in timbres." Each instrument, he says, maintains its own character "in a special set of melodic and harmonic intervals and of rhythms that result in four different patterns of slow and fast tempi with associated types of expression."

To emphasize the distinction of the parts, the composer suggests that the players "be more widely spaced than usual on the stage so that each is clearly separated from the others." This, he feels, makes not only for a more spacious play of sound, but allows the four semi-independent parts to interact dramatically while maintaining their separate identities in a four-way "conversation and argumentation."

Each instrument is thus typecast, "for each fairly consistently invents its own material out of its own special attitude and its own repertory of musical speeds and intervals." The first violin, the composer says, "should exhibit the greatest variety of character, sometimes playing with insistent rigidity (where indicated) but more often in bravura style." It also has its intervallic motifs. While all instruments use major and minor seconds, the first violin plays mainly in minor thirds, perfect fifths, major ninths, and major tenths. "Throughout the entire Quartet," Carter continues, "the second violin acts as a moderating influence, using its pizzicato [plucked] and arco [bowed] notes to mark regular time, its half, or double—always at the same speed." The second fiddle therefore becomes the "square" of the group contributing an attitude of "regularity and steadiness." A marked preference for major thirds, sixths, and sevenths is noted. The viola is "entrusted with the most expressive passages featuring glissandos [slides] and portamentos [slurs]," while using the more pungent augmented fourths, minor sevenths, and minor ninths. The composer conceives of the role of the cello as a "firmer, less fickle counterpart of the first violin."

Carter's Second Quartet might be described as a string-quartet player's quartet. Condensed and concentrated, the piece is concerned with "behavioral patterns" that the composer defines as an "ever-changing series of motives and figures having certain internal relationships with each other." Carter here reveals an enormous knowledge in building up his structure in rhythmic layers with the role of the tempo being modified at each different level. As such, this masterly quartet is a reflection of the thought and meticulous craftsmanship of a major musical mind—a model for the reconciliation of the opposites of individualism and group action, of improvisatory freedom under thoughtful formal controls. Carter's reputation grows with each new work, and he now ranks as one of America's greatest living composers.

In conclusion, this review of avant-garde developments should be qualified by recalling that at the present stage of expanded historical horizons, contemporary music in the larger context is what contemporary audiences choose to listen to. Concert programs as well as recording collections reveal that Bach, Beethoven, and other classic masters enjoy a greater following on the current scene than do Karlheinz Stockhausen, John Cage, Milton Babbitt, and Elliott Carter. The approach to recent developments in music leads in many directions. It is possible to feel secure in savoring tried-and-true classics. But modern listeners, like contemporary composers, can find adventure in exploring unfamiliar pathways.

The New Architecture

The shrill arguments between the pure functionalism of the international style and the more humanistic direction of Frank Lloyd Wright's organic structures have become muted in architectural developments since 1945. While Le Corbusier's "machines for living" still hum and whir (see Fig. 501) and Wright's more personal designs for living continue to grow (see Figs. 495, 496), both sides have had to give ground when confronted in the new environment with the problems of increasing urbanization.

Even the once-despised element of decoration has gained new respectability in overall architectural designs. Today's architect has once again become the partner of the painter, sculptor, and mosaicist. From the bleak utilitarianism of the early international style, architecture has turned once more to the principle of ornamentation—not, however, extraneous embellishment or mere architectural embroidery, but the inclusion of sculptures and murals as basic parts of the larger architectural statement. Well-placed sculptural groups, frescoes, or mosaics as points of interest can always give definition to exteriors and interiors and serve as symbols of human involvement. An unexpected turn here or a twist there can create an element of fantasy, warmth, and delight.

The Fifties

Bunshaft, Miës van der Rohe, and Johnson
The continuity of the international tradition, appropriately modified in the 1950s, can be seen on the New York skyline in two striking examples—Lever House (Fig. 538) and the Seagram Building (Fig. 539). Here, the architects have offset the pronounced verticality of early skyscrapers by limiting the number of stories, setting the structures back from the street, and adding to them a horizontal base on which the buildings are balanced.

Lever House (Fig. 538) is cantilevered outward beyond its structural supports to allow the great rise of gleaming translucent glass walls to reflect the city and sky with mirrorlike brightness. By omitting the ground floor and reducing the supporting steel shafts to a minimum, the architects created a small public garden and open passageway at the street level.

The Seagram Building (Fig. 539) has been called by its designers, Miës van der Rohe and Philip John-

right: 538.
Gordon Bunshaft,
with Skidmore,
Owings & Merrill.
Lever House, New York.
1952.

far right: 539.
Ludwig Miës van der Rohe
and Philip Johnson.
Seagram Building,
New York. 1958.

below: **540.** Le Corbusier. Notre-Dame-du-Haut, Ronchamp, France. View from southeast. 1950–55.

right: **541.** Le Corbusier. Interior south wall, Notre-Dame-du-Haut.

son, the "Tower of Light." Open at the ground level, the building is supported by stilts the functionalism of which is offset by outdoor pools and gardens sunk into a pink granite platform. The tower of smoky amber glass is cantilevered over bronze-colored steel piers to impart airiness to the soaring mass. With a taste for the structurally spare, Miës van der Rohe went beyond mere practicality and delighted in the proportions of his buildings and revelled in the beauty of their materials. While baser metals would have been equally functional, the architect showed extreme sensitivity to the qualities and potentialities of his chosen materials. In the Seagram Building the bronze finish of the rising lines is alternately smooth and textured to provide a contrapuntal pattern.

Le Corbusier   Also a painter of note, Le Corbusier allowed more color, poetry, and freedom to enter the designs of his later architecture. His pilgrimage church of Notre-Dame-du-Haut at Ronchamp (Fig. 540), high up in the Vosges Mountains of southeastern France, is a delightful fantasy of free sculptural forms in ferroconcrete and stained glass. A prowlike roof harks back to the early Christian meaning of the word *nave,* which signified a "ship" steering its way through the stormy seas of life toward a haven of refuge.

The grandeur of the exterior of Ronchamp has the power to rival the splendid natural setting, but the interior (Fig. 541) offers the intimacy of human scale. Years before, Le Corbusier and his associates

had devised a proportional system based on 7½ feet (2.2 meters), the approximate height attainable by an average man when standing with an arm raised. Using this dimension as a basic module, or unit of measure, the architect felt confident of achieving in his structures a scale suitable to human beings.

On the interior, the south wall (Fig. 541) may well be one of the great surfaces in the history of architecture. The pitch, curve, and massiveness of the wall suggest living strength and vitality. Its fine, expressive beauty, however, derives from the inspired subtlety with which the openings have been coordinated through their differences not only in scale, proportion, color, and decoration but also in the angles of their niches. Here and there on the stained glass have been painted those ancient praises of the Virgin: *Je vous salue Marie, pleine de grâce* ("Hail Mary, full of grace"). At Ronchamp, Le Corbusier achieved an interior whose richness and complexity are functionally appropriate to the enactment of the rites of holy mystery.

Frank Lloyd Wright   In the closing years of his notable career, Frank Lloyd Wright finally received a commission to construct a building in his country's largest city—the Solomon R. Guggenheim Museum (Fig. 542), a gallery for abstract art. For Wright a museum should never be a group of boxlike compartments but a continuous flow of floor space in which the eye encounters no obstruction. To achieve this ideal, he designed a single round room of rein-

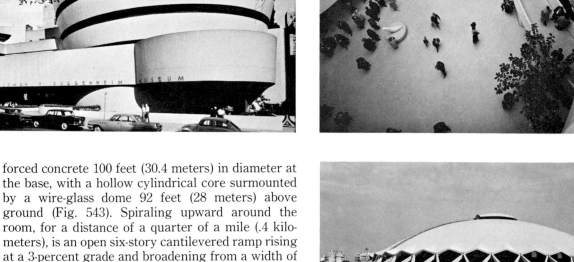

forced concrete 100 feet (30.4 meters) in diameter at the base, with a hollow cylindrical core surmounted by a wire-glass dome 92 feet (28 meters) above ground (Fig. 543). Spiraling upward around the room, for a distance of a quarter of a mile (.4 kilometers), is an open six-story cantilevered ramp rising at a 3-percent grade and broadening from a width of 17 feet (5.2 meters) at its lowest level to almost 35 feet (10.7 meters) at the top.

Throngs of spectators can be accommodated without congestion as they move easily up or down the ramp. Visitors can take the elevator to the top level and wind downward at leisure, or they can start at the bottom and walk up. They can inspect part of the exhibit at close range and at eye level or view three levels simultaneously across the open room.

The Sixties

Nervi and Saarinen Pier Luigi Nervi and Eero Saarinen, in their imaginative solutions to the problems of contemporary building, have achieved a working synthesis by providing for the functional needs of the many without sacrificing beauty of design and style. Nervi's Palazzetto dello Sport (Figs. 544, 545) is, as the title suggests, a sports palace erected in Rome for the 1960 Olympic games. The Y-shaped ferroconcrete columns are like caryatids in their suggestion of human forms whose outstretched arms seem to converge in a concerted muscular effort to support the spreading shell.

above: **544.** Pier Luigi Nervi.
Palazzetto dello Sport, Rome. 1960.

below: **545.** Pier Luigi Nervi.
Interior, Palazzetto dello Sport.

For his Trans World Flight Center at Kennedy International Airport in New York (Figs. 502, 546), Saarinen designed flowing concrete forms and dynamic stresses to convey the idea of flight while providing an airline terminal facility. Four large concrete shells resting on supports of abstract shape enclose an interior remarkable for its elastic space and sculpturesque plasticity. The complete absence of angularity makes both the interior and exterior a festival of curvilinear forms.

In his Gateway Arch for the Jefferson Westward Expansion Memorial at St. Louis (Fig. 547), Saarinen threw a sublimely simple, gleaming stainless-steel arch soaring 630 feet (192 meters) into space to mark the movement toward the western frontier. Technically it is a *catenary curve*–the shape of a chain suspended freely between two points–with height equal to width. The hollow triangular legs enclose elevator shafts and a winding stairway leading to an observatory at the apex. Set in an 85-acre (34.4-hectare) park on the banks of the Mississippi, this highest arch in the world is visible at a distance of 30 miles (48 kilometers).

above: 546. Eero Saarinen.
Interior, Trans World Flight Center,
Kennedy International Airport, New York. 1962.

below: 547. Eero Saarinen.
Jefferson Westward Expansion Memorial (Gateway Arch),
St. Louis. 1967. Stainless steel; height 630′ (192.02 m),
width at base 630′ (192.02 m).

Kahn and Venturi   Heir to the romanticism of Frank Lloyd Wright, Philadelphia architect Louis I. Kahn was one of the first Americans to make a significant break from the international-style tall boxes of glass and steel (see Figs. 538, 539) that in the postwar period of the 1950s came to line both sides of New York's Park Avenue, as well as many other streets all over the nation. While the Bauhaus-inspired architects strove to make their buildings look light and airy by denying and defying the weight of the materials and structure that hold them together, Kahn designed massive structures the monumentality of which has the grandeur of Gothic cathedrals and Egyptian temples. Indeed, they proclaim the drama the architect finds in the materials and processes of building. Kahn wanted his buildings to be "legible," and because they reveal how they were made, he believed they could be "read." Considered one of the great "form givers" of his time, Kahn looked to the knuckles, joints, and unfinished materials of his structures and there found the true basis of richness and ornament.

Among architects, Kahn identified not with those who pretend to solve problems presented by the client but with the designer-artists who want to provide "a society of spaces the client never dreamed of." Thus, he demanded complete freedom to program the life that would take place in his buildings. He received this from Dr. Jonas Salk, who specified for the Salk Institute for Biological Studies (Fig. 548) only that the laboratory provide 10,000 square feet (930 square meters) of work space for each of ten

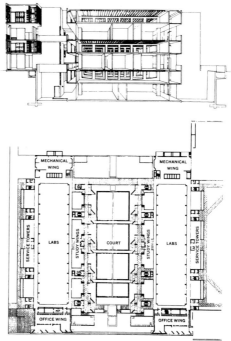

left: 548. Louis I. Kahn.
Salk Institute of Biological Studies,
La Jolla, Calif. 1968.

above: 549. Louis I. Kahn.
Plan and section of Salk Institute of Biological Studies.

scientists. Thus, when Kahn found he disagreed with the biologists on the program for their work, he set about to redirect their attitudes:

> I did not follow the dictates of the scientists, who said they are so dedicated to what they are doing that even when lunchtime comes, all they do is clear test tubes away from the benches and eat their lunches right there. I asked them: "Isn't it a strain to always hear the noises of the refrigerator and the centrifuges and the air conditioners?" "Yes," they said, "the noises are terrible." So I refused to listen to them about what should be done. I realized there should be a clean-air and stainless-steel area, and a rug and oak-table area.

To work out his program, Kahn posed such simple and direct questions as: "What does the space want to be?" "What is a wall?" "What is the use of this building?" His purpose was to discover the right program and convert it to architectural life: "When I am designing a school, I am seeking the nature of school, not just the solution for a school. This is before the many problems of the spaces and their services may be brought into unity."

Such fresh and fundamental thinking inevitably arrived at new solutions to what Kahn considered the

two basic problems in the design of buildings: the relationship of both natural light and the building's "guts" (elevators, air-conditioners, wind braces, toilets, and so on) to the main living and working spaces. The former he saw as the "servant" spaces. While ordering the servant spaces around the served areas, he also integrated them into the design aesthetic so that not only does the housing for air-conditioners and wind braces complement the living spaces but often it also creates the striking forms that give Kahn buildings their distinctive appearance.

At the Salk Institute in La Jolla, California, two laboratories face each other across a court and are "yoked together underground by a massive mechanical system" (Fig. 549). Each of three floors of open laboratory space is topped by a floor the 9-foot (2.7-meter) ceiling space of which exists solely to serve the needs of the biological research being conducted on the floor below. This permits service and research to function without the one interrupting the other. Ringing the laboratories are smaller-scale units: on the court side, a stretch of study rooms; away from the court, toward the ocean, a series of service towers; at one end, offices; at the opposite end, a mechanical wing.

550. Venturi & Rauch, with Cope & Lippincott, associate architects, and the assistance of Gerod Clark. Guild House, Philadelphia. 1965.

The special look of the building comes from the geometric slabs of concrete the surfaces of which retain the pockmarks made by the plywood pouring forms. Embellishing this are plugs of lead that fill the tie-holes left when the forms were removed. Kahn designed the structure to function but also to have a human quality. In the Salk Institute at La Jolla he provided an environment to engage its occupants' full capacities for awareness.

In revolt against the entire myth and tradition of hero-architects and of their work as monuments sublimely aloof from all that surrounds them is Kahn's former student Robert Venturi, of the Philadelphia firm of Venturi & Rauch, along with his wife, planner Denise Scott Brown. The title of Venturi's book—*Complexity and Contradiction in Architecture* (1966)—and those of two studies—*Learning from Las Vegas* and *Learning from Levittown*—suggest the challenge that these new architect-designers have put to modernist dogma.

Noting that environment, more than monuments, is the reality of human experience, the Venturis declare that "the world can't wait for the architect to build his utopia, and the architect's concern ought not to be with what it ought to be but with what it is—and with how to help improve it now. This is a humbler role for architects than the modern movement has wanted to accept." Thus, the Venturis have sought out the urban environment on its own terms, because it is there. And because it is there, they have studied the highway strip and the subdivision, to see why and how these despised features of the modern scene may have the vigor to make chaos work.

With insight and analysis, the Venturis have reasoned back through the history of style and symbolism so as to come forward with a concept of a new architecture capable of responding to the speed and mobility of a society caught in the never-ending cycle of changing life styles. Admirers of pop art, the Venturis accept the premise of the commonplace and of the cheap, efficient and practical ways that mass culture serves its needs. But like the pop artists, they possess the education, wit, and irony to deal in paradox and perversity. The Venturis point out that having renounced decoration, modernist architects manipulate structural forms until the entire building takes on the quality of decorative sculpture. Using the theory of the building as a symbol, they cite as an example a building on the highway in the shape of a duck (the sales outlet for a duck farm)—and say they design "ducks" and "decorated sheds." The Venturis even think Main Street with its mixture of the old and new, its collection of drug stores, banks, and fast-food stands, "is almost all right." The motto of Miës van der Rohe was "Less is more." The Venturis turn this inside out and assert "More is not less."

Taking the label meant as an insult from an outraged modernist, the Venturis call their work "dumb and ordinary," all the while they are filtering the ordinary through their taste and knowledge until it becomes the extraordinary. A case in point is Guild House (Fig. 550), an apartment building sponsored by the Society of Friends to house elderly tenants who wanted to remain in the old neighborhood, a lower-middle-class district of Philadelphia.

With utmost candor, the building recalls "traditional Philadelphia row houses, or even tenement backs of Edwardian apartment houses." But all sorts of mannered elements—the emphatic façade; the notched shadow of the recessed entrance; the extreme left and right alignment of trimless, slightly overscaled but "standard" double-hung windows; the single, central arch form in an otherwise rectilinear design; the narrow white band running horizontally at the next-to-top story; the color of the materials; the pop sign mounted like a movie marquee; and the

551. Joern Utzon.
Sydney Opera House.
1959–72. Reinforced concrete,
height of highest shell
200′ (60.96 m).

purely decorative and nonfunctional wire rooftop sculpture formed like a television antenna—make it clear that a highly personal, idiosyncratic intelligence has been at work. The effect is to make the educated viewer feel compelled to look again, to discover why the commonplace seems so uncommon.

This is contradictory and complex, like life. However, in a time when construction costs make the dumb and ordinary inevitable, it may prove a valid response to the complex and contradictory needs of modern life.

The Seventies

Three major buildings of the 1970s have commanded international acclaim: the Sydney Opera House in Australia; the Pompidou National Center for Arts and Culture in Paris, commonly called Beaubourg; and the new East Building of the National Gallery in Washington, D.C. Each is a cultural center with constant ongoing activities.

Utzon The Sydney Opera House (Fig. 551) sits astride a point jutting out into Sydney Bay, one of the world's finest and busiest harbors. At first sight its unique shape looms up as a massive piece of outdoor sculpture. From some angles it suggests a group of interlocking shell formations, from others a group of great white sails skimming over the rippling water. An edifice of startling beauty, it has also risen to the status of a symbol for both Sydney and Australia, thus taking its place with the Eiffel Tower for Paris, the Empire State Building for New York, and the Gateway Arch (Fig. 547) for St. Louis.

Despite its accepted name, the Sydney Opera House is really a performing arts and recreation center. The complex includes three large auditoriums—the Concert Hall, the Opera Theater, and the

Recording Studio—and two smaller halls, an exhibition space for art shows and trade exhibits, plus two restaurants. The activities it accommodates include orchestral and choral concerts; opera, ballet, and recital performances; jazz, pop, and folk concerts and variety shows; lectures and films; and conventions, meetings and conferences.

The Danish architect Joern Utzon won the international competition for the Sydney Opera House in 1957. His daring design, however, proved to be far ahead of the technology needed to construct it. It then took some twenty years to build, equip, and furnish. Mounting costs (over $100 million) and disputes with the government led to his resignation in 1966. The interior was finished off by a team of Australian architects.

The building was one of the most difficult construction jobs ever undertaken, calling for daring feats of structural technology. The immense poured-concrete foundation was first put in place over the natural sandstone bedrock of the site. Over this rise the three sets of roof vaults or shells of enormous size and bold curvature. If it had to be built from the ground up, the costs would have been astronomical. So a system of prefabricated units was devised by which precast segments made on the spot were hoisted into place by high tower cranes. The sections are held together by tensioned cables.

The Concert Hall and Opera Theater have rows of four shells each that form both the roof and the walls of the space they enclose. Covering the shells is a continuous skin of cream-and-white ceramic tiles. The mouths of the shells have two layers of thick amber-tinted glass to keep out the harbor and traffic noises. They also serve the spacious interior lobbies with windows that offer panoramic views.

Except for the elegance and quality of the materials and the free play of structural forms there is no

552. Renzo Piano and Richard Rogers. Georges Pompidou National Center for Art and Culture (Beaubourg), Paris. 1977.

conscious attempt at decoration. In the tradition of Saarinen's Trans World Flight Center (Fig. 502) and Le Corbusier's church at Ronchamp (Fig. 540), the whole building becomes an ornament in itself, and the architect assumes the role of form giver. However, the form here does not follow the function. The high-pitched Gothic vaults, so effective on the exterior, proved disastrous acoustically. The various halls then had to have acoustic ceilings and wood-paneled walls to compensate. The building frankly is a return to the elitist concept of form for form's sake. Yet who is to quibble when the form is of such surpassing elegance and surprising beauty?

Piano and Rogers From its 1977 opening in Paris the Pompidou National Center for Arts and Culture (Fig. 552) has been an instant popular success. The design by the Italian architect Renzo Piano and his British colleague Richard Rogers is both daring and functional. As a spectacle it has become the new Eiffel Tower, attracting the Parisians themselves, sightseers from the provinces, and tourists from all countries by the millions. Beaubourg, as it is called from the plateau it occupies, is structurally an open glass box supported by steel-skeleton scaffolding. The first surprise is that it is all turned inside out. Things that normally are hidden in a basement or central core—building supports, heating and air conditioning ducts, freight elevators—are transferred to the outside, painted in strong colors, and made visible to all. The interior has no breakdown for separate rooms, no walls or supporting columns, only temporary partitions that can be shifted at will. The plumbing, in other words, becomes the façade, and the building's "guts" cover its skin.

The "boiler-room façade," as it has been called, achieves continuous action as freight elevators rise and fall, and as people snake up and down the Plexiglas-enclosed escalators (Fig. 553). Kinetic architecture is one name for it, brutalism another. At any rate, the structure has produced lively controversy. This "let it all hang out" design is what Frank Lloyd Wright had characterized as indecent architectural exposure. Other critics point out that it has the aesthetics of an oil refinery. Establishment Parisians call it municipal assassination and consider it an affront to the historic grandeur of their city, just as they shouted in 1889 when the Eiffel Tower rose up.

More sympathetically and enthusiastically Beaubourg has been hailed as a science-fiction fantasy. With its bubble dome, transparent glass walls, whirring machinery, and spectacular lighting, it has been dubbed the first building of the space age. The stated purpose of Beaubourg was to move the cultural center of gravity away from New York and back to Paris. It was to be not only a museum, but also a center for the creating of art, music, drama, and films.

The complex contains the French National Museum of Modern Art, the largest collection of 20th-century painting and sculpture in existence; the Institute for Acoustical and Musical Research under the direction of composer-conductor Pierre Boulez, a scientific laboratory where teams of engineers, acousticians, computer specialists, and theoreticians of all kinds will explore new approaches to sound and music; the Public Information Library that, for the first time in France, makes newspapers, periodicals, books, slides, musical cassettes, and video tapes available to all. In addition, there is an Industrial Arts Center, an experimental theater, a poetry gallery, a cinema, a sales area, bars, and restaurants.

Beaubourg was conceived from the first as a people's palace that would break down the barriers between art and life, a cultural supermarket where both artists and visitors could get into the act. Its director has characterized it as "a creative, changing, multimedia, kinetic, cross-cultural presentation of the arts of our time." Together with the interior activities and lively exterior plaza where jugglers, fireaters, and folk singers perform, it has become a perpetual happening. In this sense Beaubourg is the modern counterpart of the medieval cathedral, which was a museum of stained glass and sculpture. It also housed the serious pursuits of religious observances, musical performances, and university lectures, while in front the plaza served as a marketplace and a theater for miracle plays, among other things.

I. M. Pei   The National Gallery's new East Building in Washington, D.C., is a structure on a grand scale that has become one with the art it houses. The masterly interplay of geometrical unity and variety derive initially from the trapezoid-shaped site the building occupies. The architect, I. M. Pei, first divided the area diagonally into two triangular sections, one to house the art collection, the other for the newly established Center for Advanced Study in the Visual Arts complete with a library and six-story reading room. The geometrical motifs are all taken from this basic division, and Pei's slashing shapes and startling diagonal accents combine high drama with dignified restraint.

Inside, the drama heightens as the space expands into a triangular court (Fig. 554) where tall trees alternate with the massive sculptures to provide a simultaneous indoor-outdoor feeling. Smaller alcoves branch out from this central hall to provide space for viewing art of more intimate dimensions. The large court is lavishly ornamented by works especially commissioned from the best-known, internationally accepted names on the contemporary scene. They include a Joan Miró tapestry, a Henry Moore bronze, and a splendid welded metal sculpture by Anthony Caro. All are scaled to harmonize with the space they occupy, which means they are large. From the roof hangs what must be Alexander Calder's biggest and liveliest mobile (Fig. 554). The constant circular movement against the structure's sharp geometrical patterns provides a dramatic dimension of its own.

The massive scale, lofty posture, and pink granite exterior of the East Building harmonizes surprisingly well with the older neoclassical Gallery opposite. The intention was to widen the scope of the National Gallery's activities. The older building will still house the superb historical collection of major masterpieces. The East Building can now concentrate on living masters, current art interests, special exhibits, and traveling shows. In its short lifetime since its 1978 opening, the building has already become a contemporary classic.

above: **553.** Georges Pompidou Center, night view of escalator side.

below: **554.** I. M. Pei. East Wing, National Gallery of Art, Washington, D.C. 1978. Interior view of the triangular court with mobile by Alexander Calder.

Ideas: Existentialism

The 20th century has witnessed vast advances in scientific knowledge, the development of nuclear energy, the expansion of electronic communications, the convenience of jet transportation, the computerization of knowledge, the exploitation of the wealth of nations, the exploration of the moon and planets, and significant breakthroughs in the ways people perceive their world through art, music, poetry, and literature. At the same time the same century has seen butchery on the unparalleled scale of two world wars plus the Korean and Indochina conflicts, attempted genocide of massive proportions, and an ever-widening gulf between the benefits of wealth for some and the deprivations of poverty for others. There is also the confrontation with the possibility of the imminent end of the human race.

The bomb, in fact, has confronted everyone with a doomsday frame of mind, and it haunts present-day life and art like a specter at the feast. The potential ruin of the planet has torn apart the sense of vital continuity and futurity, whether this may be sought in the biosphere by living on through one's children, or in theology by belief in life after death, or through nature, which will go on into eons of geological time, or in creativity by which one's work can influence unborn generations to come.

The possibility of a sudden end to the human species has led to a psychological dislocation that makes the past seem obsolete if not abhorrent since it appears to have produced this state of affairs. The present then might seem futile and meaningless, and any future ridiculous and fanciful. Certainly such an attitude is reflected in the arts, where the critical measurement of contemporary works by past standards of classical craftsmanship and excellence has broken down, and where traditional forms have fragmented and disintegrated.

Artists may now feel that they are creating only for the moment rather than for the future, and a neodadaist sense of absurdity and futility pervades many of their works. Ultimately, if nothing is going to last, why bother to write it down, paint it, or compose it? Why not just consider art as a strategy of the imagination, as the inspiration or fantasy of a pipe dream. What else is a happening except something that is experienced, then ceases to exist?

The Existentialist Challenge

Such a confrontation with extinction can be the greatest challenge to the affirmation of life. As expressed in the pursuit of knowledge and enjoyment of the arts, living on the brink makes each moment count. No one is more aware of this challenge than the artist. Whether poet, painter or composer, the will to create works that reveal the infinite possibilities in human attitudes, insights, and lifestyles is irresistible. Art, in the view of the French philosopher André Malraux, has replaced religion as the last defense against death.

Of all recent philosophies, *existentialism* perhaps comes closest to comprehending the overall current artistic situation. The rational minds of Aristotle and Descartes declared: "I think, therefore I am." A more emotional and romantic counterpart might say: "I feel, therefore I am." All that the existentialist can do is utter: "I exist, therefore I am." Getting down to bare essentials, deeds, actions, and attitudes are the affirmation of being.

Existentialism spreads a large umbrella over the broadest range of choices, possibilities, and contingencies. It can include pessimism and optimism, tragedy and comedy, despair and hope, skepticism and faith, destruction and construction, the absurd and the serious, the trivial and the sublime, negation and affirmation, rejection and conviction, together with all degrees in between.

In music existentialism allows the improvisatory happenings of a John Cage to coexist alongside the mathematical computerization of Milton Babbitt's programmed compositions. Existential thought also allowed the abstract expressionists to develop individual styles within the field of abstraction. Theirs was a solemn style involving deep commitment to the image of order through sweeping statements of epic scope. Existentialist philosophy also makes room for the reduction to absurdity of neodadaism and pop art, as well as for the surrealistic assemblages of objects found in the works of Robert Rauschenberg.

Existentialism is essentially the ultimate humanism. For one must constantly ask: What does it mean to exist? What is human existence like? How does it feel to be human? In this world of infinite possibilities, any choice or action is of necessity not derived from, directed toward, or done for the sake of anything else. Everything can be, but nothing has to be, or must be. With existentialism all art might be said to approach the condition of still-life painting—everything is, nothing is becoming, nor does it have any need to become.

Sartre   In the world of Jean Paul Sartre existence precedes essence. That is, first one must exist, then project a self-image or define oneself through actions taken and works of art created. Human beings are condemned to be free; the only limit to their freedom is freedom itself.

One of the corollaries of Sartre's thought is the essential absurdity of life. As the notion of the absurd appears in existentialist art and drama, it takes on a

555. Scene from Samuel Beckett's
Waiting for Godot.
Production by Roger Blin
at the Théâtre de l'Odéon, Paris. 1961.

very grim coloration. There is nothing lighthearted about it. Samuel Beckett's 1953 play *Waiting for Godot* (a paraphrase of the existentialist philosopher Martin Heidegger's pronouncement "waiting for God") unfolds in a series of inconsequential episodes that reveal the endless boredom and futility of life (Fig. 555). As Macbeth says when tragedy closes in on him,

> Tomorrow, and tomorrow, and tomorrow,
> Creeps in this petty pace from day to day,
> To the last syllable of recorded time;
> And all our yesterdays have lighted fools
> The way to dusty death. Out, out, brief candle!
> Life's but a walking shadow; a poor player,
> That struts and frets his hour upon the stage,
> And then is heard no more: it is a tale
> Told by an idiot, full of sound and fury,
> Signifying nothing.

For Sartre death is the ultimate absurdity. He would agree with Leonardo da Vinci, who observed that when he thought he was learning to live, he was only learning to die. Paradoxically, one cannot know life until confronted with death, or experience affirmation until one encounters negation. All life, human or otherwise, has a death sentence hanging over it. There can be no sunshine without shadow, no light without darkness. In life there is always the imminent presence of death, in victory the specter of defeat, and every joy is haunted by sadness.

The Scientific Dimension More recently, existentialism and its more systematic companion *phenomenology* have faced up to the full implications of the objective knowledge produced by modern science. Most astronomers theorize that the multiverse surrounding the earth was produced by one or more cosmic explosions, which yielded the solar system as a mere byproduct. Any order that is perceived becomes not a part of things out there but a mental construct that an individual mind may impose upon it.

Biochemists have proposed that life is also the result of one or more biological accidents. In a well-argued and challenging book entitled *Chance and Necessity* (1970) the Nobel-Prize-winning biochemist Jacques Monod points out that eons ago quite by chance certain proteins and nucleic acids somehow combined to create metabolism and the reproduction of cells. As he remarks, "We would like to think ourselves necessary, inevitable, ordained from all eternity. All religions, nearly all philosophies, and even a part of science testify to the unwearying, heroic effort of mankind desperately denying his own contingency."

Human beings, then, face an environment that is oblivious to their hopes and fears, blind to their arts, deaf to their poetry and music. They stand alone in the immensity of a multiverse that is neither hostile nor friendly, but totally indifferent. Gone with the existentialist winds are the gods and original sin, gone are the heroes and villains, gone is the tribal fiction of a chosen people, gone are the determinisms of heredity and environment, and equally gone are the preconceptions of the past.

Suddenly, all taboos, religious beliefs, moral codes, and traditional folkways have been swept away. Despite all the mythical, religious, and philosophical ideologies that have arisen over the ages to affirm the existence of cosmic eternal laws; despite the incredible growth of knowledge in all fields over the past centuries; despite all histories that unfold according to some evolutionary, necessary, and favorable plan that affirms the ascent of the human race—all that the sum total of human knowledge and experience can show is that human beings face an endless gulf, utter solitude, and complete isolation.

So if we meet the challenge of the existentialist view, we can look ourselves directly in the eye as does Gregory Gillespie in his penetrating self-portrait (Fig. 535). We can make our own decisions freely and assume the responsibility for our own heritage and future directions. We alone control the meanings and values we choose to accept or reject. We are, in fact, right back to primeval chaos. Indeed, the great illusion is that we ever left it. Faced with an infinity of choices, we can create a new set of values, a new humanism, new expressions in the arts—new because these values are not imposed from on high, valid for all time and eternity, but because they are ours and ours alone. They constitute a new covenant in a new world in which we choose to live, move, and have our being. We are alone, we simply *are*. But being can mean that we can choose to be creative animals. The spiritual kingdom, the creative power, and the full glory are now within ourselves.

Choices for Artist and Audience

In the existentialist world view, all works of art are creative acts in the face of nothingness. The artist can do something or nothing, become god or beast, Prometheus or Lucifer. Mythology becomes fact insofar as metaphor and fiction are products of the human imagination and because people have believed in them, acted upon them, written, built, carved, and composed because of them.

What is relevant for the contemporary audience and the modern artist is the great growth of knowledge about past and present, plus the easy access to the vast body of literature, art, and music across the ages. So with the many media at their command, with the tremendous extension in the span of human experience, with so many levels of taste and frames of reference, the artist and the modern audience have an unlimited number of choices.

These choices range from the traditional to the experimental, from the manipulation of mathematical formulas to chance and random happenings, from logical and cyclical wholes to fragmented reflections of a broken and distorted world. More concretely, they range from the historical repertory in recorded and live performances to acoustical jungles and electronic collages, from the revival of ancient media such as frescoes and mosaics to exploring Plexiglas and plastic fantasies, from static sculptures that rest securely on pedestals to mobiles and kinetic art in mechanical motion, from works in a single medium to multimedia mixtures of all the arts. So when it comes to doing our own thing, the bewildering problem is that there are so many possible things to do and so many ways to do them.

All art past and present becomes contemporary by virtue of its living presence in the here and now. In the larger picture, 20th-century art is not only abstraction. Cubism and expressionism, aleatory and computerized music, soaring structures of steel and glass are but a few within the wide range of choices. For all the arts, over all ages of time, all reaches of space are now contemporary art. The Parthenon, Chartres Cathedral, the Sistine Chapel, quite as much as the Guggenheim Museum, Lincoln Center, and the Trans World Flight Center, the paintings of Giotto, Rembrandt, and Picasso, the music of Bach, Wagner, and Stravinsky—all exist in the expanded present. Ultimately it is up to the contemporary reader, viewer, and listener to choose whether to read Plato or Sartre, to look at Praxiteles' statues or at those of David Smith, to listen to Gregorian chant or to Babbitt's computerized compositions. The outlines of the past, present, and future have become blurred, just as in cubist and abstract-expressionist painting space has flattened out. In modern literature, music, and films time is experienced in a flowing continuum as in dreams, with flashes backward and forward. Foreground, middle ground, background; beginning, middle, end; past, present, future—are all telescoped together. The new is also the old, and the old ever new.

Now that humanity can rekindle the fires of faith and reassert creative forces, the arts become focal points in the act of reaffirmation. In the brave new world that stretches ahead, visual artists have found scope for their pictorial projections, modern architects regard the needs of the pluralistic society as a renewed challenge to their powers, writers have discovered many new avenues for communication in the new media, and contemporary composers have reveled in the possibilities of novel sound.

This, then, is the exciting and exhilarating challenge of our time. For we can pursue the trivialities or sublimities of life, leap into the gaping void, wallow in the primordial ooze, or else create some mode of order in a world of arts and ideas. As the philosopher Nietzsche said in *So Spake Zarathustra,* you must have chaos in you to give birth to a dancing star. "I say unto you: you still have chaos in yourselves." So it becomes possible to foresee a shining creative future, a whole galaxy of dancing stars. Because when we look at the world around us, the supply of chaos seems truly inexhaustible.

If any message comes through the mists and mazes of history, it is that we should never underestimate the power and creative capacity of the human mind. As long as the challenge is there, it is the eternal quest of the artist, scientist, or philosopher to envision the invisible, comprehend the incomprehensible, understand the unintelligible.

Glossary

Within the definitions *italics* have been used to indicate terms that themselves are defined in the glossary and, in a few instances, to distinguish terms that fundamentally belong to languages other than English.

a

abacus In an architectural *column,* the uppermost member of the *capital;* the slab upon which rests the *architrave.*

abstraction In the *visual arts,* the essential rather than the particular, in certain instances even the *ideal.* The process of subordinating the real appearance of *forms* in nature to an *aesthetic* concept of form composed of *shapes, lines, colors, values,* etc. Also, the process of analyzing, simplifying, and distilling the essence from nature and sense experience. See *nonrepresentational* art.

academy Derived from the name of the grove, the Akademeia, where Plato held his philosophical seminars; in modern history, from the French Académie des Beaux-Arts, the term has often been applied to conservative and traditional *forms.* It came to signify the *cultural* and artistic establishment exercising teaching and standard-maintaining responsibilities.

a cappella Italian for "in chapel style." *Choral* music without *instrumental accompaniment.*

accompaniment The music supporting a soloist or group of performers; music subordinate to the *melody.*

acoustics That having to do with the nature and character of sound.

acrylic, acrylic resin A clear plastic used as a *vehicle* in paints and as a *casting* material in *sculpture.*

action theater A contemporary phenomenon in which *plays,* happenings, and other types of performance are strongly committed to broad moral and social issues with the overt purpose of effecting a change for the better in society. The actors may actually confront the audience directly, even move among its members, to engage them in dialogue and debate.

adagio Italian for "slow"; in musical *composition* an instruction to the performer.

aerial perspective See *perspective.*

aesthetic Having to do with the pleasurable and beautiful as opposed to the useful, practical, scientific, etc. The distinctive vocabulary of a given *style.* An aesthetic response is the perception and enjoyment of a work of art.

aesthetics A branch of philosophy having to do with the nature of beauty and art and their relation to human experience.

agitato Italian for "agitated" or "restless."

agora In ancient Greek cities, an open marketplace where the population could assemble and hold meetings.

air A simple *song,* not to be confused with *aria.*

aisle In church *architecture,* the longitudinal *spaces* situated parallel to the *nave* and *formed* by *walls, arcades,* and *colonnades.* See Fig. 114.

aleatory music From the Latin for "gamble," a music that is uncontrolled or left to chance. Whatever the elements introduced by the *composer,* their arrangement is left to the performer or to circumstance.

allegory *Expression* by means of *symbols* to make a more effective generalization or moral commentary about human experience than could be achieved by direct or literal means.

allegro Italian for "lively," "brisk," or "merry."

altar Originally a stone slab or table where offerings were made or victims sacrificed; in the Christian era, a raised *structure* in a church at which the sacrament of the Holy Eucharist is consecrated; a center of worship and ritual.

altarpiece A painted or *sculptured panel* placed above and behind an *altar* to inspire religious devotion.

alto The lowest *range* of the female *voice;* also known as *contralto.* Too, the *line* in musical writing corresponding to the alto range, or an *instrument* with this range.

ambulatory A covered passage for walking, found around the *apse* or *choir* of a church, in a *cloister,* or along the *peristyle* of an ancient Greek temple. See Fig. 138.

analogous forms Forms that relate to each other *compositionally* because of their *size, shape, color, texture,* etc.

andante Italian for "moderately slow."

animism The belief that objects as well as living organisms are endowed with soul.

anthem An inspirational *song,* usually nationalistic; a *choral* selection performed as part of a sacred service.

anthropomorphic Human characteristics attributed to nonhuman things.

antiphony Music in which two or more groups of *voices* or *instruments* alternate with one another.

apotheosis Deification, or the realization of divine status.

apse A large *niche*like *space*—usually semicircular in *shape* and *domed* or *vaulted*—projecting from and extending the interior space of such architectural *forms* as Roman and Christian *basilicas.* Most often found at the eastern end of a church *nave* and serving to house the high *altar.* See Fig. 114.

apsidal See *apse.*

arcade A series of *arches supported* by *piers* or *columns;* passageway with arched roof.

arch See Figs. 103, 179.

architectonic Overall *design* and *composition;* that which has *structure.*

architecture The science and art of building for human use, including *design,* construction, and decorative treatment.

architrave In *post-and-lintel architecture,* the *lintel* or lowest division of the *entablature* that rests directly upon the *capitals* of *columns.* See Fig. 31.

archivolt The *molding* that frames an *arch.*

area Extent, *range,* or scope, having the character of *space,* whether two- or three-dimensional.

aria An elaborate solo *song* (or duet) with *instrumental accompaniment* used usually in *cantatas, oratorios,* and *operas.* A *da capo aria* has the basic *ternary* form ABA. The first section (A) concludes on the *tonic* and is followed by the second section (B), which is contrasting in *key* and character. The singer then returns to the beginning (*da capo*), repeating the A section, usually with some *improvisation.* A *continuo aria* is an aria with continuo *accompaniment.*

arpeggio The *notes* of a *chord* played successively rather than simultaneously, in either ascending or descending order and throughout one or more *octaves.*

ars antiqua Latin for "the ancient art." A term used for the music of the 12th and 13th centuries, as opposed to the music of the 14th century, *ars nova.* Chief composers were Leonin and Perotin; principal musical innovations were stabilization of *meter* and the advancement of *polyphony* from two-voice to three- or four-voice writing.

ars nova Latin for "the new art." The title of an early 14th-century treatise by Philippe de Vitry, dealing with musical notation, which gave its name to the musical style of 14th-century France and Italy. Music of the *ars nova* (as opposed to the *ars antiqua*) has a more *secular* orientation, greater *rhythmic* complexity, independent part writing, and creativity.

ars perfecta Latin for "the perfect art." A name used to describe the music of Josquin des Prez and other 15th-century Flemish composers.

assemblage The technique of creating three-dimensional works of art by combining a variety of elements—such as *found objects*—into a unified *composition.*

atmospheric perspective See *perspective.*

atonality A type of music in which no particular *pitch* serves as the *tonic* or *key note.*

atrium An open court constructed within or in relation to a building; found in Roman villas and in front of Christian churches built from late antiquity through Romanesque times. See Fig. 114.

augmentation In music, a technique for slowing down a phrase or *theme* by increasing (usually doubling) its *note values.*

avant-garde French meaning "advanced guard"; a term used to designate innovators whose experimental art challenges the *values* of the *cultural* establishment or even those of the immediately preceeding avant-garde *styles.*

axis An imaginary *line* passing through a figure, building, or group of *forms* about which component elements are organized, their direction and focus actually establishes the axis.

b

background In *pictorial* art, that part of the *composition* which appears to be behind *forms represented* as close to the viewer; the most distant of the three zones conceived in *linear perspective* to exist in deep *space,* beyond the *foreground* and *middle ground.* See *perspective, relief.*

balance In *composition,* the equilibrium of opposing or interacting forces.

ballad A narrative *song* usually set to relatively simple music.

ballet A theatrical performance of artistic *dancing* involving a plot or narrative sequence, costumes, scenery, and musical *accompaniment.*

balustrade An architectural *form* that is a continuous row of abbreviated shafts (balusters) surmounted by a handrail to make a low fence.

band A music *ensemble* consisting of *woodwind, brass,* and *percussion instruments,* but no *strings.*

bar See *measure.*

baritone The male vocal *range* between the high of the *tenor* and the low of the *bass.*

barrel vault See Fig. 103.

basilica A rectangular-*plan* building, with an *apse* at one or both ends, originating in Roman *secular architecture* as a hall and early adopted as the *form* most suited to the needs of Christian architecture.

bas-relief See *relief.*

bass The lowest *range* of the male *voice.* Also, the lowest vocal or *instrumental line* in musical writing, or, an instrument with the range to play these *notes.* The notes to the music in this range appear on a *staff* identified by a *bass clef* (𝄢).

basso Italian for *bass.*

basso continuo See *continuo.*

bay In *architecture,* the *space* defined at four corners by the principal upright structural members, with the character of the space usually established by the need to sustain aloft the great weight of a *vault.* See Fig. 179.

beat In music, the unit for measuring time.

binary form A basic two-part musical structure in which the second part differs from the first and both parts are usually repeated.

binder See *painting, vehicle.*

biomorphic In the *visual* or *plastic arts, imagery* derived from, but not necessarily an imitation of, the *forms* of living things.

bitonality A musical technique in which melodies in two *tonalities* are played simultaneously.

brass instruments The trumpet, French horn, trombone, and tuba, all of which have metal mouthpieces for blowing and a tube *shape* that flares into an opening like a bell.

buttress A *support,* usually an exterior projection of *masonry* or wood, for a *wall, arch,* or *vault,* that opposes the lateral *thrust* of these structural members.

c

cadence A point of rest, pause, or conclusion in a musical *composition;* a strong, regular *rhythm* as in a march.

cadenza In music for solo *voice* or *instrument* a free or florid passage inserted by the *composer* or *improvised* by the performer, usually toward the end of an *aria* or *movement,* whose purpose is to display the performer's technical brilliance.

campanile In Italy, a bell tower, especially one that is freestanding, often next to but separate from a church building.

canon A body of principles, rules, standards, or norms; a criterion for establishing *measure, scale,* and *proportion.* In music, a type of strict *imitative counterpoint,* wherein the *melody* stated by one *voice* is imitated in its entirety by a second voice, which enters before the previous one has finished.

cantata Italian for music that is "sung," as opposed to music that is played, which in Italian goes by the term *sonata.* In the 17th-century sense of Bach, Scarlatti, and Handel, a multi*movement composition* for solo *voices, chorus,* and *orchestra* consisting of *recitatives* and arias for performance in church or chamber. Briefer than *oratorio* but, like oratorio, differs from *opera* in being mainly nontheatrical.

cantilever In *architecture,* a *lintel* or beam that extends beyond its *supports.*

cantus firmus Latin for "fixed song," a preexisting *melody* that medieval and Renaissance *composers* used as the basis for *polyphonic* pieces in which they added new melodies above and/or below the cantus firmus.

canvas A fabric woven of cotton or linen and used as the *support* for *painting.* Also called *duck,* especially when made of cotton.

capital The upper member of a *column,* serving as transition from shaft to *lintel* or *architrave.* See Fig. 31.

caricature An amusing distortion or exaggeration of something so familiar it would be recognized even in the distortion.

cartoon A full-*scale,* preparatory *drawing* for a *pictorial composition,* usually a large one such as a *wall painting* or a tapestry. Also a humorous drawing or *caricature.*

caryatid A *sculptured* female figure standing in the place of a *column.*

casein Made of milk protein, a *binder* for paint.

cast The molded replica made by the *casting* process.

casting A process using plaster, clay, wax, or metal that, in a liquid form, is poured into a mold. When the liquid has solidified, the mold is removed, leaving a replica of the original work of art from which the mold was taken.

catharsis The cleansing or purification of the emotions through the experience of art, the result of which is spiritual release and renewal.

cathedra An episcopal throne, or throne for a bishop; also known for its Latin name *sedes* or *"see."*

cathedral The official church of a bishop containing his *cathedra* or throne; a church that traditionally has been given *monumental* and magnificent architectural *form.*

cella An enclosed windowless chamber, the essential feature of a *classical* temple, in which the *cult* statue usually stood.

central plan In *architecture,* an organization in which *spaces* and structural elements are *ordered* round a central point.

chamber music Music for small groups.

chamber opera An *opera* with a small cast and small orchestra designed for intimate surroundings rather than for a large opera house.

chanson de geste French for "song of heroic deeds"; an *epic* poem written in Old French during the 11th to 13th centuries and designed to be performed by *minstrels* and *jongleurs.*

chant A single *liturgical melody* for voice or *chorus* that is *monophonic, unaccompanied,* and in free *rhythm.* Various types are Byzantine, *Gregorian,* Ambrosian, Milanese, Visigothic (Mozarabic), Gallican.

chapel A small church or compartment within a church, castle, or palace containing an *altar* consecrated for ritual use.

choir An organized group of singers or *instrumentalists* of the same class. In church *architecture,* the complex at the east end beyond the *crossing,* which could include *apse, ambulatory,* and radiating *chapels.*

choral That having to do with *chorus.*

chorale A *hymn* tune introduced in the German Protestant Church by Martin Luther, who frequently wrote the texts and sometimes the *melodies.*

chorale prelude An organ piece based on a Protestant *chorale,* usually played before the congregation sings the chorale or *hymn.*

chord Any combination of three or more *tones* sounded simultaneously.

chordal See *chord.*

chorus In ancient Greek drama, a group of singers and dancers commenting on the main action. In modern times, a *choir* or group of singers organized to perform in *concert* with one another. Music *composed* for such a group.

chroma In *color,* the purity of a *hue;* synonymous with *intensity* and *saturation.*

chromatic From *chroma;* in the *visual arts,* that which has a full or broad *range* of color.

chromatic scale In Western music, the full set of *tones* or *pitches* available in an *octave,* or all the piano's white and black *notes* for an octave. The opposite of the *diatonic scale,* whose pitches would be sounded by the piano's white notes within an octave.

chromaticism Raised or lowered notes introduced into *diatonic* music, or used instead of the normal diatonic degrees of the *scale,* are called *chromatic notes;* chords involving their use are *chromatic chords;* harmony saturated with chromatic chords is *chromatic harmony;* and music overgrown with chromaticism is *chromatic music.* The *chromatic scale* is a twelve-note scale dividing the *octave* into twelve half-*tone* intervals—the seven diatonic tones plus the five altered degrees, as C, C *sharp*, D, D sharp, E, F, F sharp, G, G sharp, A, A sharp, B.

civilization A *culture* in an advanced state of self-realization, thought to be characterized by marked efficiency and achievement in such realms as art, science, and letters, as well as in personal security and dignity.

classical All that relates to the *civilizations* of Greece and Rome, and subsequent *stylistic* imitations of Western antiquity. Classical can also mean established excellence, whatever the period, *style,* or *form.*

clavecin A harpsichord.

clef French for "key"; in musical *composition,* a sign placed at the beginning of a *staff* to determine the placement of *notes.* See *bass, treble.*

clerestory A row of windows in the upper part of a *wall;* also, in church *architecture,* the upper portion of the interior walls pierced by windows for the admission of light. See Figs. 115, 177.

cloister A *monastic* establishment; more particularly, a covered passage, usually *arcaded,* at the side of or surrounding a courtyard within a monastery complex.

coda Italian for "tail"; a section at the end of a *movement* of *composition* that serves as a "summing up" by using previously heard thematic material. A short coda is usually known as a *codetta.*

coffer In *architecture,* a recessed panel in a ceiling. Coffering can lighten both the actual and apparent weight of a massive ceiling and provide a decorative effect.

collage From *papiers collés,* the French for "pasted papers"; a *composition* deriving from cubism and made by pasting together on a flat *surface* such originally unrelated materials as bits of newspaper, wallpaper, cloth, cigarette packages, and printed photographs.

colonnade A row of *columns* usually spanned or connected by *lintels.*

colonnette A small *column,* performing a decorative as well as a structural function.

color A perceived quality in direct light or in objects reflecting light that varies with the wavelength of the light energy, the brilliance of the light source, and the degree to which objects reflect or absorb the light energy falling on them. In paint, color is the light-reflecting and -absorbing characteristic, which is a function of the *pigment* giving the paint its primary visual identity.

column A cylindrical post or *support* which often has three distinct parts: base, shaft, and *capital.*

comedy A light and amusing *play* or other literary work whose purpose is to arouse laughter in the beholder.

complementary colors Two contrasting *hues* that are found opposite each other on a color wheel, which hues neutralize one another when combined (such as red and green) and mutually intensify when placed adjacent to one another.

composer The writer of music or of musical *composition.*

Composite A *classical order* of temple *architecture* introduced by the Romans and combining elements from *Ionic* and *Corinthian* orders, as the acanthus-leaf motif of the Corinthian order topped by the *volutes* of the Ionic. See Fig. 86.

composition An organization or arrangement imposed upon the component elements within an individual work of art.

compound pier In *architecture,* a *pier* with *columns* and *pilasters* bundled or clustered together, with each component usually corresponding to a member in the *ribs* and *vaults.*

compression In *architecture,* stress that results from two forces moving toward each other, as in dead weight or squeezing.

concert In music, artists performing together for an audience, or a single artist performing for an audience (a situation also known as a *recital*). Agreement or *harmony* among two or more factors.

concerting style A style that developed in 16th-century Venice by pitting *choirs, ensembles,* or soloists against each other in a variety of contrasting manners, as slow *tempo* vs. fast; *polyphony* vs. *homophony;* soft vs. loud.

concertino The small or solo *ensemble* in a *concerto grosso.*

concerto An *instrumental composition* featuring a soloist (violin, piano, cello, flute, etc.) pitted against a full *orchestra* and usually written in three *movements.*

concerto grosso An *orchestral composition* in which the *instruments* are divided into two contrasting tonal bodies: a large (*ripieno,* or grosso) and a small (*concertino*) *ensemble.*

connoisseurship A discriminating knowledge of the qualities of art works and their *styles.*

consonance and dissonance Consonance occurs in an established tonal system when only the *tones* of that system are used. Use of a *note* outside the established tonal system creates a point of friction or *dissonance.* Consonance thus achieves stability or repose, while dissonance causes tension and the feeling of motion toward a consonant resolution.

construction In *sculpture,* the process of making a *form* by assembling and joining a wide variety of materials, such as wood, cardboard, plastic, paper, and metal. See *assemblage.*

content See *expressive content.*

continuo (basso continuo) A *contrapuntal* concept favored by baroque composers. It is a continuous *bass* line defined sharply enough to function as a clearly distinguishable level within the musical complex. The common effect in continuo writing is the opposition set up between the continuo part in the *bass* and the upper parts. The continuo bass line is commonly played on a *keyboard instrument* by the left hand, while the right hand supplies filler parts *improvisationally.* Since numbers are often placed beneath the bass line to guide

the player in realizing the filler parts, the continuo is also called figured bass. Because the continuo is a bass complex, other bass instruments (lute, viola da gamba, cello, bassoon) usually supplement (or may substitute for) the keyboard.

continuo aria See *aria.*

contour In the *pictorial* arts, an outline that forms the boundary of one *shape* and defines it in relation to other shapes and is *expressively* handled so as to suggest fullness and recession of *forms* and varieties in *texture,* such as those in body *structure* and soft tissue. Contrasts with simple outline, which is no more than the boundary of a form defining a *silhouette.*

contralto Female voice part with low range; also called *alto.*

contrapposto The placement of the human figure in which one part is turned in a direction opposite that of the other (usually hips and legs one way, shoulder and chest another); a counterpositioning of the body about its central *axis.*

contrapuntal The adjectival *form* of *counterpoint.*

convention A formula, rule, or practice developed by artists to create a usage or *mode* that is individual to the artist, yet communicable to the *culture* they partake of. Conventions exist in both *form* and *subject matter,* and they constitute the vocabulary and syntax of the artist's language. Conventions can simplify certain *pictorial* problems, as when a single tree serves as a *symbol* and substitute for an entire forest.

cool color A *hue* generally in the blue, green, and violet section of the *spectrum.* Psychologically, cool colors tend to be calming and unemphatic; optically they often appear to recede.

Corinthian The *classical order* of temple *architecture* characterized by slender fluted *columns* topped by highly carved, ornate *capitals* whose decorative *forms* derive from the acanthus leaf.

cornice Any horizontal architectural member projecting from the top of a *wall;* in *classical architecture* the crowning member of the *entablature.*

counterpoint The combination of two or more independent *melodic lines* into a single musical fabric; *polyphony.*

crescendo A continuous increase in loudness.

crossing In a *cruciform* church, the *space* formed by the intersection of *nave* and *transept.*

cross vault See Fig. 103.

cruciform Arranged or *shaped* like a cross.

crypt A *vaulted* chamber; wholly or partly underground, that usually houses a *chapel* and is found in a church under the *choir.*

cult A system of religious belief and its adherents.

culture The *values* and the system of their interrelationships that inform a society, motivate its behavior, and cause it to be functional to the general satisfaction of its members and to have a distinctive quality and character.

d

da capo Italian for "from the beginning." Return to or repetition of the beginning.

da capo aria See *aria.*

daguerreotype An early form of photograph in which the image is produced on a silver-coated plate.

dance A *rhythmic* and patterned succession of bodily movements, usually performed to music.

decrescendo A progressive decrease in the level of loudness.

dentil From the French for "small tooth"; one of a series of small decorative blocks projecting just below the *cornice* of an *Ionic* or *Corinthian entablature.*

design A comprehensive scheme, plan, or conception. In *painting,* the pattern organization of a *composition,* usually seen in the arrangement of *lines* or the light-and-dark elements, rather than in *color.*

deus ex machina Latin for "a god from a machine"; a device in ancient Greek and Roman drama whereby a god is introduced by means of a crane to solve a plot that has thickened to such an extent that human solutions are impossible. Figuratively, any sudden and contrived solution to what appears to be an impossible situation.

development See *sonata form.*

diatonic The seven *tones* of a *major* (or *minor) scale,* corresponding to the piano's white *keys* in an *octave. Diatonic chords* are chords built of *diatonic notes;* harmonies composed mainly of such chords are *diatonic harmonies.* The opposite of *chromatic.*

diminuendo Diminishing in *intensity* or *dynamic level.*

diminution Decreasing (usually halving) the *note values* of a phrase or section to achieve a quickening effect.

dissonance A discord or *interval* that creates a feeling of tension that demands resolution. See *consonance and dissonance.*

divertimento See *serenade.*

dome A hemispherical *vault;* theoretically, an *arch* rotated on its vertical *axis.* See Fig. 103.

dominant The fifth *note* of a *diatonic scale;* a *chord* built on the dominant.

Doric The oldest of the *classical styles* of temple *architecture,* characterized by simple, sturdy *columns* that rise without a base to an unornamented, cushionlike *capital.*

dramatis personae Actors or characters in a drama.

drawing A process of visualization by which an artist, using such *media* as pencil, chalk, or watercolor, delineates *shapes* and *forms* on a *surface,* typically paper or *canvas.*

duck See *canvas.*

duple meter A marchlike *rhythm* based on two *beats* or some multiple thereof, as 2/8, 2/4, or 4/4 time.

duplum The second voice part counting upward from the *tenor* or *cantus firmus* in medieval *organum.*

e

dynamics The various levels of loudness and softness of sounds and the increase and decrease of *intensities.*

earthwork In the *visual arts* of the contemporary period, an intervention in open nature by the artist for no purpose other than the enactment of personal ideas of art.

eclecticism The practice of selecting from various sources, usually to form a new system or *style.*

elevation An architectural *drawing* of the side of a building without *perspective* distortion.

empirical Based on experiments, observation, and practical experience without regard to science and theory.

encaustic A paint *medium* in which the *vehicle* is wax.

engaged column A *column*like *form* projecting from a *wall* and punctuating it visually.

engraving A form of printmaking in which grooves cut into a metal plate are filled with ink and the plate pressed against absorbent paper after its surface has been wiped clean.

ensemble A group of two or more musicians performing the same *composition.*

entablature In *architecture,* that portion of a building between the *capitals* of the *columns* and the roof, including in *classical* architecture the *architrave, frieze, cornices,* and *pediment.* See Fig. 31.

entasis The slight convex curving on *classical columns* to correct the optical illusion of concavity, which would result if the sides were left straight. See Fig. 31.

epic A long narrative poem in heightened *style* about the deeds and adventures of a hero. Also, simply heroic.

etching A form of printmaking requiring a metal plate coated with an acid-resistant wax, which is scratched to expose the metal to the bite of the acid. Lines eaten into the plate by the acid are subsequently filled with ink and transferred to paper after the surface of the plate has been wiped clean of excess ink.

ethos Greek meaning "custom" or "character." In art, that which gives a work *tone* or character and distinguishes it from other works. Also understood to mean the *ideal* or an ethical character. In music, the Greeks associated this with the lyre.

Evangelist One of the authors of the four *Gospels* in the Bible: Matthew, Mark, Luke, and John. Respectively, their *symbols* are an angel, a lion, an ox, and an eagle.

exposition See *sonata form.*

expression Having to do with those factors of *form* and *subject* that together give the work of art its *content* and meaning.

expressive content The fusion of *form* and *subject* that gives art its meaning and significance.

f

façade Usually the front of a building; also, the other sides when they are emphasized architecturally.

ferroconcrete A building material composed of concrete with rods or webs of steel imbedded in it. Also known as *reinforced concrete.*

figuration In the *visual arts,* the *representation* of *forms* and objects seen in nature, however *abstracted* and *schematized* the representations may be. That having to do with the human figure.

figurative See *figuration.*

figure-ground In the *pictorial* arts, the relationship between *imagery* and the *plane, background,* or generalized *space* against which the *images* are seen. Modern artists who use *abstraction* tend to regard figure and ground as a relationship between positive and negative *volumes.* An issue or problem in the *aesthetics* of *form,* it has proved fundamental to the pictorial arts of the modern period.

finale The final *movement* of a large *instrumental composition;* in *opera,* the *ensemble* terminating an act.

flat A symbol (♭) signifying that the *note* it precedes should be lowered by one half-step.

fluting Vertical channeling, concave in shape, used principally on *columns* and *pilasters.*

flying buttress A *masonry* support or segment of an *arch* that carries the *thrust* of a *vault* to a *buttress* positioned away from the main portion of the building; an important element of *structure* in the *architecture* of Gothic *cathedrals.* See Fig. 177.

foreground In the *pictorial* arts, that part of the *composition* which appears to be closest to the viewer. See *middle ground* and *background.*

foreshortening The effect of three-dimensionality made in two dimensions by basing *representation* on the principle of continuous decrease in size along the entire length of a *form* whose bulk is intended to be seen as receding in *space.*

form In the *visual arts,* a *shape* or *mass,* or, more comprehensively, the total arrangement of shapes, *structure,* and *expressiveness.* In music, the overall organization, structure, or *design* of a piece; the *ordering* in time of a *composition's* component sections. To give shape to something or achieve *style* in it.

formal See *form* and *style.*

format In the *pictorial* arts, the *shape* (usually rectangular) of the *support* at its edges; also the encompassing *volume* of *space* in relation to which a *sculpture* or building seems to have its *formal order.*

forte Italian for "loud"; *fortissimo* means "very loud"; *fortississimo,* "extremely loud."

found object An object discovered and

selected by an artist and exhibited without alteration as an *aesthetic* object, or incorporated without alteration into a more complex *composition* intended to create an aesthetic experience.

French overture An introductory *instrumental* piece first used at the 17th-century French court and characteristically in two sections: a slow stately march with dotted *rhythms* in *duple meter,* and a livelier mood with *fugal texture* and triple meter.

fresco A process of *painting* on plaster, either wet or dry, wherein the *pigments* are mixed with water and become one with the plaster; a *medium* perfected during the Italian Renaissance.

frieze The central portion of the *entablature* between the *architrave* and the *cornice;* any horizontal decorative or *sculptural* band. See Fig. 31.

fugal See *fugue.*

fugue A *polyphonic composition* characterized primarily by the *imitative* treatment of a single *subject* or subject complex.

g

gallery A long and narrow room or passage, such as that in the *nave walls* above the *aisles* of a church. See *triforium.*

genre In the *pictorial* arts and *sculpture,* the casual *representation* of everyday life and surroundings. Also, a type, *style,* or category of art.

geodesic Architectural *structure* based on light, straight elements suspended together in a state of *tension.* Used mainly in the *design* and construction of *domes.*

Gesamtkunstwerk German for a "complete," "total," or "consummate work of art"; a term coined in the late 19th century by Richard Wagner to characterize his *music dramas,* in which he brought about an alliance of all the arts—music, literature, theater, and the *visual arts*—to realize a program of ideas.

glaze In *oil painting,* a transparent film of paint laid over dried underpainting; in ceramics, a thin glassy coating fused to a clay body by firing in a kiln.

Gospels Ascribed to Matthew, Mark, Luke, and John, the four biblical accounts of the birth, life, death, and resurrection of Jesus Christ. See *Evangelists.*

gouache Watercolor made opaque by the addition of chalk.

graphic Demonstration and description by visual means.

graphic arts Vaguely related to the *linear* element, a term that identifies the *visual arts* of *drawing,* printmaking, typographic *design,* advertising design, and the technology of printing.

Greek cross A cross in which all arms are the same length.

Gregorian chant *Liturgical* music named for Pope Gregory I (590–604), who codified

the various *chants* prevalent in his time into a single body of music. Also known as *plainsong,* these chants are *monophonic,* un*accompanied melodies* in free *rhythm* sung partly by soloists and partly by *choir.*

groin See Fig. 103.

groin vault See Fig. 103.

ground A coating, such as *priming* or *sizing,* applied to a *support* to prepare the *surface* for *painting;* also *background.*

ground bass See *ostinato.*

ground plane In the *pictorial* arts, the *surface represented* as that on which figures seem to stand.

h

harmonics High-*pitched,* otherworldly *tones* produced by touching the string of an *instrument* lightly with the finger so that it vibrates in segments rather than as a whole. Also called overtones.

harmony The vertical or *chordal structure* of musical *composition;* the study of all relationships that can exist between simultaneously sounding *pitches* and the progressions of chords.

hierarchy Any system of persons or things that has higher and lower ranks.

hieroglyphic A picture or a *symbol* of an object standing for a word, idea, or sound; developed by the ancient Egyptians into a system of writing.

high relief See *relief.*

holistic An entity in which significance derives from the *organic* and irreducible relationship between the parts and the whole they make—in which the total arrangement is what counts.

homophonic See *homophony.*

homophony Music in which a principal *melody* is supported by *accompaniment* in a *chordal* or *harmonic style.*

horizon line A real or implied *line* across the *picture plane* parallel with its top and bottom edges, which, like the horizon in nature, tends to fix the viewer's eye level, and toward which in *linear perspective* all receding parallel lines seem to converge.

hubris Arrogance, as in a prideful act designed to supplant God with self.

hue The property of *color* that distinguishes one color from another as red, green, violet, etc. See *saturation, value.*

hymn A religious *song* meant to give praise and adoration.

hypostyle In Egyptian temple *architecture,* *columns* with a flat roof resting directly upon them to create a hall.

i

icon Greek for *image,* used to identify *panel paintings* made under Greek Orthodox influence that *represent* the image of a holy

person—Christ, Mary, or a saint; such works often imbued with sanctity.

iconography In the *pictorial arts* and *sculpture,* the meaning of the *images* and *symbols* depicted; *subject* matter.

ideal The *representation* of objects, individuals, and events according to a *stylized,* perfected, preconceived model; a kind of *aesthetic* distortion of perceived reality.

idealize See *ideal.*

idée fixe French for "fixed idea." Berlioz' name for a recurring *melodic motif* identified with the heroine in his *Fantastic* Symphony. In each *movement* the motif varies slightly to coincide with the musical and *programmatic* circumstances.

idol A *representation* or *symbol* of a deity used as an object of worship.

illusion See *illusionism.*

illusionism The attempt of artists to *represent* as completely as their *formal* means permit the visual phenomena of a palpably real world, even if imaginary, as in a scene of muscular and voluptuous bodies floating high in the sky.

image A *representation* of an object, an individual, or event. An image may also be an evocation of a state of being in representational or *nonrepresentational* art.

imagery In the *visual arts,* the particular *subjects* and objects chosen by an artist for depiction in a work, or, in the instance of totally abstract or *nonrepresentational* art, the particular *forms* and *shapes* with which the artist has *composed* a work.

imitation In musical *composition, the successive* restatement of a *theme* or *motif* in different *voice parts* of a *contrapuntal* complex. A *canon* is an example of strict imitation; modified forms occur by *inversion, augmentation,* and *diminution.*

imitative See *imitation.*

impasto Paint laid on in richly *textured* quantities.

improvisation On the spur of the moment, spontaneous musical *composition* for *voice* or an *instrument.* Also, in the performance of music, adding to the basic composition such decorative embellishments as *chords* and new *melodies;* a major aspect of baroque music and *jazz.*

incising Cutting into a *surface* with a sharp instrument.

instrument In music, a mechanism capable of generating the vibrations of musical sound. See *string instruments, woodwind instruments, brass instruments,* and *percussion instruments.*

instrumental See *instrument.*

instrumentation The practice by *composers* of organizing all *instrumental* possibilities for *expression.* It may also refer to the types and numbers of instruments used in a *composition.*

intensity In the *visual arts,* the relative purity or brillance of a *hue.* In music, the relative softness or loudness of a *tone.*

interval In music, the distance between two *notes* as determined by *pitch.* A *melodic interval* occurs when two notes are sounded successively; a *harmonic* interval occurs when two notes sound simultaneously. In the *visual arts,* the distance—real, represented, or implied—between things, such as measurable extent from *foreground* to *middle ground* to *background* or from one *form* to another on the same *plane.*

intervallic See *interval.*

intonazione Italian for "intonation." The 16th-century name for a *prelude* in which organists, by running their fingers rapidly over the keys and coming to a definite *chordal cadence,* established the *pitch* and *mode* for the *choir* prior to their singing a *motet.*

intrinsic Belonging to a thing by its very nature.

inversion In musical *composition,* a means of *imitation* by which the original ascending (or descending) *voice* is imitated by a descending (or ascending) voice at an equivalent *intervallic* distance.

Ionic One of the Greek *classical styles* of temple *architecture,* which developed in Ionia in Asia Minor and is distinguished by slender, fluted *columns* and *capitals* decorated with volutes or scrolls.

isocephaly In *pictorial composition,* figures arranged so that all heads align at the same level.

isorhythmic *Polyphonal* music in which the *forms* are compounded of sections unified by an identity of *rhythmic* relationships but not necessarily of *melodic* patterns.

j

jamb The upright piece forming the side of a doorway or window frame; on the portals of Romanesque and Gothic church *architecture* the place where sculptural decorations sometimes appear.

jazz An American music, originating in the black community early in the 20th century, in which *players improvise* on a *melodic theme, expressing* it in a highly personal way with *syncopated rhythms* and *contrapuntal ensemble* playing.

jongleur See *minstrel.*

k

key The *pitch* of the *tonic* (or *tonal* center within the *tonality*) established by the *composer* for a particular piece of music. It is the sum of all the musical relationships that can be perceived by constant comparison with a given pitch level. Also, a mechanism by which an *instrument* (piano, organ, clarinet, etc.) can be caused to sound.

keyboard The arrangement of *keys* on such *instruments* as the piano, the spinet, and the organ; therefore, "keyboard instruments."

keystone See Fig. 103.

l

lancet window A tall, narrow, pointed window used in Gothic *architecture.* See Fig. 177.

Ländler An Austrian peasant *dance* similar to a *waltz* and popular in the late 18th and early 19th centuries.

landscape In the *pictorial* arts, the *representation* of scenery in nature.

lantern tower A tower added above a dome to light the interior.

Latin cross A cross in which the vertical arm is longer than the horizontal arm, through whose midpoint it passes.

leading tone In music, the seventh degree of a *major* or *minor scale;* it pulls toward or "leads" to the *tonic* a half-step above.

legato Italian for "tied"; in music, the performance of *notes* in a smooth, continuous line: the opposite of *staccato.*

leitmotif German for "leading motif"; a *melodic theme* introduced by Richard Wagner into *orchestral* writing to characterize an individual, an idea, an inanimate object, etc., and *developed* to reflect transformations in the person, idea, or thing, recalling the past, prophesying the future, or explaining the present.

lento Italian for "slow."

libretto (pl. **libretti**) Italian for "little book"; the text, words, or "book" of an *opera, oratorio,* or other musico-dramatic work.

lied An art *song* in the German language.

line A mark left in its path by a moving point, or anything, such as an edge, a boundary, or a horizon, that suggests such a mark; a succession of *notes* or ideas, as in a *melodic* line or a line of thought. The *linear* might be considered one-dimensional, as opposed to the *spatial,* which is either two- or three-dimensional.

linear See *line.*

linear perspective See *perspective.*

lintel In *architecture,* a structural member that spans an opening between posts or *columns.* See *post-and-lintel* and Fig. 103.

lithography A printmaking medium based upon the antipathy of grease and water. With a grease crayon or waxy liquid, a drawing is made on a slab of grained limestone or on a grained metal plate. The drawing is treated chemically so that each grain of the plate touched by the drawing medium can accept a greasy ink and each untouched grain can accept water and repel the ink. When the plate has been wetted and charged with ink, an image in ink is retained that essentially reproduces the drawing. The printmaker then covers the plate with a sheet of paper and runs them both through a press, which offsets the drawing onto the sheet, thus producing the print.

liturgical That having to do with *liturgy.*

liturgy A rite or body of rites prescribed for religious worship.

local color The identifying *color* of an object when it is perceived without shadows under a standard light source.

loggia A *gallery* open on one or more sides, sometimes with *arches* or with *columns.*

low relief See *relief.*

lyric Of or relating to the lyre, such as a *song* to be performed to lyre *accompaniment.* In a modern sense, that which is intensely personal, ecstatic, and exuberant, even poetic. Also (in the plural) words or verses written to be set to music. The lyric theater is that involving words and music, such as *opera* and musical *comedy.*

m

madrigal In the early 14th century, a *secular* two- or three-*voice* song with a fixed *form:* two or three verses set to the same music plus a concluding two-line *ritornello* with different music. The upper voices are usually in a florid *style,* with the lower *notes* written for longer *values.* In the 16th century, a secular four- or five-voice *composition* based on love poetry or *lyrics,* with no set form but highly *imitative* and often *homophonic* in passages.

major A type of *diatonic scale* in which half-*tones* or semitones occur between the third and fourth, and seventh and eighth degrees of the scale (as opposed to the natural *minor,* in which the semitones occur between the second and third, and fifth and sixth degrees). A *key* or *tonality* based on such a scale.

masonry In *architecture,* stone or brickwork.

mass In the *visual arts,* the actual or implied physical bulk, weight, and density of three-dimensional *forms* occupying real or suggested *spatial* depth. Also, the most solemn rite of the Catholic liturgy consisting of both sung and spoken sections. It combines sections of the Ordinary (texts that do not change) in alternation with sections of the Proper (texts that vary for certain occasions or seasons). The sung sections of the Ordinary are Kyrie, Gloria, Credo, Sanctus, and Agnus Dei. The sung sections of the Proper are Introit, Gradual, Alleluia or Tract, Offertory, Communion, and Post-Communion. A cyclical mass contains sections of the Ordinary structurally coordinated by the presence of the same *melody* (i.e., *cantus firmus*) in the *tenor.* A *polyphonic mass* is the Ordinary set to music with two or more voice parts. The *requiem mass* is the mass for the dead.

measure A standard of comparison; in musical *composition,* a regular division of time, set off on the *staff* by vertical *bars.* In *rhythm* and *metrics,* "measured" means slow and stately.

medium (pl. **media**) In general, the process employed by the artist; in a more strict sense the binding substance or *binder* used to hold pigments together, such as linseed oil for *oil paint.* See *vehicle.*

melisma An extended sequence of *notes* sung to one syllable of text.

melismatic See *melisma.*

melodic See *melody.*

melody Single *tones* organized successively to create a musical *line.*

meter In poetry, the scheme of accented and unaccented *beats.* In music, the basic grouping of *beats* and accents into *measures,* e.g., the triple *meter* of a *waltz* is recognized by recurring patterns of three beats with an accent on the first beat.

metrical, metrics See *meter.*

mezzo Italian for "half," "middle," or "medium"; thus, *mezzoforte* means "medium loud" and *mezzo-soprano* means "middle soprano" or a female *voice* with a *range* between *soprano* and *contralto.*

middle ground In the *pictorial arts,* that part of the *composition* that appears to exist between the *foreground* and the *background;* the intermediate of the three zones of recession in *linear perspective.*

minnesingers German for "love singers"; German musicians of the aristocratic class who composed love songs in the medieval period. See *troubadours, trouvères.*

minor In music, a type of *diatonic scale* in which the *interval* between the first and third *notes* or *pitches* contains three semitones (as opposed to four in a *major* scale). A *key* or *tonality* based on such a scale.

minstrel In the 12th and 13th centuries, a professional singing actor or mime in the service of a castle or wandering from town to town and from castle to castle. Also known as *jongleur,* and in an expanded meaning refers to *troubadours, trouvères,* and *minnesingers.*

minuet An elegant 17th-century French *dance* in moderate triple *meter* incorporated first into the *suite* and eventually into the *sonata, symphony,* and *string quartet* as the third *movement.* In the latter usage a minuet is in *ternary form* (ABA) employing a middle section called a trio, which is followed by a repeat of the minuet.

mobile A *constructed sculpture* whose components have been connected by joints to move by force of wind or motor.

mode A particular *form, style,* or manner. In music, the *ordering* of *pitches* into a *scale* pattern; also, a pattern of *rhythm.*

model See *modeling.*

modeling The *shaping* of three-dimensional *forms* in a soft material such as clay; also, the *representation* on a flat *surface* of three-dimensional forms by means of variations in the use of *color* properties.

modulation Movement from one *key* to another.

module A standardized two- or three-dimensional unit that is intended as a unit of *measure* in *architecture* or *sculpture.*

molto Italian for "much," meaning "very."

monastery A dwelling place where monks live in a community for spiritual purposes.

monastic That having to do with monks and *monasteries.*

monochrome A single *color* or the *value* variations of a single *hue.*

monophonic See *monophony.*

monophony Music in which one *voice* or a group of voices sings the same *melody.*

montage In the *visual arts,* a *composition formed* of pictures or portions of pictures previously photographed, painted, or drawn.

monumental A work of art or *architecture* that is grand, noble, timeless, and essentially simple in *composition* and execution, whatever its actual *size.*

motet A composition that developed in the 13th century when words (*mots*) were added to the *duplum* (which became known as the *motetus*) of a *melismatic organum.* In the usual three-voice motets the *tenor* retained fragments of the original *Gregorian melody* and to each of the two upper voices new and different Latin texts were added. The 16th-century Renaissance motet is a four or five-voice sacred *composition* developed by the Flemish composers and based on a Latin text. The musical *texture* is usually *polyphonic* with *imitation* between voice parts.

motif In music, a *melodic* or *rhythmic* fragment or *theme* capable of being developed into different and larger contexts. In the *visual arts,* the *subject* or idea of an art work, such as *still life* or *landscape,* or an individual feature of a subject or *form,* usually one that recurs or predominates in the *composition.*

movement A self-contained section of a larger piece of musical *composition,* such as a *symphony.*

mullions Vertical elements dividing windows into separate "lights" or glazed sections.

multiple An art work realized by a duplication process, such as printmaking and *casting.*

mural A *painting* on a *wall,* usually large in *size.*

mystical Having a spiritual meaning or reality that can be known only by intuition, insight, or similar subjective experience.

myth A legend or story that seems to express the world view of a people or explain a practice or historical tradition.

n

narthex The porch or vestibule of a church. See Fig. 114.

natural In musical *composition,* a sign (♮) meaning that, for the *note* to which it is attached, any previous indications of *sharp* (♯) *or flat* (♭) should be canceled.

nave The great central *space* in a church; in rectangular *plans* the space extending from the entrance to the *apse,* or to the *crossing* or *choir,* and usually flanked by *aisles.* See Fig. 114.

niche A hollow recess or indentation in a wall for a statue or other ornament.

nonobjective A synonym for *nonrepresentational* art, or art without recognizable *subject matter.*

nonrepresentational In the *visual arts,* works so abstract as to make no reference whatever to the world of persons, places, and the objects associated with them; art from which all identifiable *subject matter* has been eliminated.

notation The system and process for writing out music in characters and *symbols* so that it can be read for performance.

note A musical sound of a certain *pitch* and duration; the sign in written music for such a sound; a *key* on an *instrument* such as the piano or organ that when pressed makes a specific musical sound.

O

obbligato Italian for "obliged," meaning, in music, *parts* that must not be omitted; also, a decorative *line* of music meant to be heard as a foil to the main *melody.*

obelisk A tapering shaft of stone ending with a pyramidal top.

octave The *interval* from one *note* to the next of the same *pitch* name (as from C to C), either higher or lower, which is a span of eight *diatonic* notes.

oculus A round eyelike opening or window.

oeuvre French for "work"; the whole of an artist's production, or lifework.

oil painting The process of *painting* with a *medium formed* of ground *colors* held together with a *binder* of oil, usually linseed.

opera Theater in which music is the central dramatic agent. A typical opera involves a drama or *play* with scenery and acting with the text usually sung to the *accompaniment* of an *orchestra.* Various types exist: *opera buffa* (It.), is characterized by a light simple plot with prominent comedy elements and spoken dialogue; *opera seria* (It.) normally employs *recitative* in place of spoken dialogue and involves a dramatic or serious plot; *number operas* employ a sequence of self-contained musical "numbers" (*arias,* duets, *choruses,* etc.); *music drama* is the term used for Wagnerian operas, which substitute a continuous chain of music for musical numbers. See *chamber opera.*

opus Latin for "work"; in music a term used with a number to distinguish a particular *composition* or group of compositions within the chronology of the *composer's* total *oeuvre* or output.

oratorio A musical *composition* written for soloists, *chorus,* and orchestra, and usually based on a religious story or text. The latter may involve a plot or be purely meditative and nonnarrative. Oratorios are usually performed in concert halls or churches without scenery, staging, or costumes.

orchestra In Greek theaters, the circular *space* before the *proscenium* used by the *chorus.* Also a group of *instrumentalists,* including *string players,* joined together to perform *ensemble* music.

orchestration The art and technique of arranging or *scoring* a musical *composition* for performance by the *instruments* of an *orchestra* or *band.*

order In *classical architecture,* a *style* represented by a characteristic *design* of the *column* and its *entablature;* see *Doric, Ionic, Corinthian,* and *Composite.* Also the arrangement imposed upon all elements within a *composition;* in addition, a harmonious arrangement. To arrange or organize something, give it order.

organic That which is living, such as plants; that which is integral to the whole; a system in which all parts are coordinated with one another.

organum From the 9th through the 13th centuries, the earliest *form* of *polyphonic* music, in which one or more *lines* of *melody* sound simultaneously along with the *plainsong* of *Gregorian chant.* In *parallel organum* (9th–10th centuries) an added *voice* runs exactly parallel and below the Gregorian melody. In free organum (c. 1050–1150) the main melody occurs in the lower voice while the upper voice moves in a combination of parallel and contrary motion. In *melismatic* organum (c. 1150–1250) a few *notes* of the main chant or melody are prolonged and sustained in the lower voice while the upper voice moves freely through the melismatic melody with numerous notes occurring for each note in the main chant. Two-part organum is known as organum *duplum;* three-part organum as organum *triplum.*

ostinato Italian for "obstinate," which in musical *composition* is the persistent repetition usually in the *bass,* of a clearly defined musical figure or phrase, while other *parts* or *voices* change around and above it. Also called *basso ostinato* or *ground bass.*

overture *Instrumental* music written usually to precede an *opera, oratorio,* or *ballet.* It may be an entity unto itself or directly related to the music that follows. Also, a *concert piece* in one *movement,* often with an extramusical reference.

p

painterly *Painting* in which the buttery substance of the *medium* and the gestural aspect of paint application constitute a principal aspect of the art's quality.

painting Traditionally, *painting* has been thought of as an art *form* in which *colors* are applied through a liquid *medium* to a flat *surface,* called a *ground* or *support.* A dry powder called *pigment* is the coloring agent in painters' colors, and, depending on the binding agent or *binder* used, pigments can produce such media of painting as *oil, tempera,* watercolor, *fresco, encaustic, casein,* and *acrylic resin.* These can be worked on such grounds or supports as paper, *canvas,* wood *panel,* and plaster. If the support has been given a preparatory coating, by *priming* and *sizing,* the surface thus *formed* is considered to be the *ground,* which intervenes between the painting and its support.

palette A tray or *shaped planar surface* on which a painter mixes *colors;* also the characteristic *range* and combination of colors typical of a painter or a *style* of *painting.*

panel Any rigid, flat *support* for *painting,* such as wood, usually prepared with a *ground.* Any flat, slablike *surface,* usually rectangular in shape.

pantheon Greek meaning all the gods of a people; a temple dedicated to them; a public building containing tombs or memorials of the illustrious dead.

papiers collés See *collage.*

parallel organum See *organum.*

part In musical *composition,* the writing for a single *instrument* or *voice* or a group of them; also, a section of a composition.

pathos Greek meaning the experience of emotion, grief, or passion. In art, an element that evokes pity or sympathy. Also that which deals with personal and transitory experience or emotions, as opposed to those which are universally significant.

pediment In *architecture,* the triangular *space* or gable at the end of a building, *formed* in the *entablature* by the sloping roof and the *cornice.* See Fig. 31.

pendentive In *architecture,* a triangular segment of masonry whose plane is hemispherical, four of which can form a transition from a square to a circular base of a *dome.* See Fig. 123.

percussion instruments Drums, celesta, chimes, triangle, tambourine, castanets, gongs, cymbals, glockenspiel, etc., all of which must be struck or shaken to make a musical sound.

performing arts The arts that have their full existence only in time and that to realize full existence must be played: music, *dance,* and drama.

peristyle A *colonnade* surrounding a temple or court.

perspective A *pictorial* technique for simulating on a *flat,* two-dimensional *surface,* or in a shallow *space,* the three-dimensional characteristics of *volumetric forms* and deep space. During the Renaissance in Italy, a quasi-mathematical scheme called *linear perspective* developed from the fact that parallel lines going in one direction away from the viewer must be seen as converging toward a single point on the horizon known as a *vanishing point.* Placed, in this system, at *intervals* along the assumed and converging parallels, objects are *scaled* in their *sizes* to diminish in relation to their distance from the *picture plane.* In northern Europe, at about the same time, painters developed a perspective system known long before to the Romans and the Chinese. Called *atmospheric* or *aerial perspective,* the system employed blurred outlines, loss of detail, alteration of *hues* toward the *cool colors,* and the diminution of color *saturation* and *value* contrast—all in proportion to the distance of the object from the viewer. See *foreshortening.*

phenomenology The study of the progressive development of the human mind, from a philosophical point of view; the description of the actual physical appearance of things as these can be perceived by the senses.

piano Italian for "soft"; *pianissimo* means "very soft"; *pianississimo,* "extremely soft."

pictorial That having to do with the flat arts of *painting* and *drawing* and, to a certain extent, with the art of *low relief,* in that its three-dimensional *subject matter* and *imagery* are *composed* in relation to a flat rear *plane* that physically is parallel to and only slightly behind what would be a *picture plane* and whose edges constitute a frame or *format* of specific *shape* like that of a picture. Picture or pictorial *space* is that of the *support,* which is a flat *surface* defined by a specific shape, usually rectangular. To achieve here, at the picture plane on the support, the appearance of deep space, the artist must employ such *illusionistic* devices as *modeling, foreshortening,* and *perspective* so that, in a *still life* or *landscape,* for instance, objects and *forms* seem to rest firmly on a *ground plane* at *intervals* beginning in the *foreground* and moving through the *middle ground* to the *background* and beyond.

picture plane An imaginary vertical *plane* assumed to be at the front *surface* of a *painting.*

picturesque A pictorial situation that awakens thoughts of the *sublime,* magnificent, quaint, vivid, or rugged as opposed to the orderly, symmetrical, or beautiful.

pier A *mass* of *masonry* rising vertically to *support* an *arch, vault,* or other roofing member. See Figs. 103, 177.

pietà A devotional *image* of the sorrowing Virgin holding the dead Christ.

pigment Finely powdered coloring matter mixed or ground with various *vehicles* to *form* paint, crayons, etc.; also a term used loosely to mean *color* or paint.

pilaster In *architecture,* a shallow, flat, vertical member projecting from a *wall surface* and, like a *column,* composed of base, shaft, and *capital.* Usually more decorative than structural.

pillar Any vertical architectural member—*pier, column,* or *pilaster.*

pitch A musical *tone,* or its relative highness or lowness as fixed by the frequency of the vibrations occurring per second within it.

pizzicato Italian for "plucked"; in musical *composition* an instruction to the performer to pluck the *strings* of an *instrument* instead of bowing.

plainsong From early medieval Christian worship, a type of sacred music or *liturgical chant, monophonic* in *style* and set to a Latin text. See *Gregorian chant.*

plan An architectural *drawing* that reveals in two dimensions the arrangement and distribution of interior *spaces* and *walls,* as well as door and window openings, of a building as seen from above.

planar See *plane.*

plane A *surface* that is defined and measurable in two dimensions.

plastic That which is capable of receiving physical *form;* therefore, the *visual arts.* More narrowly, that which is pliant and malleable enough to be *modeled;* therefore, the material of *sculpture.*

plasticity The three-dimensional quality of a *form,* its roundness and apparent solidity; the capability of material for being *shaped, modeled,* and manipulated.

play A literary text consisting of dialogue *composed* to be acted out in dramatic *form* for the benefit of an audience.

player One who performs.

plot In literature, the plan or scheme of the story and its unfolding action.

poco Italian for "little."

podium A platform, base, or pedestal for a building or a monument.

polychoral style *Compositions* in this style employ a *chorus* (with or without *orchestra*) divided into two or more groups, which sing and play in alternation (*antiphonally*). Venetian music at the end of the 16th century featured this style.

polychrome Several *colors* rather than one (*monochrome*).

polymeter The use of different *metrical* units in successive bars of a *composition.*

polyphony A *texture* created by the interweaving of two or more *melodic* lines heard simultaneously. *Counterpoint* is the technique used for composing polyphonic music.

polyrhythm Two or more *rhythms* combined in such a way that they are heard simultaneously, as duple rhythm or two *beats* in the treble, triple rhythm or three beats in the *bass.*

polytonal Music in which two or more *keys* or *tonalities* are heard simultaneously.

portal An imposing door and the whole architectural *composition* surrounding it.

portico A porch with a roof supported by *columns* and usually with a *entablature* and a *pediment.*

post-and-lintel In *architecture,* a structural system employing two uprights or posts to *support* a member, the *lintel* or beam, that spans the *space* between the uprights.

prelude A musical *composition* designed to introduce the main body of a work, such as an *opera;* a separate *concert* piece for piano or *orchestra,* usually based on a single *theme.* See *chorale prelude.*

presto Italian for "fast."

primary colors *Colors* that in various combinations are capable of creating any other color or *hue.* In artists' *pigments* these are red, yellow, and blue; in natural or "white" light, they are red, green, and blue. See *color, complementary colors.*

prime To prepare a *canvas* or *panel* for *painting* by giving it a *ground* of white paint or one made with a gluey or resinous substance called *size.*

program music Broadly speaking, music that consciously imitates sound effects (bird calls, bells), describes natural or social events (thunderstorms, hunting scenes), or narrates a sequence of dramatic episodes derived from poetic and dramatic sources. In the 19th century, it refers principally to *instrumental* music based on a series of actions or a sequence of episodes designed to make narrative or dramatic sense, and declared by the composer to be subject to

some sort of literary, *pictorial,* or philosophic interpretation.

proportion The relation, or ratio, of one part to another and of each part to the whole with regard to *size,* height, width, length, or depth.

proscenium From the Greek meaning "before the *skene*"; the proscenium *arch* is that which is set before the stage *space* and frames it in traditional theaters.

prosody The art of setting words to music. Also, a particular system or *style* of versification.

prototype An original *model,* archetype, or primary form from which other artists make copies or adaptations.

psalter A book of the psalms (*hymns*) found in the Bible.

pylon In Egyptian *architecture,* a monumental gateway shaped in profile like a truncated pyramid and leading to the forecourt of a temple.

r

range The extent and limitation of a *series,* such as the *notes* that a human *voice* is capable of singing, or a sequence or *values* from light to dark.

realism A mid-19th-century style of *painting* and *sculpture* based upon the belief that the subject matter of art and the methods of *representation* should be true to life without *stylization* or *idealization.* Impressionism emerged from the desire to achieve in art an absolute fidelity to human perception of physical reality.

recapitulation See *sonata form.*

recital See *concert.*

recitative In *opera, oratorio,* and *cantata,* a *form* of declamation that, although highly *stylized* and set to music, follows the *pitch* and *rhythms* of speech more than a *melodic line.* Recitative tends to serve a narrative function and often leads into an *aria* or connects arias and *ensembles.*

register A *range* (upper, middle, lower) within the capacity of the *voice,* human or *instrumental.*

reinforced concrete See *ferroconcrete.*

relief A *plane* that exists three-dimensionally as a projection from a *background.* Also, *sculpture* that is not freestanding but projects from a *surface* of which it is a part. When the projection is relatively slight, it is called *bas-relief* or *low relief;* when the projection is very pronounced, it is called *high relief.*

reliquary A small box, casket, or shrine for keeping sacred relics, usually made and decorated of precious materials.

render To reproduce or *represent* by *graphic* means.

represent See *representation.*

representation The depiction or illustration by the *graphic* means of the *visual arts* (*lines, values, colors,* etc.) of *forms* and *images* in such a way that the eye would perceive a correspondence between them

and their sources in the real world of *empirical* experience.

representative style A type of *word painting* by which the descriptive *imagery* of the text is reflected in the *shape* and turn of the *melodic lines.*

requiem See *mass.*

responsorial singing Alternate singing between a soloist and a group.

retrograde A term that indicates the employment of a *theme* or phrase in reverse order, starting on the last *note* of the *melody* and ending with the first.

rhythm In the *visual arts,* the regular repetition of a *form.* In music, all factors pertaining to temporal organization in music, including the comparative duration of *tones, meter,* and *tempo.*

rhythmic See *rhythm.*

rib In *architecture,* a slender *arched support* that in a *vault* system typically projects from the *surface* along the *groins* where semicircular vaults intersect each other. Ribs both reinforce the vaults and unify them *aesthetically.*

ribbed groin vault A *groin vault* reinforced with *ribs.* See Fig. 179.

ricercar An *instrumental composition* that developed in the 16th and 17th centuries as a counterpart to the vocal *motet.* It is characterized by the periodic recurrence of the first subject, and as each subsequent subject or subject complex appears, it ushers in a new section featuring *contrapuntal imitations* and *variation* techniques. The ricercar is the *prototype* of the later *fugue.*

ripieno The large *ensemble* in a *concerto grosso.*

ritardando In music, the gradual slowing of *tempo.*

ritornel, ritornello Italian for "refrain"; a recurrent passage in a *concerto, rondo, operatic* scene, etc.

rondo A musical *form* in which one main *theme* recurs to alternate with other themes, making a *structure* that can be diagrammed as ABACADA.

round A type of *canon* in which all *voices* enter at the *unison.*

rubato The fluctuation or *variation* of *tempo* within a bar or phrase without destroying the basic *meter.*

rusticate In *masonry* work, to build a wall of rough-hewn stone for bold *texture* and strong light-and-shade contrasts.

S

sanctuary A consecrated, sacred, or holy place; in Christian *architecture,* that part of the building where the *altar* is placed; also a refuge.

sarcophagus A stone coffin.

satire A witty exposure of vice and folly, the purpose of which is to effect moral reform.

saturation The purity, vividness, or *intensity* of a *color.*

scabellum Latin for "cymbal."

scale Relative or proportional *size.* In

music, a succession of tones usually arranged in ascending or descending order and either a whole *tone* or a half tone apart.

schematize The process of reducing the identifying characteristics of a *form*—the human head, a plant, a building, etc.—to its diagrammatic essentials; a process of *abstraction.*

scherzo Italian for "joke"; in *sonatas, symphonies,* and quartets, a *movement* substituted for the *minuet* and, like the minuet, *composed* in triple *meter* but at a faster *tempo.* Normally, the scherzo is linked with a trio in a sequence of scherzo, trio, and scherzo repeat.

score The written version of music, with all *parts* indicated both separately and in relation to one another. To prepare music in written *form.*

scriptorium In a medieval *monastery,* the workroom for the copying and illumination of manuscripts.

sculptural That which is *plastic* or has to do with *sculpture.*

sculpture A type of three-dimensional art in which *form* is created by subtractive or additive methods. In subtractive sculpture the form is found by removing (as in carving) material from a block or *mass.* In additive sculpture, the form is built up by *modeling* in clay, by *constructing* with materials as a carpenter or welder might, or by *assembling* such preexistent forms as *found objects.* Whatever the method, the final form can be *cast* in a material, such as bronze, that modifies from a liquid state to a hard and permanent one. Sculpture can be freestanding or *relief.*

section An architectural *drawing* showing the side of a building without *perspective* distortion.

secular Not religious, but relating to the worldly or temporal.

sedes See *cathedra.*

sequence In musical *composition* the repetition of a *melody* or *motif* at different *pitch* levels. Historically, sequence refers to a musical style that first came into use in the 9th century by adding text syllabically to the long *melismas* on the final vowel of an *alleluia.* Eventually the melismas were elaborated or altered musically and the sequences became highly developed as separate *compositions.* All but four were banished from the *liturgy* by the 16th-century Council of Trent.

serenade, divertimento *Instrumental compositions* that originated in the 18th century for use at festive occasions, outdoor performances, or evening gatherings. Such works contain from two to six or more *movements* consisting of marches, dances, spritely *allegros,* and at least one *andante.* They are usually *scored* for *woodwinds* when intended for outdoor performance and for a combination of *strings* and woodwinds, or strings alone, for use indoors.

serial music A collective term applied to 20th-century music that not only uses a *tone* row or series as its basic structural component, but also serializes *rhythms, timbres, dynamics,* etc. See *twelve-tone technique.*

sforzando (sforzato) A strong *dynamic* accent.

shade, shaded See *shading, value.*

shading The property of *color* that makes it seem light or dark. See *value.*

shape A two-dimensional *area* or *plane* with distinguishable boundaries, such as a square or a circle, which can be *formed* whenever a *line* turns or meets, as in an S-shape or a T-shape.

sharp A sign (♯) in musical *composition* instructing the performer to raise the *note* it precedes one half-step higher.

silhouette A *form* as defined by its outline.

size The physical magnitude of objects, *forms,* elements, and quantities. See *scale;* also *prime.*

skene In the theaters of ancient Greece, which were open-air, the small building that provided for performances both a stage and a background. It is the root word for "scene" and "scenery."

sonata Italian for "sounded"; in musical *composition,* an *instrumental* work usually written in three or four *movements.*

sonata form A structural principal employed in a *movement* of *instrumental* music. It consists of three main divisions: the *exposition,* during which the musical materials of the movement are presented or "exposed" in the *tonic key* and a new key (the entire section is usually repeated); the *development,* in which the musical ideas of the exposition are worked out and explored in various keys to provide tension and contrast; and the *recapitulation* (reprise), which resolves the tension and contrast of the development by restating the exposition, but with all the *themes* in the tonic and usually with minor changes in *orchestration* or musical materials. A *coda* may be added in conclusion.

song The simultaneous presentation of a literary text and a musical setting. The basic types are strophic, in which the *melody* is repeated over and over to different stanzas of the poem, and *through-composed,* in which the *melody* and *accompaniment* vary for each successive stanza.

song cycle A group or series of *songs* sharing a common thought, theme, or musical treatment, and intended to be sung consecutively.

soprano Vocal or *instrumental* register with the highest range. Soloists may be designated as coloratura soprano, a vocalist with great agility in the high register capable of performing rapid, dazzling, *cadenza*like passages typical of 18th- and 19th-century *operatic arias;* dramatic soprano, a powerful and declamatory voice that extends downward to the *mezzo* region; or lyric soprano, a voice with light *texture,* considerable brilliance and a capacity for sustained *melodic* singing.

space A *volume* available for occupation by a *form;* an extent, measurable or infinite, that can be understood as an *area* or a distance capable of being used both negatively and positively.

spandrel A triangular *space* above a *clerestory* window in a *barrel-vault* ceiling; also the *surface* between two *arches* in an *arcade.*

spatial, spatiality That having to do with *space.*

spectrum The full array of rainbow *colors* that appear when white light (sunlight) has been refracted into its component wavelengths by means of a transparent substance, such as a prism.

springing See Fig. 103.

squinch See Fig. 124.

staccato Italian for "detached"; in musical *composition* an instruction to perform *notes* in a short and detached manner. The opposite of *legato.*

staff The five horizontal *lines* and four intervening *spaces* on which musical *notation* can be written out. See *clef, bass, treble.*

stele A stone slab carved in *relief* and set upright to commemorate a person or event.

stereotype Something conforming to a fixed or general pattern.

still life In the *pictorial* arts, an arrangement of inanimate objects—fruit, flowers, pottery, etc.—taken as the *subject* or *motif* of a work of art.

stoa In the *agoras* of ancient Greece, a building of one or two stories in the *form* of a *colonnade* or roofed porch providing *space* for a walkway and shops, offices, and storerooms.

stretcher A wooden or metal framework upon which a painter's *canvas* can be stretched.

stretto Literally, a narrowing or quickening process achieved by a faster *tempo* or *diminution* of the *note values.* In a *fugue,* stretto is the *imitation* of a *subject* in two or more *voice* parts in rapid succession so that the statements overlap, causing an increase of *intensity.*

string instruments The violin, viola, violoncello (or cello), and double bass, all of which are equipped with strings capable of generating musical sound when either stroked with a bow or plucked.

string quartet An *ensemble* of two violins, viola, and cello; a *composition* in *sonata form* written for such an ensemble.

structure The compositional relationships in a work of art; a building or other constructed architectural unity; the operative framework that *supports* a building.

style The terms *form* and *style,* "formal analysis" and "stylistic analysis" serve interchangeably in any discussion of the way artists work or the way their art works once it has been accomplished. Both form and style are concerned with those measurable aspects of art that caused the elements, principles, and materials to come together as a *composition;* but they are equally concerned with the *expressive content* of a work. They signify a sensitive, knowing, trained, and controlled *shaping* and *ordering* of ideas, feelings, elements, and materials. Style can be the identifying characteristic of the work of a single artist, of a group of artists, or of an entire society or culture.

stylize To simplify or generalize *forms* found in nature for the purpose of increasing their *aesthetic* and *expressive content.*

stylobate In Greek temple *architecture,* the upper step of the base that forms a platform for the *columns.*

subject In the *visual arts,* the identifiable objects, incidents, and situations represented. See *iconography.* In music, the *theme* or *melody* used as the basic element in the *structure* of a *composition,* as in a *fugue.*

subject matter See *subject.*

sublime The *representation* of the violent, wild, and awesome aspects of nature as opposed to beauty, which is based upon *symmetry, proportion,* and elegance.

suite In music, a collection of various *movements* without specific relationships in *key* or musical material. The music usually is *dance*like, since suites before 1750 consisted almost invariably of four principal dance movements: the allemande, the courante, the sarabande, and the gigue. Often, simply excerpts from *scores* for *ballet* and *opera.*

summa An encyclopedic summation of a field of learning, particularly in theology or philosophy.

support In the *pictorial* arts, the physical material serving as a base for and sustaining a two-dimensional work of art, such as paper in the instance of *drawings* and prints, and *canvas* and board *panels* in *painting.* In *architecture,* a weight-bearing structural member.

surface The two-dimensional exterior *plane* of a *form* or object.

symbol A *form, image,* sign, or *subject* standing for something else; in the visual arts, often a visible suggestion of something invisible.

symmetry An arrangement or balanced *design* in which similar or identical elements have been organized in comparable *order* on either side of an *axis.*

symphonic poem (tone poem) A term first applied by Liszt to a one-*movement orchestral* work of the late 19th century based on an extramusical idea (illustrative, literary, *pictorial,* etc.). A symphonic poem is a type of *program music.*

symphony An *orchestral composition* commonly written in three or four *movements.* In a typical symphony the first movement is fast and in *sonata form;* the second is slow and can be in sonata, *binary, ternary,* or *variation* form. The third movement (sometimes omitted) is a *minuet* (scherzo) and trio; the *finale,* usually in sonata or *rondo* form, is in a lively tempo.

syncopation Stressing a *beat* that normally should remain weak or unaccented.

synoptic Affording a general, comprehensive, broad, or common view.

synthesis The deduction of independent factors or entities into a compound that becomes a new, more complex whole.

t

tabernacle A receptacle for a holy or precious object; a container placed on the *altar* of a Catholic church to house the consecrated elements of the Eucharist.

taste The evidence of preference having to do with enjoyment and appreciation.

tempera A *painting* technique using as a *medium pigment* mixed with egg yolk, glue, or *casein.*

tempo In music, the pace or rate of speed at which the *notes* progress.

tenor The highest *range* of the male *voice,* or an *instrument* with this range. In medieval *organum* the voice that sustains the notes of the *chant* or *cantus firmus.* More generally, the *line* in musical writing corresponding to the tenor range.

tensile In *architecture, structure* that is capable of sustaining *tension.*

tension *Balance* among opposing forces; a state of unrest. In *architecture,* stress from two forces moving in opposite directions, like the pulling and stretching imposed on bridge cables.

ternary form A common three-part musical *structure* consisting of three self-contained sections with the second specifically in contrast to the first and the third a repeat or modified repeat of the first: ABA or statement, contrast, restatement.

terracotta Italian meaning "baked earth"; baked clay used in ceramics, *sculpture,* and architectural decoration; also a reddish-brown *color* similar to baked clay.

texture In the *visual* or *plastic arts,* the tactile quality of a *surface* or the *representation* of that surface. In music, the relationship of the *melodic* elements and the elements that accompany them, and the particular blend of sound these create.

thematic See *theme.*

theme In music, a short *melodic* statement or an entire self-contained melody; *subject matter* to be treated in a *composition* through *development, imitation,* contrast, *variation,* expansion, juxtaposition, etc.

through-composed An *opera* with the whole of its text set to music; music that varies according to the needs of the text, instead of following a preconceived pattern of repeats and contrasts.

thrust A strong continued pressure, as in the force moving sideways from one part of a *structure* against another.

timbre *Tone color,* or the particular quality of sound produced by a *voice* or an *instrument.*

toccata Italian for "touched"; music composed for *keyboard instruments,* written in a free *style* with running passages, *chords,* and sometimes *imitative* sections.

tonality See *key.*

tone In music, a *note;* that is, a sound of definite *pitch* and duration. In the *visual arts,* a general coloristic quality, as this might be expressed in a degree of *saturation* and *value.*

tone poem See *symphonic poem.*

tonic The first and principal *note* of a *key,* functioning as a place of rest or home base and acting as a point of departure and return.

tragedy A serious drama or other literary work in which conflict between a protagonist and a superior force (often fate) concludes in calamity for the protagonist, whose sorrow excites pity and terror in the beholder and produces *catharsis.*

transept In a *cruciform* church, the whole arm set at right angles to the *nave,* which makes the *crossing.* See Fig. 114.

treble In music, the higher *voices,* both human and *instrumental,* the *notes* to whose music appear on a *staff* identified by a treble *clef* (𝄞).

triad In music, the simultaneous sounding of three *notes* to make a *chord* of only three *pitches* built up in thirds from the root note.

triforium In church *architecture,* an *arcaded* area in the *nave wall* system that lies below the *clerestory* and above the *gallery,* if there is one, and the nave *arcade.* It can be open like a gallery or be sealed (blind). See Figs. 115, 177.

triplum In the music of medieval *organum,* the third *voice part* counting upward from the *tenor* or *cantus firmus.*

trompe-l'oeil French for "fool the eye"; a type of *representation* in *painting* in which the *illusion* of *form, space,* light, and *texture* has been so cunningly contrived as to convince observers that what they perceive is the actual *subject matter* and not a two-dimensional equivalent.

troubadours, trouvères French musicians of noble lineage who flourished in the 12th and 13th centuries composing secular songs dealing with chivalry, knighthood, the Crusades, woman, and historical subjects. *Troubadours* stemmed from southern France, *trouvères* from the north. Their German counterparts were the *minnesingers.*

trumeau A post or *pillar* placed in the center of a portal to help *support* the *lintel* above, especially in medieval *architecture.* See Fig. 186.

tune A *song* or *melody;* a musical *key;* the correct *pitch* or *tonality.*

tunnel vault A *barrel vault.* See Fig. 103.

twelve-tone technique A 20th-century method of *composition* devised by Schoenberg in which the seven *diatonic* and five *chromatic tones* are treated equally so that no *tonal* center is apparent. Compositions are based on an arbitrary arrangement of these twelve tones, and their sequence is known as a tone row or series. The *notes* of a row must always be used in the established order, but may be repeated or moved from one *octave* position to another. The row may also be used in *inversion, retrograde* form, retrograde inversion, or be transposed to any step of the *chromatic scale.* A series may also be arranged vertically to form *chords.*

tympanum In medieval *architecture,* the *surface* enclosed by a *lintel* and an *arch* over a doorway; in *classical* architecture, the recessed face of a *pediment*.

u

unison The "zero" interval that occurs when two voices or different *instruments* simultaneously play a *note* or *melody* at the same *pitch*.

unity The quality of similarity, shared identity, or consistency to be found among parts of a *composition;* a logical connection between separate elements in a work of art; the opposite of *variety*.

upbeat The *note* that occurs before the first accented *tone*.

v

value The property of *color* that makes it seem light or dark; *shading*. In music, the duration of a *note*. In general, the relative worth accorded to an idea, a concept, or an object.

vanishing point In *linear perspective,* that point on the horizon toward which parallel *lines* appear to converge and at which they seem to vanish.

variations A theme and variations is a musical *form* that consists of the statement of a *melody* or *theme* followed by various modifications of it.

variety Contrast and difference, the lack of sameness among separate elements in a *composition;* the opposite of *unity*.

vault A *masonry* or concrete roof constructed on the principles of an *arch*. See Fig. 103.

vehicle The liquid in which *pigments* are dispersed to make paint. See *binder, medium*.

verisimilitude The appearance of being true to the reality of the tangibly present world; in the *visual arts,* a kind of naturalism or *realism*. See *illusionism, representation, trompe-l'oeil*.

vibrato Fluctuation of *pitch* achieved by string players through a shaking motion on the string. Vocalists often employ a similar wavering pitch to increase the emotional quality of their *tone*.

visual arts Those arts that appeal to the optical sense—*painting, sculpture, drawing,* printmaking, *architecture,* etc.

vivace Italian for "lively" or "vivacious."

voice The sound made by the human throat or by a musical *instrument;* the *part* in music written for that sound.

void A hollow or empty *space*.

volume Any three-dimensional quantity that is bounded or enclosed, whether solid or *void*.

volumetric See *volume*.

votive From the Latin for "vow," an offering made to God or in His name in petition, in fulfillment of a vow, or in gratitude or devotion.

voussoir See Fig. 103.

w

wall In *architecture,* a *plane*like upright *structure* and *surface* capable of serving as a *support,* barrier, or enclosure.

waltz A *dance* in moderate triple meter that developed from the Austrian *Ländler* in the early 19th century.

warm colors *Hues* in the red, yellow, orange, and sometimes violet sections of the *spectrum*. Psychologically, warm colors tend to excite and stimulate; optically, they appear to advance.

wind instruments See *woodwind* and *brass instruments*.

woodwind instruments The flute, oboe, English horn, clarinet, bass clarinet, bassoon, contrabassoon, and saxophone, all of which are pipes with holes in the side and can produce musical sound when blowing causes their columns of air to vibrate. Several of the woodwinds have mouthpieces fitted with reeds.

word painting See *representative style*.

Index

References are to page numbers, except for illustrations, which are also identified by figure numbers. Works have been listed under the names of their creators—composers, painters, poets, sculptors, etc. Architectural works and the paintings, sculptures, mosaics, etc. associated with them—in other words the visual arts not collected into museums—have additionally been listed under the cities where they are now to be found. The purpose of this feature is to serve the reader who may have the opportunity to travel and wish to use *Arts & Ideas* as a handbook-guide to the monuments it discusses. The Table of Contents should be consulted for further guidance to passages on periods, styles, media, and ideas. Unless repeated in the text, the events, births, and deaths cited in the Chronologies at the opening of chapters have not been indexed. Many technical terms are included in the Index with citations where they are defined in the text. For a more complete list of terms the reader should consult the Glossary, which commences on page 483.

(Fig. 539), 472; Solomon R. Guggenheim Museum, 472, 473 (Figs. 542, 543); Trans World Flight Center, 474 (Fig. 546), 478; Trinity Church, 377; as world art capital, 444-445

New York School, 442-453

Nietzsche, Friedrich, 41, 45, 334, 421, 437; *So Spake Zarathustra,* 482

nihilism, 423

Nîmes, France, Maison Carrée, 80, 81 (Fig. 93); Pont du Gard, 83 (Fig. 99), 85, 94

Nolde, Emil, 415; *Dancing around the Golden Calf,* 415 (Fig. 463)

nominalism, 188

nonobjectivism, 410, 431, 448

Norman Conquest, 138-142, 147

notation, musical, development of, 129-130, 136

number theory, Gothic, 171

Oceanic art, 410, 411, 413

octastyle, defined, 27

Octavian, *see* Augustus, Emperor

oculus, defined, 85

Ockeghem, Johannes, 229

Odo, Abbot of Cluny, 120, 129-130, 140

Odo, Bishop of Bayeux, 140, 148

Odoacer, 96-98

Ognissanti church, *see* Florence

Old Market Woman, 73 (Fig. 82), 464

Olympic games, 48

op art, 453, 456

opera, 249; chamber, 317; comic, 333; French baroque, 289-291; 17th-century English, 317-319

optical realism, 385

Oratorian Fathers, 234, 259

oratory, Roman, 90

orchestra, 18th-century development of, 288-289, 310, 322, 441

organ, baroque expansion of tonal space, 322; hydraulic, *see* hydraulus

organic architecture, 433-434

organum duplum, defined, 168

Orozco, José Clemente, 429; *Gods of the Modern World,* 429 (Fig. 488)

Orpheus, 45, 54, 113, 117

Orpheus among the Thracians, 45 (Fig. 61)

Oseberg burial ship, 141 (Fig. 161)

Ostia, Italy, 76

ostinato aria, defined, 317, 318

otherworldliness, Romanesque, 132

Oud, J. J. P., 436

Ovid, *Metamorphoses,* 427

Oxford Movement, 377

Pachelbel, Johann, 257

Padua, Italy, Arena Chapel, Giotto frescoes, 179 (Fig. 195), 189 (Fig. 206), 190

Paganini, Niccolò, 373, 374

Paisiello, Giovanni, 343, 354; *Te Deum,* 354

Palermo, Italy, Palace of the Normans, 137, 139 (Fig. 157)

Palestrina, Giovanni da, 230, 259, 260, 274, 276

Palladio, Andrea, 215, 250, 251, 257, 357; *Four Books of Architecture,* 238, 240, 241; Il Redentore, 239 (Figs. 265, 266), 240; Olympic Theater, 240 (Fig. 267); Villa Rotonda, 238, 241 (Figs. 262, 263)

Panathenaic Festival, 29, 31, 33

Pannini, Giovanni Paolo, *Interior of the Pantheon, Rome,* 84 (Fig. 101)

Pantheon, *see* Rome

parallel organum, explained, 131

Paris, France, 150, 151, 277, 343-346, 359, 382; Arc de Triomphe de l'Étoile, 346, 357, 364; Arc de Triomphe du Carrousel, 345 (Fig. 392), 357; Chamber of Deputies, 343; Eiffel Tower, 404; Hôtel de Soubise, Salon de la Princesse, 323 (Fig. 368); Île de France, 151; Library of Ste. Geneviève, 376, 397 (Fig. 447); Louvre, 277, 279 (Fig. 317), 285, 314; Luxembourg Gardens, *The Bronze Age,* 394, 395 (Fig. 443); La Madeleine, 343, 344 (Figs. 389-391), 345, 357; Museum of Decorative Arts, 395; National Library, 398; Notre Dame, 150, 152, 154, 167, 342, 366, 367; Opera, 376; Place de Charles de Gaulle (Place de l'Étoile), 346; Place de la Concorde, 343-344 (Fig. 388); Pompidou Center (Beaubourg), 478-479 (Figs. 552, 553); Rue de Rivoli, 343; Ste. Chapelle, 367; Ste. Clotilde, 367 (Fig. 414), 397; St. Denis, 150, 151, 164; Vendôme Column, 89, 346 (Fig. 393), 357

Parthenon, *see* Athens

Pascal, Blaise, 320, 322

passacaglia, defined, 318

patristic tradition, 95

patronage of arts, aristocratic baroque, 278-279, 284; bourgeois baroque, 308, 329, 338; Counter-Reformation, 266; Early Christian, 114; feudal Romanesque, 135; medieval Gothic, 164; Napoleonic, 354; 19th century, 383; Renaissance, 173, 174, 214; revolutionary, 373; WPA, 444

Pausanias, 65

Pauson, 51

Paxton, Joseph, 398, 402, 404; Crystal Palace, 398, 399 (Figs. 450, 451)

Pazzi Chapel, *see* Florence

peacock, early Christian symbolism of, 110

Pearlstein, Philip, *Two Female Models in the Studio,* 462 (Fig. 532), 463

pediment, defined, 26 (Fig. 31), 27, 29, 32-36 (Figs. 43-47)

Pei, I. M., National Gallery of Art, 479 (Fig. 554)

pendentives, defined, 105-106 (Fig. 123)

peplos, defined, 34

Pepys, Samuel, 311

Percier, Charles, 343, 357; Arc de Triomphe du Carrousel, 345 (Fig. 392); Vendôme Column, 346 (Fig. 393)

Pergamon, Turkey, 55-56, 77; acropolis, 55-57 (Fig. 65), 73; agora, 57; Altar of Zeus, 57, 59, 61-64 (Figs. 68-71), 72, 73, 75; gymnasium, 57; library, 58, 75; monument of Attalus I, 58, 59, 60 (Figs. 66, 67), 61; mosaics from, 66-67 (Figs. 73, 75); music at, 67-70; royal residence, 58, 65, 66; Temple of Athena Polias, 57 (Fig. 65), 58; theater, 58

Pergolesi, Giovanni Battista, 426

Peri, Jacopo, 247

Pericles, 16, 19-21, 23, 25, 28, 29, 49, 72

peristyle, defined, 27

Perotin the Great, 152, 168

Perrault, Claude, 292; Louvre, 279-280 (Fig. 317), 311, 357

perspective, 65, 200, 214; atmospheric, 201-202, 204, 213, 327; linear, 204, 214, 418

Persuis, Louis Luc Loiseau de, *Tri-*

omphe de Trajan, 358; *L'Inauguration du Temple de la Victoire,* 358

Perugino, 223; *Christ Delivering Keys of Kingdom to St. Peter,* 214 (Fig. 236)

Petrarch, 181, 190, 197, 237, 368

phenomenology, 481

Phidias, 24, 26, 27, 29, 32, 48, 75; *Athena Lemnia,* 40 (Fig. 55); *Lapith and Centaur,* 32 (Fig. 39)

Philadelphia, Pa., Society of Friends Guild House, 476 (Fig. 550), 477

Philip II of Spain, 234, 266-268, 274, 290, 321

Philip Augustus of France, 150, 152

Philip of Macedon, 55

Philippe de Vitry, *Ars Nova,* 189

photography, color, 6, 408; daguerreotype process, 385; journalistic, 5

Phrygian musical mode, 67-70

Piano, Renzo, Pompidou Center, 478-479 (Figs. 552, 553)

Picasso, Pablo, 348, 406, 411, 413, 419, 425, 426, 427, 430, 431, 439, 445, 453; *Les Demoiselles d'Avignon,* 10, 408 (Fig. 455), 409, 412, 418; *Guernica,* 431 (Fig. 492); *The Love of Jupiter and Semele,* 427 (Fig. 485); *Persephone,* 427; *Pipes of Pan,* 427 (Fig. 484); *Pulcinella,* 426; *Stravinsky* (portrait), 412 (Fig. 460); *Three Graces,* 427 (Fig. 483); *Three Musicians,* 419 (Fig. 469); *Woman in the Garden,* 407 (Fig. 454); *Woman's Head* (bust), 419 (Fig. 470); *Woman's Head* (painting), 10 (Fig. 13)

Pico della Mirandola, 203, 206; *Dignity of Man,* 215

Piero della Francesca, 220; *Resurrection,* 204 (Fig. 227)

Pilkington, Francis, *First Booke of Ayres,* 304, 305 (Fig. 351)

Pinturicchio, Bernardino, 216

Pisa, Italy, Baptistry, pulpit detail, 181 (Fig. 198); Campo Santo fresco (Traini), *Triumph of Death,* 184 (Fig. 204), 185; Cathedral, pulpit detail, 181 (Fig. 199)

Pisano, Andrea, 178, 191, 197

Pisano, Giovanni, 181; *Nativity and Annunciation to the Shepherds,* pulpit detail, 181 (Fig. 199), 182

Pisano, Nicola, 181, 190, 210; *Annunciation and Nativity,* pulpit detail, 181 (Fig. 198), 182

plague, *see* Black Death

plainsong, Gregorian, 131

Plateresque architectural style, 269

Plato, 19, 23, 44, 46, 47, 50, 53, 54, 70, 224, 337; Academy of, 57; *Republic,* 44, 45, 50, 209, 230, 438; *Timaeus,* 46, 226, 231. *See also* neoplatonism

Pliny the Elder, 67

Plutarch, 47; *Parallel Lives,* 343, 347

podium, defined, 62

Poe, Edgar Allan, 366

pointillism, 391

Poliziano, Angelo, 203, 206-209, 231

Pollaiuolo, Antonio, 211, 212; *Hercules Strangling Antaeus,* 200 (Fig. 220), 255

Pollock, Jackson, 445-446 (Fig. 505), 447-450; *Lucifer,* 447-448 (Figs. 506, 507), 449, 452-453

Polyclitus, 24, 54; *Doryphorus,* 37 (Fig. 49), 38, 39, 48

Polyclitus the Younger, 41

Polydorus, *see* Laocoön Group

Polygnotus, 24, 51, 65

Polynesian art, *see* Oceanic art

polyphony, Dutch preeminence in, 296; Gothic, 153, 167-168; Renais-

sance, 247; Romanesque, 131-132

polytonality, 438

Pompeii, Italy, 67, 249, 357; House of the Faun, *The Battle of Alexander,* 66 (Fig. 74)

Pont du Gard, *see* Nîmes

Ponte, Lorenzo da, 334

pop art, 442, 453-454, 480

Porcia and Cato, 81 (Fig. 95)

Porta, Giacomo della, Il Gesù, 261-262 (Figs. 291, 292); St. Peter's dome, 216 (Fig. 237), 259

portal, defined, 26

portico, defined, 26

Poseidon, 29, 35

Poseidon (Zeus?), 38 (Fig. 52), 39

Poseidon and Apollo, 33 (Fig. 42), 34

post-and-lintel construction, 26, 58, 406

postimpressionism, 390-394, 402

Potsdam, Germany, Sans-souci, 323

Poussin, Nicolas, 285-288, 292, 321, 347, 358, 393; *Et in Arcadia Ego,* 287 (Fig. 329); *Rape of Sabine Women,* 286 (Fig. 328)

Pozzo, Andrea, 260, 264, 276; *St. Ignatius in Glory,* 264 (Fig. 299)

Prandtauer, Jakob, Benedictine Abbey Church, 327 (Figs. 372, 373)

Praxiteles, 39, 69, 211; *Aphrodite of Cnidos,* 39 (Fig. 56), 40; *Aphrodite of Cyrene,* 74 (Fig. 83); *Hermes and the Infant Dionysus,* 37 (Fig. 50)

prehistoric art, *see* Stone Age art

printing, 173; silk screen, 408

Procopius, 107

Prokofiev, Sergei, *Love of Three Oranges,* 426

Promethean idea, 355

Pronomos painter, *Actors Holding Their Masks,* 42 (Fig. 59)

Propylaea, *see* Athens

Protagoras, 47

Protestantism, 275, 306-307, 321; Anglican, 307; Calvinist, 293, 295, 305, 307; Lutheran, 305, 307. *See also* Reformation

Proust, Marcel, 396, 403; *Remembrance of Things Past,* 403

psychic automatism, 424, 425, 446-447

Ptolemy, 162

public works projects, Roman, 90-93. *See also* Works Progress Administration

Puget, Pierre, *Milo of Crotona,* 283 (Fig. 324), 284

Pugin, A. W. N., Houses of Parliament, 366 (Fig. 413)

Purcell, Henry, 309, 310, 312, 321, 322; *Dido and Aeneas,* 317-318, 322

pyramids, Egyptian, 12 (Fig. 16), 13

Pythagoras, 19, 45, 46, 51, 466

Pythios, Mausoleum at Halicarnassus, 70 (Fig. 79)

quadruplum, defined, 167

quantum theory, 340

Quinault, Philippe, 289

Quintilian, 90

Rachmaninoff, Sergei, 373

Racine, Jean, 279, 281, 289-292, 357

Rameau, Jean Philippe, 323, 401

Rameses II, 2; colossi of, 12 (Fig. 17), 13

Raphael (Raffaelo Sanzio), 211, 214-218, 223, 250-252, 272, 343; *Julius II* portrait, 217 (Fig. 238); *Leo X with Two Cardinals,* 218, 219 (Fig. 239); *School of Athens,* 226-227 (Fig. 252)

Spontini, Gasparo, 343, *La Vestale,* 354, 358
Squarcialupi, Antonio, 193, 194, 209, 214
stained glass windows, Gothic, 163–166 (Figs. 187–189), 172
stasimon, defined, 46
Steen, Jan, 308; *Merry Family,* 308 (Fig. 352)
Stein, Gertrude, 426, 443
Steinbach, Erwin von, Strasbourg cathedral, 366
Stella, Frank, 463; *Singerli Variation IV,* 458 (Fig. 524), 459; *Tuftonboro,* 458 (Fig. 523), 459
Still, Clyfford, 445
Stockhausen, Karlheinz, 8, 466–467, 471; *Gesang der Jünglinge,* 466; *Opus 1970, Study I,* 466; *Study II,* 466
stoicism, 70–71, 74, 93
Stone Age art, 3, 6, 9–10
Stonehenge, 411
Storm-and-Stress movement, 325, 333, 334, 336, 338
Strasbourg, France, cathedral, 154
Strauss, Richard, 416; *Elektra,* 416; *Salomé,* 416
Stravinsky, Igor, 406, 422, 426, 427, 438, 439, 443, 466, 469; *Etude for Pianola,* 422; *Firebird,* 373; *Oedipus Rex,* 427; *Pulcinella,* 426; Picasso portrait, 412 (Fig. 460); *Rite of Spring,* 373, 406, 413, 426, 438
Stuart and Revett, *Antiquities of Athens,* 341
stylobate, defined, 26 (Fig. 31), 27, 28
Suger, Abbot, 96, 150–152, 164
Sullivan, Louis, 433, 434; Wainwright Building, 433 (Fig. 494)
Sumerian royal tombs, 4
surrealism, 405, 410, 422, 424–426, 444–447, 449, 480
Sweelinck, Jan Pieterszoon, 257, 296, 304
Swift, Jonathan, *Gulliver's Travels,* 330
Sydney, Australia, Opera House, 477 (Fig. 551), 478
symbolism, early Christian, 107, 110, 116–118, medieval, 132–133, 187, 188; 19th-century, 392, 399, 400, 402, 405
synaesthesia, 400
synthesizer-computer music, *see* electronic music

Tate, Nahum, *Dido and Aeneas,* 317
temenos, defined, 62
tempera, defined, 208
Terborch, Gerard, 308; *Gallant Scene,* 308 (Fig. 353)
Teresa of Avila, St., 234, 259, 265–266, 275, 276
tesserae, defined, 67
theater of the absurd, 441, 442
Theodora, Empress, 107
Theodore, Archbishop, sarcophagus of, 111 (Fig. 131)
Theodoric, Emperor, 96–99, 101, 102, 103, 112
Thomas, Dylan, 445, 468, 469
Thomas of Celano, *Dies Irae,* 185. *See also Dies Irae*
Thomson, Virgil, 443, 468
Thorvaldsen, Bertel, Villa Carlotta salon, 358 (Fig. 404)
Thucydides, 49
tibia, defined, 90
Tiepolo, Giovanni Battista, *Apollo*

Presenting to Frederick Barbarossa His Bride, Beatrice of Burgundy, 337 (Fig. 385)
timbre, defined, 401
Timotheus, 46
Tintoretto, 241, 244, 257; *Last Supper,* 244 (Fig. 275); *Marriage of Bacchus and Ariadne,* 250, 251 (Fig. 280)
Titian, 254, 257, 266, 272, 285; *Assumption of the Virgin,* 242 (Fig. 273), 243, 244, 250, 270; *Bacchus and Ariadne,* 243 (Fig. 274), 244, 250
Titus, Arch of, *see* Rome
toccata, 247
Toledo, Juan Bautista de, 267; Escorial Palace, 266–269 (Figs. 303–305)
Toledo, Spain, San Tomé, *Burial of Count Orgaz,* 270–271 (Fig. 310)
Toulouse, France, St. Sernin church, 120, 123 (Fig. 139), 125
Toulouse-Lautrec, Henri de, 404; *At the Moulin Rouge,* 404 (Fig. 452)
Traini, Francesco, *Triumph of Death,* 184 (Fig. 204), 185
Trajan, Emperor, 20, 58, 76–80, 82, 85–89
Tralles, Turkey, music of, 69
transept, defined, 100 (Fig. 114)
triglyph, defined, 26 (Fig. 31), 27, 28, 30, 32
triplum, defined, 167
triptych, defined, 208
troubadours, 144
trouvères, defined, 144
trumeau, defined, 162; 163 (Fig. 186)
tuba, classical Roman, 89
Turner, Joseph Mallord William, 379, 448; *Rain, Steam, and Speed: The Great Western Railway,* 379, 380 (Fig. 423)
Tutankhamon, 4, 13; throne of, 14 (Fig. 19)
Tuthmosis, *Queen Nefertiti,* 13 (Fig. 18)
twelve-tone music, 420, 438, 468, 469
tympanum, defined, 125; of Vézelay church, 124–126 (Figs. 141–143)

Uccello, Paolo, 193, 197; *Battle of San Romano,* 204 (Fig. 226)
Urban II, 120, 122
Urban VIII, Pope, 263
utilitarianism, Roman, 93–94
Utzon, Joern, Sydney Opera House, 477 (Fig. 551), 478

Valéry, Paul Ambroise, 428; *Fragments of Narcissus,* 428
van der Goes, Hugo, *Portinari Altarpiece,* 208 (Fig. 232)
van de Velde, Jan Jansz., *Still Life: Fruit Piece,* 295 (Fig. 335)
van Dyck, Anthony, 257, 292; *Five Children of Charles I,* 309, 311 (Fig. 356)
van Eyck, Jan, *Giovanni Arnolfini and His Wife,* 207 (Fig. 231), 208
van Gogh, Vincent, 292, 391, 404, 413, 415; *Starry Night,* 391 (Fig. 437), 391
Varèse, Edgar, 422; *Intégrales,* 422; *Density 2.15,* 422; *Ionization,* 422
Vasari, Giorgio, 215, 222, 251
vaulting, barrel or tunnel, 86 (Fig. 103); cross or groin, 82, 86 (Fig. 103). *See also* arch-and-vault construction

Velázquez, Diego, 244, 272–274, 292, 321; *Las Meninas,* 272–273 (Fig. 313), 439; *Water Carrier of Seville,* 272 (Fig. 312)
Veneziano, Domenico, 204
Venice, 136, 235–238; as crossroads, 252, 253; Doge's Palace, 235, 235; Il Redentore, 239 (Figs. 264–266); music at, 247–250; Library of St. Mark, 237, 238 (Fig. 261); music at, 247–250; Procuratie Nuove, 240, 241 (Fig. 268); St. Mark's Cathedral, 235–237 (Fig. 260), 247, 248, 346; Santa Maria della Salute, 240, 241 (Fig. 270)
Venturi, Robert, 476–477; *Complexity and Contradiction in Architecture,* 476. *See also* Venturi and Rauch
Venturi and Rauch, Society of Friends Guild House, 476 (Fig. 550), 477
Venus, 80–81, 231
Venus of the Vatican, 217
Venus of Willendorf, 9, (Fig. 11), 10
Verdi, Giuseppe, *Aïda,* 381
Vergil, 81, 358, 368, 370; *Aeneid,* 93, 190, 224, 318, 377
Vermeer, Jan, 292, 302, 208, 321; *Artist in His Studio,* 302, 303 (Fig. 349); *Concert,* 304 (Fig. 350), 432; *Officer and Laughing Girl,* 302, 303 (Fig. 348); *View of Delft,* 302 (Fig. 347), 432
Veronese, Paolo, 241, 245, 246, 250, 251; *Feast in the House of Levi,* 246 (Fig. 277), 247; *Marriage at Cana,* 245 (Fig. 276), 246
Verrocchio, Andrea del, 200, 211, 212, 215
Versailles Palace, 279–282 (Figs. 318–322), 291 (Figs. 332, 333); gardens, 280 (Fig. 319), 281 (Fig. 321), 282–283; Hall of Mirrors, 280 (Fig. 320), 281; Marie Antoinette's country cottage, 379; music at, 289–290
Vesalius (Andries van Wesel), *Anatomy,* 297, 300, 307
Vespucci family, 207
vestibule, defined, 313
Vézelay, France, Abbey Church of La Madeleine, 120, 124–126 (Figs. 141–143), 133 (Figs. 152–153), 134
Vicenza, Italy, Olympic Theater, 240 (Fig. 267); Villa Rotonda, 85, 238, 241 (Figs. 262, 263)
Victoria, Tomás Luis de, 266, 274–276; *Offices for Holy Week,* 275
Vienna, Austria, Belvedere Palace, 326 (Fig. 371), 327; Hofburg Palace, 326 (Fig. 370); Schönbrunn Palace, 324, music at, 332
Vigée-Lebrun, Élisabeth, 338; *Marie Antoinette,* 338 (Fig. 386)
Vignola, Giacomo, 259; Church of Il Gesù, 261–262 (Figs. 291, 292)
Vignon, Pierre Alexandre, 357; Church of La Madeleine, 343, 344 (Figs. 389–391), 345, 357
Vikings, 145, 149
Vincent of Beauvais, 187; *Speculum Majus,* 160, 172
Vingt-quatre Violons, 288–289, 310, 322
Viollet-le-Duc, Eugène, 125, 367, 374; projected cathedral, 151 (Fig. 171), 367
Virgin Mary, cult of, 96; in Gothic cathedrals, 152, 159–162
Virgin Portal, Chartres, 160–162,

170 (Figs. 183–185)
virtù, defined, 215
Vitruvius, 37, 46, 212, 231, 251
Voltaire, 324, 329, 337, 365; *Candide,* 330, 337; Houdon bust of, 332, 333 (Fig. 383)
volutes, 26 (Fig. 31), 30, 31
voussoir, defined, 86

Wagner, Richard, 374, 401, 403; *Faust,* 371; *Forest Murmurs,* 379; *Lohengrin,* 366; *Parsifal,* 366; *Rienzi,* 376; Ring Cycle, 403; *Tannhäuser,* 366; *Tristan and Isolde,* 380–381, 416
Walpole, Horace, *Castle of Otranto,* 365, 374
Warhol, Andy, 454; *Green Coca Cola Bottles,* 455 (Fig. 518)
Wartburg Castle, 137
Washington, D.C., Capitol rotunda, 85; city plan of, 282; Lincoln Memorial, 81; National Gallery, East Wing, 479 (Fig. 554); Smithsonian Institution, 353 (Fig. 403), 354; Union Station, 83; Washington Monument, 81; White House, 241
Washington, George, Greenough statue of, 353 (Fig. 403), 354, 358; Houdon statue of, 332
watercolors, 389
Watteau, Antoine, 292, 323, 326–329, 336, 338; *Garden of Bacchus,* 326 (Fig. 369); *Gersaint's Signboard,* 330 (Fig. 378); *Music Party,* 327 (Fig. 374), 328
Weber, Carl Maria von, 370, 375; *Der Freischütz,* 334, 379
Werfel, Franz, 428; *The Trojan Women,* 428
Wilde, Oscar, 416
Willaert, Adrian, 247
William and Mary, 314, 316
William of Malmesbury, 142, 167
William the Conqueror, 138–141, 147, 148
Winckelmann, J. J., 337, 353, 357, 358; *History of Ancient Art,* 341, 347; Kauffmann portrait of, 341 (Fig. 387)
wind instruments, Roman, 89–90
women's rights movement, 339
Works Project Administration (WPA), 444, 445
Wren, Christopher, 257, 309, 312, 216; Hampton Court Palace, 316 (Fig. 363); plan for London, 314–315; St. Mary-le-Bow, 315 (Fig. 361); St. Paul's Cathedral, 312–314 (Figs. 357–360)
Wright, Frank Lloyd, 406, 433, 434, 436, 437, 439, 471, 478; "Falling Water" (Kaufmann House), 434 (Fig. 496); Price Tower, Bartlesville, Okla., 433 (Fig. 495); Solomon R. Guggenheim Museum, 472, 473 (Figs. 542, 543)
Wyatt, James, Fonthill Abbey, 365 (Figs. 411, 412), 366
Wyeth, Andrew, 430; *Mother Archie's Church,* 430 (Fig. 491)

Zarlino, Gioseffe, 257
Zeus, 35, 44, 47, 51, 62; Altar of, 57, 59, 61–64 (Figs. 68–71); Temple of Olympian, 22, 31 (Fig. 38)
Zeus (Poseidon?), 38 (Fig. 52), 39
Zeus Hurling Thunderbolts, 63 (Fig. 70)
Zola, Émile, 330, 383, 399, 401, 402
Zwinger, The, *see* Dresden
Zwingli, Ulrich, 258

502 Index